A Judeo-Christian

Approach to

Business Ethics

beyond
integrity

second edition

Scott B. Rae and Kenman L. Wong

GRAND RAPIDS, MICHIGAN 49530 USA

ZONDERVAN™

Beyond Integrity
Copyright © 1996, 2004 by Scott B. Rae and Kenman L. Wong

Requests for information should be addressed to:
Zondervan, *Grand Rapids, Michigan 49530*

Library of Congress Cataloging-in-Publication Data

Beyond integrity : a Judeo-Christian approach to business ethics / [edited by] Scott B. Rae and
    Kenman L. Wong.—2nd ed.
        p. cm.
    Includes bibliographical references and index.
    ISBN 0-310-24002-6 (hardcover)
    1. Business ethics. 2. Business—Religious aspects—Christianity. 3. Business—Religious
    aspects—Judaism. I. Rae, Scott B. II. Wong, Kenman L., 1964–
    HF5387.B49 2004
    174'.4—dc22   2004010289

This edition printed on acid-free paper.

Interior design by Nancy Wilson

Printed in the United States of America

08 09 10 /❖ DC/ 10 9 8 7 6 5

Contents in Brief

Contents

Part II: Ethics, Corporations, and the Global Economy

Part III: Contemporary Ethical Issues in Business

ACKNOWLEDGMENTS

Many of our colleagues, friends, and family members have played an important role in seeing this new edition come to completion. We would be remiss if we did not recognize their contributions and express our gratitude to them.

Kenman wishes to express many thanks to his exceptional colleagues in the School of Business and Economics at Seattle Pacific University, who provide an environment conducive to scholarship and community and continue to help sharpen his thinking. They provide a source of encouragement for which he is very appreciative.

Scott expresses gratitude for his colleagues in the philosophy department at Talbot School of Theology, Biola University, for their intellectual stimulation, rich friendship, and partnership in the cause of Christ. Scott particularly appreciates his team-teaching partner in business ethics at Biola University, Tom Wilson, for encouragement and insight over the past few years of teaching this material together.

We are grateful for the people who gave various portions of the book thoughtful reading and critique, especially Bill West, who significantly shaped the material dealing with ethics in accounting and finance.

We are very appreciative of the efforts of Tina Gamponia, who coordinated the administrative side of the book for this second edition, especially in obtaining permissions for the various readings. Many thanks for her time and the organization that she brought to the book.

We are grateful to our editor at Zondervan, Jim Ruark, and his team for their work in making our material clearer, for the design of the book, and for their helpfulness in various ways.

And many thanks to our students over the years who have played a significant role in this work. Although too numerous to be named here, they have sharpened us by providing insightful comments and challenges to our ideas. Their wise questions and observations are woven throughout these pages.

Finally, our families deserve a great deal of credit for their roles in making this work possible. Scott thanks his father, Walter B. Rae, for powerfully modeling a successful businessman who operated "beyond integrity." Our immediate families, Kenman's wife Marika and children Callan and Elise, and Scott's wife Sally and children Taylor, Cameron, and Austin, all help keep us balanced and remind us what a good life is all about.

INTRODUCTION

This is the second edition of a book devoted to the application of Christian ethics to the commercial marketplace. Many changes have occurred in business since the first edition was published in 1996 to convince us that this is truly a remarkable time to reflect on topics in this exciting field. During the past decade or so, the moral climate of business seems to be pulling in opposite directions. Some unfortunate events make the need for better ethics much more apparent and, quite unintentionally, seem to welcome attempts to establish them. However, other developments make the study and actual practice of sound behavior in business much more complex and multifaceted.

When we first started teaching university students and addressing business audiences on ethics-related topics, we spent a lot of time trying to convince people (Christians too) why ethics was important to their careers, to their organizations, and to the health of the broader economy. Because of recent events, few business people (and students) now have to be persuaded that the development of sound ethics in business is not merely a detached "academic" exercise with little actual impact or importance.

Millions of individual investors who have recently suffered large-scale reductions in the values of their investment portfolios can attest to the tangible value of trustworthy behavior. Financial markets lost much ground as a direct result of misleading statements by analysts employed by highly respected investment firms and by corporate bankruptcies such as Enron and WorldCom, precipitated by fraudulent accounting statements.

These events and the ensuing media images of executives being led away in handcuffs have helped teach a hard but important lesson: that a solid moral foundation is necessary to our well-being as individuals and as a broader community with strong economic and moral interconnections. As a result, the climate of business seems to be open, once again, to discussion and action concerning moral matters. However, countervailing forces, such as short-term expectations and global competition, have also been at work to make the ability to actually practice good behavior in the marketplace more difficult. These forces seem to make the climate of business more hostile to ethical change.

Investor fixation on quarterly financial results, coupled with technology and its ensuing culture of speed, can work to push corporate decision makers into short-term thinking. As some of the recent scandals reveal, the pressure can be overwhelming even for executives long known for their character and devotion to their faith tradition. Corporate leaders find they have to appease investors by focusing on quarterly returns rather than long-term value. This provides tempting incentives to cut a wide variety of ethical corners along the way in order to "make the numbers." CEOs who dare to go against the grain and take a longer term approach may find their positions in jeopardy.

Global competition has also rapidly increased, seemingly reducing the margin to maneuver and pursue ethical considerations. Domestic companies must compete not only with each other to achieve quarterly benchmarks, but also with foreign firms, many of which may be provided with competitive advantages as a result of operating under different cultural and legal expectations on issues such as employee pay, safety, and environmental stewardship. Firms attempting to uphold higher standards than their competitors potentially face higher costs, lower profits, and the threat of "punishment" by the short-term orientation of financial markets.

The fate of one company and its leader, who has often and rightfully been upheld as a model of good corporate leadership, reflects these new challenges. The company is Malden Mills, makers of Polartec, a popular fleece material used in outerwear. Two weeks before Christmas in 1995, the people of the town of Methuen, Massachusetts, watched a devastating fire destroy three of four of the company's factories, the core of one of the last remaining large-scale textile mills in the region and the town's key employment and economic lifeline. The fire injured 24 people, left 1,400 workers unemployed, and confirmed fears that the town would be destroyed economically, the plight suffered by many New England towns as other mills shut down in search of more cost-efficient labor sources overseas.

In a stunning surprise, the company's majority owner, Aaron Feuerstein (then seventy years old), who could have simply retired on the insurance money, immediately announced plans to rebuild with the goal of having his workers back in the mill within a few months. Furthermore, Feuerstein gave every employee a $275 Christmas bonus and a $20 coupon for food at a local supermarket. Amid cheers from his employees, he then announced that for at least the next thirty days he would pay every workers' salary in full and that their health insurance had been paid for the next ninety days. Citing his faith and his belief that difficult circumstances provide the real test of moral convictions, Feuerstein stated that collecting the insurance money and retiring was never a thought that crossed his mind. "My commitment is to Massachusetts and New England. It's where I live, where I play, where I worship. Malden Mills will rebuild right here," he said at the time.[1]

[1] David Lamb, "Massachusetts Mill Town Gets Angel for Christmas," *Los Angeles Times,* 19 December 1995, A24.

After the announcement, Feuerstein followed through on his promises, receiving national attention for his actions. In the immediate years after rebuilding, the company experienced increased employee loyalty and production in the form of lower turnover and error rates. The Malden Mills story was often shared as an example of extraordinary business citizenship and how it "pays" to prioritize people over profits.

Recently, however, the story took an unfortunate and complex turn. Due in part to competitive forces and to the cost of rebuilding and paying wages to idle workers, the company became mired in debt and filed for Chapter 11 bankruptcy in late 2001. While the company emerged from bankruptcy in late 2003, Feuerstein's ownership of the company was significantly reduced, with banks and other creditors (who may not share Feuerstein's sense of social responsibility) assuming a controlling interest in the company. Moreover, the company may have to turn to more overseas production (in China) to remain competitive.

To be sure, the message here is not that nice guys finish last or that it is impossible to exercise leadership that attends to matters other than profits. However, this story does put us on appropriate notice that ethics applied to competitive markets is more complex than simple, often used platitudes such as "do the right thing" or "it all comes down to character" portray. Improving the ethical climate of business is a challenging and multidimensional task, and one that requires attentiveness to ethical norms and economic realities.

The underlying premise of this book is that ethics derived from the Christian tradition has much to contribute to this endeavor. While the world of commerce may not be "Christian" and may not readily accept ethical guidance couched in faith-based language, many businesspeople seek and take guidance from their faith traditions. These are some of the very people whose everyday decisions influence the values and conduct within the marketplace. Furthermore, many of the ethical constructs derived from the Christian faith can also be communicated in language that appeals to the broader marketplace.

Most importantly, Christian ethics and the worldview on which it is based offer a truthful lens from which to view, interpret, and critique values and events. A Christian worldview accounts for the realities of fallen human nature and the culture at large, providing a sense of realism in terms of what can be achieved. Yet it is not devoid of ideals, basing its hopefulness on the fact that our work here on earth has ultimate significance and that even the imperfect aspects of the world we live in will one day be redeemed.

We have attempted to revise and structure the second edition of this book in such a way that it is grounded in Christian theology and yet takes realistic account of the complexity and changing nature of the practice of business. The reading selections include a wide variety of perspectives, some explicitly Christian and some that merely (but clearly) reflect Christian values. Other readings will present viewpoints that are inimical to the Christian worldview but were included because they represent influential views worth engaging. Our goals are to make you think rigorously, to foster more dialogue with the world around you, and to instill values that are based soundly on the Christian faith.

Part I

Foundations for Christian Ethics in Business

ONE

Christian Ethics in Business: Tensions and Challenges

A sudden submission to Christian ethics by businessmen would bring about the greatest economic upheaval in history!

A chief executive officer, quoted in
"Is Business Bluffing Ethical?" by Albert Z. Carr

INTRODUCTION

Recently, there has been exploding interest in the idea of "spirituality" in the workplace. Major business magazines such as *Business Week* and *Fortune* have run cover stories on the topic, and academic conferences, corporate programs, and executive retreats have been organized around this theme. Understandably, the concept of integrating one's faith and values into the workplace is important and rightfully deserves such attention.

However, actual attempts to bring faith-based values into the workplace can be challenging and riddled with tension when the "darker" aspects of business and the reality of economic competition are factored into the equation. In fact, some research supports the suspicion that many business people do, in fact, live with two conflicting sets of rules: one for business, and one for their lives outside of work.

Some observers of commercial life have gone so far as to claim that virtue and success have an inverse relationship. Unless individual participants leave "private" morality at the door, financial gain will prove elusive. Business demands shrewdness and the bending, if not outright breaking, of rules, the argument typically goes. Play "softly" and you will soon be surpassed. Not that "good" behavior is nonexistent. When it occurs, however, the motivation behind it is self-interest, not ethics per se.

[1]For a more thorough discussion of the power of competitive forces, see David Korten, *When Corporations Rule the World* (West Hartford, Conn.: Kumarian Press, 1995). See also John Dobson, "The Feminine Firm: A Comment," *Business Ethics Quarterly* 6 (April 1996): 227–31.

Organizations are trapped by similar deterministic rules. A "nice" company that engages in "restrained" competition or sacrifices profits for the benefit of employees or the local community beyond motivational or public relations value will soon find itself in decline if competitors don't operate with similar rules and intentions.[1]

The idea that business demands different standards for behavior is particularly problematic for those who adhere to a belief system that holds that a unified set of values should be applicable to life in its totality. The thought that the very virtues that govern their lives outside of work could be the ones that jeopardize the ability to succeed within it is deeply troubling. Moreover, if the construct is true, we are lead to the inevitable conclusion that all who have achieved success in business from a financial standpoint have somehow compromised their moral standards in the process.

In stark contrast to the belief that financial success requires ethical compromise, a popular sentiment has it that good ethics *is* good business. Behavioral compromises are unnecessary and are the product of short-sightedness. After all, honesty and fairness will only enhance economic well-being. Customers prefer to deal with individuals and organizations with a rock-solid reputation for honesty. Therefore, ethics and self-interest do not clash at all. Sound strategy and prudence require only the short-term sacrifice of gain.

The central focus of this chapter is to examine some of the tensions and challenges of bringing Christian ethics to bear on business. Do traditional virtues such as honesty and compassion facilitate the prospect for successful participation in business? Or, conversely, do such characteristics doom a business to fail in the "competitive jungle" of economic affairs?[2]

[2] For a discussion of the inadequacies of the "jungle" metaphor for business, see Brian Griffiths, *The Creation of Wealth: A Christian's Case for Capitalism* (Downers Grove, Ill.: InterVarsity Press, 1984).

In "Is Business Bluffing Ethical?" Albert Z. Carr takes the posture that two sets of morals, one for business and one for private life, is an inescapable reality. Using the game of poker as an analogy to business, Carr argues that practices such as "bluffing" should be judged by business rules and not by "the ethical principles preached in churches." He concludes that those who try to apply their private morals at the workplace will likely fail to be successful as business people.

Based on qualitative research, authors Amar Bhide and Howard H. Stevenson in their article entitled "Why Be Honest If Honesty Doesn't Pay?" attempted to find evidence to support the popular notion that good ethics and good business are synonymous. In a somewhat surprising and optimistic conclusion, Bhide and Stevenson find that while the idea that "honesty is the best policy" makes intuitive sense, it is an unsubstantiated claim from a rational, economic standpoint. They point to cases in which breaking one's word is actually handsomely rewarded or, at the very least, seldom punished. Even so, they argue that the trust necessary for business relationships is alive and well, because for many business people honesty is a matter of conscience and morality rather than strategy.

In "Companies Are Discovering the Value of Ethics," author Norman Bowie contradicts the view that ethics and profits are inversely related. While he does not make the claim that good ethics always lead to higher profit margins, Bowie provides multiple examples in which ethics have had a positive impact on the bottom line. This is the case, he argues, because attention to ethics can provide firms with a source of competitive advantage.

The case studies in this chapter provide windows through which one can see some of these tensions and challenges illustrated. "Borland's Brave Beginning" presents a true-to-life scenario in which truth telling and financial success seem to be in conflict. "Keeping Secrets" divides a manager's loyalty between an organization and a freindship.

READINGS

Is Business Bluffing Ethical?

Albert Z. Carr

Harvard Business Review (January–February 1968). Copyright © 1967.

The ethics of business are not those of society, but rather those of the poker game.

Foreword

"When the law as written gives a man a wide-open chance to make a killing, he'd be a fool not to take advantage of it. If he doesn't, somebody else will," remarked a friend of the author. Mr. Carr likens such behavior to the bluffing of the poker player who seizes every opportunity to win, as long as it does not involve outright cheating. "No one thinks any the worse of you on that account," says the author. "And no one would think any the worse of the game of business because its standards of right and wrong differ from the prevailing traditions of morality in our society."

Mr. Carr became interested in this subject when he was a member of a New York firm of consultants to large corporations in many fields. The confidences of many stress-ridden executives made him aware of the extent to which tensions can arise from conflicts between an individual's ethical sense and the realities of business. He was struck also by the similarity of the special ethical attitude shown by many successful and stress-free businessmen in their work to that of good poker players.

Mr. Carr was Assistant to the Chairman of the War Production Board during World War II and later served on the White House staff and as a

Special Consultant to President Truman. He is now writing full-time. Among his books is *John D. Rockefeller's Secret Weapon*, a study of corporate development. This article is adapted from a chapter in his newest book, *Business As a Game*, to be published by New American Library in March 1968.

—————

A respected businessman with whom I discussed the theme of this article remarked with some heat, "You mean to say you're going to encourage men to bluff? Why, bluffing is nothing more than a form of lying! You're advising them to lie!"

I agreed that the basis of private morality is respect for truth and that the closer a businessman comes to the truth, the more he deserves respect. At the same time, I suggested that most bluffing in business might be regarded simply a game strategy—much like bluffing in poker, which does not reflect on the morality of the bluffer.

I quoted Henry Taylor, the British statesman who pointed out that "falsehood ceases to be falsehood when it is understood on all sides that the truth is not expected to be spoken"—an exact description of bluffing in poker, diplomacy, and business. I cited the analogy of the criminal court, where the criminal is not expected to tell the truth when he pleads "not guilty." Everyone from the judge down takes it for granted that the job of the defendant's attorney is to get his client off, not to reveal the truth; and this is considered ethical practice. I mentioned Representative Omar Burleson, the Democrat from Texas, who was quoted as saying, in regard to the ethics of Congress, "Ethics is a barrel of worms"[1]—a pungent summing up of the problem of deciding who is ethical in politics.

I reminded my friend that millions of businessmen feel constrained every day to say *yes* to their bosses when they secretly believe *no* and that this is generally accepted as permissible strategy when the alternative might be the loss of a job. The essential point, I said, is that the ethics of business are game ethics, different from the ethics of religion.

He remained unconvinced. Referring to the company of which he is president, he declared: "Maybe that's good enough for some businessmen, but I can tell you that we pride ourselves on our ethics. In 30 years not one customer has ever questioned my word or asked to check our figures. We're loyal to our customers and fair to our suppliers. I regard my handshake on a deal as a contract. I've never entered into price-fixing schemes with my competitors. I've never allowed my salesmen to spread injurious rumors about other companies. Our union contract is the best in our industry. And, if I do say so myself, our ethical standards are of the highest!"

He really was saying, without realizing it, that he was living up to the ethical standards of the business game—which are a far cry from those of private life. Like a gentlemanly poker player, he did not play in cahoots with others at the table, try to smear their reputations, or hold back chips he owed them.

But this same fine man, at that very time, was allowing one of his products to be advertised in a way that made it sound a great deal better than it actually was. Another item in his product line was notorious among dealers for its "built-in obsolescence." He was holding back from the market a much-improved product because he did not want it to interfere with sales of the inferior item it would have replaced. He had joined with certain of his competitors in hiring a lobbyist to push a state legislature, by methods that he preferred not to know too much about, into amending a bill then being enacted.

In his view these things had nothing to do with ethics; they were merely normal business practice. He himself undoubtedly avoided outright falsehoods—never lied in so many words. But the entire organization that he ruled was deeply involved in numerous strategies of deception.

Pressure to Deceive

Most executives from time to time are almost compelled, in the interests of their companies or themselves, to practice some form of deception when negotiating with customers, dealers, labor unions, government officials, or even other departments of their companies. By conscious misstatements, concealment of pertinent facts, or exaggeration—in short, by bluffing—they seek to persuade others to agree with them. I think it is fair to say that if the individual executive refuses to bluff from time to time—if he feels obligated to tell the truth, the whole truth, and nothing but the truth—he is ignoring opportunities permitted under the rules and is at a heavy disadvantage in his business dealings.

But here and there a businessman is unable to reconcile himself to the bluff in which he plays a part. His conscience, perhaps spurred by religious idealism, troubles him. He feels guilty; he may develop an ulcer or a nervous tic. Before any executive can make profitable use of the strategy of the bluff, he needs to make sure that in bluffing he will not lose self-respect or become emotionally disturbed. If he is to reconcile personal integrity and high standards of honesty with the practical requirements of business, he must feel that his bluffs are ethically justified. The justification rests on the fact that business, as practiced by individuals as well as by corporations, has the impersonal character of a game—a game that demands both special strategy and an understanding of its special ethics.

The game is played at all levels of corporate life, from the highest to the lowest. At the very instant that a man decides to enter business, he may be forced into a game situation, as is shown by the recent experience of a Cornell honor graduate who applied for a job with a large company:

This applicant was given a psychological test which included the statement, "Of the following magazines, check any that you have read either regularly or from time to time, and double-check those which interest you most. *Reader's Digest, Time, Fortune, Saturday Evening Post, The New Republic, Life, Look, Ramparts, Newsweek, Business Week, U.S. News & World Report, The Nation, Playboy, Esquire, Harper's Sports Illustrated.*"

His tastes in reading were broad, and at one time or another he had read almost all of these magazines. He was a subscriber to *The New Republic*, an enthusiast for *Ramparts*, and an avid student of the pictures in *Playboy*. He was not sure whether his interest in *Playboy* would be held against him, but he had a shrewd suspicion that if he confessed to an interest in *Ramparts* and *The New Republic*, he would be thought a liberal, a radical, or at least an intellectual, and his chances of getting the job, which he needed, would greatly diminish. He therefore checked some of the more conservative magazines. Apparently it was a sound decision, for he got the job.

He had made a game player's decision, consistent with business ethics.

A similar case is that of a magazine space salesman who, owing to a merger, suddenly found himself out of a job:

This man was 58, and, in spite of a good record, his chance of getting a job elsewhere in business where youth is favored in hiring practice was not good. He was a vigorous, healthy man, and only a considerable amount of gray to his hair suggested his age. Before beginning this job search he touched up his hair with a black dye to confine the gray to his temples. He knew that the truth about his age might well come out in time, but he calculated that he could deal with that situation when it arose. He and his wife decided that he could easily pass for 45, and he so stated his age on his résumé.

This was a lie; yet within the accepted rules of the business game, no moral culpability attaches to it.

The Poker Analogy

We can learn a good deal about the nature of business by comparing it with poker. While both have a large element of chance, in the long run the winner is the man who plays with steady skill. In both games ultimate victory requires intimate knowledge of the rules, insight into the psychology of the other players, a bold front, a considerable amount of self-discipline, and the ability to respond swiftly and effectively to opportunities provided by chance.

No one expects poker to be played on the ethical principles preached in churches. In poker it is right and proper to bluff a friend out of the rewards of being dealt a good hand. A player feels no more than a slight twinge of sympathy, if that, when—with nothing better than a single ace in his hand—he strips a heavy loser, who holds a pair, of the rest of his chips. It was up to the other fellow to protect himself. In the words of an excellent poker player, former President Harry Truman, "If you can't stand the heat, stay out of the kitchen." If one shows mercy to a loser in poker, it is a personal gesture, divorced from the rules of the game.

Poker has its special ethics, and here I am not referring to rules against cheating. The man who keeps an ace up his sleeve or who marks the cards is more than unethical; he is a crook, and can be punished as such—kicked out of the game or, in the Old West, shot.

In contrast to the cheat, the unethical poker player is one who, while abiding by the letter of the rules, finds ways to put the other players at an unfair disadvantage. Perhaps he unnerves them with loud talk. Or he tries to get them drunk. Or he plays in cahoots with someone else at the table. Ethical poker players frown on such tactics.

Poker's own brand of ethics is different from the ethical ideals of civilized human relationships. The game calls for distrust of the other fellow. It ignores the claim of friendship. Cunning deception and concealment of one's strength and intentions, not kindness and open-heartedness, are vital in poker. No one thinks any the worse of poker on that account. And no one should think any the worse of the game of business because its standards of right and wrong differ from the prevailing traditions of morality in our society.

Discard the Golden Rule

This view of business is especially worrisome to people without much business experience. A minister of my acquaintance once protested that business cannot possibly function in our society unless it is based on the Judeo-Christian system of ethics. He told me:

I know some businessmen have supplied call girls to customers, but there are always a few

rotten apples in every barrel. That doesn't mean the rest of the fruit isn't sound. Surely the vast majority of businessmen are ethical. I myself am acquainted with many who adhere to strict codes of ethics based fundamentally on religious teachings. They contribute to good causes. They participate in community activities. They cooperate with other companies to improve working conditions in their industries. Certainly they are not indifferent to ethics.

That most businessmen are not indifferent to ethics in their private lives, everyone will agree. My point is that in their office lives they cease to be private citizens; they become game players who must be guided by a somewhat different set of ethical standards.

The point was forcefully made to me by a Midwestern executive who has given a good deal of thought to the question:

"So long as a businessman complies with the laws of the land and avoids telling malicious lies, he's ethical. If the law as written gives a man a wide-open chance to make a killing, he'd be a fool not to take advantage of it. If he doesn't, somebody else will. There's no obligation on him to stop and consider who is going to get hurt. If the law says he can do it, that's all the justification he needs. There's nothing unethical about that. It's just plain business sense."

This executive (call him Robbins) took the stand that even industrial espionage, which is frowned on by some businessmen, ought not to be considered unethical. He recalled a recent meeting of the National Industrial Conference Board where an authority on marketing made a speech in which he deplored the employment of spies by business organizations. More and more companies, he pointed out, find it cheaper to penetrate the secrets of competitors with concealed cameras and microphones or by bribing employees than to set up costly research and design departments of their own. A whole branch of the electronics industry has grown up with this trend, he continued, providing equipment to make industrial espionage easier.

Disturbing? The marketing expert found it so. But when it came to a remedy, he could only appeal to "respect for the golden rule." Robbins thought this a confession of defeat, believing that the golden rule, for all its value as an ideal for society, is simply not feasible as a guide for business. A good part of the time the businessman is trying to do unto others as he hopes others will *not* do unto him.[2] Robbins continued:

"Espionage of one kind or another has become so common in business that it's like taking a drink during Prohibition—it's not considered sinful. And we don't even have Prohibition where espionage is concerned; the law is very tolerant in this area. There's no more shame for a business that uses secret agents than there is for a nation. Bear in mind that there already is at least one large corporation—you can buy its stock over the counter—that makes millions by providing counterespionage service to industrial firms. Espionage in business is not an ethical problem; it's an established technique of business competition."

"We Don't Make the Laws"

Wherever we turn in business, we can perceive the sharp distinction between its ethical standards and those of the churches. Newspapers abound with sensational stories growing out of these distinctions:

- We read one day that Senator Philip A. Hart of Michigan has attacked food processors for deceptive packaging of numerous products.[3]
- The next day there is a Congressional to-do over Ralph Nader's book, *Unsafe at Any Speed*, which demonstrates that automobile companies for years have neglected the safety of car-owning families.[4]
- Then another Senator, Lee Metcalf of Montana, and journalist Vic Reinemer show in their book, *Overcharge*, the methods by which utility companies elude regulating government bodies to extract unduly large payments from users of electricity.[5]

These are merely dramatic instances of a prevailing condition; there is hardly a major industry at which a similar attack could not be aimed. Critics of business regard such behavior as unethical, but the companies concerned know that they are merely playing the business game.

Among the most respected of our business institutions are the insurance companies. A group of insurance executives meeting recently in New England was startled when their guest speaker, social critic Daniel Patrick Moynihan, roundly berated them for "unethical" practices. They had been guilty, Moynihan alleged, of using outdated actuarial tables to obtain unfairly high premiums. They habitually delayed the hearings of lawsuits against them in order to tire out the plaintiffs and win cheap settlements. In their employment policies they used ingenious devices to discriminate against certain minority groups.[6]

It was difficult for the audience to deny the validity of these charges. But these men were business game players. Their reaction to Moynihan's attack was much the same as that of the automobile manufacturers to Nader, of the utilities to Senator Metcalf, and of the food processors to Senator Hart. If the laws governing their businesses change, or if public opinion becomes clamorous, they will make the necessary adjustments. But morally they have in their view done nothing wrong. As long as they comply with the letter of the law, they are within their rights to operate their businesses as they see fit.

The small business is in the same position as the great corporation in this respect. For example:

- In 1967 a key manufacturer was accused of providing master keys for automobiles to mail-order customers, although it was obvious that some of the purchasers might be automobile thieves. His defense was plain and straightforward. If there was nothing in the law to prevent him from selling his keys to anyone who ordered them, it was not up to him to inquire as to his customers' motives. Why was it any worse, he insisted, for him to sell car keys by mail, than for mail-order houses to sell guns that might be used for murder? Until the law was changed, the key manufacturer could regard himself as being just as ethical as any other businessman by the rules of the business game.[7]

Violations of the ethical ideals of society are common in business, but they are not necessarily violations of business principles. Each year the Federal Trade Commission orders hundreds of companies, many of them of the first magnitude, to "cease and desist" from practices which, judged by ordinary standards, are of questionable morality but which are stoutly defended by the companies concerned.

In one case, a firm manufacturing a well-known mouthwash was accused of using a cheap form of alcohol possibly deleterious to health. The company's chief executive, after testifying in Washington, made this comment privately:

"We broke no law. We're in a highly competitive industry. If we're going to stay in business, we have to look for profit wherever the law permits. We don't make the laws. We obey them. Then why do we have to put up with this 'holier than thou' talk about ethics? It's sheer hypocrisy. We're not in business to promote ethics. Look at the cigarette companies, for God's sake! If the ethics aren't embodied in the laws by the men who made them, you can't expect businessmen to fill the lack. Why, a sudden submission to Christian ethics by businessmen would bring about the greatest economic upheaval in history."

It may be noted that the government failed to prove its case against him.

Cast Illusions Aside

Talk about ethics by businessmen is often a thin decorative coating over the hard realities of the game:

Once I listened to a speech by a young executive who pointed to a new industry code as proof that his company and its competitors were deeply aware of their responsibilities to society. It was a code of ethics, he said. The industry was going to police itself, to dissuade constituent companies from wrongdoing. His eyes shone with conviction and enthusiasm.

The same day there was a meeting in a hotel room where the industry's top executives met with the "czar" who was to administer the new code, a man of high repute. No one who was present could doubt their common attitude. In their eyes the code was designed primarily to forestall a move by the federal government to impose stern restrictions on the industry. They felt that the code would hamper them a good deal less than new federal laws would. It was, in other words, conceived as a protection for the industry, not for the public.

The young executive accepted the surface explanation of the code; these leaders, all experienced game players, did not deceive themselves for a moment about its purpose.

The illusion that business can afford to be guided by ethics as conceived in private life is often fostered by speeches and articles containing such phrases as, "It pays to be ethical," or, "Sound ethics is good business." Actually this is not an ethical position at all; it is a self-serving calculation in disguise. The speaker is really saying that in the long run a company can make more money if it does not antagonize competitors, suppliers, employees, and customers by squeezing them too hard. He is saying that over-sharp policies reduce ultimate gains. That is true, but it has nothing to do with ethics. The underlying attitude is much like that in the familiar story of the shopkeeper who finds an extra $20 bill in the cash register, debates with himself the ethical problem—should he tell his partner?—and finally decides to share the money because the gesture will give him an edge over the s.o.b. the next time they quarrel.

I think it is fair to sum up the prevailing attitude of businessmen on ethics as follows:

We live in what is probably the most competitive of the world's civilized societies. Our customs encourage a high degree of aggression as the individual's striving for success. Business is our main area of competition, and it has been ritualized into a game of strategy. The basic rules of the game have been set by the government, which attempts to detect and punish business frauds. But as long as a company does not transgress the rules of the game set by law, it has the legal right to shape its strategy without reference to anything but its profits. If it sets a long-term view of its profits, it will preserve amicable relations, so far as possible, with those with whom it deals. A wise businessman will not seek advantage to the point where he generates dangerous hostility among employees, competitors, customers, government, or the public at large. But decisions in this area are, in the final test, decisions of strategy, not of ethics.

The Individual and the Game

An individual within a company often finds it difficult to adjust to the requirements of the business game. He tries to preserve his private ethical standards in situations that call for time strategy. When he is obliged to carry out company policies that challenge his conception of himself as an ethical man, he suffers.

It disturbs him when he is ordered, for instance, to deny a raise to a man who deserves it, or fire an employee of long standing, to prepare advertising that he believes to be misleading, or conceal facts that he feels customers are entitled to know, to cheapen the quality of materials used in the manufacture of an established product, to sell as new a product that he knows to be rebuilt, to exaggerate the curative powers of a medicinal preparation, or to coerce dealers. There are some fortunate executives who, by the nature of their work and circumstances, never have to face problems of this kind. But in one form or another the ethical dilemma is felt sooner or later by most businessmen. Possibly the dilemma is most painful not when the company forces the action on the executive but when he originates it himself—that is, when he has taken or is contemplating a step which is of his own interest but which runs counter to his early moral conditioning. To illustrate:

- The manager of an export department, eager to show rising sales, is pressed by a big customer to provide invoices which, while containing no overt falsehood that would violate a U.S. law, are so worded that the customer may be able to evade certain taxes in his homeland.
- A company president finds that an aging executive, within a few years of retirement and his pension, is not as productive as formerly. Should he be kept on?

- The produce manager of a supermarket debates with himself whether to get rid of a lot of half-rotten tomatoes by including one, with its good side exposed, in every tomato six-pack.
- An accountant discovers that he has taken an improper deduction on his company's tax return and fears the consequences if he calls the matter to the president's attention, though he himself has done nothing illegal. Perhaps if he says nothing, no one will notice the error.
- A chief executive officer is asked by his directors to comment on a rumor that he owns stock in another company with which he has placed large orders. He could deny it, for the stock is in the name of his son-in-law and he has earlier formally instructed his son-in-law to sell the holding.

Temptations of this kind constantly arise in business. If an executive allows himself to be torn between a decision based on business considerations and one based on his private ethical code, he exposes himself to a grave psychological strain.

This is not to say that sound business strategy necessarily runs counter to ethical ideals. They may frequently coincide; and when they do, everyone is gratified. But the major tests of every move in business, as in all games of strategy, are legality and profit. A man who intends to be a winner in the business game must have a game player's attitude.

The business strategist's decisions must be as impersonal as those of a surgeon performing an operation—concentrating on objective and technique, and subordinating personal feelings. If the chief executive admits that his son-in-law owns the stock, it is because he stands to lose more if the fact comes out later than if he states it boldly and at once. If the supermarket manager orders the rotten tomatoes to be discarded, he does so to avoid an increase in consumer complaints and a loss of goodwill. The company president decides not to fire the elderly executive in the belief that the negative reaction of other employees would in the long run cost the company more than it would lose in keeping him and paying his pension.

All sensible businessmen prefer to be truthful, but they seldom feel inclined to tell the *whole* truth. In the business game truth-telling usually has to be kept within narrow limits if trouble is to be avoided. The point was neatly made a long time ago (in 1888) by one of John D. Rockefeller's associates, Paul Babcock, to Standard Oil Company executives who were about to testify before a government investigating committee: "Parry every question with answers which, while perfectly truthful, are evasive of *bottom* facts."[8] This was, is, and probably always will be regarded as wise and permissible business strategy.

For Office Use Only

An executive's family life can easily be dislocated if he fails to make a sharp distinction between the ethical systems of the home and the office—or if his wife does not grasp that distinction. Many a businessman who has remarked to his wife, "I had to let Jones go today" or "I had to admit to the boss that Jim has been goofing off lately," has been met with an indignant protest. "How could you do a thing like that? You know Jones is over 50 and will have a lot of trouble getting another job." Or, "You did that to Jim? With his wife ill and all the worry she's been having with the kids?"

If the executive insists that he had no choice because the profits of the company and his own security were involved, he may see a certain cool and ominous reappraisal in his wife's eyes. Many wives are not prepared to accept the fact that business operates with a special code of ethics. An illuminating illustration of this comes from a Southern sales executive who related a conversation he had had with his wife at a time when a hotly contested political campaign was being waged in their state:

"I made the mistake of telling her that I had had lunch with Colby, who gives me about half my business. Colby mentioned that his company had a stake in the election. Then he said, 'By the way, I'm treasurer of the citizens' committee for Lang. I'm collecting contributions. Can I count on you for a hundred dollars?'

"Well, there I was. I was opposed to Lang, but I knew Colby. If he withdrew his business I could be in a bad spot. So I just smiled and wrote out a check then and there. He thanks me, and we started to talk about this next order. Maybe he thought I shared his political views. If so, I wasn't going to lose any sleep over it.

"I should have had sense enough not to tell Mary about it. She hit the ceiling. She said she was disappointed in me. She said I hadn't acted like a man, that I should have stood up to Colby.

"I said, 'Look, it was an either-or situation. I had to do it or risk losing the business.

"She came back at me with, 'I don't believe it. You could have been honest with him. You could have said that you didn't feel you ought to contribute to a campaign for a man you weren't going to vote for. I'm sure he would have understood.'

"I said, 'Mary, you're a wonderful woman but you're way off the track. Do you know what would have happened if I had said that? Colby would have smiled and said, "Oh, I didn't realize. Forget it." But in his eyes from that moment I would be an oddball, maybe a bit of a radical. He would have listened to me talk about his order and would have promised to give it consideration. After that I wouldn't hear from him for a week. Then I would telephone and learn from his secretary that he wasn't yet ready to place the order. And in about a month I would hear through the grapevine that he was giving his business to another company. A month after that I'd be out of a job.'

"She was silent for a while. Then she said, 'Tom, something is wrong with business when a man is forced to choose between his family's security and his moral obligation to himself. It's easy for me to say you should have stood up to him—but if you had, you might have felt you were betraying me and the kids. I'm sorry that you did it, Tom, but I can't blame you. Something is wrong with business!"

This wife saw the problem in terms of man's obligation as conceived in private life; her husband saw it as a matter of game strategy. As a player in a weak position, he felt that he could not afford to indulge an ethical sentiment that might have cost him his seat at the table.

Playing to Win

Some men might challenge the Colbys of business—might accept serious setbacks to their business careers rather than risk a feeling of moral cowardice. They merit our respect—but as private individuals, not businessmen. When the skillful player of the business game is compelled to submit to unfair pressure, he does not investigate himself for moral weakness. Instead, he strives to put himself into a strong position where he can defend himself against such pressures in the future without loss.

If a man plans to take a seat in the business game, he owes it to himself to master the principles by which the game is played, including a special ethical outlook. He can then hardly fail to recognize that an occasional bluff may well be justified in terms of the game's ethics and warranted in terms of economic necessity. Once he clears his mind on this point, he is in a good position to match his strategy against that of the other players. He can then determine objectively whether a bluff in a given situation has a good chance of succeeding and can decide when and how to bluff, without a feeling of ethical transgression.

To be a winner, a man must play to win. This does not mean that he must be ruthless, cruel, harsh, or treacherous. On the contrary, the better his reputation for integrity, honesty, and decency, the better his chances of victory will be in the long run. But from time to time every businessman, like every poker player, is offered a choice between certain loss or bluffing within the legal rules of the game. If he is not resigned to losing, if he wants to rise in his company and industry, then in such a crisis he will bluff—and bluff hard.

Every now and then one meets a successful businessman who has conveniently forgotten the small or large deceptions that he practiced on his way to fortune. "God gave me my money," old John D. Rockefeller once piously told a Sunday school class. It would be a rare tycoon in our time who would risk the horse laugh with which such a remark would be greeted.

In the last third of the twentieth century even children are aware that if a man has become prosperous in business, he has sometimes departed from the strict truth in order to overcome obstacles or has practiced the more subtle deceptions of the half-truth or the misleading omission. Whatever the form of the bluff, it is an integral part of the game, and the executive who does not master its techniques is not likely to accumulate much money or power.

Notes

[1]*The New York Times*, March 9, 1967.
[2]See Bruce D. Henderson, "Brinkmanship in Business," HBR March-April 1967, 49.
[3]*The New York Times*, November 21, 1966.
[4]New York, Grossman Publishers, Inc., 1965.
[5]New York, David McKay Company, Inc., 1967.
[6]*The New York Times*, January 17, 1967.
[7]Cited by Ralph Nader in "Business Crime," *The New Republic*, July 1, 1967, p. 7.
[8]Babcock in a memorandum to Rockefeller (Rockefeller Archives).

Questions for Discussion:

1. Do you agree with the executive's statement that "a sudden submission to Christian ethics would produce the greatest economic upheaval in history"? What do you think he means by that statement?
2. How do you evaluate Carr's analogy of business to a poker game, with its own distinct set of rules?

Why Be Honest If Honesty Doesn't Pay?

Amar Bhide and Howard H. Stevenson

Harvard Business Review (September–October 1990): 121–29. Copyright © 1990.

Business men and women keep their word because they want to, not because honesty pays.

We bet on the rational case for trust. Economists, ethicists, and business sages had persuaded us that honesty is the best policy, but their evidence seemed weak. Through extensive interviews we hoped to find data that would support their theories and thus, perhaps, encourage higher standards of business behavior.

To our surprise, our pet theories failed to stand up. Treachery, we found, can pay. There is no compelling economic reason to tell the truth or keep one's word—punishment for the treacherous in the real world is neither swift nor sure.

Honesty is, in fact, primarily a moral choice. Businesspeople do tell themselves that, in the long run, they will do well by doing good. But there is little factual or logical basis for this conviction. Without values, without a basic preference for right over wrong, trust based on such self-delusion would crumble in the face of temptation.

Most of us choose virtue because we want to believe in ourselves and have others respect and believe in us. When push comes to shove, hard-headed business-folk usually ignore (or fudge) their dollars-and-cents calculations in order to keep their word.

And for this, we should be happy. We can be proud of a system in which people are honest because they want to be, not because they have to be. Materially, too, trust based on morality provides great advantages. It allows us to join in great and exciting enterprises that we could never undertake if we relied on economic incentives alone.

Economists and game theorists tell us that trust is enforced in the marketplace through retaliation and reputation. If you violate a trust, your victim is apt to seek revenge and others are likely to stop doing business with you, at least under favorable terms. A man or woman with a reputation for fair dealing will prosper. Therefore, profit maximizers are honest.

This sounds plausible enough until you look for concrete examples. Cases that apparently demonstrate the awful consequences of abusing trust turn out to be few and weak, while evidence that treachery can pay seems compelling.

The moralists' standard tale recounts how E. F. Hutton was brought down by its check-kiting fraud.[1] Hutton, once the second largest broker in the nation, never recovered from the blow to its reputation and finances and was forced to sell out to Shearson.

Exxon's Valdez disaster is another celebrated example. Exxon and seven other oil companies persuaded the town of Valdez to accept a tanker terminal by claiming that a major spill was "highly unlikely." Their 1,800-page contingency plan ensured that any spill would be controlled within hours. In fact, when Exxon's supertanker spewed forth over 240,000 barrels of oil, the equipment promised in the cleanup plan was not available. The cost? According to recent (and still rising) estimates, Exxon's costs could exceed $2 billion, and the industry faces severe restrictions on its operations in Alaska.

But what do these fables prove? Check-kiting was only one manifestation of the widespread mismanagement that plagued Hutton and ultimately caused its demise. Incompetently run companies going under is not news. Exxon's under-preparedness was expensive, but many decisions turn out badly. Considering the low probability of a spill, was skimping on the promised cleanup equipment really a bad business decision at the time it was taken?

More damaging to the moralists' position is the wealth of evidence against trust. Compared with the few ambiguous tales of treachery punished, we can find numerous stories in which deceit was unquestionably rewarded.

Philippe Kahn, in an interview with *Inc.* magazine, described with apparent relish how his company, Borland International, got its start by deceiving an ad salesman for *BYTE* magazine.

Inc.: The story goes that Borland was launched by a single ad, without which he wouldn't be sitting here talking about the company. How much of that is apocryphal?

Kahn: It's true: one full-page ad in the November 1983 issue of *BYTE* magazine got the company running. If it had failed, I would have had nowhere else to go.

Inc.: If you were so broke, how did you pay for the ad?

Kahn: Let's put it that we convinced the salesman to give us terms. We wanted to appear only in *BYTE*—not any of the other microcomputer magazines—because *BYTE* is for programmers, and that's who we wanted to reach. But we couldn't afford it. We figured the only way was somehow to convince them to extend us credit terms.

Inc.: And they did?

Kahn: Well, they didn't *offer.* What we did was, before the ad salesman came in—we existed in two small rooms, but I had hired extra people so we would look like a busy, venture-packed company—we prepared a chart with what we pretended was our media plan for the computer magazines. On the chart we had *BYTE* crossed out. When the salesman arrived, we made sure the phones were ringing and the extras were scurrying around. Here was this chart he thought he wasn't supposed to see, so I pushed it out of the way. He said, "Hold on, can we get you in *BYTE*?"

I said, "We don't really want to be in your book, it's not the right audience for us." "You've got to try," he pleaded. I said, "Frankly, our media plan is done, and we can't afford it." So he offered good terms, if only we'd let him run it just once. We expected we'd sell maybe $20,000 worth of software and at least pay for the ad. We sold $150,000 worth. Looking back now, it's a funny story; then it was a big risk.[2]

Further evidence comes from professional sports. In our study, one respondent cited the case of Rick Pitino, who had recently announced his decision to leave as coach of the New York Knicks basketball team with over three years left on his contract. Pitino left, the respondent wrote, "to coach the University of Kentucky (a school of higher learning, that like many others, is a party in breaking contracts)." Pitino was quoted in the *New York Times* the week before as saying that he never broke a contract. But he's 32 years old and has had five jobs. What he neglected to say is that he's never completed a contract. The schools always let him run out, as they don't want an unhappy coach.

"The same thing is done by professional athletes every year. They sign a long-term contract and after one good year, they threaten to quit unless the contract's renegotiated. The stupidity of it all is that they get their way."

Compared with the ambiguity of the Hutton and Exxon cases, the clear causality in the Kahn and Pitino cases is striking. Deceiving the *BYTE* salesman was crucial to Kahn's success. Without subterfuge, Borland International would almost certainly have folded. And there is a hard dollar number (with lots of zeros in it) that professional athletes and coaches gain when they shed a contract.

What of the long term? Does treachery eventually get punished? Nothing in the record suggests it does. Many of today's blue chip companies were put together at the turn of the century under circumstances approaching securities fraud. The robber barons who promoted them enjoyed great material rewards at the time—and their fortunes survived several generations. The Industrial Revolution did not make entirely obsolete Machiavelli's observation, "Men seldom rise from low condition to high rank without employing either force or fraud."[3]

Power can be an effective substitute for trust. In theory, Kahn and Coach Pitino should suffer the consequences of their deceits and incomplete contracts: scorned by its victims and a just society, Borland shouldn't be able to blow a whistle. But they continue to prosper. Why do reputation and retaliation fail as mechanisms for enforcing trust?

Power can be an effective substitute for trust.

Power—the ability to do others great harm or great good—can induce widespread amnesia, it appears. Borland International's large ad budget commands due respect. Its early deceit is remembered, if at all, as an amusing prank. Pitino's record for winning basketball games wipes out his record for abandoning teams in midstream.

Prestigious New York department stores, several of our respondents told us, cavalierly break promises to suppliers:

"You send the department store an invoice for $55,000 and they send you $38,000. If you question it they say, 'Here is an $11,000 penalty for being two days late; here is the transportation tax and a dockage fee.... You didn't follow our shipping instructions, Clause 42, Section 3C. You used the wrong carrier.' And half the time they call the order in and send the 600-page confirming document later, and they say you didn't follow our order."

"Department stores are horrible! Financial types have taken control, the merchants are out. The guy who keeps beating you down goes to his boss at the end of the year and says 'Look at the kind of rebates I got on freight reduction— $482,000. I delayed payments an average of 22 days from my predecessor at this kind of amount, and this is what I saved.'"

Nevertheless, suppliers still court their tormentors' orders.

"Don't tell me that department stores will go out of business because they treat their suppliers like that! I don't believe that at all. They have too much power—they screw one guy, and guys are waiting in line to take a shot at them again."

Heroic resistance to an oppressive power is the province of the students at Tiananmen Square, not the business-folk in the capitalist societies the students risk their lives to emulate. Businesspeople do not stand on principle when it comes to dealing with abusers of power and trust. You have to adjust, we were told. If we dealt only with customers who share our ethical values, we would be out of business.

A real estate developer we interviewed was blunt:

People are really whores. They will do business with someone they know they can't trust if it suits their convenience. They may tell their lawyers: "Be careful, he's dishonest; he's not reliable and he will try to get out of the contract if something happens." But those two do business with each other.... I've done transactions with people knowing that they were horrible and knowing that I'd never talk to them. But the deal was so good, I just accepted it, did the best I could, and had the lawyers make triply sure that everything was covered.

Sometimes the powerful leave others no choice. The auto parts supplier has to play ball with the Big Three, no matter how badly he or she has been treated in the past or expects to be treated in the future. Suppliers of fashion goods believe they absolutely have to take a chance on abusive department stores. Power here totally replaces trust.

Usually, though, power isn't quite that absolute, and some degree of trust is a necessary ingredient in business relationships. Pitino has demonstrated remarkable abilities in turning around basketball programs, but he isn't the only coach available for hire. Borland International's business is nice to have, but it can't make or break a computer magazine. Nevertheless, even those with limited power can live down a poor record of trustworthiness. Cognitive inertia—the tendency to search for data that confirm one's beliefs and to avoid facts that might refute them—is one reason why.

To illustrate, consider the angry letters the mail fraud unit of the U.S. Post Office gets every year from the victims of the fake charities it exposes. Apparently donors are annoyed that they can't keep sending contributions to a cause they believed in. They want to avoid information that says they have trusted a fraud.

When the expected reward is substantial and avoidance becomes really strong, reference checking goes out the window. In the eyes of people blinded by greed, the most tarnished reputations shine brightly.

Many a commodity broker's yacht has been financed by cleaning out one customer after another. Each new doctor or dentist who is promised the moon is unaware of and uninterested in his or her predecessor's fate. Such investors want to believe in the fabulous returns the broker has promised. They don't want references or other reality checks that would disturb the dreams they have built on sand. Thus can the retail commodity brokerage business flourish, even though knowledgeable sources maintain that it wipes out the capital of 70% of its customers every year.

The search for data that confirm wishful thinking is not restricted to naive medical practitioners dabbling in pork bellies. The *Wall Street Journal* recently detailed how a 32-year-old conglomerateur perpetrated a gigantic fraud on sophisticated financial institutions such as Citibank, the Bank of New England, and a host of Wall Street firms. A Salomon Brothers team that conducted due diligence on the wunderkind pronounced him highly moral and ethical. A few months later—

Even with a fully disclosed public record of bad faith, hard-nosed businesspeople will still try to find reasons to trust. Like the proverbial "other woman," they'll reason, "It's not his fault." And so it comes to pass that Oscar Wyatt's Coastal Corporation can walk away from its gas-supply contracts;[4] then, with the consequent lawsuits not yet settled, issue billions of dollars of junk bonds. Lured by high yields, junk bond investors choose to believe that their relationship will be different: Wyatt *had* to break his contracts when energy prices rose; and a junk bond is so much more, well, *binding* than a mere supply contract.

Similarly, we can imagine, every new Pitino employer believes the last has done Pitino wrong. Their relationship will last forever.

Ambiguity and complexity can also take the edge off reputational enforcement. When we trust others to keep their word, we simultaneously rely on their integrity, native ability, and favorable external circumstances. So when a trust appears to be breached, there can be so much ambiguity that even the aggrieved parties cannot apprehend what happened. Was the breach due to bad faith, incompetence, or circumstances that made it impossible to perform as promised? No one knows. Yet without such knowledge, we cannot determine in what respect someone has proved untrustworthy: basic integrity, susceptibility to temptation, or realism in making promises.

The following example, in which we hear the buyer of a company who was taken in by the seller's representations, is instructive:

"The seller said: 'We have a technology that is going to be here for a long time. We own the market.' We liked this guy so much, it was funny. He's in the local area, he knew my father. He's a great guy to talk to, with all sorts of stories.

"He managed to fool us, our banks, and a mezzanine lender, and he ended up doing quite well on the deal. Then the company went on the skids. The funny thing is, afterwards he bought the business back from us, put a substantial amount of his own capital in, and still has not turned it around. I'm just not sure what was going on.

"I guess he believed his own story and believed it so much that he bought the business back. He was independently wealthy from another sale anyway, and I think he wanted to prove that he was a great businessman and that we just screwed the business up. If he was a charlatan, why would he have cared?"

Where even victims have difficulty assessing whether and to what extent someone has broken a trust, it is not surprising that it can be practically impossible for a third party to judge.

That difficulty is compounded by the ambiguity of communication. Aggrieved parties may underplay or hide past unpleasantness out of embarrassment or fear of lawsuits. Or they may exaggerate others' villainies and their own blamelessness. So unless the victims themselves can be trusted to be utterly honest and objective, judgments based on their experiences become unreliable and the accuracy of the alleged transgressor's reputation unknowable.

Businesspeople learn not to get hung up about other people's pasts.

A final factor protecting the treacherous from their reputations is that it usually pays to take people at face value. Businesspeople learn over time that "innocent until proven guilty" is a good working rule and that it is really not worth getting hung up about other people's pasts.

Assuming that others are trustworthy, at least in their initial intentions, *is* a sensible policy. The average borrower does not plan million-dollar scams, most coaches do try to complete their contracts, and most buyers don't "forget" about their suppliers' bills or make up reasons for imposing penalties.

Even our cynical real estate developer told us:

"By and large, most people are intrinsically honest. It's just the tails, the ends of the bell-shaped curve, that are dishonest in any industry, in any area. So it's just a question of tolerating them."

Another respondent concurred:

"I tend to take people at face value until proven otherwise, and more often than not, that works. It doesn't work with a blackguard and a scoundrel, but how many total blackguards and scoundrels are there?"

Mistrust can be a self-fulfilling prophecy. People aren't exclusively saints or sinners; few adhere to an absolute moral code. Most respond to circumstances, and their integrity and trustworthiness can depend as much on how they are treated as on their basic character. Initiating a relationship assuming that the other party is going to try to get you may induce him or her to do exactly that.

Overlooking past lapses can make good business sense too. People and companies do change. It is more than likely that once Borland International got off the ground, Kahn never pulled a fast one on an ad salesman again. Today's model citizen may be yesterday's sharp trader or robber baron.

Trust breakers are not only unhindered by bad reputations, they are also usually spared retaliation by parties they injure. Many of the same factors apply. Power, for example: attacking a more powerful transgressor is considered foolhardy.

"It depends on the scale of the pecking order," we were told. "If you are a seller and your customer breaks promises, by and large you don't retaliate. And if you are an employee and your employer breaks promises, you usually don't retaliate either."

Where power doesn't protect against retaliation, convenience and cognitive inertia often do. Getting even can be expensive; even thinking about broken trusts can be debilitating. "Forget and move on" seems to be the motto of the business world.

Businesspeople consider retaliation a wasteful distraction because they have a lot of projects in hand and constantly expect to find new opportunities to pursue. The loss suffered through any individual breach of trust is therefore relatively small, and revenge is regarded as a distraction from other, more promising activities.

Retaliation is a luxury you can't afford, respondents told us.

"You can't get obsessed with getting even. It will take away from everything else. You will take it out on the kids at home, and you will take it out on your wife. You will do lousy business."

"It's a realization that comes with age: retaliation is a double loss. First you lose your money; now you're losing time."

"Bite me once, it is your fault; bite me twice, my fault. . . . But bite me twice, and I won't have anything to do with you, and I'm not going to bite back because I have better things to do with my life. I'm not going to litigate just for the pleasure of getting even with you."

Only those who have their best years behind them and see their life's work threatened actively seek to retaliate. In general, our interviews suggested, businesspeople would rather switch than fight. An employee caught cheating on expenses is quietly let go. Customers who are always cutting corners on payments are, if practicable, dropped. No fuss, no muss.

Our interviewees also seemed remarkably willing to forget injuries and to repair broken relationships. A supplier is dropped, an employee or sales rep is let go. Then months or years later the parties try again, invoking some real or imaginary change of circumstances or heart. "The employee was under great personal strain." "The company's salesman exceeded his brief." "The company is under new management." Convenience and cognitive inertia seem to foster many second chances.

What about the supposed benefits of retaliation? Game theorists argue that retaliation sends a signal that you are not to be toyed with. This signal, we believe, has some value when harm is suffered outside a trusting relationship: in cases of patent infringement or software piracy, for example. But when a close trusting relationship exists, as it does, say, with an employee, the inevitable ambiguity about who was at fault often distorts the signal retaliation sends. Without convincing proof of one-sided fault, the retaliator may get a reputation for vindictiveness and scare even honorable men and women away from establishing close relationships.

Even the cathartic satisfaction of getting even seems limited. Avenging lost honor is passé, at least in business dealings. Unlike Shakespeare's Venetian merchant, the modern businessperson isn't interested in exacting revenge for its own sake and, in fact, considers thirsting for retribution unprofessional and irresponsible.

"There is such a complete identification in my mind between my company's best interests and what I want to do that I am not going to permit anything official out of spite. If I can't rationalize [retaliation] and run it through my computer brain, it will be relegated to my diary and won't be a company action."

> **"Retaliation is a double loss. First you lose your money; then you lose your time."**

We would be guilty of gross exaggeration if we claimed that honesty has no value or that treachery is never punished. Trustworthy behavior does provide protection against the loss of power and against invisible sniping. But these protections are intangible, and their dollars-and-cents value does not make a compelling case for trustworthiness.

A good track record can protect against the loss of power. What if you stop being a winning coach or your software doesn't sell anymore? Long-suppressed memories of past abuses may then come to the fore, past victims may gang up to get you.

A deal maker cited the fate of an investment bank that was once the only source of financing for certain kinds of transactions.

"They always had a reputation for being people who would outline the terms of the deal and then change them when it got down to the closing. The industry knew that this is what you had to expect; our people had no choice. Now that the bank has run into legal problems and there are other sources of funds, people are flocking elsewhere. At the first opportunity to desert, people did—and with a certain amount of glee. They are getting no goodwill benefit from their client base because when they were holding all the cards they screwed everybody."

Another entrepreneur ascribed his longevity to his reputation for trustworthiness:

"The most important reason for our success is the quality of my [product] line. But we wouldn't have survived without my integrity because our lines weren't always very successful. There are parabola curves in all businesses, and people still supported me, even though we had a low, because they believed in me."

Trustworthiness may also provide immediate protection against invisible sniping. When the abuse of power banishes trust, the victims often try to get their own back in ways that are not visible to the abuser: "I'm not in business just to make a profit. If a client tries to jerk me around, I mark up my fees." "The way to get even with a large company is to sell more to them."

On occasion, sniping can threaten the power it rebels against. The highhandedness of department stores, for example, has created a new class of competitors, the deep discounter of designer apparel.

"Ordinarily, manufacturers don't like to sell their goods at throwaway prices to people like us," says one such discounter. "But our business has thrived because the department stores have been systematically screwing their suppliers, especially after all those leveraged buyouts. At the same time, the manufacturers have learned that we treat them right. We scrupulously keep our promises. We pay when we say we'll pay. If they ask us not to advertise a certain item in a certain area, we don't. If they make an honest mistake in a shipment, we won't penalize them.

"The department stores have tried to start subsidiaries to compete with us, but they don't understand the discount business. Anyone can set up an outlet. What really matters is the trust of the suppliers."

How can you quantify the financial repercussions when suppliers you have abused ship hot items to your competitors first?

Neither of these benefits can be factored easily into a rational business analysis of whether to lie or keep a promise. Sniping is invisible; the sniper will only take shots that you cannot measure or see. How could you possibly quantify the financial repercussions when suppliers you have abused refuse your telephone orders or ship hot items to your competitors first?

Assessing the value of protection against the loss of power is even more incalculable. It is almost as difficult to anticipate the nature of divine retribution as it is to assess the possibility that at some unknown time in the future your fortunes *may* turn, whereupon others *may* seek to cause you some unspecified harm. With all these unknowns and unknowables, surely the murky future costs don't stand a chance against the certain and immediate financial benefits from breaking an inconvenient promise. The net present values, at any reasonable discount rate, must work against honoring obligations.

Given all this, we might expect breaches of trust to be rampant. In fact, although most businesspeople are not so principled as to boycott powerful trust breakers, they do try to keep their own word most of the time. Even allowing for convenient forgetfulness, we cannot help being swayed by comments like this:

"I've been in this business for 40 years. I've sold two companies; I've gone public myself and have done all kinds of dealings, so I'm not a babe in the woods, OK? But I can't think of one situation where people took advantage of me. I think that when I was young and naive about many things, I may have been underpaid for what my work was, but that was a learning experience."

One reason treachery doesn't swamp us is that people rationalize constancy by exaggerating its economic value.

"Costs have been going up, and it will cost me a million dollars to complete this job. But if I don't, my name will be mud and no one will do business with me again."

"If I sell this chemical at an extortionate price when there is a shortage, I will make a killing. But if I charge my customers the list price, they will do the right thing by me when there is a glut."

Just as those who trust find reasons for the risks they want to run, those who are called on to keep a difficult promise cast around for justification even when the hard numbers point the other way. Trustworthiness has attained the status of "strategic focus" and "sustainable competitive advantage" in business folklore—a plausible (if undocumented) touchstone of long-term economic value.

But why has it taken root? Why do business men and women want to believe that trustworthiness pays, disregarding considerable evidence to the contrary? The answer lies firmly in the realm of social and moral behavior, not in finance.

The businesspeople we interviewed set great store on the regard of their family, friends, and the community at large. They valued their reputations, not for some nebulous financial gain but because they took pride in their good names. Even more important, since outsiders cannot easily judge trustworthiness, businesspeople seem guided by their inner voices, by their consciences. When we cited examples to our interviewees in which treachery had apparently paid, we heard responses like:

"It doesn't matter how much money they made. Right is right and wrong is wrong."

"Is that important? They may be rich in dollars and very poor in their own sense of values and what life is about. I cannot judge anybody by the dollars; I judge them by their deeds and how they react."

"I can only really speak for myself, and to me, my word is the most important thing in my life and my credibility as an individual is paramount. All the other success we have had is secondary."

The importance of moral and social motives in business cannot be overemphasized. A selective memory, a careful screening of the facts may help sustain the fiction of profitable virtue, but the fundamental basis of trust is moral. We keep promises because we believe it is right to do so, not because it is good business. Cynics may dismiss the sentiments we heard as posturing, and it is true that performance often falls short of aspiration. But we can find no other way than conscience to explain why trust is the basis for so many relationships.

At first, these findings distressed us. A world in which treachery pays because the average businessperson won't fight abusive power and tolerates dishonesty? Surely that wasn't right or efficient, and the system needed to be fixed! On further reflection, however, we concluded that this system was fine, both from a moral and a material point of view.

The moral advantages are simple. Concepts of trust and, more broadly, of virtue would be empty if bad faith and wickedness were not financially rewarding. If wealth naturally followed straight dealing, we would only need to speak about con-

flicts between the long term and the short, stupidity and wisdom, high discount rates and low. We would worry only about others' good sense, not about their integrity. It is the very absence of predictable financial reward that makes honesty a moral quality we hold dear.

Trust based on morality rather than self-interest also provides a great economic benefit. Consider the alternative, where trust is maintained by fear.

A world in which the untrustworthy face uncertain retribution is a small world where everyone knows (and keeps a close eye on!) everyone else. A village, really, deeply suspicious not only of commodities brokers but also of all strangers, immigrants, and innovators.

No shades or ambiguities exist here. The inhabitants trust each other only in transactions in which responsibilities are fully specified—"deliver the diamonds to Point A, bring back cash"—and breaches of trust are clear. They do not take chances on schemes that might fail through the tangled strands of bad faith, incompetence, overoptimism, or plain bad luck.

A dark pessimism pervades this world. Opportunities look scarce and setbacks final. "You can't afford to be taken in even once" is the operating principle. "So when in doubt, don't."

In this world, there are no second chances either. A convicted felon like Thomas Watson, Sr. would never be permitted to create an IBM. A Federal Express would never again be extended credit after an early default on its loan agreements. The rules are clear: an eye for an eye and a tooth for a tooth. Kill or be killed.

Little, closed, tit-for-tat worlds do exist. Trust is self-reinforcing because punishment for broken promises is swift—in price-fixing rings, loan-sharking operations, legislative log rolling, and the mutually assured destruction of nuclear deterrence. Exceed your quota and suffer a price war. Don't pay on time and your arm gets broken. Block my pork barrel project and I'll kill yours. Attack our cities and we'll obliterate yours.

At best such a world is stable and predictable. Contracts are honored and a man's word really does become his bond. In outcome, if not intent, moral standards are high, since no one enters into relationships of convenience with the untrustworthy. On the other hand, such a world resists all change, new ideas, and innovations. It is utterly inimical to entrepreneurship.

Fortunately, our world is full of trusting optimists—a Steve Jobs with no track record to speak of can start an Apple.

Fortunately, the larger world in which we live is less rigid. It is populated with trusting optimists who readily do business with strangers and innovators. A 26-year-old Steve Jobs with no track record to speak of or a 52-year-old Ray Kroc with nearly ten failures behind him can get support to start an Apple or a McDonald's. People are allowed to move from Maine to Montana or from plastics to baked goods without a lot of whys and wherefores.

Projects that require the integrity and ability of a large team and are subject to many market and technological risks can nonetheless attract enthusiastic support. Optimists focus more on the pot of gold at the end of the rainbow than on their ability to find and punish the guilty in case a failure occurs.

Our tolerance for broken promises encourages risk taking. Absent the fear of debtors' prison and the stigma of bankruptcy, entrepreneurs readily borrow the funds they need to grow.

Tolerance also allows resources to move out of enterprises that have outlived their functions. When the buggy whip manufacturer is forced out of business, we understand that some promises will have to be broken—promises that perhaps ought not to have been made. But adjustments to the automobile age are more easily accomplished if we don't demand full retribution for every breach of implicit and explicit contract.

Even unreconstructed scoundrels are tolerated in our world as long as they have something else to offer. The genius inventors, the visionary organizers, and the intrepid pioneers are not cast away merely because they cannot be trusted on all dimensions. We "adjust"—and allow great talent to offset moral frailty—because we know deep down that knaves and blackguards have contributed much to our progress. And this, perhaps unprincipled, tolerance facilitates a dynamic entrepreneurial economy.

Since ancient times, philosophers have contrasted a barbaric "state of nature" with a perfect, well-ordered society that has somehow tamed humankind's propensity toward force and fraud. Fortunately, we have created something that is neither Beirut nor Bucharest. We don't require honesty, but we honor and celebrate it. Like a kaleidoscope, we have order and change. We make beautiful, well-fitting relationships that we break and reform at every turn.

We should remember, however, that this third way works only as long as most of us live by an honorable moral compass. Since our trust isn't grounded in self-interest, it is fragile. And, indeed, we all know of organizations, industries, and even whole societies in which trust has given way either to a destructive free-for-all or to inflexible rules and bureaucracy. Only our individual wills, our determination to do what is right, whether or not it is profitable, save us from choosing between chaos and stagnation.

Notes

[1]The HBR Collection *Ethics in Practice* has six citations (Boston: Harvard Business School Press, 1989).

[2]"Management by Necessity," *Inc.*, March 1989, p. 33. Reprinted with permission. Copyright © 1989 by Goldhirsh Group, Inc., 38 Commercial Wharf, Boston, Mass. 02310.

[3]*The Discourses*, Chapter XIII, Book 2, Modern Library Edition, 1950.

[4]"In the early 1970s," reports *Forbes* (Toni Mack, "Profitable If Not Popular," May 30, 1988, 34), "Wyatt found himself squeezed between rising natural gas prices and low-priced contracts to supply gas to cities like San Antonio and Austin. His solution? Renege. He simply refused to honor the contract."

Questions for Discussion:

1. Do you agree with Bhide and Stevenson that honesty doesn't pay? Why or why not?
2. What do you think is the connection between good ethics and good business ("good business" being defined as profitability)?

Companies Are Discovering the Value of Ethics

Norman Bowie

USA Today Magazine (January 1998): 22–24. Copyright © 1998 Society for the Advancement of Education. Copyright © 2000 Gale Group.

Most discussion of business ethics focuses on ethics as a constraint on profit. From this view, ethics and profit are related inversely: the more ethical a business is, the less profitable it is; the more profitable, the less ethical. Certainly, there are times when doing the morally correct thing will reduce profits. Not using an "agent" to provide bribes when doing business abroad is one example. Nonetheless, the traditional characterization of an inverse relationship between ethics and profits is only part of the story at best. A more balanced view points out that there frequently is a positive relation between ethics and profits; normally, ethics enhances the bottom line, rather than diminishing it.

The best news is that the conventional cynical view about business ethics provides a money-making opportunity and can be the source of a competitive advantage. Other things being equal, a firm known for its high ethical standards can have an above-average profit. An auto repair shop known for its honesty is a busy and prosperous one.

Ethical behavior contributes to the bottom line by reducing the cost of business transactions, establishing trust among stakeholders, increasing the likelihood of successful teamwork, and preserving the social capital necessary for doing business.

First, an ethical firm reduces the cost of business transactions. For instance, most economic exchanges have a period of time between the payment for a good or service and delivery, or, conversely, a period of time between the delivery of a good or service and payment for it. This time gap can stand in the way of a profitable transaction. Perhaps the supplier will not deliver or the vendor will fail to pay. A small supplier is offered a large contract by a major manufacturer. Although one might think that the small supplier would be overjoyed by such an arrangement, it should be cautious. It can be held hostage by the much larger manufacturer, which can delay payment for the product or demand other concessions.

Recently, a number of large firms in the U.S. unilaterally announced an increase in the time that they would settle their accounts. Obviously, this fact makes future suppliers more reluctant to do business with these firms. The major manufacturer with a reputation for prompt payment will get the small supplier to provide the quality product. The major manufacturer that lacks a reputation for prompt payment will not.

Yet another illustration concerns the acceptability of checks as a means of payment. A seafood shop in Ocean City, Md., had the following notice posted on the wall: "We will not accept checks and here is why." Below the notice was a row of checks stamped "Insufficient funds." That seafood shop no longer would do business with those who wanted to pay by check.

There are vast regional differences in the acceptability of checks as a means of payment. In the Upper Midwest, they are accepted routinely. In most grocery stores and in some other businesses, the customer even may make the check out for an amount larger than the purchase and thus get both the purchase and some cash. On the East Coast, checks are not accepted routinely as a means of payment. Instead, credit cards are. Since most credit card sales represent additional costs, merchants in the Upper Midwest have lower costs of doing business than those merchants in other parts of the country.

Employee and customer theft is a major problem for business, as are shirking on the job and a declining work ethic. A culture of drug abuse exacerbates the problem. Business incurs great costs in dealing with these issues. Elaborate security systems are put into place. Employees are asked to submit to "honesty tests" and expensive drug screening.

Yet, businesspeople, along with most everyone else, recognize differences in the propensity of individuals to steal, take drugs, or shirk their responsibilities on the job. Again on a statistical basis, there are regional differences. During the 1980s, firms moved to the Upper Midwest despite the harsh climate and high taxes to take advantage of a workforce that had a high work ethic. Recently, the shift has been to Utah, a state with a large percentage of Mormons—a highly religious group that has a strong work ethic. Such examples are not limited to the U.S. In Budapest, Hungary, a large number of managers prefer to hire only those under the age of 30 because these younger employees are less likely to be infected by the bad work habits that existed under communism.

What these examples show is that those motivated by strong moral and religious values are less likely to behave opportunistically and, thus, will be more productive and more profitable. Employees and customers with the right values need less monitoring and fewer honesty and drug tests. Consequently, employers will try to hire people who statistically are more likely to be honest.

Ethical behavior builds trust, which increases the likelihood of profit. As a company builds trust, customers, employees, and suppliers are less likely to behave opportunistically. A reputation for trust will attract like-minded customers, employees, and suppliers. Thus, trust is reinforcing in a kind of virtuous circle.

Moreover, a firm characterized by high-trust stakeholder relationships is likely to have competitive advantages. If trust is defined as keeping one's word and not taking undue advantage (behaving opportunistically) when one has the capability of doing so, the competitive advantage gained by a trusting organization will be clear.

Human resource management will be very different in a trusting organization. The essential point is that trusting relationships change the nature of monitoring. In nontrusting relationships, the supervisor functions as a policeman; in trusting relationships, as a mentor, the way a professor functions with a doctoral student or a coach develops a young pitcher. The kind of monitoring a mentor does is very different from that which a policeman does. A mentoring relationship allows qualitative criteria and uses fewer quantitative measures, is less frequent, and requires less in the way of detail.

Lately, there has been much discussion about teamwork and about eliminating layers of management. Workers are to be "empowered"—i.e., more responsibility and discretion as the layers of management control wither away. If teamwork and empowerment are not to be empty rhetoric, the nature of supervision must be more of a mentoring than a policing type. Greater trust will be a key element in any cost savings that result from eliminating layers of management and the empowerment of employee teams.

Trust also reduces the amount of bias in forecasts and overstatement of need in budgetary requests. Nearly every person in a business organization has experience with the budget game: A number of budgetary units report to a higher authority that sets the budget for each unit. The authority asks what each of the units need. Each unit knows that there are not sufficient funds to meet all the needs; therefore, the requests of each unit will not be granted fully. Each unit then overstates its need so that the failure to meet the requests will not cause as much pain. As a result, the central authority engages in long costly negotiations with each unit to arrive at a figure that is fairly close to what each unit would have expected to receive. Transaction costs could have been reduced greatly if the information to the central budget authority had reflected true need more accurately. If the various units could agree to make accurate requests and trust one another to keep their promises, these traditional transaction costs could be slashed.

A more trusting organization could help American manufacturing enterprises overcome two disadvantages. Traditionally, the engineering team that designs a product does its work separately. Those who manufacture the product have little, if anything, to say about its design. As a result, some problems with a prototype do not appear until the manufacturing stage. Much time is lost as the prototype is redesigned to meet the requirements of mass production.

The sales unit of a firm and the manufacturing unit often work at cross-purposes. The sales force has incentives to sell as much of a product as it can. Indeed, the commission system is what provides the incentive. However, if quality is to be maintained and backlogged orders are to be kept to a minimum, sales must not exceed the ability of the manufacturing process to produce the goods in question. Given the commission system. there is no incentive for the sales staff to take these limitations into account and to cooperate with manufacturing to secure the optimal amount of sales at any given time.

As the result of Japanese competition, these defects have been recognized, and American companies have realized that there must be greater cooperation among units within the firm. Trust among the units and a supportive compensation scheme are required for greater cooperation. To build that trust, managers need to speak differently about other units in the firm than they do about its competitors. The unit that manufactures the product is not the enemy of the salesperson. Failure to understand that distinction undermines the trust needed to achieve a competitive advantage.

What holds true within a firm will continue to do so as various companies enter into joint ventures. With such cooperation among firms from different countries becoming increasingly common and successful, one would expect to see more joint ventures between corporations that have higher levels of trust. The rationale for this is fairly clear. If one member of the joint venture fails to keep its contract, behaves opportunistically, or provides a shoddy product or service, all parties will suffer. The unhappy customer will blame all alike. Thus, a trustworthy partner is the best partner in a business sense. Picking a moral partner may be the most important decision to be made when setting up a joint venture.

Finally, trust is needed for successful research and development. The rationale for this contention is based on the knowledge of the environment needed for creative thought, particularly scientific research. Some corporations have adopted a competitive strategy of introducing new products at such a rate that goods created in the last few years account for a certain percentage of the firm's sales. Such companies refuse to rest on their laurels.

How can such a strategy be achieved? There is considerable evidence that creative people are most productive in an environment with minimal monitoring and control. It is counterproductive to have laboratory scientists filling out weekly reports asking them what they discovered that week. Providing research scientists with the freedom and independence necessary to stimulate creative thinking requires a great deal of trust on the part of management. Firms with a culture of trust are likely to be more adaptive and innovative.

Yet another benefit of ethical behavior is that it provides a solution to what theorists call collective action problems. A collective action problem occurs when an obvious public good can not be achieved because it is not in the self-interest of any individual who is a part of the problem to take steps to resolve it. Thus, large cities throughout the world suffer from traffic congestion. All would benefit if many more people used public transportation. For any individual, though, the reduction in congestion resulting from his or her taking the bus is very small, while the inconvenience, especially given its imperceptible effect on congestion, is large. Therefore, this individual, and every other automobile owner, will tend to drive and traffic congestion will remain horrible.

There are many ways of tackling a collective action problem. One traditional means is to provide incentive so that the cost-benefit ratio is reversed. For instance, instituting tolls for cars that greatly increase the cost of driving to work would force drivers onto the bus or train.

Collective action problems exist in business as well. Assume that, in certain situations, production of a good or service requires a team effort and that the individual contribution of each team member can not be isolated and measured. Any team member who acts in a purely self-interested manner would free ride off the others. This free-riding phenomenon explains why many hard-working students complain bitterly about group projects that are graded on the productivity of the group.

Indeed, if enough members free ride, the gain in potential productivity from teamwork would be lost. In such situations, the benefits of group activity are optimized only when there is no free riding. For that to occur, each member of the group must make a commitment not to free ride. This commitment is most likely in a moral community where the members are bound together by common values and mutual respect.

Social capital

A final benefit of ethical corporate behavior is that it preserves the social capital that makes a free market possible. A market system does not operate in a vacuum, but coexists with many other institutions in society, including the family, the church, and the political, criminal justice, and educational systems. Each of these institutions contributes toward making capitalism possible: The court system enforces contracts; the political system provides monetary stability; and the educational system trains future employees and prepares them for the workforce.

Corporate misconduct raises the cost and reduces the amount of social capital. The more businesspeople try to avoid the terms of their agreement, the greater the number of disputes that end up in court. More and more umpires are needed. When the environment is despoiled or misleading advertising occurs, the public demands more regulation. Increased governmental activity adds to the cost of government.

A market system needs moral capital as well. If capitalism is to be successful, there must be both within society and within capitalism a widespread acceptance of certain moral norms, such as truthtelling, bill-paying, and fair play. When these norms are perceived as being violated, a vicious circle begins. If other people will not play by the rules, then each person reasons there is no longer gain from following the rules. As more and more people abandon these moral forms, the social capital that makes market activity possible is depleted.

A major concern about Russia is whether the criminal element has gotten such a hold on business activity that capitalism becomes impossible. What some commentators refer to as "wild capitalism" is doomed to failure. Once again, ethical behavior contributes to the bottom line, but in this case to the bottom line of capitalism itself, rather than to the bottom line of an individual firm.

Some may object to this analysis. They might say that businesspeople should do the right thing because it is right, rather than because such actions contribute to the bottom line.

Philosophers are familiar with the hedonic paradox: "The more you consciously seek happiness, the less likely you are to find it." If you do not believe this, just get up some morning and resolve that every act will be done in order to achieve happiness. You soon will be miserable. Happiness is the result of successful achievement, but is not itself something you try to achieve. According to Aristotle, self-realization is what you try to achieve, and happiness is the result of achieving it.

Perhaps, to some extent, profits are like that. If your focus on them is excessive, you are less likely to achieve them. The conventional wisdom is that managers should focus on the bottom line. There is an obsession in America with quarterly reports—one that forces managers to focus on the short run, rather than the long run. If corporations took the moral point of view, they would focus on meeting the needs of their stakeholders. For instance, they might focus on providing secure work for employees and quality products for customers. If they did that, profits likely would follow.

Second, employees are very suspicious of management's motives when new concepts like empowerment or quality circles are introduced. If the employees think that these ideas are being implemented to increase profits, they often will attempt to sabotage them, even if the workers would be better off. Thus, quality circles and empowerment only can succeed if all those affected believe such practices are being introduced for the right reasons.

Third, media reports of corporate good works frequently are greeted with public scorn because the public is suspicious of the corporation's motives. "They are just trying to buy good will" is a phrase that is heard often. Corporate executives who really do act from ethical motives are frustrated when their motives are questioned. Yet, it is hard for the public to determine motives, which is why reputation, corporate character, and a record of altruistic acts are important. If Johnson & Johnson proclaims moral motives for what the pharmaceutical company does, it tends to be believed. The public remembers how Johnson & Johnson handled the Tylenol poisonings. Not only did the firm do the right thing—pulling the product from the market and repackaging it in a more secure manner—it did so for the right reason. Moreover, Johnson & Johnson profited as a result.

What of the future? All capitalist systems are not alike. Japanese capitalism differs from German capitalism and both differ from the American version. Which will be most successful in the next century? The answer depends on many factors. One is ethics because, as has been shown, ethical behavior can lower costs, increase productivity, and preserve the social capital that makes capitalism possible. It is in our national interest to ensure that American capitalism is a leader in ethics as well as in product development and cheap capital.

––––––

Dr. Bowie is Elmer L. Andersen Chair in Corporate Responsibility, University of Minnesota, Minneapolis.

Questions for Discussion:

1. Do you agree with Bowie that companies are taking ethics more seriously today? If so, what do you think accounts for this?
2. Do you think that "high-trust stakeholder relationships" make a company more competitive? Why or why not?

CASE STUDIES

Case 1.1: Borland's Brave Beginning

Philipe Kahn, the colorful former CEO and current chairman of Borland International built a powerful software company from the ground up with a series of brilliant business moves, including the 1991 acquisition of Ashton-Tate, one of the software industry's biggest companies, for $440 million. Until very recently, the company was extremely successful, culminating in the building of a palatial headquarters complex costing nearly $100 million. At one point Kahn even entertained thoughts of challenging Microsoft as the world's top software manufacturer.[3] While the company has recently fallen on hard times, its beginning is what interests us. Some would consider it morally questionable, while others would denote it as being "smart moves within the game."

In an interview with *Inc.* magazine, Kahn told the story of Borland's humble beginnings. Operating out of two small rooms and strapped for cash, he couldn't afford to place an ad in *BYTE* magazine, the best forum to reach his target market. In order to convince the ad salesman to extend credit terms, Kahn hired extra people to scurry around and made sure the phones were ringing so they would look busy. He prepared a media plan on a chart in which *BYTE* was crossed out, but he made sure the salesman "accidentally" saw the chart. When the salesman asked if they wanted to advertise in *BYTE*, Kahn replied that it was not the right audience and that they couldn't afford it. The salesman pleaded with him and eventually gave him good terms of credit. The ad ran once and sold $150,000 worth of software, launching a successful venture.[4]

3 Julie Pitta, "The Barbarian Steps Down," *Los Angeles Times*, 12 January 1995, D1.

4 "Managing by Necessity," *Inc.*, March 1989, 33.

Questions for Discussion:

1. Are Kahn's actions unethical in any way? Is this deception or just shrewd business sense at work? How would Carr and Bowie respond?

2. One could argue that it was the salesman's responsibility to check Kahn's financial documents and it is therefore his fault that he was lured into lending credit. Do you agree? What

would be the reasonable responsibilities of the salesman, according to the "rules of the game"?

3. Many would argue that everyone benefited and no one was hurt, thus the action was moral. Do you agree? Why or why not?

Case 1.2: Keeping Secrets

Rumors have been swirling among employees after officials of a major airplane manufacturing company announced that a significant number of employees will be receiving layoff notices in the coming weeks. The economic recession and the negative impact on the travel industry caused by the September 11 terrorist attacks have greatly reduced the number of commercial airplane orders, forcing the company to downsize.

While it is known that a specific number of employees will be laid off, the names of those who will be given notice are held in strict confidence. After the initial announcement, many employees have felt vulnerable and have been searching for employment at other firms. Given the status of the economy, jobs have been hard to find.

Only a few top executives, select members of the human resources department, and "group managers" know the names of those who have been targeted for layoff until the day the actual R.I.F. (reduction in force) notices are issued (three weeks from now). As a group manager whose department will be affected, you are one of the few people in the firm privy to the names on the list. Once the layoffs are announced, employees have roughly four to six weeks to finish their tasks and look for other employment.

The company has a policy of strict confidentiality when it comes to layoffs. When word has gotten out early in the past, some employees left early to take other positions, leaving the company in the lurch. A few employees even resorted to sabotage of company equipment and computers during their last weeks on the job to "get even."

Normally your contractual obligation to uphold confidentiality is not a problem. However, you currently find yourself in a difficult situation. Seeing the name of one of your employees, named John, on the list has made you somewhat depressed and wishing you could let him know his status ahead of time.

John is a computer systems analyst who has worked for the company for seven years. His area and level of expertise on his current project are critical to the company. If he were to leave early and not finish his tasks, your department would be hard pressed to finish the project according to schedule. This would result in substantial delays that could jeopardize future contracts with this particular client, a major airline, whose executives are already upset about delays in earlier stages of the project.

You and John have become close friends. In part, this is due to the fact that he is in a similar stage of life as you, in his mid-thirties and married with three children. Your daughters also play together on a soccer team, and your families have frequent social outings.

John and his wife Margie are about to welcome their fourth child into the world. At a soccer game one evening, John mentions that he has received an offer for employment by another company. "All things being equal, I would rather stay where I'm at. The pay and the commute are better," he states. "Knowing when the layoff announcement is coming, I tried to get more time to decide, but they need to fill the position. I need to let them know in a week. Do you think I should accept the position?" he states with a wink.

Understanding the level of confidentiality required by your position (and employment contract), you remain silent. John replies, "I know you can't say anything directly about the layoffs, but am I safe to assume that your 'non-response' is good news? Given our relationship over the years, you would probably at least warn me in a roundabout way if the news were the opposite, right? Besides, by giving me some indication, you would be doing much more good than harm. No one gets hurt if you let me know. Think of what I stand to lose if you don't tell me."

Questions for Discussion:

1. What will you do? Why?
2. Do you have to choose between confidentiality and loyalty to a friend?

COMMENTARY

Many businesspeople feel the acute and uneasy tension between the moral values that seem to permeate commercial dealings and the behavioral standards that should govern their lives in total. Indeed, the suspicion that economic success may actually *require* a compromise of values is one of the most troubling aspects of participating in business. Make honesty and/or compassion a central virtue of business, you may secretly fear, and you will find yourself (or your organization) at a great disadvantage. Situations such as the Borland case poignantly illustrate how such tensions may arise in the specific form of a trade-off between virtue (truth telling) and financially successful business strategy.

Yet an important question to ask is whether or not a case such as this accurately depicts the predominant ethos of business. In fact, there are good reasons to conclude that it does not and that a somewhat more optimistic account of the moral character of economic life is more accurate. Contrary to popular belief, trust and honesty are probably more the norms of business practice than the exceptions, as authors Bhide and Stevenson conclude in "Why Be Honest If Honesty Doesn't Pay?"

While a natural extension of their conclusion might be that good ethics *is* good business, and that at times morally sound behavior works to one's advantage, to see a perfect relationship here would be overstating the case. We are firmly convinced, however, that although it may be difficult, Christian businesspeople can and should live with a unified set of ethical guidelines. They can do so with the confidence that "success" will not be compromised in the process, but only if a broader definition of the term is used.

Albert Carr obviously sees things quite differently, arguing that poker is a fitting analogy for business. On the issue of deception, he is correct in observing that poker should be judged by its own set of rules and that "bluffing" is a morally acceptable strategy. This is the case because each person who plays poker is aware of the rules. However, Carr falls short in not asking whether or not the same can be said for business.

The game analogy is not a good fit for commerce because, unlike poker, not all participants or those who are affected are "at the table" by choice. Take for example, consumers who are innocently harmed by dangerous products, or those who are swindled out of their retirement savings. Furthermore, even if everyone participates by choice, not all of the "players" are aware of, nor can they reasonably be expected to be aware of, the operative rules.

Bluffing

Borland's launch is a nice story; however, former CEO Phillipe Kahn's actions illustrate the inadequacy of Carr's poker analogy for business. Although the outcome was "good" for everyone, judging the morality of a decision or action based on consequences alone is inadequate. If the outcome had been different and Borland could not pay for the space, there would be nothing endearing about the tale at all. *BYTE* would have lost $20,000, and the salesman would have suffered some consequences too. While these are arguably small losses, it is the principle that is at stake.

In probing deeper, one has to wonder if success at deception, even on a small scale, is truly beneficial, especially in the long term. Will an even more desperate situation lead to more lies but on a grander scale? Will employees adhere to sound ethics when a story about how the company's founder behaved circulates as a part of the company's lore?

Some readers will undoubtedly argue that the salesman should not have been so naive as to have been persuaded into extending credit without a thorough check of Borland's financial documents. However, a reasonable and competent salesperson does not anticipate being mislead in such a manner. Nor are salespersons usually expected to approve credit, given the fact that there would be a built-in conflict of interest if they were.

Another story should serve to reinforce these points. Barry Minkow was touted as a wonder boy for launching a company called ZZZBest in the 1980s. By age 20, Minkow had become a millionaire through the seemingly overnight success of his building restoration business. Just as quickly as the company soared, however, came its demise.

After applying for a multimillion-dollar loan, Minkow cleverly deceived the bank's auditors by falsely inflating the financial promise of his business. He brought the auditors to a large building during off-hours to show them a large company account. In reality, the building was not a ZZZBest account at all. Minkow paid off a security guard to gain access to a building and had several colleagues wear company uniforms in order to trick the auditors. In the end, Minkow served several years in prison for his role in defrauding investors and lenders of more than $100 million. While former Borland CEO Philippe Kahn's actions may not amount to illegal fraud and the stakes were significantly lower in his case, the ethical principles seem parallel.

In other well-defined instances, however, Carr's support of "bluffing" seems acceptable because no deception has occurred. Consider advertisements in which the performance of a product is grossly exaggerated for entertainment or attention grabbing purposes.

Although much care should be exercised, "bluffing" is justifiable in some very narrow situations. When access to the standards of conduct is widely available and no reasonable participant is deceived, the principle of truthfulness has not been violated. In these well-defined and specific instances, there is no real conflict of moral standards.

Good Business

While the issue of "bluffing" makes for a valuable and interesting discussion, the broader contextual question of whether or not success in business *requires* ethical compromise such as the use of deceptive tactics is important to examine. On this issue, some of Carr's observations are particularly provocative. Most notable is his statement that "a sudden submission to Christian ethics by businessmen would bring about the greatest economic upheaval in history." To be sure, Carr is not claiming a complete lack of actions that resemble kindness and honesty. The point is that when they occur, they are motivated more by financial interests than by moral sentiments. Clearly, for Carr ethics is not the pathway to success.

In sharp contrast to Carr's perspective, a popular view holds that ethical compromises in business are unnecessary since good ethics are actually good business, especially in the long-term financial horizon. Authors Bhide and Stevenson ("Why Be Honest If Honesty Doesn't Pay?") argue that while this idea makes intuitive sense, there is no empirical evidence to back the claim. In most cases, they assert, violations of honesty go unpunished because many victims refuse to acknowledge that they have been duped or choose to simply move on with their lives rather than being tied up in costly litigation. Furthermore, they cite several examples of cases where transgressors of the principle of truth telling are actually handsomely rewarded for their efforts because of inequities in power. However, the encouraging note in their findings is that businesspeople do practice honesty despite the fact that there may not be an economically rational reason to do so.

Norman Bowie offers many examples that work to support the claim that attention to ethical matters can enhance the bottom line. While acknowledging that in some cases profits may have to be sacrificed for the sake of ethics, Bowie correctly points out how ethical behavior reduces transaction costs, establishes trust, and preserves the "social capital" necessary to sustain an efficient economy.

Considering the examples provided by Bowie, the relationship between ethics and the bottom line is complicated and multilayered. Although honesty and practices such as "values-based management" are commendable and can perhaps lead to economic gains more often than not, ethical behavior is not a magical blueprint for a successful business in the economic sense. While numerous careers and businesses have indeed been built upon reputations for honesty and fairness, there is no perfect correlation between good ethics and business success. If such a relationship existed, the need for business ethics would not exist since nearly everyone would practice solid moral behavior.

While connecting ethics to profitability may help to convince skeptics, business professionals and organizations must act ethically because it is the right thing to do, not because it "pays." Doing right often has real costs. In fact, many companies promoting themselves as "socially responsible" have failed to live up to their claims and have paid a dear price in the form of heightened public criticism.

More importantly, truly virtuous acts are those that are done with the proper motivation. While acknowledging the very real tensions and possible trade-offs, priority should be given to sound ethical behavior because a Christian worldview judges and measures "success" in light of eternity, not by the accumulation of money and power. This is the true spirit in which faith and spirituality should be brought into the world of business.

TWO

Christian Engagement in Business

The challenge is not so much to bring Christ with us into our work, but to discover his presence already there.

Robert Sirico

Tough business is a place where heaven and earth meet and tussle just like any other point we occupy. Some of us are called to be there, working in the tensions that will only be resolved in glory.

Steve Brinn

INTRODUCTION

Historically, Christians have had an uneasy relationship with business. In fact, Augustine flatly declared, "Business is in itself an evil," and Tertian observed that trade is "scarcely adapted for a servant of God." More recently, debates about the potentially pernicious effects of globalization, coupled with troubling revelations about corporate misconduct, have raised centuries-old questions about the essential compatibility of Christianity and business. Can commerce be a legitimate means of participating in divine work in the world when it appears to be conducted within a system riddled with values that are in tension with the Christian tradition?

The focus of this chapter will be on the development of a theologically informed perspective on Christian engagement with business. In particular, the important issue of how Christians in business-oriented work should thoughtfully and faithfully approach their work will be addressed. Should commercial activity be abandoned for the sake of moral and spiritual purity, be seen instrumentally as primarily a means to support the "real" or "proper" work of the church, or be embraced as a legitimate spiritual vocation/calling?

A theologically informed view of business also serves as an important foundation for the material covered in later parts of this book.

Christian ethics are derived from theology. Our understanding of God's character, purposes, and will form the foundation for who we ought to be and how we should live. Christian *business* ethics also rests on these foundational concepts.

The context in which engagement with business will be investigated is within the broader discussion of how Christians should interact with contemporary culture, of which business is a part. Different theological traditions within Christianity hold widely diverging views about the relationship between Christianity and culture. Some traditions (and theologians who have influenced them) emphasize the gap between Christian values and those of the surrounding culture, and lean toward separatist tendencies in their interactions. Others see harmony between the values of Christ and those of culture and tend to emphasize common moral ground between them. Still others fall somewhere in between, giving different emphasis on the fallen, the "graced," and the "to be redeemed" aspects of culture, and participate within it accordingly.

The first essay in this chapter, "Christ and Business: A Typology for Christian Business Ethics" by Louke van Wensveen Siker, sets the stage for examining appropriate Christian engagement with business by creating a set of organizing categories.[1] Based on H. Richard Niebuhr's classic book *Christ and Culture*, Van Wensveen Siker develops a typology that categorizes a range of beliefs about the relationship between the competing moral authorities of "Christ" and "Business." She describes five "ideal types" in which patterns of thought regarding this relationship are detected. The remaining essays in this chapter bear distinctive marks of the various strands of thought described by Van Wensveen Siker.[2]

The second essay presents an optimistic account of business and of the sanctity of participation within it. Robert Sirico's "The Entrepreneurial Vocation" attempts to correct some unflattering assumptions about the world of commerce. In so doing, he undermines the tacit assumption that business is not an arena in which the "proper work" of the church can take place. Sirico argues that business has *intrinsic* value because entrepreneurial activity (broadly understood) is reflective of God's creative nature.

In the third essay, "Tough Business: In Deep, Swift Waters," executive Steve Brinn states that we should accept difficult ethical tensions as a fact of life in the fallen, imperfect world of business. However, he asserts that Christians should not leave an arena simply because there is moral danger. The model lived by Christ, Brinn observes, is one of cultural engagement rather than abandonment.

[1] Note: Due to editorial error, in the first edition (1996) two categories (4 and 5) in the typology were reversed and several subtitles (in types 1, 2, and 3) were inadvertently added. The errors have been corrected in this edition. The publisher and editors extend their apologies to the author.

[2] To be sure, the remaining essays do not perfectly fit the categories developed in the typology. Any typology has limits, and it is quite likely that many authors (and readers) hold parts of two or more of the types simultaneously. However, typologies are extremely helpful tools to categorize and describe basic thought patterns.

The first case study, "Business as a Calling," presents a scenario in which two students discuss over lunch whether or not business has spiritual legitimacy as a proper vocation. The second case, "The Assignment," probes the issue of Christian involvement in controversial activities. Under what conditions should an employee accept a controversial project in order to improve the ethical environment? Is this an example of what author Steve Brinn refers to as "deep, swift waters"?

As you read the case studies, assess which type or types (as presented in the essay "Christ and Business") your thinking most closely resembles. Given what you have read in this chapter, how has your thinking been challenged, changed, or confirmed?

READINGS

Christ and Business: A Typology for Christian Business Ethics

Louke van Wensveen Siker

Journal of Business Ethics 8 (1989): 883–88. Copyright © 1989 Kluwer Academic Publishers.

Introduction

As the field of business ethics is becoming more defined, the sub-discipline of Christian business ethics is taking on a multi-faceted shape. In this paper I shall take stock of the variety of ways in which Christian business ethicists currently conceive of ethical change in business. In order to do so, one needs an appropriate set of organizing categories. Simply adopting the traditional categories used by applied philosophers to organize the field—utilitarian, Kantian, etc.—will not do, for Christian ethicists rarely structure their work along these lines. Rather, I shall show that traditional theological categories can go a long way in helping one appreciate the scope and variety of Christian business ethics as a relatively new area of inquiry. The categories I have chosen are inspired by the typology set forth in H. Richard Niebuhr's classic study, *Christ and Culture*.[1]

The Typology

Before I proceed, let me briefly call to mind the main features of Niebuhr's typology. The book *Christ and Culture* explores how Christians over the centuries have dealt with what Niebuhr calls "the enduring problem of the relation between the authorities of Christ and culture."[2] Niebuhr discerns a pattern of recurring answers to this problem, which he proceeds to organize in the form of five types. First he presents the most extreme answers. Here one finds the views of radical Christians, who stress the presence of evil in culture to such a degree that they can see Christ only in opposition to it ("Christ Against Culture"). At the opposite end of the spectrum one finds the position of cultural Christians, who see no basic contradiction between the demands of culture and the demands of Christ ("The Christ of Culture"). Between these extremes, Niebuhr locates three other typical positions. So-called synthesist Christians tend to establish a hierarchy in which the authority of culture is affirmed, yet also superseded by the authority of Christ ("Christ Above Culture"). Dualist Christians struggle with the ambivalence created by seeing culture as both fallen and preserved by God ("Christ and Culture in Paradox"). Finally, conversionist Christians tend to affirm culture insofar as it is the arena of Christ's transforming work ("Christ the Transformer of Culture").

Niebuhr's typology is well suited to serve as a heuristic device for understanding the rich variety inherent in the work of Christian business ethicists. Its focus, the relation between the authorities of Christ and culture, must naturally also be a main theme in an area of inquiry characterized as both Christian and concerned with business. In fact, for the purposes of this study, Niebuhr's five types can simply be narrowed down into the following subset: Christ Against Business, The Christ of Business, Christ Above Business, Christ and Business in Paradox, and Christ the Transformer of Business. In each case, "Business" refers to the prevailing capitalist business culture. These categories will provide a uniquely theological way of identifying various approaches in Christian business ethics. While the categories used by applied philosophers reflect different foundations of moral authority, an adaptation of Niebuhr's typology will show various ways in which *one* ultimate moral authority, Christ, is thought to relate to an area of life that also claims human loyalty, business. In other words, these categories will highlight a range of beliefs about the ramifications of Christ's work and being for the possibility and dynamics of ethical change in business.

As we shall see, each of Niebuhr's five types is indeed clearly represented among Christians reflecting on ethics in business. This is not to say, however, that any one approach exactly fits a particular type. As Niebuhr observes, "when one returns from the hypothetical scheme to the rich complexity of individual events, it is evident at once that no person or group ever conforms completely to a type."[3] Yet to the extent that the typology can provide a rough background against which various approaches may be grouped (and exceptions noted!), it will serve a useful purpose. Given this qualification, I will now proceed to show what a Niebuhrian typology of Christian business ethics might look like.

Type I: Christ Against Business

At some point in time, every Christian business ethicist is likely to encounter the skepticism or even opposition of those among the faithful who assume that the business world can never be salvaged from its corruption. The arguments sound familiar, all variations on the theme, "Business ethics, isn't that an oxymoron?" Niebuhr himself points to an early proponent of this attitude, the church father Tertullian, who argued that trade "is scarcely 'adapted for a servant of God,' for apart from covetousness, which is a species of idolatry, there is no real motive for acquiring."[4]

The skepticism of the radical Christian about ethical change in business seems to be a permanent motif among the various ways of relating Christ and business, akin to the attitude Niebuhr has described with his "Christ Against Culture" type. Theologically speaking, such skepticism is rooted in the assumption that the current business culture must be marked off as a realm of evil and idolatry, a realm that must be destroyed, rather than changed. As a Christian, one must dissociate oneself as much as possible from the corruption of the business world, while focusing on the new order established by Christ. A modern example of such radical skepticism about ethical change in business can be found in the writings of Franz Hinkelammert, a Marxist theologian who has been working in Costa Rica. Hinkelammert describes a capitalist business world marked by idolatry, where commodities and corporations are treated as independent agents, requiring the total subjection of all business people. He concludes that Christians confessing faith in God clearly have no choice but to repudiate this realm of idolatry.[5]

Overall, it is fair to say that the "Christ Against Business" type forms the anti-type of any method in Christian business ethics. It denies the validity of the discipline, because it denies the legitimacy of anything resembling the prevailing form of business enterprise.

Type II: The Christ of Business

In a scene from *The Power of Ethical Management* by Kenneth Blanchard and Norman Vincent Peale, a minister says to a bewildered businessman, "When you have patience, you realize that if you do what is right—even if it costs you in the short run—it will pay off in the long run."[6] The minister also explains that having patience means trusting in the timing of a higher power, which could be called God. If you do that, things will always work out. This scene epitomizes the assumption that God's aims and the aims of business are essentially in harmony. While the business world may still contain a fair share of corruption, the argument goes, in essence it bears the stamp of goodness. Overcoming the corruption is not only possible, but also relatively easy. After all, most business people have good intentions and basically know right from wrong. They only need some guidance in making concrete moral decisions. Business ethicists, in the role of consultants, can provide such guidance and thus facilitate ethical change. This familiar approach to business ethics can be classified as the "Christ of Business" type.

Niebuhr's observations regarding cultural Christians help to highlight further the features of the "Christ of Business" type. Niebuhr notes, for example, that "the cultural Christians tend to address themselves to the leading groups in a society."[7] Similarly, the "Christ of Business" approach involves targeting mainly top-level managers as the agents of ethical change. Niebuhr notes also that cultural Christians use the language of these sophisticated circles. Similarly, Christian business ethicists often swap theological categories for a mixture of generally accepted ethical terms and the straight business talk of the corporations they consult. A most notable example of this kind of adaptation is the catch phrase "good ethics means good business." Finally, Niebuhr notes that, in their zeal to recommend Christ to the cultured,

cultural Christians "want to make discipleship easy."[8] Similarly, the "Christ of Business" approach makes ethics look simple and attractive, a matter of positive thinking, a message that sells at a two-day management retreat. All in all, Niebuhr's "Christ of Culture" type helps us to understand how the specific features of this widely practiced approach to business ethics flow from the basic assumption that Christ and business are essentially aligned.

Type III: Christ above Business

Niebuhr's third type, "Christ Above Culture," helps us gain perspective on a somewhat less optimistic, yet even more widespread Christian approach to business ethics. The so-called synthetic type is based on the largely Thomistic assumption that ethical change resembles step-for-step elevation to a higher level of existence, a process guided by the rational discernment and application of natural law and, ultimately, divine law. In Christian business ethics, this assumption finds expression in the method of applying general norms to specific situations by means of careful, deductive reasoning. The general norms, such as human dignity, justice, and co-creation, are thought to have universal moral authority. They provide the unequivocal basis for the field of business ethics. The main task of the discipline is to guide the transformation of business according to these ultimate foundations, usually by means of rationally developed medial norms, such as subsidiarity and proportionality. A perfect example of this approach can be found in an essay by Theodore V. Purcell, S.J., entitled "Management Development: A Practical Ethical Method and a Case."[9]

In sum, unlike the radical Christians, synthesist business ethicists do not assume that the modern business world needs to be destroyed. After all, it is still part of the created order. Nor, on the other hand, do they follow the cultural Christians in believing that business already carries the full potential of goodness within its own laws. Rather, they assume that business life needs to be elevated by means of authoritative, external guidelines.

This may not be an easy task. For example, as Thomas McMahon has asked, how does one apply the justice-based concept of a family living wage in a business world guided by the notion of compensation based on comparable worth?[10] Yet despite such difficulties, adherents of the synthesist view of transformation believe that with thorough and imaginative reasoning, it is possible to find authoritative direction.

Type IV: Christ and Business in Paradox

"Christ and culture stand in a relation of paradox," observes Robert S. Bachelder, a congregational pastor. As a result,

> executives should expect that their general and personal callings will exist in tension. But this tension need not create defeatism and cynicism. It can give rise to alertness and moral imagination. What executives must do is accept the moral ambiguities of their companies and yet fully participate in them, trusting all the while in God to open the way to new moral possibilities.[11]

Niebuhr's "Christ and Culture in Paradox" type could not have been more adequately expressed in relation to a business context. And, as we shall see, Bachelder is not the only one to perceive ethical change in business as a matter of tension and paradox. Once again, we are dealing with a distinctive motif in Christian business ethics.

In describing the paradox type, Niebuhr observes that dualist Christians are highly sensitive to the fallenness of culture. Yet at the same time they feel called to participate in culture. After all, God continues to sustain the world in its sin, so to escape it would mean to counter God's plan. Living with this tension between judgment and participation, dualist Christians tend to have only limited expectations of social transformation. The sins of this world can be kept in check through laws and countervailing force, yet the Kingdom of God is not of this world. Meanwhile, God's grace does work transformation in individuals. Yet even forgiven sinners are left to juggle the imperfect options of social life, being always forced again to "sin boldly" with no positive rules to guide their actions.

In a business context, one finds this type expressed in various ways. One manifestation, at a social level, is the activist attempt to channel the power of big business by means of external pressure, such as strikes, boycotts, shareholder resolutions, publicity, and legislation. I am thinking, for example, of the work of the Interfaith Council on Corporate Responsibility under the direction of Tim Smith. At a personal level, one recognizes the type when business ethicists, like Robert Bachelder, stress the necessity to live with compromise and ambiguity, and the need to use one's best personal judgment in the absence of clear-cut rules. My favorite example along these lines comes actually not from a business ethicist, but from Dietrich Bonhoeffer, who observes in his *Ethics* that in extreme situations, one may sometimes have to opt for "the destruction of human livelihoods in the interest of the necessities of business."[12]

All in all, dualist business ethicists are likely to speak the realistic language of power struggles and necessary compromises. Yet with all the stress on freedom of judgment and the absence of fixed rules, this realism can just as easily express itself in liberal as in conservative recommendations (witness the examples mentioned above!). Thus dualist business ethicists are not likely to excel in predictability. But then, of course, their strength lies in providing a witness to the courage and freedom found in a living faith.

Type V: Christ the Transformer of Business

Niebuhr's fifth type, the conversionist approach to the problem of Christ and culture, is marked by nuances rather than tensions. It expresses awareness of the perversion of culture, combined with affirmation of culture as the arena of God's transforming work. Conversionists see transformation as a process which begins with a conversion of the human spirit, and ends in action and social change. Given these inner-worldly possibilities of change, they believe, it is appropriate for Christians to focus more on positive practice than on negative action toward sin.

Conversionist business ethicists will combine awareness of serious evil in the business world with hope for actual, historical transformation of business life. In their attempts to seek out this transformation, they will try to work *with* business, rather than always *against* it. Also, they will take a holistic approach, paying attention to the spiritual as well as the material, the individual as well as the communal. Notions such as character, embodiment, and story may well appear in their work.

A good example of a conversionist approach can be found in Max Stackhouse's book *Public Theology and Political Economy*.[13] In chapter 7, entitled "Spirituality and the Corporation," Stackhouse argues:

> the ideal of social democracy borne by the ecumenical church ... must, without extensive political [*sic*], economic, or technological power, develop a new spirituality, based on a public theology, to transform the materialist and reductionist preoccupation of all present economic forms and ideologies. This is possible because already within the modern corporation are residual ecclesiological elements wherein spiritual matters are intrinsically related to social ones, and therefore are potentially related to new patterns of material and organizational embodiment.[14]

This brief passage captures the main features of the conversionist type in almost a textbook manner, showing both concern for economic distortions and hope for a spirit-based, yet fully historical transformation.

Evaluation

... Now let me turn to the payoff for Christian business ethics. Most obviously, Niebuhr's typology could assist Christian business ethicists in their efforts at maintaining methodological self-awareness in a new area of inquiry. Taken one step further, Niebuhr's typology could also provide fresh opportunities for approaching the work of colleagues in the field. After all, the nuances of the various types prevent the kind of black-and-white vision that does not do justice to the work of another. For example, one is less liable to lump together dualists with the radical approach, or conversionists with the cultural approach, to mention some common errors. On that basis, the typology may even become the occasion for an open discussion on the relative adequacy of each approach....

This leads to my final observation. Niebuhr's typology may ultimately challenge Christian business ethicists to investigate how their methods may be complementary. Niebuhr himself carefully avoided designating any one of his types as the most authoritative answer to the enduring problem of the relation between Christ and culture.[15] He advocated what we might nowadays call a reflective equilibrium approach, arguing that each type contributes something indispensable and yet insufficient in itself. Thus the radical Christian reminds one of the force of Christ's authority, the cultural Christian shows how the gospel can be brought to leading groups in society, the synthesist reminds one that salvation affirms creation, the dualist adds a healthy dose of suspicion and realism, and the conversionist calls one to positive, confessional action. In a similar vein, the various theological approaches to seeking ethical change in business may well complement each other in unexpected ways. In that case, we should be listening carefully to Norman Vincent Peale as well as to Tim Smith!

Notes

[1] H. Richard Niebuhr, *Christ and Culture* (Harper & Row, New York, 1951).

[2] *Christ and Culture*, 11. Niebuhr's statement of the problem can be criticized for implying that Christ and human life may potentially be conceived of apart from culture. Yet, as Charles Scriven argues in his recent study, *The Transformation of Culture* (Herald Press, Scotsdale, PA, 1988), Niebuhr generally seems to refer to the authority of the *prevailing* culture. Given this understanding, statements concerning Christ's opposition to culture, or Christian withdrawal from culture, make more sense.

[3] *Christ and Culture*, 43–44.

[4] *Ibid.*, 54. Citation from Tertullian, *On Idolatry*, xi.

[5] Franz Hinkelammert, "The Economic Roots of Idolatry: Entrepreneurial Metaphysics," in *The Idols of Death and the God of Life: A Theology*, ed., Pablo Richard et al. (Orbis Books, Maryknoll, NY, 1983), 165–93.

[6]Kenneth Blanchard and Norman Vincent Peale, *The Power of Ethical Management* (William Morrow, New York, 1988), 60.

[7]*Christ and Culture*, 104.

[8]*Ibid.*, 126.

[9]Theodore V. Purcell, S.J., "Management Development: A Practical Ethical Method and a Case," in *Doing Ethics in Business*, ed. Donald G. Jones (Oelgeschlager, Gunn & Hain, Cambridge, MA, 1982), 187–202.

[10]Thomas F. McMahon, "The Contributions of Religious Traditions to Business Ethics," *Journal of Business Ethics* 4 (1985): 344.

[11]Robert S. Bachelder, "Ministry to Managers," *The Christian Ministry* 15 (September 1984): 14.

[12]Dietrich Bonhoeffer, *Ethics* (Macmillan, New York, 1955), 239.

[13]Max L. Stackhouse, *Public Theology and Political Economy: Christian Stewardship in Modern Society* (Eerdmans, Grand Rapids, 1987).

[14]Ibid., 131. In this passage Stackhouse uses dialectical language to throw a different light on an earlier developed argument. Overall, his argument does not depend on a dialectical reading of history.

[15]Yet, personally Niebuhr seems to prefer the conversionist type. See, for example, Paul Ramsey, *Nine Modern Moralists* (Prentice-Hall, Englewood Cliffs, N.J., 1962), 149–79.

Questions for Discussion:

1. What are the primary ways that Van Wensveen Siker views the relationship between Christianity and business?
2. Which of these do you think of as the dominant paradigm of the Christian business person today?
3. Which of these do you think is most consistent with the Bible, and why?

The Entrepreneurial Vocation

Fr. Robert Sirico

Unpublished paper of the Acton Institute for the Study of Religion and Liberty. Copyright © 1996 Fr. Robert Sirico.

I. The Entrepreneurial Vocation

One may say, without fear of contradiction, that prejudice against minorities is unpopular in modern society. And with good reason: the idea that people are judged merely by the group that they happen to belong to, without any regard for their person and individual qualities, is properly odious to anyone with moral sensibilities.

Yet despite this laudable attitude prevalent throughout the popular culture, there remains one minority group upon which an unofficial open-season has been declared: the entrepreneur!

One sees evidence of this prejudice everywhere about us, and one need only look at the popular culture's means of communications to see the prejudice made abundantly clear. Consider the books (say of Dickens or Sinclair Lewis), television programs (like *Dallas* or *Dynasty*), films (*China Syndrome, Wall Street*, or even some versions of *A Christmas Carol*), cartoons strips (like "Doonesbury") and even sermons that you've heard in which the business person is depicted. Meditate on the image that is being projected.[1] Does even one positive image emerge?

Even when opinion makers, especially moral leaders, are not occupied with denouncing the "rapacious appetite" and "obscene and conspicuous consumption" of these capitalists, the best one comes to expect of them is that they might tolerate business merely as a necessary evil which is in need of a broad and complicated network of controls in order to force it to serve human needs. And this is, all too often, the attitude of even capitalism's friends! In this presentation I hope to offer a differing point of view.

> *It is as though business people and those who work for the church employ two different models in their day-to-day operations—and indeed they do.*

My particular concern here is the prevalent bias against capitalism among religious leaders. Why the negative attitude of entrepreneurs on the part of religious leaders? Not very long ago an article of mine was published in the *Wall Street Journal* in which I criticized the anti-free market sentiments of the Sandinista regime in Nicaragua. I pointed to this bias as the primary reason that the nation was suffering from heartrending poverty. A very curious thing began to happen the next day. I began to receive phone calls from people all throughout the U.S. The strange thing about this series of phone callers was the similar profile they shared. After some perfunctory remarks about Nicaragua, I found that most of these callers really weren't interested in talking about Latin America at all. Each was a relatively successful business person; each had deep moral and religious convictions; and each of them was utterly astounded that a Catholic priest would explicitly defend the free market as a morally preferable system.

These people represented a variety of Christian traditions and told me that they each felt disenfranchised and alienated from their churches. I recall one man in particular, who described himself as a conservative Catholic, saying that he no longer attended Mass because he refused to sit and be condemned from the pulpit for his business skills.

A recent book by former Ambassador Michael Novak tells of his experience at a conference on economics where a group of Latin American priests were participants. The conference went for several days during which time cogent and fact filled arguments were presented demonstrating the ways in which a free economy can lift the poor from poverty by the production of wealth. The priests said nothing until the final day of the conference. Mr. Novak recounts the experience: "At the last session of what had been a happy seminar, one of the priests arose to say that his colleagues had assembled the night before and asked him to make a statement on their behalf. . . ." "We have," he said, "greatly enjoyed this week. We have learned a great deal. We see very well that capitalism is the most effective means of producing wealth, and even that it distributes wealth more broadly and more evenly than the economic systems we see in Latin America. But we still think that Capitalism is an immoral system."[2]

My guess is that many of you sitting here have heard similar things in your congregations. Why does this state of affairs exist? Why is it that the very best you business people get to hear from a religious leader so often is, "Well, the way to redeem yourself is to give us your money"? Why does there appear to be such ignorance on the part of clergy and religious leaders about the realities of the market and how it operates, and its moral basis?

One very obvious reason is the sheer lack of any course in virtually all the seminaries I am acquainted with, in economics. This, of course, has not deterred religious leaders from pronouncing on economic matters.

In addition to this intellectual gap, there is a practical gap. There seems to be such a gap between religious leaders and business people in their understanding of market operations because the two groups tend to operate out of two very different worlds and proceed from two very different sets of assumptions. It is as though business people and those who work for the church employ two different models in their day-to-day operations—and indeed they do.

It will help to bridge this gap by proving the religious model and the business model briefly. Simply put, people who work in the church operate from a distributivist economic model. By this I mean that on Sunday morning a collection basket is passed. On Monday the bills are paid, acts of charity are attended to, etc. If Sunday collections come up short on a regular basis, making it difficult to pay the bills, most preachers begin to turn up the screws a notch or two and lay on another layer of guilt. Thus, in the minds of many clergy, the economic world they see is like a pie that is in need of being divided up. They view the world of money as static, so in order for one to obtain a larger piece of that pie, it will be necessary for someone else to get a somewhat smaller piece.

Now the business person operates from a very different model. The entrepreneur talks of *making* money, not collecting it. In other words, for the business person, who must consider the needs, wants and desires of the consumer, the way to get money is to offer something of value. The world of money for these people is dynamic. It is this process, which we call the free market that is responsible for the "wealth of nations," a phrase associated in the popular mind with the title of Adam Smith's classic book, but which was first employed in the Book of Isaiah (60:5).

Let me be clear that I am not advocating that religion adopt a bottom line mentality with regard to its mission. There are some matters which simply do not fit within an economic calculus and which cannot be evaluated in terms of "dollar and cents." What I am saying, however, is that before religious leaders choose to pronounce on economic matters, they do well to become informed.

Another factor that plays into the hostility one frequently encounters regarding capitalism in religious circles comes from a noble, if mistaken, source. Many religious leaders spend a great deal of their lives confronting the wretchedness of poverty in close proximity. Anyone here who has traveled in Third World countries knows the cry of the human heart that yells "Stop!" when confronted with such human misery. Unnecessary poverty angers us, and we want to put an end to it. This sentiment is an exactly proper Christian sentiment.

The problem results when this sentiment is combined with the economic ignorance I described previously. When this happens the cry against poverty is easily converted into a rage against wealth, which, while understandable, is ill-informed and even deadly. It is deadly because it fails to see that the amelioration of poverty can only be achieved by the production of wealth. It is deadly because it seeks to kill the goose that will lay the golden egg; indeed, it will kill the goose that will hatch other golden-egg-laying geese!

II. Toward a Positive View of Entrepreneurial Activity

As the lady in the musical once said, let's begin at the very beginning, which is a very good place to start. And, I don't mean our Do Re Mes, I mean the book of Genesis and the creation of the world.

A. The Creation

I am sure that you all know the dramatic account of God making the heavens and the earth, the ocean and the dry land, the stars of the heavens, all of the creeping things of the earth, and finally the apex of his creation: Man and Woman. Do you recall God's reaction after each act of creation? Over six times on the first page of Scripture one refrain is repeated over and over again: "God saw that it was good."

This view of the created order, specifically the goodness of the material world that God made, has not been accepted without controversy, even within the Christian tradition. When we look back into the first centuries of Christianity we see that a movement developed which regarded that material world as fundamentally evil, created by a demigod. This movement was known as Gnosticism, and the Gnostic impulse has surfaced and resurfaced under many guises throughout Christian history.

B. The Incarnation

Of course, no orthodox Christian can be agnostic, if for no other reason than the fact of the Incarnation of Christ. The Incarnation is the breaking into human history of the Divine. We Christians believe that it is through the Incarnation that God has elected to reconcile the world to Himself.

The implications of this are astounding, and throughout history, believers have been uncomfortable with them. In the fourth century the Arians believed that Jesus was certainly man; so much did they believe that Jesus was man that they could not bring themselves to believe that he was God; in the second century the Docetists believed that Jesus was divine; so much did they believe Jesus was divine that they couldn't bring themselves to believe that he was really man.

In the face of these two errors, what Scripture scholar Raymond Brown calls "the Great Church," pronounced that Jesus was *both* God and man, thus showing that the Incarnation radically accomplishes the creation, enabling the creation to discover its meaning. Jesus is true God and true man; authentic anthropology, then, is Christology; for, to use the words of the Second Vatican Council and the present Pope, it is "Christ the Redeemer" who "fully reveals man to himself."[3]

C. Two Approaches

I have taken us on this rather technical theological excursion because, in a real sense, it is the fundamental goodness of this material dimension of human existence that is at the root of the conflict over the morality of capitalism, the free market and what I call, the entrepreneurial vocation. There are two potential mistakes that can develop with regard to the proper relation of the human person to the material world. Both stem from the Gnostic-inspired view that sees the material world as evil and unrelated to spirituality.

The first view reasons that because all matter is evil, its possession and use is likewise evil. Throughout the centuries this tendency has recurred in various forms; from radical proponents of apostolic poverty like the Spiritual Franciscans of the middle ages to the Marxist inspired Liberation Theologians of today. For these, poverty is the only way to spirituality (unlike other orders that take a vow of poverty who say only that God is calling *them* to poverty, not everyone). The implication here is that wealth is axiomatically sinful, and that the wealthy must be relieved of their money in order to be absolved from their sin.

A second branch from the same root takes an opposite twist. This is seen in what are called the "Prosperity Gospel" people. They say that wealth is a sign of God's blessing, and that poverty is a result of sin. An appreciation of the balanced view of man's relation to the material world held by the majority of Christians throughout the ages can offer a corrective to such imbalances.

D. The Uniqueness of Human Nature

An entrepreneur is a kind of *impressairo*, one who organizes numerous factors, and brings things into connection so as to produce. It is this creative aspect of the entrepreneur that is so akin to God's creative activity as we read it in the book of Genesis. In this sense, I would argue, the entrepreneur participates in that call to productivity that God gives to the whole human race. It is a distinct call, this entrepreneurial vocation, to be sure, like that of being a parent. But if it is not quite as sublime as, say, Motherhood, the keenness of insight required of the entrepreneur remains sacred.

In order to carry out this creative enterprise, the entrepreneur must have access to the material factors of production; he must be permitted to acquire and trade property. Santayana once said, "to be is to be something in particular," and it is with this focus that we can explore what it is about humans that justifies their having rights, specifically the right to private property. One thing that the human person is "in particular" is a concrete body which puts the human person into some kind of relation with the material order, as noted above. Observe how humans are related to the material way uniquely different than are animals. Animals are bound to things by instinct; humans are related to things by reason, and this is the other thing that humans are in particular: We are self-reflecting, thinking beings who survive by the use of our reason. The mind is the predominant element which makes humans distinctly human. (The fact that some humans have a diminished capacity to reason in no way changes the fact that human nature has this rational component.) Thus, we are generically and essentially distinct from the animal which cannot reason.

The rational relationship between the human person and nature is what gives rise to property. It is our capacity to reason, our rational faculty, which causes us to relate to the material order in a way that is more than immediate and temporary: our relation to the material is, rather, general and permanent. Stability and permanency are the expression in time of the universality of the relationship of humans to things. Nor is ours merely a relationship of consumption, but possession and production.

Property is the foundation and context of this relationship. By the relationship of the human person to nature, we leave the imprint of our individuality upon nature by means of the time, effort, and ability we extend which in turn produces wealth and property. Wealth and property do not exist in a state of nature, where Hobbes said, "life is brutish, mean, nasty and short; red in claw and tooth." They come into existence only when people place value on things. This is seen in that black, sticky, smelly, unpleasant substance that was mostly an annoyance until a way was found to process and refine it in such a way that petroleum was produced.

When seen in this light, property rights are really an expression and a safeguard to personal rights. The defense of the right to property, then, ought not be seen as the defense of detached material objects in themselves, but of the dignity, liberty and very nature of the human person who, to allude to John Locke, has mixed his labor with nature to produce property. The right to property, then, is an extension and exercise of human rights.

Perhaps the greatest economist of this century, Lugwig von Mises, drew the connection between economic and personal liberty very clearly when he said, "Choosing determines all human deci-

sions. In making his choice man chooses not only between various material things and services. All human values are offered for option."

Another writer put it this way: "Choice is fundamental to economics because it is fundamental to the moral nature of man. It is crucial to recall that before becoming what some have called "the first economist," Adam Smith was a moral philosopher. Although he authored the famous *Wealth of Nations*, which I mentioned earlier, few people realize that its companion work is entitled *Theory of Moral Sentiments*.

III. The Sanctity of the Entrepreneurial Vocation

The total dynamism of the Christian life of necessity encompasses the material order—including the world of business and finance—by virtue of the Creation and the Incarnation, as outlined above. There are two popular but mistaken views of the role of the laity in the Christian vocation of the apostolate. One view implies that if you can't be a full-time minister or priest you have to settle for second best; the second view says that if you can't be a full-time minister or priest your call is to pay the bills, which your business will enable you to do.

I remember when I was a seminarian assigned to work one summer in Austin, Texas I met a lady who asked why I wanted to become a priest (never an easy question to answer). As we drove along the freeway with the top down she appeared to be in a nostalgic mood and said, "My husband had a vocation once, and then he met me."

This view seems to assume that lay people don't really have vocations, but that they do the best they can under the circumstances. Or, if they do have vocations, this view tends to think that it is less than, and inferior to that of the full-time missionary.

A second view that firmly believes that business people have a defined and God-appointed vocation, I believe is equally problematic. Simply put, this view sees the task of the business person as paying the bills that the clergy run up. These views are superficial, as are my descriptions of them, yet they both have some truth to them, even while they essentially lack depth.

Of course the vocation of the business person is different than that of the ordained minister, in much the same way that the vocation of being a mother is distinct from being a father. Likewise, it *is* the responsibility of lay people to make possible the practical dimensions of the apostolate, even as it is the responsibility for the clergy to do the same. The manner in which each fulfills that vocation will depend upon the concrete circumstances of the individuals involved.

To hear some people speak you would get the impression that the vocation of the entrepreneur is somehow prompted by the shortage of priests, or ministers, or missionaries, which would mean, of course, that if there were no shortage, the laity would have nothing to do with the Church's apostolate. I am reminded here of a conversation that my spiritual mentor Cardinal Newman had with Bishop Ullathorne over 100 years ago. The bishop is reported as having bemoaned, somewhat haughtily, "The laity, the laity. What are the laity?" To which Newman replied, "Without them, my lord, the hierarchy would look rather foolish."

You see, the vocation of the business person, the vocation of those who have the talent to produce wealth, to use their abilities to build the kingdom of God in conjunction with their leaders, is nothing new. The vocation of the laity, Yves Congar reminds us in his classic work *Lay People in the Church*, "existed from the beginning of the Church, and today it takes new forms, better adapted to the present era."[4] We must find new ways to present, Isaac Hecker (founder of the Paulist Fathers) once said, "Old truths in new forms"—ways to reproduce, consecrate and give new qualification to the apostolic already incumbent upon the faithful by virtue of the sacrament of initiation: Baptism and confirmation.

The challenge, then, is not so much to bring Christ with us into our work, but to discover his presence already there, precisely through the natural order that he created in the first instance, because, of course, God is no stranger to the world he made. The task of the lay person, the special challenge of the entrepreneur, is to allow grace to "build upon nature," as Aquinas tells us.

The task is less one of "Christianizing" as much as it is to "Christofinalize." We are called to bring our fullest potential to all that God has gifted us with. The great philosopher Etienne Gilson said it much better than I ever could. Permit me to quote him at length:

> If one wants to practice science for God's sake, the first condition is to practice it for its own sake, or as if for its own sake, because that it is the only way to learn it. . . . It is the same with an art: one must have it before one can put it to God's service. We are told that faith built the medieval cathedrals: no doubt, but faith would not have built anything had there been no architects and craftsmen. If it be true that the west front of Notre Dame is a raising of the soul to God, that does not prevent its being a geometrical composition as well: to build a front that will be an act of charity, one must first understand geometry. We . . . who acclaim the high worth of nature because it is God's work, should show our respect for it by taking as our first rule of action *that piety is never a substitute for technique;* for technique is that without which the most fervent piety is powerless to make use of nature for God's sake. Nothing and nobody obliges a Christian to occupy himself with science, art or philosophy, for there is no lack of other ways of serving God; but *if he has chosen this way of serving him*, the end he puts before himself obliges him to excel; the very intention that guides him compels him to be a good scholar, a good philosopher, a good artist: it is the only way he can become a good servant.[5]

What does this call mean to those of you in the vocation of enterprise? It will mean that you must strive to be more fully what you are, to display more fully the virtue of inventiveness; to act more boldly with the virtue of creativity; to continue to be other-regarding as you anticipate market demands, as you develop in yourselves and school others in the virtue of thrift; not to merely share your wealth with those in need, but to tutor others, by your example and your mentorship, how to become independent and to produce wealth themselves.

"By themselves brilliant ideas do not serve humankind; to be brought into service to man, they must be transformed through complex processes of design and production."

Your entrepreneurial vocation will require of you that you continue to be watchful practitioners in the art of discovery, for by it you will create employment opportunities for those who would otherwise go without. In a reflection on the faith dimensions of the American economy, a group of leading lay people penned these lines: "By themselves brilliant ideas do not serve humankind; to be brought into service to man, they must be transformed through complex processes of design and production. The talent to perform this transformation is as rare and as humanly precious as talent in any other field."[6]

In the pursuit of your vocation you will be tempted in many ways. You may be tempted to give up and think that the sometimes mundane world of finances, business and materialism has no spiritual dimension or meaning. Or perhaps you will be tempted in the opposite direction: to think that all that matters is the bottom line, and that no other values can have any bearing.

In those moments, this priest prays that you will remember the Incarnation, and the cost that was paid by the Son of God in that freely chosen action to enter the material world and to sanctify it. In those moments, when you are buffeted, when you are judged and condemned, and when even those you'd hoped would offer understanding, guidance and support seek to intervene into your creative endeavor, I urge you to remember the Parable of the Talents and be refreshed.

Know that it is God who has entrusted you with His talents, and that he expects you to be industrious with them; to be productive with them; to be creative with them.

If you will be faithful to this sacred call, then He shall say to you, on that Great Day when all wrongs will be made right, what He said to those servants in Matthew's Gospel: "Well done, good and faithful servant; you have shown yourself faithful in small ways . . . come and join your master's happiness" (chapter 25).

Notes

[1]For a fuller description of how the businessman has been depicted in literature see Michael McTague, *The Businessman in Literature: Dante to Melville* (New York: Philosophical Library, 1979).

[2]Michael Novak, *This Hemisphere of Liberty* (Washington, D.C.: The AEI Press, 1990), 38.

[3]Vatican Council II: Pastoral Constitution on the Church in the Modern World *Guardium et Spes*, 22: AAS 58 (1966), 1042–43; as quoted by John Paul II in *Redemptor Hominis*, #10.

[4]Yves Congar, O. P., *Lay People in the Church* (Westminster, MD: Newman Press, 1965).

[5]Etienne Gilson, "L'Intelligence au service du Christ-Roi," in *Christianisme et Philosophie* (Paris, 1936), 155–56, cited in Congar, Op. Cit., 388.

[6]*Toward the Future—Catholic Social Thought and the U.S. Economy* (New York: American Catholic Committee, 1984), 28.

Questions for Discussion:

1. Do you agree with Sirico in the way he sees business, especially entrepeneurial activity, as a "sacred" vocation? Why or why not?
2. Do you agree with Sirico that churches and businesses operate under very different views of money?

Tough Business: In Deep, Swift Waters

Steve Brinn

Vocatio 2, no. 2 (July 1999): 3–6. Copyright © 1999.

"Tough business" is the stuff that causes us to say, "There must be a fifth solution to this, because the first four stink." Or it causes us to say, "God, I don't really know the right answer—I see a range of options and not one of them gives me any comfort that I know the right thing to do." Put yet another way, tough business is the kind of business engagement that, in spite of our very best effort, causes some other Christian bystander to say, "And she considers herself a Christian!"

Tough business is a tough road to travel. Still, Christ calls many of his followers to this journey. More pilgrims on this path should talk honestly about our experiences, including fears and failures. To that end, I would like to address three "tough business" questions.

Why Not Tough Business?

The first question is "Why shouldn't Christians be up to their ears in tough stuff—and aren't most of our reasons for shying away from it shallow or false?"

From the time I entered business more than 22 years ago, Christ to me has been a model of engagement. Dangerous engagement in life, where there was high exposure with questionable people and complicated issues, entailing prospects for great conflict and trouble. Christ's invitation to be like him led me, in the business context, from safe harbors to open water. Do we, as Christians, belong out there, where we are bound, often, to get wet?

I row a scull. Usually novice rowers, on a river, will cleave to the shore. The water is shallower there, and the currents are less strong. By custom, rowers on one side of the river row upstream and on the other side downstream, so collisions are far less likely. Should you pitch out of your boat, by chance, the swim to shore is easier. All in all, it is a place to begin, with much less exposure than out in the middle.

As rowers progress, they are challenged to move to deeper water. They do this because the shortest, fastest run is down the middle of a river; there, the current is swifter. Rowers are moving in both directions, so the chance for collision is greater (especially as scullers face backward!) and, if you go for a swim, it is much further away to the safety of the shore.

If Jesus were a rower, he would move to deeper water as his skills progressed. If Jesus were a businessman, he would get his feet down and learn the basics. Then he would push out and take his faith to the place where the action is. But is this what Christians do? Too often, I think, people come into the church, experience its safe harbor—and then just stay there, rather than moving out in faith. This is true in every direction. And it seems to be very true in the case of Christians in the marketplace.

> *If Jesus were a businessman, he would get his feet down and learn the basics. Then he would push out and take his faith to the place where the action is.*

Why is this? I suppose the reasons are as diverse as people in the church. But it seems clear that for many people of faith stepping into business at all is stepping into Babylon, and "less is better." In this spirit, Christians may steer away from large-stakes, fast-paced transactional situations, controversy, or exposure by their selection of employment—or by their response to team members, if these circumstances arise.

Here is an example of these predicaments from my own experience. Some years ago, just after I joined the company where I am now a senior executive, it came to my attention that one of our associates was proposing a deal involving our property on a river and riverboat gambling. I was stunned and unsure what to do. Though I do not believe gambling to be a categorical sin, participating in a gaming enterprise even indirectly was about the last thing under heaven I would choose to do.

Tough business situation: Do I (1) resign, (2) threaten to resign if the proposal is adopted or (3) keep my place at the table and express my own strong reservation, using my business sense as well as my moral convictions, and see how things actually develop?

I chose option (3). Another executive who is a Christian immediately resigned from his position as CFO and from the board in order to "hear no evil," and, presumably, avoid participating directly in one.

As things played out over months, I was teased as a prude, told of my hypocrisy, and accused of worrying about my reputation. But I held my ground, asked tough-minded questions about the durability of the business, the business implications, and the involvement in gaming and how it fit with the core principles of our company. In the end, the deal faded—and the proponent left the company.

The moral of the story isn't that, if you stay at the wheel and don't abandon ship bad things won't happen. (I've stayed at the wheel other times, and the thing I disliked still came to pass.) But it does illustrate how I was able to retain a vote, while my colleague surrendered his chair and, in my view, made it even more difficult for our shared objections to be spoken with greatest force.

I think Christ wanted my voice in that discussion. What's more, I think he wants our voices in many "tough business" exchanges which may never have ideal outcomes, but only relatively better rather than worse results in the best case. But Christians shy away from these situations, consciously and subconsciously every day. They abdicate the role and think they are avoiding the chance of failure and sin. In the past few years, I've come to see that this crucible, this highwire

act of being in but not of the world, just can't be avoided. We all face it, in different roles. And counting degrees is only within the ken of God himself.

This last point is crucial. For 20 years I have struggled to reconcile my heart for heaven with the reality of the work world and its chances and outcomes. I could never put them together! I never experienced resolution of the tension, and therefore thought I was in the wrong place, which led me to consider career changes, new tactics, different decision-making strategies, and leaving the marketplace altogether! Then it finally struck me: We are children of God living our lives in a world hostile to our Father, and we are never in our lifetime going to experience a resolution of the conflict between the Kingdom of God and the powers of this earth. In other words, this is not heaven—but we are not in the wrong place.

Jesus incarnated this truth. Wherever he went, the will of heaven and the will of the world confronted each other, kicking up all kinds of disturbances and storms. Our lives will, in a fractional way, resemble His walk. Tough business is a place where heaven and earth meet and tussle just like any other point we occupy. Some of us are called to be there, working in the tensions that will only be resolved in glory.

Avoiding tough business out of concern for our reputation is ungodly, if we are called to the role by God. Abdicating the role is also a false solution if we do so to escape the tension basic to our existence, between the will of God and the powers controlling this world. (There is no place really to escape it!) Finally, though there is little support for, or understanding of, tough business in the church, the church's failure in this area is not an excuse for shunning God's call.

Christians should be right in the middle of tough business, as followers of the one true God. Who better to make tough choices without any good outcomes?

Where God Is

The second question worth pondering is: "Will God meet us there?"

Obviously, from what already has been said, the answer is "Yes!" God calls many Christians into these situations. Followers of Jesus aren't supposed to go spoiling for trouble, but if we put our oars into deeper water we are going to get drawn into situations involving pain, disappointment, and compromise. Other believers may end up saying "And he calls himself a Christian!"

To judge from church practices, there is little grace available to followers of Jesus who understand their calling to be tough business. Much in church is said about the difficulties of marriage and family, health, aging and poverty, and as to those things words and symbols all say grace abounds. But what about reducing, but not stopping, adverse impacts of logging, or providing two weeks rather than one week of severance pay to 100 people laid off in a corporate restructuring? Are these kinds of issues ever the stuff of group prayer? Do sermons ever recognize the compromises all of us who are in the marketplace face daily? When they do, do they provide assurances that our work has meaning—and when we fail, that we may receive grace? Sadly, across the church, these supports for marketplace Christians are lacking.

> *God will meet Christians in the crucible of tough business as often as they follow Him there in faith.*

Oddly, we may feel more confidence in God's mercy toward the penitent assassin than the slick but reportedly reborn casino manager. Yet the God who can wash cardinal sins white as snow is more than capable of forgiving the businesswoman implicated in a corporate injury to a third party resulting from a breached contract! And despite the compunctions about business in the North American church today, church-goers who do engage in business can receive both God's guidance and forgiveness as they wrestle with limited options, misinformation and misunderstanding, the painful reality of scarce resources and the zero-sum games endlessly played out in a competitive economy. God will meet Christians in the

crucible of tough business as often as they follow Him there in faith.

C. Everett Koop, the former Surgeon General of the United States, once commented that his most painful injuries, while attempting with all his heart to perform his best in office as a person of faith, arose from the vicious insults of Christian critics. Those of us who follow Jesus, who always push into deep water, should thank God when we see a person of faith tackling tough jobs in the marketplace or in government. And we should hope for their courage, wisdom and perseverance, rather than thinking the worst and attacking like jackals.

We have a long way to go. God is already there, waiting for us.

> *We should thank God when we see a person of faith tackling tough jobs in the marketplace. And we should hope for their courage, wisdom and perseverance, rather than thinking the worst and attacking like jackals.*

Tips and Tools

It is dangerous to prescribe any nostrum for the troubles confronted in tough business. But we all learn lessons that may be helpful to other pilgrims. So here are a few my own life freely offers the reader:

- We should figuratively stand on our heads every morning, to remember all the mystery in the world before we enter the 20th century business realm, which is so much predicated on science and efficiency. In fact, the daily sacrament of this kind of irreverence on the way into the office gets us oriented toward heaven's part in all that will face us the rest of the day, no matter how mundane or hopelessly separated from heaven itself.
- Read fairy tales. This is a complement to standing on one's head. Fairy tales defy limits. Up can suddenly meet down. Animals can talk. And, if we restore our belief in heaven's ability

to exceed all rules, we start to lift our sights away from the way it is done, to truly be "in, but not of" the world in which we are working. Deals, then, can be at least partly shaped by mercy. Hopes for improving a hopelessly tarnished prospect may not be abandoned, but rather rekindled. Nothing is ever completely over when we look at things through the eyes of faith. Fairy tales help restore the child, even in business people.

- Don't flee from the scenes of your failure. Christian businesspeople hate failures as much as anyone, and perhaps more, because we feel called to results not achievable in this lifetime. It is tempting to sweep our failures out of sight and rush on to the next challenge. Yet, by admitting our shortcomings and experiencing forgiveness for them, we find our relationship with God in tough business grows. And He will give us new visions, which often grow out of the ashes of our failures.
- Give yourself time. It takes time to find out what really is your calling, and then to learn the ropes. This may take decades. I am 46 and just beginning to get a clearer sense of the gifts I've been given and where to put them to work.

- Beware of life-style enclaves. Just like every other "group" in our society, business folks tend to hang out too much with each other. Find friends who aren't called to tough business and let your world overlap with theirs. Both of you will be better off.
- Join a revolutionary movement at some point. Sooner or later business causes anyone to become established, just as professional ministry does. Do something that shocks your friends and tests your own fences.
- Never give up on things that matter. God doesn't. Why should we?
- Finally, carry a token. It will go with you into the marketplace and call you back to the memory of God when you would least expect it.

I imagine that many of you soon will be in the knot-hole of tough business again, alone and wondering why you can't build a bridge that really works between heaven and earth. That's not your job. That job belongs to Jesus. But my prayer is that He will meet you in the bind, give you courage and wisdom there, and heal your wounds and worries as you stay in the world, where you are meant to be, as salt and light.

Questions for Discussion:

1. What does Brinn mean by "tough business"?
2. What would you have done if your company were considering the property deal that involved riverboat gambling?
3. How do you balance Brinn's notion of tough business with the command to "keep oneself from being polluted by the world" (James 1:27)?

CASE STUDIES

Case 2.1: Business as a Calling

The following discussion takes place over lunch:

Student #1: I heard a thought-provoking guest speaker in one of my classes today. He issued a direct challenge to all business majors or those intending to go into business after graduation, asking, "Why don't you forget about profit and do something meaningful with your life?" I have often wondered about the same thing. Since business is based on capitalism, and capitalism is rooted in greed (the pursuit of profit), the whole realm seems to be corrupt. How can you justify majoring in something like business (or intend to go into business)? Business is so corrupt that you have to give up trying to be ethical in order to succeed! In fact, I've heard that an old saying in business is "Do unto others *before* they do unto you!"

Student #2: Hey, wait a minute! Business is a legitimate calling! Lots of people make a real difference in the world through their involvement in it. An elder at my church owns a medium-sized business, and he seems to be able to uphold sound ethics. The difference he makes in our community and in the lives of his employees is significant. He also gives a lot of money away to charitable causes. Without earning a profit, he couldn't do these things.

Student #1: Maybe so, but I look at most of my friends in business, and I can't see much good that they are doing in the world. Sure, some of them get to talk about their faith, and most even give away some of their income, but this fact alone doesn't justify what they do to earn it. If a mobster donated money to charity, would that make the means by which he acquired it acceptable? To me, the moral nature of the work itself has to stand on its own merits. My roommate from last year graduated and took a job in the marketing department of a company that operates a chain of fancy executive gadget stores. All he does is contribute to crass consumerism by working for a company that gets people to buy stuff they don't really need!

I can't see how God would call anyone to the profit-oriented business world when there are so many other needs around us. I think Christians who are sincere about serving God should go into work that has more direct social benefits. It's in these other lines of work that one can see God's grace in the world.

Question for Discussion:

Now it's your turn to respond. Based on the selections in this chapter, how would you answer? Is your friend correct in his assumptions about the nature of business (greedy and crass) and whether or not it can be a legitimate calling?

Case 2.2: The Assignment

Upon graduation from college, Sarah takes a position at a small firm (20 employees) that specializes in Web design and management services for business clients. Sarah loves both the work that she does and her place of employment. The owners of the company have treated her well, and her co-workers are very collegial and fun to be around.

After nine months on the job, she is given the opportunity to take the lead role on a project for a new client that everyone around the firm has referred to as "the big Kahuna." It's an honor to be asked to take this role since it is very clear that if this client is impressed with the work done on the initial project much more work may be directed to the firm.

Sarah is well aware of the positive light in which senior executives of the firm view her and the career opportunities presented by being asked to lead the design team on this particular project. However, the nature of the client company's business and some of its past marketing campaigns are troubling to her. The company is a leading apparel manufacturer and retailer that has sought to create an edgy, somewhat rebellious image. One marketing campaign, which used posters in dormitories and full page ads in college newspapers, featured "drinking games" and "party drink" mixes, prompting some activists to accuse the company of encouraging under-age drinking. While the company was initially concerned about the negative publicity, clothing sales actually increased.

At an initial conceptual design meeting, Sarah meets marketing executives from the client company who express their desire for a website that "attracts a lot of traffic by capitalizing on the brand identity and image we have worked so hard to successfully create." After the meeting, Sarah meets with a senior executive of her firm named Lynn, a seasoned veteran of the advertising industry who has served as an informal mentor to Sarah. She shares with Lynn that this assignment is especially giving her trouble because her cousin was killed a few years ago in a car accident in which under-age drinking was involved.

Lynn replies, "I understand your reservations, Sarah, but consider the positive impact you can make on the campaign. Someone will end up directing the design work. It may as well be someone with a conscience. For years I worked on ad campaigns for a tobacco company and was able to help curb some possible 'spill-over' that would have impacted kids. I suggest you accept the assignment."

Question for Discussion:

In light of concepts developed in this chapter, should Sarah accept the assignment? Why or why not?

COMMENTARY

Integrative Perspectives: Christian Engagement in Business

The weight of historical Christian thought seems to lean against wholehearted participation in business. Comments such as those by Augustine and Tertullian cited in this chapter's introduction portray commerce as "worldly" and unsanctified. Since many of these types of negative sentiments were written within the context of premodern economies, which were essentially zero-sum in nature, they are understandable.

Even today, however, Christian involvement in business is still viewed with skepticism. At best, business is commonly seen as a means of supporting the "real" work of the church. This is reflected in the fact that many Christian businesspeople justify their involvement in business by citing opportunities for evangelism or by what they do "on the side," whether it is volunteering, giving money, or going out of their way to assist a troubled colleague or employee. In contrast, they have difficulty explaining how business activity by itself can be proper "kingdom" work. Current headlines and negative portrayals of business only contribute to nagging suspicions that business is spiritually suspect work.

The commercial marketplace is often seen as a murky realm fraught with values and activities that run counter to traditional Christian ethics. Practices that appear essential for success, such as hiding negative aspects of products, ruthlessly undermining the competition, and eliminating jobs held by people who need employment, are difficult to reconcile with values such as honesty, civility, and compassion. Such negative depictions of the marketplace are troublesome for those attempting to live their lives under the guidance of Christian ethics.

If negative anecdotal depictions and recent headlines about corporate conduct tell the whole story, the case for business as a legitimate calling would undoubtedly be difficult to make. However, even if business were as dark and "fallen" as portrayed, this alone may not be reason enough to abandon it as a place of Christian engagement. In "Tough Business: In Deep, Swift Waters" Steve Brinn insightfully points out that Christians should be at the forefront of business *because* (and not despite the fact that) moral tensions exist.

Furthermore, pessimistic accounts of business, though common, may not present a comprehensive or truthful picture. As Robert Sirico eloquently states in "The Entrepreneurial Vocation," "Christ is no stranger to the world he has created." To some degree, the world of business already bears the imprint of the goodness of its creator. For example, sound ethics in business are probably more the rule than the exception. Underneath the headlining scandals (which make for high entertainment value), an efficient economy rests upon a largely invisible but solid moral foundation. Since it is largely taken for granted, we are most aware of this foundation when it is undermined. Indeed, recent stock market declines perpetuated by corporate accounting scandals remind us of the existing but fragile trust needed to buoy an efficient economy.

Furthermore, good ethics, in some cases, make sound long-term financial sense. Although not a guarantee or a proper motive for ethical behavior, a reputation for honesty can be a strategic asset. While far from aligned (the tendency of Type 2 in "Christ and Business"), there is undoubtedly some degree of overlap between Christian values and most common business practices.

If, in fact, these more optimistic accounts are true, and Christian values are woven to some extent into the fabric of business, eager participation in business is far less problematic. However, a proper theology of business and cultural engagement must move well beyond the mere avoidance of evil and into a deeper realization of how economic activity may be a "calling" that directly participates in God's work in the world.

The primary or general calling of all Christians is to live a godly life. In addition, Christians may have specific callings into occupations, many of which are "worldly" in nature. In contrast to the view widely held during the medieval period, in which only clergy and monks were called, the Protestant Reformers (and many subsequent scholars) have pointed out that since all of creation is the theater for God's glory, all biblically lawful work can serve as a legitimate vocation.

On what basis can business be considered a specific calling? First, business activity can help fulfill the creation mandate given in Genesis 1:26–28, which contains community ordering and co-creativity with God as key components. Theologian R. Paul Stevens has pointed out that the creation mandate has been tragically separated from the Great Commission, leading to the erroneous conclusion that evangelism is all that matters.[3]

Second, business is one means by which God provides for his people. Business provides goods and services, creates employment opportunities, and with market capitalism's unique ability to create new wealth, may (if properly done) be the best means of mitigating poverty in the world.

Third, one's work in business may reflect two other related and important but generally under-emphasized theological concepts. Theologian Miroslav Volf makes a strong case that one's calling is an outworking of spiritual giftedness (pneumatological) and a means of active participation in God's transforming work of the world in preparation for the new creation (eschatological).[4]

While each of the "types" presented in the essay "Christ and Business" contribute important insights, Type 5, "Christ the *Transformer* of Business," is most helpful in terms of giving us a proper understanding of Christian engagement with business. It both acknowledges the fallen nature of business and its institutions and recognizes God's work in transforming and redeeming the world he created. Christians then bear a significant responsibility to participate in business (and other parts of culture) in order to contribute to this transformative agenda.[5]

A Multifaceted Calling

Especially since it is a highly influential part of our culture, business should be viewed as a legitimate place of calling for Christians. If Christians were simply to pull out of stained parts of the culture, the invariable course would be further decline. A strategy of withdrawal also neglects the fact that there are no "pure" venues in which one can participate. The whole world bears the staining effect of the Fall.

This is not to say that every part of business is in need of transformation. With respect to practices and areas of commerce that already reflect Christian values, the task is to uphold and promote them. Neither is it correct to state that Christians can or should be involved in every aspect of business. Clearly, some values, practices, and even some entire industries would be more appropriately engaged

3 R. Paul Stevens, "The Marketplace: Mission Field or Mission?" *Crux* 37, no. 3 (September 2001): 11.

4 Miroslav Volf, *Work in the Spirit: Toward a Theology of Work* (Oxford: Oxford University Press, 1991).

5 For a more complete discussion of this idea, see James Skillen, "Conclusion" in Bob Goudzwaard, *Globalization and the Kingdom of God* (Grand Rapids: Baker, 2001).

and changed through external "prophetic" means, such as withdrawal and/or modeling a different way of thinking and acting.

Business activity should not be seen as second class in terms of its spiritual value if proper aims and motives are kept in mind. In fact, it should be seen as a legitimate and important calling and as a proper venue to exercise one's giftedness and, above all, to advance God's kingdom on earth by serving others.

THREE

Christian Ethics for Business: Norms and Benchmarks

An ethical man is a Christian holding four aces.

Mark Twain[1]

He has told you, O mortal, what is good; and what does the LORD *require of you but to do justice, and to love kindness, and to walk humbly with your God?*

Micah 6:8 NRSV

1 Cited in Alexander Hill, *Just Business: Christian Ethics for the Marketplace* (Downers Grove, Ill.: InterVarsity Press, 1997): 11.

INTRODUCTION

In chapter 1, we suggested that the culture of business presented numerous challenges to men and women aspiring to conduct business ethically. Business, it seems, has its own set of rules by which it is played, rules that can be very different from the norms governing one's private life. The temptation is great to compartmentalize one's life and to live life as a dichotomy, with different standards for each sphere, in order to succeed in business. Such a dichotomy, we suggested, is contrary to Christian ethics, which takes as the norm Christ as Lord over all areas of life. Thus, in contrast to Carr, who argued that one must separate workplace morality from the morality of private life, we suggest that this is neither necessary nor desirable.

Though we agree with Bhide and Stevenson that good ethics is not necessarily good business, there are numerous examples of men and women of integrity who are succeeding in their work and leading profitable companies. We further agree with Bhide and Stevenson in their primary argument that good ethics is inherently valuable and should be pursued because it is right, not because it is profitable. We would urge a unified view of life and morality, not only because it is consistent with the Bible, but because such a dichotomy is harmful to one's soul. We think there is good reason to question whether the dichotomy proposed by Carr is even possible to maintain over the long-run of one's career. Such a dichotomy is clearly not desirable, nor is it necessary to succeed.

In this chapter we want to spell out in more detail what a Christian ethic for business entails. The readings for this chapter introduce you to some of the main concepts in Christian ethics and its application to business. The article on business ethics by Alexander Hill synthesizes Christian ethics into three primary principles: holiness, justice, and love. Hill insightfully applies these to business and shows how they can be kept in balance. His goal is not to present a comprehensive Christian ethic, however, and as a result, he assumes many things about Christian ethics, such as how the Bible is used.

By contrast, Bernard Adeney shows in his article how the Bible is to be interpreted and applied. That can be more complicated than we might think because the culture in which the Bible was written is so different than our own. This makes a significant difference in reading the Bible correctly and accurately and in applying it to business as well as to other areas of life. Adeney's background as a cross-cultural missionary gives him a rich framework to address the subject of culture and the Bible. We are committed to the notion that when the Bible addresses a subject, it does so with authority and should be taken seriously. But accounting for cultural differences between the world of the Bible and the world of today is not always easy or straightforward.

We realize, however, that not everyone approaches ethics in the workplace from the perspective of the Bible. In fact, there are numerous ways that people make moral decisions. We want to introduce you to the ones most frequently used and to provide some critique of them before presenting an alternative framework of Christian ethics. We use a roundtable discussion format to help you grasp the essentials of the different ways people make moral decisions. To build a foundation for a Christian ethic for business, we will offer guidelines for using the Bible properly in ethics. Once that foundation is laid, we will then suggest some important concepts for Christian business ethics.

An Introduction to Ethical Reasoning

In our contemporary culture, people use a wide variety of methods of moral reasoning. They employ different ethical systems at different times as they wrestle with what is right or wrong, or what one's moral obligation is in any specific instance. One place to see these various modes of moral reasoning is in the way the debate over various social issues is conducted. In fact, one of the reasons that so many of these debates seem unresolvable is that the participants in them are using drastically different methods of arriving at their conception of right and wrong. Take for example the following scenario:

Imagine that you are the CEO for a company that is launching into a new market, expanding your service to parts of Asia that your company has not previously served. You and your staff have prepared a proposal for a project that could amount to a fifty-million-dollar contract over the next five years for your firm. The contract is to provide your services to a government agency in Southeast Asia. You are now flying to meet with government officials to bid on the deal. When you arrive to meet with the officials, you are told that you must submit a "pledge" to certain officials, in cash, in order to remain competitive in the bidding. When you ask if other bidders are also required to submit such pledges, you are told that that is not your concern. You must submit the money if you are to have any chance of securing the contract. You quickly realize that you have been asked to bribe the officials under the table in order to be considered for the contract. Your company has done this in the past before you became CEO.

Your principles tell you that this is wrong, but there are many other considerations, such as the jobs that will be created as well as those that will be saved by getting this contract, the cultural context in which bribery is a routine practice, and the fact that your interests would be clearly served by securing the contract. You agree to pay the bribe and submit your bid accordingly. On the flight home, you are troubled that you may not have done the right thing. Yet, not only is your career in jeopardy if you fail to win the contract, but hundreds of jobs are also at stake for your company. Upon returning home, you are still bothered as you await word about the contract, so you bring the situation up for discussion at the next local chamber of commerce meeting. Many of your closest friends and associates are among the participants. However, they seem to only add to your confusion as each approaches moral problems with a radically different methodology. The participants (with their respective approaches in parenthesis) respond to you in the following way:

Participant #1: The President of a Community Business (ethical egoist)

"Why is this a moral discussion at all? I would have no problem doing anything that you have just stated. You see, for me it all boils down to the fact that I have a business to run, and the only thing that matters is if I can make a profit, provided I stay within the bounds of the law. In fact, the only business ethic worth its weight is 'Do unto others before they do unto you.' There is no doubt that my competitors would also do this. After all, if my own job is dependent on this contract, what's my family going to do? Starve, so that I can feel good about myself? Forget it! My mortgage is not paid with someone else's moral principles. Aside from all this, isn't capitalism based on self-interest anyway? You guys are so naive. I mean, it's a rough and tumble world. If I don't look out for my needs, who will? A book that you should all read is *Looking Out for Number One*. Its says it all!"

Participant #2: The Head of the Local Chamber of Commerce (a Utilitarian):

"Wow, what a scenario! I admit, the prospect of bribing officials would bother me a bit. But if I were you, I think I could justify my actions based on the good that it will do for my employees and for the local community. Just think, without this contract, hundreds of jobs are at stake. That could devastate our local economy. But if we were to secure the deal, we could create jobs, expand our tax base, and go forward with those badly needed community improvement projects. I know that the competing company would be hurt, but their business doesn't depend on government contracts to the degree that yours does. You see, I believe that it is not necessarily principles that determine right and wrong, but the consequences produced by the actions in question. If a particular course of action or decision produces the best set of consequences, then it seems to me that it should be allowed. To put it another way, the action that produces the greatest balance of benefits over harms is the one that is the most moral. So in this case, what is important is whether or not taking the information would produce the greatest good for the greatest number of people. As I just pointed out, this could produce a lot of good for the people in your company. Now, there may be situations in which a similar action may produce, on balance, more negative than positive consequences. In those cases, it should not be allowed. We should be careful of setting hard-and-fast rules that don't take the consequences into account."

Participant #3: The President of the Area Christian Businesswomen's Chapter (Deontologist, or principle-based ethics):

"Hey, wait a minute, doesn't this simply come down to simple bribery, which is designed to create an unlevel playing field for competition? This is clearly wrong. My moral authority, the Bible and common Western morality is clearly opposed to this. Thus, it doesn't matter to me how many people would lose their jobs or what our community would gain from the contract. It equally doesn't matter if I might lose my job! Bribery is wrong, period! If torn between loyalty to my employer and loyalty to God, there's no question as to who I will honor first. Likewise, you should instead trust that God will provide if you honor his principles first."

Participant #4: Local Television Talk Show Host (emotivist):

"I hate to throw a monkey wrench into this whole discussion, but in my view, all the participants so far are trying to do the impossible. Each person so far has attempted to make some kind of determination of what is right or wrong in this case. I don't think that's possible. They are really just using the language of right and wrong to mask their own personal preferences. What I mean is that anytime a person says that something is right or wrong, all they are saying and can say about it is that they either like or dislike the action or position under consideration. We should be honest and admit that we're only talking about our preferences, and using moral language to give greater persuasive power to our argument. In this specific case, you should ask yourself how you feel about it. Feelings are more important than any reasoning you could do. In my own view, my feelings would not be bothered by any of this, so I think it's okay."

Participant #5: An Anthropology Professor (relativist):

"I clearly reject what my friend from the Christian businesswomen's society says because the Bible is not my moral authority! Now I'm not prepared to say that there is no such thing as genuine right and wrong, but I do think that there is no universal, absolute standard of right and wrong. What is moral depends on the situation and on what the cultural consensus of right and wrong is at that time. In this case, if the culture has reached a consensus that it should be allowed, then I see no reason why it should not be allowed. Conversely, if the culture is opposed to the practice, I see no good reason why any particular standard should be forced on them. I know that in most parts of the non-Western world, bribery is just a part of the game. Even though it may seem terrible to us, who are we to judge what is right for them? We should simply respect their norms. So the operative question that we should be asking is whether or not this is an acceptable part of the business culture as opposed to the morality of other parts of life. You know, what is the right thing to do while in Rome?"

Participant #6: A Minister (virtue theory):

"I'd like to put a slightly different slant on this issue. You see, I believe that there's more to morality than simply arguing about correct decisions when a person is faced with a moral dilemma. There is more to the moral life than simply doing the right thing and making the correct decision. Being the right type of person is more important. Thus, we cannot neglect the place of an individual's character, or virtue, when considering ethical questions. Simply debating issues is powerless if we continue to ignore the character traits that give people the ability to actually do the right thing. After all, most of the recent business ethics scandals in the headlines involved participants that were educated at the nation's elite universities. So it couldn't have been just a matter of knowing right from wrong. It was plainly a matter of character. As such, I believe that there are more important questions that need to be asked in this situation. For example, what does a person's attitude toward fair competition tell us about his or her character? What does support for paying the bribe or opposition to it say about our society? Does it say that as a society we no longer value fair competition on the merits of the product or the service? Besides, as I mentioned earlier, what good is only debating about ethics when our schools and communities no longer agree about, or seek to equip our children with, the character necessary to carry out what they know to be right? These are very important questions that cannot be ignored in any discussion of ethics in business."

Whew! A bit confusing, isn't it? No wonder we have so many disagreements about morality in society. Each person in this discussion has argued using a distinctive style of moral reasoning from a specific ethical system. They represent each of the predominant modes of moral reasoning that are used in the debates over today's current moral issues. Examples of the various styles of moral reasoning discussed in this chapter appear frequently in the media during discussions of moral issues. You will likely find most of these systems employed regularly if you watch for them. A notable exception, however, is the approach taken by the last participant, the virtue or character approach. Though it has made somewhat of a resurgence in recent years, it is a view that is still largely absent from public debate. However, it is an approach that we believe is essential to the very functioning and survival of the free-market system. We will say more about this in the last part of this chapter. In what follows, we will analyze each of the ethical systems used by the participants in this panel, spelling out the positive elements of each system as well as offering a critique of each system.

Ethical Egoism

Ethical egoism is the theory that the morality of an act is determined by one's self-interest. Those actions that advance self-interest are moral, and those that do not are not moral. To say that one is an ethical egoist is not to say that they are egotistical. This is a common confusion. The ethical egoist simply uses self-interest to make moral decisions. Participant #1 in the discussion above is a clear example of an ethical egoist because he was making his moral decision based strictly on his self-interest.

Although egoism has its appeal in the contemporary culture, there are problems with it as an all-encompassing ethical system. First, egoism does not provide any way to umpire conflicting interests without appeal to some other system. What happens when my self-interest conflicts with yours? All the egoist can do to resolve that conflict is to reassert his basic premise of self-interest. It is naive to think that interests never conflict. Yet this assumption seems to be necessary if ethical egoism is to be a workable system.

A second problem with ethical egoism as a sufficient system of ethics is that the Scripture calls believers and unbelievers both to a balance of self-interest and altruism. We are called to care about the needs of others because they are comparable to our own and because a significant part of being a disciple of Christ is following his altruistic example. Believers are called to be servants, and that invariably involves periodically putting others' needs ahead of our own. This does not, however, obligate believers to neglect their legitimate self-interest. The Bible does not condemn the pursuit of self-interest. Philippians 2:4 makes this very clear when it says, "Each of you should look not only to your own interests, but also to the interests of others." The Bible condemns exclusive pursuit of self-interest, not self-interest balanced by concern for the interests of others. The Bible does not call its followers to the kind of extreme altruism that ethical egoists claim it does. One should remember that at times even Jesus walked away from the crowds in order to get time alone with his heavenly Father. Thus, there is a place for legitimate self-interest, to which the Bible periodically appeals, only it must be balanced by a compassionate concern for the interests of others.

Utilitarianism

Utilitarianism is known as a teleological system (taken from the Greek word *telos*, meaning "end"), in which the end produced determines the morality of an act. In fact, sometimes utilitarianism and teleological ethics are used interchangeably. The most common form of utilitarianism today asserts that the act that produces the greatest good for the greatest number, that is, that produces the greatest balance of good consequences over harmful ones, is the one to choose. Thus, this type of moral reasoning is also called consequentialism, because of its overriding emphasis on the consequences of an action.

Utilitarian modes of moral reasoning are widely applied in many of the current moral issues under debate. As was evident from Participant #2 in the discussion, a good deal of the discussion about morals in business is conducted on utilitarian grounds, where the principles take a backseat to consideration of the consequences. If, on balance, the action provides more beneficial consequences for more people, then it is considered by advocates to be the most moral course of action. A further example of this type of reasoning is involved when companies consider closing plants or laying off workers to maintain their competitive position in the marketplace. Often the firm will justify these measures by acknowledging that they are producing harm for some but asserting that, on balance, they are safeguarding the jobs of the rest of the employees by keeping the company in business, thus producing a greater balance of benefit over harms.

Though utilitarianism has its appeal, especially in a secular society, it also has its shortcomings. The most common charge against utilitarianism is that it cannot protect the rights of minorities and that it sometimes can justify obvious injustices because the greater good is served. For example, slavery in the South during the Civil War era was clearly justifiable from a utilitarian point of view. It provided cheap labor that made the South very prosperous and clearly benefited more people than it harmed. But no one today would justify slavery on any grounds, let alone utilitarian ones, and the good consequences that it produced appear not only irrelevant but callous toward the suffering that so many slaves endured. The reason that slavery was immoral has little to do with the balance of consequences. Rather, it has to do with a universal principle that directs us to safeguard the basic rights and dignity of each individual, ultimately because they are made in the image of God.

As with egoism, even though utilitarianism has wide popular appeal and is the basis for much public policy, other problems remain for this system. First, it requires that the decision maker be a good prophet, capable of predicting and measuring harms and benefits, which is difficult to do. Second, the notions of benefit and harm are not value neutral. For example, why is it a harm when someone is laid off or killed? It is clearly because of a prior commitment to a moral principle of human dignity and the sanctity of life that says it is wrong to kill someone, regardless of the benefit. In order to explain why something should count as a benefit or a harm, one must appeal to principles. There is as much diversity and pluralism about what constitutes a benefit and a harm as there is about the definition of the good. Nevertheless, although there are problems with utilitarianism, it is important to take the consequences of actions and decisions seriously since there may be times when appeal to principles does not resolve a dilemma.

Emotivism

Emotivism is an approach to morality that has made a significant resurgence in recent decades. Listening to callers and guests of popular radio and television talk shows, one could easily conclude that this is one of the dominant methods to address ethical questions today.[2] Participant #4 in our discussion above represents this approach. According to the emotivist, personal feelings are the most important determinant of right and wrong. Since feelings differ from individual to individual, however, morality quickly breaks down into a matter of personal preference. The emotivist holds that the judgments expressed by moral language simply communicate a person's emotions about a subject, and thus nothing anyone says in moral language can be true or false. Ethical statements are considered by the emotivist as attitudes masquerading as facts.

One of the primary criticisms of emotivism is that it cannot account for the place of reason in ethics. Emotivism sets up a false dichotomy that is as follows:

a) Either there are moral facts, like there are facts about the sciences, or

b) Values are nothing more than expressions of our subjective feelings.

But there is another critical possibility: that moral truths are truths of reason, or a moral judgment is true if it is backed up by better reasons than the alternatives. As Christians, we would also say that moral truths are truths of revelation and that there is a strong connection between the facts of creation and the facts of morality. Good reasons usually resolve moral disagreements, but for the emotivist, giving good

2 For further commentary on this, see Thomas Sowell, "The Mushing of America," *Forbes*, 18 July 1994, 69.

reasons and manipulation would amount to much the same thing. There is no good reason to assume that moral language is not also factual language and that moral judgments are cognitive statements, not just expressions of emotion or preference. It should not be surprising that ethical statements are not empirically verifiable, since right and wrong are not empirically observable qualities. But neither are they simply emotive expressions.

Deontological Systems

In contrast to teleological forms of moral reasoning, deontological moral systems are based on principles. Deontological is derived from the Greek term *dei* meaning "it is necessary." From this comes the notion of moral obligations that are inherently necessary, not because of the ends or consequences they produce. Deontological obligations are one's moral duties because they are inherently the right thing to do. The deontologist would say, for example, that theft is wrong, period, irrespective of who benefits from it. The consequences of actions are not relevant for determining right and wrong since moral obligations come from principles, not ends. Participant #3 takes this approach in the previous discussion.

There are a variety of types of deontological systems, both from religious perspectives and from more secular views of the world. In fact, most religious traditions that are centered around a book, such as Judaism, Christianity, and Islam, are strongly deontological in their ethical outlook because their principles come from either the words or the ideas (or both) of their sacred book. This is usually called the "divine command theory" of ethics, where the divine commands recorded in the inspired literature form the primary source of moral guidance for the particular religion's followers. The Bible is clearly foundational for Christian ethics, and we will discuss how to use the Bible in ethics later in this chapter.

A second form of deontological morality is found in the use of natural law. In general, natural law refers to broad, general, objective, and widely shared moral values that are consistent with Scripture and revealed apart from Scripture. Justice, fairness, respect for an individual's dignity, the obligation not to harm another, truth telling, and the respect for life in prohibitions against killing are some examples of virtually universally shared values that had an origin that predated Scripture.[3] Oxford University theologian John Macquarrie has put it this way: "In fact the very term 'natural law' is misleading if it is taken to mean some kind of code. The natural law is not another code or system of laws in addition to all the actual systems, but is simply our

3 For a catalog of these values traced historically, see the appendix in C. S. Lewis, *The Abolition of Man* (New York: Macmillan, 1947).

rather inaccurate way of referring to those most general moral principles against which particular rules or codes have to be measured."[4] To call them natural *laws* can be misleading, since they are the general principles on which our specific laws are based.

Perhaps the central passage in the Bible that affirms natural law is in Romans 2:1–16. After Paul appeals to creation to point out the sin of the nonreligious, and, interestingly, to oppose homosexuality in Romans 1:18–32, he proves in Romans 2:1–16 that the moralistic person is also condemned before God because of his sin. The heart of this passage as it applies to natural law is in verses 14–15, where Paul states, "Indeed, when Gentiles, who do not have the law, do by nature things required by the law, they are a law for themselves, even though they do not have the law, since they show that the requirements of the law are written on their hearts, their consciences also bearing witness, and their thoughts now accusing, now even defending them."

God appears to hold those without the law accountable for their sin in the same way that he holds the Jews accountable (Romans 2:17–29). It is difficult to see how this could be just unless those without the law had some way in which they could know what was right and wrong. In other words, for God to legitimately hold the world accountable for sin, they must have access to God's standard of morality, even if they are without special revelation. This would be natural law or general revelation applied to morality. God has revealed these values outside of Scripture and made them accessible to those without access to Scripture. Paul's teaching in Romans 2 is parallel to the oracles to the nations (Isaiah 13–27; Jeremiah 46–51; Ezekiel 25–32; Amos 1–2), in which the prophets condemn Israel's pagan neighbors, who did not have the law, for many of the same things for which he condemned Israel, who did have the law. Unless the nations had some access to God's law outside of the written law, it is hard to see how God can be just in holding people accountable for that which they have no knowledge.[5]

To illustrate how natural law can apply to business ethics, consider employee rights. One of the most widely held universal moral principles is the dignity of the individual person and the corresponding duty to respect it. Human dignity is ultimately grounded in the image of God, but one does not need to be a religious believer to uphold the right to human dignity. This principle undergirds much of the American Bill of Rights and declarations of human rights made around the world in this century. It is also the fundamental moral principle that obligates employers to provide safe and humane working conditions for employees. Workplaces that carry risk of injury to workers are problematic because this signifies a lack of respect for the

4 John Macquarrie, "Rethinking Natural Law," in Charles E. Curran and Richard A. McCormick, eds., *Readings in Moral Theology, No. 7: Natural Law and Theology* (New York: Paulist Press, 1991), 239.

5 For further exegetical study on the biblical basis for natural law, see Alan F. Johnson, "Is There Biblical Warrant for Natural Law Theories?" *Journal of the Evangelical Theological Society* 27 (June 1982): 185–99.

dignity of the individual worker. Firms employing workers in third world countries have the responsibility to provide wages and working conditions that are consistent with respect for human dignity. Furthermore, when living arrangements are provided as part of the compensation, those quarters need to be consistent with human dignity. That is not to say that employers overseas must provide conditions similar to those in the United States, but the conditions must not violate basic norms of human dignity. This principle comes from natural law and is central to the discussion of employee rights. The need of firms to make a reasonable profit must also be considered alongside of respect for worker dignity. Of course, if workers willingly choose to work in substandard conditions, they are responsible for that choice. But in countries where workers have few employment choices, their vulnerability increases the moral obligation of employers to provide humane working conditions.

Respect for human dignity is also at the heart of society's concern over sexual harassment and workplace discrimination. Because both men and women possess fundamental dignity from being made in God's image, they are not to be the objects of sexual harassment. They are not to be treated as objectified sexual objects to be used for pleasure but are to be respected as persons, significant because they bear God's image. Though there is disagreement on the definition of sexual harassment, whether the emphasis on it has gone too far, and how to protect the rights of the accused, virtually everyone agrees that sexual harassment is immoral because it violates a person's essential dignity. Similarly, discrimination on the basis of race, gender, or disability violates the respect for each person's dignity.

Virtue Theory

As we previously noted, virtue approaches to ethics have been strangely absent from today's public discussion over moral issues. However, the consideration of character in ethics has made a resurgence as of late. There have been a host of academic works on the topic, and works such as *Habits of the Heart* by Robert Bellah and colleagues and *The Book of Virtues* by William J. Bennett are evidence that the approach is making a comeback in popular circles as well. As is evident from the comments offered by Participant #6 in the previous discussion, the virtue approach greatly differs from the other methods.

All of the normative theories examined to this point are action-oriented ethical systems. Every participant in the chamber of commerce discussion except the last participant uses one of these methods. Most ethical theories in modern times have focused on doing the right action or making the right decision when confronted by a moral dilemma. Many of the major debates in ethics have revolved around the basis for determining what is the right action, whether consequences or principles provide that basis, and whether the right action is universal or relative. The virtue theorist holds that there is more to morality than simply doing the right thing. The foundational moral claims made by the virtue theorist are those about the person doing the action, not the act that he or she performs. The tradition of virtue theory is a long one, going back to Plato and Aristotle, and includes the Gospels, the Stoics and Epicureans, and Thomas Aquinas.

Some of the main differences between virtue ethics and standard act-oriented ethics include an emphasis on being over doing, an emphasis on who a person should become over what a person should do, the importance of following exemplary people over following moral rules, an emphasis on a person's motive or attitude over action, and a stress on developing character over obeying rules. Virtue theory is an ethics of character, not of duty. These emphases are certainly consistent with the biblical emphasis on emulating the character of Christ.

The virtue approach is essential to business ethics for several reasons. First, Participant #6 in the above discussion is correct in his statement that many of the most egregious business ethics scandals have involved participants who graduated from some of the country's elite schools and who almost certainly knew right from wrong. Thus, ethics has much to do with character. For example, whether one wants to call his character flaw greed or pride, many of us tend to forget that convicted insider Michael Milken was earning over $350 million a year when he cheated to get even more. There is no question of Milken's intelligence; he was a financial genius who graduated from an Ivy League university. Moreover, he knew his actions were wrong because he engaged in numerous actions to cover up his transgressions. Thus, it is not just a matter of moral reason, but of the will working in conjunction with knowledge of matters of right and wrong. It has been said that "reason without virtue is powerless, while virtue without reason is blind."[6] Thus, there is a need for both reason and virtue in a comprehensive approach to ethics.

Second, as a system that requires virtues such as trust, honesty, and cooperation for its very functioning, the foundations of capitalism may be doomed without the character necessary to exercise self-restraint on the part of the participants. Indeed, the founders of our nation believed that the democratic experiment would only work if the citizens were virtuous. Contrary to popular belief, total liberty was never their intent. Rather, their vision was one of "ordered" or "restrained" liberty, that is, freedom tempered by morals and character.

6 Adapted from William Frankena, *Ethics*, 2nd ed. (New York: Prentice Hall, 1973), 65.

The alarming direction of many recent trends and their impact on society reveals the truthfulness of what they envisioned. Since business in a free-enterprise system is a cornerstone of democracy, we should all be worried about the future of the free-market economy if virtue is not once again taken seriously in the public dialogue about morality.

Most of these systems are still widely in use in the contemporary culture. As you read and hear about the different pressing moral issues being debated in public, be sure to watch for which of these styles of moral reasoning are used. The Bible does employ different types of moral reasoning from time to time, but nowhere does it suggest that any of the systems mentioned in this chapter are all-sufficient. The biblical emphasis seems to be strongly deontological (a blend of divine commands and natural law); that is, God has revealed his moral principles primarily but not exclusively in the Bible. His principles are also evident in the world as he has revealed them through general revelation. Furthermore, as mentioned above, Scripture also places a strong emphasis on moral character. Thus, the Bible seems to support a total approach to ethics that is based on moral principles that are guided by the virtues exemplified by Christ in their application.

READINGS

The Bible and Culture in Ethics

Bernard T. Adeney

From *Strange Virtues: Ethics in a Multicultural World* (Downers Grove, Ill.: InterVarsity Press, 1995), chapter 4: 79–105.

Christians believe that the Bible is the primary, authoritative guide to faith and life. Cultural conventions do not have an authority that overrules Scripture. When Christians differ, whatever their culture, they rightly search the Scriptures to find wisdom.

William Dyrness has argued that "it is scripture, and not its 'message,' that is finally transcultural."[1] The message of the Bible, or the way it is interpreted, is always perceived and stated in human language that reflects the priorities of particular people in a particular culture. The entire canon of the Bible, on the other hand, is constitutive of what it means to be a Christian in every time and place. David Kelsey writes that to call a text "scripture" is to say:

1) that its use in certain ways in the common life of the Christian community is essential to establishing and preserving the community's identity. . . . 2) It is authority for the common life of the Christian community. . . . 3) It is to ascribe some kind of

'wholeness' to it.... 4) The expression, "Scripture is authoritative for theology" has self-involving force.[2]

The term *scripture* implies commitment. In every time and place, believers define themselves in relation to Scripture. Whatever their differences in doctrine or practice, all accept a common written source as the vehicle of the revelation of God in Christ.

Yet the Bible is not self-interpreting. While all accept the text,[3] what they think it means differs widely.

The Cultural Context of the Bible

Not only the culture of the reader but also the many different cultures that lie within and behind the text compound the task of understanding. We can understand what we read only in relation to our cultural experience. But everything that is written in the Bible is located within the cultural experience of its author or editor.

There is an overlap between the cultures of the Bible and the cultures of its readers in every age. If there weren't, the task of reading such a foreign text would be impossible. But there are also pervasive differences. If we do not understand these differences, the ethical teaching of the Bible remains incomprehensible.

Christian commitment to the Bible reflects the conviction that God is revealed through this text. As Robert McAfee Brown has commented,

> Christians make the initially bizarre gamble that "the strange new world within the Bible" is a more accurate view of the world than our own and that we have to modify our views as a result. This means engaging in dialogue with the Bible—bringing our questions to it, hearing its questions to us, examining our answers in its light, and taking its answers very seriously, particularly when they conflict with our own, which will be most of the time.[4]

The problem comes when the Bible's questions and its answers seem totally foreign and incomprehensible to us. Whatever their doctrine of Scripture, most Christians simply ignore the parts that seem irrelevant. But more difficult to ignore are differences in interpretation between different believers or even in the same person at different times.

Devout Christians sometimes marvel that each time they come to a familiar passage they learn something new. The Holy Spirit opens their eyes to new insight. Whenever a person reads a text again, she comes to it from a slightly different context. This week she has different problems and concerns from those she faced a year ago. As the context of her interpretation changes, she sees new things in the text. Just as two photographs of the same scene can look dramatically different because of how they are framed, what focus is used, the light setting chosen and the type of film and camera used, so a text looks different to us as we visualize it from different vantage points. With dramatically different cultures, the range of vantage points widens.

This does not mean that the text changes. The number and types of legitimate interpretations are controlled by what is really in the text.[5] What is in the text itself is ruled by the finite number of meanings possible in its original context. Ethical instructions, laws, examples, and narratives cannot be abstracted from the context without affecting their meaning. Whether the Bible says, "do not kill," "greet one another with a holy kiss" or "Jesus wept," the meaning of the text cannot be understood without the context.

Without this understanding, much of the Bible would be even more puzzling than it is. For example, in Exodus 23:19 the Israelites are commanded, "You shall not boil a kid in its mother's milk." Knowing that "a kid" means a baby goat does not get us much closer to understanding why there should be such a prohibition. While animal-rights activists might be delighted with this verse, it is unlikely that prevention of cruelty to animals was the motive for the law. Archaeological discoveries concerning Canaanite fertility practices provide a much more plausible explanation. Boiling a kid in its mother's milk was evidently part of a common fertility rite. Thus the law should be understood as forbidding syncretism with Canaanite religions. Those who have no connection with fertility rites may find the literal meaning of the law irrelevant. On the other hand, insofar as we can find analogies in our own culture, we may still learn from this rule.

In many parts of the world, rites to appease spirits and assure fertility are common. In such a context this law is very relevant. It teaches us how God viewed fertility magic in the context of ancient Canaan. Even in contexts where such rites are rare, the meaning within this law may have relevance today. For example, a cosmopolite might extrapolate that in some situations, use of a dangerous fertility drug (trust in the magic of science to manipulate what rightly belongs to God) is an unwarranted means of increasing fertility. Perhaps Asians who hunt the rhinoceros (and are threatening its extinction) because of the purported powers of its horn in Chinese medicine should also take note.

Some biblical commands cannot be understood apart from their original context. Others are clear enough but should not be followed in most places today because the cultural condition that gave them meaning are no longer pertinent. Whether the command is Peter's instruction to "greet one another with a kiss of love" (1 Pet 5:14), Paul's observation that "any woman who prays or prophesies with her head unveiled disgraces her head— it is one and the same thing as having her head shaved" (1 Cor 11:5), or the Deuteronomic law that rebellious children should be stoned (Deut 21:18–21), the commandments of Scripture must be understood for what they meant to people in a specific time and place before we can begin to understand what they might mean in *our* time and place.

In the Old Testament, God does or commands many things that appear abhorrent today. It is hard to imagine anything good that can be learned from a law that allows parents to have their children executed. We might speculate that since the law provided for a legal procedure that involved the whole community, it was unlikely to be used except in very extreme cases. Thus in addition to

protecting the community from a youth who was entering life of crime, the law protected children from arbitrary execution by parents who in that culture had unlimited power over their offspring. At the very least, the law required the agreement and participation of the entire community in the death sentence.

The meaning of the law can be understood only in relation to the actual conditions of its context. Possibly the law was intended to prevent even crueler practices. If so, like the divorce law ("because you were so hard-hearted," Mt 19:8), it did not legislate something good but only prevented something worse.

Even so, I am not happy with this law and do not pretend to fully understand it. I don't think that under any circumstances disobedient children should be killed. Apart from the hazard of allowing my modern consciousness to stand in judgment on Scripture, I am culturally too distant from the events reported to fully understand them. But it is clear that the meaning of goodness is sometimes understood differently by the authors of the original text from the way we understand it today.

For example, in Numbers 15 Moses is instructed by God to have a man stoned to death for gathering wood on the sabbath. Functionally the man was doing exactly the same thing as Jesus and his disciples did when they plucked grain to eat on the Sabbath (Mt 12:1–8). But Moses, in accordance with the law, had the wood-gatherer stoned.

Korah, one of Israel's leaders, was outraged by Moses' seeming abuse of power. Korah said, in effect, "Moses, you have gone too far. Why should you have such power to act unilaterally? Are you the only one who knows the mind of God?" (Num 16:3).

Korah was not alone in his concern. He brought with him 250 well-known community leaders who had been appointed members of the council, a group meant to serve as judges of the people. Korah argued that all of God's people are holy. "All the congregation are holy, every one of them, and the LORD is among them. So why then do you exalt yourselves above the assembly of the LORD?" (Num 16:3). As far as I know, this is the first biblical approximation of an argument for the priesthood of all believers.

When we read with modern eyes, Korah was admirable. He didn't grumble off in a corner but responsibly brought his concern to an appointed council. His concerns were ethical and related to human rights; his instincts were democratic; his methods were responsible; and his theological arguments were sophisticated by modern standards. Ah, therein lies the rub. Korah's actions cannot be judged by modern standards. Their meaning can be accessed only within the context of the birth of the nation of Israel in the early bronze age.

The meaning of Korah's action, in his cultural context, was rebellion against Moses and against God, threatening the very existence of the nation of Israel as a unified people of God. In this context, not only was Moses' leadership challenged, but God's leadership, God's law and the discipline required for the formation of a nation were at stake. Apparently the Ten Commandments were also at stake, as gathering wood was a violation of the sabbath.

According to the account in Numbers, God considered Korah's sin so grave that Moses had to plead before God for the survival of the whole nation. As it was, God created an earthquake that scared the Israelites half to death. "The ground under [Korah and his family and followers] was split apart. The earth opened its mouth and swallowed them up. . . . And fire came out from the LORD and consumed the two hundred fifty men offering the incense" (Num 16:31–32, 35).

The point here is not whether Moses was intrinsically right or wrong to cast a death sentence on someone for gathering wood on the sabbath, but that Korah was horribly wrong to challenge Moses' leadership at this pivotal moment in the formation of Israel. Korah's action cannot be judged in itself, apart from his cultural context. This is the story of a power struggle. The action of God leaves no question that Korah's action was wrong in that time and in that place.

It does not follow from this that stoning people who gather wood on the sabbath is a good idea today. The conditions that existed during the time of the exodus will never be repeated. Does this mean that the passage has nothing to teach us? Of course not.

We might learn that keeping the sabbath is very important in the eyes of God—an important lesson for those enslaved by the twin gods of workaholism and materialism. We might learn that democracy is not an absolute good—an important lesson for those who think liberal political culture is the apex of civilization. We might learn that community solidarity and respect for leadership can be more important than individual human rights or even the deaths of 251 people—an important lesson for those who have elevated individualistic autonomy to the central place in ethics.

The story is rich with ethical content. But the content cannot be abstracted into timeless truths that are alienated from real times and places. The story as a whole is far more fertile for ethical learning than any principles abstracted from it. The principles may prove false if they are applied at the wrong time, in the wrong place, by the wrong person. Fortunately, the lessons I drew from the story of Korah are not absolute. From other stories we might learn opposite kinds of lessons.

From the story of the disciples plucking grain we might learn that human need can be more important than legalistic forms. From the story of Nathan the prophet's rebuke of David we might learn that leadership should not have unlimited power and that it is important to stand up against leaders when they violate the rights of individuals (2 Sam 11–12). From the story of Jesus and the woman taken in adultery we might learn that mercy in the judgment of sinners is wise for leaders who are also sinners (Jn 8:2–11). Even from other stories in the life of Moses we might learn lessons balancing the story of Korah.

For example, when the people worship the golden calf, Moses pleads for their lives: "Alas, this people has sinned a great sin; they have made for themselves gods of gold. But now, if you will only forgive their sin—but if not, blot me out of the book you have written" (Ex 32:31–32). Presumably worshiping a golden calf was more serious than gathering firewood on the Sabbath, but in a different context, in a different life situation for God's people, a different ethical judgment is brought into play.

Does this mean that biblical ethics are relativistic, that there are no absolutes and we must make all our decisions according to subjective criteria? By no means! Ethics in the Bible are contextual. They are incarnated words. But they derive from the character and will of God, which do not change.

Eugene Nida, followed by Charles Kraft, suggests that the Bible teaches a "relative cultural relativism."[6] The point is not that all truth is relative, but that all truth is enfleshed in specific language that relates it to specific cultural concerns. We can have an adequate but never an absolute understanding of moral principles: adequate because we can clearly see goodness and evil at work in biblical and modern times, never absolute because goodness and evil are grounded in specific realities of which we know only a tiny part. Nida goes so far as to say,

> The only absolute in Christianity is the triune God. Anything which involves [a human being], who is finite and limited, must of necessity be limited, and hence relative. Biblical cultural relativism is an obligatory feature of our incarnational religion, for without it we would either absolutize human institutions or relativize God.[7]

The poles of absolutism and relativism in ethics will be explored further [elsewhere]. For now we must turn to the question of how ethics are learned from the Bible.

Learning to See the World Through the Stories of the Bible

The primary way we learn goodness from the Bible is by making the story of the Bible the interpretive framework through which we view all of life. This approach does not deny that we learn propositions or doctrines from the Scriptures. But unlike traditional conservative theology, we do not view these doctrines as propositions that we learn and then apply to various contexts. Rather, they are a lens through which we see reality. They help us to see the truth. The lens is not the truth, but it helps us to describe what is true.

George A. Lindbeck writes,

> A comprehensive scheme or story used to structure all dimensions of existence is not primarily a set of propositions to be believed, but is rather the medium in which one moves, a set of skills that one employs in living one's life. Its vocabulary of symbols and its syntax may be used for many purposes, only one of which is the formulation of statements about reality.[8]

Like a culture or language, it is a communal phenomenon that shapes the subjectivities of individuals rather than being primarily a manifestation of those subjectivities.[9]

Christians are inescapably influenced to see and experience the world through the lens of their culture. The reality we experience is socially constructed. It is difficult for even a strong-minded individual to maintain a belief that is contradicted by everyone else. There is a well-known story of an anthropologist who went to study a tribe and ended up becoming an animist. The story of reality the tribe told became the interpretive framework through which the anthropologist perceived all of reality.

A friend of mine experienced a radical loss of faith while studying for his Ph.D. One day he looked out the window in Cambridge and was overwhelmed with the feeling that the buses below, and all the material things he saw, were all that mattered, all that existed. The story of the universe he imbibed day after day from the university and from popular culture was in stark contradiction to his faith. The result was radical doubt.

Our lived morality is a result of the way we perceive reality. People usually act in relation to their interpretation of the way the world really is, far more than from a set of beliefs or principles.

Iris Murdoch has observed that "we are not isolated free choosers, monarchs of all we survey, but benighted creatures sunk in a reality whose nature we are constantly and overwhelmingly tempted to deform by fantasy."[10] In this situation, morality is, as Simone Weil suggested, a matter of attention. We act in accordance with what we think matters, what we see as true. Our actions toward our family or colleagues, or employees or bosses, are more a natural outflowing of the story we are living than a rational choice of good or evil.

Our perception of reality derives from a tradition. In modern liberal culture, reality is perceived as an object accessible to universal, scientific, liberal rationality. In contrast, Alasdair MacIntyre argues that rationality itself is determined by particular traditions and by the social institutions and relationships that embody them. He writes, "What each person is confronted with is at once a set of rival intellectual positions, a set of rival traditions embodied more or less imperfectly in contemporary forms of social relationship and a set of rival communities of discourse, each with its own specific modes of speech."[11]

Modern liberals reject this position and continue to impose their own brand of rationality on everyone. The great temple to universal, scientific rationality is the modern university. Adherence to any particular tradition, especially if it is explicitly religious, is ruled out of the classroom. In contrast, "postmodern" thinkers have radically "deconstructed" or destroyed the pretensions of universal, scientific rationality, along with its liberal institutions. They acknowledge diversity along with the assumption that there is no truth and every tradition is equally untenable.

MacIntyre critiques both the pretensions of liberalism and the cynicism of some forms of postmodernism.[12] He argues that we can be coherent about reality only if we perceive it out of a coherent way of seeing the world. Much of the incoherence of the modern world derives from the fact that people live out of half-believed liberalism, an incoherent mixture of traditions or no tradition at all. The fact that we need a tradition, along with its community of practices, does not

imply that only one tradition is true or that all are false (or equally true). All traditions are limited by the perspective of their histories, their institutions and their standpoint in time and place.

In order to escape the deformed fantasies of our age, Christians believe we must see the world from the perspective of God's work in history.[13] The stories of the Bible provide the language and categories through which we see the world truly. Lindbeck says,

> It is important to note the direction of interpretation. Typology does not make scriptural contents into metaphors for extra scriptural realities but the other way around. It does not suggest, as is often said in our day, that believers find their stories in the Bible, but rather that they make the story of the Bible their story. The cross is not to be viewed as a figurative representation of suffering nor the messianic kingdom as a symbol for hope in the future; rather, suffering should be cruciform, and hopes for the future messianic. . . . It is the text, so to speak, which absorbs the world, rather than the world the text.[14]

Christians learn to be good from the Bible by telling themselves and each other the story of their lives as a part of the story of the Bible. More important than the stories believers tell are the stories they live. Goodness comes by the work of the Holy Spirit when a person lives as part of the people of God. That happens when she has learned the story of Israel, of Jesus, and of the church so well that her life becomes a continuation of the story. Then a Christian becomes "a letter of Christ . . . written not with ink but with the Spirit of the living God, not on tablets of stone but on tablets of human hearts" (2 Cor 3:3).

The great problem for ethics is, of course, *How* do we learn the story of the Bible? There seem to be many stories in the Bible. The stories that are there do not all seem consistent with each other. The cultural contexts of the stories are often strange to us. And the way the same stories are related by different parts of the Christian community are sometimes unrecognizable to each other. These are very large questions, which are beyond the scope of this book. As a start, however, let's consider several of the many ways in which we are formed by the biblical narratives.

Ethics in the Context of a Narrative

Stanley Hauerwas once commented that we can learn more ethics from reading novels than from reading ethics books. The Bible is not an ethics book. It does not contain many systematic treatises on ethics. Where ethics are explicitly addressed, it is usually in the context of a story. The Old Testament law is recounted in the context of the saga of the exodus; the Sermon on the Mount is an integral part of the story of Jesus. To borrow an expression that David Kelsey uses to describe Karl Barth's view of Scripture, the Bible is like a "vast, loosely structured, non-fictional novel."[15]

We learn ethics from a story by allowing its way of seeing the world to become our own symbolic structure of meanings. For example, when we read the story of the prodigal son we may identify with the father, the prodigal, the elder brother, or even the riotous friends. As we identify with one or more characters, their behavior and relationships become symbols of our own behavior and relationships. The meaning and moral evaluation of our own behavior are clarified by the meaning assigned to the actions of the characters in the story. The prodigal son's riotous living may symbolize our own rebellion and teach us that forgiveness is really possible.

Within the biblical narrative we see a moral outlook on life that is expressed in many literary forms. In stories, poetry, history, prophecy, apocalypse, law, sermons, proverbs, letters, songs, biography, prayers and other kinds of literature, good and evil are revealed and symbolized within a particular cultural context.

When Christians read the rich profusion of biblical material, four common questions emerge: (1) How do we deal with all the intense and messy emotions expressed by biblical authors? (2) How relevant are biblical commandments for life today? (3) Are biblical principles the heart of

Christian ethics? (4) Does the Bible tell us *why* we should live in one way rather than in another?[16] Many other questions could be added to these four, such as the place of moral examples (positive and negative), visions, aesthetic expression, tragedy and so on. All are best understood in the context of a story. Nevertheless, in order to limit my task I will examine these four questions.

1. *Expressions of emotion.* The Bible is full of emotions. From the fear of Adam and Eve to the exultation of David, from the erotic love of Solomon to the anguish of Jeremiah, from the depression of Job to the calm courage of Esther, from the tears of Jesus to the joy of his disciples, every book of the Bible bears the mark of breathing human beings whose moral lives are expressed with emotion.

At the emotional level there can be no precise formulation of what are appropriate responses to specific situations. Usually such responses are recorded without comment. Emotional responses cannot be easily labeled good or bad. They are more amenable to the terms *honest* or *dishonest*, *appropriate* or *inappropriate*. For a priori reasons, only Jesus' emotive responses may be labeled good. The psalmist who expressed happiness at the thought of Babylonian babies' having their brains smashed in is clearly not a guide for our emotional response to our enemies (Ps 137:9).

Nevertheless, the scope and range of emotions expressed by biblical writers gives valuable insight into the way God's people saw the world around them. In their emotions we see their honest response to what they saw as God's work in the world. Because they did not always see clearly, their emotions were not always appropriate. In many cases we are not able to judge whether the responses were appropriate. Their situation is too far from us. Their experience is too foreign. Even so, in most cases the emotions expressed enable us to identify with the biblical writer. While we may not uncritically imitate biblically expressed emotions, those emotions often provide a window into the heart of the situations the writers faced.

Sometimes within a story we see the destructive effects of negative emotions. Sometimes we see how God addresses human beings in the midst of their emotions. And sometimes human emotions are vehicles for the revelation of the heart of God. In Jeremiah, the prophet's own feeling of anguish at the coming destruction of Jerusalem is not distinguished from the Word of Yahweh. Gerhard von Rad comments that Jeremiah's unwanted vision contains a "darkness so terrible . . . that it constitutes a menace to very much more than the life of a single man; God's whole way with Israel hereby threatens to end in some kind of metaphysical abyss."[17]

Unlike Jeremiah, we are not meant to curse ourselves and our parents and wish we had never been born. But if we ever do, if we ever experience despair that is even remotely like Jeremiah's, then his story and the way that God dealt with him in it may become vitally important to our moral life. Although Jeremiah's specific responses to his situation are not presented as a model for us to follow, within the context of the story of his life with God his emotions reveal the depths of evil and despair that exist in the world. We cannot judge him. Perhaps his response was far more appropriate than that of anyone else in the city of Jerusalem at the time. Certainly he saw more than anyone else. His emotions teach us to see.

2. *Moral rules and law.* It is tragic how many Christians try to reduce the Bible's moral teaching to the level of rules, commandments and laws. When ethics and law are equated, the primary questions for biblical interpretation become, Am I bound by this law or may I safely ignore it? Is this commandment absolute, or is it relative to its original context? Is this instruction a commandment for all times and places, or is it a specific rule for a particular culture? Is this law relevant or irrelevant? Is this a moral or a ceremonial law?

The problem is not that these questions are invalid. But they do not go deep enough. Jesus said,

Do not think that I have come to abolish the law or the prophets; I have come not to abolish but to fulfill. For truly I tell you, until heaven and earth pass away, not one letter, not one stroke of a letter, will pass from the law until all is accomplished. Therefore whoever breaks one of the least of these commandments, and teaches others to do the same, will be called least in the kingdom of heaven; but whoever does them and teaches them will be called great in the kingdom of heaven. For I tell you, unless your righteousness exceeds that of the scribes and Pharisees, you will never enter the kingdom of heaven. (Mt 5:17–20)

There is no part of the law that is irrelevant. The common distinction between ceremonial and moral law has no substantiation in the Old or New Testament. So-called ceremonial laws are interspersed with clearly moral commandments. The ancient Israelites knew no distinction between the two. The religious and moral life of Israel were a single tapestry. Furthermore, as we have seen, some of the "moral" laws, including those calling for capital punishment, are the most difficult for modern people to understand.

The attempt by some "theonomists" to argue that all the laws of the Bible must be literally followed is in stark contradiction to a narrative reading of Scripture. When we abstract the laws from their context, their very source of meaning is lost. At the other extreme, some dispensationalists would discard some of the most profound teachings of Scripture by assigning them to a dispensation or period that does not concern Christians. For example, some say that the "Sermon on the Mount" is addressed only to Jews who will remain on the earth after the rapture.[18] The narrative structure of the law is honored, but at a cost of deleting some of its greatest insights. Theological liberals sometimes do the same but with different criteria.

Perhaps the most common and damaging "criticism with a penknife"[19] is the practice of rejecting the "difficult" Old Testament law in favor of New Testament grace. Not only does this contradict the practice and teaching of Jesus, but it deprives the believer of a great portion of the Old Testament. New Testament commandments are not necessarily more authoritative than Old Testament laws. Neither can be understood or blindly followed apart from their context. Their meaning is their source of authority and derives from God's will for God's people in a particular time and place.

Christopher Wright has classified the Old Testament law into five categories, each of which functioned within a specific sphere of ancient Jewish life. These categories include criminal law, civil law, family law, cultic law and charitable law.[20] Each of these areas of law was relative to the specific social structures of Israel. The law helped create and maintain these social structures. Today our social structures are different. Insofar as our societies are not agrarian, monarchical, slave-based, patriarchal, tribal, theocratic, polygamous, Middle Eastern and so on, we will have to develop our own laws to govern ourselves.

Laws are functional within their spheres of authority. They reflect an orientation toward love of God and neighbor within a specific social setting. Insofar as our setting is similar, these laws provide wisdom and instruction to us today.

Jesus said, "'You shall love the Lord your God with all your heart, and with all your soul, and with all your mind.' This is the greatest and first commandment. And a second is like it: 'You shall love your neighbor as yourself.' On these two commandments hang all the law and the prophets" (Mt 22:37–40). Every kind of biblical literature must be understood both in relation to its context and in relation to the great love commandments. These commandments are the motive that lies behind every other commandment. We can learn from every law in the Bible when we understand how each law makes the love commandment specific in a particular context.

Biblical moral rules are usually simple and outline the boundaries of acceptable conduct rather than the specifics. For example, the prohibitions of the Decalogue (Ten Commandments) mark the edges of God's will and must be understood within the context of God's liberation of the people from Egypt and their revelatory purpose for Israel. The command not to steal, for example, does not elucidate the details of Christian economic relations. It does provide a basic boundary

for acceptable economic behavior which has significance for every society. But the meaning of stealing may differ from culture to culture with varying definitions of property rights.

The prohibition of theft, like the other nine commandments, is not a timeless ethical principle that we must translate into different cultural idioms. Still less is it a criminal law code. The Decalogue includes no detailed legislation or penalties. Rather it is a commandment that derives its meaning from the countless rules and regulations that are given in the criminal, civil, family, cultic and charitable law. Taken together, these laws provide a picture of the kind of community God wanted Israel to be in the early bronze age.

In order to understand the kind of community God wants us to be today, we must understand the picture drawn by the biblical narrative of the people of God. The laws enflesh that paradigmatic picture. We are not freed from the laws in the sense that we need not follow them. Rather, we are bound to follow the *meaning* of the law as it is contained in the account of God's will for Israel. As we can see from Jesus' commentary on the prohibition of adultery, that task may be far more rigorous than merely obeying the law. Jesus suggested that the meaning of adultery encompasses all male lust which objectifies women in the secret of the heart (Mt 5:27–28).

All of the classic "four uses of the law" may be understood as elucidating the symbolic structure of meaning revealed in the biblical story. (1) The theological or revelatory use of the law shows us the nature of the world and the meaning of our relationships and actions. (2) The moral use of the law convicts us of sin and drives us to Christ. (3) The political/social use of the law utilizes the paradigm of society revealed by the law to help create modern legal norms that will function in our society with similar purposes to the biblical law. (4) The didactic, teaching use of the law seeks concrete, applicable rules that are as relevant today as when they were first given by God, because the contextual meaning of the law still holds.

Luther and Calvin had a classic debate over the four uses of the law. Both accepted the first three, but Luther argued that because of grace we are freed from the fourth. My position combines the two Reformers' positions. Like Calvin, I do not think we are freed from the law. Like Luther, I do not believe we are bound by its particulars without consideration of context. Insofar as we can discover it, we are bound to the *meaning* to which the law points. The meaning of the law can be understood only in relation to the story of which it is a part.

3. *Moral principles and themes.* A common approach to ethics is to seek the basic moral principles that lie behind all the rules, laws and instructions of the Bible. The rule may then be disregarded in favor of the principle. The strength of this approach is that it seeks the meaning of the law. The principles of the great commandment to love God and your neighbor are the foundation of all Christian ethics. We are to interpret all the moral instruction of the Bible through the lens of these great principles.

Jesus is very harsh in his condemnation of those who meticulously follow every biblical rule but have forgotten the meaning and purpose of the law: "Woe to you, scribes and Pharisees, hypocrites! For you tithe mint, dill and cummin, and have neglected the weightier matters of the law: justice and mercy and faith. It is these you ought to have practiced without neglecting the others. You blind guides! You strain out a gnat but swallow a camel!" (Mt 23:23–24).

Justice, mercy and faith are foundational to a moral life. Through them we can understand the meaning of the law. But there is danger in seeing them as the basic meaning behind the law. Even the greatest principles are abstractions that live primarily in the world of thought and words. What does it mean to love God and do justice? The law tells you how in a specific situation. Even better, a story tells you how. If the great principles that may be deduced from the parable of the good Samaritan or the parable of the prodigal son are listed, some might think we have clearer teaching. But the principles listed are not *more* than the story. They are very much less. The idea that God loves sinners may leave a person cold. But the image of the father rushing to embrace his rebellious son grips the heart. It tells us how God loves us by giving us an image that relates to our experience and imagination.

Principles are indispensable to biblical ethics, but they should not be elevated to become the central source, still less the *only* source, of ethics. Principles are a tool for understanding the meaning of God's will, divorced from any specific situation or context. They lack the specificity of contact with cultural reality. Christians who make principles central often attempt to prioritize them to overcome situations of value conflict. For example, if the principle of protecting life is higher than the principle of telling the truth, then Rahab's lie can be justified.[21] Others absolutize certain principles in such a way that a sociocultural interpretation of the principle is treated like a moral rule that gives the same answer in every possible situation.[22]

With the exception of the great commandment, principles should not be rigidified into a strict hierarchy. It is not clear from the biblical record that a life is always of more value than the truth, or that, to quote Norman Geisler, "a complete person is more valuable than an incomplete person."[23] Nor should a particular cultural interpretation of a principle be taken as a rule for all time. Honoring parents (a principle) does not necessarily mean patriarchy (a sociocultural structure).

Just as principles help us see the meaning of biblical laws, so laws reveal the meaning of principles in a particular context. The real meaning of a principle can be understood only as it touches reality. But where it touches different realities, its incarnated meaning changes. The principle does not change at the level of abstract words. Justice and love remain the ideals. But whether they mean a person should be forgiven or stoned depends on the context.

Often moral rules point beyond themselves to principles. Take this moral rule: "If you take your neighbor's cloak in pawn, you shall return it to him by sunset, because it is his only covering. It is the cloak in which he wraps his body; in what else can he sleep? If he appeals to me, I will listen, for I am full of compassion" (Ex 22:26 NEB; this is categorized by Wright among the "charitable laws"). Taken as a moral rule, this may not give us much direct help for specific economic relations in the modern world. Coats are not usually taken in pawn today, and even if they were, they are not usually the only thing in which a person can sleep.[24] The law points beyond itself to the principle of compassion for the poor. The principle teaches us that God cares about the poor and how we treat them.

The meaning of the principle of care for the poor is derived from this and many other rules about how one should treat a poor person in a particular situation. Principles are tools to help us reincarnate moral practice from one context to another. By abstracting some of the meaning from a law in simple form, they help us see how God's will in the biblical context might be relevant to us, even though our context is different. But the real meaning of the principle is revealed only in good practices in actual life.

The prophets continually appeal to ethical principles that go beyond the limited scope of moral rules. Often these appeals come in the form of warnings against evil practices. For example, "Woe . . . to those who issue oppressive decrees, to deprive the poor of their rights and withhold justice from the oppressed of my people. . . . What will you do on the day of reckoning, when disaster comes from afar?" (Is 10:1–4 NIV). Legal oppression is denounced with an appeal to the principle of justice for the poor. The meaning of the principle derives from specific practices of oppression.

Moral rules and commandments should not be stripped of their power by abstraction into principles or dispositions, as if the rule could then be discarded as merely local. The rules put flesh on principles. It is more helpful to think of principles as abstractions from rules rather than rules as applications of principles. A theological, narrative understanding of the commandments protects them from ahistorical legalism and makes possible their application in altered form to new historical situations. Principles help transfer the meaning of good and evil from one context to another.

Principles lack the sharp definition of laws but provide an intermediate step through which contextual laws can be "reincarnated" in another cultural context. A good biblical example of this process is provided by Jesus in the Sermon on the Mount. "Eye for eye, tooth for tooth" (Ex 21:24) was an Old Testament law meant to protect a neighbor from excessive retaliation in the context of tribal warfare. Jesus does not simply discard the law but reformulates its deep, original meaning in terms of love for one's enemy. The original law protected the people against feuds and extremes of vengeance. Its meaning was rooted in respect for the rights of the enemy. Jesus does not eliminate that meaning but shows its logical implication.

4. *Why should we be good?* The fourth level of moral discourse has been called the "postethical" or "meta-ethical" level. Here the question is asked, Why be moral? What is the foundation and meaning of goodness?

There is an extensive philosophical debate over whether theology and morality are interdependent.[25] The Bible does not offer logical or philosophical arguments for the meaning or basis of morality. Nor does it offer such arguments for the existence of God. Without entering into the debate over whether all morality is logically dependent on theology,[26] we can say it is clear that faith in the God of the Bible requires or entails moral behavior. In both testaments those who identify themselves as God's people are called to be like God in character and moral practice. God's people are to be holy because God is holy (Lev 11:45). They are to be merciful because God is merciful (Num 14:18–19; compare Hos 6:6). Jesus said, "Be perfect, therefore, as your heavenly Father is perfect" (Mt 5:48; compare 5:43–47).

But the basis of biblical morality is not an abstract demand that we imitate God; it is an appeal to respond to the inherent nature of who

God is and what God has done. God is first of all presented in the Bible as our creator. Because God is both loving and creator, we are to be good because God made us to be good. Goodness is good for us because we were made in the image of God and can become who we are meant to be only by being like God. God created us as cultural creatures; therefore, our goodness must be expressed in and through our cultures.

The Bible also pictures God as our parent. The Bible simply assumes that certain responses to one's creator and parent are appropriate and good. The definitions of creator, father and mother are assumed to carry self-evident moral requirements. In the West, with its tremendous emphasis on individual autonomy and personal freedom, some may find this assumption more difficult to follow than those in other parts of the world. The majority of cultures in the world see obedience to parents as basic to membership within the community. Those who have been abandoned or abused by their father or mother may find the analogy of obedience to God as Father and Mother less than self-evident.[27] Nevertheless, whether or not the assumption of God's rights as parent are accepted, in the Bible they are assumed as universal for all God's created offspring.

The biblical story of God's love for his children is the paradigmatic story from which we are to understand our rights and responsibilities in human families. God is pictured as both a father and mother to us, but we are not to see God primarily as like our earthly mother or father, who may or may not be good.[28] Rather, we should be parents who love our children the way God loves us. The image is transcultural and rooted in biology, even though its realization on earth will vary according to different cultural patterns of family structure. Matriarchal, patriarchal, egalitarian, nuclear, extended and other family structures are all capable of reflecting God's love through the parents to the children.

Third, we are to be good because God is the lawgiver and judge of all the earth. God reserves the right as our creator and parent to judge the whole earth. As judge, God demands obedience.

Richard Mouw has written a carefully nuanced book that argues that all Christian morality is founded on the idea of "moral surrender to the divine will."[29] As Mouw points out, surrender to God's authority need not be founded on fear of judgment; nevertheless, God's judgment is an inevitable aspect of God's authority. This image is prominent in Islam, which means submission.

The biblical picture of God as judge assumes that morality makes sense because there is goodness and justice at the heart of the universe. Justice and righteousness in the present make sense because, in the biblical story, God will someday establish them on earth. The coming kingdom of God is both motive and goal of Judeo-Christian ethics. The God of justice and the God of mercy are one and the same. God will judge the earth because God loves the earth.

Fourth, we are to be good because we are partners with God in a covenant. There is a paradox in the Bible on this point. On the one hand this covenant is a gift. It is unearned and eternal. On the other hand it is a mutual agreement that entails promises. The requirements of the covenant are religious fidelity (God is pictured as a husband and Israel as his bride) and social justice. In the New Testament, God's people have been accepted and forgiven through the new covenant sealed with the blood of Christ. Membership in this covenant is confirmed by obedience to Christ (Jas 2:17; see also Mt 25:31–46; Heb 6:4–8).

This points us to what I take as the central ethical image in the biblical story. We are to live well as the fitting response to God as our lover and redeemer.[30] Morality in the Bible is fundamentally seen as a response to God's grace in choosing, liberating, blessing, forgiving and judging us. The focal point of revelation is the mystery of the incarnation. God's Son, Jesus, took upon himself the agony of history and died to set God's people free. If we are really free, then we must live in the true freedom of obedience (Gal 5:1).

Biblical goodness is linked to gratitude, reverence, loyalty, faith and hope. These virtues transcend all cultures. Above all, goodness is revealed in love. The law of love opposes and denies the validity of every cultural custom that restricts the flow of God's love in the community. God's love in Christ breaks down all ethnic, social, economic and sexual barriers that lead to the oppression of one group by another (Gal 3:28). The Bible tells us a story in historical, cultural terms of God's character and action in history. This story tells us why we should be good.

The Cultural Context of the Reader

It is not possible for us to understand the story of the Bible "objectively." As I have already indicated, all of knowledge is "subjective" in the sense that whatever we know, we know from a particular perspective. The goal of biblical understanding is not the formulation of some transcultural set of ethical principles but obedience to God in a particular time and place. People in different sociocultural situations may understand different things from the same story, in part because the will of God (but not the character of God) is different in different contexts.

The following story illustrates how a new cultural setting may raise disturbing new questions about a situation that had previously seemed clear and simple.

"Jane" taught English in a university in China. One day she saw "Kwei-feng" looking at someone else's paper on the final examination. Kwei-feng had often been in Jane's apartment, teaching her how to cook and engaging in deep conversations. They had become good friends. Jane had threatened failure to anyone caught cheating, but if she failed Kwei-feng, she knew Kwei-feng's job prospects might well be destroyed for life. If Kwei-feng failed this class she would be dismissed from the university with very slim possibilities for another chance at higher education or a decent job. Failure in the university could result in life-long economic dependence on her parents. Her whole future might hang on this one exam. Besides, Kwei-feng was one of the most capable of Jane's students.

Jane could not recall any direct biblical passages on cheating, but she knew that dishonesty is

wrong. The rules were clear, and academic standards were at stake. But was Kwei-feng really cheating, checking her answer with a friend or just allowing her eyes to wander? If she was cheating, did it really warrant dismissal from the university? Did cheating mean the same thing here as in America? If it did, was it valued differently? Jane knew that her Chinese colleagues were very lax on cheating. But did the fact that they were lax mean she should be too?

What was the real meaning of Kwei-feng's wandering eyes? What was Jane's responsibility in the situation as a young American visiting teacher? Jane had gone to China with a very black-and-white view of right and wrong: rules should never be broken. But in this situation she was all at sea. When she confronted Kwei-feng in the hall and saw the anguished horror in her eyes, Jane's heart felt leaden and her rules hollow. Kwei-feng was her most promising student. How could she know what was good in this situation?

The question whether Kwei-feng was right to allow her eyes to wander is only a small part of the ethical dilemma in this story. In her own context, Jane would not have hesitated to fail a student caught cheating. She felt strongly about the biblical principle of honesty. Failure for cheating was simple justice. But did justice demand the same action in China?

Jane had to make a portentous decision quickly in a situation that she did not fully understand. If she had had more experience as a teacher in China, if she had understood the nature of the Chinese educational system better, if she had perceived a wider range of possible responses, if she had been able to consult a trusted Chinese Christian teacher, she would have been in a better position to know the will of God in this situation.

Jane approached the dilemma not only as a teacher in China but also as a North American with a well-established set of norms on things like cheating, plagiarism, intellectual property rights, academic competition, educational opportunity and vocational freedom. None of these norms can be directly derived from the Bible, because in the biblical narrative there is no comparable sociocultural educational structure as now exists in the West. Nor, for that matter, is there a biblical educational structure comparable to that of China. Jane had to decide what to do based on a synthesis of educational values from her culture of origin, an understanding of the values of her new social situation and a critical assessment of both, based on the biblical story.

Since Jane's cultural situation in China was so far from the structures of education in the Bible, there were no concrete biblical laws or rules to tell her what to do.[31] General principles like honesty and justice seemed to be in tension with other principles like gentleness and mercy. Jane's emotions seemed to be in conflict with her rational, rule-oriented side. Perhaps of greatest importance was what kind of person Jane had become as a result of living her life in accordance with the Scriptures. If Jane was a person of integrity and compassion, a person of prayer and sensitivity, a person of self-control and wisdom, then she had a much greater chance of acting rightly in the situation. There is no law against the fruits of the Spirit (Gal 5:22–23). The guidance of the Holy Spirit might make up for her lack of cultural knowledge. On the other hand, even a godly person can make horrible mistakes. She would do well to learn the ropes of the Chinese educational system.[32]

The Bible is not an ancient puzzle to be solved but a narrative of God's action in history. As Brevard Childs has explained, "The central task is not the objective understanding of the Bible's ethical passages but the understanding of God's will."[33] It is impossible to know God's will apart from doing it in a particular human context. Knowledge is partial and dangerous when divorced from obedience and experience.[34] We cannot blithely say that we know what the Bible means before we have actually tried to do it.[35] In many instances we cannot know how to do God's will before we understand the sociocultural context in which we are placed.

The Sociocultural Context of the Bible: Model or Paradigm?

One of the knottiest problems for biblical social ethics is how to interpret the social structures assumed in the Bible. Are the structures of Israel an essential part of God's revelation? What is their ethical significance for us? The social, economic, political and cultural structures assumed in the Bible are very foreign to most of us in the modern world. Most of us no longer live in a world of absolute monarchies, slavery, tribal and clan warfare, patriarchy (in its ancient Middle Eastern form) and animal sacrifice.

The entire Old Testament assumes that God's people are a political entity who are ideally ruled by God. Today most Christians assume that a theocracy is both impossible and undesirable. Apart from a few Islamic states, most countries of the world now assume a religious pluralism that is foreign to the world of the Bible.

Instead of the agrarian world assumed in much of the Old Testament, the world today is undergoing rapid urbanization. Instead of a world of assumed male superiority, many parts of the world have vigorous movements for women's equality. Instead of absolute monarchy, democracy is a pervasive ideal. Instead of an all-encompassing religious, economic, political and social legal system, we have a patchwork of laws that govern different aspects of life in relation to social realities that are very different from those assumed in the Bible. Instead of face-to-face economic relations in which usury was forbidden, most of the world is structured around credit.

It is tempting to respond to these pervasive differences by simply rejecting at least the Old Testament as irrelevant to our time. The extent to which this is done by Christians of all theological convictions is one of the great tragedies of the church. Equally unacceptable are the attempts to require that all the Old Testament be literally followed or to limit the Old Testament to a source of "spiritual" typologies of Christ.

Christopher J. H. Wright offers a persuasive argument that the social shape of Israel is an essential part of its biblical theological significance.[36] The social laws of Israel cannot be easily separated from their theological motivation. Jewish law is continually justified with reference to the character of God. The revelation of God in the

Bible is inseparable from an understanding of the kind of society Israel was meant to be. The story of God's work in the world cannot be divorced from the way God is revealed in the peculiar social structures of Israel.

In his massive study of the sociological world of the Old Testament prior to 1050 B.C., Norman Gottwald concludes that Israel was

> an egalitarian, extended family, segmentary, tribal society with an agricultural-pastoral economic base ... characterized by profound resistance and opposition to the forms of political domination and social stratification that had become normative in the chief cultural and political centers of the ancient Near East.[37]

With the ancient law, God offered Israel an opportunity to be different from the surrounding nations. Within the context of a social structure based on slavery, Israel was to free all slaves and give them a nest egg every seven years (Deut 15). Within the context of a political system of monarchy, Israel was to know that monarchy would become a vehicle of oppression (1 Sam 8) and that even its greatest king was not above the law of God (2 Sam 12). Within the context of an agricultural economy, Israel was to ensure that everyone had a fair share of land and that both land and animals would be respected (Lev 25). Within the context of patriarchy and polygamy, Israel was to protect the rights of women (Deut 21:10–14; 22:13–29).

It would be nice if all these points were unambiguous—even better, if the institutions that we find abhorrent were simply outlawed. The seeds of the destruction of monarchy, slavery, racism, sexism and polygamy are all found in the Old and New Testaments. But these seeds were beyond the perception of most of the biblical writers. In the Law and Prophets and the letters of Paul, structures of oppression are questioned, denounced and ameliorated, but there are few calls for their abolition. In fact, these structures were usually embedded in the thought patterns of the biblical writers.

The commandments of the Old and New Testament do not assume an ideal social structure for all time. Rather, they assume the social structure

of *their own* time and outline ways in which Israel, or the church, was to be different. Israel provides a paradigm of God's will in relation to actual social conditions. Israel is not a model of how the church, still less any secular state, should be structured. The Old Testament tells a story of God's work in the ancient Near East that is relevant not only to the church but also to modern politics.

Theologians like Elisabeth Schüssler Fiorenza have argued that we need a "hermeneutic of suspicion" that ferrets out the influence of sexism on the biblical writers.[38] Fiorenza's hermeneutic of suspicion comes dangerously close to making her own subjective view of feminism into the critical standard by which everything else is judged. Nevertheless, a carefully used hermeneutic of suspicion can reveal how the social structures of the cultures of the Bible shaped its message in ways that are not relevant to our culture. Fiorenza suggests that in order to do this we must

> not understand the New Testament as an archetype but as a prototype. Both archetype and prototype denote original models. However, an archetype is an ideal form that establishes an unchanging timeless pattern, whereas a prototype is not a binding timeless pattern or principle. A prototype, therefore, is critically open to the possibility of its own transformation.[39]

The cultures of the Bible are no more authoritative than our own. Most of the Bible's moral exhortations were practically directed to people who were not living by idealized structures but according to the pagan practices around them. I suspect that things are not too different today. Biblical patterns of the extended family, home education, agriculture, usury, defense and medicine are rarely seen as authoritative today. One of the great tasks of biblical interpretation is to distinguish between the will of God and the particular cultural homes in which it was biblically incarnated.

Bridging the Gap Between Text and Today

The basic argument of this chapter has been that the biblical story, understood in context, teaches us to become good as we learn to see our lives as part of the same story. By guiding our interpretation, the story leads us to experience reality in a way that is consistent with God's work in the world. The story of God's work with Israel and revelation in Christ is our story too.

But it is not our only story. There is also the story of our lives that is inseparable from our cultural context. Our culture provides us with a symbolic meaning system from which we can never fully escape. We read the story of the Bible through cultural eyes. Our own cultural experience is not higher in authority than the Scriptures, but it is our starting place. It is also our goal. The Bible's teaching must be lived in our own cultural experience before we fully understand it.

This requires a process that is often called contextualization We do not translate the Bible directly into a new cultural setting. Nor do we even "transculturate" it, as if the message of the gospel were an abstraction that could simply be expressed in different cultural forms.[40] It is the Bible, not an abstract interpretation of its message, that is authoritative. The message of the Bible can be understood only as it is perceived from a specific cultural standpoint. God's Word is always incarnated, and different parts of the church may incarnate it differently.[41] In other words, the content of the gospel cannot be separated from its cultural form.

The Reverend Nelly Hutahaean is a Barak pastor from North Sumatra, Indonesia. The following story relates how she tried to obey the God of the Bible in her own cultural context.[42]

One day Ari, a close friend of Nelly, came to her to ask for help. Ari's father had been killed and her mother imprisoned for many years because of involvement with the communists. Ari was rescued as a baby and raised by a foster family. She was now eighteen years old and only two months away from graduation from high school. Ari was a conscientious student, well respected by her teachers and friends. Recently she had been chosen to represent the school in a traditional Batak dance performance. As Nelly met Ari, she saw that her eyes were swollen and her body covered with black and blue marks from the most recent beating she had received from her foster father.

Every day Ari was required to come straight home from school and work in the house: washing clothes, cleaning, ironing, cooking, washing dishes, etc. She had been forbidden to take part in any extracurricular activities. Ari's foster father had very strict rules for her, and any deviation brought severe punishment. When the foster father found out she had accepted the honor of representing the school in the traditional dance, he locked all her school uniforms and books in the closet and forbade her to return to school.

Ari could not stand the pain and degradation of her position in that house any longer. She received regular beatings and now was being denied the chance to finish high school. She asked Nelly to help her escape and run away to Jakarta. There she hoped to see her mother in prison and start a new life. Nelly's dilemma was over whether or not she should help Ari escape.

My first response to this story was outrage against the foster father and the conviction that Nelly should help Ari escape from such abuse. From my (Western) perspective, an eighteen-year-old had every right to flee from such a situation. Ari's foster family treated her like a slave. They would not allow her to finish high school. Her foster father abused her. And she wanted to meet her long-lost mother.

But Nelly was not so sure. She wanted to make sure that her response would be faithful to Scripture and wise in relation to the cultural situation. She pointed out that if Ari ran away and broke her relationship with her foster family, it would have a grave impact on the rest of her life. It would also bring severe repercussions on the whole foster family and even the whole community. Fleeing from the family would break one of the most basic taboos of the Batak people. It would be considered the greatest possible sin. Ari would be excommunicated not only from the family but from the entire community. Not only would she not finish high school, but she would be an outcast for life. As part of a Batak family, she was guaranteed material security for the future by the clan. If she ran away, she would become as one who is dead.

By breaking the most basic *adat* (tradition) of the society, Ari would also bring irreparable shame on the family and father who had raised her. Within the patriarchal, close-knit family structure of the clan, the father would be seen as having failed in his duty, and the whole family would suffer. He would be shunned. His business might well be boycotted and go bankrupt. The whole community would be divided and suffer the loss of his participation. The *adat* was so strong that no woman had ever dared flee before.

Nelly wanted to understand what she should do, both within this context and in the context of the Bible. On the one hand, the biblical story highly values the family. The fifth commandment requires that father and mother be honored and suggests that such honor brings with it a long and fruitful life (Deut 5:16). For almost eighteen years this family had raised Ari and paid for her schooling.

On the other hand, Ari seems to come under the category of an oppressed orphan. The Bible is full of commands like "Seek justice, rescue the oppressed, defend the orphan, plead for the widow" (Is 1:17). The God of the Bible is the defender of the weak.

Within the context of Batak culture, how could Nelly honor both themes in the Bible? Nelly believed that honor was due to the foster family that had raised Ari. On the other hand she knew Ari needed help and could not be abandoned to face her suffering alone.

After a process of reflection, biblical study, counsel with trusted members of the community, study of possible alternatives and repercussions, and planning,[43] Nelly arranged for Ari to be hidden with another local family. An elder of the community was selected to approach the foster father, reassure him of Ari's safety, tell him Ari's perspective, and ask him to forgive her and give his permission for her to finish school. Meanwhile, Nelly prayed that God would forgive her for her boldness and help Ari to be able to meet her mother. She also prayed for eventual reconciliation between Ari and her foster father.

In retrospect, Nelly reflected that within a paternalistic, collective and family-oriented society such as hers, conflict such as this can seldom be solved by an individual. The leaders of the community are the only ones able to bring about a tolerable solution.

I learned much from this story. I saw that my Western, individualistic, human rights approach to a solution was inadequate. I also saw an example of a wise woman who took her culture and her faith very seriously. Nelly did not accept the patriarchal assumption that a father has unlimited power over his daughter. But she did not reject the communal resources of her culture for problem-solving. Nelly did not approach the Bible as a narrow rule book requiring a daughter always to obey. Nor did she simply resort to the popular "poor-and-oppressed" passages without consideration of the importance of family and communal structures. In her values and actions Nelly combined respect for authority, loyalty to the oppressed and cultural sensitivity.

Because we live in a fallen world, we cannot be assured that stories such as this will all turn out right. In Ari's case the results were mixed. Ari is still not reconciled with her foster father, but she was able to finish high school and go on to university without being alienated from the community. Her mother is now free, and Ari is married and has children of her own. Nelly's story provides an example of someone who interpreted a moral crisis in her own culture through the lens of the biblical narrative. Nelly combined the story of the Bible with the story of her culture in such a way that her praxis was the product of wisdom.

Those of us who live in a foreign culture have a double task. We must continue to integrate the biblical story with the perspectives of our culture of origin. Beyond that, we must begin to understand our new home deeply enough so that its story may be seen and transformed through the Word of God.

Notes

1. William A. Dyrness, *Learning About Theology from the Third World* (Grand Rapids, Mich.: Zondervan, 1990), p. 28. Of course the Bible itself is culturally located, but its original text functions cross-culturally for all Christians.

2. David Kelsey, *The Uses of Scripture in Recent Theology* (Philadelphia: Fortress, 1975), p. 89. Kelsey argues for an essentially functional definition of Scripture. That is, the Bible, or at least parts of the Bible, are Scripture because they function as authoritative for the Christian community. One may accept Kelsey's functional definition without denying (as Kelsey does) that "authoritative" is a judgment about Scripture in and of itself. I would hold that the entire canon of the Bible functions as authoritative for the Christian community because Christians believe God has made it the authoritative vehicle of revelation.

3. For the purpose of this chapter I ignore the problems raised by textual criticism. There are extensive debates about just what is the original text of Scripture. These debates are important but lie beyond the scope of this chapter and the competence of its author. I do not think they would substantially change my argument. There are also very significant differences in doctrines of the authority of Scripture, but whatever their differences, most Christians account for their beliefs and behavior in relation to Scripture.

4. Robert McAfee Brown, *Unexpected News: Reading the Bible with Third World Eyes* (Philadelphia: Westminster Press, 1984), p. 13. "The strange new world within the Bible" is a term borrowed from Karl Barth.

5. Unfortunately, sometimes translations of the text enshrine the interpretation of the (usually white male) translator. The text may then be narrowed in its meaning or even made to say what is not there, based on the cultural bias of the translator.

6. Kraft writes, "The Scriptures are like the ocean and supra cultural truth like the icebergs that float in it. Many icebergs show at least a bit of themselves above the surface, some lie entirely beneath the surface. Much of God's [self] revelation . . . in the Scriptures is at least partially visible to nearly anyone who is willing to see it. . . . But much lies beneath the surface, visible only to those who search to discover what supra cultural truth lies beneath the specific cultural applications in Scripture" (Charles H. Kraft, *Christianity in Culture* [Maryknoll, N.Y.: Orbis, 1979], p. 131). Kraft's discussion of hermeneutical issues in chapter 7, "Supra Cultural Meanings via Cultural Forms," is very helpful. Still, I am not sure there are any "supracultural meanings" that exist denuded of cultural flesh. Every word of Scripture is itself a cultural form. If so, "supracultural meanings" may be more like molecules than like icebergs! Marvin Mayers, followed by Paul Hiebert, tries to improve on Eugene Nida's "relative cultural relativism" and proposes a model of ethical reflection based on "biblical absolutism and cultural relativism." While Mayers's approach has many helpful insights, it lacks the hermeneutical rigor dis-

played by Kraft. See chapter 16, "Cross-Cultural Ethics," in Marvin K. Mayers, *Christianity Confronts Culture*, 2nd ed. (Grand Rapids, Mich: Zondervan, 1987), pp. 241–60. Also see Paul G. Hiebert, *Cultural Anthropology* (Grand Rapids, Mich.: Baker Book House, 1983), pp. 251–62.

7. Eugene A. Nida, *Customs, Culture and Christianity* (New York: Harper & Brothers, 1954), p. 282; see also pp. 48–53. Actually even this statement is questionable, since our understanding of the Triune God is far from absolute. But Nida's intention is to locate all that is infinite and absolute with God.

8. George A. Lindbeck, *The Nature of Doctrine* (Philadelphia: Westminster Press, 1984), p. 35.

9. Ibid., p. 33.

10. Iris Murdoch, "Against Dryness: A Polemical Sketch," in *Revisions*, ed. Stanley Hauerwas and Alasdair MacIntyre (Notre Dame, Ind.: University of Notre Dame Press, 1983), p. 49.

11. Alasdir MacIntyre, *Whose Justice? Which Rationality?* (Notre Dame, Ind.: University of Notre Dame Press, 1988), p. 393.

12. For the sake of brevity I am simplifying MacIntyre considerably.

13. "The Christian tradition" is in fact many different traditions, each of which describes the world differently. When I speak of "Christians" as if they were all from one tradition, I am simplifying in order to make a point. By the word *Christians* I assume a broad, central stream of the Christian tradition, including both Protestants and Catholics, which treats the Bible as Scripture.

14. Lindbeck, *Nature of Doctrine, p.* 118.

15. Kelsey, *Uses of Scripture*, p. 48. To approach the Bible like this is not to ignore the insights of biblical critical scholars. They may help us understand the story contained in the Bible. But the focus is not on some revelatory event that lies behind the text (as in Gerhard von Rad) nor on the experience of the community that transmitted it (as in Rudolf Bultmann), nor even on revelatory experience of the modern reader (as in Karl Barth), but on the story in the text of the canon as it now stands (see the work of Brevard Childs, such as *Introduction to the Old Testament As Scripture* [Philadelphia: Fortress, 1979]).

16. These four "levels of moral discourse" were first distinguished by Henry David Aiken but have been adapted many times since. Henry David Aiken, *Reason and Conduct* (New York: Alfred Knopf, 1962), pp. 65–87. Compare Allen Verhey, "The Use of Scripture in Ethics," *Religious Studies Review* 4 (January 1978); James Gustafson, *Theology and Christian Ethics* (Philadelphia: United Church Press, 1974), pp. 130–33. As a typology of ways of relating ethics to Scripture, the four levels are far too simplistic. We learn goodness from the Bible in many more ways than this. However, the four levels still capture four questions that trouble many Christians.

17. Gerhard von Rad, *Old Testament Theology* (San Francisco: Harper & Row, 1965), 2:204.

18. I have no written reference for this view but have often heard it expressed by believers within Plymouth Brethren circles. The dispensationalist approach pioneered by J. N. Darby has the advantage of trying to fit the law into a narrative structure of God's work in the world. On the other hand, some of Darby's followers have propagated an extreme literalism that does violence to the original meaning of the text in its context and results in a narrow legalism. Every instruction of the Bible that is not assigned to another dispensation must be followed to the letter.

19. The practice of cutting out any parts of Scripture that a person does not like. The prototypical example of this practice was the heretic Marcion (second century A.D.), who deleted the Old Testament and significant parts of the New which did not meet his approval.

20. Christopher J. H. Wright, *Living As the People of God* (Leicester, U.K.: InterVarsity Press, 1983), pp. 151–52; also published as *An Eye for an Eye* (Downers Grove, Ill.: InterVarsity Press, 1984). Wright's classification of the law was first proposed by A. Phillips, *Ancient Israel's Criminal Law: A New Approach to the Decalogue* (London: Blackwell, 1970).

21. Joshua 2:1–7. See John Jefferson Davis, *Evangelical Ethics* (Phillipsburg, N.J.: Presbyterian and Reformed, 1985), pp. 15–16. Norman L. Geisler is also an exponent of what he calls "ethical hierarchicalism"; see *Ethics: Alternatives and Issues* (Grand Rapids, Mich.: Zondervan, 1971).

22. Bill Gothard's popular teaching on the principle of family hierarchy falls in this category. Gothard absolutizes the sociocultural system of patriarchy in the name of biblical principles.

23. Geisler, *Ethics*, p. 117. Geisler makes the absurd statement concerning those with physical limitations that "a person who is physically complete has a better manifestation of humanity than one who is not." By this measure Hitler showed more humanity than Helen Keller!

24. This observation does not apply to street people. But street people's coats are not usually worth enough to take in pawn. If they were, this rule might well be authoritative in its literal sense.

25. See, for example, Ian T. Ramsey, ed., *Christian Ethics and Moral Philosophy* (London: SCM Press, 1966), and Gene Outka and John P. Reeder Jr., eds., *Religion and Morality* (Garden City, N.Y.: Anchor/Doubleday, 1973).

26. This is a fundamental question of epistemology. It appears to me that the argument hinges on an evaluation of David Hume's familiar dictum "No Ought from an Is; no ethical conclusions from non-ethical premises." It is certainly possible to argue that the conception of a biblical God in itself requires some ethical conclusions. See Dewi Z. Phillips, "God and Ought," in *Christian Ethics and Moral Philosophy*, ed. Ian T. Ramsey (London: SCM Press, 1966), pp. 140–44. On the other hand, some argue that religious belief is itself dependent upon a priori moral judgments. See Kai Nielsen's article in the same volume, "Some Remarks on the Independence of Morality from Religion." Both of these positions may be argued without con-

tradition. A person can certainly make moral decisions about the goodness or existence of God without having belief or formal theology. But that does not imply that the person's moral ability or awareness did not come from God. If we begin with the assumptions of the biblical narrative, it is clear that God is the source of all morality. William Frankena is probably right in his assertion that a rational justification of ethics is possible without logically requiring a religious premise. See Frankena, "Is Morality Logically Dependent on Religion?" in *Religion and Morality*, ed. Gene Outka and John P. Reeder Jr. (Garden City, N.Y.: Anchor/Doubleday, 1973), p. 259. I would argue, however, that from Christian premises the ultimate meaning of both morality and reason is founded in the character of God. See C. S. Lewis, *Miracles* (New York: Macmillan, 1947).

27. Those with painful family relationships should be reassured that God is not a parent like their parents, but rather their *mother* and *father* ought to be like their heavenly Father and Mother.

28. Images of God as father are pervasive in both Testaments. Images of God as mother are more rare because of the patriarchal structures of Israel. Nevertheless, there are a few mother images of God. See, for example, Isaiah 66:12–13. The terms *father* and *mother* are human symbols or signs of what God is like. Since God is a spirit and has no sexual organs, neither image should be taken as literal (see Jn 4:24).

29. Richard J. Mouw, *The God Who Commands* (Notre Dame, Ind.: University of Notre Dame Press, 1990), p. 2. Mouw is careful not to base such surrender primarily on God's power to judge the earth, but God's absolute authority over the earth clearly entails judgment as one aspect of God's authority. Mouw's book helpfully restores obedience to a central place in ethics. Unlike Mouw, I do not think it is the central moral image of the biblical narrative.

30. This is a pervasive theme in the writings of H. Richard Niebuhr.

31. Perhaps the closest analogy is found in the book of Daniel, where Daniel is a student and teacher in a foreign context in which he must meet the demands of the Babylonian educational structure or face death. We are told that Daniel "responded with prudence and discretion" (Dan. 2:14). But this is still a far cry from Jane's situation.

32. In this case Jane gave Kwei-feng a stern warning and allowed her to finish the examination in a different seat. But even a year later she was unsure if she had done the right thing. One reason cheating is common in many communal cultures is that individuals often have very little sense of the private ownership of ideas. An African student once commented, "Cheating is when one person withholds that which another person has need of."

33. Brevard Childs, *Biblical Theology in Crisis* (Philadelphia: Westminster Press, 1970), p. 126.

34. See, for example, the results of Pharaoh's "knowledge" of God's will prior to his obedience to God's will. The result of knowledge without obedience was "So the heart of Pharaoh was hardened" (see Ex. 9:27–35).

35. The influence of Latin America theology can be discerned in these thoughts. For example, José Míguez Bonino says, "Correct knowledge is contingent on right doing," and "faith is always a concrete obedience" (*Doing Theology in a Revolutionary Situation* [Philadelphia: Fortress, 1975], pp. 89–90). The emphasis of liberation theology is on the movement from action (praxis) to thought (biblical ethics). This emphasis is good as a corrective but must not obscure the fact that the movement is dialectical and goes both ways.

36. Wright, *Living As the People of God*.

37. Norman K. Gottwald, *The Tribes of Yahweh: A Sociology of the Religion of Liberated Israel 1250–1050 BCE* (London: SCM Press, 1979), p. 10.

38. Elisabeth Schüssler Fiorenza, *In Memory of Her: A Feminist Reconstruction of Christian Origins* (New York: Crossroad, 1983).

39. Ibid., p. 33. This short discussion only scratches the surface of the hermeneutical issues raised. Fiorenza's book includes a very helpful overview of different feminist approaches. See also Phyllis Trible, *God and the Rhetoric of Sexuality* (Philadelphia: Fortress, 1978), and Letty Russell, *Human Liberation in a Feminist Perspective* (Philadelphia: Westminster Press, 1974).

40. Charles H. Kraft, *Christianity in Culture* (Maryknoll, N.Y.: Orbis, 1979). See pp. 280–89.

41. I understand this as one of the major points argued persuasively in Dyrness, *Learning About Theology from the Third World*.

42. Nelly is a graduate student at Satya Wacana Christian University. She wrote out this story in Indonesian as one of the requirements for an ethics course I taught in the spring of 1992. With her permission I have paraphrased her story in English, shortening it and emphasizing portions that suit the needs of this chapter.

43. These are elements in the well-known "hermeneutical circle."

Questions for Discussion:

1. What do you think are the main points Adeney is trying to make about the use of the Bible in ethics? Do you agree with these points?
2. How do you think the Old Testament is relevant to ethics today? What does Adeney suggest?
3. What do you think Adeney means when he says, "It is not possible for us to understand the Bible 'objectively'"? Do you agree with his view?
4. How does Adeney use biblical principles in ethics? Do you agree that principles need to be balanced by an understanding of the culture from which they came? Do you agree that "the prohibition of theft, like the other nine commandments, is not a timeless ethical principle that we must translate into different cultural idioms"? Why or why not?

Business Ethics

Alexander Hill

From *The Complete Book of Everyday Christianity*, ed. by Robert Banks and R. Paul Stevens (Downers Grove, Ill.: InterVarsity Books, 1998). Copyright © 1997.

Business is often compared to a poker game. Both, it is argued, require nondisclosure and distrust in order to succeed, with only the naive showing their true intentions. Mark Twain's observation that "an ethical man is a Christian holding four aces" reflects a notion still in vogue today—that ethics and competitive environments like business or winner-takes-all games rarely mix.

A Separate Business Ethic?

The poker metaphor serves to legitimize business behavior that would be considered immoral in the personal realm—bluffing, deception and contributing to another's harm. All of these behaviors are justified in the name of their "real world" contexts.

Advocates of dual morality, that is, applying one set of ethics in the marketplace and another in the home and church, expect employees to lay aside personal values and to focus solely on generating corporate profits. Everything possible, except perhaps breaking the law, must be done to enhance the bottom line. Subordinates have no right to interject personal values, such as environmental protection, fairness to fellow workers or contempt for dishonest sales techniques, into corporate matters. A century ago businessman Dan Drew, founder of Drew Seminary, smartly summed up this philosophy: "Sentiment is all right up in the part of the city where your home is. But downtown, no. Down there the dog that snaps the quickest gets the bone. I never took any stock in a man who mixed up business with anything else" (quoted in Steiner and Steiner, p. 333).

A soul mate of Drew was oil baron John D. Rockefeller. Influenced by his devout Baptist mother, he developed on the one hand a strong personal religious ethic. His shrewd father taught him on the other hand to win at any cost in business, once boasting, "I cheat my boys every chance I get. I want to make them sharp." Rockefeller resolved this contradiction by compartmentalizing his life into two separate realms. Ruthless in business, he gave kickbacks to railroads, violently suppressed labor unrest and bribed competitors' employees to give him inside information. However, in his personal life he donated nearly half a billion dollars to a countless variety of worthy causes. One writer concludes that "Rockefeller was a conscientious Christian who struggled to end the livelihood of his every rival" (Steiner and Steiner, p. 27).

Such a segmented ethical system is inherently unchristian because it ignores the twin doctrines of creation and sovereignty. The apostle Paul argues that no realm of life is beyond the lordship of Christ. Indeed, all things were created "through him," "in him," and "for him." His authority sustains the created order, extending over "thrones,

or dominions, or principalities, or powers" (Col 1:16 KJV).

As such, Christ has power over all beings and institutions. No human activity—including the practice of business—falls outside of his lordship. To argue otherwise is to denigrate his authority. The sacred-secular split embodied by Drew and Rockefeller must be rejected because Christian ethics cannot be relegated to part-time status, applied only on evenings and weekends. On the contrary, Martin Luther correctly asserted that Christian vocation is best expressed in life's most common experiences.

It must also be noted that business is no mere poker game but a major social institution. To compare it to a game is to trivialize its importance. Further, not all of its so-called players understand the unwritten dog-eat-dog rules. Many, including immigrants, family members, the elderly and the young, do not have their guards up and are easy prey. Finally, to argue that employees must turn off their consciences when they enter their workstations is to ignore the lessons of Nuremberg and My Lai (Konrad, pp. 195–97).

God's Character and Human Nature

How then should Christians, having rejected dual morality, behave in the workplace? Simply put, we are called to imitate God. But what does this mean? Three divine characteristics repeatedly emphasized in Scripture are holiness, justice and love. Of course, such imitation is easier said than done. Despite our noblest intentions, we regularly exaggerate, break promises and hide our errors. Why? We do so because we are sinners whose moral grip is weak and whose moral vision is clouded. This is particularly problematic in the hothouse of the marketplace where financial stakes are high, career destinies are decided and the temptation to rationalize is strong.

Even as sinners, however, we generally aspire for wholeness and regret when we fall short. Our consciences, though less reliable than originally designed, are still operative. Personal redemption and the guidance of the Holy Spirit also contribute significantly to our efforts.

Holiness in Business

During the Middle Ages *holiness* was construed to mean separation from ordinary life in order to pursue otherworldly contemplation. Hence business—perhaps the most fleshy of all human enterprises—was viewed as being "dirty," even antithetical to holiness. Fortunately, this is not an accurate definition of biblical holiness.

Holiness has three primary attributes: zeal for God, purity and accountability. The first attribute, zeal for God, requires that all human concerns—material goods, career goals and personal relationships—be considered of secondary importance. As Jesus observed, only one master can be primary (Mt 6:24). Does this mean that God is opposed to business success? No, the crucial point is that holiness is fundamentally about priorities. As long as business is a means of honoring God rather than an end in itself, the concept of holiness is not violated. What holiness prevents is making business, or any other human activity, an idol.

The second attribute of holiness is purity. Ethical purity reflects God's moral perfection and separation from anything impure. Jesus beckons his followers to "be perfect . . . as your heavenly Father is perfect" (Mt 5:48), and Paul encourages believers to be "holy and blameless" (Eph 5:27). In business such purity means being morally different from one's peers. This includes, but is by no means limited to, purity in communication (not skewing financial reports, not manipulating contract language and not using innuendo to undercut others) and purity in sexuality (not making lewd comments, not engaging in flirting and not participating in sexual discrimination).

The third attribute of holiness is accountability. Scripture abounds with illustrations of righteousness being rewarded and of sin being punished. The analogy may be rough, but accountability is not solely a theological concept. It is an economic principle as well. For while the market neither credits righteousness nor sanctions sin per se, it does tend to reward companies that keep promises and are honest while punishing enterprises that regularly miss deadlines and produce substandard products.

Many false perceptions of holiness exist. J. I. Packer writes, "Partial views abound. Any lifestyle based on these half-truths ends up looking grotesque rather than glorious; one-sided human development always does" (p. 163). Three such misguided views of holiness are legalism, judgmentalism and withdrawal. Legalism reduces holiness to rule keeping. Like the Pharisees of Jesus' day, legalistic managers tend to be procedurally rigid, emphasizing policies and petty rules over employee welfare. Judgmentalists justify themselves by pointing out even greater moral lapses in others, having long memories of subordinates' errors. Ironically, they are doomed to lives of hypocrisy because of their inability to measure up to their own standards. Finally, those who define holiness as withdrawal from society are guilty of confusing moral separation, which Scripture endorses, and physical separation, which it generally does not. Judging from the company Jesus and Paul kept, they would feel quite comfortable mingling with today's stockbrokers, IRS agents and sales representatives.

Justice in Business

On his conversion to Judaism, entertainer Sammy Davis Jr. commented, "Christianity preaches love your neighbor while Judaism preaches justice. I think that justice is the big thing we need." Fortunately, he was only partially correct. Christianity also emphasizes justice. Four key concepts are procedural rights, substantive rights, meritorious justice and contractual justice.

Procedural rights focus on fair processes. Scripture requires a decision-maker to be impartial, having neither preexisting biases nor any conflict of interests. Nepotism is a classic violation of this principle. Another occurs when a corporate board member fails to disclose her personal financial interest in another company with which the board is negotiating. Procedural justice also mandates that adequate evidence be marshaled and that each person affected by a decision be afforded the opportunity to tell his or her side of the story. Thus, auditors must be thorough and able to authenticate all findings. In like manner, supervisors should hesitate before dismissing employees for theft, disloyalty or incompetence solely on the word of a coworker or circumstantial information. In the New Testament both Jesus and Stephen were denied such simple due process (Mt 26:60; Acts 6:13).

Substantive rights are ones such as the right to own property, to physical safety, to prompt payment for work completed and to be told the truth. Hence employees must steal neither time nor material, because such behavior violates their employer's property rights. Likewise, employers must neither deceive nor discriminate against their employees, because this would infringe on their right to be told the truth and to be treated with dignity. When parties fail to respect substantive rights, the government is often called in to remedy the harm (Rom 13:1–7).

Meritorious justice links the concepts of cause and effect. Good choices (for example, working hard or selecting trustworthy business partners) bring success, while bad choices (for example, hiring a mediocre manager or expanding too rapidly) produce failure. Merit earns its own rewards. Proverbs concurs: "He who works his land will have abundant food, but the one who chases fantasies will have his fill of poverty" (28:19). Similarly, Jesus states, "With the measure you use, it will be measured to you" (Mt 7:2), and Paul advises: "A man reaps what he sows" (Gal 6:7).

Contractual justice recognizes that individuals may agree to take on additional duties vis-à-vis each other. This may be as simple as a seller and buyer transferring title to a house or as sophisticated as the merging of two multinational corporations. Each party's performance is conditioned on the performance of the other. Examples of such expanded duties include business partners who agree to divide their earnings. By contrast, neighbors assume no such obligations. Likewise, while employers pay their workers and retain the right to bring disciplinary action against them for poor performance, friends possess no such rights. The difference is that contractual justice permits the creation of additional duties. Similarly, God's covenant with Israel extended extraordinary rights

to Abraham's progeny but also imposed additional responsibilities. Compliance was rewarded by peace and prosperity; breaches were met with severe sanctions (Lev 26:3–39).

As central as justice is to the core of Christian ethics, it must, however, never be separated from holiness and love. Isolated, it becomes harsh, permitting no second chances for those who fail. None of us cherishes working for a company that fires staff for minor breaches of corporate policy or that reacts in knee-jerk fashion with a lawsuit for every noncompliance by a supplier or dealer. Of course, the problem is not with justice or holiness, but with us. We stumble over their high standards due to our moral imperfections (Rom 7:1–25). A third characteristic—love—is therefore vital to complete our picture of Christian business ethics.

Love in Business

Many consider love to be the apex of Christian ethics. Paul identified it as the greatest human virtue, and Martin Luther thought it best described the essence of God's character (Bloesch, p. 42). Jesus ranks love for God first and love for neighbor second. It is important to note that his definition includes both holiness (making God our highest priority) and justice (always taking the interests of others into account).

Love's primary contribution to the holiness-justice-love mix is its emphasis on relationships. By way of example, imagine an embezzler who now regrets what she has done. While holiness causes her to feel unclean and justice creates a fear of getting caught, love produces a sense of grief over the harm caused to others. Breaching relationships causes such pain.

While it is tempting to define *love* as a "soft" virtue, concluding that it has no place in the rough and tumble of the marketplace, we need only note that business history is littered with companies ruined by fractured relationships. Indeed, commercial ventures depend more upon cooperation than competition. To be successful, partners must get along with each other; supervisors must engender loyalty among their subordinates; and suppliers must be brought into a supportive network.

Love has three primary characteristics: empathy, mercy and self-sacrifice. *Empathy* is the capacity to celebrate others' joys and shoulder their burdens, that is, to sincerely feel what others feel. Of course, it would strain credibility to argue that modern capitalism operates primarily on the basis of empathetic love. Backs are scratched to mutual advantage, and perhaps achieving reciprocal respect is the best that can be expected. Christian empathy goes far beyond this, however, encouraging corporate executives to demonstrate concern for the less fortunate, to take personal interest in the fate of deathly ill associates and to sympathize with sales staff who miss quotas due to unexpected personal problems.

Mercy is empathy with legs. It takes the initiative in forgiving, redeeming and healing. Christian mercy seeks reconciliation, even to the extent of loving one's enemy (Mt 5:38–44). Other ethical systems refuse to go so far. Aristotle and Confucius, for example, taught that the duty to love is conditioned on the other person's response. The Christian position demands much more, requiring us to live not according to the golden rule but beyond it (Bloesch, p. 33).

Self-sacrifice means that love willingly sacrifices the very rights that justice bestows. For example, an employee motivated by love may voluntarily relinquish her office in order to accommodate a disabled peer. Or a spouse may consent to move so that his wife's career is enhanced. Saint Francis of Assisi was so sacrificial in giving his clothes to the poor that his disciples had difficulty keeping him dressed. Sacrificial love frightens us because it appears to be a blank check with no limits. While soldiers who jump on hand grenades to save the lives of their comrades and Jesus' sacrificial death are admired, business leaders understandably balk at such extreme vulnerability.

Are there any limits to such love? Clergyman Joseph Fletcher, author of *Situation Ethics*, thinks not. He contends that love is Christianity's sole ethical principle and that holiness concepts (for example, zeal for the truth, ethical purity and concern for right and wrong) are to be cast aside when they impede love. Fletcher's approach provides minimal guidance as to what actions should be taken in a morally unclear situation. Does love really provide moral cover for falsifying a document in order to protect a fellow worker? Does an executive's concern for shareholder wealth and employee job security justify his bribing government officials? For Fletcher, "altruistic sinning" is the order of the day. This emasculated definition of love not only ignores holiness but flouts justice as well. What good are the rights of property ownership and due process if they can be willy-nilly disregarded in the name of love? Justice prohibits such behavior by providing a base line set of rights—dignity being primary—that can neither be given or taken away in the name of love.

Love places limits upon itself. Is it really loving to lie for a peer who is using drugs? Serving as a doormat in such situations may actually cause more long-term harm to the person being "helped." King David's slavish devotion to his son Absalom resulted in a selfish, and ultimately self-destructive, personality (2 Sam 15). Biblical self-love calls us to love our neighbor as ourselves (Lk 10:27). The ethical rule of thumb regarding self-love is an inverted golden rule: if we would feel ethically uncomfortable asking another to do a particular act, then we ought not consent to do it for others. Christian self-love does not condone abuse or servility. Rather, incorporating the concepts of holiness, justice and love, it produces healthy reciprocal relationships.

Holiness, Justice and Love in Business

A balanced view requires that holiness, justice and love be respected equally. Without holiness, love degenerates into permissiveness. Nearly anything can be justified in the name of love—defamation, price fixing, industrial espionage. Conversely, holiness without love produces unforgiving perfectionism. Who would want to work for a supervisor who embodies such an ethic? But holy love produces the highest and purest form of integrity and compassion.

Likewise, love without justice lapses into favoritism and a short-term perspective. Imagine an employee being given a day off with full compensation without regard to the perception of partiality by other staff. Justice without love is equally unacceptable. To twist the facts of the prior example, what do we think of supervisors who always go by the book, never acknowledging exceptional individual circumstances? Such a harsh approach leaves us feeling cold. Only when combined do justice and love form "tough love," a disciplined balancing of long-term interests.

Finally, holiness without justice drifts toward withdrawal from the marketplace and a privatized form of religion. Conversely, justice without holiness results in an amoral form of procedural fairness that lacks moral substance. Decision-makers become absorbed in procedural details (for example, time lines, required signatures, waivers) and fail to focus on the deeper rights and duties involved. Only through holy justice can ethical integrity and procedural justice both be ensured.

The ultimate goal is to produce practitioners who imitate God's holy, just, loving character in the marketplace. This is the true character of biblical business ethics.

References and Resources

T. Beauchamp and N. Bowie, *Ethical Theory and Business*, 4th ed. (Englewood Cliffs, N.J.: Prentice Hall, 1993); D. Bloesch, *Freedom for Obedience: Evangelical Ethics for Contemporary Times* (San Francisco: Harper & Row, 1987); R. Chewning, *Biblical Principles and Business*, vols. 1–4 (Colorado Springs: NavPress, 1989); R. Chewning, J. Eby and S. Roels, *Business Through the Eyes of Faith* (New York: Harper & Row, 1990); J. F. Fletcher, *Situation Ethics: The New Morality* (Philadelphia: Westminster Press, 1966); A. Hill, *Just Business: Christian Ethics in the Marketplace* (Downers Grove, Ill.: InterVarsity Press, 1997); A. Hill, "Colossians, Philemon and the Practice of Business," *Crux* 30, no. 2 (1994): 27–34; A. Konrad, "Business Managers and Moral Sanctuaries," *Journal of Business Ethics*, 1 (1982): 195–200; J. Packer, *Rediscovering Holiness* (Ann Arbor, Mich.: Servant, 1992); L. Smedes, *Mere Morality* (Grand Rapids: Eerdmans, 1983); G. Steiner and J. Steiner, *Business, Government and Society* (New York: Random House, 1983); J. Stott, *Christian Counter-Culture: The Message of the Sermon on the Mount* (Downers Grove, Ill.: InterVarsity Press, 1978); O. Williams and J. Houck, *Full Value: Cases in Christian Business Ethics* (San Francisco: Harper & Row, 1978).

Questions for Discussion:

1. How does Hill respond to the advocates of a dual morality, that is, one set of moral rules for business and a different set of moral rules for one's private life? Compare Hill's response with the conclusions drawn in chapter 1.
2. Do you agree that holiness, justice, and love are the three fundamental moral principles in Christian ethics? Why or why not? If not, what other principles would you add?
3. What difficulties arise if any one of the three principles is followed and not balanced by the other two? What does Hill say is the result when holiness is not balanced by justice and love? If justice is not balanced by holiness and love? If love is not balanced by holiness and justice?
4. How is Hill's understanding of love different from Joseph Fletcher's situation ethics as described by Hill?

CASE STUDIES

Case 3.1: Payroll Pressures

You are the director of a small, faith-based, nonprofit organization that began as a ministry of your local church and has grown to a size sufficient to operate independently of the church. Your income is derived from delivery of services to inner-city residents and includes literacy, job training, family counseling, and other educational programs. You have three primary clients from whom the majority of your income depends: the school district, the department of justice, and the city. All contracts with your organization are cost-reimbursable; that is, they cannot be invoiced and reimbursed until the services are rendered. Similarly, all equipment expenses relating to the services cannot be billed until they are paid for.

The organization began a new project for one of these clients a few months ago. The work was billed as it was completed, but reimbursement is now four months delayed. You have sent letters and made phone calls, but nothing you have tried has worked to get reimbursement paid to you. Most reimbursements are received within 30 days of billing, and you structure your cash flow accordingly. As is the case with many faith-based nonprofits, cash flow is continually a problem. Since this is a major contract, the client's delay has created a situation in which you anticipate that you will not be able to make your payroll within the next month or so. In the past, when payroll was in jeopardy, you could borrow short-term funds from the church. But the church is in the midst of a major building project and has its own cash flow problems.

One option would be to bill your more reliable clients for upcoming work or equipment expenses prior to completing the work or paying for the equipment. For example, you need to purchase computer equipment for employment training but have not done so yet. You could bill the client for that equipment and get reimbursed in two to three weeks, in time to make the payroll. But you would be communicating to the client that you have already paid for the equipment. You could probably do the same with other forthcoming work for the client. The chances of this being detected are very low. You have been in operation for a number of years and have never been audited. In fact, your reputation for integrity is one reason the clients keep using your services. On the other hand, you feel a responsibility to your employees to pay them on time and do not want to ask them to wait until you receive payment from a troublesome client to pay them. You also realize that if they are paid late, they may quit and you would lose good employees.

Questions for Discussion:

1. What options do you have in order to make your payroll? Are there any options that do not involve moral tensions?
2. If the only option was to engage in advance billing, thus violating the cost reimbursable agreement you have with these government clients, would that be a problem morally? Why or why not?
3. How do the principles of holiness, justice, and love have a bearing on this situation? How would you balance the demands of the above principles?

Case 3.2: Not So Amusing

For three generations your family has run a popular amusement park. In doing so, your family is known for operating out of a set of values consistent with their Christian faith. You have grown up with these values, you are a Christian yourself, and you believe that your family's business really stands for something. Your father was quite conservative in this regard and was considered a "pillar" of the community. When he died, it fell to you to take over the family business.

Now you are facing a lawsuit brought by two homosexual men who have sued your company because they were not allowed to dance (quite suggestively) together at one of the dances in the amusement park. They have offered to drop the lawsuit if you will change the park policy and allow same-sex dancing to take place. You have received an enormous amount of mail, some supportive of the present policy and some very opposed to it. Your lawyers advise you that you will almost certainly lose the lawsuit, that it will be expensive, and that public opinion will be against you. You wonder if, after all these years, the business will suffer a decline while you are at the helm. You wonder about the employees and their families, what your father would have done, and what your faith mandates you to do.

Questions for Discussion:

1. What course of action would you take here? What message are you sending to the community by your decision?

2. Is it possible, or desirable, to have a business that reflects Christian values when it comes to the behavior of consenting adults? Why or why not?
3. By changing the park policy, are you in some way condoning homosexuality, which you believe violates your faith?
4. How would you balance holiness, justice, and love in this case?

COMMENTARY

Use of the Bible in Ethics

Christian ethics begins with God's revealing his character and corresponding moral principles in the Bible. The goal of Christian ethics is to emulate that character (Matthew 5:48, "Be perfect . . . as your heavenly Father is perfect"), and the specific moral principles and rules help spell out more precisely what that involves. As a result, Christian ethics will be a blend of virtue ethics and deontological ethics—that is, a mixture of virtues that reflect God's character and principles that are derived from God's character. God's revelation of his character and commandments is not confined strictly to the Bible, as the discussion of natural law suggests. Natural law functions as a supplement to the Bible, however, so when the Bible speaks to a moral issue, it does so with authority.

Yet, it is one thing to recognize that the Bible is the authoritative source for Christian ethics and quite another to use it correctly. To insist on the centrality of the Bible does not justify simplistic proof-texting, often done out of context, to address complex business ethics problems. Rather, one goes to the Scripture primarily to discover broader principles that can then be applied to specific situations encountered in business.

It is true that the Bible has a good deal to say about money and materialism—especially what people do with their wealth and their attitude toward it. But the business practices described in the Bible occurred in the ancient world, which had an economic system very different from the globalized market economy of the twenty-first century. Thus, applying the Bible in business ethics can be complicated. Even though we may agree on the Bible's authority for ethics, we may disagree on whether and how a biblical teaching applies to the issue at hand. That is not to justify skepticism about the Bible, but only to appreciate the complexity of using the Bible properly in addressing business ethics issues.

The Bible was written in a context in which life was predominantly agricultural. Most people lived in small villages, centered around their extended families. Government was usually by a monarch, and individuals had little if any input into the laws that regulated their lives. There were no stock markets, no sophisticated financial tools, no equivalent of the banking system, and nothing remotely resembling a mass communications network like the Internet. Though there was international trade, most economic activity was directed at subsistence. There were economic abuses, exploitation of the vulnerable, and resulting cries for economic justice, as recorded in the Bible.

Because that economic world was so different from today's, it is unreasonable to expect the Bible to directly address complex issues such as insider trading, mergers and acquisitions, and consumer safety. Yet the Bible does have a good deal to say about general principles of economic justice, fairness, and integrity in one's business dealings.

We also should recognize that the Bible was written in different literary types, each with its own distinctives. Much of the Bible was written in narrative format, making its point by telling a story. Other parts, including the Psalms and much of the Prophets, were written in poetry, using vivid figurative language to evoke an emotional as well as rational reaction from the reader. Wisdom literature, especially the Proverbs, often took the form of short, pithy sayings whose primary goal was to be memorable, not technically precise. The Proverbs are intended as "rules of thumb" that have occasional exceptions.

The books of Exodus–Deuteronomy record the law of Moses, which was God's legislation to set up the nation of Israel. It was written in a unique time in biblical history, when Israel was a theocracy, that is, when the law of God was automatically the law of the land. By contrast, the epistles of the New Testament were written in the form of pastoral letters and use a combination of warm personal comments and compelling rational arguments to make their point.

In general, the goal of interpretation of any biblical passage is to discern the intention of the original author for the original audience. That is, we want to ask: What is the point that the original author was trying to make to his original audience? Only after we have clearly answered that question are we ready to ask how a passage applies to contemporary life. The question asked in so many informal discussions of the Bible—What does this passage mean to me?—is premature and irrelevant until the more foundational question of the intent of the original author to the original audience is considered.

To understand the original intent of a biblical passage, we must recognize its specific cultural context. Bernard Adeney is certainly correct when he insists that the Bible was enmeshed in a cultural context, so that some commandments make no sense at all unless you understand that context. Adeney's example of the Hebrew commandment "You shall not boil a kid [baby goat] in its mother's milk" is a clear case in point. That command is impossible to grasp without knowing its background in Canaanite religious rituals, which Israel was prohibited from practicing. Likewise, the command to wash one another's feet makes little sense in today's culture, since today roads are paved, we don't wear sandals as our primary footwear, and we don't walk long distances to get somewhere. Numerous commands in the Bible fit in this category. Some of the commands that apply most clearly to business practices, such as the year of Jubilee (which required that all land be returned to its original owners every fifty years—think of what that would do to today's real estate markets!), need to be understood within the context of a predominantly agricultural society in which raw land was the principal—and often the only—tangible asset a person would have.

Adeney is also correct to insist that in applying the Bible into a specific context we also read it through the lenses of our own culture. Most people are not aware of their cultural framework until they come into contact with a different culture. Though it sounds like relativism, Adeney is right that no one is purely objective when it comes to reading and applying the Bible. This doesn't mean we shouldn't try our best to overcome our cultural biases; in many cases, we can. Reading the Bible in a community of people, preferably from other cultures, helps to minimize the bias. However, Adeney probably goes too far when he insists that the prohibitions, as against theft, given in the Ten Commandments are not timeless principles. It would be more accurate to say that what constitutes theft may vary from culture to culture, depending on how property rights are viewed. But however theft is defined, it is prohibited by the command "You shall not steal."

To apply the Bible correctly, Adeney states, we must distinguish between general principles and specific practices. Many times the specific practice mentioned in the Bible is conditioned by the culture and is not normative for today. But the general principle is usually a moral norm that can be applied in a different specific situation today. For example, in the New Testament, believers are commanded to "greet one another with a holy kiss," to "wash one another's feet," and to "work with their hands." A holy kiss applied the principle of hospitality, footwashing applied the principle of willingness to perform lowly service, and manual labor applied the principle of working hard to support oneself and one's family. To apply the principle of hospitality, we greet with handshakes instead of kisses.

As a general rule, if the practice still communicates the underlying principle, the practice is probably to be taken as a norm for today. To put it another way, the greater the similarities between the ancient context and today, the more likely it is that a command of the Bible is still a norm. For example, since in many cultures a greeting kiss does not communicate hospitality, the principle can be expressed in another culturally appropriate way. And working hard to support one's family can be expressed in many different ways, not simply through manual labor. The goal of application is to seek the underlying principle and attempt to apply it to today's setting. As Adeney states, "principles are the tools that help us reincarnate moral practice from one context to another." Principles are the intermediate step between specific practices in the ancient setting and specific practices in today's setting.

We also have to take into account some theological differences between the Old and New Testaments. For example, the ceremonial laws (laws dealing with the sacrifices and religious festivals) of the Old Testament no longer apply specifically to Christians because of the death of Christ (Hebrews 8–10). Also, the New Testament is clear that the food laws of the Old Testament no longer apply specifically (Acts 8–12) and that no one is under the Old Testament civil law (Romans 7:1–4). Thus, numerous laws that were mandated for Israel are not *directly* applicable to Christians today. However, they are *indirectly* applicable through the use of broader principles as intermediate steps. The challenge is to reapply them in a way that is relevant to today's culture and faithful to the intent of the law in the Old Testament. For example, we are not to offer the sacrifice of thanksgiving literally, but instead we are to express thanksgiving to God in a variety of ways, including public testimony, generous giving, and private prayer.

Some of the most challenging laws to reapply include those that governed economic life, such as the Jubilee. We will examine those laws more fully in chapter 4.

Theological Norms for Business Ethics

As we argued in the introduction to this chapter, the person committed to Christian ethics for the workplace should reject the dual morality of the poker game. Alexander Hill insightfully points out that even some well-known Christian businessmen, such as Dan Drew and John D. Rockefeller, separated their work lives from their private lives. Hill reinforces our belief that a sacred-secular split is not justifiable from the perspective of Christian ethics. He also rightly insists that the goal of Christian ethics is for the believer to imitate the character of God. To spell this out further, he reduces this to three fundamental traits that he correctly insists are central to Christian ethics. These traits are holiness, justice, and love. We can think of these as the legs on a three-legged stool; each is essential, because if you remove any leg, the stool won't stand up. Let's spell out in more detail why these traits are central to Christian ethics and what is meant by each trait.

Holiness

The Bible is very clear that holiness—being set apart for a distinctive reason—is a central component of Christian ethics. In ethics, being holy refers to being set apart in terms of purity and behavior from one's surrounding culture and environment. That is, those who are holy stand out as different and have the sense that God has set them apart so that by the way they live, people notice something distinctive. That difference is designed to bear witness to the reality of God in the person's life. God called Israel to be a holy nation (Exodus 19:6) and the individuals in the nation to be holy as God himself is holy (Leviticus 19:2). Holiness is clearly a central attribute of God, and the command to be holy is based on this character trait of God (1 Peter 1:16). In fact, some have suggested that holiness is the unifying element for all of Old Testament ethics.[7] In the Old Testament, Israel was to be a nation set apart for God, and its moral conduct as a nation was to be different from its surrounding neighbors'. The Law of Moses gave numerous commands that were designed to set a different standard for Israel for that very purpose—that their neighbors might see this difference and recognize that God was in their midst. Likewise in the New Testament, Christians are to be holy—that is, set apart for God's purposes so that the people with whom they came into contact would see their distinctiveness and be drawn to God as a result (1 Peter 1:16; 2:9).

As Hill points out, holiness was taken at times to mandate separation from the world, particularly from the world of business and commerce, which was viewed as the antithesis of holiness. But in reality, the practice of holiness assumed contact with the world, not withdrawal from it; it meant living out a different way of life in the midst of numerous ethical and religious challenges. For example, the demands of holiness might involve treating employees whom you have laid off differently—that is, better—than the "industry standard." Or holiness might mean not giving in to conflicts of interest that might compromise your decision-making objectivity. Or it might mean handling your expense accounts accurately, refusing to pad the accounts

7 See, for example, Walter C. Kaiser Jr., *Toward Old Testament Ethics* (Grand Rapids: Zondervan, 1983).

even though that may be customary in the company you work for. Or it might mean that you cannot take part in some company activities that involve moral compromise or cannot service accounts in enterprises that you believe are fundamentally immoral, such as the pornography industry.

We should be careful to keep holiness balanced by the other central virtues and to be sure that our pursuit of holiness does not become separation from the world. For example, there may be some advertising accounts that make egregious use of sexual persuasion, such as ad campaigns for Abercrombie & Fitch. But we should be careful not to be so sensitive that every ad that appeals to sex is objectionable. The result of that would likely be that there is no place in the advertising industry for someone who cares about being ethical. In our view, that would be a form of separation from the world that is not necessary in order to fulfill the demands of holiness. Holiness does not mean having *no* contact with the world, only not assimilating its values.

Justice

In the Bible, justice is also one of the principal virtues that should characterize those who desire to follow God. In one of the most direct biblical texts, the prophet Micah reminded the rebellious nation of Israel what God required of them. He put it this way: "He [God] has told you, O mortal, what is good; and what does the LORD require of you but to do *justice*, and to love kindness, and to walk humbly with your God?" (Micah 6:8 NRSV). This text also encompasses the final leg of our three-legged stool: love. The term that Micah uses for *kindness* is the Hebrew term for *love*. Perhaps the best way to understand this concept is "unconditional loyalty" (which we discuss further in the next section). Here God commands his people to "do justice," that is, to live lives characterized by justice. This is clearly one of the most central concepts of Christian ethics.

The core idea behind justice is that the just person is the one who meets the standards set by God's character. For example, in the ancient world, it was easy to cheat someone to whom you sold agricultural goods. To measure out products, people used a simple system of weights and measures. The weights would be used to counterbalance a scale. On one side would be the grain or other product being purchased, and on the other side would be the weights, to tell the seller how much of the product the buyer had agreed to buy. But if the weights were not accurate, a seller could systematically cheat the buyer and sell less than promised. The law of Moses prohibited this kind of business practice. In Leviticus 19:35–36, the law is clear: "You shall do no wrong in judgment, in measurement of weight, or capacity. You shall have *just* balances, *just* weights, a *just* ephah, and a *just* hin; I am the LORD your God, who brought you out from the land of Egypt" (NASB). Here the idea of justice involves meeting the standard—that is, if a weight or balance says it weighs a certain amount, that had better be the amount it actually weighs.

This idea is also applied to courts of law in the Old Testament. The same term for *justice* is translated "innocent" when used in a legal setting. For example, in Exodus 23:7 the law commands, "Keep far from a false charge, and do not kill [through capital punishment] the *innocent* [normal term for *just*] and those in the right, for I will not acquit [same term, meaning to proclaim someone innocent, or just] the guilty" (NRSV). Here the innocent person was in court, and it was proven that he was innocent (just); that is, the person had met the standard of the law. The standard is the civil law, and the court case was to determine whether or not the person was "up to standard" of the law. Thus, justice has to do with meeting up to standard.

Hill focuses his discussion on a single standard of fairness that is an important element of justice although it does not exhaust the idea. He emphasizes meeting the standard of fairness in providing due process (procedural justice), keeping contracts (contractual justice), upholding fundamental rights (substantive justice), and rewarding merit (meritorious justice). These reflect later philosophical categories of justice in common use today and are consistent with the biblical notion of justice as meeting up to standard.

When it comes to business practices, justice involves treating people fairly, according to the standard of what they deserve. It would mean giving people clear and truthful explanations of the reasons for their termination, not hiding behind the common explanation, "We're eliminating your position." In addition, it would mean not giving preferential treatment to employees based on race, family status, gender, or close personal/family relationship (that is, nepotism). It would mean recognizing fundamental rights in the workplace such as the right to privacy, thus not viewing employees' email or listening to their voice mail unless there were a compelling business reason or a suspicion of wrongdoing. It would also mean not covering for someone who asks you to lie for him or her, not signing off on something that is misleading, or not enabling someone to steal time or equipment from the company. It would further mean holding people accountable for doing what they contractually say they are going to do and not covering for them when they cannot or will not fulfill their contract.

We should be careful about emphasizing justice at the expense of the other virtues, particularly love, lest the workplace become a rigid, harsh place with no room for grace, mercy, or second chances. As Hill mentions, no one wants to work around people who apply justice without holiness or love—where, for example, people are fired for minor violations of company policy. Justice must be balanced by love.

Love

It may sound strange to think of love in the context of business relationships, but the Bible leaves no doubt about the centrality of love for Christian ethics. When Jesus was asked about the most important commandments, he was very clear—it was love for God and for one's neighbor (Matthew 22:36–40). According to Jesus, the law of Moses could be summarized in those two commands. The rest of the New Testament echoes how important love is for Christian ethics. The apostle Paul insists that love is the greatest of the virtues (1 Corinthians 13:13) and that the entire law of Moses can be summarized as the command to love (Romans 13:8–10; Galatians 5:16). In addition, love is the critical distinguishing mark of Christian ethics, the mark of whether or not someone knows God (1 John 4:7–8), a mark that identifies someone as a follower of Christ (John 13:34–35).

In the Bible, love is not a sentimental feeling but rather an action that seeks the best interests of another. In the Old Testament the concept is often rendered by the term "covenant loyalty" and has the idea of sticking by someone, accepting the person, and seeking his or her best without any strings attached. You don't necessarily have to like someone in order to love him. In regard to ethics, if holiness and justice emphasize distinctiveness and standards, then love focuses on relationships. The motivation to do what is right that comes from love is not so much a desire to be pure or to meet up to the standard as it is to avoid hurting someone about whom you care deeply.

Contrary to popular opinion, love is very important to a well-run business. Hill is certainly right when he points out that many companies have come apart due to problems in relationships among the company leadership, board of directors, employees, suppliers, or customers. Money is not the sole motivation for people to do their jobs well—management consultants have pointed out for some time that people need to feel loved and cared for, to feel that they belong and are valued, in order to function at their best. Love in the workplace involves giving a second chance to employees who might not work out or who have violated company policy, particularly if they would be hard hit by the loss of the job. It may mean showing some flexibility in meeting performance standards or sales quotas rather than rigidly holding to the numbers. It may mean giving flex time to employees facing family crises such as caring for sick children or elderly relatives. It may involve being more generous with severance pay than is customary for laid-off employees.

One clear example of love in action occurred with a group of American companies operating manufacturing plants just across the border in Mexico. Companies routinely move operations that do not require skilled labor to countries where wage rates are lower. The workers who make up the labor force in many of these factories in Mexico and other Latin American countries are called *maquiladoras*, and in general, both the employees and the government are grateful for the jobs and income. When the Mexican government devalued the peso, the purchasing power of these employees was diminished because their wages were now worth less than previously. The companies wanted to raise their wages to compensate for the devaluation, a loving thing to do in itself. But the government prohibited companies from raising wages to avoid fueling further inflation. So the companies went further than they were contractually obligated to by providing a variety of non-monetary benefits to the employees, such as nonperishable food, clothes, and blankets.

Or take the case of Aaron Feuerstein, mentioned in the introduction to this book. After his Polartec manufacturing plant burned down, he could have taken the insurance settlement, invested it, and retired. But out of love for his employees and the community, he used the insurance money to rebuild the plant, thus saving their jobs and enabling the community to stay together. Though he would have been doing nothing unjust or wrong by taking the money and retiring, he expressed his loyalty to the employees by putting their interests ahead of his own and rebuilding the plant.

Balancing Holiness, Justice, and Love

Hill insightfully points out that if any one of these three primary virtues is allowed to dominate the other two, the three-legged stool becomes unstable. For example, as he suggests, holiness alone can produce withdrawal from the world, a judgmental attitude toward others because of pride, or a grinding legalism in which rules take precedence over all other considerations. Moreover, justice alone can produce harshness and rigidity, leaving no place for someone to recover and learn from failure. Finally, love alone can degenerate into permissiveness or favoritism, wherein maintaining relationships counts for everything at the expense of upholding standards. If taken to an extreme, we can easily become a doormat, neglecting even our own needs and interests.

We encourage you to use these parameters of holiness, justice, and love in making moral decisions that you face in business. When approaching a specific moral decision, ask yourself what is demanded by these three traits and how they can be balanced. As you work through the cases in this chapter and the chapters to follow, think about how your decisions reflect these three virtues. We believe these character traits are central to a Christian ethic for business.

Part II

Ethics, Corporations, and the Global Economy

FOUR

Corporate Social Responsibility

You're not in business to make friends. Neither am I. We're here to succeed. If you want a friend, get a dog. I'm not taking any chances, I've got two dogs.

Al Dunlap, former CEO of Sunbeam, in *Mean Business*

Our mission is to do four essential things: obey the law . . . take care of our customers . . . take care of our people . . . and respect our suppliers. If we do these four things and do them consistently, we will succeed as a business enterprise that is profitable and rewarding to our shareholders.

Jim Sinegal

INTRODUCTION

Some years ago, executives of Herman Miller, Inc., a leading office furniture manufacturing company, faced a difficult decision. The company had acquired a stellar reputation for its commitment to environmentally friendly practices, but now executives were informed that wood used in producing the company's signature piece, the Eames chair, was contributing to the destruction of rain forests.

A decision to use materials from another species of tree may not have been so difficult if it were not for the fact that the wood in question gave the chair its distinctive "rosewood" finish. In fact, the suggestion to use a substitute product prompted one company executive to state that the market for the chair would be destroyed. Complicating the matter further, the company was struggling financially at the time and could not easily afford to jeopardize the value of its share price by risking the market position of its most well-known product.

To a large degree, significant questions related to corporate social responsibility were at the heart of this dilemma. Questions such as:

What is the role and purpose of the corporation in society, and what is the scope of its responsibilities? Should it primarily seek to maximize profit for shareholders, or should it function to serve other constituents and broader social goals, even when these pursuits may reduce financial gain?

Public concern about the broader responsibilities of corporations has accompanied their rapidly increasing political and economic power. In addition to environmental protection, issues such as transparency in accounting, product safety, third world labor conditions, and duties to help solve pressing social problems have raised questions that seek to clarify the nature and responsibilities of corporations.

While public attention to these questions has been renewed, the topic has long been debated by economists and management scholars. The first reading in this chapter is the classic essay, "The Social Responsibility of Business Is to Increase Its Profits" by Milton Friedman. Friedman, a Nobel laureate in economics, argues that the primary duty of managers of a publicly held company is to increase wealth for its shareholders. When managers act in "socially responsible" ways that effectively reduce profits, they violate their fiduciary duties to the owners of the enterprise. Friedman's theory has become known as the "shareholder wealth" or "custodian of wealth" model of social responsibility.

An alternative philosophy of corporate responsibility or "theory of the firm" is the "stakeholder" approach, which has gained much popularity in recent years among both academicians and corporate executives.[1] Proponents of this model argue that the lone consideration of shareholder interests is morally insufficient. Instead, corporations must broaden their obligations to a wide group of "stakeholders."

Kenneth Goodpaster's essay "Business Ethics and Stakeholder Analysis" lays out the basic contours of this approach. In essence, corporations have responsibilities to those who have a vested interest or "stake" in the company, rather than to owners exclusively. Since business transactions affect many constituents, corporations also have a moral obligation to consider the interests of consumers, suppliers, employees, and other members of the broader community.

The third article in this chapter is a conversation with Jim Sinegal, CEO of Costco. Interviewers Albert Erisman and David Gill pose thoughtful questions about how ethics and corporate responsibility play out in the retailing business. Sinegal gives clear, honest answers about the centrality of corporate values in building a sustainable enterprise that benefits a wide group of stakeholders, including shareholders.

[1] R. Edward Freeman notes that it may be more accurate to speak of stakeholder "theories," since organizations can choose from a number of viable "normative cores" to guide the process of balancing the claims of various stakeholder groups. See R. E. Freeman, "Stakeholder Theory of the Modern Corporation," in T. Donaldson, P. Werhane, M. Cording, *Ethical Issues in Business: A Philosophical Approach*, 7th ed. (Englewood Cliffs, N.J.: Prentice-Hall, 2002).

The case studies in this chapter give a concrete context to these issues by examining situations in which highly profitable products may produce negative consequences for their users and broader communities. What, then, are the responsibilities of the firms who produce, market, and sell them?

READINGS

The Social Responsibility of Business Is to Increase Its Profits

Milton Friedman

New York Times Magazine (13 September 1970), 33: 122–26. Copyright © 1970.

When I hear businessmen speak eloquently about the "social responsibilities of business in a free-enterprise system," I am reminded of the wonderful line about the Frenchman who discovered at the age of 70 that he had been speaking prose all his life. The businessmen believe that they are defending free enterprise when they declaim that business is not concerned "merely" with profit but also with promoting desirable "social conscience" and takes seriously its responsibilities for providing employment, eliminating discrimination, avoiding pollution and whatever else may be the catchwords of the contemporary crop of reformers. In fact they are—or would be if they or anyone else took them seriously—preaching pure and unadulterated socialism. Businessmen who talk this way are unwitting puppets of the intellectual forces that have been undermining the basis of a free society these past decades.

The discussions of the "social responsibilities of business" are notable for their analytical looseness and lack of rigor. What does it mean to say that "business" has responsibilities? Only people can have responsibilities. A corporation is an artificial person and in this sense may have artificial responsibilities, but "business" as a whole cannot be said to have responsibilities, even in this vague sense. The first step toward clarity in examining the doctrine of the social responsibility of business is to ask precisely what it implies for whom.

Presumably, the individuals who are to be responsible are businessmen, which means individual proprietors or corporate executives. Most of the discussion of social responsibility is directed at corporations, so in what follows I shall mostly neglect the individual proprietor and speak of corporate executives.

In a free-enterprise, private-property system, a corporate executive is an employee of the owners of the business. He has direct responsibility to his employers. That responsibility is to conduct the business in accordance with their desires, which generally will be to make as much money as possible while conforming to the basic rules of the society, both those embodied in law and those embodied in ethical custom. Of course, in some cases his employers may have a different objective. A group of persons might establish a corporation for an eleemosynary purpose—for example, a hospital or a school. The manager of such a corporation will not have money profit as his objective but the rendering of certain services.

In either case, the key point is that, in his capacity as a corporate executive, the manager is the agent of the individuals who own the corporation or establish the eleemosynary institution, and his primary responsibility is to them.

Needless to say, this does not mean that it is easy to judge how well he is performing his task. But at least the criterion of performance is straightforward, and the persons among whom a voluntary contractual arrangement exists are clearly defined.

Of course, the corporate executive is also a person in his own right. As a person, he may have many other responsibilities that he recognizes or assumes voluntarily—to his family, his conscience, his feelings of charity, his church, his clubs, his city, his country. He may feel impelled by these responsibilities to devote part of his income to causes he regards as worthy, to refuse to work for particular corporations, even to leave his job, for example, to join his country's armed forces. If we wish, we may refer to some of these responsibilities as "social responsibilities." But in these respects he is acting as a principal, not an agent; he is spending his own money or time or energy, not the money of his employers or the time or energy he has contracted to devote to their purposes. If these are "social responsibilities," they are the social responsibilities of individuals, not of business.

What does it mean to say that the corporate executive has a "social responsibility" in his capacity as businessman? If this statement is not pure rhetoric, it must mean that he is to act in some way that is not in the interest of his employers. For example, that he is to refrain from increasing the price of the product in order to contribute to the social objective of preventing inflation, even though a price increase would be in the best interests of the corporation. Or that he is to make expenditures on reducing pollution beyond the amount that is in the best interests of the corporation or that is required by law in order to contribute to the social objective of improving the environment. Or that, at the expense of corporate profits, he is to hire "hardcore" unemployed instead of better-qualified available workmen to contribute to the social objective of reducing poverty.

In each of these cases, the corporate executive would be spending someone else's money for a general social interest. Insofar as his actions in accord with his "social responsibility" reduce returns to stockholders, he is spending their money. Insofar as his actions raise the price to customers, he is spending the customers' money. Insofar as his actions lower the wages of some employees, he is spending their money.

The stockholders or the customers or the employees could separately spend their own money on the particular action if they wished to do so. The executive is exercising a distinct "social responsibility," rather than serving as an agent of the stockholders or the customers or the employees, only if he spends the money in a different way than they would have spent it.

But if he does this, he is in effect imposing taxes, on the one hand, and deciding how the tax proceeds shall be spent, on the other.

This process raises political questions on two levels: principle and consequences. On the level of political principle, the imposition of taxes and the expenditure of tax proceeds are governmental functions. We have established elaborate constitutional, parliamentary and judicial provisions to control these functions, to assure that taxes are imposed so far as possible in accordance with the preferences and desires of the public—after all, "taxation without representation" was one of the battle cries of the American Revolution. We have a system of checks and balances to separate the legislative function of imposing taxes and enacting expenditures from the executive function of collecting taxes and administering expenditure programs and from the judicial function of mediating disputes and interpreting the law.

Here the businessman—self-selected or appointed directly or indirectly by stockholders—is to be simultaneously legislator, executive and jurist. He is to decide whom to tax by how much and for what purpose, and he is to spend the proceeds—all this guided only by general exhortations from on high to restrain inflation, improve the environment, fight poverty and so on and on.

> *The conflict of interest is clear when union officials are asked to subordinate the interest of their members to some more general social purpose.*

The whole justification for permitting the corporate executive to be selected by the stockholders is that the executive is an agent serving the interests of his principal. This justification disappears when the corporate executive imposes taxes and spends the proceeds for "social" purposes. He becomes in effect a public employee, a civil servant, even though he remains in name an employee of a private enterprise. On grounds of political principle, it is intolerable that such civil servants—insofar as their actions in the name of social responsibility are real and not just window-dressing—should be selected as they are now. If they are to be civil servants, then they must be selected through a political process. If they are to impose taxes and make expenditures to foster "social" objectives, then political machinery must be set up to guide the assessment of taxes and to determine through a political process the objectives to be served.

This is the basic reason why the doctrine of "social responsibility" involves the acceptance of the socialist view that political mechanisms, not market mechanisms, are the appropriate way to determine the allocation of scarce resources to alternative users.

On the grounds of consequences, can the corporate executive in fact discharge his alleged "social responsibilities"? On the one hand, suppose he could get away with spending the stockholders' or customers' or employees' money. How is he to know how to spend it? He is told that he must contribute to fighting inflation. How is he

to know what action of his will contribute to that end? He is presumably an expert in running his company—in producing a product or selling it or financing it. But nothing about his selection makes him an expert on inflation. Will his holding down the price of his product reduce inflationary pressure? Or, by leaving more spending power in the hands of his customers, simply divert it elsewhere? Or, by forcing him to produce less because of the lower price, will it simply contribute to shortages? Even if he could answer these questions, how much cost is he justified in imposing on his stockholders, customers and employees for this social purpose? What is his appropriate share and what is the appropriate share of others?

And, whether he wants to or not, can he get away with spending his stockholders', customers' or employees' money? Will not the stockholders fire him? (Either the present ones or those who take over when his actions in the name of social responsibility have reduced the corporation's profits and the price of its stock.) His customers and his employees can desert him for other producers and employers less scrupulous in exercising their social responsibilities.

This facet of "social responsibility" doctrine is brought into sharp relief when the doctrine is used to justify wage restraint by trade unions. The conflict of interest is naked and clear when union officials are asked to subordinate the interest of their members to some more general social purpose. If the union officials try to enforce wage restraint, the consequence is likely to be wildcat strikes, rank-and-file revolts and the emergence of strong competitors for these jobs. We thus have the ironic phenomenon that union leaders—at least in the U.S.—have objected to Government interference with the market far more consistently and courageously than have business leaders.

The difficulty of exercising "social responsibility" illustrates, of course, the great virtue of private competitive enterprise—it forces people to be responsible for their own actions and makes it difficult for them to "exploit" other people for either selfish or unselfish purposes. They can do good—but only at their own expense.

Many a reader who has followed the argument this far may be tempted to remonstrate that it is all well and good to speak of government's having the responsibility to impose taxes and determine expenditures for such "social" purposes as controlling pollution or training the hardcore unemployed, but that the problems are too urgent to wait on the slow course of political processes, that the exercise of social responsibility by businessmen is a quicker and surer way to solve pressing current problems.

Aside from the question of fact—I share Adam Smith's skepticism about the benefits that can be expected from "those who affected to trade for the public good"—this argument must be rejected on grounds of principle. What it amounts to is an assertion that those who favor the taxes and expenditures in question have failed to persuade a majority of their fellow citizens to be of like mind and that they are seeking to attain by undemocratic procedures what they cannot attain by democratic procedures. In a free society, it is hard for "good" people to do "good," but that is a small price to pay for making it hard for "evil" people to do "evil," especially since one man's good is another's evil.

I have, for simplicity, concentrated on the special case of the corporate executive, except only for the brief digression on trade unions. But precisely the same argument applies to the newer phenomenon of calling upon stockholders to require corporations to exercise social responsibility (the recent G.M. crusade for example). In most of these cases, what is in effect involved is some stockholders trying to get other stockholders (or customers or employees) to contribute against their will to "social" causes favored by the activists. Insofar as they succeed, they are again imposing taxes and spending the proceeds.

The situation of the individual proprietor is somewhat different. If he acts to reduce the returns of his enterprise in order to exercise his "social responsibility," he is spending his own money, not someone else's. If he wishes to spend his money on such purposes, that is his right, and I cannot see that there is any objection to his

doing so. In the process, he, too, may impose costs on employees and customers. However, because he is far less likely than a large corporation or union to have monopolistic power, any such side effects will tend to be minor.

If the individual proprietor acts to reduce the returns of his enterprise in order to exercise his "social responsibility," he is spending his own money, not someone else's.

Of course, in practice the doctrine of social responsibility is frequently a cloak for actions that are justified on other grounds rather than a reason for those actions.

To illustrate, it may well be in the long-run interest of a corporation that is a major employer in a small community to devote resources to providing amenities to that community or to improving its government. That may make it easier to attract desirable employees, it may reduce the wage bill or lessen losses from pilferage and sabotage or have other worthwhile effects. Or it may be that, given the laws about the deductibility of corporate charitable contributions, the stockholders can contribute more to charities they favor by having the corporation make the gift than by doing it themselves, since they can in that way contribute an amount that would otherwise have been paid as corporate taxes.

In each of these—and many similar—cases, there is a strong temptation to rationalize these actions as an exercise of "social responsibility." In the present climate of opinion, with its widespread aversion to "capitalism," "profits," the "soulless corporation" and so on, this is one way for a corporation to generate goodwill as a byproduct of expenditures that are entirely justified in its own self-interest.

It would be inconsistent of me to call on corporate executives to refrain from this hypocritical window-dressing because it harms the foundations of a free society. That would be to call on them to exercise a "social responsibility"! If our institutions, and the attitudes of the public, make it in their self-interest to cloak their actions in this way, I cannot summon much indignation to denounce them. At the same time, I can express admiration for those individual proprietors or owners of closely held corporations or stockholders of more broadly held corporations who disdain such tactics as approaching fraud.

Whether blameworthy or not, the use of the cloak of social responsibility, and the nonsense spoken in its name by influential and prestigious businessmen, does clearly harm the foundations of a free society. I have been impressed time and again by the schizophrenic character of many businessmen. They are capable of being extremely farsighted and muddleheaded in matters that are outside their businesses but affect the possible survival of business in general. This shortsightedness is strikingly exemplified in the calls from many businessmen for wage and price guidelines or controls or incomes policies. There is nothing that could do more in a brief period to destroy a market system and replace it by a centrally controlled system than effective governmental control of prices and wages.

The shortsightedness is also exemplified in speeches by businessmen on social responsibility. This may gain them kudos in the short run. But it helps to strengthen the already too prevalent view that the pursuit of profits is wicked and immoral and must be curbed and controlled by external forces. Once this view is adopted, the external forces that curb the market will not be the social consciences, however highly developed, of the pontificating executives; it will be the iron fist of Government bureaucrats. Here, as with price and wage controls, businessmen seem to me to reveal a suicidal impulse.

The political principle that underlies the market mechanism is unanimity. In an ideal free market resting on private property, no individual can coerce any other, all cooperation is voluntary, all parties to such cooperation benefit or they need not participate. There are no "social" values, no "social" responsibilities of individuals. Society is a collection of individuals and of the various groups they voluntarily form.

The political principle that underlies the political mechanism is conformity. The individual must serve a more general social interest—whether that be determined by a church or a dictator or a majority. The individual may have a vote and a say in what is to be done, but if he is overruled, he must conform. It is appropriate for some to require others to contribute to a general social purpose whether they wish to or not.

Unfortunately, unanimity is not always feasible. There are some respects in which conformity appears unavoidable, so I do not see how one can avoid the use of the political mechanism altogether.

But the doctrine of "social responsibility" taken seriously would extend the scope of the political mechanism to every human activity. It does not differ in philosophy from the most explicitly collectivist doctrine. It differs only by professing to believe that collectivist ends can be attained without collectivist means. That is why, in my book *Capitalism and Freedom*, I have called it a "fundamentally subversive doctrine" in a free society, and have said that in such a society, "there is one and only one social responsibility of business—to use its resources and engage in activities designed to increase its profits so long as it stays within the rules of the game, which is to say, engages in open and free competition without deception or fraud."

Questions for Discussion:

1. Do you agree with Friedman that the sole goal of a corporation is to increase shareholder wealth? Why or why not?
2. When management gives to charity (for more than public relations purposes), do you think that management is actually stealing from shareholders, as Friedman asserts (he also calls it "taxation without representation")? How would you react if a company in which you had an investment was giving to organizations involved in activities you thought were immoral?

Business Ethics and Stakeholder Analysis

Kenneth E. Goodpaster

Business Ethics Quarterly 1, no. 1 (January 1991): 53–73. Copyright © 1991.

So we must think through what management should be accountable for; and how and through whom its accountability can be discharged. The stockholders' interest, both short- and long-term is one of the areas. But it is only one.

Peter Drucker, 1988, Harvard Business Review

What is ethically responsible management? How can a corporation, given its economic mission, be managed with appropriate attention to ethical concerns? These are central questions in the field of business ethics. One approach to answering such questions that has become popular during the last two decades is loosely referred to as "stakeholder analysis." Ethically responsible management, it is often suggested, is management that includes careful attention not only to stockholders *but to stakeholders generally* in the decision-making process.

This suggestion about the ethical importance of stakeholder analysis contains an important kernel of truth, but it can also be misleading. Comparing the ethical relationship between managers and stockholders with their relationship to other stakeholders is, I will argue, almost as problematic as ignoring stakeholders (ethically) altogether—presenting us with something of a "stakeholder paradox."

Definition

The term "stakeholder" appears to have been invented in the early '60s as a deliberate play on the word "stakeholder" to signify that there are other parties having a "stake" in the decision-making of the modern, publicly-held corporation in addition to those holding equity positions. Professor R. Edward Freeman, in his book *Strategic Management: A Stakeholder Approach* (Pitman, 1984), defines the term as follows:

A stakeholder in an organization is (by definition) any group or individual who can affect or is affected by the achievement of the organization's objectives. (46)

Examples of stakeholder groups (beyond stockholders) are employees, suppliers, customers, creditors, competitors, governments, and communities. . . .

Another metaphor with which the term "stakeholder" is associated is that of a "player" in a game like poker. One with a "stake" in the game is one who plays and puts some economic value at risk.[1]

Much of what makes responsible decision-making difficult is understanding how there can be an ethical relationship between management and stakeholders that avoids being too weak (making stakeholders mere means to stockholders' ends) or too strong (making stakeholders quasi-stockholders in their own right). To give these issues life, a case example will help. So let us consider the case of General Motors and Poletown.

The Poletown Case[2]

In 1980, GM was facing a net loss in income, the first since 1921, due to intense foreign competition. Management realized that major capital expenditures would be required for the company to regain its competitive position and profitability. A $40 billion five-year capital spending program was announced that included new, state-of-the-art assembly techniques aimed at smaller, fuel-efficient automobiles demanded by the market. Two aging assembly plants in Detroit were among the ones to be replaced. Their closure would eliminate 500 jobs. Detroit in 1980 was a city with a black majority, an unemployment rate of 18% overall and 30% for blacks, a rising public debt and a chronic budget deficit, despite high tax rates.

The site requirements for a new assembly plant included 500 acres, access to long-haul railroad and freeways, and proximity to suppliers for "just-in-time" inventory management. It needed to be ready to produce 1983 model year cars beginning in September 1982. The only site in Detroit meeting GM's requirements was heavily settled, covering a section of the Detroit neighborhood of Poletown. Of the 3,500 residents, half were black. The whites were mostly of Polish descent, retired or nearing retirement. An alternative "green field" site was available in another midwestern state.

Using the power of eminent domain, the Poletown area could be acquired and cleared for a new plant within the company's timetable, and the city government was eager to cooperate. Because of job retention in Detroit, the leadership of the United Auto Workers was also in favor of the idea. The Poletown Neighborhood Council strongly opposed the plan, but was willing to work with the city and GM.

The new plant would employ 6,150 workers and would cost GM $500 million wherever it was built. Obtaining and preparing the Poletown site would cost an additional $200 million, whereas alternative sites in the midwest were available for $65–80 million.

The interested parties were many—stockholders, customers, employees, suppliers, the Detroit community, the midwestern alternative, the Poletown neighborhood. The decision was difficult. GM management needed to consider its competitive situation, the extra costs of remaining in Detroit, the consequences to the city of leaving for another part of the midwest, and the implications for the residents of choosing the Poletown site if the decision was made to stay. The decision about whom to talk to and *how* was as puzzling as the decision about *what* to do and *why*.

I. Stakeholder Analysis and Stakeholder Synthesis

Ethical values enter management decision-making, it is often suggested, through the gate of stakeholder analysis. But the suggestion that introducing "stakeholder analysis" into business decisions is the same as introducing ethics into those decisions is questionable. To make this plain, let me first distinguish between two importantly different ideas: stakeholder analysis and stakeholder synthesis. I will then examine alternative kinds of stakeholder synthesis with attention to ethical content.

The decision-making process of an individual or a company can be seen in terms of a sequence of six steps to be followed after an issue or problem presents itself for resolution.[3] For ease of reference and recall, I will name the sequence PASCAL, after the six letters in the name of the French philosopher-mathematician Blaise Pascal (1623–62), who once remarked in reference to ethical decision-making that "the heart has reasons the reason knows not of."

1. PERCEPTION or fact-gathering about the options available and their short- and long-term implications;
2. ANALYSIS of these implications with specific attention to affected parties and to the decision-maker's goals, objectives, values, responsibilities, etc.;
3. SYNTHESIS of this structured information according to whatever fundamental priorities obtain in the mindset of the decision-maker;
4. CHOICE among the available options based on the synthesis;
5. ACTION or implementation of the chosen option through a series of specific requests to specific individuals or groups, resource allocation, incentives, controls, and feedback;
6. LEARNING from the outcome of the decision, resulting in either reinforcement or modification (for future decisions) of the way in which the above steps have been taken.

. . . Now, by *stakeholder analysis* I simply mean a process that does not go beyond the first two steps mentioned above. That is, the affected parties caught up in each available option are identified and the positive and negative impacts on each stakeholder are determined. But questions having to do with processing this information into a decision and implementing it are *left unanswered*. These steps are not part of the *analysis* but of the *synthesis, choice,* and *action.*

Stakeholder analysis may give the initial appearance of a decision-making process, but in fact it is only a *segment* of a decision-making process. It represents the preparatory or opening phase that awaits the crucial application of the moral (or nonmoral) values of the decision-maker. So, to be informed that an individual or an institution regularly makes stakeholder analysis part of decision-making or takes a "stakeholder approach" to management is to learn little or nothing about the ethical character of that individual or institution. It is to learn only that stakeholders are regularly identified—*not why and for what purpose.* To be told that stakeholders are or must be "taken into account" is, so far, to be told very little. Stakeholder analysis is, as a practical matter, morally *neutral.* It is therefore a mistake to see it as a substitute for normative ethical thinking.[4]

What I shall call "stakeholder synthesis" goes further into the sequence of decision-making steps mentioned above to include actual decision-making and implementation (S, C, A). The critical point is that stakeholder synthesis offers *a pattern or channel by which to move from stakeholder identification to a practical response or resolution.* Here we begin to join stakeholder analysis to questions of substance. But we must now ask: What kind of substance? And how does it relate to *ethics?* The stakeholder idea, remember, is typically offered as a way of integrating *ethical* values into management decision-making. When and how does substance become *ethical* substance?

Strategic Stakeholder Synthesis

We can imagine decision-makers doing "stakeholder analysis" for different underlying reasons, not always having to do with ethics. A management team, for example, might be careful to take positive and (especially) negative stakeholder effects into account for no other reason than that offended stakeholders might resist or retaliate (e.g., through political action or opposition to necessary regulatory clearances). It might not be *ethical* concern for the stakeholders that motivates and guides such analysis, so much as concern about potential impediments to the achievement of strategic objectives. Thus positive and negative effects on relatively powerless stakeholders may be ignored or discounted in the synthesis, choice, and action phases of the decision process.[5]

In the Poletown case, General Motors might have done a stakeholder analysis using the following reasoning: our stockholders are the central stakeholders here, but other key stakeholders include our suppliers, old and new plant employees, the city of Detroit, and the residents of Poletown. These other stakeholders are not our direct concern as a corporation with an economic mission, but since they can influence our short- or long-term strategic interests, they must be taken into account. Public relations' costs and benefits, for example, or concerns about union contracts or litigation might well have influenced the choice between staying in Detroit and going elsewhere.

I refer to this kind of stakeholder synthesis as "strategic" since stakeholders outside the stockholder group are viewed instrumentally, as factors potentially affecting the overarching goal of optimizing stockholder interests. They are taken into account in the decision-making process, but as external environmental forces, as potential sources of either good will or retaliation. "We" are the economic principals and management; "they" are significant players whose attitudes and future actions might affect our short-term or long-term success. We must respect them in the way one "respects" the weather—as a set of forces to be reckoned with.[6]

It should be emphasized that managers who adopt the strategic stakeholder approach are not necessarily *personally* indifferent to the plight of stakeholders who are "strategically unimportant." The point is that *in their role as managers,* with a fiduciary relationship that binds them as agents to principals, their basic outlook subordinates other stakeholder concerns to those of stockholders. Market and legal forces are relied upon to secure the interests of those whom strategic considerations might discount. This reliance can and does take different forms, depending on the emphasis given to market forces on the one hand and legal forces on the other. A more conservative, market-oriented view acknowledges the role of legal compliance as an environmental factor affecting strategic choice, but thinks stakeholder interests are best served by minimal interference from the public sector. Adam Smith's "invisible hand" is thought to be the most important guarantor of the common good in a competitive economy. A more liberal view sees the hand of government, through legislation and regulation, as essential for representing stakeholders that might otherwise not achieve "standing" in the strategic decision process.

What both conservatives and liberals have in common is the conviction that the fundamental orientation of management must be toward the interests of stockholders. Other stakeholders (customers, employees, suppliers, neighbors) enter the decision-making equation either directly as instrumental economic factors or indirectly as potential legal claimants. . . . Both see law and regulation as providing a voice for stakeholders that goes beyond market dynamics. They differ about how much government regulation is socially and economically desirable.

During the Poletown controversy, GM managers as individuals may have cared deeply about the potential lost jobs in Detroit, or about the potential dislocation of Poletown residents. But in their role as agents for the owners (stockholders) they could only allow such considerations to "count" if they served GM's strategic interests (or perhaps as legal constraints on the decision). . . .

The essence of a strategic view of stakeholders is not that stakeholders are ignored, but that all but a special group (stockholders) are considered on the basis of their actual or potential influence on management's central mission. The basic nor-mative principle is fiduciary responsibility (organizational prudence), supplemented by legal compliance. . . .

Multi-Fiduciary Stakeholder Synthesis

In contrast to a strategic view of stakeholders, one can imagine a management team processing stakeholder information by giving the same care to the interests of, say, employees, customers, and local communities as to the economic interests of stockholders. This kind of substantive commitment to stakeholders might involve trading off the economic advantages of one group against those of another, e.g., in a plant closing decision. I shall refer to this way of integrating stakeholder analysis with decision-making as "multi-fiduciary" since all stakeholders are treated by management as having equally important interests, deserving joint "maximization" (or what Herbert Simon might call "satisficing").

Professor Freeman, quoted earlier, contemplates what I am calling the multi-fiduciary view at the end of his 1984 book under the heading *The Manager as Fiduciary to Stakeholders*:

> Perhaps the most important area of future research is the issue of whether or not a theory of management can be constructed that uses the stakeholder concept to enrich "managerial capitalism," that is, can the notion that managers bear a fiduciary relationship to stockholders or the owners of the firm, be replaced by a concept of management whereby the manager *must* act in the interests of the stakeholders in the organization? (249)

As we have seen, the strategic approach pays attention to stakeholders as to factors that might affect economic interests, so many market forces to which companies must pay attention for competitive reasons. They become actual or potential legal challenges to the company's exercise of economic rationality. The multi-fiduciary approach, on the other hand, views stakeholders apart from their instrumental, economic, or legal clout. It does not see them merely as what philosopher John Ladd once called "limiting operating conditions" on management attention.[7] On this view, the word "stakeholder" carries with it, by the deliberate modification of a single phoneme, a dramatic shift in managerial outlook.

In 1954, famed management theorist Adolf Berle conceded a longstanding debate with Harvard law professor E. Merrick Dodd that looks in retrospect very much like a debate between what we are calling strategic and multi-fiduciary interpretations of stakeholder synthesis. Berle wrote:

> Twenty years ago, [I held] that corporate powers were powers in trust for shareholders while Professor Dodd argued that these powers were held in trust for the entire community. The argument has been settled (at least for the time being) squarely in favor of Professor Dodd's contention. (Quoted in Ruder, see below.)

The intuitive idea behind Dodd's view, and behind more recent formulations of it in terms of "multiple constituencies" and "stakeholders, not just stockholders" is that by expanding the list of those in whose trust corporate management must manage, we thereby introduce ethical responsibility into business decision-making.

In the context of the Poletown case, a multi-fiduciary approach by GM management might have identified the same stakeholders. But it would have considered the interests of employees, the city of Detroit, and the Poletown residents *alongside* stockholder interests, not solely in terms of how they might *influence* stockholder interests. This may or may not have entailed a different outcome. But it probably would have meant a different approach to the decision-making process in relation to the residents of Poletown (talking with them, for example).

We must now ask, as we did of the strategic approach: How satisfactory is multi-fiduciary stakeholder synthesis as a way of giving ethical substance to management decision-making? On the face of it, and in stark contrast to the strategic approach, it may seem that we have at least arrived at a truly moral view. But we should be cautious. For no sooner do we think we have found the proper interpretation of ethics in man-

agement than a major objection presents itself. And, yes, it appears to be a *moral* objection!

It can be argued that multi-fiduciary stakeholder analysis is simply incompatible with widely-held moral convictions about the special fiduciary obligations owed by management to stockholders. At the center of the objection is the belief that the obligations of agents to principals are stronger or different in kind from those of agents to third parties.

The Stakeholder Paradox

Managers who would pursue a multi-fiduciary stakeholder orientation for their companies must face resistance from those who believe that a strategic orientation is the only *legitimate* one for business to adopt, given the economic mission and legal constitution of the modern corporation. This may be disorienting since the word "illegitimate" has clear negative ethical connotations, and yet the multi-fiduciary approach is often defended on ethical grounds. I will refer to this anomalous situation as the *Stakeholder Paradox*:

> It seems essential, yet in some ways illegitimate, to orient corporate decisions by ethical values that go beyond strategic stakeholder considerations to multi-fiduciary ones.

I call this a paradox because it says there is an ethical problem whichever approach management takes. Ethics seems both to forbid and to demand a strategic, profit-maximizing mindset. The argument behind the paradox focuses on management's *fiduciary* duty to the stockholder, essentially the duty to keep a profit-maximizing promise, and a concern that the "impartiality" of the multi-fiduciary approach simply cuts management loose from certain well-defined bonds of stockholder accountability. On this view, impartiality is thought to be a *betrayal of trust*. Professor David S. Ruder, a former chairman of the Securities and Exchange Commission, once summarized the matter this way:

> Traditional fiduciary obligation theory insists that a corporate manager owes an obligation

of care and loyalty to shareholders. If a public obligation theory unrelated to profit maximization becomes the law, the corporate manager who is not able to act in his own self-interest without violating his fiduciary obligation, may nevertheless act in the public interest without violating that obligation.[8] (226)

Ruder continued:

Whether induced by government legislation, government pressure, or merely by enlightened attitudes of the corporation regarding its long range potential as a unit in society, corporate activities carried on in satisfaction of public obligations can be consistent with profit maximization objectives. In contrast, justification of public obligations upon bold concepts of public need without corporate benefit will merely serve to reduce further the owner's influence on his corporation and to create additional demands for public participation in corporate management. (228–29)

Ruder's view appears to be that (a) multi-fiduciary stakeholder synthesis *need not* be used by management because the strategic approach is more accommodating than meets the eye; and (b) multi-fiduciary stakeholder synthesis should not be invoked by management because such a "bold" concept could threaten the private (*vs.* public) status of the corporation.

In response to (a), we saw earlier that there were reasonable questions about the tidy convergence of ethics and economic success. Respecting the interests and rights of the Poletown residents might really have meant incurring higher costs for GM (short-term as well as long-term).

Appeals to corporate self-interest, even long-term, might not always support ethical decisions. But even on those occasions where they will, we must wonder about the disposition to favor economic and legal reasoning "for the record." If Ruder means to suggest that business leaders can often *reformulate* or *represent* their reasons for certain morally-grounded decisions in strategic terms

having to do with profit maximization and obedience to law, he is perhaps correct. In the spirit of Milton Friedman's famous essay, we might not summon much indignation to denounce them. But why the fiction? Why not call a moral reason a moral reason?

This issue is not simply of academic interest. Managers must confront it in practice. In one major public company, the C.E.O. put significant resources behind an affirmative action program and included the following explanation in a memo to middle management:

I am often asked why this is such a high priority at our company. There is, of course, the obvious answer that it is in our best interest to seek out and employ good people in all sectors of our society. And there is the answer that enlightened self-interest tells us that more and more of the younger people, whom we must attract as future employees, choose companies by their social records as much as by their business prospects. *But the one overriding reason for this emphasis is because it is right.* Because this company has always set for itself the objective of assuming social as well as business obligations. Because that's the kind of company we have been. And with your participation, that's the kind of company we'll continue to be.[9]

In this connection, Ruder reminds us of what Professor Berle observed over twenty-five years ago:

The fact is that boards of directors or corporation executives are often faced with situations in which they quite humanly and simply consider that such and such is the decent thing to do and ought to be done. . . . They apply the potential profits or public relations tests later on, a sort of left-handed justification in this curious free-market world where an obviously moral or decent or humane action has to be apologized for on the ground that, conceivably, you may somehow make money by it. (*Ibid.*)

The Problem of Boldness

What appears to lie at the foundation of Ruder's cautious view is a concern about the "boldness" of the multi-fiduciary concept [(b) above].[10] It is not that he thinks the strategic approach is always satisfactory; it is that the multi-fiduciary approach is, in his eyes, much worse. For it questions the special relationship between the manager as agent and the stockholder as principal.

Ruder suggests that what he calls a "public obligation" theory threatens the private status of the corporation. He believes that what we are calling multi-fiduciary stakeholder synthesis *dilutes* the fiduciary obligation to stockholders (by extending it to customers, employees, suppliers, etc.) and he sees this as a threat to the "privacy" of the private sector organization. If public obligations are understood on the model of public sector institutions with their multiple constituencies, Ruder thinks, the stockholder loses status.

There is something profoundly *right* about Ruder's line of argument here, I believe, and something profoundly *wrong*. What is right is his intuition that if we treat other stakeholders on the model of the fiduciary relationship between management and the stockholder, we will, in effect, make them into quasi-stockholders. We can do this, of course, if we choose to as a society. But we should be aware that it is a radical step indeed. For it blurs traditional goals in terms of entrepreneurial risk-taking, pushes decision-making towards paralysis because of the dilemmas posed by divided loyalties and, in the final analysis, represents nothing less than the conversion of the modern private corporation into a public institution and probably calls for a corresponding restructuring of corporate governance (e.g., representatives of each stakeholder group on the board of directors). Unless we believe that the social utility of a private sector has disappeared, not to mention its value for individual liberty and enterprise, we will be cautious about an interpretation of stakeholder synthesis that transforms the private sector into the public sector.

On the other hand, I believe Ruder is mistaken if he thinks that business ethics requires this kind of either/or: either a private sector with a strategic stakeholder synthesis (business without ethics) or the effective loss of the private sector with a multi-fiduciary stakeholder synthesis (ethics without business).

Recent debates over state laws protecting companies against hostile takeovers may illustrate Ruder's concern as well as the new challenge. According to one journalist, a recent Pennsylvania anti-takeover law

> does no less than redefine the fiduciary duty of corporate directors, enabling them to base decisions not merely on the interests of shareholders, but on the interests of customers, suppliers, employees and the community at large. Pennsylvania is saying that it is the corporation that directors are responsible to. Shareholders say they always thought they themselves were the corporation.

Echoing Ruder, one legal observer quoted by Elias[11] (*ibid.*) commented with reference to this law that it "undermines and erodes free markets and property rights. From this perspective, this is an anticapitalist law. The management can take away property from the real owners."

In our terms, the state of Pennsylvania is charged with adopting a multi-fiduciary stakeholder approach in an effort to rectify deficiencies of the strategic approach which (presumably) corporate raiders hold.

The challenge that we are thus presented with is to develop an account of the moral responsibilities of management that (i) avoids surrendering the moral relationship between management and stakeholders as the strategic view does, while (ii) not transforming stakeholder obligations into fiduciary obligations (thus protecting the uniqueness of the principal-agent relationship between management and stockholder).

II. Toward a New Stakeholder Synthesis

We all remember the story of the well-intentioned Doctor Frankenstein. He sought to improve the human condition by designing a powerful, intelligent force for good in the community. Alas, when he flipped the switch, his creation turned out to be a monster rather than a marvel! Is the concept of the ethical corporation like a Franken-stein monster?

Taking business ethics seriously need not mean that management bears *additional* fiduciary relationships to third parties (non-stockholder constituencies) as multi-fiduciary stakeholder synthesis suggests. It may mean that there are morally significant *nonfiduciary* obligations to third parties surrounding any fiduciary relationship (See *Figure 1*). Such moral obligations may be owed by private individuals as well as private-sector organizations to those whose freedom and wellbeing is affected by their economic behavior. It is these very obligations in fact (the duty not to harm or coerce and duties not to lie, cheat, or steal) that are cited in regulatory, legislative, and judicial arguments for constraining profit-driven business activities. These obligations are not "hypothetical" or contingent or indirect, as they would be on the strategic model, wherein they are only subject to the corporation's interests being met. They are "categorical" or direct. They are not rooted in the *fiduciary* relationship, but in other relationships at least as deep.

Figure 1. Direct Managerial Obligations

It must be admitted in fairness to Ruder's argument that the jargon of "stakeholders" in discussions of business ethics can seem to threaten the notion of what corporate law refers to as the "undivided and unselfish loyalty" owed by managers and directors to stockholders. For this way of speaking can suggest a multiplication of management duties *of the same kind* as the duty to stockholders. What we must understand is that the responsibilities of management toward stockholders are of a piece with the obligations that *stockholders themselves* would be expected to honor in their own right. As an old Latin proverb has it, *nemo dat quod non habet*, which literally means "nobody gives what he doesn't have." Freely

translating in this context we can say: No one can expect of an *agent* behavior that is ethically less responsible than what he would expect of himself. I cannot (ethically) *hire* done on my behalf what I would not (ethically) *do* myself. We might refer to this as the "Nemo Dat Principle" (NDP) and consider it a formal requirement of consistency in business ethics (and professional ethics generally):

(NDP) Investors cannot expect of managers (more generally, principals cannot expect of their agents) behavior that would be inconsistent with the reasonable ethical expectations of the community.[12]

The NDP does not, of course, resolve in advance the many ethical challenges that managers must face. It only indicates that these challenges are of a piece with those that face us all. It offers a different kind of test (and so a different kind of stakeholder synthesis) that management (and institutional investors) might apply to policies and decisions.

The foundation of ethics in management—and the way out of the stakeholder paradox—lies in understanding that the conscience of the corporation is a logical and moral extension of the consciences of its principals. It is *not* an expansion of the *list* of principals, but a gloss on the principal-agent relationship itself. Whatever the structure of the principal-agent relationship, neither principal nor agent can ever claim that an agent has "moral immunity" from the basic obligations that would apply to any human being toward other members of the community.

Indeed, consistent with Ruder's belief, the introduction of moral reasoning (distinguished from multi-fiduciary stakeholder reasoning) into the framework of management thinking may *protect* rather than threaten private sector legitimacy. The conscientious corporation can maintain its private economic mission, but in the context of fundamental moral obligations owed by any member of society to others affected by that member's actions. Recognizing such obligations does *not* mean that an institution is a public institution. Private institutions, like private individuals, can be and are bound to respect moral obligations in the pursuit of private purposes.

Conceptually, then, we can make room for a moral posture toward stakeholders that is both *partial* (respecting the fiduciary relationship between managers and stockholders) and *impartial* (respecting the equally important nonfiduciary relationships between management and other stakeholders). As philosopher Thomas Nagel has said, "In the conduct of life, of all places, the rivalry between the view from within and the view from without must be taken seriously."[13]

Whether this conceptual room can be used *effectively* in the face of enormous pressures on contemporary managers and directors is another story, of course. For it is one thing to say that "giving standing to stakeholders" in managerial reasoning is conceptually coherent. It is something else to say that it is practically coherent.

Yet most of us, I submit, believe it. Most of us believe that management at General Motors *owed* it to the people of Detroit and to the people of Poletown to take their (nonfiduciary) interests very seriously, to seek creative solutions to the conflict, to do more than use or manipulate them in accordance with GM's needs only. We understand that managers and directors have a special obligation to provide a financial return to the stockholders, but we also understand that the word "special" in this context needs to be tempered by an appreciation of certain fundamental community norms that go beyond the demands of both laws and markets. There are certain class-action suits that stockholders ought not to win. For there is sometimes a moral defense.

Conclusion

The relationship between management and stockholders is ethically different in kind from the relationship between management and other parties (like employees, suppliers, customers, etc.), a fact that seems to go unnoticed by the multi-fiduciary approach. If it were not, the cor-

poration would cease to be a private sector institution—and what is now called business ethics would become a more radical critique of our economic system than is typically thought. On this point, Milton Friedman must be given a fair and serious hearing.

This does not mean, however, that "stakeholders" lack a morally significant relationship to management, as the strategic approach implies. It means only that the relationship in question is different from a fiduciary one. Management may never have promised customers, employees, suppliers, etc. a "return on investment," but management is nevertheless obliged to take seriously its extralegal obligations not to injure, lie to or cheat these stakeholders *quite apart from* whether it is in the stockholders' interests.

As we think through the *proper* relationship of management to stakeholders, fundamental features of business life must undoubtedly be recognized: that corporations have a principally economic mission and competence; that fiduciary obligations to investor and general obligations to comply with the law cannot be set aside; and that abuses of economic power and disregard of corporate stewardship in the name of business ethics are possible.

But these things must be recognized as well: that corporations are not solely financial institutions; that fiduciary obligations go beyond short-term profit and are in any case subject to moral criteria in their execution; and that mere compliance with the law can be unduly limited and even unjust.

The *Stakeholder Paradox* can be avoided by a more thoughtful understanding of the nature of moral obligation and the limits it imposes on the principal-agent relationship. Once we understand that there is a practical "space" for identifying the ethical values shared by a corporation and its stockholders—a space that goes beyond strategic self-interest but stops short of impartiality—the hard work of filling that space can proceed.

Notes

[1]Strictly speaking the historical meaning of "stakeholder" in this context is someone who literally *holds* the stakes during play.

[2]See Goodpaster and Piper, *Managerial Decision Making and Ethical Values*, Harvard Business School Publishing Division, 1989.

[3]See Goodpaster, *PASCAL: A Framework for Conscientious Decision Making* (1989).

[4]Actually, there are subtle ways in which even the stakeholder identification or inventory process might have *some* ethical content. The very process of *identifying* affected parties involves the use of the imagination in a way that can lead to a natural empathetic or caring response to those parties in the synthesis, choice and action phases of decision-making. This is a contingent connection, however, not a necessary one.

[5]Note that including powerless stakeholders in the analysis phase may indicate whether the decision-maker cares about "affecting" them or "being affected by" them. Also, the inclusion of what might be called secondary stakeholders as advocates for primary stakeholders (e.g., local governments on behalf of certain citizen groups) may signal the values that will come into play in any synthesis.

[6]It should be mentioned that some authors, most notably Kenneth R. Andrews in *The Concept of Corporate Strategy* (Irwin, Third Edition, 1987) employ a broader and more social definition of "strategic" decision-making than the one implied here.

[7]Ladd observed in a now-famous essay entitled "Morality and the Ideal of Rationality in Formal Organizations" (*The Monist*, 54, 1970) that organizational "rationality" was defined solely in terms of economic objectives: "The interests and needs of the individuals concerned, as individuals, must be considered only insofar as they establish limiting operating conditions. Organizational rationality dictates that these interests and needs must not be considered in their own right or on their own merits. If we think of an organization as a machine, it is easy to see why we cannot reasonably expect it to have any moral obligations to people or for them to have any to it." (507)

[8]"Public Obligations of Private Corporations," *Univ. of Pennsylvania Law Review*, 114 (1965). Ruder recently (1989) reaffirmed the views in his 1965 article.

[9]Business Products Corporation—Part 1 HBS Case Services 9–377–077.

[10]"The Business Judgement Rule" gives broad latitude to officers and directors of corporations, but calls for reasoning on the basis of the long-term economic interest of the company. And corporate case law ordinarily allows exceptions to profit-maximization criteria only when there are actual or potential *legal* barriers, and limits charitable and humanitarian gifts by the logic of long term self-interest. The underlying rationale is accountability to investors. Recent work by the American Law Institute, however, suggests a rethinking of these matters. See *Exhibit 2*.

[11](Christopher Elias, "Turning Up the Heat on the Top," *Insight*, July 23, 1990).

[12]We might consider the NDP in broader terms that would include the relationship between "client" and "professional" in other contexts, such as law, medicine, education, government, and religion, where normally the community's expectations are embodied in ethical standards.

[13]T. Nagel, *The View from Nowhere*, Oxford Univ. Press (1986), p.163.

Questions for Discussion:

1. How is the stakeholder thesis of Goodpaster different from the ideas put forth by Friedman?
2. On what basis does Goodpaster suggest that non-fiduciary interests of stakeholders be taken seriously? Do you agree?

A Long Term Business Perspective in a Short Term World

A Conversation with Jim Sinegal

An Interview with James D. Sinegal by Albert Erisman and David Gill

Ethix (March/April 2003): 6–9, 16. Copyright © 2003.

Low Prices and High Wages: Why?

Al Erisman: Costco is distinctive among its competitors with its policies of never marking anything up more than 14 percent (with an average mark-up of only 10%). You have been known to lower prices on items when the wholesale price went down—even if market competition and customer awareness didn't require it, even if you had purchased the item at an earlier, higher price. Costco also is determined that its employee wages and benefits lead the industry. Business Week reported that a Costco cashier with four years experience can earn more than $40,000 with full benefits. Where do these policies come from? How did you decide to run your business this way?

Jim Sinegal: Part of it is just sound business thinking. It shouldn't surprise anyone that if you find good people, give them good jobs, and pay them good wages, good things will happen.

Part of the reason may also have to do with the kind of business we have. When we opened our first warehouse in downtown Seattle with forklifts running through stacks of tires and electronics, food and mayonnaise and cranberry juice, people would naturally ask the question, how can they sell things for such low prices? What are these guys doing?

We decided that we would take away any objections or questions a customer might have, such as perhaps we could be treating our employees unfairly in order to sell things at low prices. We also decided to establish a stronger and better "guarantee of satisfaction" on every product we sold, that would exceed the warrantee offered by any other company.

We have the same attitude toward our suppliers and everyone else who has contact with our business. We operate this way because we believe philosophically that this is what we should be doing—but we also do it because of the nature of our business. People would always ask "What's the catch?" We wanted to make it clear that there were no catches.

David Gill: Don't investors pressure you to increase quarterly profits and raise shareholder value by cutting wages and raising prices as the market dictates or allows? How do you and your Board resist that?

Sinegal: We get it every day. That's not an unreasonable question for someone in the business of making money. Their job is to buy low and sell high. But that's not our job. Our job is to build the company, hopefully one that's going to be here fifty years from now. You don't do that by changing every time the wind blows in a different direction.

The things that we do are basic and intrinsic to our business and our company. Our reputation for pricing is an example. We have sweated over this for years. Why would we sacrifice that just to make a quarterly target? It wouldn't make sense—sacrificing everything, risking our whole reputation. We believe our strategy will maximize shareholder value over the long term.

> ### We have a reputation for pricing. Why would we sacrifice that just to make a quarterly target?

Gill: Customers have price and quality incentives to come to Costco. Employees have wage and satisfaction incentives to work at Costco. What is the incentive for investors? Must they always share your long term view?

Sinegal: The record shows clearly that we are successful over the long term. I don't know what the exact number is but look at our return over the past five or ten or fifteen years. Our mission is to do four essential things: obey the law. . . . take care of our customers . . . take care of our people . . . and respect our suppliers. If we do these four things, and do them consistently, we will succeed as a business enterprise that is profitable and rewarding to our shareholders.

It is possible for some to ignore these things and reward their shareholders in the short term—but not for the long term. We feel an obligation to build businesses so that communities can count on us being there, suppliers can count on us being there, employees can count on the security of jobs, and customers who shop with us know that they can count on us. When they buy a washing machine or a television, we're still going to be around a couple of years from now.

Erisman: This all seems pretty obvious but many are not doing business this way. Why?

Sinegal: In the past year public attention has been focused on the "crooks in business" and how to stop them. The result has been a bunch of new legislation and rules. You know as well as I do that the crooks are going to go on "crooking"—they're going to figure it out. But I believe that, by and large, most businesses are running on a basis similar to ours.

The Good CEO

Gill: Business Week called you one of the good CEOs. What in your view makes a good CEO? As you look for a successor some day at Costco, what characteristics matter most?

Sinegal: I'm flattered of course that *Business Week* included me in that group. Characteristics? Good leaders make the determination how to run the company and then communicate it to everyone in the company so that they all understand it. Honesty and doing the right thing cannot be the responsibility of management alone. Every level of the company should understand what the rules are and every employee in the company should be mortified if the company and its people don't do

what they are supposed to do. The attitude has got to be pervasive throughout the organization: "We don't do that kind of stuff around here! Period!"

Gill: So first you're looking for character and ethics?

Sinegal: You're looking for a lot of things. You look for intelligence, industriousness, integrity, for someone faster than a speeding bullet—all of those things you want in a manager. If you start off with integrity, financial integrity as well as intellectual integrity, you're starting on a pretty good base.

Values and Integrity through the Ranks

Erisman: How do you make sure that integrity and company values are part of the culture all the way down to the forklift driver and the mail delivery person?

Sinegal: As an organization, make sure that you are consistent. You put in place simple guidelines on how you run your business and then follow them. One guideline we follow at Costco is that no employee who has been with us for more than two years can be fired without the approval of a senior officer in the company. We think an employee who has been with us two years is entitled to that. No manager can come in on a bad day and decide some employee is history. There has got to be a review process. Is it perfect? Of course not. We're fallible. But it is one of the things that we do to show respect to our employees.

Another example is our open-door policy. People have a way to voice their grievances and get them addressed. All 100,000 employees cannot run to me (although sometimes it feels like they do) but I do take on some. It would be a very rare day that I don't get a couple of calls from employees. But think about this: if warehouse managers know that their own regional bosses have open door policies and will talk to any employees about their issues, then they are going to be a little faster to talk to the troubled employees themselves. They don't want the problems to come back to them through their bosses. They are smart enough to figure out that it is their responsibility to take care of things at their level.

Gill: You can't know 100,000 employees personally and you can't visit all your stores as frequently. What do you do differently now to maintain consistency in your culture and values?

Sinegal: It's clearly much more difficult than in the early days. That rule about the two-year employee termination review used to apply just to my partner Jeff Brotman and me. When the company got too big we had to say the review will be by one of our senior officers. I used to pride myself on visiting every one of our warehouses between October and December. Now that is impossible. Some locations take two days of travel just to get there. I still try to get to every warehouse at least once a year. Why? That's what I do for a living. I love the business and I enjoy doing it. It is important that those in management get out there and understand where the business is. Otherwise your business is going to fall apart on you.

Technology at Costco

Gill: Does information technology help you to stay in communication?

Sinegal: Technology has made us much more productive. With computers, fax machines, and cell phones we have more productive time during the course of the whole day and can react to situations more immediately.

Erisman: When I think of technology and retail, I think of what Amazon has done at the front end of their business—and what WalMart has done at the back end of their business. How does Costco's use of technology compare with what Amazon and Wal-Mart have done?

Sinegal: We have a relatively sophisticated computer system and lots of technology. We have wireless recording of purchases and can go into any of our warehouses anywhere and check on how any given item is selling during the day. Sometimes we have so much information it's more than we can deal with. Our web site and our e-commerce business are also profitable on a fully allocated basis, and that is somewhat of a milestone.

Technology helps us become more efficient and productive but our business still has a lot of art as opposed to strictly science. The reason that the dot-com companies didn't succeed is that they were very good at the science end but they didn't understand anything about the art of buying and selling merchandise. They thought that was the easy part but it turned out to be the most difficult. Time will tell whether Amazon.com is going to turn a profit. My guess is that they will succeed. They are pretty sophisticated guys and there is a reason why they survived when the others were falling by the wayside. But buying and selling merchandise is the business. These other things augment your running the business but they aren't the driving force. If you don't have the right merchandise in the right place at the right time you can forget about everything else. All the satellites in the world aren't going to help you.

The reason the dot-com companies didn't succeed is that they were very good at the science end but they didn't understand anything about the art of buying and selling merchandise.

Retail in the Future

Erisman: How do you see the retail world thirty years from now? Any dramatic changes?

Sinegal: I think there will continue to be the huge hypermarket types of businesses. People have been going to the marketplace for thousands of years for its social significance as much as for replenishing household needs.

Erisman: It won't all be done on-line?

Sinegal: I don't think so. People are still going to want to go out and have that social exchange. I think there probably will be more hypermarkets. I think that WalMart-style, 200,000 square foot, superstores that carry everything will become the norm as time goes on. We could see shopping malls turn into superstores where there are independent stations within one superstore with one check-out. The expertise within those walls will reside in the little stores and boutiques inside the superstore.

Gill: Part of it is that people want to associate with people. But another part must be that people want to see and touch the merchandise. I'm not sure that even if you could make something holographically present in my living room it would be a satisfying substitute for going to a store and seeing and touching the thing itself.

Sinegal: A good example of that is that ninety percent of our book sales are unplanned. A customer walks by the book table, sees a book, picks it up, looks at the jacket, says "hey this looks kind of interesting," and buys it.

Gill: Is anything being lost, in your view, by the replacement of local merchants by huge national franchises in cookie cutter malls everywhere you go? There are certainly some efficiencies of scale with the Home Depots, SportMarts, Office Maxes, and Costcos in every community but can the smaller neighborhood store survive? Should we mourn its loss?

Sinegal: It comes down to the quality of the individual merchant. Those who run their businesses in an efficient manner are going to survive. But we need to ask also, what's the difference between a 200,000 square foot WalMart superstore and a 200,000 square foot shopping center with shops carrying the same merchandise?

Gill: It may be that most traditional downtown shopping districts, especially in rural America, were smaller than the typical WalMart or Costco.

Sinegal: Some of these power centers have a drugstore, a supermarket, a sporting good store, a coffee shop, a clothier, and a couple of restaurants. All together they add up to a lot of square footage.

Costco and Small Businesses

Gill: How big is your emphasis on supplying small businesses? Maybe Costco is actually supplying (and preserving) small businesses rather than replacing them entirely.

Sinegal: The business customer is the key member that we service. We also supply a lot of nonprofits like churches, schools, and sports teams. Sixty percent of our business is with business customers.

Gill: Where Home Depot comes in, local hardware stores disappear. But where Costco comes in, it sounds like you might replace some stores, but you're also helping others to survive by being their supplier.

Sinegal: Our business was founded so that small businesses could come in and buy essentially everything they needed for their business under one roof. Café owners could purchase all of their food and drink, cigarettes and candy, cleaning supplies, pots and pans, toilet paper and towels, pads and pencils, and so on. They also might buy a television set for home or work.

Gill: Would you sell them a pick-up truck to drive all their stuff back to the office or home also?

Sinegal: Actually, I think on a referral basis we sell about 100,000 cars a year. That's pretty substantial.

Erisman: In the December 2002 issue of your magazine, The Costco Connection, *I noticed an article about ethics in business. Is this to help small businesses improve their operating structure? Is that part of your work with small businesses?*

Sinegal: Absolutely. Small businesses are our key customers and you will find articles in most issues that revolve around the businesses: advice on how to run a business, how to get staff, how to hire consultants, and so on.

Globalization Challenges

Erisman: Costco has gone global both in terms of its supply chain and its sales outlets. What challenges have you seen in moving from an American company to a global company?

Sinegal: Every country is different. The one constant is value. Value is appreciated no matter where you go, though how you make it work can vary by country.

After we started our business in Seattle we had an opportunity to go up to Canada. We thought "Canada is only 140 miles away, how different could it be?" Well, we found out! They have a different system of weights and measurements, a different currency system, different laws, and a different language. Everything had to be printed in two languages. We found out very quickly that there was a lot to doing business in a different country even if it was only 140 miles away.

That experience helped prepare us to do business in countries that are much more difficult than Canada. Today we do business in 61 Costcos in Canada and we have 15 in the UK. We have 21 in Mexico, three in Japan, five in South Korea, and three in Taiwan. So, we've got an international presence in various places and we will continue to grow internationally, especially in Japan, the UK and Mexico.

The keys to doing international business are to understand local rules and laws, recognize what customers want to buy, and take care of our employees. Whether in the UK or Canada or in Mexico, we're going to measure ourselves against every other retailer and make sure that we're paying higher wages than anyone else. We would like to be able to turn our inventory faster than our people because excessive turnover of people is very costly.

Expanding into New Product Areas

Gill: You manufacture some of the things that you sell, such as bakery goods. How do you decide what to make. For example, have you thought about becoming a book publisher? Is the process simply that somebody in your organization gets the idea, proposes it, and then you decide whether its cost-effective or not?

Sinegal: That's pretty generally the way it starts.

Gill: Do you have a strategy to go out and aggressively build up your own manufacturing industry?

Sinegal: We get calls all the time from people who want us to do ancillary businesses and all sorts of deals or proposals coming to us about getting involved in salons or healthcare in our warehouses. It's not our business and we think that probably it winds up just taking up valuable parking spaces. We do have a strategy of trying to bring new products and new services to our customers on an ongoing basis. The question in our minds is whether we can we do it well and provide value for the customer. If we think we can, we're prepared to try it.

Ethical Screening of Products

Gill: Are there products where you could make money, but you would not pursue for ethical reasons.

For example, how would you decide whether to sell pornography? Do you have stated policies on these things?

Sinegal: Yes, we do. We determined that we're not going to carry any pornographic materials. We also don't carry violent video games. We don't carry guns or ammunition. These decisions came from those of us who run the company.

Erisman: But you do have cigarettes.

Sinegal: We do have cigarettes. Obviously it's a dilemma today. But it was a big portion of how we started our business taking care of wholesale customers. A lot of them sell tobacco in their stores, cafes, machines, and lunch trucks.

Gill: Do you have policies for your buyers to investigate how products are manufactured, i.e., that there is no child labor or slave labor? How would you enforce this?

Sinegal: There are lots of laws in the US and other countries. We also have a code of conduct for our suppliers that demands that they have to meet the laws of their own country, pay the right wages, and not use child, slave, or prison labor, etc.

Gill: What about bribery?

Sinegal: Bribery is clearly the worst. As an American company we can't get involved in bribery because of the Foreign Corrupt Practices Act. We have a conduct policy for our suppliers. We visit our supplier factories on a regular basis to make certain they are complying with our standards and values.

> *If you don't have the right merchandise in the right place at the right time you can forget about everything else. All the satellites in the world aren't going to help you.*

What Went Wrong in Corporate America?

Gill: As you look back on the corporate scandals of the last couple years, what would you say has gone wrong in American business? What is the problem and the solution from where you sit?

Sinegal: I think the gates were too wide open, with too many opportunities. Clearly that's something that has to be taken care of. But no matter what types of rules and regulations, no matter how many committees are set up, bad guys are still going to figure out some way to do wrong. The good news is that there aren't that many bad guys. Most business leaders are trying to run their businesses in an ethical fashion. I think the biggest single thing that causes difficulty in the business world is the short-term view. We become obsessed with it. But it forces bad decisions.

Erisman: But you can't regulate against it.

Sinegal: It's a process. It's the way our system works. The system is a very good one. I'm not knocking it. The pressure from analysts and Wall Street is good because it forces us to think carefully about our business. Reflection and thinking from another point of view is not bad at all.

Finding Time to Reflect

Erisman: How do you find time for reflection, given the pace of life, the quantity of information, and competitive pressures?

Sinegal: You have to schedule it. You have to plan the opportunity to think about your business and plan what you're going to do. Otherwise you're just a hamster running on a treadmill; you're never going to get anywhere. You've got to schedule it. Strategic planning is an important part of running any business and the more so for businesses that are operating in multiple states and countries.

Erisman: In the future, will Costco be in the Middle East, Africa, South America—or other places that might be a little more difficult than Mexico, Japan, or the UK?

Sinegal: There are lots of places for us to go that don't have really severe problems but I could see a time where we might enter areas of greater challenge.

Gill: Do you have a grand vision for what you'd like to do with this company before you hand it off to somebody else?

Sinegal: We're not kamikaze pilots. We want to do things in a sensible fashion. If we can speed up our growth, without outdistancing our management team, and provide a quality product, then we will do so. Aside from the quality issues and wanting to grow the business in a sensible fashion, we don't have any grand scheme that says, for example, that we have to be in Latin America by the year 2015 or have 1000 Costco's in ten years.

Questions for Discussion:

1. How well do you think Jim Sinegal has done in integrating good business practice with being a good corporate citizen?
2. What do you think of Costco's decision not to carry potentially profitable products such as pornography, guns, and violent video games? Are they being consistent in their decision to sell cigarettes? Why or why not?

CASE STUDIES

Case 4.1: Violent Video Games

"Shoot a snitch in the kneecaps, or snuff out a rival with a single head shot and watch them bleed" (from the jacket of the video game, *Kingpin*).

As computer games become more realistic in graphical appearance and more violent in thematic content, controversy is growing. One popular game, *Grand Theft Auto: Vice City*, has participants scoring points by killing people, stealing cars, and dealing drugs. Players receive new life by having implied sexual relations with prostitutes. An ad for the teen rated game *Wargasm* reads, "Kill your friends guilt free."

Of course, not all video games contain questionable content. Many games, including several top sellers, have educational or other nonviolent themes. However, many violent games that push the envelope on tastefulness and morality sell well and provide solid profits for their manufacturers.

There are thousands of studies linking violent behavior among children to watching violence on television. While research to examine the effect of computer-simulated violence on real-world violence is in its beginning stages, experts say that computer activity is much more compelling than other forms of media because the players participate and become engaged in the game through the role of one of the characters. Pomona College professor Brian Stonehill claims that this is a big change from other types of spectator violence because "this takes you out of the role of spectator and into the role of murderer."[2]

Some electronic gaming industry executives respond that their products should not be taken so seriously. Steve Race, a former president of Sony Computer Entertainment, once told a reporter, "I just sell games, lady. To make me responsible for the mores or values of America, I don't think I'm ready for that."[3] Other industry spokespersons state that the more violent "M" (Mature) rated games are intended for 19–22-year-old males, who clearly know the difference between fantasy and reality.

The industry has also adopted a self-imposed rating system (www.esrb.com) to help parents make informed choices to keep the games in the hands of age appropriate audiences. Defenders of the industry state that given the rating system, parents are at fault if the games wind up in the wrong hands, since they are the ones who purchase the games for their children. But critics of these types of

2 Amy Harmon, "Fun, Games, Gore," *Los Angeles Times*, 12 May 1995, A28.

3 Ibid.

games point out that enforcement of the rating system is spotty at best. Some retailers don't enforce the code at all, while others do so in an inconsistent manner. Moreover, the industry isn't really sincere about working with parents, as seen by the way the games are marketed. Ads for violent teen-rated games have been placed in *Sports Illustrated for Kids*. And games rated for all ages are often sold right next to those earning an "M" rating.[4]

4 Susan Nielsen, "A Beginners Guide to Becoming a Video Game Prude," *Seattle Times*, 21 February 1999.

Questions for Discussion:

1. Despite the demand for these games and the high profit margins they create, are these companies being socially irresponsible?
2. Do these companies have any responsibilities to (non-shareholder) stakeholders?

Case 4.2: Starbucks and Fair Trade Coffee

After receiving much publicized pressure from activist organizations such as *Transfair USA*, Starbucks officials announced in April 2000 that the company would begin to sell Fair Trade coffee in all of its retail stores. Specifically, the company announced that it would sell coffee certified by the Fair Trade Federation by the pound and would feature it as its "coffee of the day" on the twentieth day of every month.

Starbucks is a company that prides itself on being "socially responsible." The company is heavily involved in community service and philanthropic activities and has its own charitable foundation, the Starbucks Foundation.

The concept behind Fair Trade originated as a faith-based initiative in Europe during the late 1980s. The goal is simply to ensure that suppliers and growers of products in poor countries receive fair prices for their goods.

Fair Trade coffee beans are purchased directly from cooperatives owned by Latin American farmers. In effect, profit-taking by export middlemen, often labeled "coyotes," has been greatly reduced, and the growers are allowed to take home a much higher profit from the sales of beans. For example, under traditional trade arrangements, coffee sells for a variable price on the world market (as low as 50 to 60 cents per pound recently). Farmers in Central America receive as little as 25 to 40 cents per pound of coffee, which (after roasting and packaging) sells in stores in the United States for as much as $9 to $10 retail.

In contrast, coffee beans are sold at guaranteed and precontracted prices (recently $1.26 to $1.62 per pound) under Fair Trade purchase agreements. Growers receive up to 50 to 60 cents more per pound than they would receive under traditional arrangements, allowing many farming families to escape poverty.

Promoters of Fair Trade coffee claim that another important benefit of the product is that a high percentage of it is organically grown through sustainable and earth-friendly farming practices.

Starbucks's announcement was initially seen as a leadership stance. However, some critics still believe that the company continues to "exploit" coffee farmers in Latin America, since the total amount of Fair Trade coffee used comes to less than 1 percent of total sales. These critics are pressuring Starbucks (and other coffee retailers) to use more Fair Trade coffee.

The reluctance on the part of coffee retailers such as Starbucks to carry more Fair Trade coffee may be partially explained by the readiness and willingness of consumers to pay more. Since Fair Trade coffee is more expensive to purchase, some (or most) of the cost is usually passed along to consumers in the form of higher prices. For example, a pound of "house blend" retails for approximately $10 in Starbucks stores. The price of a Fair Trade blend is approximately $11.45. While the company could use much more Fair Trade coffee, prices would have to be raised, and price-conscious consumers could simply purchase coffee from competing retailers. Alternatively, Starbucks could "absorb" some of the higher costs, leading to a reduction in profit.

Critics of Fair Trade coffee claim that the practice has some inconsistencies. For example, some cooperatives set a size limit (i.e., twelve acres) to the farms that qualify for the programs. Farmers who exceed that amount of land may not qualify for some Fair Trade programs even though they may treat workers fairly and otherwise qualify.

Also, some critics argue that the additional money going to farmers amounts to an artificial "wage support" that is not sustainable over time, and that rather than teaching farmers how to compete in the global marketplace, this creates an unhealthy dependence.

Finally, Fair Trade coffee often comes up short in taste tests, which likely means that most current purchasers buy the product for the social benefits rather than for quality or price. Critics claim that pre-negotiated higher prices may effectively create disincentives to improve quality.

Resources:

Transfair website: http://www.transfair.org

Bradley Meachean, "How Fair Is Fair Trade Coffee?" *Seattle Times,* 11 September 2002.

Questions for Discussion:

1. How should Starbucks proceed?
2. How should Starbucks executives resolve the classic dilemma of trying to determine whether it is best (and most important) to act on behalf of shareholder wealth (profit) or to benefit other corporate stakeholders?

COMMENTARY

When corporate managers are confronted with decisions that seem to jeopardize earnings for shareholders in order to avoid harm to another party or to attain another public good, should they decide to maximize profit, take a course of action that favors the other goal, or attempt to strike some sort of a balance?

In large part, the answer depends on how the legitimate purposes and aims of corporations are conceptualized. The day-to-day moral latitude that managers have in making decisions is determined in part by these ideas since they play an important role in shaping corporate identity and mission, consumer purchasing and employment decisions, and the legal and regulatory context in which business operates.

Christian Ethics and Corporate Responsibility

Developing a flawless model of corporate social responsibility from a Christian perspective is a challenging task, given the fact that modern shareholder-owned corporations did not exist when the Scriptures were written. However, there is clear biblical teaching given to individuals and whole communities on topics such as justice, stewardship, and duties to others. While a corporation is neither an individual person nor a true "community," the Bible does not neatly separate individual ethics from group ones. As ethicist Sondra Ely Wheeler states, "There is just righteousness and unrighteousness."[5] Furthermore, in the Hebrew scriptures, there are many behavioral standards given to farmers, who some believe to be the equivalent of modern corporations in their day.[6] As such, there are sufficient theological resources to help provide guidelines for the appropriate aims and purposes of corporations.

5 Sondra Ely Wheeler, "Christian Character: A Different Approach to Business Ethics," *Vital Speeches of the Day*, New York, 15 October 2002.

6 See Hershey H. Friedman, "Biblical Foundations of Business Ethics," *Markets & Morality* 3, no.1 (Spring 2000).

One popular approach, in both theory and practice, to corporate responsibility has been articulated by Milton Friedman and other advocates for what has come to be known as the "custodian of wealth" model. Friedman argues that as agents, managers have a moral duty to maximize wealth for owners of the company, the shareholders. Exceeding standards set by law and "ethical custom," such as fraud, and directly spending corporate profits on social causes represents a form of "taxation without representation."

It should be noted that Friedman has no quarrel with owners of *privately* held companies, such as Levi Strauss or Patagonia, that wish to forgo profits for the sake of other social endeavors. However, managers of publicly held companies should not use corporate funds on a social agenda if shareholders have not given their explicit consent.

Friedman's theory would be at odds with behavior that considers the interests of non-shareholders if company profit would benefit from goodwill or positive publicity. For example, many corporations today prominently feature their community service activities in their advertising campaigns, improving customer perception and perhaps attracting talented workers who wish to be employed by a "corporation with a conscience."

While Friedman's approach has been the target of much criticism for its narrow conception of corporate responsibility, it merits some support from a Christian perspective. By itself, the goal of increasing shareholder wealth is not morally problematic, though it is worth noting the irony that firms focusing too narrowly on achieving it often find it illusive.

The biblical tradition recognizes some special privileges that come with ownership. The commandment against theft surely implies that someone has ownership (in an earthly sense) of an object or a piece of property, entitling him or her to direct its usage within limits. While "property" today is quite different than in Old Testament times, taking the form of paper representation rather than tangible physical assets, the concept is still applicable.

As investors, shareholders have legally recognized ownership of publicly held corporations. Increasing the value of their financial investment should be a high priority item on the managerial decision-making agenda. In fact, as a practical matter, without solid returns on investment, a corporation risks losing its ability to attract investment capital, recruit and retain top-notch employees, and invest in capital improvements and research and development efforts.

It is also important to note that "shareholders" are often institutions such as charitable foundations or ordinary working people who have invested their money in college savings, retirement, and pension funds. Contrary to common perceptions, shares of companies are not only exclusively held by wealthy "fat cats." Many investors are ordinary folks counting on investment income for retirement, for philanthropic purposes, or for financing their children's education.

Profit is an important aim for corporations for other reasons too. At the risk of stating the obvious, even organizations working for the primary benefit of other (non-shareholder) stakeholder groups need to earn a profit, perhaps even a significant one, in order to have adequate resources to give. As the old saying goes, "No margin, no mission."

Friedman's approach also correctly raises the issue of corporate charitable giving that does not reflect the values of shareholders. Several years ago some well-known corporations came under public protest for supporting nonprofit organizations engaged in controversial activities or decisions. For example, several companies were criticized for contributions made to Planned Parenthood and to the Boy Scouts of America because of its rejection of gay leaders.

Weaknesses of Friedman's Approach

When examined from a Christian viewpoint, however, the custodian of wealth model has some serious limitations. These problems become obvious in cases in which the quest for profit might produce harm to an innocent party or when it comes into conflict with other social goods. While Scripture does recognize and legitimize the idea of private property, it is a limited "right."[7] Along with the privileges of ownership come special duties or social responsibilities for the larger community.

In the Hebrew scriptures, land owners were instructed to avoid harm by not exploiting workers and to advance the common good by making provisions for impoverished members of their surrounding community. Scripture also makes it clear that God retains "transcendental title" to "private" property. Humans are merely stewards, which greatly curtails our freedom to simply view our use of property as an exclusively individualistic or private matter. From the biblical tradition, ownership is a spiritual and moral matter. Property is to be used in service to God, primarily for the benefit of others. In modern economies, this implies that shareholders should not exercise a "right" and expect corporate managers to act in harmful ways to maximize profits.

In addition to unduly elevating ownership rights, Friedman's model has other weaknesses. First, he makes broad assumptions about the economic "rationality" of shareholders, assuming that they are only interested in maximizing profit. This runs counter to a Christian

7 To be clear, the emphasis on "rights" in contemporary dialogue is more a product of the Enlightenment than of the biblical tradition.

understanding of human nature as fallen but still capable of goodness because it reflects God's image.

While some shareholders may favor increased profit at any social cost, most support a more tempered approach. Consistent with a Christian understanding of human nature, moral concerns often accompany self-interested pursuits. Among them are concern for the well-being of others. Any theory that reduces human motivations and behaviors to narrow self-interested economic interests is inconsistent with the Christian tradition.[8] In fact, some research into voting patterns confirms that shareholders value contributions to social causes over financial gain. They will often cast votes for courses of action that produce social benefits at the expense of profit.[9] The growth of socially responsible mutual funds that screen companies out of investment portfolios due to controversial practices, products, or services provides another piece of evidence that humans are not motivated solely by economic concerns.

Another notable problem is that Friedman seems to advocate law as the standard for corporate behavior. While he does mention "ethical custom" as another restraining force, he certainly implies that going beyond legal standards and financial prudence is unnecessary and even unethical, given shareholder ownership of the corporation. Given corporate lobbying efforts to shape legal and regulatory standards and the time lag between the need for a law and its actual passage, the adequacy of using law as the primary standard for business behavior must be viewed skeptically. From a Christian perspective, higher, transcendent "laws," in the form of ethics, must serve as guiding standards.

Assessing the Stakeholder Approach

While Friedman's model falls short, does the "stakeholder" approach more closely fit with Christian ethics? This approach was developed in partial response to the shortcomings in the wealth maximization philosophy of the firm. To be certain, it can come in several different forms, prompting scholars such as R. Edward Freeman to observe that it may be more accurate to refer to stakeholder "models."

Kenneth Goodpaster's article, "Business Ethics and Stakeholder Analysis" provides us with a basic description of the approach. According to Goodpaster, shareholders do have a special place in managerial decision making, but not at the expense of duties to other stakeholders. While he does not place shareholders and other stakeholder groups on equal ground, he does argue that the nature of the principle-agency relationship necessitates that stakeholder groups be given significant moral consideration in decision making.

8 For a thoughtful critique of economic reductionism, see Robert H. Nelson, "Economic Religion versus Christian Values," *Markets & Morality* 1, no. 2 (October 1998).

9 See Petra Rivoli, "Ethical Aspects of Investor Behavior" *Journal of Business Ethics* 14 (1995): 265–77. For a further discussion of complex human motivations and behavior, see Robert Frank, "Can a Socially Responsible Firm Survive in a Competitive Environment?" in David Messick and Ann Tenbrunsel, *Codes of Conduct: Behavioral Research into Business Ethics* (New York: Russell Sage Foundation, 1996), 86–103.

The stakeholder approach conceives of social responsibility in terms that reach beyond profit maximization for shareholders and allows for duties to non-shareholder interests. Furthermore, it creates much more "elbow room" for managers to make decisions that refrain from harm or contribute to other social objectives, providing an "escape hatch" from conflicts of conscience in the workplace. This is particularly appealing if the value system of the firm is consistent with Christian values and ethics.

Since the stakeholder approach can come in many models, depending on the "normative core" or philosophy that drives and guides the process of balancing stakeholder interests and decision making, and has insufficiencies of its own, it is far from perfect. However, from our perspective, its general shape and direction is more consistent with the spirit of Christian ethics.

Various Christian theological traditions construe social institutions such as government, schools, and families as entities ordained by God to promote his purposes in the world. Since business is another one of these entities, profit should be viewed as a means to promote other goods, such as human well-being. Depending upon the central guiding philosophy employed as the "normative core," stakeholder theory permits this possibility to exist in theory and in practice.

Problems with the Stakeholder Approach

While the stakeholder approach leaves more room for ethical considerations and has many points of agreement with Christian ethics, it too suffers from some limitations. Foremost of these is that objectives for managerial decision making may be less clear when compared to the seemingly formulaic nature of the wealth maximization view of the firm. More specifically, the criticism has been raised that the stakeholder approach, without a well-defined governing philosophy or "normative core" at its center, creates too much room and gives managers too little guidance as to how they should balance the competing claims of stakeholder groups.

For example, the timber industry continues to be controversial in areas such as the Pacific Northwest. While timber harvesting provides vital economic lifelines for some small towns, some interest groups want to end logging because of its adverse impact on the environment. Managers are left without clear direction in terms of achieving a proper balance. The result is likely to be some type of consensus among the competing interests. While not problematic in its own right, the consensus reached may or may not reflect company values

10 For a thoughtful discussion of these and other shortcomings of the stakeholder approach, see Helen Alford and Michael Naughton, *Managing as if Faith Mattered* (Notre Dame, Ind.: University of Notre Dame Press, 2001).

and may not be ethically defensible in terms of broader conceptions of the common good.[10]

These shortcomings need to be acknowledged. The stakeholder model provides "space" for managers and is thereby necessary, but it is not sufficient. Managers still need other sources of moral guidance to make good decisions. To be certain, there may be times when perfect answers may not be available, and the appropriate balance between profit and other social goods could fit into a range of morally defensible options.

Despite its weaknesses, the stakeholder approach pushes the concept of corporate responsibility in the right direction. A philosophy of the firm that broadens the scope of moral duties to a wider range of constituents is much more consistent with the biblical tradition.

Social Responsibility in the "Real World" of Competitive Markets

Several serious objections to conceptions of corporate responsibility that extend duties to non-shareholders need to be addressed. Foremost is the criticism that these approaches seem to go against the Western tradition of emphasizing the primacy of private property rights. Shareholders are the owners of the firm, and within legal boundaries, their interests should receive the highest priority. In fact, managers' duties to shareholders are recognized by law to the extent that the management of a firm can be sued for practices that are significantly detrimental to shareholder interests.

While shareholders should undoubtedly receive significant consideration, other stakeholder interests also merit attention, primarily when harm may accrue to them. Legal standards for corporations are currently evolving to allow for these broader concerns.[11]

11 See Richard Marens and Andrew Wicks, "Getting Real: Stakeholder Theory, Managerial Practice, and the General Irrelevance of Fiduciary Duties Owed to Shareholders," *Business Ethics Quarterly* 9, no. 2 (April 1999): 273–93.

A second criticism of a broader approach to corporate responsibility is that it is naive and not representative of the "real world." Despite rhetorical claims to the contrary, most, if not all, firms exist to maximize profit. In fact, some theorists argue that competition forces firms to do so. Executives who do not maximize profit or at least give it a very high priority will soon find the organizations they are entrusted with run out of business by other firms who do not expend similar levels of resources on "socially responsible" endeavors. Rhetoric to the contrary is only window dressing to seek a competitive advantage, given the public's taste for dealing with socially responsible firms.

The concept of a firm's taking a broader view of social responsibility is not just a scholarly fiction or ideal. Many companies allow values to drive strategy, leading them to make decisions with broader obligations in mind. While good public relations may have ensued or profit increased in the long run with respect to some of these decisions, it would be difficult to make a rational case for these decisions based on cost-benefit analysis before the fact. For example, the Herman Miller, Inc. executives facing the difficult dilemma discussed in this chapter's introduction made the risky decision to change the wood in the company's signature product in order to be true to the company's values.

A third and related objection is that holding corporations to high moral ideals, particularly those derived from a Christian worldview, is an exercise in futility. In light of the power that corporations hold, our individual beliefs about what they "should" be doing seem meaningless. There is no doubt that the best efforts of individuals can sometimes feel futile. However, the views and actions of individuals may have some powerful practical ramifications. For example, consumers will often make choices consistent with socially responsible practices. With the speed of information available on the Web, consumers can punish and reward businesses with much greater force. Employees will also sacrifice income to work for organizations with which they share values and a sense of mission. Many individual executives also hold a Christian worldview and work to shape their firm's culture to reflect such values.[12]

12 For profiles of some of these leaders, see Laura Nash, *Believers in Business* (Nashville: Thomas Nelson, 1994).

Furthermore, if held broadly enough by enough individuals, the values of the wider culture can be changed, which can then drive reactionary changes from organizations, can work toward shaping public policy, and, if necessary, can change the legal environment of business. Therefore, we should not be too quick in dismissing the utility of articulating high standards for the conduct of business corporations. Even if it falls on deaf ears, however, sometimes "prophecy" matters more than efficacy. A limited prospect for change does not negate the Christian obligation to point out injustice and to provide living examples of a more ethical and truthful way of doing business.

A final objection is that economic reality makes true social responsibility an unreachable ideal. According to the theory of competitive markets, the forces of economics place severe restraints on a firm's ability to choose to act in a manner that is not self-interested. In "real" business settings, stiff competition demands that managers consider the firm's survival and not engage in costly behaviors no matter the social benefit, especially if competing firms are not engaging in similar behavior. Moreover, the pressure to produce attractive quarterly financial reports makes moral considerations a secondary consideration at best.

While competitive and financial pressures should not be minimized, there is some evidence to support the idea that socially responsible behavior may result in financial gains, sometimes in unanticipated and indirect ways. For example, corporations may attain advantages in recruiting and retaining talented employees who wish to work for an organization that shares their values. Or consumers or business partners may be attracted to the firm for similar reasons.[13] While considering stakeholder interests for the sake of profit is not "socially responsible" behavior in the true sense, there is some evidence to discount the idea that the "real world" of economics is comprised of a set of iron-clad laws that prevent ethical considerations.

Costco serves as an outstanding example of a firm that is trying to honor the interests of a broad range of stakeholders while managing shareholder expectations and the tensions produced by operating in competitive markets. CEO Jim Sinegal clearly describes the importance of emphasizing company values in building an organization that is sustainable and profitable for the long term.

Norman Bowie has observed a dynamic of irony in the pursuit of profit. Much like the way individuals find the intentional pursuit of happiness illusive, firms who focus only on profit may never acquire it. Rather, those who focus on treating stakeholders well, and for its own sake, may well achieve it, much as individuals who focus on other matters find happiness as a by-product. Borrowing from an old philosophical idea known as the "Hedonic paradox," Bowie has referred to this dynamic as the "profit paradox."[14]

Bowie's observations find some support in the conclusions drawn in the well-known book *Built to Last*, in which authors Jim Collins and Jerry Porras find that companies managed around a deep sense of mission and core values are often more profitable than those operated with the direct goal of profit maximization.[15]

From a Christian perspective, corporate social responsibility entails much more than the pursuit of profit. While profit is a necessary and highly important part of the life of an organization, the direction of the causal arrow should be reversed. Instead of treating stakeholders well for instrumental reasons, profit should be seen as a means toward broader goals of service or as a reward for paying attention to other mission-related objectives. Profit should not be seen as *the* goal of business.

13 See R. Frank, "Can a Socially Responsible Firm Survive in a Competitive Environment?" and Manuel Velasquez, "Why Ethics Matter: A Defense of Ethics in Business Organizations." *Business Ethics Quarterly* 6, no. 2 (April 1996): 201–22.

14 Norman E. Bowie, "New Directions in Corporate Social Responsibility." *Business Horizons* 34 (July/August 1991): 55–65.

15 Jim Collins and Jerry Porras, *Built to Last: Successful Habits of Visionary Companies* (San Francisco: HarperCollins, 1994).

FIVE

Globalization, Economics, and Judeo-Christian Morality

There is not a necessary opposition between doing well and doing good, between taking care of business and taking care of each other. They may actually need one another.

Richard John Neuhaus, in *Doing Well and Doing Good: The Challenge to the Christian Capitalist*

Market forces, if they are given complete authority even in the purely economic and financial arenas, produce chaos and could ultimately lead to the downfall of the global capitalist system.

George Soros, Soros Fund Management, in *The Crisis of Global Capitalism*

INTRODUCTION

Religious groups throughout the centuries have had a great deal to say about materialism and about people's economic lives. For instance, the Bible has more material on wealth and possessions than on the concepts of heaven and hell combined. Other religious traditions have also addressed economics in varying degrees of detail. Until the advent of the Industrial Revolution, religious teaching on economic life was predominantly individualistic, mostly applying to the way the individual gained or used wealth. Very little was addressed to the institutional economic system because the economies, for the most part, were simple agrarian and trade-guild-oriented systems. Well-developed industrial economies had yet to come on the historical scene. With the industrial age came new economic and social arrangements and new challenges that religious groups sought to address.

Sociologist Max Weber, in his classic work *The Protestant Ethic and the Spirit of Capitalism*, defended the idea that Calvinist faith was a key element in the development of capitalist industrial society. Since the publication of this work in the nineteenth century, and since the growth of the capitalist economic system, scholars and religious authorities have debated the question of whether capitalism is Christian or not. As you read on this subject on your own, you will find a wide spectrum of opinions on the subject. There are those who hold that the Bible condemns capitalism as an inherently immoral system, and they want nothing to do with such a system. On the other hand are those who insist that capitalism is entirely consistent with biblical values and that virtually any criticism of capitalism is unbiblical.

The language of the debate in Christian circles is no less acrimonious than that in nonreligious arenas. There are those who have more theological reservations about capitalism than others and advocate a greater degree of government intervention to correct some of the abuses they believe are inherent in the free-market system. With the rise of the global economy and increasing economic interdependence among nations, the impact of economic decisions and market forces is felt more dramatically and more rapidly. Some argue that global capitalism raises new problems for which market solutions only make things worse, not better.

Until the late nineteenth century, most religious leaders endorsed capitalism with little reservation. Some of the abuses of the industrial age were becoming apparent in England and were the subject of critics like the novelist Charles Dickens, with some churchmen joining in the criticism. But it was not until the 1890s, with the rise of the Social Gospel and the advent of Catholic social encyclicals such as *Rerum Novarum*, that Catholic and Protestant leaders began to speak out against the abuses of capitalism. To be sure, capitalism had its defenders, mostly conservative Protestants, but the religious mood at the time was critical of the system, with many critics advocating forms of socialism that nations of Europe were trying.

More recently, in the past thirty years the debate over capitalism has raged in evangelical Christian circles, echoing many of the themes first raised around the turn of the twentieth century. Evangelicals who tend to be more on the political left led the criticism of capitalism in more explicitly biblical terms than the earlier debates. They observed that many of the correctives proposed by the New Deal legislation of the 1930s had not worked, and they concluded that the problems with capitalism were systemic. However, in the current debate, evangelicals on the political right have responded aggressively and defended capitalism as the system most consistent with important biblical values.

Some have even observed that Catholic critics of capitalism have softened and recent papal encyclicals such as *Centesimus Annus* have guardedly endorsed the market system. With the economic collapse of socialism in the late 1980s, most of the critics of capitalism no longer have a ready alternative to which they can turn. They have not embraced capitalism but only admitted that there must be a third way, an alternative to both systems.

The two readings in this chapter provide a view of economics and economic systems from a biblical perspective. The Oxford Declaration is the collaborative statement of evangelical theologians written in the aftermath of the fall of the Berlin Wall, which signified the collapse of socialism in Eastern Europe. It provides general principles of political economy from an evangelical worldview. For a bit more detail, the second reading gives a thorough biblical basis for economic justice. It offers some helpful insights that will echo what you read in chapter 2 on the use of the Bible in social ethics. But the majority of the article deals with the biblical parameters for a just economic system. The authors, Stephen Mott and Ronald J. Sider, are theologians who have long been sensitive to the abuses of the free-market system, while at the same time appreciating its strengths. Their article provides a balanced perspective on the intersection of Christian theology and economics.

Economics 101

Before you get into the readings in this chapter, we want to introduce some of the primary concepts that define an economic system. One writer has creatively called this "economics for *prophets*" in his book by that title.[1] Keep in mind that every economic system in the world today is a mixed system. When we say that the market system or the command system is characterized by x or y, we are referring to what is called an "ideal type." Since the collapse of socialism in the late 1980s, there is no longer any debate between the merits of capitalism and socialism. Rather, the debate concerns whether economic and social problems can be solved by more or less reliance on the market or, to put it conversely, more or less government intervention in the market. That debate has taken a turn few people expected in the aftermath of the September 11 attacks and has propelled government to more involvement in economic matters due to the increasing connection between economic and national security.

In any economy, there are basic questions that the system must address. The most basic have to do with how the goods of society will be distributed and on what basis. That is, as long as theft is illegal,

[1] Walter L. Owensby, *Economics for Prophets: A Primer on Concepts, Realities, and Values in Our Economic System* (Grand Rapids: Eerdmans, 1988).

trading of goods and services in the marketplace remains the most effi-cient way of distributing those goods and services. Other important questions concern ownership of property, deciding which goods and services get produced and what price is charged for them, what wages will be, how to ensure for quality and safety in products, how wealth will be distributed, what level of unemployment is acceptable, and how competition is viewed. In pure market systems, property, partic-ularly the means of production and businesses, is all privately owned. In pure command systems, which characterize socialism, most busi-nesses are owned publicly, specifically, by the state. In most systems, there are degrees of private ownership, and the differences in the sys-tems has to do with how much is owned by the state and how much is owned privately. An economy in which government owns a sizeable portion of economic assets or controls certain markets is more com-mand-oriented. For example, countries that have nationalized health care are command-oriented in that segment since government is the employer and supplier of health care. In some European countries, governments own large portions—and in some cases all—of the air-line industry and the energy industries.

In the United States, business tends to be far more privately owned, and government tends not to be a shareholder in American companies. In market-oriented systems, the forces of supply and demand determine what goods and services will be produced, how much they cost, and what workers will be paid; that is, the market determines these elements. In pure command systems, the state or whatever authority is responsible for economic central planning decides what will be produced, the price level, and the wage scale for workers. Again, most economic systems are a mixture of market and command styles when it comes to prices and wages. For example, wages are not entirely determined by market forces in most industri-alized countries due to minimum wage laws set by government. Though formal price controls are rare, tariffs are routinely imposed to protect domestic markets from outside competition, which in effect helps determine what products are produced and their price.

In pure market systems, competition ensures product safety and quality, since consumers will not continue to buy from manufacturers who produce shoddy or unsafe products, ultimately driving them out of business if they do not meet the standards of the marketplace. In command systems, the state with its regulatory agencies is responsible for ensuring safety. In the United States, which has a predominantly market system, this aspect of ensuring safety is highly command-oriented. This is even more the case in Europe and Japan. There is rel-atively little confidence that the market will guarantee consumer safety. Even in market systems where society trusts competition to effect product safety, there is an information time lag during which consumers are unprotected. That is, it takes time for a company's reputation for building unsafe products to become widely known in the marketplace, during which time consumers are unknowingly buying risky products.

In pure market systems, wealth is distributed according to merit as measured by the market. As a result, wealth tends to be more concentrated in fewer hands in this system. In pure command-oriented systems, wealth is distributed more equally, often based on need or on a person's social contribution, such as the way Olympic athletes were rewarded in former communist countries. But most systems are mixed. In the Western industrialized world, wealth is redistributed through a progressive tax system, and need plays a significant role in determining who gets certain resources. Politics as well as need influences the distribution of wealth, as the decades of "corporate welfare" indicate. The more wealth is distributed on grounds other than merit, the fewer incentives there are for people to take risks in starting or expanding businesses, because the tax system takes a higher share of their income the more successful they are. In market systems, roughly 5 percent unemployment is considered optimal. Should unemployment drop below that level, that is usually an indication that the economy is growing too fast, thereby running the risk of inflation. In fact, the central bank in many market economies will try to control the money supply in order to keep the economy from becoming inflationary from heating up too rapidly, thus keeping unemployment at a level where substantial numbers of people will be unemployed at any given time. In command economies, everyone has a job and there is 0 percent unemployment. However, there is less choice in what job a person will have, and people frequently end up being "underemployed," that is, doing jobs that are well beneath their skill level or doing "make work" jobs that lack dignity and could be eliminated without any loss or anyone noticing.

In market systems, competition is viewed as one of the chief positive elements, encouraging quality and innovation, thus giving consumers access to better and cheaper goods and services. Even though competition can at times be cutthroat and go beyond the bounds of civility and even beyond the law, the benefits of having an economy based on competition far outweigh the costs. Advocates of command economies would argue that the costs outweigh the benefits. Some of the costs would be that some would lose, affecting them negatively and causing social dislocations, and that there would be wasteful duplication of goods and services. Again, most systems are mixed, and governments frequently restrict competition or minimize its harmful effects. Trade is frequently restricted in order to protect domestic industry. Governments subsidize what they consider key businesses, and in some cases, government subsidies actually give incentives for people *not* to produce, as in the case of farm supports for agriculture around the Midwest. Governments also intervene periodically to "bail out" companies hurt by normal market forces. For example, in the 1980s the U.S. government rescued Chrysler from near-bankruptcy and it became profitable again after being threatened by competition from Japan. And in the aftermath of the September 11 terrorist attacks, the U.S. government offered massive subsidies to the airline industry to keep carriers from going into bankruptcy.

A primer on economics would not be complete without mention of the trend toward a global economy. In the past few years the world economy has taken dramatic strides toward becoming more integrated and interdependent. *Globalization* refers to the process of tighter economic, political, and social integration/cooperation. This involves a more free flow of products, services, investment, and employees and has been made possible by technological advances such as the Internet. For example, due to the prevalence of electronic communications, companies can employ people around the world and it matters less where they live. Electronic and data technology have also enabled the virtually instantaneous flow of investment capital around the world. Barriers to trade have been lowered, and the world economy is more integrated than ever before. Entrepreneurial activity now has a global focus, and technology can be distributed globally and efficiently, thus lowering prices and making more goods and services available to more people. This has allowed the benefits of economic growth to spread to regions that have heretofore had relatively stagnant economies.

Critics of globalization have argued that the process has left the poor further behind and simply increased the profits of already large, profitable, and powerful corporations. Further caution about the pace of globalization has also come in the aftermath of the September 11 attacks, as concerns about the vulnerability of such a highly interdependent economy have grown. It is likely that the trend toward globalization will slow and become more expensive as companies are increasingly concerned about security and countries are more cautious about having open borders, both for goods and for immigration, in the post–September 11 world.

READINGS

The Oxford Declaration on Christian Faith and Economics

First published in *Transformation* (April/June 1990): 1–8.
From *Christianity and Economics in the Post-Cold War Era,* edited by Herbert Schlossberg, Vinay Samuel, and Ronald J. Sider (Grand Rapids: Eerdmans, 1991), 11–30.

Preamble

This **Oxford Declaration on Christian Faith and Economics** of January 1990 is issued jointly by over one hundred theologians and economists, ethicists and development practitioners, church leaders and business managers who come from various parts of the world. We live in diverse cultures and subcultures, are steeped in differing traditions of theological and economic thinking, and therefore have diverse notions as to how Christian faith and economic realities should intersect.[1] We have found this diversity enriching even when we could not reach agreement. At the same time we rejoice over the extent of unanimity on the complex economics of today made possible by our common profession of faith in our Lord Jesus Christ.

We affirm that through his life, death, resurrection, and ascension to glory, Christ has made us one people (Galatians 3:28). Though living in different cultures, we acknowledge together that there is one body and one Spirit, just as we are called to the one hope, one Lord, one faith, one baptism, and one God and Father of us all (Ephesians 4:4).

We acknowledge that a Christian search for truth is both a communal and also an individual effort. As part of the one people in Christ, each of us wants to comprehend the relevance of Christ to the great issues facing humanity today together "with all the saints" (Ephesians 3:18). All our individual insights need to be corrected by the perspectives of the global Christian community as well as Christians through the centuries.

We affirm that Scripture, the word of the living and true God, is our supreme authority in all matters of faith and conduct. Hence we turn to Scripture as our reliable guide in reflection on issues concerning economic, social, and political life. As economists and theologians we desire to submit both theory and practice to the bar of Scripture.

Together we profess that God, the sovereign of life, in love made a perfect world for human beings created to live in fellowship with God. Although our greatest duty is to honour and glorify God, we rebelled against God, fell from our previous harmonious relationship with God, and brought evil upon ourselves and God's world. But God did not give up on the creation. As Creator, God continues patiently working to overcome the evil which was perverting the creation. The central act of God's redemptive new creation is the death, resurrection, and reign in glory of Jesus Christ, the Son of God, and the sending of the Holy Spirit. This restoration will only be completed at the end of human history and the reconciliation of all things. Justice is basic to Christian perspectives on economic life.

Justice is rooted in the character of God. "For the Lord is righteous, he loves justice" (Psalm 11:7). Justice expresses God's actions to restore God's provision to those who have been deprived and to punish those who have violated God's standards.

A. Creation and Stewardship

God the Creator

1. From God and through God and to God are all things (Romans 11:36). In the freedom of God's eternal love, by the word of God's omnipotent power, and through the Creator Spirit, the Triune God gave being to the world and to human beings which live in it. God pronounced the whole creation good. For its continuing existence creation is dependent on God. The same God who created it is present in it, sustaining it, and giving it bountiful life (Psalm 104:29). In Christ, "all things were created . . . and all things hold together" (Colossians 1:15–20). Though creation owes its being to God, it is itself not divine. The greatness of creation—both human and non-human—exists to glorify its Creator. The divine origin of the creation, its continued existence through God, redemption through Christ, and its purpose to glorify God are fundamental truths which must guide all Christian reflection on creation and stewardship.

Stewardship of Creation

2. God the Creator and Redeemer is the ultimate owner. "The earth is the Lord's and the fullness thereof" (Psalm 24:1). But God has entrusted the earth to human beings to be responsible for it on God's behalf. They should work as God's stewards in the creative, faithful management of the world, recognising that they are responsible to God for all they do with the world and to the world.

3. God created the world and pronounced it "very good" (Genesis 1:31). Because of the Fall and the resulting curse, creation "groans in travail" (Romans 8:22). The thoughtlessness, greed, and violence of sinful human beings have damaged God's good creation and produced a variety of ecological problems and conflicts. When we abuse and pollute creation, as we are doing in many instances, we are poor stewards and invite disaster in both local and global eco-systems.

4. Much of human aggression toward creation stems from a false understanding of the nature of creation and the human role in it. Humanity has constantly been confronted by the two challenges of selfish individualism, which neglects human community, and rigid collectivism, which stifles human freedom. Christians and others have often pointed out both dangers. But only recently have we realised that both ideologies have a view of the world with humanity at the centre which reduces material creation to a mere instrument.

5. Biblical life and world view is not centred on humanity. It is God-centred. Non-human creation was not made exclusively for human beings. We are repeatedly told in the Scripture that all things—human beings and the environment in which they live—were "for God" (Romans 11:36; 1 Corinthians 8:6; Colossians 1:16). Correspondingly, nature is not merely the raw material for human activity. Though only human beings have been made in the image of God, non-human creation too has a dignity of its own, so much so that after the flood God established a covenant not only with Noah and his descendants, but also "with every living creature that is with you" (Genesis 9:9). Similarly, the Christian hope for the future also includes creation. "The creation itself will be set free from its bondage to decay and obtain the glorious liberty of the children of God" (Romans 8:21).

6. The dominion which God gave human beings over creation (Genesis 1:30) does not give them licence to abuse creation. First, they are responsible to God, in whose image they were made, not to ravish creation but to sustain it, as God sustains it in divine providential care. Second, since human beings are created in the image of God for community and not simply as isolated individuals (Genesis 1:28), they are to exercise dominion in a way that is responsible to the needs of the total human family, including future generations.

7. Human beings are both part of creation and also unique. Only human beings are created in the image of God. God thus grants human beings dominion over the non-human creation (Genesis 1:28–30). But dominion is not domination. According to Genesis 2:15, human dominion over

creation consists in the twofold task of "tilling and taking care" of the garden. Therefore all work must have not only a productive but also a protective aspect. Economic systems must be shaped so that a healthy ecological system is maintained over time. All responsible human work done by the stewards of God the Sustainer must contain an element of cooperation with the environment.

Stewardship and Economic Production

8. Economic production results from the stewardship of the earth which God assigned to humanity. While materialism, injustice, and greed are in fundamental conflict with the teaching of the whole Scripture, there is nothing in Christian faith that suggests that the production of new goods and services is undesirable. Indeed, we are explicitly told that God "richly furnishes us with everything to enjoy" (1 Timothy 6:17). Production is not only necessary to sustain life and make it enjoyable; it also provides an opportunity for human beings to express their creativity in the service of others. In assessing economic systems from a Christian perspective, we must consider their ability both to generate and to distribute wealth and income justly.

Technology and Its Limitations

9. Technology mirrors the basic paradox of the sinfulness and goodness of human nature. Many current ecological problems result from the extensive use of technology after the onset of industrialization. Though technology has liberated human beings from some debasing forms of work, it has also often dehumanised other forms of work. Powerful nations and corporations that control modern technology are regularly tempted to use it to dominate the weak for their own narrow self-interest. As we vigorously criticise the negative effects of technology, we should, however, not forget its positive effects. Human creativity is expressed in the designing of tools for celebration and work. Technology helps us meet the basic needs of the world population and to do so in ways which develop the creative potential of individuals and societies. Technology can also help us reverse environmental dev-

astation. A radical rejection of modern technology is unrealistic. Instead we must search for ways to use appropriate technology responsibly according to every cultural context.

10. What is technologically possible is not necessarily morally permissible. We must not allow technological development to follow its own inner logic, but must direct it to serve moral ends. We acknowledge our limits in foreseeing the impact of technological change and encourage an attitude of humility with respect to technological innovation. Therefore continuing evaluation of the impact of technological change is essential. Four criteria derived from Christian faith help us to evaluate the development and use of technology. First, technology should not foster disintegration of family or community, or function as an instrument of social domination. Second, persons created in the image of God must not become mere accessories of machines. Third, as God's stewards, we must not allow technology to abuse creation. If human work is to be done in cooperation with creation then the instruments of work must cooperate with it too. Finally, we should not allow technological advancements to become objects of false worship or to seduce us away from dependence on God (Genesis 11:1–9). We may differ in what weight we ascribe to individual criteria in concrete situations, and therefore our assessment of particular technologies may differ. But we believe that these criteria need to be taken into consideration as we reflect theologically on technological progress.

11. We urge individuals, private institutions, and governments everywhere to consider both the local, immediate, and the global, long-term ecological consequences of their actions. We encourage corporate action to make products which are more "environmentally friendly." And we call on governments to create and enforce just frameworks of incentives and penalties which will encourage both individuals and corporations to adopt ecologically sound practices.

12. We need greater international cooperation between individuals, private organisations, and nations to promote environmentally responsible action. Since political action usually serves the

self-interest of the powerful, it will be especially important to guarantee that international environmental agreements are particularly concerned to protect the needs of the poor. We call on Christians everywhere to place high priority on restoring and maintaining the integrity of creation.

B. Work and Leisure

Work and Human Nature

13. Work involves all those activities done, not for their own sake, but to satisfy human needs. Work belongs to the very purpose for which God originally made human beings. In Genesis 1:26–28, we read that God created human beings in his image "in order to have dominion over . . . all the earth." Similarly, Genesis 2:15 tells us that God created Adam and placed him in the garden of Eden to work in it, to "till it and keep it." As human beings fulfil this mandate, they glorify God. Though fallen, as human beings "go forth to their work" (Psalm 104:23) they fulfil an original purpose of the Creator for human existence.

14. Because work is central to the Creator's intention for humanity, work has intrinsic value. Thus work is not solely a means to an end. It is not simply a chore to be endured for the sake of satisfying human desires or needs, especially the consumption of goods. At the same time, we have to guard against over-valuation of work. The essence of human beings consists in that they are made in the image of God. Their ultimate, but not exclusive, source of meaning and identity does not lie in work, but in becoming children of God by one Spirit through faith in Jesus Christ.

15. For Christians, work acquires a new dimension. God calls all Christians to employ through work the various gifts that God has given them. God calls people to enter the kingdom of God and to live a life in accordance with its demands. When people respond to the call of God, God enables them to bear the fruit of the Spirit and endows them individually with multiple gifts of the Spirit. As those who are gifted by the Spirit and whose actions are guided by the demands of love, Christians should do their work in the service of God and humanity.

The Purpose of Work

16. In the Bible and in the first centuries of the Christian tradition, meeting one's needs and the needs of one's community (especially its underprivileged members) was an essential purpose of work (Psalm 128:2; 2 Thessalonians 3:8; 1 Thessalonians 4:9–12; Ephesians 4:28; Acts 20:33–35). The first thing at issue in all fields of human work is the need of human beings to earn their daily bread and a little more.

17. The deepest meaning of human work is that the almighty God established human work as a means to accomplish God's work in the world. Human beings remain dependent on God, for "unless the Lord builds the house, those who build it labour in vain" (Psalm 127:1a). As Genesis 2:5 suggests, God and human beings are co-labourers in the task of preserving creation.

18. Human work has consequences that go beyond the preservation of creation to the anticipation of the eschatological transformation of the world. They are, of course, not ushering in the kingdom of God, building the "new heavens and a new earth." Only God can do that. Yet their work makes a small and imperfect contribution to it— for example, by shaping the personalities of the citizens of the eternal kingdom which will come through God's action alone.

19. However, work is not only a means through which the glory of human beings as God's stewards shines forth. It is also a place where the misery of human beings as impeders of God's purpose becomes visible. Like the test of fire, God's judgment will bring to light the work which has ultimate significance because it was done in cooperation with God. But it will also manifest the ultimate insignificance of work done in cooperation with those evil powers which scheme to ruin God's good creation (1 Corinthians 3:12–15).

Alienation in Work

20. Sin makes work an ambiguous reality. It is both a noble expression of human creation in the image of God, and, because of the curse, a painful testimony to human estrangement from God.

Whether human beings are tilling the soil in agrarian societies, or operating high-tech machinery in information societies, they work under the shadow of death, and experience struggle and frustration in work (Genesis 3:17–19).

21. Human beings are created by God as persons endowed with gifts which God calls them to exercise freely. As a fundamental dimension of human existence, work is a personal activity. People should never be treated in their work as mere means. We must resist the tendency to treat workers merely as costs or labour inputs, a tendency evident in both rural and urban societies, but especially where industrial and post-industrial methods of production are applied. We encourage efforts to establish managerial and technological conditions that enable workers to participate meaningfully in significant decision-making processes, and to create opportunities for individual development by designing positions that challenge them to develop their potential and by instituting educational programmes.

22. God gives talents to individuals for the benefit of the whole community. Human work should be a contribution to the common good (Ephesians 4:28). The modern drift from concern for community to preoccupation with self, supported by powerful structural and cultural forces, shapes the way we work. Individual self-interest can legitimately be pursued, but only in a context marked by the pursuit of the good of others. These two pursuits are complementary. In order to make the pursuit of the common good possible, Christians need to seek to change both the attitudes of workers and the structures in which they work.

23. Discrimination in work continues to oppress people, especially women and marginalised groups. Because of race and gender, people are often pushed into a narrow range of occupations which are often underpaid, offer little status or security, and provide few promotional opportunities and fringe benefits. Women and men and people of all races are equal before God and should, therefore, be recognised and treated with equal justice and dignity in social and economic life.

24. For most people work is an arduous good. Many workers suffer greatly under the burden of work. In some situations people work long hours for low pay, working conditions are appalling, contracts are nonexistent, sexual harassment occurs, trade union representation is not allowed, health and safety regulations are flouted. These things occur throughout the world whatever the economic system. The word "exploitation" has a strong and immediate meaning in such situations. The God of the Bible condemns exploitation and oppression. God's liberation of the Israelites from their oppression served as a paradigm of how God's people should behave towards workers in their midst (Leviticus 25:39–55).

25. Since work is central to God's purpose for humanity, people everywhere have both the obligation and the right to work. Given the broad definition of work suggested above (cf. para 13), the right to work here should be understood as part of the freedom of the individual to contribute to the satisfaction of the needs of the community. It is a freedom right, since work in its widest sense is a form of self-expression. The right involved is the right of the worker to work unhindered. The obligation is on every human being to contribute to the community. It is in this sense that Paul says, "if a man will not work, let him not eat."

26. The right to earn a living would be a positive or sustenance right. Such a right implies the obligation of the community to provide employment opportunities. Employment cannot be guaranteed where rights conflict and resources may be inadequate. However the fact that such a right cannot be enforced does not detract in any way from the obligation to seek the highest level of employment which is consistent with justice and the availability of resources.

Rest and Leisure

27. As the Sabbath commandment indicates, the Biblical concept of rest should not be confused with the modern concept of leisure. Leisure consists of activities that are ends in themselves and therefore intrinsically enjoyable. In many parts of the world for many people, life is "all work

and no play." While masses of people are unemployed and thus have only "leisure," millions of people—including children—are often overworked simply to meet their basic survival needs. Meanwhile, especially in economically developed nations, many overwork to satisfy their desire for status.

28. The first pages of the Bible tell us that God rested after creating the universe (Genesis 2:2–3). The sequence of work and rest that we see in God's activity is a pattern for human beings. In that the Sabbath commandment interrupted work with regular periods of rest, it liberates human beings from enslavement to work. The Sabbath erects a fence around human productive activity and serves to protect both human and non-human creation. Human beings have, therefore, both a right and an obligation to rest.

29. Corresponding to the four basic relations in which all people stand (in relationship to non-human creation, to themselves, to other human beings, and to God), there are four activities which we should cultivate in leisure time. Rest consists in the enjoyment of nature as God's creation, in the free exercise and development of abilities which God has given to each person, in the cultivation of fellowship with one another, and above all, in delight in communion with God.

30. Worship is central to the Biblical concept of rest. In order to be truly who they are, human beings need periodic moments of time in which God's commands concerning their work will recede from the forefront of their consciousness as they adore the God of loving holiness and thank the God of holy love.

31. Those who cannot meet their basic needs without having to forego leisure can be encouraged by the reality of their right to rest. The right to rest implies the corresponding right to sustenance for all those who are willing to work "six days a week" (Exodus 20:9). Modern workaholics whose infatuation with status relegates leisure to insignificance must be challenged by the liberating obligation to rest. What does it profit them to "gain the whole world" if they "forfeit their life" (Mark 8:36)?

C. Poverty and Justice

God and the Poor

32. Poverty was not part of God's original creation, nor will poverty be part of God's restored creation when Christ returns. Involuntary poverty in all its forms and manifestations is a result of the Fall and its consequences. Today one of every five human beings lives in poverty so extreme that their survival is daily in doubt. We believe this is offensive and heart breaking to God.

33. We understand that the God of the Bible is one who in mercy extends love to all. At the same time, we believe that when the poor are oppressed, God is the "defender of the poor" (Psalm 146:7–9). Again and again in every part of Scripture, the Bible expresses God's concern for justice for the poor. Faithful obedience requires that we share God's concern and act on it. "He who oppresses a poor man insults his maker, but he who is kind to the needy honours Him" (Proverbs 14:31). Indeed it is only when we right such injustices that God promises to hear our prayers and worship (Isaiah 58:1–9).

34. Neglect of the poor often flows from greed. Furthermore, the obsessive or careless pursuit of material goods is one of the most destructive idolatries in human history (Ephesians 5:5). It distracts individuals from their duties before God, and corrupts personal and social relationships.

Causes of Poverty

35. The causes of poverty are many and complex. They include the evil that people do to each other, to themselves, and to their environment. The causes of poverty also include the cultural attitudes and actions taken by social, economic, political and religious institutions, that either devalue or waste resources, that erect barriers to economic production, or that fail to reward work fairly. Furthermore, the forces that cause and perpetuate poverty operate at global, national, local, and personal levels. It is also true that a person may be poor because of sickness, mental or physical handicap, childhood, or old age. Poverty is also caused by natural disasters such as earthquakes, hurricanes, floods, and famines.

36. We recognise that poverty results from and is sustained by both constraints on the production of wealth and on the inequitable distribution of wealth and income. We acknowledge the tendency we have had to reduce the causes of poverty to one at the expense of the others. We affirm the need to analyse and explain the conditions that promote the creation of wealth, as well as those that determine the distribution of wealth.

37. We believe it is the responsibility of every society to provide people with the means to live at a level consistent with their standing as persons created in the image of God.

Justice and Poverty

38. Biblical justice means impartially rendering to everyone their due in conformity with the standards of God's moral law. Paul uses justice (or righteousness) in its most comprehensive sense as a metaphor to describe God's creative and powerful redemptive love. Christ, solely in grace, brought us into God's commonwealth, who were strangers to it and because of sin cut off from it (Romans 1:17–18; 3:21–26; Ephesians 2:4–22). In Biblical passages which deal with the distribution of the benefits of social life in the context of social conflict and social wrong, justice is related particularly to what is due to groups such as the poor, widows, orphans, resident aliens, wage earners and slaves. The common link among these groups is powerlessness by virtue of economic and social needs. The justice called forth is to restore these groups to the provision God intends for them. God's law expresses this justice and indicates its demands. Further, God's intention is for people to live, not in isolation, but in society. The poor are described as those who are weak with respect to the rest of the community; the responsibility of the community is stated as "to make them strong" so that they can continue to take their place in the community (Leviticus 25:35–36). One of the dilemmas of the poor is their loss of community (Job 22:5; Psalm 107:4–9, 33–36). Indeed their various needs are those that tend to prevent people from being secure and contributing members of society. One essential characteris-

tic of Biblical justice is the meeting of basic needs that have been denied in contradiction to the standards of Scripture; but further, the Bible gives indication of how to identify which needs are basic. They are those essential, not just for life, but for life in society.

39. Justice requires special attention to the weak members of the community because of their greater vulnerability. In this sense, justice is partial. Nevertheless, the civil arrangements in rendering justice are not to go beyond what is due to the poor or to the rich (Deuteronomy 1:17; Leviticus 19:15). In this sense justice is ultimately impartial. Justice is so fundamental that it characterises the personal virtues and personal relationships of individuals as they faithfully follow God's standards. Those who violate God's standards, however, receive God's retributive justice, which often removes the offender from society or from the divine community.

40. Justice requires conditions such that each person is able to participate in society in a way compatible with human dignity. Absolute poverty, where people lack even minimal food and housing, basic education, health care, and employment, denies people the basic economic resources necessary for just participation in the community. Corrective action with and on behalf of the poor is a necessary act of justice. This entails responsibilities for individuals, families, churches, and governments.

41. Justice may also require socio-political actions that enable the poor to help themselves and be the subjects of their own development and the development of their communities. We believe that we and the institutions in which we participate are responsible to create an environment of law, economic activity, and spiritual nurture which creates these conditions.

Some Urgent Contemporary Issues

42. Inequitable international economic relations aggravate poverty in poor countries. Many of these countries suffer under a burden of debt service which could only be repaid at an unacceptable price to the poor, unless there is a radical

restructuring both of national economic policies and international economic relations. The combination of increasing interest rates and falling commodity prices in the early 1980s has increased this debt service burden. Both lenders and borrowers shared in creating this debt. The result has been increasing impoverishment of the people. Both lenders and borrowers must share responsibility for finding solutions. We urgently encourage governments and international financial institutions to redouble their efforts to find ways to reduce the international indebtedness of the Third World, and to ensure the flow of both private and public productive capital where appropriate.

43. Government barriers to the flow of goods and services often work to the disadvantage of the poor. We particularly abhor the protectionist policies of the wealthy nations which are detrimental to developing countries. Greater freedom and trade between nations is an important part of reducing poverty worldwide.

44. Justice requires that the value of money be reliably known and stable, thus inflation represents poor stewardship and defrauds the nations' citizens. It wastes resources and is particularly harmful to the poor and the powerless. The wealthier members of society find it much easier to protect themselves against inflation than do the poor. Rapid changes in prices drastically affect the ability of the poor to purchase basic goods.

45. Annual global military expenditures equal the annual income of the poorest one-half of the world's people. These vast, excessive military expenditures detract from the task of meeting basic human needs, such as food, health care, and education. We are encouraged by the possibilities represented by the changes in the USSR and Eastern Europe, and improving relations between East and West. We urge that a major part of the resulting "peace dividend" be used to provide sustainable solutions to the problems of the world's poor.

46. Drug use and trafficking destroys both rich and poor nations. Drug consumption reflects spiritual poverty among the people and societies in which drug use is apparent. Drug trafficking undermines the national economies of those who produce drugs. The economic, social, and spiritual costs of drug use are unacceptable. The two key agents involved in this problem must change: the rich markets which consume drugs and the poorer countries which produce them. Therefore both must urgently work to find solutions. The rich markets which consume drugs must end their demand. And the poorer countries which produce them must switch to other products.

47. We deplore economic systems based on policies, laws, and regulations whose effect is to favour privileged minorities and to exclude the poor from fully legitimate activities. Such systems are not only inefficient, but are immoral as well in that participating in and benefitting from the formal economy depends on conferred privilege of those who have access and influence to public and private institutions rather than on inventiveness and hard work. Actions need to be taken by public and private institutions to reduce and simplify the requirements and costs of participating in the national economy.

48. There is abundant evidence that investment in small scale enterprises run by and for the poor can have a positive impact upon income and job creation for the poor. Contrary to the myths upheld by traditional financial institutions, the poor are often good entrepreneurs and excellent credit risks. We deplore the lack of credit available to the poor in the informal sector. We strongly encourage governments, financial institutions, and Non-Governmental Organisations to redouble their efforts to significantly increase credit to the poor. We feel so strongly about this that a separate statement dedicated to credit-based income generation programmes has been issued by the conference.

D. Freedom, Government, and Economics

The Language of Human Rights

49. With the United Nations Declaration of Human Rights, the language of human rights has become pervasive throughout the world. It expresses the urgent plight of suffering people whose humanity is daily being denied them by their oppressors. In some cases rights language has

been misused by those who claim that anything they want is theirs "by right." This breadth of application has led some to reject rights as a concept, stating that if everything becomes a right then nothing will be a right, since all rights imply corresponding responsibilities. Therefore it is important to have clear criteria for what defines rights.

Christian Distinctives

50. All human interaction is judged by God and is accountable to God. In seeking human rights we search for an authority or norm which transcends our situation. God is that authority; God's character constitutes that norm. Since human rights are a priori rights, they are not conferred by the society or the state. Rather, human rights are rooted in the fact that every human being is made in the image of God. The deepest ground of human dignity is that while we were yet sinners, Christ died for us (Romans 5:8).

51. In affirmation of the dignity of God's creatures, God's justice for them requires life, freedom, and sustenance. The divine requirements of justice establish corresponding rights for human beings to whom justice is due. The right to life is the most basic human right. God created human beings as free moral agents. As such, they have the right to freedom—e.g., freedom of religion, speech, and assembly. Their freedom, however, is properly used only in dependence on God. It is a requirement of justice that human beings, including refugees and stateless persons, are able to live in society with dignity. Human beings therefore have a claim on other human beings for social arrangements that ensure that they have access to the sustenance that makes life in society possible.

52. The fact that in becoming Christians we may choose to forego our rights out of love for others and in trust of God's providential care does not mean that such rights cease to exist. Christians may endure the violation of their rights with great courage but work vigorously for the identical rights of others in similar circumstances. However it may not be appropriate to do so in some

circumstances. Indeed this disparity between Christian contentment and campaigning on behalf of others in adverse situations is a witness to the work and love of God.

53. All of us share the same aspirations as human beings to have our rights protected—whether the right to life, freedom, or sustenance. Yet the fact of sin and the conflict of competing human rights means that our aspirations are never completely fulfilled in this life. Through Christ, sin and evil have been conquered. They will remain a destructive force until the consummation of all things. But that in no way reduces our horror at the widespread violation of human rights today.

Democracy

54. As a model, modern political democracy is characterised by limited government of a temporary character, by the division of power within the government, the distinction between state and society, pluralism, the rule of law, institutionalisation of freedom rights (including free and regular elections), and a significant amount of non-governmental control of property. We recognise that no political system is directly prescribed by Scripture, but we believe that Biblical values and historical experience call Christians to work for the adequate participation of all people in the decision-making processes on questions that affect their lives.

55. We also recognise that simply to vote periodically is not a sufficient expression of democracy. For a society to be truly democratic, economic power must be shared widely and class and status distinctions must not be barriers preventing access to economic and social institutions. Democracies are also open to abuse through the very chances which make them democratic. Small, economically powerful groups sometimes dominate the political process. Democratic majorities can be swayed by materialistic, racist, or nationalistic sentiments to engage in unjust policies. The fact that all human institutions are fallen means that the people must be constantly alert to and critical of all that is wrong.

56. We recognise that no particular economic system is directly prescribed by Scripture. Recent history suggests that a dispersion of ownership of the means of production is a significant component of democracy. Monopolistic ownership, either by the state, large economic institutions, or oligarchies is dangerous. Widespread ownership, either in a market economy or a mixed system, tends to decentralise power and prevent totalitarianism.

The Concentration of Economic Power

57. Economic power can be concentrated in the hands of a few people in a market economy. When that occurs political decisions tend to be made for economic reasons and the average member of society is politically and economically marginalised. Control over economic life may thus be far removed from a large part of the population. Transnational corporations can also wield enormous influence on some economies. Despite these problems, economic power is diffused within market-oriented economies to a greater extent than in other systems.

58. In centrally planned economies, economic decisions are made for political reasons, people's economic choices are curtailed, and the economy falters. Heavy state involvement and regulation within market economies can also result in concentrations of power that effectively marginalise poorer members of the society. Corruption almost inevitably follows from concentrated economic power. Widespread corruption so undermines society that there is a virtual breakdown of legitimate order.

Capitalism and Culture

59. As non-capitalist countries increasingly turn away from central planning and towards the market, the question of capitalism's effect on culture assumes more and more importance. The market system can be an effective means of economic growth, but can, in the process, cause people to think that ultimate meaning is found in the accumulation of more goods. The overwhelming consumerism of Western societies is testimony to the fact that the material success of capitalism encourages forces and attitudes that are decidedly non-Christian. One such attitude is the treatment of workers as simply costs or productive inputs, without recognition of their humanity. There is also the danger that the model of the market, which may work well in economic transactions, will be assumed to be relevant to other areas of life, and people may consequently believe that what the market encourages is therefore best or most true.

The Role of Government

60. Government is designed to serve the purposes of God to foster community, particularly in response to our rebellious nature (Romans 13:1, 4; Psalm 72:1). As an institution administered by human beings, government can exacerbate problems of power, greed, and envy. However, it can, where properly constructed and constrained, serve to limit some of these sinful tendencies. Therefore it is the responsibility of Christians to work for governmental structures that serve justice. Such structures must respect the principle that significant decisions about local human communities are usually best made at a level of government most directly responsible to the people affected.

61. At a minimum, government must establish a rule of law that protects life, secures freedom, and provides basic security. Special care must be taken to make sure the protection of fundamental rights is extended to all members of society, especially the poor and oppressed (Proverbs 31:8–9; Daniel 4:27). Too often government institutions are captured by the economically or socially powerful. Thus, equality before the law fails to exist for those without power. Government must also have regard for economic efficiency and appropriately limit its own scope and action.

62. The provision of sustenance rights is also an appropriate function of government. Such rights must be carefully defined so that government's involvement will not encourage irresponsible behaviour and the breakdown of families and communities. In a healthy society, this fulfilment of rights will be provided through a diversity of

institutions so that the government's role will be that of last resort.

Mediating Structures

63. One of the phenomena associated with the modern world is the increasing divide between private and public sectors. The need for a bridge between these two sectors has led to an emphasis on mediating institutions. The neighbourhood, the family, the church, and other voluntary associations are all such institutions. As the early church did in its context, these institutions provide citizens with many opportunities for participation and leadership. They also provide other opportunities for loyalty in addition to the state and the family. Their role in meeting the needs of members of the community decreases the need for centralised government. They also provide a channel for individuals to influence government, business, and other large institutions. Therefore Christians should encourage governments everywhere to foster vigorous voluntary associations.

64. The future of poverty alleviation is likely to involve expanded microeconomic income generation programmes and entrepreneurial development of the so-called "informal sector" as it becomes part of the transformed formal economy. In this context, there will most likely be an even greater role for Non-Governmental Organisations. In particular, church bodies will be able to make a significant and creative contribution in partnership with the poor, acting as mediating institutions by virtue of the churches' longstanding grass-roots involvement in local communities.

Conclusion

65. As we conclude, we thank God for the opportunity God has given us to participate in this conference. Through our time together we have been challenged to express our faith in the area of economic life in practical ways. We acknowledge that all too often we have allowed society to shape our views and actions and have failed to apply scriptural teaching in this crucial area of our lives, and we repent.

We now encourage one another to uphold Christian economic values in the face of unjust and subhuman circumstances. We realise, however, that ethical demands are often ineffective because they are reinforced only by individual conscience and that the proclamation of Christian values needs to be accompanied by action to encourage institutional and structural changes which would foster these values in our communities. We will therefore endeavour to seek every opportunity to work for the implementation of the principles outlined in this **Declaration,** in faithfulness to God's calling.

We urge all people, and especially Christians, to adopt stewardship and justice as the guiding principles for all aspects of economic life, particularly for the sake of those who are most vulnerable. These principles must be applied in all spheres of life. They have to do with our use of material resources and lifestyle as well as with the way people and nations relate to one another. With girded loins and burning lamps we wait for the return of our Lord Jesus Christ when justice and peace shall embrace.

Notes

1. In January 1987, 36 Christians from all continents and a broad range of professions and socio-political perspectives came together at Oxford to discuss contemporary economic issues in a way that was both faithful to the scriptures and grounded in careful economic analysis. (The papers from that conference were published in *Transformation* 4 [1987], nr. 3.4.) They authorized a three-year process to attempt to draft a comprehensive statement on Christian faith and economics.

In this project, groups of economists and theologians met all over the world in regional conferences and addressed issues under four headings: Stewardship and Creation; Work and Leisure; The Definition of Justice and Freedom; Government and Economics. A separate paper on micro enterprise was also undertaken. These regional discussions and studies were then drawn together to form the issues for analysis and debate at the Second Oxford Conference on January 4–9, 1990.

Questions for Discussion:

1. Does the Oxford Declaration accurately represent biblical teaching on economic life? Can it be relevant to economic life today?
2. Do you think the Declaration adequately takes into account the differences between economic life in the ancient world and the global information-based economy of today?
3. Do you agree with the Declaration on the role of government in economic life? Why or why not?

Economic Justice: A Biblical Paradigm

Stephen Mott and Ronald J. Sider

From *Toward a Just and Caring Society: Christian Responses to Poverty in America,* edited by David P. Gushee (Grand Rapids: Baker, 1999), 15–45.

Introduction[1]

Values shape economics. Economic thinking combines empirical analysis and normative beliefs. Whether or not persons realize it, some normative system of values partially determines every economic decision.

Economic thinking, in fact, combines three components: normative beliefs, empirical analysis, and a political philosophy.[2] Fundamental beliefs about things like the nature of persons, history, the creation of wealth, and the nature of just distribution, guide economic decisions. So do complex analyses of economic data and economic history. Each time one wants to make a specific economic decision, however, one cannot stop and rethink all one's normative beliefs on the one hand and undertake elaborate socioeconomic analyses on the other. One needs a road map, a handy guide, so one can make quick but responsible decisions about economics and politics. Such a road map, often called an ideology or a political philosophy, is "a pattern of beliefs and concepts (both factual and normative) which purports to explain complex social phenomena with a view to directing and simplifying socio-political choices facing individuals and groups."[3] Marxist communism and democratic capitalism, of course, have been the two dominant political philosophies of the twentieth century.

Christians, like everyone else, require a political philosophy or ideology. But they dare not adopt an ideology uncritically or they risk violating their most basic confession that Jesus is Lord of all—including economics and politics. That means that Christian truth must determine the shape of a Christian's ideology. Since analysis of the world and normative beliefs are the two essential components that shape any ideology or political philosophy, a Christian must construct his or her political philosophy by combining the most accurate, factual analysis that is available with normative Christian truths.

Where should Christians go for these normative principles and ideas that guide their thinking about economics? The fall has not destroyed all knowledge of truth and goodness given by the Creator to all persons made in God's image (e.g., Rom. 1:18–25); therefore, some Christians look to natural law as a source for the norms needed to guide economic and political life.[4] Sin, however, has profoundly distorted our total being, including our minds. Therefore, in this study we turn to the revealed truth of the Bible as the primary source for our normative framework.

The Bible provides norms for thinking about economics in two basic ways: the biblical story and the biblical paradigm on economic justice.

The biblical story is the long history of God's engagement with our world that stretches from creation through the fall and the history of redemption to the culmination of history when Christ returns. This biblical story offers decisive insight into the nature of the material world, the dignity and character of persons, and the significance and limitations of history. For example, since every person is a body-soul unity made by God for community, no one will ultimately be satisfied with material abundance alone or with material abundance kept only for oneself. Since every person is so important that God became flesh to die for her sins and invite her to live forever with the living God, economic life must be ordered in a way that respects this God-given dignity. We need to explore systematically these and other implications of the biblical story for economic life.

The Bible also provides norms in a second way. It is true that there is no biblical passage with a detailed systematic treatise on the nature of economic justice. But throughout the Bible, we find materials—commands, laws, proverbs, parables, stories, theological propositions—that relate to all the normative questions that economic decisions require. For example, should everyone own productive capital or should just a few? Is justice only concerned with fair procedures or does it include a fair distribution of wealth? In what sense is equality a central goal? What about the creation of wealth? Should we care for those unable to provide for themselves? Every book of the Bible offers material relevant to these kinds of questions.

The same is true of the various types of justice that different thinkers over the years have sought to define. Some of the most important are:

- procedural justice, which specifies fair legal processes for deciding disputes between people
- commutative justice, which defines fair means of exchange of goods (e.g., honest weights and measures)
- distributive justice, which specifies a fair allocation of a society's wealth, resources and power
- retributive justice, which defines fair punishment for wrongs committed
- restorative justice, which is an aspect of distributive justice and specifies fair ways to correct injustice and restore socioeconomic wholeness for persons and communities.

Here, too, of course, there are no lengthy systematic discourses on these topics. But there is much relevant biblical material.

Since there is no detailed systematic treatise on economic justice, we must construct a biblical paradigm on economic justice by looking carefully at all the relevant canonical texts that stretch from Genesis to Revelation. These texts represent many different literary genres, from history to poetry to prophetic declaration. They were written over many hundreds of years and addressed to people in dramatically different cultures, all of which differ from our own complex civilization at the beginning of the third millennium A.D. In order to develop a faithful biblical paradigm on economic justice, we must in principle first examine every relevant biblical text using the best exegetical tools to understand its original meaning and then, secondly, construct an integrated, systematic summary of all this diverse material in a way that faithfully reflects the balance of canonical teaching. In this short chapter, unfortunately, space does not permit examination of every relevant passage. But we seek to include important, representative texts. Mistakes, of course, are possible at any point, either in our specific exegesis or our overall summary. But our aim is fidelity to the text and to the balance of canonical teaching. To the extent that critics—friendly or hostile—can help us approach closer to that goal, we will be grateful.

The interpretive task, of course, does not end when one completes even the most faithful biblical paradigm. We should not take biblical mechanism like the return of the land every fifty years (Leviticus 25) and apply them mechanically to our very different culture and economy. A literal, mechanical application would neither fit our different settings nor even speak to many of our urgent questions. There is not a word in Scripture about the merits of a flat tax, the activity of the International Monetary Fund, or the Earned Income Tax Credit. We must apply the biblical framework paradigmatically, allowing the biblical worldview, principles, and norms to provide the normative framework for shaping economic life today.

Our goal in this essay is to present a faithful biblical paradigm on economic justice. We offer this summary of biblical teaching in the hope that all Christians, starting with ourselves, will allow biblical revelation, rather than secular ideas of left or right, to provide the decisive normative framework for their thinking about economics. We also hope the biblical paradigm on economic justice will even prove attractive to those who do not claim to be Christians.

The Biblical Story

The biblical story of creation, fall, redemption, and· eschaton teaches us many things about the world, persons, and society that are foundational for Christian economic thought.

The World

Because it is created out of nothing *(ex nihilo)* by a loving, almighty Creator, the material world is both finite and good.

The material world is not divine. The trees and rivers are not, as animists believe, divinities to be worshiped and left as unchanged as possible. Biblical faith desacralizes the world, permitting stewardly use of the material world for wise human purposes.

Nor is the material world an illusion to be escaped, as some Eastern monists claim. It is so good in its finitude (Genesis 1) that the Creator of the galaxies becomes flesh and even promises to restore the groaning creation to wholeness at his Second Coming (Rom. 8:19–23). Although not as important as persons, who alone are created in the image of God, the non-human creation has its own independent worth and dignity (Gen. 9:8–11). Persons therefore exercise their unique role in creation as caring stewards who watch over the rest of the created order (Gen. 2:15).

The biblical vision of the world calls human beings to revel in the goodness of the material world, rather than seek to escape it. It invites persons to use the non-human world to create wealth and construct complex civilizations—always, of course, in away that does not destroy the rest of creation and thereby prevent it from offering its own independent hymn of praise to the Creator.

The Nature of Persons

Created in the image of God, made as body-soul unities formed for community, and called to faithful stewardship of the rest of creation, persons possess an inestimable dignity and value that transcends any economic process or system.

Because our bodies are a fundamental part of our created goodness, a generous sufficiency of material things is essential to human goodness. Any economic structure that prevents persons from producing and enjoying material well-being violates their God-given dignity. Because our spiritual nature and destiny are so important that it is better to lose even the entire material world than lose one's relationship with God, any economic system that tries to explain persons only as economic actors or that offers material abundance as the exclusive or primary way to human fulfillment contradicts the essence of human nature. Any economic structure that subordinates labor to capital thereby subordinates spiritual reality to material reality in contradiction to the biblical view of persons.[5] For persons invited to live forever with the living God, no material abundance, however splendid, can satisfy the human heart. Because human beings are body-soul unities, definitions of human rights should include both freedom rights and socioeconomic rights.

People are made both for personal freedom and communal solidarity. The God who cares so much about each person that the incarnate Creator died for the sins of the whole world and invites every person to respond in freedom to the gift of salvation, demands that human economic and political systems acknowledge and protect the dignity and freedom of each individual. Any economic order that denies economic freedom to individuals or reduces them to a factor of production subordinated to mere economic goals, violates their individual dignity and freedom.

Since persons are free, their choices have consequences. Obedient, diligent use of our gifts normally produces sufficiency of material things (unless powerful people oppress us). Disobedient, lazy neglect of our responsibilities normally increases the danger of poverty. Totally equal economic outcomes are not compatible with human freedom.

The first few chapters of Genesis underline the fact that we are also created for community. Until Eve arrived, Adam was restless. Mutual fulfillment resulted when the two became one flesh.[6] God punished Cain for violating community by killing his brother Abel, but then allowed Cain to enjoy the human community of family and city (Genesis 4).[7] As social beings, we are physically, emotionally, and rationally interdependent and have inherent duties of care and responsibility for each other. Authority, corporate responsibility, and collective decision-making are essential to every form of human life.[8] Therefore, economic and political institutions are not merely a consequence of the fall.

Because our communal nature demands attention to the common good, individual rights, whether of freedom of speech or private property, cannot be absolute. The right to private property dare not undermine the general welfare. Only God is an absolute owner. We are merely stewards of our property, called to balance personal rights with the common good.[9]

Our communal nature is grounded in God. Since persons are created in the image of the triune personal God who is Father, Son and Holy Spirit, "being a person means being united to other persons in mutual love."[10] Any economic system that emphasizes the freedom of individuals without an equal concern for mutual love, cooperation and responsibility neglects the complex balance of the biblical picture of persons. Any economic system that exaggerates the individual right of private property in a way that undermines mutual responsibility for the common good defies the Creator's design for human beings.

The biblical view of persons means that economic injustice is a family problem. Since we are all "God's offspring" (Acts 17:29; cf. all of vv. 24–29), we all have the same Father. Therefore all human beings are sisters and brothers. "Exploitation is a brother or sister treating another brother or sister as a mere object."[11] That is not to overlook differentiation in human society.[12] We do not have exactly the same obligations to all children everywhere that we have to those in our immediate biological family. But a mutual obligation for the common good of all people follows from the fact that all persons are sisters and brothers created in the image of our Heavenly Father.

Human rights specify minimal demands for how we should treat people to whom God has given such dignity and worth. Human institutions cannot create human rights. They can only recognize and protect the inestimable value of every person which flows from the central truths of the biblical story: every person is made in the image of God; every person is a child of the Heavenly Father; every person is loved so much by God that the eternal Son suffers crucifixion because God does not desire that any should perish (2 Peter 3:9); every person who accepts Christ, regardless of race, gender or class, is justified on exactly the same basis: unmerited grace offered through the cross. Since that is the way God views people, that is the way we should treat each other.

Statements of human rights spell out for individuals and communities the fixed duties which implement love for neighbor in typical situations of competing claims. Rights extend the gaze of love from spontaneous responses to individual needs to structured patterns of fair treatment for everyone. Vigorous commitment to human rights for all helps societies respect the immeasurable dignity and worth that the Creator has bestowed on every person.

Stewardship of the Earth

Persons alone are created in the divine image. Persons alone have been given the awesome responsibility of exercising dominion over the non-human creation (Gen. 1:28). This stewardly dominion, to be sure, must be that of the loving gardener who thoughtfully cares for, and in a sense serves, the garden (Gen. 2:15). It dare not be a destructive violation of the independent worth of the rest of creation. But God's earthly stewards rightly cultivate and shape the earth placed in our care in order to produce new beauty, more complex civilizations, and greater wealth.

Creation of Wealth

The ability to create wealth is a gift from God. The One in whose image we are made creates astounding abundance and variety. Unlike God, we cannot create *ex nihilo;* we can only retrace the divine design. But by giving us minds that can study and imitate his handiwork, God has blessed human beings with awesome power not only to reshape the earth but to produce things that have never been.

The Creator could have directly created poetry, plays, sonatas, cities and computers. Instead, God assigned that task to us, expecting us to cultivate the earth (Gen. 2:15), create new things, and expand human possibilities and wealth. Adam and Eve surely enjoyed a generous sufficiency. Just as surely, the Creator intended their descendants to probe and use the astoundingly intricate earth placed in their care to acquire the knowledge, power, and wealth necessary, for example, to build vast telescopes that we can use to scan the billions of galaxies about which Adam and Eve knew nothing. In a real sense, God purposely created human beings with very little so that they could imitate and glorify their Creator by producing vast knowledge and wealth. Indeed, Jesus' parable of the talents sharply rebukes those who fail to use their skills to multiply their resources.[13] Just,

responsible creation of wealth is one important way persons obey and honor the Creator.

The Glory of Work

God works (Gen. 2:1–2). God Incarnate was a carpenter. St. Paul mended tents. Even before the fall, God summoned Adam to cultivate the earth and name the animals (Gen. 2:15–20). Work is not only the way we meet our basic needs. In addition, it is both the way we express our basic nature as co-workers with God and also a crucial avenue for loving our neighbors. Meaningful work by which persons express their creative ability is essential for human dignity. Any able person who fails to work disgraces and corrodes his very being. Any system that could but does not offer every person the opportunity for meaningful work violates and crushes human dignity.

The Lord of Economics

There is only one God who is Lord of all. God is the only absolute owner (Lev. 25:23). We are merely stewards summoned to use the wealth God allows us to enjoy for the glory of God and the good of our neighbor. We cannot worship God and Mammon. Excessive preoccupation with material abundance is idolatry. No economic task, however grand, dare claim our full allegiance. That belongs to God alone who consequently relativizes the claims of all human systems. God's righteous demands for justice judge every economic system. As the Lord of history, God works now with and through human co-workers to replace economic injustice with more wholesome economies that respect and nurture the dignity and worth of every human being.

The Importance of History

Modern secular thinkers absolutize the historical process even while they say it is meaningless. Even if life is absurd, our time here is all we have. Medieval thinkers sometimes belittled history, viewing earthly existence merely as a preparation for eternity. The biblical story affirms the importance of history while insisting that persons are also made for life eternal. It is in history that the

Redeemer chooses to turn back the invading powers of evil by launching the Messianic kingdom in the midst of history's sin. It is in history that persons not only respond to God's call to eternal life, but also join the Lord's long march toward justice and righteousness. And it is because we know where history is going and are assured that the Redeemer will return to complete the victory over every evil and injustice that we do not despair even when evil achieves sweeping, temporary triumphs. So we work for better economic systems, knowing that sin precludes any earthly utopia now, but rejoicing in the assurance that the kingdom of *shalom* that the Messiah has already begun will one day prevail, and the kingdoms of this world will become the kingdom of our Lord.

The Tragedy of Sin

Nothing on God's good earth has escaped sin's marauding presence. Sin has twisted both individual persons and the ideas and institutions they create. Rebelling against their Creator's instructions, people either exaggerate or belittle the significance of history and the material world. Exaggerating their own importance, they regularly create economic institutions—complete with sophisticated rationalizations—that oppress their neighbors. Workable economic systems must both appeal to persons' better instincts which sin has not quite managed to obliterate, and also hold in check and turn to positive use the pervasive selfishness which corrupts every act.

Sin, Power, and Justice

One of the important ways that God has chosen to restrain and correct evil, including economic injustice, is through the use of power by human beings.[14] Power is the ability to realize one's own will in a communal action even against the resistance of others.[15] Power itself is not evil. It is essential to human life and precedes the fall. It is God's gift to each person so that they can act in freedom as a co-worker with God to shape their own life and that of their community and world. By using power, we make actual our possibilities of being, which God presents as a particular gift designed for each life.[16] God wants persons to have power to control the material necessities of life. God gives power over wealth and property for human enjoyment (Eccles. 5:19).

The special attention which Scripture gives to the plight of the widow, the orphan, the poor, and the resident alien reflects the awareness in Scripture that when persons lack basic power, evil frequently follows. Thus, in the center of Job's declaration of the injustices to these groups is the statement: "The powerful possess the land" (Job 22:8, NRSV; cf. Job 35:9; Eccles. 4: 1). In the real world since the fall, sinful actions against others pervert the intention of the Creator. Sinful persons and evil forces which thwart the divine intention greatly restrict the ability to act in accordance with one's created being. This fallen use of power to impede the Creator's intentions for the lives of others is *exploitative power*. Exploitative power allows lust to work its will.[17] "Alas for those who devise wickedness and evil deeds upon their beds! When the morning dawns, they perform it, because it is in their power. They covet . . . they oppress . . ." (Micah 2:1–2, NRSV). Unequal power leads to exploitation.

The biblical understanding of human nature also warns us about the potential for evil afforded by sharp differences in power among individuals and groups in society. John Calvin described a "rough equality" in the Mosaic Law. In commenting upon the canceling of debts in the sabbatical year, he wrote,

> In as much as God had given them the use of the franchise, the best way to preserve their liberty was by maintaining a condition of rough equality [*mediocrem statum*], lest a few persons of immense wealth oppress the general body. Since, therefore, the rich if they had been permitted constantly to increase their wealth, would have tyrannized over the rest, God put a restraint on immoderate power by means of this law.[18]

A Christian political philosophy and economic theory accordingly must be based on a realism about human nature in light of the universality of sin. Powerful forces prey upon the weak. Human selfishness resists the full costs of communal obligations. Individual egoism is heightened in group conflict, and sin is disguised and justified as victims are blamed for their own plight.

An *intervening power* is necessary to limit exploitative power.[19] Power can demand and enforce political and economic change that corrects exploitation. Power produces changes which guarantee basic human needs and resist the forces that deny them. Intervening power is creative as it defeats exploitative power and reestablishes the creative power God wills for each person.

The source and model is God, who in common grace and in special grace restores persons' creative power by overcoming the forces which pervert the creation. God exerts power as the defender of the poor. Yahweh does "justice for the orphan and the oppressed" (Ps. 10:18, NRSV) by "break[ing] the arm [i.e., power] of the wicked" (v. 15) "so that those from earth may strike terror no more" (v. 18).

God's normal way of exerting power is through human creatures, who are God's lieutenants on the earth. Sometimes, when human justice fails and there is "no one to intervene," God acts in more direct and extraordinary ways (Isa. 59:15–18). But God's intention is for institutions, including government, to be the normal channels of God's intervening power.

Justice determines the proper limits and applications of intervening power. Justice provides the right structure of power. Without justice, power becomes destructive.[20]

Power, on the other hand, provides fiber and grit for justice. "I put on justice . . . I championed the cause of the stranger. I broke the fangs of the unrighteous, and made them drop their prey from their teeth" (Job 29:14, 16–17).

Biblical justice relates to both power (see Ps. 71:18–19) and love (Ezek. 34:16, 23–24; Ps. 146:7). As Martin Luther King stated, "Power without love is reckless and abusive and . . . love without power is sentimental and anemic. Power at its best is love implementing the demands of justice."[21]

One criterion of the legitimacy of power is whether it is being used for justice. The deliverance from Egypt was carried out by power ("out-stretched arm") with great acts of justice (*sepatim*, Exod. 6:6–7; 7:4). As in the stories of the judges, so in the exodus God "is acting in history as the one who uses his power to see that justice is done."[22] Power is used against power.[23] God upholds the poor and needy (Isa. 41:17) by His "just power" (vv. 10, 20). God works "justice to the fatherless and oppressed" by breaking the arm (power) of the evildoer to eliminate the source of oppression (Ps. 10:15–18). In our sinful world, intervening power is essential to correct exploitative power.

Thus far, we have seen how the biblical story provides important insight into the nature of the world, persons, history, the creation of wealth, sin and power. All this offers important elements of a biblical framework for thinking about economics. But we need more. We need a more detailed understanding of justice, equity (and equality), God's attitude toward the poor, and the role of government in fostering economic justice. For that we turn to a more detailed analysis in order to develop a biblical paradigm on economic justice.

A Biblical Paradigm

Justice identifies what is essential for life together in community and specifies the rights and responsibilities of individuals and institutions in society. What does the Bible tell us about the nature of justice?

Earlier, we noted several different types of justice. It is clear from biblical material that procedural justice is important. Legal institutions should not be biased either toward the rich or the poor (Deut. 10:17–18; Lev. 19:15; Exod. 23:3). Everyone should have equal access to honest, unbiased courts. Similarly, scriptural teaching on honest weights and measures (Lev. 19:35–36; Amos 8:5; Prov. 11:1) underlines the importance of commutative justice in order that fair, honest exchange of goods and services is possible.

Distributive Justice

There is less agreement, however, about the nature of distributive justice. Are the resources of society justly distributed, even if some are very poor and others very rich, as long as procedural and commutative justice are present? Or does a biblically informed understanding of distributive justice demand some reasonable standard of material well-being for all?

Calvin Beisner is typical of those who define economic justice in a minimal, procedural way:

> Justice in economic relationships requires that people be permitted to exchange and use what they own—including their own time and energy and intellect as well as material objects—freely so long as in so doing they do not violate others' rights. Such things as minimum wage laws, legally mandated racial quotas in employment, legal restrictions on import and export, laws requiring "equal pay for equal work," and all other regulations of economic activity other than those necessary to prohibit, prevent, and punish fraud, theft, and violence are therefore unjust.[24]

Carl Henry provides another example. In a fascinating chapter on the nature of God and social ethics, he argues that modern theological liberalism's submerging of God's wrath in God's love has led to a parallel disaster in society. Both in God and society, love and justice are very different and should never be confused. The state should be responsible for procedural justice, not love. In dire emergencies (the Great Depression, for example), it may be proper for the government to assist the poor and jobless, but normally, voluntary agencies like the church should perform such acts of love or benevolence. "In the New Testament view," Henry argues, "the coercive role of the State is limited to its punitive function."[25]

Henry is surely right that the biblical God is both searing holiness and amazing love. The one dare not be collapsed into the other. But does that mean that love is not connected with economic justice? Does it mean that economic justice exists, as Beisner argues, as long as procedural justice prevents fraud, theft, and violence?

Others argue that the biblical materials point to a much closer relationship between justice and love. If justice is understood to be in continuity with love, it takes on the dynamic, community-building character of love. Rather than having primarily a minimal, punitive and restraining function, justice in the biblical perspective has a crucial restorative character, identifying and correcting areas of material need. The debate over whether human rights includes economic rights is an extension of the debate over the continuity of love and justice. Are human rights essentially procedural (freedom of speech, religion, etc.) or do they include the right to basic material necessities?

To treat people equally, this second view argues, justice looks for barriers which interfere with the opportunity for access to productive resources needed to acquire the basic goods of society or to be dignified, participating members in the community. Justice takes into consideration certain handicaps which are hindrances to pursuing the opportunities for life in society. The handicaps which justice considers go beyond individual physical disabilities and personal tragedies. Significant handicaps can be found in poverty or prejudice. A just society removes any discrimination which prevents equality of opportunity. Distributive justice demands special consideration to disadvantaged groups by providing basic social and economic opportunities and resources.[26]

Is there biblical data to help us decide how to define distributive justice? Again, there is no systematic treatise on this topic anywhere in the Scriptures. But there is considerable relevant material. This is especially true in the Old Testament which, unlike the New Testament, usually addresses a setting where God's people make up the whole society, not just a tiny minority. (Therefore it is strange for Carl Henry to make his case for a minimal, procedural definition of justice on the basis of the New Testament alone, rather than the full canonical revelation.)

Several aspects of biblical teaching point to the broader—rather than the narrower, exclusively procedural—understanding of justice.[27] Frequently the words for *love* and *justice* appear together in close relationship. Biblical justice has a dynamic, restorative character. The special concern for the poor running throughout the Scriptures moves beyond a concern for unbiased procedures. Restoration to community—including the benefit rights that dignified participation in community require—is a central feature of biblical thinking about justice.

Love and Justice Together

In many texts we discover the words for love and justice in close association. "Sow for yourselves justice, reap the fruit of steadfast love" (Hos. 10:12).[28] Sometimes, love and justice are interchangeable: ". . . [It is the Lord] who executes *justice* [*mišpāt*] for the orphan and the widow, and who *loves* the strangers, providing them food and clothing" (Deut. 10:18, NRSV; see Isa. 30:18).[29]

Justice's Dynamic, Restorative Character

In the Bible, justice is not a mere *mitigation* of suffering in oppression, it is a *deliverance*. Justice involves rectifying the gross social inequities of the disadvantaged. The terms for *justice* are frequently associated with *yasaʿ, yᵉšûʿâ* the most important Hebrew word for deliverance and salvation: " . . . God arose to establish justice [*mišpāt*] to save [*hôšiaʿ*] all the oppressed of the earth" (Ps. 76:9; see Isa. 63:1).[30] "Give justice to the weak" and "maintain the right of the lowly" are parallel to "rescue the weak and the needy and snatch them out of the power of the wicked" (Ps. 82:3–4).[31]

Justice describes the deliverance of the people from political and economic oppressors (Judg. 5:11),[32] from slavery (1 Sam. 12:7–8; Micah 6:4), and from captivity (Isa. 41:1–11 [cf. v. 2 for *sedeq*]; Jer. 51:10). Providing for the needy means ending their oppression, setting them back on their feet, giving them a home, and leading them to prosperity and restoration (Pss. 68:5–10; 10:15–18).[33] Justice does not merely help victims cope with oppression; it removes it. Because of this dynamic, restorative emphasis, distributive justice requires not primarily that we maintain a stable society, but rather that we advance the well-being of the disadvantaged.

God's Special Concern for the Poor

Hundreds[34] of biblical verses show that God is especially attentive to the poor and needy. God is not biased. Because of unequal needs, however, equal provision of basic rights requires justice to be partial in order to be impartial. (Good firefighters do not spend equal time at every house; they are "partial" to people with fires.) Partiality to the weak is the most striking characteristic of biblical justice.[35] In the raging social struggles in which the poor are perennially victims of injustice, God and God's people take up the cause of the weak.[36] Rulers and leaders have a special obligation to do justice for the weak and powerless.[37] This partiality to the poor provides strong evidence that in biblical thought, justice is concerned with more than fair procedures.

The Scriptures speak of God's special concern for the poor in at least four different ways.[38]

1. Repeatedly, the Bible says that the Sovereign of history works to lift up the poor and oppressed. Consider the exodus. Certainly God acted there to keep the promise to Abraham and to call out the chosen people of Israel. But again and again the texts say God also intervened because God hated the oppression of the poor Israelites (Exod. 3:7–8; 6:5–7). Annually, at the harvest festival, the people of Israel repeated this confession: "The Egyptians mistreated us. . . . Then we cried out to the Lord, the God of our fathers, and the Lord heard our voice and saw our misery, toil and oppression. So the Lord brought us out of Egypt" (Deut. 26:6–8). Or consider the Psalms: "But the Lord says, 'I will now rise up because the poor are being hurt'" (12:5). "I know the Lord will get justice for the poor and will defend the needy in court" (140:12). God acts in history to lift up the poor and oppressed.

2. Sometimes, the Lord of history tears down rich and powerful people. Mary's song is shocking: "My soul glorifies the Lord. . . . He has filled the hungry with good things but has sent the rich away empty" (Luke 1:46, 53). James is even more blunt: "Now listen, you rich people, weep and wail because of the misery that is coming upon you" (James 5:1).

Since God calls us to create wealth and is not biased against the rich, why do the Scriptures warn again and again that God sometimes works in history to destroy the rich? The Bible has a simple answer. It is because the rich sometimes get rich by oppressing the poor. Or because they have plenty and neglect the needy. In either case, God is furious.

James warned the rich so harshly because they had hoarded wealth and refused to pay their workers (5:2–6). Repeatedly, the prophets said the same thing (Ps. 10; Jer. 22:13–19; Isa. 3:14–25). "Among my people are wicked men who lie in wait like men who snare birds and like those who set traps to catch men. Like cages full of birds, their houses are full of deceit; they have become rich and powerful and have grown fat and sleek.... They do not defend the rights of the poor. Should I not punish them for this?" (Jer. 5:26–29).

Repeatedly, the prophets warned that God was so outraged that he would destroy the nations of Israel and Judah. Because of the way they "trample on the heads of the poor ... and deny justice to the oppressed," Amos predicted terrible captivity (2:7; 5:11; 6:4, 7; 7:11, 17). So did Isaiah and Micah (Isa. 10:1–3; Mic. 2:2; 3:12). And it happened just as they foretold. According to both the Old and New Testaments, God destroys people and societies that get rich by oppressing the poor.

But what if we work hard and create wealth in just ways? That is good—as long as we do not forget to share. No matter how justly we have acquired our wealth, God demands that we act generously toward the poor. When we do not, God treats us in a similar way to those who oppress the poor. There is not a hint in Jesus' story of the rich man and Lazarus that the rich man exploited Lazarus to acquire wealth. He simply neglected to share. So God punished him (Luke 16:19–31).

Ezekiel contains a striking explanation for the destruction of Sodom: "Now this was the sin of your sister Sodom: She and her daughters were arrogant, overfed and unconcerned; they did not help the poor and needy.... Therefore I did away with them as you have seen" (16:49–50). Again, the text does not charge them with gaining wealth by oppression. It was because they refused to share their abundance that God destroyed the city.

The Bible is clear. If we get rich by oppressing the poor, or if we have wealth and do not reach out generously to the needy, the Lord of history moves against us. God judges societies by what they do to the people at the bottom.

3. God identifies with the poor so strongly that caring for them is almost like helping God. "He who is kind to the poor lends to the Lord" (Prov. 19:17). On the other hand, one "who oppresses the poor shows contempt for their Maker" (14:31).

Jesus' parable of the sheep and goats is the ultimate commentary on these two proverbs. Jesus surprises those on the right with his insistence that they had fed and clothed him when he was cold and hungry. When they protested that they could not remember ever doing that, Jesus replied: "Whatever you did for one of the least of these brothers of mine, you did for me" (Matt. 25:40). If we believe his words, we look on the poor and neglected with entirely new eyes.

4. Finally, God demands that his people share his special concern for the poor. God commanded Israel not to treat widows, orphans, and foreigners the way the Egyptians had treated them (Exod. 22:21–24). Instead, they should love the poor just as God cared for them at the exodus (Exod. 22:21–24; Deut. 15:13–15). When Jesus' disciples throw parties, they should especially invite the poor and disabled (Luke 14:12–14; Heb. 13:1–3). Paul held up Jesus' model of becoming poor to show how generously the Corinthians should contribute to the poor in Jerusalem (2 Cor. 8:9).

The Bible, however, goes one shocking step further. God insists that if we do not imitate God's concern for the poor, we are not really God's people—no matter how frequent our worship or how orthodox our creeds. Because Israel failed to correct oppression and defend poor widows, Isaiah insisted that Israel was really the pagan people of Gomorrah (1:10–17). God despised their fasting because they tried to worship God and oppress their workers at the same time (Isa. 58:3–7). Through Amos, the Lord shouted in fury that the very religious festivals God had ordained made God angry and sick. Why? Because the rich and powerful were mixing worship and oppression of the poor (5:21–24). Jesus was even more harsh. At the last judgment, some who expect to enter heaven will learn that their failure to feed the hungry condemns them to hell (Matthew 25). If we do not care for the needy brother or sister, God's love does not abide in us (1 John 3:17).

Jeremiah 22:13–19 describes good king Josiah and his wicked son Jehoiakim. When Jehoiakim became king, he built a fabulous palace by oppressing his workers. God sent the prophet Jeremiah to announce a terrible punishment. The most interesting part of the passage, however, is a short aside on this evil king's good father: "He defended the cause of the poor and needy, and so all went well. *'Is that not what it means to know me?'* declares the Lord" (v. 16; our italics). Knowing God is *inseparable* from caring for the poor. Of course, we dare not reduce knowing God only to a concern for the needy as some radical theologians do. We meet God in prayer, Bible study, worship—in many ways. But if we do not share God's passion to strengthen the poor, we simply do not know God in a biblical way.

All this biblical material clearly demonstrates that God and God's faithful people have a great concern for the poor. Earlier, we argued that God is partial to the poor, but not biased. God does not love the poor any more than the rich. God has an equal concern for the well-being of every single person. Most rich and powerful people, however, are genuinely biased; they care a lot more about themselves than about their poor neighbors. By contrast with the genuine bias of most people, God's lack of bias makes God appear biased. God cares equally for everyone.

How then is God "partial" to the poor? Because in concrete historical situations, equal concern for everyone requires special attention to specific people. In a family, loving parents do not provide equal tutorial time to a son struggling hard to scrape by with "D's" and a daughter easily making "A's." Precisely in order to be "impartial" and love both equally, they devote extra time to helping the more needy child. In historical situations (e.g., apartheid) where some people oppress others, God's lack of bias does not mean neutrality. Pre-

cisely because God loves all equally, God works against oppressors and actively sides with the oppressed.

We see this connection precisely in the texts that declare God's lack of bias: "For the Lord your God is God of gods and Lord of lords, the great, the almighty, the terrible God, who is not partial and takes no bribe. He executes justice for the fatherless and the widow, and loves the sojourner, giving him food and clothing" (Deut. 10:17–18). Justice and love are virtual synonyms in this passage. There is no suggestion that loving the sojourner is a benevolent, voluntary act different from a legal demand to do justice to the fatherless. Furthermore, there is no indication in the text that those needing food and clothing are poor because of some violation of due process such as fraud or robbery. The text simply says they are poor and therefore God, who is not biased, pays special attention to them.

Leviticus 19 is similar. In verse 15, the text condemns partiality: "You shall not be partial to the poor or defer to the great." The preceding verses refer to several of the Ten Commandments (stealing, lying, blasphemy [v. 11]). But special references to the poor are in the same passage. When harvesting their crops, God's people must leave the grain at the edge of the field and not pick up the grapes which fall in the vineyard: "You shall leave them for the poor and the alien" (v. 10). This is a divine command, not a suggestion for voluntary charity, and it is part of the same passage that declares God's lack of bias.[39]

Precisely because God is not biased he pays special attention to the poor. Consequently, an understanding of justice that reflects this biblical teaching must be concerned with more than procedural justice. Distributive justice which insists on special attention to the poor so they have opportunity to enjoy material well-being is also crucial.

Justice as Restoration to Community

Justice is restoration to community—and to the benefit rights necessary for dignified participation in community. Since persons are created for community, the Scriptures understand the good life as sharing in the essential aspects of social life. Therefore, justice includes restoration to community. Justice includes helping people return to the kind of life in community which God intends for them. Leviticus 25:35–36 describes the poor as being on the verge of falling out of the community because of their economic distress. "If members of your community become poor in that their power slips *with you*, you shall make them strong . . . that they may live *with you*" (Lev. 25:35–36 [our translation]). The word translated as "power" here is "hand" in the Hebrew. "Hand" *(yad)* metaphorically means "power."[40] The solution is for those who are able to correct the situation to do so and thereby restore the poor to community. The poor in fact are their own flesh or kin (Isa. 58:7). Poverty is a family affair.

In order to restore the weak to participation in community, the community's responsibility to its diminished members is "to make them strong" again (Lev. 25:35). This translation is a literal rendering of the Hebrew, which is the word "to be strong" and is found here in the causative (Hiphil) conjugation and therefore means "cause him to be strong." The purpose of this empowerment is "that they may live *beside you*" (v. 35, emphasis added). According to Psalm 107, God's steadfast love leads God to care for the hungry so they are able to "establish a town to live in; they sow fields and plant vineyards. . . . By his blessing they multiply greatly" (vv. 36–38, NRSV). Once more the hungry can be active, participating members of a community. The concern is for the whole person in community and what it takes to maintain persons in that relationship.

Community membership means the ability to share fully, within one's capacity and potential, in each essential aspect of community.[41] Participation in community has multiple dimensions. It includes participation in decision-making, social life, economic production, education, culture, and religion. Also essential are physical life itself and the material resources necessary for a decent life.

Providing the conditions for participation in community demands a focus on what are the basic needs for life in community. Achieving such justice includes access to the material essentials of life, such as food and shelter. It is God "who executes justice for the oppressed; who gives food to the hungry" (Ps. 146:7 NRSV). "The Lord . . . executes justice for the orphan and the widow and loves the strangers, providing them food and clothing" (Deut. 10:18, NRSV). "Food and clothing" is a Hebraism for what is indispensable.[42]

Job 24, one of the most powerful pictures of poverty in the Bible, describes the economic benefits that injustice takes away. Injustice starts with assault on the land, the basis of economic power (v. 2). It moves then to secondary means of production, the donkey and the ox (v. 3). As a result, the victims experience powerlessness and indignity: "They thrust the needy off the road; the poor of the earth all hide themselves" (v. 4, NRSV). The poor are separated from the bonds of community, wandering like wild donkeys in the desert (v. 5). They are denied basic needs of food (vv. 6, 10), drink (v. 11), clothing, and shelter (vv. 7, 10). Elsewhere in Job, failure to provide food for the needy is condemned as injustice.[43] Opportunity for everyone to have access to the material resources necessary for life in community is basic to the biblical concept of justice.

As we shall see at greater length in the following section, enjoying the benefit rights crucial to participation in community goes well beyond "welfare" or "charity." People in distress are to be empowered at the point where their participation in community has been undercut. That means restoring their productive capability. Therefore restoration of the land, the basic productive resource, is the way that Leviticus 25 commands the people to fulfill the call to "make them strong again" so "they may live beside you" in the land (v. 35). As the poor return to their land, they receive a new power and dignity that restores their participation in the community.

Other provisions in the Law also provide access to the means of production.[44] In the sabbatical laws, the lands remain fallow and unharvested so that the poor may eat" (Exod. 23: 10–11). The means of production were to be given over to the poor in entirety every seven years, recognizing, as Walter Rauschenbusch correctly noted,[45] that the entire community had rights in the land. We also see this general right of all the people to be fed from the land in the laws which allow people to eat grain or fruit as they walk through someone else's field or orchard (Deut. 23:24f.). Similarly, the farmer was not to go back over the first run of harvesting or to harvest to the very corners of the field, so that the poor could provide for themselves (Deut. 24:19–22; Lev. 19:9–10).

There are also restrictions on the processes which tear people down so that their "power slips" and they cannot support themselves. Interest on loans was prohibited; food to the poor was not to be provided at profit (Lev. 25:36f.). A means of production like a millstone was not to be taken as collateral on a loan because that would be "taking a life in pledge" (Deut. 24:6, RSV). If a poor person gave an essential item of clothing as a pledge, the creditor had to return it before night came (Exod. 22:26). All these provisions are restrictions on individual economic freedom that go well beyond merely preventing fraud, theft, and violence. The Law did, of course, support the rights of owners to benefit from their property, but the Law placed limits on the owners' control of property and on the quest for profit. The common good of the community outweighed unrestricted economic freedom.

The fact that justice in the Scriptures includes benefit rights[46] means that we must reject the concept of the purely negative state, which merely protects property, person, and equal access to the procedures of the community. That is by no means to deny that procedural justice is important. A person who is denied these protections is cut off from the political and civil community and is not only open to abuse, but is diminished in his or her ability to affect the life of the community. Procedural justice is essential to protect people from fraud, theft, and violence.

Biblical justice, however, also *includes positive rights*, which are the responsibility of the community to guarantee. Biblical justice has both an economic and a legal focus. The goal of justice is not primarily the recovery of the integrity of the legal system. It is the restoration of the community as a place where all live together in wholeness.

The wrong to which justice responds is not merely an illegitimate process (like stealing). What is wrong is also an end result in which people are deprived of basic needs. Leviticus 19:13 condemns both stealing and withholding a poor person's salary for a day: "You shall not defraud your neighbor; you shall not steal; and you shall not keep for yourself the wages of a laborer until morning." Isaiah 5:8–10 condemns those who buy up field after field until only the rich person is left dwelling alone in his big, beautiful house. Significantly, however, the prophet here does not denounce the acquisition of the land as illegal. Through legal foreclosing of mortgages or through rough debt bondage, the property could be taken within the law.[47] Isaiah nevertheless condemns the rulers for permitting this injustice to the weak. He appeals to social justice above the technicalities of current law. Restoration to community is central to justice.

From the biblical perspective, justice is both procedural and distributive. It demands both fair courts and fair economic structures. It includes both freedom rights and benefit rights. Precisely because of its equal concern for wholeness for everyone, it pays special attention to the needs of the weak and marginalized.

None of the above claims, however, offers a norm that describes the actual content of distributive justice. The next two sections seek to develop such a norm.

Equity as Adequate Access to Productive Resources

Equality has been one of the most powerful slogans of our century. But what does it mean? Does it mean equality before the law? One person, one vote? Equality of opportunity in education? Identical income shares? Or absolute identity as described in the satirical novel, *Facial Justice?*[48]

As we saw earlier, equality of economic results is not compatible with human freedom and responsibility. Free choices have consequences; therefore, when immoral decisions reduce someone's earning power, we should, other things being equal, consider the result just. Even absolute equality of opportunity is impossible unless we prevent parents from passing on any of their knowledge or other capital to their children.

So what definition of equality—or better, equity—do the biblical materials suggest?

Capital in an Agricultural Society

The biblical material on Israel and the land offers important clues about what a biblical understanding of equity would look like. The contrast between early Israel and surrounding societies was striking.[49] In Egypt, most of the land belonged to the Pharaoh or the temples. In most other Near-Eastern contexts a feudal system of landholding prevailed. The king granted large tracts of land, worked by landless laborers, to a small number of elite royal vassals. Only at the theological level did this feudal system exist in early Israel. Yahweh the King owned all the land and made important demands on those to whom he gave it to use. Under Yahweh, however, each family had their own land. Israel's ideal was decentralized family "ownership" understood as stewardship under Yahweh's absolute ownership. In the period of the judges, the pattern in Israel was, according to one scholar, "free peasants on small land holdings of equal size and apportioned by the clans."[50]

Land was the basic capital in early Israel's agricultural economy, and the Law says the land was divided in such a way that each extended family had the resources to produce the things needed for a decent life.

Joshua 18 and Numbers 26 contain the two most important accounts of the division of the land.[51] They represent Israel's social ideal with regard to the land. Originally, the land was divided among the clans of the tribes so that a relatively similar amount of land was available to all the family units. The larger tribes got a larger portion and the smaller tribes a smaller portion (Num. 26:54). By lot the land was further subdivided

among the protective association of families, and then (Joshua 18–19) among the extended families. The criterion of the division was thus equality, as is stated directly in Ezekiel's vision of a future time of justice. In this redistribution of the land, it is said to be divided "equally" (NRSV, literally, "each according to his brother," Ezek. 47:14). The concern, however, was not the implementation of an abstract ideal of equality, but the empowerment of all the people. Elie Munk, a French, Jewish Old Testament scholar, has summarized the situation this way: "The point of departure of the system of social economy of Judaism is the equal distribution of land among all its inhabitants."[52]

The concern for empowerment was not merely for the first generation but for all subsequent generations. Several institutions had the purpose of preserving a just distribution of the land. The *law of levirate* served to prevent the land from going out of the family line (Deut. 25:5). The provision for a *kinship redeemer* meant that when poverty forced someone to sell his land, a relative was to step in to purchase it for him (Lev. 25:25).

The picture of land ownership in the time of the judges suggests some approximation of equality of land ownership—at least up to the point where every family had enough to enjoy a decent, dignified life in the community if they acted responsibly. Albrecht Alt, a prominent Old Testament scholar, goes so far as to say that the prophets understood Yahweh's ancient regulation on property to be "one man—one house—one allotment of land."[53] Decentralized land ownership by extended families was the economic base for a relatively egalitarian society of small landowners and vinedressers in the time of the judges.[54]

The story of Naboth's vineyard (1 Kings 21) demonstrates the importance of each family's ancestral land. Frequent Old Testament references about not moving ancient boundary markers (e.g., Deut. 19:14; 27:17; Job 24:2; Prov. 22:28; Hos. 5:10) support the concept that Israel's ideal called for each family to have enough land so that they had the opportunity to acquire life's necessities.

"Necessities" is not to be understood as the minimum necessary to keep from starving. In the nonhierarchical, relatively egalitarian society of small farmers depicted above, families possessed resources to earn a living that would have been considered reasonable and acceptable, not embarrassingly minimal. That is not to suggest that every family had exactly the same income. It does mean, however, that every family had an equality of economic opportunity up to the point that they had the resources to earn a living that would enable them not only to meet minimal needs of food, clothing, and housing, but also to be respected participants in the community. Possessing their own land enabled each extended family to acquire the necessities for a decent life through responsible work.

The Year of Jubilee

Two astonishing biblical texts—Leviticus 25 and Deuteronomy 15—show how important this basic equality of opportunity was to God. The Jubilee text in Leviticus demanded that the land return to the original owners every fifty years. And Deuteronomy 15 called for the release of debts every seven years.

Leviticus 25 is one of the most radical texts in all of Scripture,[55] at least it seems that way to people committed either to communism or to unrestricted capitalism. Every fifty years, God said, the land was to return to the original owners. Physical handicaps, death of a breadwinner, or lack of natural ability may lead some families to become poorer than others. But God does not want such disadvantages to lead to ever-increasing extremes of wealth and poverty, with the result that the poor eventually lack the basic resources to earn a decent livelihood. God therefore gave his people a law to guarantee that no family would permanently lose its land. Every fifty years, the land returned to the original owners so that every family had enough productive resources to function as dignified, participating members of the community (Lev. 25:10–24). Private property was not abolished. Regularly, however, the means of producing wealth was to be equalized—up to the

point of every family having the resources to earn a decent living.

What is the theological basis for this startling command? Yahweh's ownership of everything is the presupposition. The land cannot be sold permanently because Yahweh owns it: "The land shall not be sold in perpetuity, for the land is mine; for you are strangers and sojourners with me" (Lev. 25:23).

God, the landowner, permits his people to sojourn on his good earth, cultivate it, eat its produce, and enjoy its beauty. But we are only stewards. Stewardship is one of the central theological categories of any biblical understanding of our relationship to the land and economic resources.[56]

Before and after the year of Jubilee, land could be "bought" or "sold." Actually, the buyer purchased a specific number of harvests, not the land itself (Lev. 25:16). And woe to the person who tried to get more than a just price for the intervening harvests from the date of purchase to the next Jubilee!

> If the years are many you shall increase the price, and if the years are few you shall diminish the price, for it is the number of the crops that he is selling to you. You shall not wrong one another, but you shall fear your God; for I am the Lord your God (Lev. 25:16–17, RSV).

Yahweh is Lord of all, even of economics. There is no hint here of a sacred law of supply and demand that operates independently of biblical ethics and the Lordship of Yahweh. The people of God should submit to God, and God demands economic justice among his people.

The assumption in this text that people must suffer the consequences of wrong choices is also striking. A whole generation or more could suffer the loss of ancestral land, but every fifty years the basic source of wealth would be returned so that each family had the opportunity to provide for its basic needs.

Verses 25–28 imply that this equality of opportunity is a higher value than that of absolute property rights. If a person became poor and sold his land to a more prosperous neighbor but then recovered enough to buy back his land before the Jubilee, the new owner was obligated to return it. The original owner's right to have his ancestral land to earn his own way is a higher right than that of the second owner to maximize profits.

This passage prescribes justice in a way that haphazard handouts by wealthy philanthropists never will. The year of Jubilee was an institutionalized structure that affected all Israelites automatically. It was the poor family's right to recover their inherited land at the Jubilee. Returning the land was not a charitable courtesy that the wealthy might extend if they pleased.[57]

Interestingly, the principles of Jubilee challenge both unrestricted capitalism and communism in a fundamental way. Only God is an absolute owner. No one else has absolute property rights. The right of each family to have the means to earn a living takes priority over a purchaser's "property rights" or a totally unrestricted market economy. At the same time, Jubilee affirms not only the right but the importance of property managed by families who understand that they are stewards responsible to God. This text does not point us in the direction of the communist model where the state owns all the land. God wants each family to have the resources to produce its own livelihood. Why? To strengthen the family (this is a very important "pro-family" text!); to give people the freedom to participate in shaping history; and to prevent the centralization of power—and the totalitarianism which almost always accompanies centralized ownership of land or capital by either the state or small elites.

One final aspect of Leviticus 25 is striking. It is more than coincidental that the trumpet blast announcing Jubilee sounded on the Day of Atonement (Lev. 25:9). Reconciliation with God is the precondition for reconciliation with brothers and sisters.[58] Conversely, genuine reconciliation with God leads inevitably to a transformation of all other relationships. Reconciled with God by the sacrifice on the Day of Atonement, the more prosperous Israelites were summoned to liberate the poor by freeing Hebrew slaves and by returning all land to the original owners.[59]

It is not clear from the historical books how much the people of Israel implemented the Jubilee.[60] Regardless of its antiquity or possible lack of implementation, however, Leviticus 25 remains a part of God's authoritative Word.

The teaching of the prophets about the land underlines the principles of Leviticus 25. In the tenth to the eighth centuries B.C., major centralization of landholding occurred. Poorer farmers lost their land, becoming landless laborers or slaves. The prophets regularly denounced the bribery, political assassination, and economic oppression that destroyed the earlier decentralized economy described above. Elijah condemned Ahab's seizure of Naboth's vineyard (1 Kings 21). Isaiah attacked rich landowners for adding field to field until they dwelt alone in the countryside because the smaller farmers had been destroyed (Isa. 5:8–9).

The prophets, however, did not merely condemn. They also expressed a powerful eschatological hope for a future day of justice when all would have their own land again. In the "latter days," the future day of justice and wholeness, "they shall all sit under their own vines and under their own fig trees" (Mic. 4:4; cf. also Zech. 3:10). No longer will the leaders oppress the people; instead they will guarantee that all people again enjoy their ancestral land (Ezek. 45:1–9, especially vv. 8–9).

In the giving of the land, the denunciation of oppressors who seized the land of the poor, and the vision of a new day when once again all will delight in the fruits of their own land and labor, we see a social ideal in which families are to have the economic means to earn their own way. A basic equality of economic opportunity up to the point that all can at least provide for their own basic needs through responsible work is the norm. Failure to act responsibly has economic consequences, so there is no assumption of equality. Central, however, is the demand that each family have the necessary capital (land) so that responsible stewardship will result in an economically decent life.[61]

The Sabbatical Year

God's law also provides for liberation of soil, slaves, and debtors every seven years. Again, the concern is justice for the poor and disadvantaged (as well as the well-being of the land). A central goal is to protect people against processes that would result in their losing their productive resources, or to restore productive resources after a time of loss.

Every seven years the land is to lie fallow (Exod. 23:10–11; Lev. 25:2–7).[62] The purpose, apparently, is both ecological and humanitarian. Not planting any crops every seventh year helps preserve the fertility of the soil. It also was God's way of showing his concern for the poor: "For six years you shall sow your land and gather in its yield; but the seventh year you shall let it rest and lie fallow, so that the poor of your people may eat" (Exod. 23:10–11). In the seventh year the poor were free to gather for themselves whatever grew spontaneously in the fields and vineyards.

Hebrew slaves also received their freedom in the sabbatical year (Deut. 15:12–18). Poverty sometimes forced Israelites to sell themselves as slaves to more prosperous neighbors (Lev. 25:39–40).[63] But this inequality and lack of property, God decrees, is not to be permanent. At the end of six years Hebrew slaves are to be set free. When they leave, masters are to share the proceeds of their joint labors with departing male slaves:

> And when you let him go free from you, you shall not let him go empty handed; you shall furnish him liberally out of your flock, out of your threshing floor, and out of your wine press; as the Lord your God has blessed you, you shall give to him (Deut. 15:13–14; see also Exod. 21:2–6).

As a consequence, the freed slave would again have some productive resources so he could earn his own way.[64]

The sabbatical provision on loans is even more surprising (Deut. 15:1–6) if, as some scholars think, the text calls for cancellation of debts every seventh year.[65] Yahweh even adds a footnote for those with a sharp eye for loopholes: it is sinful to refuse a loan to a poor person just because it is the sixth year and financial loss might occur in twelve months.

> Be careful that you do not entertain a mean thought, thinking, "The seventh year, the year of remission, is near," and therefore view your needy neighbor with hostility and give nothing; your neighbor might cry to the Lord against you, and you would incur guilt. Give liberally and be ungrudging when you do so, for on this account the Lord your God will bless you in all your work and in all that you undertake (vv. 9–10, NRSV).

If followed, this provision would have protected small landowners from the exorbitant interest of moneylenders and thereby helped prevent them from losing their productive resources.

As in the case of the year of Jubilee, this passage involves structured justice rather than mere charity. The sabbatical release of debts was an institutionalized mechanism to prevent the kind of economic divisions where a few people would possess all the capital while others had no productive resources. Deuteronomy 15 is both an idealistic statement of God's demand and also a realistic reference to Israel's sinful performance. Verse 4 promises that there will be no poor in Israel—*if* they obey all of God's commands! If the more wealthy had followed Deuteronomy 15, small landowners would have been far less likely to lose their productive resources. But God knew they would not attain that standard. Hence the recognition that poor people will always exist (v. 11). The conclusion, however, is not permission to ignore the needy because hordes of paupers will always exceed available resources. God commands precisely the opposite: "Since there will never cease to be some in need on the earth, I therefore command you, 'Open your hand to the poor and needy neighbor in your land'" (v. 11).

Jesus knew, and Deuteronomy implies, that sinful persons and societies will always produce poor people (Matt. 26:11). Rather than justifying neglect, however, God intends that this knowledge will be used by God's people as a reminder to show concern and to create structural mechanisms that promote justice.

The sabbatical year, unfortunately, was practiced only sporadically. Some texts suggest that failure to obey this law was one reason for the Babylonian exile (2 Chron. 36:20–21; Lev. 26:34–36).[66] Disobedience, however, does not negate God's demand. Institutionalized structures to prevent poverty are central to God's will for his people.

Does the biblical material offer a norm for distributive justice today? Some would argue that the biblical material on the land in Israel only applies to God's covenant community. But that is to ignore the fact that the biblical writers did not hesitate to apply revealed standards to persons and societies outside Israel. Amos announced divine punishment on the surrounding nations for their evil and injustice (Amos 1–2). Isaiah condemned Assyria for its pride and injustice (Isa. 10:12–19). The book of Daniel shows that God removed pagan kings like Nebuchadnezzar in the same way he destroyed Israel's rulers when they failed to show mercy to the oppressed (Daniel 4:27). God obliterated Sodom and Gomorrah no less than Israel and Judah because they neglected to aid the poor and feed the hungry. The Lord of history applies the same standards of social justice to all nations.

That does not mean, however, that we should try to apply the specific mechanisms of the Jubilee and the Sabbatical release to late-twentieth-century global market economies. It is the basic Paradigm that is normative for us today.

It would be silly to try to apply the specific mechanisms of the Jubilee and Sabbatical release of debts in today's world. Land, for example, has a very different function in an industrial economy. Appropriate application of these texts requires that we ask how their specific mechanisms functioned in Israelite culture, and then determine what specific measures would fulfill a similar function in our very different society. Since land in Israelite society represented productive power, we must identify the forms of productive power in modern societies. In an industrial society the primary productive power is the factory, and in an information society it is knowledge. Faithful application of these biblical texts in such societies means finding mechanisms that offer everyone the opportunity to share in the ownership of these productive resources. If we start with the Jubilee's call for everyone to enjoy access to productive power, we must criticize all socioeconomic arrangements where productive power is owned or controlled by only one class or group (whether bourgeois, aristocratic, or proletarian), or by a state or party oligarchy. Indeed, we saw that the prophets protested the development of a different economic system in which land ownership was shifted to a small group within society. And we must develop appropriate intervening processes in society to restore access to productive resources to everyone.

The central normative principle that emerges from the biblical material on the land and the sabbatical release of debts is this: *Justice demands that every person or family has access to the productive resources (land, money, knowledge) so they have the opportunity to earn a generous sufficiency of material necessities and be dignified participating members of their community.* This norm offers significant guidance for how to shape the economy so that people normally have the opportunity to earn their own way.

But what should be done for those—whether the able-bodied who experience an emergency or dependents such as orphans, widows, or the disabled—who for shorter or longer periods simply cannot provide basic necessities through their own efforts alone?

Generous Care for Those Who Cannot Care for Themselves

Again the biblical material is very helpful. Both in the Old Testament and the New Testament, we discover explicit teaching on the community's obligation to support those who cannot support themselves.

The Pentateuch commands at least five important provisions designed to help those who could not help themselves:[67]

1. The third year tithe goes to poor widows, orphans, and sojourners as well as to the Levites (Deut. 14:28–29; 26:12).
2. Laws on gleaning stipulated that the corners of the grain fields and the sheaves and grapes

that dropped were to be left for the poor, especially widows, orphans, and sojourners (Lev. 19:9–10; Deut. 24:19–21).

3. Every seventh year, fields must remain fallow, and the poor may reap the natural growth (Exod. 23:10–11; Lev. 25:1–7).

4. A zero-interest loan must be available to the poor, and if the balance is not repaid by the sabbatical year, it is forgiven (Exod. 22:25; Lev. 25:35–38; Deut. 15:1–11).

5. Israelites who become slaves to repay debts go free in the seventh year (Lev. 25:47–53; Exod. 21:1–11; Deut. 15:12–18). And when the freed slaves leave, their temporary "master" must provide liberally, giving the former slaves cattle, grain, and wine (Deut. 15:14) so they can again earn their own way.

In his masterful essay on this topic, John Mason argues that the primary assistance to the able-bodied person was probably the no-interest loan. This would maintain the family unit, avoid stigmatizing people unnecessarily, and require work so that long-term dependency did not result.

Dependent poor, such as widows and orphans, received direct "transfer payments" through the third-year tithe. But other provisions, such as those on gleaning, required the poor to work for the "free" produce they gleaned. The widow Ruth, for example, labored in the fields to feed herself and her mother-in-law (Ruth 2:1–23).

It is important to note the ways that the provisions for helping the needy point to what we now call "civil society." Not only did Ruth and other poor folk have to glean in the fields; more wealthy landowners had responsibilities to leave the corners of the fields and the grapes that dropped. And in the story of Ruth, Boaz, as the next of kin, took responsibility for her well-being (chapters 3, 4).

The texts seem to assume a level of assistance best described as "sufficiency for need"—"with a fairly liberal interpretation of need."[68] Deuteronomy 15:8 specifies that the poor brother receive a loan "large enough to meet the need." Frequently, God commands those with resources to treat their poor fellow Israelites with the same liberality that God showed them at the exodus, in

the wilderness, and in giving them their own land (Exod. 22:21; Lev. 25:38; Deut. 24:18, 22). God wanted those who could not care for themselves to receive a liberal sufficiency for need offered in a way that encouraged work and responsibility, strengthened the family, and helped the poor return to self-sufficiency.

Were those "welfare provisions" part of the law to be enforced by the community? Or were they merely suggestions for voluntary charity?[69] The third-year tithe was gathered in a central location (Deut. 14:28) and then shared with the needy. Community leaders would have to act together to carry out such a centralized operation. In the Talmud, there is evidence that the proper community leaders had the right to demand contributions.[70] Nehemiah 5 deals explicitly with violations of these provisions on loans to the poor. The political leader calls an assembly, brings "charges against the nobles," and commands that the situation be corrected (Neh. 5:7; cf. all of 1–13). Old Testament texts often speak of the "rights" or "cause" of the poor. Since these terms have clear legal significance,[71] they support the view that the provisions we have explored for assisting the poor would have been legally enforceable. "The clear fact is that the provisions for the impoverished were part of the Mosaic legislation, as much as other laws such as those dealing with murder and theft. Since nothing in the text allows us to consider them as different, they must be presumed to have been legally enforceable."[72]

The sociopolitical situation is dramatically different in the New Testament. The early church is a tiny religious minority with very few political rights in a vast pagan Roman empire. But within the church, the standard is the same. Acts 2:43–47 and 4:32–37 record dramatic economic sharing in order to respond to those who could not care for themselves. The norm? "Distribution was made to each as any had need" (Acts 4:35). As a result, "there was not a needy person among them" (v. 34).

The great evangelist Paul spent much of his time over several years collecting an international offering for the impoverished Christians in

Jerusalem (2 Cor. 8–9). For his work, he found a norm (2 Cor. 8:13–15)—equality of basic necessities—articulated in the exodus story of the manna, where every person ended up with "as much as each of them needed" (Exod. 16:18; NRSV).[73]

Throughout the Scriptures we see the same standard. When people cannot care for themselves, their community must provide a liberal sufficiency so that their needs are met.

A Role for Government

Thus far we have seen that the biblical paradigm calls for an economic order where all who are able to work enjoy access to appropriate productive resources so they can be creative co-workers with God, create wealth to bless their family and neighbors, and be dignified participating members of their community. For those who cannot care for themselves, the biblical framework demands generous assistance so that everyone has a liberal sufficiency of basic necessities.

But what role should government play?[74] Certainly government does not have sole responsibility. Other institutions, including the family, the church, the schools, and business, have crucial obligations.

At different points in the biblical text it is clear that the family has the first obligation to help needy members. In the great text on the Jubilee in Leviticus 25, the first responsibility to help the poor person forced by poverty to sell land belongs to the next of kin in the extended family (Lev. 25:25, 35). But the poor person's help does not end with the family. Even if there are no family members to help, the poor person has the legal right to get his land back at the next Jubilee (25:28). Similarly, 1 Timothy 5:16 insists that a Christian widow's relatives should be her first means of support. Only when the family cannot, should the church step in. Any policy or political philosophy that immediately seeks governmental solutions for problems that could be solved just as well or better at the level of the family violates the biblical framework which stresses the central societal role of the family.

But is there a biblical basis for those who seek to exclude government almost completely from the field of the economy? Not at all. The state is not some evil to be endured like an appendectomy.[75] According to Romans 13, the state is a gift from God designed for our good. Hence John Calvin denounced those who regarded magistrates "only as a kind of necessary evil." Calvin called civil authority "the most honorable of all callings in the whole life" of mortal human beings; its function among human beings is "no less than that of bread, water, sun, and air."[76]

Government is an aspect of community and is inherent in human life as an expression of our created social nature. This perspective is contrary to the social contract theory at the base of liberal political philosophy, in which warring individuals put aside their independent existence by contracting to have a society to whose government, when formed, they transfer their individual rights. Governmental action to empower the poor is one way we implement the truth that economic justice is a family affair.

Sin also makes government intervention in the economy necessary. When selfish, powerful people deprive others of their rightful access to productive resources, the state rightly steps in with intervening power to correct the injustice. When other individuals and institutions in the community do not or cannot provide basic necessities for the needy, government rightly helps.

Frequently, of course, the state contributes to social cohesion by encouraging and enabling other institutions in the community—whether family, church, non-governmental social agencies, guilds, or unions[77]—to carry out their responsibilities to care for the economically dependent. Sometimes, however, the depth of social need exceeds the capacity of non-governmental institutions. When indirect approaches are not effective in restraining economic injustice or in providing care for those who cannot care for themselves, the state must act directly to demand patterns of justice and provide vital services.

The objective of the state is not merely to maintain an equilibrium of power in society. Its purpose is not merely to enable other groups in the society to carry out their tasks. The state has a positive responsibility to foster justice. The nature of justice defines the work of government so fundamentally that any statement of the purpose of government must depend upon a proper definition of justice.

That is why our whole discussion of the biblical paradigm on the economic components of justice is so important. "The Lord has made you king to execute justice and righteousness" (1 Kings 10:9; cf. Jer. 22:15–16). These two key words *(justice* and *righteousness)*, as we have seen, refer not only to fair legal systems but also to just economic structures.

The positive role of government in advancing economic justice is seen in the biblical materials which present the ideal monarch. Both the royal psalms and the Messianic prophecies develop the picture of this ideal ruler.

Psalm 72 (a royal psalm) gives the following purpose for the ruler: "May he defend the cause of the poor of the people, give deliverance to the needy, and crush the oppressor" (v. 4, NRSV). This task is identified as the work of justice (vv. 1–3, 7), and, in this passage, justice includes using power to deliver the needy and oppressed.

According to Psalm 72 there are oppressors of the poor, separate from the state, who need to be crushed. State power, despite its dangers, is necessary for society because of the evil power of such exploiting groups. "On the side of the oppressors there was power," Ecclesiastes 4:1 declares. Without governmental force to counter such oppressive power, there is "no one to comfort" (Eccles. 4:1). Whether it is the monarch or the village elders (Amos 5:12, 15), governmental power should deliver the economically weak and guarantee the "rights of the poor" (Jer. 22:15–16; also Pss. 45:4–5; 101:8; Jer. 21:12).

Prophecies about the coming Messianic ruler also develop the picture of the ideal ruler. "With righteousness he shall judge the poor, and decide with equity for the meek of the earth; he shall smite the earth with the rod of his mouth, and with the breath of his lips he shall kill the wicked" (Isa. 11:4, NRSV).

This ideal ruler will take responsibility for the needs of the people as a shepherd: "He shall feed them and be their shepherd" (Ezek. 34:23). Ezekiel 34:4 denounces the failure of the shepherds (i.e., the rulers) of Israel to "feed" the people. Then in verses 15–16, the same phrases are repeated to describe God's promise of justice:

"I will make them lie down," says the LORD God. "I will seek the lost, and I will bring back the strayed, and I will bind up the injured, and I will strengthen the weak, but the fat and the strong I will destroy. I will feed them in justice" (NRSV).

This promise will be fulfilled by the coming Davidic ruler (vv. 23–24). Similarly in Isaiah 32:1–8, the promised just and wise monarch is contrasted to the fool who leaves the hungry unsatisfied (v. 6).

This teaching on the role of government applies not just to Israel but to government everywhere. The ideal monarch was to be a channel of God's justice (Ps. 72:1), and God's justice extends to the whole world (e.g., Ps. 9:7–9). All legitimate rulers are instituted by God and are God's servants for human good (Rom. 13:1, 4). In this passage, Paul states a positive reason for government (government acts "for your good" [v. 4]) before he specifies its negative function ("to execute wrath on the wrongdoer" [v. 4]). Romans 13 is structurally similar to Psalm 72:1 in viewing the ruler as a channel of God's authority. All people everywhere can pray with the Israelites: "Give the king thy justice, O God" (Ps. 72:1).

Daniel 4:27 shows that the ideal of the monarch as the protector of the weak has universal application. God summons the Babylonian monarch no less than the Israelite king to bring "justice and . . . mercy to the oppressed." Similarly in Proverbs 31:9, King Lemuel (generally considered to be a northern Arabian monarch) is to "defend the rights of the poor and needy" (NRSV). "The general obligation of the Israelite king to see that persons otherwise not adequately protected or provided for should enjoy fair treatment in judicial proceedings and should receive the daily necessities of life is evidently understood as the duty of all kings."[78]

The teaching on the ideal just monarch of Israel, whether in royal psalms or Messianic prophecies, cannot be restricted to some future Messianic reign. God demanded that the kings of Israel provide in their own time what the Messianic ruler would eventually bring more completely: namely, that justice which delivers the needy from oppression. God's concern in the present and in the future, within Israel and outside of Israel, is that there be a community in which the weak are strengthened and protected from their foes.

Conclusion

The traditional criterion of distributive justice which comes closest to the biblical paradigm is distribution according to needs.[79] Guaranteeing basic needs for life in community becomes more important than the criteria which are central in many worldly systems: worth, birth, social contribution, might and ability, or contract.

Some of the other criteria of distributive justice are at least assumed in the biblical approach.

Achievement (e.g., ability in the market so stressed in Western culture) has a legitimate role. It must be subordinate, however, to the central criterion of distribution according to needs for the sake of inclusion in community.

The biblical material provides at least two norms pertaining to distribution of resources to meet basic needs.

1. Normally, all people who can work should have access to the productive resources so that, if they act responsibly, they can produce or purchase an abundant sufficiency of all that is needed to enjoy a dignified, healthy life in community.

2. Those who cannot care for themselves should receive from their community a liberal sufficiency of the necessities of life provided in ways that preserve dignity, encourage responsibility, and strengthen the family.

Those two norms are modest in comparison with some ideals presented in the name of equality. A successful effort to implement them, however, would require dramatic change, both in the U.S. and in every nation on earth.

Notes

1. We want to thank two graduate assistants, Joan and Chris Hoppe-Spink, who helped to gather materials and proofread.

2. See further Ronald J. Sider, "Toward an Evangelical Political Philosophy. *Transformation* (July–September 1997): 1–10; and for a brief discussion of the use of a biblical paradigm, Christopher J. H. Wright, "The Use of the Bible in Social Ethics," *Transformation* (January–March 1984): 10.

3. Julius Gould quoted in J. Philip Wogaman, *The Great Economic Debate: An Ethical Analysis* (Philadelphia: Westminster, 1997), 10.

4. See, for example, John Courtney Murray, *We Hold These Truths: Catholic Reflections on the American Proposition* (Kansas City: Sheed and Ward, 1960). J. Budziszewski has recently published a more popular statement: *Written on the Heart: The Case for Natural Law* (Downers Grove, Ill.: InterVarsity Press, 1997).

5. John Paul II, *Laborem exercens*, Section 13.

6. Hans Walter Wolff, *Anthropology of the Old Testament* (Philadelphia: Fortress, 1974), 29. *Flesh* here represents human beings in relationship and solidarity with others.

7. Cf. also Ecclesiastes 4:8.

8. Richard J. Mouw, *Political Evangelism* (Grand Rapids: Eerdmans, 1973), 45.

9. Thomas Aquinas, *Summa Theologiae*, 2a2ae. 66, 2, 7 in Aquinas, *Selected Political Writings*, ed. D'Entrèves (Oxford: Blackwell, 1948), 169, 171; cf. 1a2ae. 94, 5, 127.

10. *Economic Justice for All: Pastoral Letters on Catholic Social Teaching and the U.S. Economy* (Washington: National Conference of Catholic Bishops, 1986), section 64, 34.

11. Wogaman, *Great Economic Debate*, 43.

12. See, for example, James W. Skillen, *Recharging the American Experiment: Principled Pluralism for Genuine Civic Community* (Grand Rapids: Baker, 1994), especially chapter 4.

13. One should not interpret the parable to refer exclusively to material wealth. It calls people to use their gifts and resources creatively and boldly to advance God's reign—which, of course, includes material well-being.

14. See further, Stephen Charles Mott, *A Christian Perspective on Political Thought* (New York: Oxford University Press, 1993), chapter 1.

15. Max Weber, *Economy and Society: An Outline of Interpretative Sociology*, 4th ed., ed. G. Roth and C. Wittick (New York: Bedminster, 1968), II, 926.

16. For this perspective on power in the writings of Paul Tillich and James Luther Adams, cf., for example, Paul Tillich, *Love, Power and Justice: Ontological Analyses and Ethical Applications* (New York: Oxford University, 1954), esp. 35–53; Adams, "Theological Bases of Social Action," in James Luther Adams, *Taking Time Seriously* (Glencoe, Ill.: Free Press, 1957), esp. 42, 50.

17. Aristotle stated that all people do what they wish if they have the power (*Politics* 1312b3, cf. 1313b32).

18. John Calvin, *The Harmony of the Last Four Books of Moses*, 8th Commandment, on Deut. 15:1, following the translation of Harro Höpfl, *The Christian Polity of John Calvin* (Cambridge: Cambridge University, Studies in the History and Theory of Politics, 1982), 158. *Mediocrem* would seem to mean here "avoiding the extremes."

19. Rahner correctly sees this use of power as justified as the consequence of the sin to which it answers. Karl Rahner, "The Theology of Power," in Karl Rahner, *Theological Investigations* (Baltimore: Helicon, 1966), 4.395.

20. Paul Tillich, "Shadow and Substance: A Theory of Power" (1965), in Paul Tillich, *Political Expectation*, ed. J. L. Adams (New York: Harper, 1971), 118.

21. Martin Luther King, Jr., *Where Do We Go from Here: Chaos or Community?* (Boston: Beacon, 1967), 37.

22. John Goldingay, "The Man of War and the Suffering Servant," *Tyndale Bulletin* 27 (1976): 84.

23. Exodus 15:6, 12 in light of v. 9. Justice as deliverance from exploitative power is seen also in 2 Sam. 18:31: "The Lord has given you justice this day from the power of all who rose up against you." The word often translated as "deliverance" in English (e.g., the NIV in this verse) is the Hebrew word for "doing justice."

24. E. Calvin Beisner, *Prosperity and Poverty: The Compassionate Use of Resources in a World of Scarcity* (Westchester, Ill.: Crossway Books, 1988), 54.

25. Carl F. H. Henry, *Aspects of Christian Social Ethics* (Grand Rapids: Eerdmans, 1964), 160.

26. See also William Frankena, "The Concept of Social Justice," in *Social Justice*, ed. R. Brandt (Englewood Cliffs, N.J.: Prentice Hall, 1962), 18–21.

27. Cf. further Mott, *A Christian Perspective on Political Thought*, 77–78.

28. Our translation.

29. See also Isa. 30:18; Jer. 9:24; Hos. 2:19; 12:6; Mic. 6:8.

30. Our translation. Cf. also Pss. 40:10; 43:1–2; 65:6; 71:1–2, 24; 72:1–4; 116:5–6; 119:123; Isa. 45:8; 46:12–13; 59:11, 17; 61:10; 62:1–2; 63:7–8 (LXX); and frequently "deliver": Pss. 31:1; 37:28, 40.

31. Cf. Job 29:12, 14; Prov. 24:11.

32. "Triumphs" in the NRSV translates the word for "justice" in the plural—i.e., "acts of justice" (cf. the NIV, "righteous acts").

33. Cf. Psalms 107; 113:7–9.

34. Literally! See the collection (about two hundred pages of biblical texts) in Ronald J. Sider, *For They Shall Be Fed* (Dallas: Word, 1997).

35. Cf. Norman H. Snaith, *The Distinctive Ideas of the Old Testament* (London: Epworth, 1944), 68, 71–72; James H. Cone, *God of the Oppressed* (New York: Seabury, 1975), 70–71.

36. This is not to ignore the fact that there are many causes of poverty—including laziness and other sinful choices (see Sider, *Rich Christians in an Age of Hunger* [Downers Grove, Ill.: InterVarsity Press, 1977], chap. 6). God wants people who are poor because of their own sinful choices to repent and be changed by the power of the Holy Spirit.

37. Ps. 72:1–4; Prov. 31:8–9; Isa. 1:10, 17, 23, 26; Jer. 22:2–3, 14–15; Dan. 4:27.

38. The following section is adapted from Ronald J. Snider, *Genuine Christianity* (Grand Rapids: Zondervan, 1996), 137–41.

39. See further, Stephen Charles Mott, "The Partiality of Biblical Justice," *Transformation* (January–March, 1993): 24.

40. Hans Walter Wolff, *Anthropology of the Old Testament* (Philadelphia: Fortress, 1974), 68. The NIV translates: ". . . becomes poor and is unable to support himself. . . ."

41. Rights are the privileges of membership in the communities to which we belong; cf. Max L. Stackhouse, *Creeds, Society, and Human Rights: A Study in Three Cultures* (Grand Rapids: Eerdmans, 1984), 5, 44, 104–5.

42. C. Spicq, *Les Épîtres Pastorales, Études Bibliques* (Paris: Gabalda, 1969), 190 (on 1 Tim. 6:8).

43. See also Job 22, where injustice includes sins of omission—i.e., failure to provide drink for the weary and bread for the hungry (v. 7; cf. 31:17), as well as the exploitative use of economic power (v. 6a). In 31:19 the omission is failure to provide clothing. Cf. the important modern statement of benefit rights by Pope John Paul XXIII, in his encyclical *Pacem in Terris*, where he says that each person has the right "to the means necessary for the proper development of life, particularly food, clothing, shelter, medical card, rest, and finally, the necessary social services." Pope John XXIII, *Pacem in Terris, 11*, in *Papal Encyclicals, Vol. 5: 1958–1981*, ed. C. Carlen (n.p. Consortium, 1981), 108.

44. See further, Stephen Mott, "The Contribution of the Bible to Economic Thought," *Transformation* (June–September/October–December, 1987): 31.

45. Walter Rauschenbusch, *Christianity and the Social Crisis* (Boston: Pilgrim 1907), 20.

46. Those who resist the recognition of economic rights sometimes argue from a distinction of a *justice proper* from a *general justice* which is voluntary. The economic materials of the Bible are then said to belong to the latter (see, for instance, the writings of Ronald H. Nash [e.g., *Freedom, Justice and the State* (Lanham, Md.: University Press of America, 1980), 37, 75.]). The confinement of economic responsibility to a general, voluntary statement of social obligation does not hold up before the biblical materials. Distributive justice in its specific or proper sense of deciding between conflicting claims about

the distribution of social benefits is involved in passages such as Jeremiah 5:28: "They judge not with justice the cause of the fatherless, to make it prosper, and they do not defend the rights (*mispat*) of the needy."

Another objection to our discussion of benefit rights comes from theonomists who argue that the kinds of texts we have used are not part of the civil law because no sanctions are provided. This objection misses the paradigmatic, and thus incomplete, nature of biblical law (Deut. 14:28). Furthermore, civil apparatus is provided for the third-year tithe in that it is to be stored in a central place, in the towns (Deut. 14:28). Micah 2:4–5, with its references to measuring and dividing the allotment of the land and casting the lot, is a prediction of a future redistribution of the land by Yahweh in which the *latifundia* of the aristocracy in Jerusalem will be ended. This new distribution will be administered by "the assembly of Yahweh" (Albrecht Alt, "Micha 2, 1–5 G's Anadasmos in Judah," in Albrecht Alt, *Kleine Schriften zur Geschichte des Volkes Israel*, Vol. 3 [Munich: Beck, 1959], 374). Theonomist theory also does not correspond to actual biblical practice (e.g., Nehemiah's enforcement of the prohibition on interest and of tithes for the Levites despite the lack of civil apparatus for these provisions in the Law [Neh. 5:7; 11:23; 12:44–47; 13:10–14]). What is decisive against the effort to remove benefit rights from justice proper is that the justice required of the ruler has the same characteristics as that required elsewhere. Justice involves deliverance. "May he defend the cause of the poor of the people, give deliverance to the needy, and crush the oppressor!" (Ps. 72:4).

47. Eryl W. Davies, *Prophesy and Ethics: Isaiah and the Ethical Traditions of Israel* (Sheffield, *Journal for the Study of the Old Testament, Supplement Series 16* [1981]), 69, 116.

48. Leslie Poles Hartley, *Facial Justice* (Hamish Hamilton, 1960).

49. See Roland de Vaux, *Ancient Israel: Its Life and Institutions*, trans. John McHugh (London: Darton, Longman, and Todd, 1961), I, 164.

50. H. Eberhard von Waldow, "Social Responsibility and Social Structure in Early Israel," *Catholic Biblical Quarterly 32* (1970): 195.

51. See the discussion and the literature cited in Mott, *Biblical Ethics and Social Change*, 65–66; and Stephen Charles Mott, "Egalitarian Aspects of the Biblical Theory of Justice," in the *American Society of Christian Ethics, Selected Papers 1978*, ed. Max Stackhouse (Newton, Mass.: American Society of Christian Ethics, 1978), 8–26.

52. Elie Munk, *La Justice sociale en Israël* (Boudry, Switzerland: Baconnière, 1948), 75.

53. Albrecht Alt, "Micah 2:1–5 G's Anadasmos in Juda," *Kleine Schriften zur Geschichte des Volkes Israel* III (Munich: C. H. Beck, 1959), 374.

54. In this study of early Israel, Norman Gottwald concluded that Israel was "an egalitarian, extended-family, segmentary tribal society with an agricultural-pastoral economic base ... characterized by profound resistance and opposition to the forms of political domination and social stratification that had become normative in the chief cultural and political centers of the ancient Near East." *The Tribes of Yahweh: A Sociology of the Religion of Liberated Israel 1250–1050 B.C.E.* (London: SCM Press, 1979), 10.

55. For a survey of the literature on Leviticus 25, see R. Gnuse, "Jubilee Legislation in Leviticus: Israel's Vision of Social Reform," *Biblical Theological Bulletin 15* (1983): 43–48.

56. See the excellent book edited by Loren Wilkinson, *Earthkeeping: Christian Stewardship of Natural Resources*, 2nd ed. (Grand Rapids: Eerdmans, 1980), esp. 232–37.

57. See in this connection the fine article by Paul G. Schrotenboer, "The Return of Jubilee," *International Reformed Bulletin* (fall 1973): 19ff., esp. pp. 23–24.

58. See also Eph. 2:13–18. Marc H. Tanenbaum points out the significance of the day of atonement in "Holy Year 1975 and Its Origins in the Jewish Jubilee Year," *Jubilaeum* (1974): 64.

59. For the meaning of the word *liberty* in Lev. 25:10, see Martin Noth, *Leviticus* (Philadelphia: Westminster, 1975), 187: "Deror, a 'liberation' ... is a feudal word from the Accadian (an)duraru—'freeing from burdens.'"

60. The only other certain references to it are in Lev. 27:16–25; Num. 36:4; and Ezek. 46:17. It would be exceedingly significant if one could show that Isa. 61:1–2 (which Jesus cited to outline his mission in Luke 4:18–19) also refers to the year of Jubilee. De Vaux doubts that Isa. 61:1 refers to the Jubilee (*Ancient Israel*, 1:176). The same word, however, is used in Isa. 61:1 and Lev. 25:10. See John H. Yoder's argument in *Politics of Jesus* (Grand Rapids: Eerdmans, 1972), 64–77; see also Robert Sloan, *The Acceptable Year of the Lord* (Austin: Scholar Press, 1977); and Donald W. Blosser, "Jesus and the Jubilee" (Ph.D. diss., University of St. Andrews, 1979). Sharon H. Ringe, *Jesus, Liberation, and the Biblical Jubilee* (Philadelphia: Fortress, 1985), 36–45, supports Luke 4:18–19 as a Jubilee text.

61. On the centrality of the land in Israel's self-understanding, see further Christopher J. H. Wright, *An Eye for an Eye: The Place of Old Testament Ethics Today* (Downers Grove, Ill.: InterVarsity Press, 1983), esp. chaps. 3 and 4. Walter Brueggemann's *The Land* (Philadelphia: Fortress Press, 1977), is also a particularly important work on this topic.

62. De Vaux, *Ancient Israel*, 1:173–75.

63. Leviticus 25 seems to provide for emancipation of slaves only every fiftieth year.

64. See Jeremiah 34 for a fascinating account of God's anger at Israel for their failure to obey this command.

65. Some modern commentators think that Deuteronomy 15:1–11 provides for a one-year suspension of repayment of loans rather than an outright remission of them. See, for example, C. J. H. Wright, *God's People in God's Land* (Grand Rapids: Eerdmans, 1990), 148, and S. R. Driver, *Deuteronomy*, International Critical Commentary, 3rd ed. (Edinburgh: T. And T. Clark, 1895), 179–80. But Driver's argument is basically that remission would have been *impractical*. He admits that verse 9 seems to point toward remission of loans. So too Gerhard von Rad, *Deuteronomy* (Philadelphia: Westminster, 1966), 106.

66. See de Vaux, *Ancient Israel* 1:174–75, for discussion of the law's implementation. In the Hellenistic period, there is clear evidence that it was put into effect.

67. See especially John Mason's excellent article, "Assisting the Poor: Assistance Programmes in the Bible," *Transformation* (April–June, 1987): 1–14.

68. Ibid., 7.

69. See *Ibid.*, 8, for some examples; cf. also the earlier discussion of Beisner and Henry.

70. Ibid., 9.

71. Mason (p. 14, n. 39) comments: "Two Hebrew words are used for 'rights' or 'cause': the predominant word is *mishpat*, which is used elsewhere to refer to the laws and judgments of God; at Ps. 140:12 (with *mishpat*), Prov. 29:7; 31:9; and Jer. 22:16 the word is *din* and means most likely 'righteous judgment' or 'legal claim'" (TDOT v. III, 190–91; TWOT v. 11, 752–55, 947–49).

72. Ibid., 9.

73. For a much longer discussion of both the passages in Acts and Paul's collection, see Sider, *Rich Christians in an Age of Hunger*, 79–89.

74. Other chapters will deal at greater length with this question. Here we want only to address the question as it relates directly to economic justice.

75. Ronald H. Nash, *Freedom, Justice and the State* (Lanham, Md.: University Press of America, 1980), 27.

76. John Calvin, *Institutes of the Christian Religion*, ed. J. McNeill (Philadelphia: Westminster, 1960), 4.20.3, 4, 22 (pp. 1488, 1490, 1510); cf. Höpfl, *The Christian Polity of John Calvin*, 44–46. Similarly for Luther, government is an inestimable blessing of God and one of God's best gifts; cf. W. D. J. Cargill Thompson, *The Political Thought of Martin Luther*, ed. P. Broadhead (Sussex: Harvester, 1984), 66.

77. The state molds the process of mutual support among the groups; Reinhold Niebuhr, *The Nature and Destiny of Man, Vol. 2: Human Destiny* (New York: Scribner's, 1964), 266.

78. Meredith G. Kline, *Kingdom Prologue* (Hamilton, Mass.: Meredith G. Kline, 1983), 34, citing Daniel 4:27 in support.

79. We insist, of course, as the previous discussion shows and the next two paragraphs indicate, on important qualifications to "distribution according to need." The able-bodied must work to earn their own way and bad choices rightly have negative economic consequences. At the same time, of course, we recognize that bad choices are frequently rooted both in unfair structures and emotional and spiritual needs.

Questions for Discussion:

1. How do you think biblical mandates such as the year of Jubilee and the Sabbatical Year apply today? Do they apply at all? If so, how?

2. Which basis for distributive justice comes closest in your view, to the biblical teaching? Is it need-based, merit-based, or some combination of other factors?

3. How do you respond to the authors' assertion that "God is on the side of the poor?" Do you think God has a special concern for the poor and vulnerable? Why or why not?

CASE STUDIES

Case 5.1: Downsizing: Efficiency or Corporate Hit Men?

As CEO of your company, you are responsible to the shareholders to produce a reasonable rate of return on their investment. Your industry is exceptionally competitive, and you are constantly looking for ways to reduce your costs. The most effective ways to do so involve taking advantage of your size in the market to drive down costs charged by your suppliers and reducing the size of your workforce. Salaries are by far the largest percentage of your costs. In some cases, mergers can help the company to force lower costs for supplies because the company is now larger, and it can help reduce salaries by eliminating overlapping positions. But at times you realize that you simply must lay off workers. This is particularly true when you experience a downturn in business, as you have observed of some of your colleagues in industries such as aerospace, where layoffs are a regular occurrence. There is little debate over layoffs when business is struggling, but you are now reviewing the possibility of laying off roughly 5 percent of your workforce for a variety of reasons that include pressure from Wall Street to show better earnings in the next year, moving some operations overseas to take advantage of lower wage rates, and a desire to keep your operation as lean as you can.

At present your company is doing well, though Wall Street thinks it can do better in the next year. You realize that the company is not struggling, not in survival mode, and layoffs are not necessary to keep the company from going out of business. As word gets out in the community that layoffs are being discussed, you are aware of criticism from community leaders who fear that people are going to be put out of work needlessly. Some even charge the company with allegations of greed and caring more for profit than for people. Critics also point out that you took a sizable bonus home at the end of last year and will likely get another one this year based on the company's performance. They wonder about the fairness of your bonus and the need to lay off workers. As a Christian, you are very sensitive to these criticisms, and you wonder about the tension between being fair to both your shareholders and your employees.

Sources: John Rothchild, "The Invisible Hand," *Worth* (June 1996): 87–92; Harry J. Van Buren, "Acting More Generously than the Law Requires: The Issue of Employee Layoffs in *Halakah*," *Journal of*

Business Ethics 19 (1999): 335–43; Allan Sloan, "The Hit Men," *Time*, 26 February 1996, 44–48.

Questions for Discussion:

1. Do you think the company would be doing anything unethical by laying off workers in this case? Do you think the charges of greed are fair? Defend your answers.
2. Is there a moral difference between a company that cuts jobs and transfers operations overseas in order to survive and a company that transfers operations overseas in order to increase its existing profit margin? Why or why not?
3. Who should bear the costs of helping displaced workers find new jobs and acquire new skills—the individual, the company, or the community? Or should it be a combination of the three? If a combination, who do you think should shoulder the major share of the cost?
4. Do you think there is such a thing as a "right to a job"? Why or why not? If you think people have such a right, how does that affect your view of the layoffs being considered in this case?

Case 5.2: Executive Compensation: Out of Control or Market Appropriate?

You are serving on the compensation committee for a large, publicly traded company. You have been on the board of the company for some time but are serving on the compensation committee for the first year. Your job as a committee is to evaluate the performance of the CEO and other top executives and make a recommendation for their salary and bonuses for the upcoming year. You have a recommendation from the compensation consultant, who has been hired by the company's management to assist them and the board in setting competitive compensation levels for the executive team. Over the past year, the company's earnings have been rather flat, and the stock price has been basically unchanged. You know that CEOs around the industry are paid in small part salary and large part stock options, which tie the CEOs compensation to his or her performance.

For some time, you have been concerned about the way CEO pay has spiraled. In your view, it is out of control, but you also realize that good CEOs are rare and that if they increase the shareholders' value, then they should be paid in accordance with their performance. You have heard of CEOs who already own the bulk of their company's stock being granted millions more stock options, and you look at the total amount of compensation in the hundreds of millions per year for top-paid CEOs, even when their companies are performing poorly. In fact, you have noticed that when the company's stock does not do well, CEOs are given that much more in terms of stock options to offset the stock's poor performance. And when a CEO is fired, usually the new one is paid more than the departing one.

> *Sources*: Geoffrey Colvin, "The Great CEO Pay Heist," *Fortune*, 25 June 2001, 64–70; Carol J. Loomis, "This Stuff Is Wrong," *Fortune*, 25 June 2001, 73–84; Justin Fox, "The Amazing Stock Option Sleight of Hand," *Fortune*, 25 June 2001, 86–92.

Questions for Discussion:

1. Do you think that CEOs are generally overpaid, or are they entitled to whatever compensation package that the market will bear?
2. Are CEOs justified in accepting bonuses when the company is not profitable or when it is downsizing significantly to cut costs? Do you think this reveals a double standard of pay for performance, or should they be compensated for making the hard choices necessary to maintain their firm's competitiveness?
3. Is executive compensation an example of a flaw in the market system, or does their pay reflect the executives' value to the company? Defend your answer.
4. How do you evaluate the role of the compensation consultant? Do you think he or she has a conflict of interest in his or her role?

Case 5.3: Selling Eggs and Embryos

If you look carefully at many college newspapers, you will find a group of advertisements that, a few years ago, you would not have seen. The ad reads something like this: "Egg donors wanted for a loving family. Must be healthy and able to handle the process of donation. Generous financial incentive offered for your time and inconvenience. Additional compensation for donors who have traits in demand by infertile couples." Those traits include athletic ability, race, physical features such as height, hair and eye color, and intelligence, measured by SAT scores. College age women are being recruited from all over the United States to "donate" their eggs to infertile couples who need them to increase their chances at achieving a pregnancy. Many infertile couples experience difficulty conceiving a child because of their age. After age 35, and especially after age 40, a woman's eggs have aged, and it becomes more challenging to become pregnant. Infertility clinics thus recruit egg donors of prime childbearing age to donate their eggs to these couples. In reality, they are selling their eggs to the clinic, which in turn sells them to the infertile couple. A resourceful college-age woman can offset many expenses of going to college by periodically donating her eggs. In addition, the embryos that are often left over after infertility treatments are also available on the open market for infertile couples willing to purchase them. A new market is now opening up for eggs and embryos.

Yet many people are uncomfortable with the notion of having eggs and embryos available for purchase and sale on the open market. The law reflects this ambivalence with selling body parts. The law has long prohibited selling organs for transplant, and adoption laws do not allow birth mothers to be paid for giving up their child for adoption, though some are advocating an open market for adoption for the sake of efficiency. Yet sperm donors are compensated, minimally, but blood donors typically are not. Surrogate mothers are generally paid for carrying a child for another couple, though some argue that there is no significant difference between a surrogate mother and a birth mother putting a child up for adoption. The question raised by the new market in body parts is this: Are there some goods and services that should be beyond the market, that is, not subject to market forces for their distribution?

Sources: Kenneth R. Weiss, "Eggs Buy a College Education," *Los Angeles Times*, 27 May 2001, A1, 38–39.

Questions for Discussion:

1. With regard to women being able to sell their eggs to infertile couples, do you consider this a valid market transaction, or should eggs and embryos not be for sale? Spell out the reasons for your view.
2. If you hold that selling eggs to infertile couples is morally acceptable, do you think there are nevertheless some goods and services that should not be distributed through the market? If so, what are they? Why should those goods and services not be subject to the market?

3. If you disagree with women selling eggs to infertile couples, do you also have a problem with sperm donors and surrogate mothers being compensated? Why should those goods and services be available outside normal market mechanisms?

COMMENTARY

Since Max Weber's controversial thesis in *The Protestant Ethic and the Spirit of Capitalism*, people have paid a great deal of attention to the intersection of religion and economics. Weber argued that Calvinism provided the ideological engine for the growth of capitalism in three primary ways. First, he argued that Calvin adopted and expanded Martin Luther's view of worldly callings, that a person could have a legitimate calling from God to work in industry and commerce, not just in the formal ministry. This is in sharp contrast to the dominant beliefs held from medieval times until the Reformation, when only the religious had callings and the rest of the population simply had jobs. Luther, and Calvin after him, argued that since God was sovereign over all, the whole world was the theater of his glory. Thus, all occupations, such as theater and even politics, were capable of demonstrating his majesty and should be pursued. Second, the habits of discipline—namely, hard work and thrift—that Calvinism encouraged were essential to a changing concept of work. People were encouraged to work for more than simply providing for their subsistence needs. Third, and perhaps most important, Calvinism, according to Weber, encouraged its adherents to "prove their election/salvation" by achieving success and prosperity in the world. This was seen as a sign of God's blessing on them and evidence that their election to salvation was secure. Though there were other factors, such as the division of labor, that also contributed to the rise of capitalism, the Calvinist ethos was a part of it.

Assumed in the Calvinist view of the world were also the virtues necessary to restrain self-interest and a concern for the common good, both necessary to keep the engine of capitalism under control. Adam Smith assumed both these elements in his classic work, *The Wealth of Nations*.[2] For him the capitalist was also the gentleman, who was bound by Judeo-Christian moral restraints on self-interest and an interest in business and commerce serving the community in which it was conducted. Few people remember that Adam Smith was not an

[2] For further reading on Smith's contribution to the intellectual foundation for capitalism, see Patricia Werhane, *Adam Smith and His Legacy for Modern Capitalism* (New York: Oxford University Press, 1991).

economist but a moral philosopher, and the capitalism that Smith advocated was not at all like its modern media portrayal in films like *Wall Street*. It is important to keep this in mind as you consider the various critiques of capitalism that the capitalism being criticized is the current practice, not the original idea proposed by Adam Smith.

Views of Wealth in the Bible and the Ancient World

The Bible's teaching on wealth and economics was set in an ancient economic system that was very different from the system of today. That doesn't mean that the Bible has nothing of relevance for today's economic world, only that we must use the Bible carefully in applying its general principles of economic life for today. As we pointed out in chapter 3, and as Mott and Sider insist, a direct application of many of the commands of the Bible relating to economic life would be impossible today, since the system to which those commands were addressed has dramatically changed. Rather, we are seeking from Scripture general principles or norms that govern economic life and that can be applied to different economic arrangements.

At first glance, the Bible appears to condemn the accumulation of wealth. Classic passages of Scripture such as "It is easier for a camel to go through the eye of a needle than for a rich man to enter the kingdom of God" (Luke 18:25), and "Blessed are you who are poor" (Luke 6:20) suggest that possession of wealth is suspect and poverty is a virtue. Of course, these texts should be balanced by others that present wealth in a different perspective. These include the sayings of the Old Testament wisdom literature, which regard wealth as God's blessing to be enjoyed (Ecclesiastes 5:18–20) and a result of one's diligence (Proverbs 10:4–5). Similarly, in the New Testament, Paul counsels Timothy to keep wealth in proper perspective (1 Timothy 6:6–19). He acknowledges that God gives liberally to his people for their enjoyment (v. 17). Yet this is balanced by admonitions not to trust in one's wealth because of the uncertainty of wealth and the temptation to arrogance (see also Ecclesiastes 5:8–6:12) and to be content with one's economic station in life.

The Bible does make a distinction between the possession of wealth and the love of wealth. Only the latter is condemned (1 Timothy 6:10). The love of wealth and the desire to become wealthy bring a variety of temptations and have the potential to shipwreck one's spiritual life (1 Timothy 6:9). Yet the members of the early church and the crowds who followed Jesus represented the socioeconomic spectrum from the very poor to the wealthy. It does not appear that the possession of wealth per se is problematic in Scripture, but hoarding one's wealth when surrounded by poverty is a sign of selfishness and greed. Throughout Scripture, the wealthy are condemned for their callousness to the needs of the poor (Amos 4:1–4; James 2:1–7).

The early days of the church were characterized by an extraordinary generosity toward the poor, who constituted the majority of the membership in the early church (Acts 2:42). Though the pattern of the early church probably did not involve a socialistic style of holding property in common, it did involve heightened sensitivity to the needs of the poor. Though the Bible does affirm the right to private property, it is not absolute. It is tempered by the responsibility to use one's wealth to meet needs of the poor in the community. It is further tempered by the notion that we are trustees, or stewards of God's property, which is entrusted to us both for our needs and enjoyment and for use for God's purposes.

The pursuit of wealth in the ancient world was fraught with potential problems, which made it easy to view those who possessed wealth with moral and spiritual skepticism. Though we should be careful not to minimize the temptations facing the pursuit of wealth today, there are some important differences between the modern and ancient economic systems that may partially account for the strong cautions about wealth. For example, in the ancient world, as a general rule, people became wealthy differently than in today's market system. The ancient economic system was largely centered around subsistence agriculture, with some commerce and trade. Real estate was the predominant productive asset. The ancient economy is best described as what is called a "zero-sum game." That is, there was a relatively fixed pool of economic resources, so that when one person became wealthy, it was usually at the expense of someone else.

To put it a different way, there was a fixed economic pie, and when someone received a larger piece, that meant that someone else received a smaller piece. This set up numerous opportunities to become wealthy at someone else's expense, either by theft, taxation, or extortion. One of the most common ways this was done in the ancient world was for those who had resources to loan money to the poor (frequently to pay for basic needs) at terms they could not repay, with what little land they owned as collateral. Then when they inevitably defaulted, the lender would appropriate their land, thereby increasing his wealth, and the debtor would become a tenant farmer or slave, or be reduced to dependence on charity. This kind of taking advantage of the poor occurred regularly in the ancient world and is why the Bible so frequently condemns exploitation of the poor.[3] In these cases, literally, the rich became richer at the expense of the poor, and when someone was wealthy, more often than not they had

3 For further discussion on this important aspect of economic life in the ancient world, see Justo L. Gonzales, *Faith and Wealth: A History of Early Christian Ideas on the Origin, Significance, and Use of Money* (New York: HarperCollins, 1990). For further reading on the theological aspects of wealth and possessions, see Craig L. Blomberg, *Neither Poverty nor Riches: A Biblical Theology of Material Possessions* (Grand Rapids: Eerdmans, 1999).

acquired it through some immoral means. Thus, the wealthy were viewed with suspicion, and there was great emphasis on the potential temptations of becoming wealthy because there were so few morally legitimate avenues to becoming wealthy in the ancient world.

In modern industrial economies, the size of the economic pie is constantly increasing. Wealth is being created instead of simply being transferred. In fact, every time a company makes a profit, wealth is created and the size of the pie grows larger. That is why the rich can become wealthy while at the same time the poor can also be better off. That is why the incomes of the poor can and have increased at the same time as the wealth of the rich accumulates, though admittedly, at very different rates.[4] But simply because someone like Bill Gates or Warren Buffet has extraordinary wealth, it does not follow that the poor are necessarily worse off because of their wealth. Nor does it necessarily follow that their wealth was gained at the expense of someone else. In a modern market economy, wealth is constantly being created, which is why it is possible for someone to become wealthy without necessarily succumbing to the temptations about which Scripture warned.

It is far easier to be wealthy and virtuous in today's market economy than it was in the ancient world. Of course, the same admonitions about not giving in to the temptations that accompany the pursuit of wealth apply today, as do the commands to share generously with those in need. One's attitude toward one's wealth as well as generosity with one's wealth are fundamentally conditions of the heart that have not changed since the ancient world. Regardless of one's level of wealth, one is still expected to depend on God, not on money for one's hope, to share God's heart for the poor and be generous toward those in need.

A Biblical Paradigm for Economic Life

As Mott and Sider point out in their article in the reading for this chapter, the Bible addresses specific economic practices, while at the same time laying out moral norms for economic life that transcend time, culture, and both Testaments. These norms form the basic principles guiding economic arrangements in whatever culture or time period is relevant. Though the practices of a fundamentally agricultural society are very different from an industrial or information economy, the norms from Scripture are applicable to a new set of practices and time.

The biblical foundations for economic justice begin in Genesis 1–2. God's creation of the world out of nothing and his pronouncement

[4] See Peter Brimelow, "Cutting a Pie: Are the Poor Getting Poorer as the Rich Get Richer? Not Exactly," *Forbes*, 4 September 2000, 86.

that the world is "good" teach that the created world is inherently good, although Genesis 3 indicates that it is also subject to the entrance of sin into the world. As the New Testament describes, creation eagerly awaits its redemption (Romans 8:19–23). From the beginning of the biblical record, human beings are a part of creation but also stewards over it. The Bible is clear that God owns all the land and that human beings are simply trustees of it. That is why in the Old Testament, real estate could not be permanently bought or sold (Leviticus 25:23–24).

Part of the dominion mandate over creation is the opportunity and responsibility to put the creation to use for the common good, particularly for the benefit of human beings. God's common grace is available to all human beings to aid them in the work of establishing dominion over the creation, bringing it under control and unlocking its potential. This responsibility gives a high place for traits such as freedom, initiative, and creativity in utilizing creation responsibly for the benefit of humankind. As Mott and Sider indicate, responsible wealth creation is a part of the dominion mandate and a tangible way in which one can honor God.

To be sure, creation is not to be worshiped. The Genesis record is clear on the distinction between the creation and its Creator.[5] Though the creation is good, it is both finite and fallen. Thus, it has value because it is God's and on account of what it can contribute to human beings' welfare. That is not to say that human beings can exploit the creation, only that it can be used for human benefit. Two extremes should be avoided, according to the fundamental principles in Genesis: worship of creation and irresponsible exploitation of creation.

Mott and Sider also point out that human beings were created both with freedom and with a fundamental need for community. Being made in God's image, human beings are more than material beings and more than merely economic agents in a marketplace. Economic systems that deny freedom and initiative are just as problematic as those that elevate individual freedom at the expense of community.

In the Bible, work was instituted prior to the introduction of sin into the world. Adam and Eve were commanded to work the garden in order to care for it and to realize its benefits (Genesis 2:15). Thus, work is inherently good and not a curse. After the Fall, work became more arduous and taxing, but that did not destroy its fundamental goodness. Work is essential to human flourishing, which suggests, as Mott and Sider insist, that economic systems must provide access to productive work for as many people as possible. All work is flawed due to sin; thus, alienation can occur in any economic system. That is,

5 See in chapter 8 a further discussion on this with regard to environmental ethics.

the criticisms of work are more due to the fallen nature of work than to any specific economic system.

Throughout the Scripture it is presumed that human beings are responsible for engaging in the work necessary to provide for themselves and their families. Adam and Eve were to work in the idyllic garden of Eden in order to gather what was necessary for their sustenance. Though the spirit of community is very strong in both Old and New Testament, people do not have a claim on the community's resources unless they are incapable of supporting themselves. The provisions for the poor in both Testaments presume that they cannot support themselves. For those capable of working, the Pauline admonition that "if a man will not work, he shall not eat" (2 Thessalonians 3:10) means that those unwilling to work have no claim on the resources of the community. This is expanded in the same context when Paul commands them to "settle down and earn the bread they eat," as opposed to idly awaiting the Lord's return (vv. 11–12).

However, the Bible makes generous provision for those who cannot support themselves and are economically vulnerable. God's heart for the poor is articulated throughout the Scripture, and Mott and Sider rightly recognize its centrality for the Bible's economic message. The Mosaic law set up institutions that provided an ample safety net for the poor, and the prophets roundly condemned those who took advantage of the economically vulnerable. The prophets regularly connect spiritual maturity to tangible commitments to caring for the poor. For instance, in Isaiah 58:6–7, the type of religious service acceptable to God is not a fast or other ceremony, but service to the poor. Likewise Isaiah identifies the signs of the coming Kingdom by the fact that the gospel is preached to the poor and the vulnerable are rescued (Isaiah 61:1–2; Luke 4:18–19). Service to the poor is that which is "just and right," according to Jeremiah (22:1–6). The wisdom literature connects one's heart for God with service of the poor. Proverbs 14:31 puts it strikingly: "He who oppresses the poor shows contempt for their Maker, but whoever is kind to the needy honors God." Similarly, Proverbs 19:17 insists that "he who is kind to the poor lends to the LORD, and he will reward him for what he has done."

Mott and Sider provide many examples of the variety of laws in Israel that were designed to promote economic justice. They focus on the economically vulnerable and provide a means of access to the resources necessary to provide for oneself and one's family. Mott and Sider insightfully summarize the notion of economic justice taken from these laws concerning the land: "Justice demands that every person or family has access to the productive resources (land, money, knowledge) so they have the opportunity to earn a generous sufficiency of material necessities and be dignified participating members of their community."

Economic justice does not suggest, as some have supposed, an equality of outcome, but rather an equality of opportunity to earn a sufficient living in order not to be dependent on the community. That is, economic justice does not presume that everyone must achieve the same level of prosperity, only that they have equal opportunity to get there. In terms of distributive justice, it would appear that the Bible uses both need and merit as criteria for distributing the goods of society. Those who can work earn their share based on their merit, consisting of their initiative, creativity, and hard work. Those incapable of self-support are entitled to a share of the goods of society on the basis of their need.

We could summarize the primary moral principles governing economic life as follows:

1. Even though marred by sin, the created world is inherently good since it is God's good creation.
2. God is the ultimate owner of all productive resources.
3. Human beings are stewards of these resources charged with responsible and productive use of them.
4. Responsible wealth creation is part of the dominion mandate and is a way of honoring God.
5. Human beings are created with freedom and a need for community, making them more than autonomous economic agents.
6. Work is inherently good, though marred by sin.
7. Human beings who are capable of working are responsible for supporting themselves and their families.
8. The community is responsible for taking care of the poor—those who cannot support themselves.
9. Human beings are not to exploit the economically vulnerable, but to take care of them.
10. Economic justice is the provision of access to the productive resources necessary for self-support.
11. Distributive justice in the Bible is based on a combination of merit and need.

Moral and Theological Critique of Capitalism

Over the years, a variety of criticisms have been leveled against capitalism as an economic system, particularly since, with a handful of socialist exceptions, it is the only viable economic system in operation.

Many of the most common criticisms of market capitalism have become more pointed due to globalization. As a result of a global economy, what happens in one country's economy can have an immediate and catastrophic impact on the rest of the world. Clear examples of this include the 1997 Asian financial crisis and the late-1990s Latin American economic meltdown. Even though the economic world has changed dramatically in the past few years, from industrial capitalism to a globalized, knowledge-based economy, the fundamental criticisms of capitalism have remained consistent.

The most common critique of capitalism concerns its foundational motive—greed. It is alleged that capitalism is a system based on greed, or on what Adam Smith called "the invisible hand of self-interest." Capitalism is run by individuals maximizing their profit, and the assumption is that to succeed they must make a useful product or perform a useful service and in so doing contribute to the common good. Yet the critics observe that greed and individual acquisitive self-interest has not contributed to the common good, but has undermined it. It has, for example, created enormous disparities in the distribution of income, and concentrated wealth in the hands of a relative few at the expense of the majority of the poor of the world. Certainly Wall Street, both in reality and in its media portrayals, has reinforced the notion that capitalism is based on greed. The prevailing ethos that "greed is good" is exemplified by corporate raider Gordon Gekko in the film *Wall Street* and by his real-life counterpart, Ivan Boesky. Critics of capitalism insist that a system fueled by a trait that Scripture clearly identifies as a vice cannot possibly be Christian. Expanding American profit and power, the rise of the consumer society, and our over-consumption all assume that greed fuels the economic system.

A second critique is that capitalism leads to an unjust concentration of wealth and global inequalities in resource use. Critics of globalization claim that the global economy has made these inequalities worse. For example, the United States has roughly five percent of the world's population, yet uses over fifty percent of the world's resources. In the developing world, the situation is the reverse, with far more people and far fewer of the world's goods at their disposal. Critics cite the growing concentration of economic and political power in the hands of a few around the world. This power is concentrated in the handful of multinational corporations that control a disproportionate amount of wealth and power and that exercise it unjustly to maintain their "empires," often at the expense of the poor.

This leads to a third major criticism of capitalism, that first world capitalism is responsible for third world poverty. The concentration of economic power in the West enables the West to dictate economic terms to the Third World and continue to exploit them in order to increase its own wealth and power. Critics of globalization suggest that the poor around the world and in this country are poor because we in the First World are rich. That is, there is a cause-and-effect relationship between the prosperity of the West and the poverty of the rest of the world. Critics argue that the poverty of the world is maintained by capitalism, not alleviated by it. They think it is preposterous to suggest that capitalism might be the solution to the problem of poverty, since they hold that it is clearly the cause.

A fourth criticism is that capitalism leads to over-consumption. Goods that would appear to have no socially redeeming value are produced and consumed simply because in the capitalist system supply follows demand. If there is market for a certain good, someone will make it, regardless of its social value. The only value of a product that counts is its economic value as measured by the market. Products like pornography, a billion-dollar business annually in the United States, and cigarettes, which (disputed only by tobacco companies) kill thousands of people each year and cost billions in medical care, are examples of products society would undoubtedly be better off without, yet are produced in mass quantities simply because the market demands it. Moreover, producers are accused of undermining autonomy through "creating" demand in the minds of consumers in order to maximize profit. As any marketing textbook will state, one way to do this is to "differentiate" basically similar products through advertising and market positioning. One can see this in the innumerable varieties of the same goods produced and marketed. For example, the average Foot Locker store has hundreds of essentially similar athletic shoes. Of course, some variety is appropriate, but critics of capitalism insist that the amount of variety demanded by the market says something negative about the character of its consumers. This kind of consumerism leaves a person and a society spiritually impoverished.

A final criticism of capitalism is that the private accumulation of wealth is prohibited by the Bible. Old Testament commands such as the Sabbatical Year, Jubilee, redemption of the land, and gleaning provision are designed to keep people from inordinately accumulating wealth. The rich young ruler is told to sell all he has and give it to the poor (Matthew 19:16–26), poverty is a virtue and the poor glorified (Luke 6:20), and the early church shared all their goods in common (Acts 2:42–47). All of these passages suggest that the accumulation of wealth that is necessary to provide the assets for capitalism is in violation of biblical principles. Critics of capitalism insist that the gospel is biased for the poor, and the rights of the rich are nonexistent in Scripture.

The defenders of capitalism have responded to each of these critiques of capitalism, arguing that its critics have either misunderstood the system or misinterpreted the Bible. First, they insist that greed and self-interest are not the same thing. When Adam Smith wrote of self-interest fueling capitalism, he had nothing like *Wall Street* in mind. He advocated *enlightened* self-interest, that is, self-interest restrained by Judeo-Christian morality and a concern for the common good, in which everyone benefits. Capitalism was never intended to operate apart from the virtue of its participants. Yet the critics of capitalism reply that the conditions under which Smith envisioned capitalism are so foreign to today's situation that perhaps capitalism is not capable of being a moral system, with self-interest properly restrained. Whether or not that is true is open to debate, but the key point here is that self-interest does not equal greed.

The second and third critiques, that the concentration of economic power inherent in capitalism is responsible for third world poverty assume that the world's supply of goods is a "zero-sum game." So if someone gets a bigger slice of the economic pie, someone else will inevitably get a smaller slice. Those "someones" have been the rich in the First World who have profited at the expense of the poor in the Third World. The defenders of capitalism have responded that the world is not a zero-sum game. In fact, capitalism is capable of making the pie bigger for everyone.

An honest assessment of capitalism should acknowledge that there are clearly situations that can be categorized as win-lose. However, once again this is an indictment of unscrupulous participants that inhabit every system rather than of capitalism itself. In fact, the great majority of transactions in the free-market create win-win conditions that increase the size of the economic pie for all parties when one participant profits. The genius of capitalism is that it is the only system that is capable of creating wealth as well as distributing it. For example, a study by Stanford economics professor Paul Krugman suggests that there is no simple cause-and-effect relationship between first world prosperity and third world poverty.[6] Thus, over-consumption is not inherently theft, nor has the First World necessarily gotten rich at the expense of the poor. Nobody has to lose when someone wins economically speaking. In fact, economic development of all parts of the world is mutually beneficial. Defenders of capitalism insist that the critics have fundamentally misunderstood capitalism at this point.

Capitalism's defenders point to decades of empirical data to show that capitalism is the best means of lifting the poor out of their poverty. They cite the Pacific Rim miracles of economic development as evidence. Nations known as the "Asian tigers," such as Singapore,

6 Paul Krugman, "Does Third World Growth Hurt First World Prosperity?" *Harvard Business Review* (July/August 1994): 113–21.

South Korea, Taiwan, and Japan have little natural resources on which to build an economy. Yet they are all prosperous because of a system that allowed initiative and creativity to flourish. On the other hand, resource-rich nations such as Brazil and the former Soviet Union are poor precisely because they have been saddled with economic systems that have discouraged initiative and risk-taking, which are essential for business development. In some Latin American countries, a patent process to protect intellectual property is notably absent. Thus, inventors have no initiative to bring designs to the market because there is no legal protection for their ideas. The contrast between the prosperity of South Korea and the continuing poverty of North Korea is another particularly vivid case in point. Both have roughly the same endowment of natural resources, yet the capitalist system has enabled people in the south to prosper, and per capita income is substantially higher in the south.[7] Thus, it is inept government policies, rather than wealth and capitalism in the industrialized countries, that has contributed to third world poverty.

On the fourth critique, the charge of over-consumption, advocates of capitalism admit that the free market allows for production of many goods and services that do not have socially redeeming value. Christian defenders of the market system would surely agree that pornography is a grievous evil without which society would clearly be better off. But they argue that the presence of such products and services is a small price to pay for the greater good of economic freedom. Having socially worthless products on the market or having far too much variety in the types of goods is an acceptable downside for the privilege of economic freedom. In addition, over-consumption is more of an indictment of the character of the people than a shortcoming of the system. We should be clear that over-consumption is not morally neutral, but is a genuine indictment on one's character. The Bible speaks clearly to the responsible use of one's wealth, but that is a matter of the heart, not the economic system. It is true that the market system does provide more goods and services, and thus increases the temptation to over-consume. But materialism can occur in any economic system because of human sin and selfishness.

The final critique, that the Bible prohibits private accumulation of wealth, gets to the heart of the biblical material on capitalism. Defenders of capitalism argue that the critics have misinterpreted and misapplied the Scripture that they cite. For example, some argue that when the early church shared their goods in common in Acts 2, that became the norm designed to prevent people from inordinately accumulating wealth. Yet the arrangement in Acts 2 can also be seen as temporary. In view of the imminent return of Christ, it made little

[7] For further reading on this, see Michael Novak, *The Spirit of Democratic Capitalism* (New York: Simon & Schuster, 1984).

sense to accumulate wealth. But as the return of Christ was delayed, that practice was abandoned in favor of the Pauline doctrine of "no work, no eat." Similarly, the Old Testament laws that protected the poor were aimed not at redistribution of income but at a renewal of opportunity for the vulnerable to support themselves.

Even if one favors the market system, it does not follow that all goods and services must be distributed according to market mechanisms. There are some limits on what the market can distribute. For example, the process by which children are adopted has been widely criticized as inefficient, and some have proposed to streamline the process by making it market practice. It is true that there is a black market for adoption, but that is illegal in most Western countries. However, there is broad consensus that human beings, particularly vulnerable newborn babies, should not be bought and sold as market commodities. Similarly, there is great debate over whether eggs, sperm, and embryos should be bought and sold on the market, in addition to reproductive services such as surrogate motherhood. Today there are a variety of online registries from which one can connect with egg, sperm, and embryo "donors" and surrogates, and even choose the traits of these donors, for a fee. There is further discussion over whether health care should be distributed according to market forces, as has become dominant in the United States through the system of managed care. There is widespread disillusionment among the medical profession with market-based medicine and a growing desire to see health care, not as a market service, but as a right. Regardless of your views on these specific goods and services, it should be clear that there are some goods that are what Stanford law professor Margaret Radin calls "market inalienable," that is, goods and services that violate human dignity by subjecting them to market forces.[8]

Conclusion

It would be difficult to maintain that the Bible is neutral when it comes to evaluating different economic practices. The prophets voiced searing criticism of the nation of Israel and its surrounding neighbors for its economic injustices, neglect of the poor, and exploitation of the economically vulnerable. Their critique was based on the foundation of the Mosaic law, which structured the social order, including economic life of the emerging nation Israel. There were clearly ideals such as the Jubilee that were to govern economic life both individually and structurally, and the prophets held the nation accountable to them when they violated both the letter and the spirit of those laws. The Bible is not to be identified with any one economic system. Rather, it

[8] Margaret J. Radin, *Contested Commodities* (Cambridge, Mass.: Harvard University Press, 2001).

stands authoritative over all social and economic systems, proclaiming God's Word on them and calling participants to adhere to the fundamental principles governing economic life.

Though there are some aspects of capitalism that are clearly cause for concern, many of the criticisms of capitalism reflect a misunderstanding of the way the system functions or misinterpret the Scripture. The Old Testament commands on economic life are probably better seen as mandates for a regular redistribution of opportunity rather than wealth and income. The fifth commandment, "Thou shalt not steal," provides the basis for private ownership and property, and the church's sharing all things in common was a temporary response to the expected imminent return of Christ. The mandate at creation gave humankind the opportunity to create wealth and so further exercise dominion over the creation. The emphasis on individual initiative, creativity, and economic freedom are rooted in the command to have responsible dominion over creation.

The Bible places great emphasis on the individual's responsibility for his own economic condition. The Proverbs stress the role of diligence and its causal relationship with economic prosperity. Paul bluntly states that if someone does not want to work, he has no right to any of society's goods (2 Thessalonians 3:6). Thus, it would appear that merit is a primary determinant of the distribution of society's goods. Need surely counts for something as well, but the poor, the object of compassion and care in Scripture, were those who were incapable of supporting themselves, not those who could work but did not, for whatever reason. Whatever was redistributed was done so voluntarily, and clearly the Bible places great stress on generous giving to those in need. Finally, the high place the Bible gives to freedom suggests that a system that maximizes freedom, within the restraints of righteousness and virtue, is more consistent with biblical values than those systems that limit freedom.

However, there are some concerns that are raised by the collision of biblical values with capitalism. There is a well-placed concern about the over-consumption and the materialism that is encouraged by the system. The Bible saves some of its clearest condemnation for the person who has succumbed to the temptation of materialism. There is a further concern about the ability of capitalism to fairly distribute the goods of society. Even if one accepts a merit-based distribution of wealth, it should be troubling to see the wide disparities in the distribution of income, especially the accumulation of wealth that is beyond what a person will ever need or is willing to give away. The principles of justice balanced by mercy taught by the Old Testament mandates on economic life are still applicable to us today. Finally, the potential abuses of capitalism illustrate the need for society in general, and religious leaders in particular, to encourage the development of virtue and character to provide the necessary internal restraints of self-interest and urge the tempering of self-interest in favor of the common good.

SIX

International Business

Many moral situations are not determined by either absolute principles or prima facie commandments. One need not be a relativist to see that many decisions are relative to a particular situation.

Bernard T. Adeney

Nothing captures the difference in mind-set between East and West more than attitudes toward sweatshops . . . sweatshops that seem brutal from the vantage points of an American sitting in his living room can appear tantalizing to a Thai laborer getting by on beetles.

Nicholas Kristof and Sheryl WuDunn

INTRODUCTION

With the rapid globalization of the economy comes increasing cultural conflicts involving business practices. Picture yourself as a business executive responsible for expanding your firm's presence into promising international markets. In some countries, you may be expected to offer small cash payments to government officials in order to operate without lengthy delays. Such payments are a normal part of doing business in some cultures, though they are considered immoral and illegal in much of the West. What will you do? Will you adhere to what you consider to be a universal standard that does not permit "bribery"? Or will you adopt the philosophy "When in Rome, do as the Romans do" and justify the payments because they are a culturally acceptable practice?

Or imagine that you are a human resources director for an apparel company asked to tour and evaluate your company's subcontracted manufacturing facilities located in several developing countries. During your visits, you see laborers working for longer hours, in far worse conditions, and for far less pay than would be deemed acceptable if the factories were located in the United States. What changes, if any, will you champion to company executives on your return? Should improved wages and working conditions be written into future agreements with subcontractors? Or should wages and working conditions simply be determined by economics and the customs of the places where the factories are located?

Conflicts over situations like these can cause a tremendous amount of confusion over the standards that should be followed when working abroad. There have been two traditional ways to address the problem. The first is to follow the edict that one should abide by the standards of the host country. Relying on arguments that all moral standards are culturally, rather than transcendentally defined, it is argued that to abide by home country standards is to engage in an unacceptable form of ethnocentrism. This appeal to "cultural relativism" asserts that moral standards are relative from culture to culture. As such, no one can say with certainty that the standards of one culture are superior to those of another.

For example, in a well-publicized case in the 1970s that involved bribery, former Lockheed CEO Carl Kotchikan testified before Congress that he had paid millions of dollars in bribes to Japanese officials in order to secure a multimillion-dollar contract for his firm. He reasoned that since these types of payments were common practice in Japan, his actions were morally acceptable although the practice is disapproved of in the United States. Moreover, he argued, if he had abided by American beliefs about bribery, his company would have lost the contract—and with it, thousands of jobs.

In sharp contrast to the "do as the Romans do" approach, others have chosen to primarily resolve these tensions by abiding by the standards of their own country. If a practice they encounter differs from the standard with which they are familiar, no matter how common it is and how openly it may be practiced, it is viewed as wrong. For those who hold that values are absolute and should govern wherever one engages in economic transactions, adapting to the ethics of different countries can lead to some unacceptable compromises of values. Conversely, maintaining the values of the home country in a simplistic manner can be culturally insensitive and can jeopardize the ability to succeed in a foreign land.

Challenging questions exist with respect to cross-cultural behavior. Should one strictly adhere to Western standards of conduct even if it means the loss of ability to engage in business? Or are ethics really no more than cultural conventions rather than objective, transcendent norms? Can we somehow balance the two traditional views and act in ways that are both culturally and morally appropriate at the same time?

While these questions are indeed difficult to resolve, the articles included in this chapter have some important insights to contribute. Bernard Adeney's "Ethical Theory and Bribery," provides important insights into the nature of cross-cultural ethical conflicts. Adeney reminds us of the importance of being aware of the role that our own cultural lenses may play in interpreting events as they occur around us. While Adeney rejects moral relativism, he accurately describes the complexity of ethics when cultural assumptions and conventions are brought into the picture.

In "Two Cheers for Sweatshops," authors Nicholas Kristof and Sheryl WuDunn, provide an interesting and provocative angle on the contemporary "sweatshop" problem that has been the source of much contentious debate. Kristof and WuDunn argue that sweatshops are seen by many local citizens as "opportunities" rather than as means of oppression. Using China as an example, Kristof and WuDunn suggest that low-wage, low-skilled industries may be necessary places in which economic development can begin to flourish.

READINGS

Ethical Theory and Bribery

Bernard T. Adeney

From *Strange Virtues: Ethics in a Multicultural World* (Downers Grove, Ill.: InterVarsity Press, 1995), chapter 7: 142–62.

In interviews with Christians from all parts of the world working in "Third World" countries, the most commonly cited moral problem is corruption or bribery.[1] This chapter explores how Western ethical theory of moral choice might contribute to a sharpened perception of the nature of moral reality in relation to this thorny issue. I will examine a case study in order to consider how classical ethical categories and more recent conceptions contribute to an understanding of what is at stake in a particular crosscultural

problem. This will provide both an in-depth ethical analysis of bribery and the outlines of an ethical method for evaluating other crosscultural dilemmas.

As an individual case, the situation presented in the following story is relatively trivial. But behind it lies a much larger problem of how to "act well" in a bureaucratic, patronage-based, social structure in which relationships, and even survival, are structured through the giving and receiving of gifts.

The Case Study: Elusive Justice

Bill looked at the police officer with uncertainty and frustration. The officer had asked him for 200,000 rupiahs for the return of his driver's license. It was Bill's twelfth weekly visit to the headquarters since the license had been confiscated, and his resentment rose as he faced the possibility of yet another wasted week clouded with uncertainty and unpleasantness, unable to use his car. Must he sacrifice his principles in order to resolve the matter?

The problem began when Bill had returned from a missionary assignment out of town. He was coming into Bandung, West Java, along the main highway from Cirebon, the same road on which he had left the city two days before. The chaotic congestion was about normal in this heavily populated part of town. Animals, trishaws, and people were weaving their way in and out among the motorized traffic that crawled along the road toward the urban open market. For some time Bill had been caught behind a slow-moving, over-crowded bus, and there was little chance of getting past it, even when it stopped to allow passengers to alight.

Suddenly Bill was jolted to attention when something hit the side of the car. Before he knew what had happened, he caught sight of a policeman approaching the car and shaking his fist. By the time the officer had picked up his baton from the street, Bill was out of the car and prepared for the worst. Fellow missionaries had warned him never to tangle with the police. In fact, it was missionary policy not to call the police, even in the case of a house burglary. Experience had shown that it was cheaper to sustain the losses of robbery than to bear the frustration of red tape and loss of further property taken to headquarters to test for fingerprints.

Bill did not have to wait long to find out what he had done wrong. For several hundred yards approaching the market area, the highway became a one-way street. Buses and other public vehicles were permitted to use it in both directions, but private vehicles had to detour around back streets and rejoin the highway several blocks beyond the market. Bill pleaded that he had seen no sign and had simply followed the bus. The officer walked Bill back twenty yards and pointed out to him a small, mud-spattered sign obscured by a large parked truck. This did not seem to concern the officer at all. There was a law and a sign—and Bill was guilty.

Officer Somojo escorted Bill to the local police post in the market. Five other officers materialized from the stalls in the market, so Somojo began to explain how very embarrassing it was for him to have to prosecute a foreigner, and how he regretted that Bill had put him in this difficult position. After some time, Somojo suggested that the whole thing might be smoothed over quietly and without further awkwardness if Bill would pay a token fine of 2,000 rupiahs ($1.20) on the spot. Bill had been expecting just such a request. Without even asking if it was a formal, legitimate fine for which a receipt would be given, Bill quickly protested that although he might be technically guilty, Indonesian law had a system of justice and courts where such matters were to be settled. He would go through proper channels and requested to be allowed to do so. The officer scowled and told Bill that he would have to hold his driver's license until the case was settled. Bill could come to the police headquarters the following week to get it back. Since no receipt was issued for the license, Bill secretly feared that he would never see it again.

The following week, Bill went to the appointed office, only to be informed that the license had been sent to another department on the other side of the city. After a slow trip by trishaw, Bill finally found his way to the other office. The policeman in charge had a record of Bill's offense and said Bill could talk to the captain who would probably be prepared to settle the issue for 4,000 rupiahs. Bill suspected dishonesty and requested an official receipt for the money. The man just smiled. Bill told the policeman that he had come to Indonesia to build efficiency, justice, and a high standard of morality in the country. He would prefer to go through official channels. At that, he was told to return in a week's time. So week followed weary week, with hours wasted in travel and more hours spent waiting in offices. Each time the amount requested for settlement rose higher.

Bill worried about what he should do. He didn't want to be a troublemaker, but as a missionary he had to take a stand for honesty. His Christian witness depended on it. His whole upbringing as the son of an evangelical pastor had been one of strict integrity, and he had managed, so far, to maintain this standard in previous encounters with immigration officers and postal clerks. Yet, while he felt he had done the right thing, he still felt uneasy, for he knew full well that government officials were so poorly paid that they had to make at least double their official salaries on the side if they were to feed and clothe their families. The whole system was unjust, and he was caught in it. Bill talked to some other missionaries. They just laughed and said, "Let us know how you get on!"

Now it was the twelfth week, and he still did not have his license. Moreover, the amount being asked to settle the case had risen to 200,000 rupiahs (U.S. $120). Should he pay the official and end the case? Or should he appeal to a higher-level officer in hopes of a just settlement? Bill looked at the officer and said . . .[2]

Responses to the Case Study

As I have presented this case study to Christians from various countries, most felt that "Bill" should have paid the bribe or fine in the first place. Others, including Indonesians, Filipinos and a few North Americans, thought "Bill" should stand firm.

Of the minority who said Bill should refuse to pay, the Americans appealed to a moral principle: "Bribery is always wrong." The Filipinos explained that the only way for Christians to escape the straightjacket of corruption is for them, as a community, to become known as people who never compromise in such matters, no matter how trivial the situation. Some Indonesians suggested that because of his role as a Westerner and a missionary Bill should not pay. But of course Indonesian Christians would just pay; they would have no choice.

The majority from all nationalities felt that in this situation the money should have been paid in the first place. Various reasons were given in justification: (1) The situation involves a conflict of values—the values to be gained by paying are greater than the values lost by compromise. (2) Since the police are paid so poorly, the money should be thought of as a tip for services rendered rather than a bribe. (3) Bribery is an accepted mechanism for legal transactions in this context. Westerners have no right to impose their own legal norms on a context in which small-scale bribery has almost the status of customary law. (4) Corruption should be fought, but you must choose your enemy. If you refuse to compromise at such a trivial level, you will waste all your time struggling with the victims of the system and have no time to address the real villains—the structures of the system and those who enforce them at a high level. (5) Unless Bill has friends in high places he has no choice. He must pay and should be considered a victim of petty extortion, not a criminal.

Sources of Moral Decision-Making in Ethical Theory

How does Western ethical theory correspond to the reasons stated in these various opinions? The concern of this chapter is to clarify why some people think one way and others another way. What follows is a brief description of theoretical ways of moral thought. I will use two traditional, philosophical approaches to moral decision-making and see how far they take us in understanding why people differ on their opinions. More recent ethical theory attempts to move beyond the "decision" by focusing on the moral qualities of the person(s) within their particular tradition and social structure.

Deontological ethics: absolute right and wrong. The first traditional approach is often called "deontological" ethics, from the Greek *ontos*, which means "that which exists by itself." A deontological approach to ethics argues that goodness and evil are intrinsic to an act or an actor. Certain actions and attitudes are right or wrong *in and of themselves*, no matter what their effect on the world. Some Christians argue that we must do or not do certain things, regardless of culture, and leave the results in God's hands.

For example, a Christian pacifist may argue that it is always wrong to kill another human being. Even if by killing a person you save ten lives, it is still wrong. Some would say the same for lying. George MacDonald said, "I would not favor a fiction to keep a whole world out of hell. The hell that a lie would keep any man out of is doubtless the very best place for him to go to. It is truth . . . that saves the world."[3]

In this quote, lying is seen as deontologically wrong. A deontological approach draws the line at a certain point and suggests that if your behavior crosses this line it is wrong, no matter what your motives are or how salutary the outcome.

A simplified deontological approach to Christian ethics is sometimes labeled "moralism." There are clear moral rules derived from Scripture, reason or society. These are moral absolutes that should never be violated under any circumstances: don't lie, don't bribe, don't kill, don't drink alcohol, turn the other cheek, and so on. A value of this approach is that it is clear, uncompromising and objective, and it precludes rationalization. Some students who argued that "bribery is always wrong" exhibit this approach.

The biggest problem with moralism is that a person's choice of moral rules is likely to be deeply related to culture. No one follows all the rules of the Bible, so determining what is absolute requires selection. Bribery may feel wrong to me because it is considered illegal and "sleazy" in my culture. To someone from another context, small-scale bribery may seem perfectly all right. One Third World pastor told me that he felt great relief and peace after paying a small bribe to a police officer who stopped him for a minor infraction. He felt that God had rescued him from a potentially very dangerous situation!

Moralism ignores the fact that sometimes moral rules conflict with each other or with broader moral principles. Moralism can lead to legalistic self-righteousness and concentration on trivial rules at the expense of larger, less definable issues. For legalists, all morality is flattened out. All rules are equally important. Those in the fourth group, who argued for ignoring the small-

scale problem and fighting against corruption at a higher level, were trying to avoid this problem. Similarly, those who felt a Westerner could afford to resist but they could not were applying different rules to different people according to their power in the situation: it is better not to pay, but for some it is just too costly.

Moralism is a shallow example of a deontological approach that insufficiently recognizes the complexity of reality. The narrow rigidity of legalism is an inherent danger of deontology.

Teleological ethics: goodness determined by the outcome. The second philosophical stream is called "teleological" ethics, from the Greek *telos*, which means end, result or goal. Teleological ethics argue that goodness lies not in an act or actor but in the act's real effect on the real world. People and actions are judged good or evil not by some inner quality but by the results of their action in human history. As Jesus said, "You will know them by their fruits" (Mt 7:20).

For example, some Christians would object to an absolutist interpretation of the commands not to kill or to lie. To kill or lie in order to save the lives of innocent people may be seen as good. Of course the results or "fruit" of an action cannot be measured only for the short term; the long term must also be considered. If the judgment of God is factored into a teleological approach, its distance from deontology is lessened. God's sovereign final judgment is the ultimate guarantee that good action produces good results and sin leads to death.

Situation ethics is a popular attempt to escape the dangers of moralism. Joseph Fletcher argued that since Christians are not "under the law," there are no moral rules, only the law of love. Every situation should be judged uniquely on the basis of love: what is the most loving thing to do in this situation? On the one hand, goodness is determined by motivation—does the action spring from love? On the other hand, it is based on realistic calculation of what action will most effectively show love to those involved. Situation ethics recognizes the primacy of love and the uniqueness of each individual circumstance. In regard to the case study above, those who considered the low pay of the police and the conventional acceptance of the system of "gift giving" exhibit a situational rather than a moralistic approach.

Situation ethics has many problems. There is the obvious danger of subjective rationalization. Almost anything can be justified by an appeal to love. As Stanley Hauerwas observed,

> The ethics of love is often but a cover for what is fundamentally an assertion of ethical relativism. It is an attempt to respond to the breakdown of moral consensus by substituting the language of love for the language of good and right as the primary determinate for the moral.... Love becomes a justification for our own arbitrary desires and likes.[4]

The short- and long-term effects of an action rarely can be accurately predicted. The true situation ethicist chooses the good by calculating what course of action will have the most loving results. Morality by calculation assumes that it is possible to know the moral results of an action. But the moral results of action are often unknowable, even after the event. What can scarcely be known in retrospect can hardly be known beforehand. Situations do not stand alone but are part of a larger historical, sociocultural and economic context that is impossible to master.

An Indonesian professor responded to the story of Bill by writing out his own hypothetical story of the policeman, showing how hard his life was and the desperate material needs of his family. His conclusion was that Bill should have paid out of love and respect for the policeman. But his imagined circumstances are just the sorts of things that a person cannot know on the spot, when a decision has to be made.

Situation ethics promotes an individualistic approach that exchanges the absolutism of rules for an absolutism of the personal conscience. By doing so, it ignores the usefulness of moral rules as a shorthand for judgments of society or the Christian community on right and wrong. Situation ethics devalues all principles except love and oversimplifies the relational meaning of morality. Love may be our highest norm, but it is not the only one. In a case of bribery, other principles such as justice, honesty, gentleness and obedience to the state cannot be ignored.

Finally, situation ethics is too time-consuming. To judge every situation afresh, without the benefit of rules, is impossible for human beings, for we must all categorize reality in order to avoid being overwhelmed by data. To be sure, emotivist situationalism is easy and quick. But if a situationalist is serious about calculating the most loving action, each decision could be long and torturous.

The dangers of a situational approach were recognized by respondents to the case study who argued for a principled rejection of all bribery. They saw a principled approach as the only way for a community to resist the enslavement of corruption. Some even argued that it was working, that officials no longer tried to receive payments from the Christian community because they knew it was futile.

On the other hand, the Indonesians who said that Bill should refuse to pay but that Indonesians would have to pay were not situationalists. Their conclusion was based not on the love commandment but on a power assessment of the situation: a Westerner might be able to get away without paying, but they could not. Furthermore, they thought it was appropriate for Bill to go through all the hassle of refusing to pay because of his role as a Western missionary who would be expected to bring unexpected values into the situation. At the very least they did not want to judge Bill in his decision to take a costly stand.

Situation ethics is a shallow example of a teleological approach that overestimates the power of an individual to calculate and bring about loving results without the restraints of law and community.

Distinctions, Synthesis and the Problem of Bribery

Deontological and teleological ethics are often treated as mutually exclusive. The polarization of means and ends, the antithesis between principles and results, is a characteristic weakness of Western dualistic thought. It leads to a war between the absolutists and the relativists. The absolutists are thought to be too narrow and rigid. The relativists are thought to be too wishy-washy.

Actually, the distinctions between deontology and teleology helpfully show two necessary and contrasting elements in moral choice. These are not contradictory, but complementary. The way they fit together cannot be determined by abstract philosophical principle. The concrete situations in which moral choices are embodied reveal the ways in which principles and results interact.

Absolute moral principles. As a Christian I believe there are absolute moral principles and rules that reflect the character of God. These moral principles underlie all human behavior and are based in the fact that we live in a moral universe. Human beings were created in the image of God and have an intrinsic value. In the words of the Westminster Confession, we were created "to glorify God and to enjoy him forever." While these deontological absolutes are expressed and emphasized differently in different places and times, they are clearly affirmed by Christians in all cultures.

The central moral absolute that follows from these Christian affirmations is "'The Lord our God, the Lord is one; you shall love the Lord your God with all your heart, and with all your soul, and with all your mind, and with all your strength.' . . . 'You shall love your neighbor as yourself.' There is no commandment greater than these" (Mk 12:29–31).

Out of love for God and neighbor come the deontological proscriptions against idolatry and covetousness. From love of neighbor and the inherent dignity of the human person (rooted in creation and confirmed by redemption) come the absolutes of beneficence (the quality of charity or kindness) and the commands to seek justice and love mercy. Most would accept the further implication that one should never torture or degrade a human being made in the image of God.[5]

Some Christians see bribery as one of these absolutes. Bribery is seen as a form of dishonesty, of cheating, which favors the rich. They reject any compromise and are willing at any cost to resist the pressure to smooth their way with money. An American businessman in the Middle East has told me some marvelous stories of his absolute refusal to compromise on the issue of bribery. Though he faced enormous obstacles to his business, he always kept his priorities straight. He knew he was there not primarily to make money but to serve God.

Bribery as a general concept may be fit into this absolute category if a moral condemnation is included in the definition of bribery. If a bribe is defined as a gift intended to corrupt an official and cause him to act unjustly, then it must always be wrong to bribe. Some have tried to rigidly define bribery as only gifts given to obtain illegal favors. Given that definition, gifts to obtain just or legal service can be called tips.

But this is an unfortunate solution to a complex dilemma, because it allows proscriptions against bribery to be considered absolute while it disregards the most common kind of bribery in the modern world.[6] By this definition there is nothing amiss when individuals or corporations pay large sums of money for special treatment, provided the treatment is not illegal.

Certainly gifts, especially large gifts given to obtain basic services, easily become a means of oppression. As a result of such gifts, those who cannot or will not pay may be denied even minimal justice. Similarly, gifts given by large foreign companies to win contracts routinely squeeze out the local industries that cannot afford such gifts. As John Noonan has observed, size is an important clue to whether a payment is a tip or a bribe.[7]

But what about small gifts? Is there anything wrong with small gifts given to induce a poverty-stricken civil servant to bypass mountains of (quite legal) red tape? Whether such gifts are considered a bribe or a legitimate tip may amount to a matter of definition. The word *bribery* has strong moral connotations. Characterizing a transaction as a gift, tip or bribe makes a great deal of difference. Our tradition, our culture and the assumptions embedded in our experience usually determine how we describe a given activity.[8]

Some Christians reject an absolute prohibition on bribes because they believe that what a Westerner calls a bribe may be a necessary mechanism for sharing wealth in poor countries. A prominent scientist of unquestionable Christian integrity suggested to me that paying a bribe in the Soviet Union is permissible if it is really an accepted part of a person's salary. Where salaries are low, everyone knows that officials must require gifts in order to survive. The money is not meant to corrupt but to expedite a sluggish process. People need money to live, and you have to make small gifts in order to get things done.

A moral distinction may be made on the basis of whether a person has the freedom to give or not to give. If a small gift is freely given to obtain better service and there is no fear or threat involved, it is possible to consider it a tip. Presumably the service would be given in any case, but would probably take a little longer. The tip speeds up the process and benefits both parties. Little or no harm is done to the poor who either do not need the service or can obtain it with a little more time.

On the other hand, if fear or force is involved, or if the expected delays are extreme, the freedom that characterizes a gift or a tip is removed.[9] A gift or a tip is never compulsory.

While a gift is never compulsory, it may be strongly expected. When my neighbors bring me a bunch of bananas from their tree, they expect that sooner or later I will share with them the papayas that grow in our yard. Yet I would never suspect them of bribery! As Anthony Gittins has pointed out, gift giving is a rule-governed activity in which obligations are a constant.[10] The obligations, however, are not usually to be seen as the requirement to pay the person back on a tit-for-tat basis. Rather, the obligation is to continue the relationship that is symbolized by the gift: "gift exchange is seen to be patterned behavior embodying clear moral values; it creates and maintains personal relationships, not simply between private individuals, but between groups and between 'moral persons' or statuses."[11]

This is a far cry from bribery, in which either the briber buys special service from the bribee through an illegal gift or the bribee forces an illegal payment by refusing to give fair treatment. A gift helps create or maintain a moral relationship, while a bribe undermines it.

Small gifts paid to poor officials are ambiguous because they occupy a gray area between a gift, a tip and a bribe. Usually they are not compulsory, but neither are they free. They may help establish a relationship of trust and mutual help, but they are also underlined with the threat of poor service and time delays. Certainly they are a part of the establishment of status relationships, but they are also sometimes a pure economic exchange that takes place outside the law.

This ambiguity was echoed by many Christians I interviewed. For example, a Christian who worked in the Dominican Republic suggested that the clear definitions we assume in the West do not apply to some other countries. He suggested,

> In the U.S. there is a clear line between a bribe and a non-bribe. But in many places it is a continuum. In the States a person may get a 30% commission while their counterpart in the third world receives only 5% but expects a bribe. Sometimes you don't know you are paying a bribe. You may receive a bill for 125% import duty where 25% of it is a bribe. The equivalent of not paying the customs officer a tip is not paying a waitress a tip. He deserves a tip as payment for his services because his salary is so low.[12]

The complexity of the meaning and value of gift giving is reflected in the book of Proverbs, where there are three negative and three positive references to bribery (Prov. 15:27; 17:8; 17:23; 18:16; 21:14; 22:16). John Noonan Jr., in his massive historical study of bribery, faults the Old Testament for having a double standard. He suggests that while the extortion of bribes is roundly condemned, the giving of bribes (or gifts to officials) is not condemned in the Old Testament.[13] Such equivocation in the Old Testament seems to reflect a recognition of the power differential between a poor person who gives a gift in order to stave off injustice and the rich who uses his power to exploit the poor. The powerful and the powerless are not judged by the same abstract absolute, but by the relationships and intentions of their situation. Thus,

> If you close your ear to the cry of the poor,
>   you will cry out and not be heard.
> A gift in secret averts anger;
>   and a concealed bribe in the bosom,
>   strong wrath.
> When justice is done, it is a joy to the
>   righteous,
>   but dismay to evildoers. (Prov 21:13–15)

The way a moral act is described is part of the texture of a narrative. If the narrative experienced is of a righteous poor person who escapes injustice by giving a culturally appropriate gift to his or her potential oppressor, the reality described is very different from the narrative of a policeman who threatens torture unless he is given a large gift. The definition of what is going on springs not from a philosophical category such as "deontology" or "teleology" but from a much larger tradition and narration of experience.

The positive references to bribery in the Bible appear to reflect a utilitarian approach to ethics for those who have no other means of receiving justice. However, Proverbs unequivocally condemns those who accept bribes in order to do wrong: "The wicked accept a concealed bribe to pervert the ways of justice" (Prov 17:23). It also warns that giving gifts does not always work: "Giving to the rich will lead only to loss" (Prov 22:16). A single perspective on bribery cannot be forced on the Bible, because different verses were written at different times for different contexts and different people.

Certainly the great majority of Old Testament references to bribery are negative. The God of the Bible is one who does not accept *šōḥad* (bribes), who judges impartially. We are called to be like God in love of righteousness. Nevertheless, there is enough ambiguity in the biblical record to allow for hesitancy in making the prohibition of bribes an absolute.

Right and wrong "on the face of it." A helpful intermediate category between the relativism of teleology and the absolutism of deontology has been developed by Roman Catholic moral theology. The concept of prima facie moral rules and principles is founded in the recognition that we live in a fallen, sinful world where what ought to be is sometimes impossible. *Prima facie* means "on the face of it" or "on first assessment." Prima facie rules ought to be absolutes in all cultures and all times. On the face of it, all things being equal, one must always obey these rules.

If you break a prima facie command or principle, you cannot escape doing evil. Nevertheless, there are tragic circumstances where, because of sin, values come into conflict and one commandment must be sacrificed if we are to uphold a higher value. Such an action, even though justified, should never be done without regret. In a real sense it still remains wrong. For there are tragic consequences from such a violation that undermine the fabric of society. Evil still clings to the act, even if it is morally justifiable.

William Frankena suggests that if certain actions are prima facie wrong, they are "intrinsically" wrong. In other words,

> They are always actually wrong when they are not justified on other moral grounds. They are not in themselves morally indifferent. They may conceivably be justified in certain situations, but they always need to be justified; and, even when they are justified, there is still one moral point against them.[14]

Commonly cited prima facie rules include the prohibitions against killing, lying, work on the sabbath and divorce. If you kill to stop a maniac gone amok, lie to save an innocent person hiding in your house, overwork to meet an urgent deadline, or divorce to end a situation of physical and mental abuse, in each case your action may be necessary and morally justifiable. But your action is not *good*; it is a necessary evil. Tragic consequences will follow. A fellow human will be dead, truth and human trust will be undermined, the quality of your inner harmony and worship will be threatened, what God has joined together will be torn apart.

The "necessary" evil that is done in all these cases will affect the actor, the immediate people involved and the broader society. Their effect is not only personal but also social. That is why these moral rules, on the face of it, should never be broken.

Some Christians deny this category and treat examples such as the above as absolutes never to be broken. But the prima facie category has the virtue of taking moral rules seriously without trivializing the power of evil to frustrate the best intentions of law. Prima facie principles may only be broken to avert some greater evil. Unlike in situation ethics, prima facie rules and principles are not nullified by moral calculation. They remain strong guides for behavior which must be reckoned with even when we tragically break them.

How can we determine when a prima facie moral law must be set aside in favor of a higher value? Some ethicists reject the implication that a Christian may face unavoidable evil. Instead of a prima facie category of morality, they suggest a fixed hierarchy of values in which to choose a higher value over a lower is not a lesser evil but a higher good. For example, to lie to save innocent life is in no sense wrong, but the highest possible good in the situation.[15] Others admit the tragedy implied by the prima facie category but also suggest a fixed hierarchy of values to guard against creeping relativism.

Unfortunately, no fixed hierarchy of values can be demonstrated from Scripture, reason or experience. Where is it written that death is worse than deceit? Is divorce worse than lying? Is neglecting the needs of your family worse than neglecting a friend in despair? Is stealing a car more honorable than allowing a criminal to escape? There is no abstract answer to such questions apart from detailed knowledge of the situations in which they are embedded. The fact that there is no fixed hierarchy of values does not imply that such values are relative, subjective or changeable. All of the actions in this paragraph are intrinsically wrong. But their relative seriousness depends on many factors not revealed in the moral principle itself. Cowardice may sometimes be worse than killing.[16]

One thing can be known for certain. The double love command does not admit exception.

Augustine suggested that every other command of God must be filtered through the eyes of the command to love God and your neighbor. "On these two commandments hang all the law and the prophets" (Mt 22:40). The love commandment does not set aside the other commands but interprets their true meaning in a concrete situation. Unlike in situation ethics, love is not all that matters, but love is a part of all that matters. All moral situations receive their true weight in relation to the love of God and neighbor.

The category of prima facie rules is helpful for thinking about bribery. If bribery is defined as the giving of gifts in exchange for privileges or services that either are illegal or are meant to be administered impartially, then bribery is a prima facie evil. Each case of bribery undermines the cause of justice in society by making it difficult for the poor to be treated fairly. Bribery is officially illegal in almost every country in the world. On the other hand, it is possible to conceive of situations where greater harm may be done by refusing to pay a bribe. In the case of Bill, were fifteen hundred rupiahs ($1.50) and the principle of not paying an unofficial gift to an impoverished police officer worth the weeks or months of frustration and the possible permanent loss of private transportation? Should Bill be fighting other battles?

Whatever your answer, the effects are not simple. The escalating amount of money required symbolizes a growing alienation between Bill and the authorities. Is this a case of justice holding out against tyranny or a case of a foolish neo-colonialist foreigner insisting that his hosts conform to his rules? In either case Bill is unable to ensure that justice is done. If he pays, he violates his own conscience and may well reinforce the structural injustice of a society that treats those with money better than those without. If he doesn't pay, he may end up without a car because he quibbled over paying less than two dollars to a poor official.

Our individual actions cannot always overcome evil that is a structural part of a situation. Many Christians have told me stories of instances where they paid a small bribe to avoid what they understood as a far greater evil. Were they without sin in doing so? Perhaps not. The prima facie category does not absolve the lawbreaker from guilt. It only allows us to recognize our weakness in the face of a sinful world. Sometimes we are not wise enough or strong enough to act well in situations of ambiguity. Sometimes we cannot see any good course of action. Sometimes the law we break seems insignificant in the face of the enormity of our situation. If so, we dare not claim innocence. Nor may we rescind or denounce our action. It throws us on the mercy of God.[17]

Relative moral situations. Many moral situations are not determined either by absolute principles or by prima facie commandments. One need not be a relativist to see that many decisions are relative to a particular situation. Those who argued that the "bribe" was really a tip with the status of customary law are suggesting that what is a bribe in a Western legal context is best considered a tip in an Indonesian context. In that case Bill simply misunderstood the meaning of his situation in a foreign context. His refusal to pay was not so much wrong as unwise.

While in the case of Bill this argument may be oversimplified, there are many moral choices we make that are unique to a particular person, time or place. Such relative situations are not trivial. They may have large moral consequences. But they are not subject to abstract definition. They require deep understanding of a context and the subject's role in it. They require calculation of what actions will bring the most good and prevent the most evil in a particular context. They require the capacity of character and the commitment to care about what matters most. And they require the wisdom of God's Spirit so that we may choose the good.

Culture plays a major role in making morally relative decisions. How do we treat time? How do we decide how to live and at what socioeconomic level? How directly and forcefully do we communicate? How individualistic or communalistic are we in decision-making? How competitive are we? How do we spend our money? When do we give to those in need? How much time do we spend with our family? How do we honor our parents? How do we plan for emergencies? How

authoritarian are we with our subordinates? Do we reach out to those in prison? How do we work for justice in society? How do we share the good news of our faith with people in need?

These, and many other questions like them, may be the most important moral questions of our lives. But there are no simple answers to them that are directly based on absolute or prima facie commandments.

An American evangelist once told a wealthy audience that a person could not be a Christian and drive a BMW luxury sedan. While such a statement could be considered neither an absolute nor a prima facie moral command, it provocatively dramatized what is at stake in our relative moral decisions. It is our relative moral decisions that demonstrate what we mean when we claim to love God and our neighbor.

In some cases the definition of a bribe and the meaning of a particular gift may be relative to the cultural intentions and expectations of those involved. In the Middle East the value of a service or a thing is often defined through emotional bargaining. The normal fee for installing a telephone may not be fixed but variable. Appeals to relationship, need, the ability to pay and other subjective factors are a vital part of defining the value of all goods and services. After all, why should we think something (like a telephone) has an objective value outside the relationships of those involved in the transaction?

A study by E. Glen, D. Witmeyer and K. Stevenson of negotiation styles within the United Nations showed that Arabs argued with an intuitive-affective style, expressing their positions through appeals to strong emotion. Compromises were often "indicated by strong expressions of personal friendship and esteem towards the intermediary."[18]

If relationships are the key to negotiations, it is not hard to see how the value of a service might be understood as contextual. For many people, relationships outweigh efficiency. If the feelings are right, for example, a seller may be willing to take a loss. While in economic terms it is a loss, in affective terms there is a gain—an established relationship of indebtedness. At the least the customer may come back, and she may encourage her friends to do so as well. On the other hand, if the feeling of relationship is wrong the seller may pass up a profit. An economic profit may not outweigh the cultural alienation of dealing with someone perceived as rude and arrogant.

What Westerners see as bribery or deceit may be understood in some countries as ways of maintaining or achieving the right relationships. The market conditions of modern capitalism are not necessarily a more moral way of setting price than a bargaining relationship between two people.

Sometimes if a right relationship is established with someone, the necessity for a monetary exchange is eliminated. The right word or the meeting of eyes (or the humble averting of eyes!) may signal the kind of respect or "in-groupness" that establishes relationship.

In our case study, Bill might have been able to avoid the situation of conflict altogether. By showing the policeman genuine love, by expressing greater respect, by demonstrating true humility, by a wise use of trust, by an appropriate invitation or nonmonetary gift, by speaking with meek authority, Bill (or Jesus) might have reached the policeman in his place of greatest need. He might have been able to avoid the request for a bribe *and* initiate a friendship.

Many situations that appear to be either-or moral dilemmas may have hidden within them a third way. A godly Indonesian pastor shared his surprise with me that one time when he was stopped by the police for a traffic infraction, he was released with no payment or charge after he had apologized with genuine humility for his error. The right word spoken by the right person in the right way at the right time may bridge the chasm to another human being.

Most people do not have such deep power for good in their character. Most do not have the wisdom to overcome the deep divisions in society which lead to conflict. Sometimes human evil or structural injustice cannot be overcome by goodness. Sometimes the best of people end up on one cross or another. The best course of action for one person may be disastrous for another.

The relative moral decisions we make are ultimately grounded in the absolute core values that guide our lives. They grow out of our habitual praxis, our knowledge (or ignorance) of our context, our relationship to a community and the gift of God's wisdom and guidance.

Bribery and Social Structure

Why is bribery so much a part of some societies and not of others? Are some countries more dishonest than others? Does poverty make people corrupt? The prevalence of bribery in poor countries may contribute to the paternalism or even racism of some Westerners who see it as evidence of "Third World" backwardness or moral inferiority.

One Englishman suggested that in India it stemmed from a Hindu culture in which there are no moral absolutes. Religion undoubtedly influences ethics, but if Hinduism is the culprit, why is there so much graft in many Roman Catholic and Muslim societies? Certainly moral relativism is no part of Catholicism or Islam. Moreover, it seems unlikely that the "Protestant" West is more honest or less greedy than other parts of the world.

A better explanation is that the social structures of some countries makes gift giving a far more extensive practice than in others. In Indonesia one seldom pays a visit without bringing a gift. In North Africa relationships are secured through mutual indebtedness. In Egypt nothing is done without a tip. In Latin America trust is ensured by a gift. In China connections are established through presents. Gift giving is not bribery; but when gifts become an obligatory mechanism for major social functions, the possibilities for corruption are obvious.

In many parts of the world, gift giving is radically shaped by a historical marriage between the structures of patronage and bureaucracy. Gift giving is an integral part of a patriarchal society. It is expected that the superior should care for the people under him by giving them gifts. Gifts are a means of buying loyalty and service. In the Marcos palace in Manila there were whole rooms full of merchandise for giving as gifts. Gifts mitigate an unjust and harsh social system. People are honored to have a patron, a protector. A person may be exploited, but he or she is also protected by the "father."[19]

The word *patron* is originally from Rome. But the idea of responsibilities that accompany patriarchy must go back to the dawn of history. When a bureaucracy is added to a patronage system, both systems are modified but continue to operate. Modern bribery is related to this historical marriage. In Latin America a semifeudalistic hacienda system was grafted onto a bureaucracy derived from the French. In Indonesia the feudalistic Javanese state was consciously married to the Dutch colonial bureaucracy. In the process, both were changed.

Bureaucracy is a different system from the hacienda system or the Javanese rule of the divine king, but a gift is still the accepted mechanism to buy loyalty or silence or service. Gifts are expected not only from the social superior but also from anyone who needs the "loyalty" or service of the bureaucrat.

In the traditional society, services were rendered and protection was given according to a strict hierarchical order. Gifts were simply a means of strengthening established relationships and rewarding good work. In a modern bureaucracy, relationships have to be established without the benefit of a clear social order. If the country is very poor, with high unemployment and a large, underpaid bureaucracy, civil servants are effectively paid with power and prestige rather than money. They must use their power to receive gifts if they are to support a family. The "patron" must demonstrate by gifts her worthiness of being served. This, of course, lends itself to corruption. But it is more than bribery in the Western sense. It also serves the social functions of sharing wealth and clarifying relationships. An Ethiopian church leader remarked,

> In Africa we do not have such a defined world as you do in the States. We give weight to different issues. It's not that bribery is OK, but it's not so central. In America money changes hands by different rules. People still get a share of the wealth that passes through their hands, but it is done by more highly defined rules. On the other hand, it can be very irritating in Africa.

When Bill refused to pay the policeman a small sum, he also refused to recognize the status and power of the man. In America a police officer is ideally a servant of the people and an agent of the law. But in Indonesia he is an important, powerful man (albeit a very poor one) whose dignity must be upheld.

The linking of patronage and bureaucracy might be considered morally neutral if it were not for the poor. Not only the relatively rich are served by the bureaucracy but the poor as well. An Indonesian professor remarked to me that the Dutch ideal was that the bureaucrat was meant to serve the people.[20] But here the bureaucrat does not serve the people, he serves the state. Or more accurately, he serves his superiors in the bureaucracy. This can become very oppressive to the poor who have nothing. It takes great sacrifice, or is simply impossible, for someone who earns fifty dollars a month to scrape together a bribe. Of course the poor are seldom expected to pay as much as the rich. To someone used to the rule of law, this too feels unjust. Actually it mitigates the injustice of the system.

The ability to break the bribery system depends on the power you have, what is at risk and what values are at stake. Those who can afford to go without the services of the bureaucrat, who can afford to wait, who have the power and education to appeal to higher levels, whose goodwill and service are needed by the country or who have connections to a powerful elite in the country can break the system. Such people also "earn" the service they receive, though they do it in an indirect manner.

Conclusion

Moral choice in every society is founded in the cultural character of a person and the way he or she sees the world. We are cultural creatures who make sense of our lives by means of a narrative that distinguishes between the good and the evil, the important and the insignificant. What we pay attention to shapes our ability to choose. This chapter suggests that neither relativism nor absolutism is an adequate approach to moral choice. The structures of society are fallen and pervaded by evil as well as infused with good. To cooperate with the good while exposing the evil is a task that requires character, sensitivity and knowledge.

First of all, we need to know our core, absolute values. These may never be compromised, though they may be expressed in different ways. Certain types of bribery are absolutely wrong. Paying money to subvert justice or hide our own evil is clearly wrong. The size of a gift is significant. Very large gifts that are given or demanded in exchange for services that are intended to be free signal serious injustice. Needless to say, gifts to secure illegal services are also wrong.

Second, we need to avoid situations of value conflict. When confronted with tragic circumstances we cannot control, we need to know how to choose higher values over lesser values. While some kinds of bribery are absolutely wrong, some may be wrong but unavoidable. They are wrong on the face of it, but less significant than the values that would be lost if we refused to pay. Some people have more power to break the bribery system than others. Therefore it is important not to judge those who make different decisions about what is a "lesser evil." Nevertheless, the greatest danger of the prima facie category is that it may become an easy way out, a means of justifying actions we know are wrong. Most of what we call bribery is evil and cannot be done without consequences that hurt other people more than the briber. If we bribe or kill or lie for what we consider a higher cause, repentance is advisable, for judgment lies ahead.

Third, we must constantly weigh our priorities and decisions on the basis of what fits our particular role in a particular context. Some things that look like bribes to Western eyes may be appropriate tips or gifts that serve a positive role in a given social structure. When there is ambiguity, the Westerner would do well to get advice from someone native to the culture. Bill might have gotten better advice from an Indonesian than he did from other missionaries. But to do so he would have to have the humility to be a learner and not a teacher in the situation.

Conversely, some kinds of payment that look perfectly legitimate to Westerners look like bribery to others. An Asian woman complained that some of the worst corruption comes when large Christian mission organizations lure gifted national leaders away from urgently needed, indigenously controlled work. The offer of a relatively enormous salary tempts gifted people to abandon locally controlled organizations to serve a Christian multinational. Local leaders may become discouraged as their gifted young leaders are made subservient to foreign organizations. Thus the power of money can perpetuate another form of colonialism.[21]

Sometimes patterns of foreign aid serve the same function as bribery. Aid brings dependence, fostered by a patronage system in which the foreigner has all the financial power. Paternalism may take the place of partnership.

Obviously these issues are not cut and dried. What may be right for one situation may be wrong for another. Gifts may be empowering or enslaving. The fact that *some* values are relative does not mean that *all* values are relative. The fact that there are some situations of structural evil where one cannot escape without fault does not suggest that whenever we feel tension we should give in.

Bribery is a serious evil in the modern world. The person who successfully navigates the shoals of corruption is likely to be someone who is living the right kind of story. At the point where we have to make a decision, we are unlikely to reflect on whether deontology, teleology or prima facie thinking is more appropriate. The kind of person we are and the way we are oriented to God, to our neighbor and to our own self-interest will most likely decide for us.

The God of Job and the God of Jesus does not accept bribes.[22] Bribes are the opposite of true gifts. Bribes seek to dominate and control. Bribes subvert justice for the poor. Gifts are given freely and establish a reciprocal relationship. Gifts are a sign of love. Gifts are at the heart of the gospel. Those who love God bring gifts, not bribes, to their neighbor.

Notes

1. This does not necessarily mean bribery is the most important ethical problem, but it fits the image of an ethical problem for many of the people I interviewed. Unlike poverty or injustice, it is a common problem that demands an immediate moral decision.

2. Case study by Keith Hinton in *Case Studies in Missions*, ed. Paul G. Hiebert and Frances Hiebert (Grand Rapids, Mich.: Baker Book House, 1987), pp. 138–40. I have adjusted the money figures to reflect approximate values in 1993.

3. *Annals of a Quiet Neighborhood*, chap. 9. Quoted in *George MacDonald: An Anthology*, ed. C. S. Lewis (London: Geoffrey Bles, 1946), p. 102.

4. Stanley Hauerwas, *Vision and Virtue* (Notre Dame, Ind.: University of Notre Dame Press, 1981), p. 124.

5. An interesting incidence of this principle as expressed in the Old Testament law is in Deuteronomy 25:1–3. Punishment is by flogging (possibly a more humane punishment than years of imprisonment), but a limit is placed on the punishment "lest he be degraded in your eyes." The type of punishment is cultural, but the limitation on it is theological. Other examples of laws that protect the dignity of the individual include Exodus 22:21–27; 23:4–9; Leviticus 19:9–10, 13–18, 23–25, 33–36; Deuteronomy 14:28–29; 15:12–14; 20:5–7, 19–20; 21:10–14; 22:1–4; 23:24–25; 24:5–6, 10–15, 17–22; 25:4; 27:18–19, 25. Organizations like Amnesty International work on the assumption that minimal human rights like freedom from torture are a crosscultural absolute. Of course there are widespread crosscultural differences over what constitutes a full "human." Some would functionally exclude slaves, women, twins, people with physical or mental disabilities, fetuses and so on. The Bible does not exclude any of these categories from human being.

6. For an example of this view of bribery see Paul G. Hiebert, *Cultural Anthropology* (Philadelphia: J. B. Lippincott, 1976), pp. 260–61. Hiebert's view is also followed by Marvin K. Mayers.

7. John T. Noonan Jr., *Bribes* (New York: Macmillan, 1984), pp. 696–98.

8. An example of this is the way the abortion debate is defined. One tradition talks about "murdering unborn babies," and another tradition talks about eliminating unwanted fetal tissue. How the act of abortion is described determines the moral conclusions.

9. The categories of "freedom to-freedom not to" and "fear-force" as concepts relevant to the moral evaluation of a bribe were suggested to me by Anthony J. Gittins after he read the manuscript of this chapter.

10. Anthony J. Gittins, *Gifts and Strangers: Meeting the Challenge of Inculturation* (New York: Paulist, 1989), especially chap. 4, "Gifts, Guile, and the Gospel," pp. 84–110. Gittins cites Marcel Mauss, *The Gift* (London: Cohen and West, 1970), as a major source of his ideas on gift-giving.

11. Gittins, *Gifts and Strangers*, p. 87.

12. This statement is greatly oversimplified. In fact the line between a gift and a bribe is less than crystal-clear, even in the United States. The legal system has attempted to make it clear, but the presence of hundreds of lobbyists with large expense accounts on Capitol Hill underlines the ambiguity in the system.

13. Noonan, *Bribes*. In spite of the immense historical and crosscultural research displayed in Noonan's book, he shows surprisingly little interest in the cultural meaning of gifts. His legal approach to knowledge is grounded in natural law theory, which shows a strong proclivity for absolute definitions of right and wrong.

14. William K. Frankena, *Ethics*, 2nd ed. (Englewood Cliffs, N.J.: Prentice-Hall, 1973), p. 55.

15. See for example, Normal Geisler, *Ethics: Alternatives and Issues* (Grand Rapids, Mich.: Zondervan, 1971).

16. This surprising conclusion was reached by both Mahatma Gandhi and Thomas Merton. This does not mean they thought killing was ever good, only that in some situations there might be something worse. In the face of horrendous injustice, if you cannot achieve nonviolent resistance, even resisting violently might be better than doing nothing at all.

17. "If we say that we have no sin, we deceive ourselves, and the truth is not in us. If we confess our sins, he who is faithful and just will forgive us our sins and cleanse us from all unrighteousness" (1 Jn 1:8–9).

18. E. Glenn, D. Witmeyer, and K. Stevenson, "Cultural Styles of Persuasion," *International Journal of Intercultural Relations* (1977), p. 64.

19. Some of these ideas came out of an excellent conversation I had with Samuel Escobar at the 1989 Lausanne II Congress in Manila.

20. Pak Nico Kana of Satya Wacana Christian University in Salatiga, Java, made this statement in a private conversation with me in November 1989.

21. For a spirited attack on the evil power of money in missions see Jonathan J. Bonk, *Missions and Money: Affluence As a Western Missionary Problem* (Maryknoll, N.Y.: Orbis, 1991).

22. See Noonan, *Bribes*, p. 705.

Questions for Discussion:

1. How does Adeney view bribery? How does he distinguish between gifts and bribes? Do you agree?

2. If you were Bill the missionary, how would you have responded to the demand for a bribe?

Two Cheers for Sweatshops

Nicholas Kristof and Sheryl WuDunn

From *New York Times Magazine* (24 September 2000).

It was breakfast time, and the food stand in the village in northeastern Thailand was crowded. Maesubin Sisoipha, the middle-aged woman cooking the food, was friendly, her portions large and the price right. For the equivalent of about 5 cents, she offered a huge green mango leaf filled with rice, fish paste and fried beetles. It was a hearty breakfast, if one didn't mind the odd antenna left sticking in one's teeth.

One of the half-dozen men and women sitting on a bench eating was a sinewy, bare-chested laborer in his late 30's named Mongkol Latlakorn. It was a hot, lazy day, and so we started chatting idly about the food and, eventually, our families. Mongkol mentioned that his daughter, Darin, was 15, and his voice softened as he spoke of her. She was beautiful and smart, and her father's hopes rested on her.

"Is she in school?" we asked.

"Oh, no," Mongkol said, his eyes sparkling with amusement. "She's working in a factory in Bangkok. She's making clothing for export to America." He explained that she was paid $2 a day for a nine-hour shift, six days a week.

"It's dangerous work," Mongkol added. "Twice needles went right through her hands. But the managers bandaged up her hands, and both times she got better again and went back to work."

"How terrible," we murmured sympathetically.

Mongkol looked up, puzzled. "It's good pay," he said. "I hope she can keep that job. There's all this talk about factories closing now, and she said there are rumors that her factory might close. I hope that doesn't happen. I don't know what she would do then."

He was not, of course, indifferent to his daughter's suffering; he simply had a different perspective from ours—not only when it came to food but also when it came to what constituted desirable work.

Nothing captures the difference in mind-set between East and West more than attitudes toward sweatshops. Nike and other American companies have been hammered in the Western press over the last decade for producing shoes, toys and other products in grim little factories with dismal conditions. Protests against sweatshops and the dark forces of globalization that they seem to represent have become common at meetings of the World Bank and the World Trade Organization and, this month, at a World Economic Forum in Australia, livening up the scene for Olympic athletes arriving for the competition. Yet sweatshops that seem brutal from the vantage point of an American sitting in his living room can appear tantalizing to a Thai laborer getting by on beetles.

Fourteen years ago, we moved to Asia and began reporting there. Like most Westerners, we arrived in the region outraged at sweatshops. In time, though, we came to accept the view supported by most Asians: that the campaign against sweatshops risks harming the very people it is intended to help. For beneath their grime, sweatshops are a clear sign of the industrial revolution that is beginning to reshape Asia.

This is not to praise sweatshops. Some managers are brutal in the way they house workers in firetraps, expose children to dangerous chemicals, deny bathroom breaks, demand sexual favors, force people to work double shifts or dismiss anyone who tries to organize a union. Agitation for improved safety conditions can be helpful, just as it was in 19th-century Europe. But Asian workers would be aghast at the idea of American consumers boycotting certain toys or clothing in protest. The simplest way to help the poorest Asians would be to buy more from sweatshops, not less.

On our first extended trip to China, in 1987, we traveled to the Pearl River delta in the south of the country. There we visited several factories, including one in the boomtown of Dongguan, where about 100 female workers sat at workbenches stitching together bits of leather to make purses for a Hong Kong company. We chatted with several women as their fingers flew over their work and asked about their hours.

"I start at about 6:30, after breakfast, and go until about 7 p.m.," explained one shy teenage girl. "We break for lunch, and I take half an hour off then."

"You do this six days a week?"

"Oh, no. Every day."

"Seven days a week?"

"Yes." She laughed at our surprise. "But then I take a week or two off at Chinese New Year to go back to my village."

The others we talked to all seemed to regard it as a plus that the factory allowed them to work long hours. Indeed, some had sought out this factory precisely because it offered them the chance to earn more.

"It's actually pretty annoying how hard they want to work," said the factory manager, a Hong Kong man. "It means we have to worry about security and have a supervisor around almost constantly."

It sounded pretty dreadful, and it was. We and other journalists wrote about the problems of child labor and oppressive conditions in both China and South Korea. But, looking back, our worries were excessive. Those sweatshops tended to generate the wealth to solve the problems they created. If Americans had reacted to the horror stories in the 1980's by curbing imports of those sweatshop products, then neither southern China nor South Korea would have registered as much progress as they have today.

The truth is, those grim factories in Dongguan and the rest of southern China contributed to a remarkable explosion of wealth. In the years since our first conversations there, we've returned many times to Dongguan and the surrounding towns and seen the transformation. Wages have risen from about $50 a month to $250 a month or more today. Factory conditions have improved as

businesses have scrambled to attract and keep the best laborers. A private housing market has emerged, and video arcades and computer schools have opened to cater to workers with rising incomes. A hint of a middle class has appeared—as has China's closest thing to a Western-style independent newspaper, *Southern Weekend*.

Partly because of these tens of thousands of sweatshops, China's economy has become one of the hottest in the world. Indeed, if China's 30 provinces were counted as individual countries, then the 20 fastest-growing countries in the world between 1978 and 1995 would all have been Chinese. When Britain launched the Industrial Revolution in the late 18th century, it took 58 years for per capita output to double. In China, per capita output has been doubling every 10 years.

In fact, the most vibrant parts of Asia are nearly all in what might be called the Sweatshop Belt, from China and South Korea to Malaysia, Indonesia and even Bangladesh and India. Today these sweatshop countries control about one-quarter of the global economy. As the industrial revolution spreads through China and India, there are good reasons to think that Asia will continue to pick up speed. Some World Bank forecasts show Asia's share of global gross domestic product rising to 55 to 60 percent by about 2025—roughly the West's share at its peak half a century ago. The sweatshops have helped lay the groundwork for a historic economic realignment that is putting Asia back on its feet. Countries are rebounding from the economic crisis of 1997–98 and the sweatshops—seen by Westerners as evidence of moribund economies—actually reflect an industrial revolution that is raising living standards in the East.

Of course, it may sound silly to say that sweatshops offer a route to prosperity, when wages in the poorest countries are sometimes less than $1 a day. Still, for an impoverished Indonesian or Bangladeshi woman with a handful of kids who would otherwise drop out of school and risk dying of mundane diseases like diarrhea, $1 or $2 a day can be a life-transforming wage.

This was made abundantly clear in Cambodia, when we met a 40-year-old woman named Nhem

Yen, who told us why she moved to an area with particularly lethal malaria. "We needed to eat," she said. "And here there is wood, so we thought we could cut it and sell it."

But then Nhem Yen's daughter and son-in-law both died of malaria, leaving her with two grandchildren and five children of her own. With just one mosquito net, she had to choose which children would sleep protected and which would sleep exposed.

In Cambodia, a large mosquito net costs $5. If there had been a sweatshop in the area, however harsh or dangerous, Nhem Yen would have leapt at the chance to work in it, to earn enough to buy a net big enough to cover all her children.

For all the misery they can engender, sweatshops at least offer a precarious escape from the poverty that is the developing world's greatest problem. Over the past 50 years, countries like India resisted foreign exploitation, while countries that started at a similar economic level—like Taiwan and South Korea—accepted sweatshops as the price of development. Today there can be no doubt about which approach worked better. Taiwan and South Korea are modern countries with low rates of infant mortality and high levels of education; in contrast, every year 3.1 million Indian children die before the age of 5, mostly from diseases of poverty like diarrhea.

The effect of American pressure on sweatshops is complicated. While it clearly improves conditions at factories that produce branded merchandise for companies like Nike, it also raises labor costs across the board. That encourages less well established companies to mechanize and to reduce the number of employees needed. The upshot is to help people who currently have jobs in Nike plants but to risk job factors for others. The only thing a country like Cambodia has to offer is terribly cheap wages; if companies are scolded for paying those wages, they will shift their manufacturing to marginally richer areas like Malaysia or Mexico.

Sweatshop monitors do have a useful role. They can compel factories to improve safety. They can also call attention to the impact of sweatshops on the environment. The greatest downside of industrialization is not exploitation of workers but toxic air and water. In Asia each year, three million people die from the effects of pollution. The factories springing up throughout the region are far more likely to kill people through the chemicals they expel than through terrible working conditions.

By focusing on these issues, by working closely with organizations and news media in foreign countries, sweatshops can be improved. But refusing to buy sweatshop products risks making Americans feel good while harming those we are trying to help. As a Chinese proverb goes, "First comes the bitterness, then there is sweetness and wealth and honor for 10,000 years."

Questions for Discussion:

1. What do you think of the countries that allow and even encourage children to work? How do you balance the need for income and the need for children to get an education?
2. What do you think of the assertion that refusing to buy goods made in sweatshops is actually harmful to those in third world countries that the first world are trying to help?

CASE STUDIES

Case 6.1: Sweatshops

You are employed in the human resources department of a large international company that manufactures athletic clothing and shoes. Over the course of several years, the company has closed down a dozen or so manufacturing plants in the United States. Most of the company's manufacturing and assembly operations have been moved overseas to subcontractor-owned factories located in third world countries. Wages are much lower and local regulations governing worker safety and factory conditions are significantly less restrictive in third world countries than in the United States.

Recently, your company has become the target of groups who protest against "globalization." Members of these groups have been quoted in major media stories and have set up websites accusing your company of "selling out" American labor by moving jobs overseas. They have also accused your organization of running "sweatshops" and exploiting poor workers by paying low wages, exposing workers to dangerous working conditions, and employing young children at some plants. You are asked by company executives to lead a team of human resources personnel to visit some of these factories and write a report offering your thoughts about the company's actions.

After visiting five different factories, you find that the average wage is $30 (U.S.) for a six-day week, which averages 55 hours (in the U.S., a worker doing comparable work earns about $17 per hour). This wage scale is in compliance with minimum wage scales set by local laws. Most workers are young women (16–22) who live in poor conditions and cannot save much money or afford many items we would consider necessities in the United States. However, the employees you interview tell you that they are satisfied with the wages they earn and the hours they work. Judging by the long line of job seekers at each factory's gates each morning, you can tell that there is heavy local demand for a job in the factories.

You also find that working conditions are much different than in the United States. One factory had inadequate ventilation and no source of clean drinking water. When you were inside this particular factory, the temperature was 98 degrees and very humid. At another factory you witnessed a number of workers handling chemicals without wearing masks or gloves, which does not necessarily violate local

laws but goes against your company's code of conduct. About 25 percent of the one hundred or so workers you interviewed at this factory
had no knowledge of your company's code of conduct, which is supposed to be posted. In fact, several workers had not even heard of your
company.

During your trip, you also speak with several youthful-appearing
employees who told you they were only 13 years old. Local laws permit them to work at this age, and it is clear to you that their families
need the income they produce. However, protesters are particularly
vocal about firms employing children under the age of 14.

Questions for Discussion:

1. Which of your company's practices can you defend in good
   conscience? Which practices are in need of modification?
2. Comment on the issues of wages, working conditions, and
   child labor. Incorporate the readings into your answer.

Case 6.2: "When in Rome, Do As the Romans Do"?

Upon graduation, you take a position with an organization setting
up Internet-coffee houses in countries with developing economies.
One of your first assignments is to spend a month in Southeast Asia
to assist in opening stores near large university campuses.

During your first week, your supervisor (a citizen of the country
you are in) asks you to look into acquiring electricity and phone service for the stores. After you stand in a long line, a local government
official informs you that the wait for such services can take 6 to 9
months, a delay that would make it impossible to open the stores by
the start of the school year. When told of the waiting period, your
supervisor informs you that the proper procedure is to go back and
recognize the government official's position and authority by offering
him a gift (approximately $5 U.S.) in order to receive faster service.

Upon hearing this suggestion, you raise the question of whether
or not such a payment would constitute bribery, since these types of
payments are not legally acceptable in the United States and seem to
contribute to corruption. Furthermore, they seem to give you an unfair
advantage over a local citizen who cannot pay the amount in question.

Your supervisor replies in a joking manner that you should take off
your "red-white-and-blue glasses" because this is the way things are
done here. "Besides," he explains in a more serious tone, "there is a vast
difference between a 'gift' or 'tip' to ensure promptness, and a true

bribe." "A gift," he explains, "is perfectly legal here, especially considering the small amount in question. It simply speeds up the process. It's like paying more for first-class service in your country," he says. "We are not corrupting anyone. It's a common, known practice. In fact, the gifts are considered part of the compensation of government employees, who are paid very poorly, so you could look at it as a form of charity." His answer sounds reasonable, but you are still troubled.

Before heading back to the government office the next morning, you recall something else that is troubling you too—the fact that many local companies hire children of current employees over and above equally or slightly more qualified candidates. Prior to your arrival, you had heard that nepotism (hiring family members) is commonly practiced since there is a strong cultural emphasis on familial ties, over and above individual merit, as the basis of social organization.

Questions for Discussion:

1. Based on the readings, which of the practices could you support from an ethical perspective? Why?
2. On what basis should we make decisions about matters of right and wrong when another culture's practices differ from our own?

COMMENTARY

With the expansion of business across global boundaries has come an increase in the level of awareness of conflicting behavioral standards between nations and cultures. For those that engage in economic transactions in international settings, a great deal of tension exists over whether they should adapt their behaviors to fit in with the dominant practices of a particular culture when there is conflict with their own familiar standards of behavior. While simply "doing as the Romans do" makes sense from a strictly practical standpoint, many are uncomfortable with the notion that engaging in practices that would constitute a compromise of their Christian moral ideals may be necessary in order to operate successfully in a different culture.

While cultural sensitivity is undoubtedly important, and cultural relativism has recently been a popular position to take on this issue, there are many instances in which simply following the popular mores of the land, including our own, is clearly wrong. However, this does not lead to the conclusion that someone trying to abide by Christian ethics cannot be successful while doing business internationally. There are many situations in which a conflict of ethics is only apparent. Upon closer examination, many instances that resemble moral conflicts may really be arguments over facts, procedures, or, as Bernard Adeney points out, culturally laden interpretation of events, instead of underlying ethical principles. In these instances, one can participate successfully in international business while consistently abiding by the norms of Christian morality.

Many who hold to the view that people should behave like the Romans while in Rome base their position on ethical relativism, which became popular as a result of the observations of cultural anthropologists, who observed that different cultures have widely varying moral codes and concepts of right and wrong. Its key advocates include primarily anthropologists, such as William Graham Sumner, who wrote his classic book *Folkways*, outlining his notion of relativism; Ruth Benedict; Melville Herskovits; and philosopher John Ladd.[1] As they studied different cultures, they were struck by the lack of a uniform concept of right and wrong. For example, some cultures practice polygamy; others practice monogamy. Some cultures consider it a moral obligation to give one of their children to an infertile couple. Some cultures, such as certain groups of Eskimos, practice euthanasia and infanticide in ways that seem ghastly and immoral to many in other cultures. Among the Auca Indians of South America, treachery was considered the highest virtue, and the missionaries who brought the gospel to them were horrified that the Aucas regarded Judas, not Jesus, as the hero. These are just a sample of the great variety of ways that morality is conceived and practiced.

As a result of these observations, new conclusions were being drawn about the nature of morality. It was suggested that in view of such moral diversity, belief in universal moral values that applied irrespective of culture could not be maintained. Such moral diversity called into question ethical systems that posited absolute, unchanging moral principles that could be universally applied. The more "enlightened" way of viewing morality was to allow for morality to be relative to the culture in which one found oneself. Rather than universal moral absolutes, morality was seen as relative to the cultural consensus.

To be sure, some anthropologists only pointed out the differences between cultures when it came to moral codes. They held to what is called *cultural relativism*, or the diversity thesis. This is simply a descriptive notion that says that there are widely differing standards of right and wrong among different cultures in the world. But many

1 Their main works in this area are as follows: William Graham Sumner, *Folkways* (New York: Ginn and Co., 1906); Ruth Benedict, *Patterns of Culture* (New York: New American Library, 1934); Melville Herskovits, *Cultural Relativism* (New York: Random House, 1972); John Ladd, ed., *Ethical Relativism* (Belmont, Calif.: Wadsworth Publishing Co., 1973).

went further and espoused a more strong form of relativism, called *ethical relativism,* or the dependency thesis. This strong form of relativism holds that all values are culturally created, and as a result there are no objective, universal moral principles that are binding on all cultures and time periods. To be sure, values are shaped by the culture in which they are practiced. The history of ethics shows how sociological conditions strongly influenced the emphases of different thinkers.[2] But the ethical relativist is saying much more than that. He or she holds that morality is dependent on the cultural context in which one finds him- or herself, and as a result there are no objective universal moral principles that are binding on all cultures and time periods.

Ethical relativism has become a popular approach to morality in the broader culture and in international business. Many executives will justify decisions to offer bribes or forgo worker and product safety standards by employing arguments based upon cultural relativity.

Despite its philosophical shortcomings, ethical relativism does have appeal. The first appeal of relativism is based on the important notion that morality does not occur in a sociological vacuum. Some of our cultural values are formed in reaction to, or affirmation of, the social conditions of the time. Unfortunately, these have been and often are mistaken for absolute/objective standards, when in reality they are little more than the biases of a particular (often dominant) culture, dressed up in moral language.

A good example of this dynamic at work is the practice of slavery during the Civil War era. Though it was clearly immoral for human beings to own other human beings and, in many cases, to treat them like animals, many in the South attempted to justify slavery as an institution, sometimes using biblical grounds. Slavery, which was created as a result of the agricultural conditions in the South, was treated as moral, and the right to own slaves was regarded as an absolute right. Of course, it was nothing of the sort, and a cultural creation was regarded as an absolute moral right, mistaking the absolute for the sociologically relative.

A second appeal of relativism comes from the way it is presented. Frequently, relativism is presented as though it and its polar opposite, called absolutism, were the only two valid alternatives. The absolutist holds to absolute moral principles rigidly and does not allow for any exceptions, regardless of the circumstances. As Adeney points out, this position simplistically "flattens out" all morality and neglects the fact that a person's choice of moral rules is often highly related to culture. This is clearly not an attractive or realistic position to hold, and if rel-

[2] See chapter 4 for a survey of the history of ethics. Each thinker is analyzed in terms of his sociological context and the contribution to his emphases.

ativism is presented as the only alternative to this kind of absolutism, it is not hard to see why people would prefer relativism.

However, it is better to see morality on a continuum, with absolutism at one extreme and relativism at the other. One can hold to objective moral principles and not be an absolutist; that is, one can be what is called a prima facie absolutist, or an absolutist "on the surface." While far from a perfect ethical theory, prima facie absolutism recognizes the importance of objective moral principles that do not change depending on how one feels about them, but it also allows for periodic exceptions to general principles, depending on the circumstances. On selected issues, most people who hold to the importance of principles would admit exceptions. For example, in the case of abortion, it is widely agreed that in the rare case in which the mother's life is at imminent risk from continuing a pregnancy, it is justifiable to end the pregnancy. Similarly, if someone comes into your house with a gun ready to shoot and asks where your husband or wife is, you are not obligated to tell him the truth. Thus the relativist's appeal rests on a false dichotomy.

A third appeal of relativism comes from the appropriate need to be sensitive to people from other cultures. While acknowledging the fine line between sensitivity and falling into moral relativism, Christian ethics upholds the values of humility and the practice of love toward others, including efforts at understanding and appreciating (not just "tolerating") legitimate cultural differences.

A fourth appeal of relativism comes from the modern emphasis on scientific objectivity. When applied to morality, this takes the form of value neutrality, presumed by the culture to be a good thing. Yet it is becoming more recognized in scholarly circles that value neutrality is actually a myth, and even if it were possible, it might not even be desirable. But in the popular culture, holding to absolute values that transcend culture is considered the equivalent of imposing one's values on other people and cultures. The person who does this is considered at best, somewhat unenlightened, and at worst, a narrow, rigid fundamentalist. Given that alternative to relativism, again, it is not surprising that relativism is appealing.

In spite of its appeal and widespread use in the popular culture, relativism has significant philosophical shortcomings, namely its vulnerability to being reduced to personal subjectivism and its inconsistency with our use of moral language and metaphors.[3] However, there are several other critical weaknesses of relativism. First, in terms of the observations of the cultural anthropologists who developed relativism, the degree of moral diversity is overstated and the high degree of moral consensus is understated. There is a good deal more moral

3 For a more detailed discussion of these weaknesses, see Norman Bowie, *Multinational Ethics* (Englewood Cliffs, N.J.: Prentice-Hall, 1989), 366–82.

consensus among cultures than was first believed. Anthropologist Clyde Kluckhohn has noted:

> Every culture has a concept of murder, distinguishing this from execution, killing in war and other justifiable homicides. The notions of incest and other regulations upon sexual behavior, the prohibitions on untruth under defined circumstances, of restitution and reciprocity, of mutual obligations between parents and children—these and many other moral concepts are altogether universal.[4]

A second shortcoming is related to the first. Many of the observations of moral diversity were differences in moral practices. But diversity in practice does not necessarily equal diversity in underlying values or principles. There is much less moral diversity than many anthropologists think they have observed. A person who holds to the reality of objective moral values can easily account for varieties in practices from the perspective of the underlying principles.

A third weakness of relativism is that ethical relativism cannot be drawn from the observations of the cultural relativist. That is, the strong form of relativism, that values are dependent on the cultural context in which one finds oneself, cannot be drawn from the weaker form or from the phenomena of moral diversity. Ethical relativism as a system does not follow from the empirical data of moral diversity among cultures. Simply because different cultures have different moral standards, even if the degree of moral diversity were not overstated, it does not follow that there is no such thing as absolute values that transcend culture.

For instance, although bribery (in its true form) is supposedly "commonly practiced," very high level government officials have been brought down by scandals in which it was involved. Moreover, if bribery is readily accepted, one wonders why it is always done in secret. And no nation that we are aware of defends bribery to the international community. When someone is accused of it, they usually deny that it occurred rather than mounting a defense of the practice.

A fourth weakness of relativism is that it provides no way to arbitrate among competing cultural value claims. This is critical as business begins to expand across national boundaries and countries are attempting to create trade agreements. In the absence of transcendent norms, the United States cannot rightfully accuse China of wrongdoing in its alleged failures to crack down on the piracy of intellectual property such as computer software. Furthermore, many countries recognize the high degree of cultural diversity within their own popula-

[4] Clyde Kluckhohn, "Ethical Relativity: Sic et Non," *Journal of Philosophy* (1955): LII. See also E. O. Wilson, *On Human Nature* (New York: Bantam Books, 1979).

tions. Thus, there must be a way to adjudicate the various moral claims that occur as a result of inevitable cultural clashes.

The fifth and most serious charge against relativism is an extension of the fourth weakness. The relativist cannot morally evaluate any clearly oppressive culture or, more specifically, any obvious tyrant. In the absence of absolutes, no one can rightfully claim the existence of international human rights. Cultures that relegate women to the status of second-class citizens cannot be evaluated by the relativist, since morality is dependent on the cultural context. Similarly, the relativist cannot pass judgment on someone like Hitler—who oppressed a minority with the permission, if not approval, of the majority—since for the relativist there is no moral absolute that transcends culture to which he or she can appeal as a basis for that judgment.

A final objection to relativism is the charge that its central premise, that there are no moral absolutes, is a self-defeating statement because that statement is an absolute itself. However, the relativist could respond that the statement is only a formal absolute, not a material one; that is, it is a statement that describes the procedure of relativism, not a moral principle that is absolute. That distinction is correct, but there is still a moral absolute for the relativist that makes the system self-defeating. That is the absolute of tolerance and respect for the values of other cultures. The relativist could not likely tolerate any culture that had intolerance as one of its central virtues.

While these objections to relativism can seem quite abstract, they are critical when considering particular situations that arise in international business settings. Clearly, some cases of doing as Romans do can violate a transcendent norm for moral behavior. As mentioned above, bribery (in its true form) is a case in point. While it may be common, all signs lead to a conclusion that it is still immoral. Thus, one should not bribe just because it seems to be a common practice.

There are other instances in which using cultural relativism to justify simply abiding by the host country standards is morally wrong. Consider the fact that unlike the industrialized countries, there are many governments that do not even attempt to consider or represent the best interests of their citizens when enacting legislation. While we take democratic government for granted, it is charitable to call the ruling parties of some countries "governments" at all, since they do little that represents what governing implies. For example, without apparent consideration of the interests of their citizens, some governments accept toxic chemicals from industrialized countries and dispose of them in unsafe ways in exchange for large sums of money. For a company to "export death" in such a manner, knowing the risks involved and that the money is probably going to the private wealth of a few government officials, is irresponsible and immoral.

Even cases in which governments do look out for the interests of their citizens can be problematic. Certain countries are in no position to enact high moral standards for their business practices. As Thomas Donaldson points out, some developing countries must accept lower standards for wages and environmental protection in order to give an incentive for foreign investment. In some instances, they have very little bargaining power with foreign governments and corporations. Often they are forced to choose between accepting these tradeoffs or forgoing economic development.[5]

Low-wage, low-skill factories (sweatshops) in developing nations provide some insight into the complex nature of behaving ethically in international business. Many factory workers have no other options than to accept low wages in exchange for their labor, which usually takes place under poor conditions. For some young women, the available alternatives are unemployment, farming, or prostitution. As Kristof and WuDunn point out in "Two Cheers for Sweatshops," a job in a factory is seen as an "opportunity" within this broader context.

With the surplus of available labor in many of these countries, these employees cannot simply quit and take another position. In some cases, when some workers tried to unionize, they were fired immediately. Thus, to treat these workers poorly and to pay them the minimum amount possible fits a textbook definition of exploitation, in which a party with all of the power forces another to abide by their rules.

However, the issue is very complex because it would be unpractical to pay a rate much higher than the market set price. The incentive to set up shop would be immediately destroyed, and the economic disruption caused by the overnight creation of a wealthy class of workers could be severe. In addition, the risk of attracting professionals, such as physicians and teachers, who may leave their positions for higher paying factory work is a real possibility.

Paying lower wages to workers based on geographical location is not necessarily immoral. In our own country, there are sometimes large wage variations for similar positions based on differences in cost of living. The goal, however, should be to provide a wage that provides a decent standard of living. Although there are clear limits, the term "decent" can be defined somewhat flexibly depending on the culture and the stage of economic development of a particular place. The issue of safe working conditions and how employees are treated, however, offers far less flexibility. On these issues, ethics demands that people be treated the same way, wherever they may live and work.

[5] Thomas Donaldson, *The Ethics of International Business* (New York: Oxford University Press, 1989).

With these examples in mind, it is undoubtedly challenging to try to adopt local standards of behavior while staying within the bounds of Christian ethics. However, we earlier stated that one could consistently abide by Judeo-Christian morals and succeed in international business settings. For example, with respect to bribery, there is no empirical evidence that it is even necessary in order to gain success in those parts of the world where it is "commonly" practiced. Research conducted by John Graham shows that American firms were never held at a disadvantage through bribery legislation.

Moreover, as the second shortcoming of relativism described above notes, many instances in which ethical conflicts appear may really be disagreements over facts and interpretations rather than underlying moral principles. The common situation of small monetary payments to government officials serves as an excellent example. On the surface, these situations pit conflicting standards against each other. However, upon closer examination, these may be conflicts over definition and/or culture, rather than underlying ethical principles. When these types of conflicts occur, the immediate question that must be asked is whether or not a real conflict of underlying moral principles is taking place. As Adeney points out, these types of payments may represent gifts, tips, bribes, or something in between all of them.

These are just a few examples of situations that lead to the question of how to act when in a cross-cultural situation. In sum, "While in Rome, do as the Romans do" is an inadequate guide to moral action while operating in different cultures. Cultural relativism as a theory has some significant shortcomings, and simply adapting to the norms of a host country can lead to some serious transgressions of Judeo-Christian morality. However, narrow "absolutism" is not the correct answer either. There are other instances in which mere apparent and not real conflicts of underlying ethical principles can be resolved (though perhaps not easily) with a closer look at the facts, including our cultural assumptions. Thus, Christians can, indeed, be successful in international business while remaining consistent with the ethical standards of their tradition, though they will have to be open-minded and cautiously but appropriately flexible in the process.

Part III

Contemporary Ethical Issues in Business

SEVEN

Human Resources Management

Treating persons with respect entails not treating them as things, objects, or tools in an effort to achieve one's own goals (as a manager, say) or the goals of the corporation.

John R. Rowan

Possibly the greatest threat to privacy [in the workplace] is posed by . . . combining the use of monitoring and surveillance devices with certain computer software and computer networks.

Seumas Miller and John Weckert

INTRODUCTION

In the last twenty-five years, there has been an explosion of discussion on the subject of employee rights. This has corresponded with an increased emphasis in society in general on individual rights, particularly the rights to privacy and free speech. Understandably, this general societal emphasis has translated into a growing concern for protection of the rights of employees in the workplace. With the publication of David Ewing's classic "employee bill of rights" in 1977, the debate over exactly what rights employees have in the workplace was sharpened.[1]

Questions of employee rights and privacy are more complicated today because of the growing use of electronic communication, including Internet usage; the increasing concern over the use of illegal drugs; the spread of the HIV virus; and the growth of genetic testing for certain catastrophic diseases, some whose onset is later in life. In addition, with the extremely competitive business environment, granting rights to workers will likely collide more frequently with the profit

[1] David Ewing, "A Proposed Bill of Rights," in *Freedom inside the Organization* (New York: E. P. Dutton, 1977): 144–51. See the Commentary section for more detail on the specifics of his bill of rights.

maximization mandate, giving employers less financial flexibility to grant broad employee rights. When the exercise of employee rights affects a firm's profitability, as it often does, employers may feel less inclined to institute changes that protect the rights of workers at the expense of the company's bottom line.

Historically, employees have had to fight hard to gain certain rights in the workplace. Companies were commonly viewed as the owners' property, with which they could dispose in any way they saw fit. This idea came to be known more formally as "employment at will"; that is, the employer had the right to hire and fire at his discretion. He owed virtually nothing to employees other than fair wages for work performed in a safe environment. For example, he did not owe workers due process when they had been fired. As a result, employees had few if any legal rights, and the differential in power favoring the employer effectively prevented employees from voicing concerns or otherwise pressuring employers to make changes in the way employees were treated.

In the first half of the twentieth century, the primary employee right for which employees fought was the right to organize into labor unions, helping balance the power differential between employer and employees. Labor unions were primarily intended to safeguard workers' rights, specifically the right to fair wages and a safe workplace. The National Labor Relations Act, passed in the mid-1930s, prohibited companies from firing workers because of union membership and generally made it easier for workers to organize. In addition, other New Deal legislation in the 1930s extended worker rights by limiting the number of hours in the regular required workweek and prohibiting child labor. With the decline of union influence in the 1980s and 90s, however, employees have increasingly had to rely on the courts and government regulators to force employers to recognize the workplace rights they believe should be protected.

The notion of employee rights and privacy is broad, encompassing many specific issues. There is great debate over what rights workers do possess when they enter the workplace and under what conditions these rights may be overridden. As an introductory exercise, consider the following short scenarios and decide whether management is justified in firing an employee when they occur. This will help you think about what rights employees have in the workplace.

1. The president of the company has a "gut feeling" that an employee is not trustworthy.
2. A high-ranking member of the company regularly and visibly purchases the competitor's products.

3. An employee openly attacks and grumbles about company management to other employees.
4. An employee "blows the whistle" on the employer for disseminating fraudulent information on product safety tests.
5. An employee refuses to service a pharmaceutical industry client that manufactures abortion-inducing drugs.

The issues in the above scenarios include the rights of employees to free speech, to follow their moral convictions, and to conduct themselves off company time however they see fit. Employee privacy is a bit more specific and is focused on what privacy rights employees possess while on the job. Again, consider the following brief scenarios and decide whether they constitute a justifiable invasion of the employee's privacy.

1. Using the company email system, an employee complains to another employee about management. Someone in management reads this and has the employee fired.
2. For safety reasons, a company mandates HIV testing for all employees.
3. A genetic test is developed that can screen a person for certain genetic diseases such as Alzheimer's, Lou Gehrig's disease, and Huntington's disease. Your employer wants you to be tested and wants access to the results.
4. The employee handbook of the company states that "employees will not date co-workers or clients of the firm"—a violation that could result in dismissal.
5. The company has a policy that it will not hire smokers because of the increased cost to the company of their health care.

The readings in this chapter introduce you to the various ethical issues in human resource management. Entire textbooks are devoted to this subject, so what we offer here is an overall justification for employee rights and some of the most controversial issues in this area. John Rowan lays out the theoretical basis for employee rights in his article, "The Moral Foundation of Employee Rights." He argues that the moral value of respect for human dignity grounds treatment of employees as persons. He suggests that such treatment of employees involves fair pay, workplace safety, due process, and privacy. Seumas Miller and John Weckert take up in more detail the controversial area of employee privacy and insist that the most frequently voiced justifications for monitoring employees and invading their privacy do not stand up to close scrutiny. They suggest that there should be a presumption of privacy in the workplace, with the burden of proof on the employer to justify overriding someone's privacy. They relate this to surveillance, monitoring of email, and Internet use as well as to electronic observation of one's computer use. Finally, J. H. Foegen addresses the still-controversial area of sexual harassment, insightfully pointing out how the efforts to identify and deal with sexual harassment in the workplace have resulted in isolating men and women at work—precisely the opposite from the effect that was intended.

READINGS

The Moral Foundation of Employee Rights

John R. Rowan

Journal of Business Ethics 24, no. 4 (April 2000): 355–61. Copyright © 2000 Kluwer Academic Publishers.

In business ethics, clear communication from theorists (academics) to practitioners (managers) is crucial if positive effects in the workplace are to be achieved. Unfortunately, such communication does not always occur. We on the academic side tend to spend time reading and reviewing substantial amounts of ethical theory, and all too often we simply relay our findings, in their complex and impractical form, to managers. Thus, what managers frequently get is often not what they need, which is theory in a workable and relatively simple format—guidelines which may be consulted when making difficult decisions or which may be implemented as company policy. If the communication is to be improved, it is we academics who must change. Managers simply have neither the time nor the inclination to attempt large-scale translations of complex ethical theories and guidelines forwarded to them.

My aim in this paper is to retain these considerations in discussing employee rights, which is one of the most important, yet complex, issues in

the field of business ethics. First, it is important because employees, generally speaking, are in a comparatively inferior bargaining position with respect to their employers. This inequality opens up possibilities for various sorts of exploitation, such as inadequate compensation, discrimination, and privacy invasions, all of which have been known to occur. Second, employee rights are complex, in that managers, as a prerequisite for making ethically sound decisions, must assess which alleged employee rights are legitimate (spurious claims surely arise at times), and must weigh them against the rights of those in other stakeholder groups.

If managers are to adequately address particular situations in which these issues arise, they must have a deeper understanding of the underlying ethical considerations. More precisely, an understanding of the moral foundation of employee rights is required. Guidelines alone can be ambiguous; the various amendments to the U.S. Constitution are examples of basic rules which, on their own (without theoretical context), can be interpreted and applied in a variety of ways. A mere list of employee rights will face similar difficulties. Thus, managers will be able to make more consistent, more ethically sound decisions when the scope of possible interpretations of rights is restricted by the particular theoretical foundation. This paper aims to provide just such a foundation, one that is defensible, practically workable, and can be grasped with relatively little time and effort. This will be achieved through a discussion of the foundation itself, followed by some examples of employee rights which it generates, and then some specific examples of policy and practice. It is hoped that this approach will provide what is currently lacking by providing a middle ground between the extremes of listing employee rights with what for managers is insufficient justification (Ewing, 1977) and an overly theoretical justification (Donaldson, 1989; Gewirth, 1996; McCall, 1996).

First, however, providing a definition of a right is in order. For our purposes, a right should be understood as a "moral claim." The first part of this definition, the stipulation that a right is moral, is meant to indicate that it is not necessarily recognized by any conventional system. A legal right, for example, is held by a certain individual or group of individuals just in case the government decides that the right is held.

Whether or not a legal right is moral is an open question. The prevailing American laws through much of the nineteenth century provided slave owners with certain legal rights, in essence property rights, over their slaves, yet we have come to think that no legitimate moral foundation for such rights ever existed. Conversely, the (moral) rights of slaves not to be treated as property (indeed the rights of persons not to be enslaved) were not recognized by American law for a long time. This discussion treats employee rights as moral, since they may or may not be conventionally recognized, either legally or in corporate policy. The foundation for such rights refers to their theoretical justification, and provides a method for assessing which alleged rights are legitimate, and which

should be overridden in cases where legitimate ones conflict.

The second part of the definition indicates that a right is a claim. The legal scholar Wesley Hohfeld (1919) was the first to use this terminology, and moral philosophers have followed this practice (Feinberg, 1989; Sumner, 1987; Thomson, 1990). A claim, according to Hohfeld, is a particular type of right, one that is correlative with a duty on the part of the person(s) against whom the right is held. My moral right not to be harmed by others is therefore to be understood as a moral duty on the part of others not to harm me. My right to private property is to be understood as a duty on the part of others not to steal or otherwise use that which is mine. This description of claims implies that they are relational, and this is what should be expected in a discussion of employee rights. In other words, an employee's right to safety in the workplace is held against her employer, since the employer has the duty to provide her with a safe work environment; she does not hold this right against members of the general public, since they have no such duty.

The moral foundation for these sorts of employee rights focuses on employees as persons. Unlike the study of science, the study of ethics is often accused of suffering from an inability to provide deductively valid conclusions. As this is the nature of ethical theory, the best we can hope for is to start with views that are sufficiently basic to warrant near-universal acceptance—"first principles" Aristotle called them. Here, two such views are offered: first, employees are persons; and second, there is something morally significant about persons, something that makes it wrong to treat them in certain ways.

The suggestion will be that the moral importance of persons is a function of their having goals and interests. Having goals is of moral relevance because of the widely held view that individuals ought to have the means for formulating and executing a minimally acceptable life plan. When such means are taken away by others or are simply unavailable, as in cases of extreme poverty, no reasonable goals are possible, and we often say that something ought to be done to rectify the situation. This is an aspect of the liberal conception of the self, espoused in the traditional philosophical literature by Locke (1960) and Mill (1991), and more recently by Rawls (1971) and Raz (1987). While it is not the case that individuals should be provided with everything they desire, possessing at least a minimally acceptable variety of options for a life plan, "personal autonomy" according to Raz, is a necessary condition merely for having goals, and thus for achieving goals. Interests are even more basic, as they may be defined as needs, which are certainly of moral importance; they are the necessary preconditions not only for life itself, but for being able to formulate and execute a life plan. For this reason, the moral importance of interests is also thought to derive from considerations of personal autonomy, and examples may include security, shelter, adequate food and water, education, and a healthful environment (Braybrooke, 1987; Copp, 1992; Shue, 1989).

If the moral importance of being a person is a function of having goals and interests, then we may postulate certain basic rights which all persons, simply by virtue of being persons, can be said to possess. The first is a right to freedom, which includes not only negative freedom, such as the right not to be physically restrained, but positive freedom, such as the rights not to be coerced or hindered by the effects of external forces (Berlin, 1984). This right follows naturally from having goals for the following reason. Having goals, as noted in the previous paragraph, is of moral importance. When individuals do not have at their disposal minimally acceptable options when formulating their goals, it is commonly thought that something ought to be done to rectify the situation. This implies that when nothing is done, something has gone wrong morally, which in turn implies a right of some sort held by the individuals in question. Because freedom pertains to availability of options, it makes [sense] to say that this is a right to freedom, positive as well as negative (as described above). This is not to say that business corporations are charged with the duty to ensure freedom for all citizens; firms are not to oversee societal welfare operations.

More mildly, the claim is that when managers choose to hire employees, they must bear in mind that they are dealing with persons, and that the (positive and negative) freedom of their employees is therefore to be respected.

Second, a right to well-being follows naturally from having interests. Understood as the necessary preconditions even for pursuing goals, interests are thought to be of moral importance for the same reason as goals; when some of those preconditions are not present, it is commonly thought that something ought to be done to rectify the situation. This implies that when nothing is done, something has gone wrong morally, and this in turn implies a right of some sort held by the individuals in question. It makes sense to say that this is a right to well-being; when preconditions are absent, interests are not satisfied, and well-being is not had.

These generic rights to freedom and well-being are not uncommon in the human rights literature (Gewirth, 1978). An additional right, implicit in the above discussion of the first two, is the right to equality. The idea is that everyone has the rights to freedom and well-being equally, to the same extent; since these rights are held by persons as persons, and since everyone is a person, this equality is inescapable. Indeed, this observation helps to explain why it is commonly thought that something ought to be done to assist those lacking freedom or well-being; as having goals and interests is the defining aspect of the moral equality of all persons, failing to assist is failing to treat those individuals as everyone wants to be treated. In the business context, as all persons have goals and interests, a manager who herself is employed in an effort to pursue her goals cannot consistently fail to recognize that her employees are doing the same. Thus, the type of job, or level of responsibility within a corporation, ought not affect the degree to which the other two generic rights are held.

The rights to freedom, well-being and equality can be summarily captured under the rubric of "respect." Persons, simply because they are persons, have a right to be treated in a way that respects these three separate rights. Conversely, we can say that it is wrong to treat people in a way that fails to respect them as persons, as moral beings with goals and interests and thus with rights to freedom, well-being and equality. Some may recognize the remarks here and in previous paragraphs as consistent with the basic Kantian idea (in the second formulation of the categorical imperative) that it is wrong to treat others as means only (Kant, 1981), and indeed this is what the foregoing discussion suggests. Treating persons with respect entails not treating them as things, objects, or tools in an effort to achieve one's own goals (as a manager, say) or the goals of the corporation.

For these reasons, the moral philosopher can offer the manager the following regarding ethical decisions pertaining to employee rights. Employees should at all times be treated in a way that respects them as persons. The basic message is simple, and the underlying reasoning can be communicated to managers without requiring them to engage in hundreds of pages of philosophy. While this approach will not always yield unique prescriptions (different people may still reach different conclusions regarding the proper course of action in particular situations), we should expect this approach to produce a divergence of solutions which is minimal, or at least less frequent than what typically seems to be the case.

Further, this approach coincides with recently developed theories of the firm that emphasize the importance of personal autonomy and the general idea that the corporation should positively contribute to the lives of individuals affected by its activities (Freeman, 1984; Hartman, 1996; Solomon, 1992). The strict distinction between work activities and personal activities is uncalled for according to these theories; there is no reason for thinking that business life must be opposed to (and thus cannot contribute to) personal life. Employees, as persons, work in order to advance their ends, and therefore are entitled to "respect" as described above. Supporting the plausibility of this view of the firm is the observation that stockholders, managers, and indeed all those contributing to the organization are involved in an effort to pursue their goals, and consistency requires managers to bear this in mind when dealing with employees.

Some examples of specific cases will be considered shortly, but first it is worth reviewing a few employee rights which should, on this understanding of the moral foundation of such rights, appear in the policy statement of any company. The first of these is the right of employees to receive fair pay, and there are at least three different contexts in which this is relevant. First, pay should be fair in an interpersonally comparative sense. Whether pay scales are based on seniority, achievement, or some other aspect(s), corporations have a duty to consider all employees equally. Hence, the cry "Equal pay for equal work" is a protest against alleged wage discrepancies (usually to the detriment of women and minorities) even when controls for seniority, achievement and other relevant factors are considered. Second, pay should be fair in an intrapersonally comparative sense; as an individual's service to a corporation grows in length of time and (perhaps) in responsibility, she should receive comparatively more in the way of compensation.

Both of these derive from equality, but the third context of fair pay, which is non-comparative and pertains to the notion of a minimum wage, derives from well-being. When we consider employees as persons who deserve respect, the justification for a minimum wage should be clear. As persons have goals and interests, a certain minimum standard of living is required. Whether this entails the existence of broader welfare rights held (against the government) by all persons, employed or not, is an open question; some claim that corporations (and others) are morally culpable for ignoring the plight of the homeless and jobless, but on the model of employees as persons, the homeless and jobless are not necessarily being treated by corporations as things because they are not being treated by corporations in any way at all. Regardless, employees are persons with whom corporations have dealt, and have contracted to perform work. To hire a person for an appallingly meager wage is to use her as a means only, to treat her merely as an item on the balance sheet, acquiring her services for as little as possible. Because many potential employees are in comparatively weak bargaining positions, the wage agreed upon, if unchecked, is likely to be very small in many situations (as was the case a century ago). An employee right to a minimum wage is a recognition that the employee is a person, with goals and interests, and also that the maximization of shareholder wealth is insufficient justification for using her as a mere tool for profit.

A second employee right is that of safety in the workplace. Employers have a duty to provide a safe work environment and to make improvements when necessary, since failing to do so risks the well-being of persons. There also exists the duty to inform workers of certain risks which cannot be avoided; not doing so amounts to a deliberate attempt to mislead in an effort to hold down labor costs.

A third employee right, more general in nature, is that of due process in the workplace (Werhane, 1985). All employees, as persons who have goals, ought to be afforded a certain degree of participation in the decision-making processes of their companies. When firings or demotions are necessary, employees ought to be informed about the reasons (and indeed about the reasons behind any action by management that affects them), and perhaps even granted an appeal or hearing.

Finally, employees as persons have a right to privacy in the workplace (and also outside the workplace). This derives from the basic right to freedom, and at a minimum this entails the right to be left alone (Werhane, 1985), including the right to withhold from employers personal information that is not relevant to the job. Therefore, practices such as forcing employees to submit to polygraph tests (in order to ensure compliance with company rules) are morally questionable. The employee's inferior bargaining position with respect to available options makes her susceptible to exploitation; the polygraph test itself may be a form of exploitation (since the employee may have no viable alternative but to comply) and further, the information learned by the employer may in certain circumstances be used against her. Such

policies therefore put employees at risk of losing viable options, and thus of losing freedom. Whether a practice such as mandatory random drug testing violates this right is debatable, since companies (especially ones which entrust employees to protect public welfare, such as those in the transportation industry) do have a legitimate interest in securing drug-free employees. Even if a strong case can be made in favor of the permissibility of drug-testing policies in certain fields, the inherent potential for employee harassment or other abuse by the employer means that acceptable guidelines must be instituted and strictly followed (Desjardins and Duska, 1987). Such testing, for example, must be truly random (to guard against discrimination), and must be conducted in such a way that the personal space of the persons being tested is not unnecessarily violated.

While rights such as these seem very general (and thus perhaps impractical), they can be utilized successfully by managers when the underlying foundation of employees as persons is understood. Recognition of the basis of these rights will enable managers to discern what, exactly, is owed to employees, and what is inordinate. Perhaps even more importantly, the foundation will provide a means for adjudication when rights conflict. In a proposed drug-testing policy, for example, one employee's right to a safe work environment may conflict with another's right to privacy. The appropriate course of action will be a function of which employee will be respected more as a person if her right is recognized. It may also be the case that some compromise can be reached that respects both employees reasonably well. The important point is that employee rights with inadequate justification or with overly theoretical justification will not provide managers with a workable framework for moral reasoning in these sorts of instances.

This short list of employee rights is certainly incomplete, but these four suggestions are examples which seem straightforward to follow from the moral foundation of employees as persons. The last one, the right to privacy, is relevant to the example of a policy prohibiting dating between persons in the same office, the same department, or even the same company. The justification for such a policy is the correlation between the existence of these sorts of relationships and a decline in job performance. However, treating employees as persons requires not grouping them in statistical categories, at least not for the purpose of restricting their personal freedom. This policy therefore violates the employee's moral right to privacy; the choice of persons with whom to associate is, in short, none of the company's business. If there is a drop in job performance, then at that time the company may take certain actions (disciplinary or otherwise) to protect its interests; but the justification for any such action is poor job performance, not dating, and at no time may the employees be required to cease the relationship.

A more specific example, as follows, is adapted from one offered by Donaldson and Dunfee (1995). An account executive, who happens to be female (Jane), is selected by a consulting firm to handle the affairs of an important client, "important" meaning very wealthy and thus potentially very beneficial for the firm's shareholders. Shortly after Jane is appointed, the client informs the firm that he prefers to deal with a male representative. What is the ethically appropriate course of action?

One possibility would be for the firm, citing its obligation to maximize shareholder wealth, to ask Jane to remove herself from the account. Another possibility, more in line with its obligation not to discriminate against employees on the basis of gender, would be to inform the client that Jane is best qualified for the job, and should he remain unsatisfied he is welcome to take his business elsewhere. Recalling the proposed foundation on which Jane's rights are based, there is a strong presumptive case in favor of the second alternative. Jane, being a person, ought not be used merely as a cog in a profit-making machine. She is more than a tool to be used to advance the firm's interests.

There may be room for some middle ground. After all, shareholders are persons, too. Losing the account would, in some sense, be failing to respect them as persons whose goals include earning a dividend on money they have invested in good faith; but brusquely dismissing Jane from the account would be a more severe violation of failing to demonstrate respect. A middle ground solution would honor the request of the client while not treating Jane as a mere object. Perhaps Jane may be removed from the account provided she is compensated in some way, though this is not to suggest that she may simply be bought off. Treating Jane as a person requires taking her goals and interests into account, and if, for example, her goals are closely tied to professional advancement within the firm, it may be appropriate to give her special attention in the future, or to negotiate a more specific arrangement to which she is agreeable. Of course, if no compromise can be reached, then the firm may have little choice (morally) but to reject the client's request.

At this point, the general process for arriving at solutions to ethical problems involving employee rights can be seen. Managers are often in difficult positions; besides employees, they have responsibilities to a variety of stakeholder groups, including shareholders, consumers, bondholders, suppliers, and sometimes even political groups and the general public. When these responsibilities are not only contractually established but are moral in nature, there are moral rights held by the various groups which correspond with the duties. The appropriate course of action will therefore be a function of which rights are strongest, and the strength of the rights can be assessed by viewing the assorted rightholders as persons who, simply because they are persons, warrant respect. The suggestion in this paper is that the rights of employees in particular can be seen in this way.

Thus, when a retail company, unfortunate enough to have a delivery to its warehouse delayed until the day before a big sale, must decide whether to require its employees to work late into the night loading trucks and driving the merchandise to the stores, the deliberation should involve a weighing process of sorts. What is the strength of the company's duty to its customers, incurred through advertising, to get the goods to the stores by the promised date? What is the strength of the company's duty to its shareholders to accomplish this task, and the strength of its duty to its employees not to require them (via some sort of threat) to work extra hours? The answers to these questions can be found by looking to the framework of employees as persons, and also considering consumers and shareholders as persons. An immediate observation, perhaps evident from the foregoing discussion, is that the employee's rights are sufficiently strong that the company cannot simply order the extra work. Perhaps it may offer bonuses or incentives for anyone willing to stay late and help the company. Again, though, without the development of an arrangement which the employees deem acceptable, it must allow the employees to leave work on time (without penalty), issue "rainchecks" to customers who show up at the stores the next day, and (in the interests of both the customers and shareholders), do as much in the way of customer service as is reasonable under the circumstances.

Again, the hope is that managers, equipped with a reasonable and practical understanding of the moral foundation of employee rights, will be able to put theory into practice when confronted with difficult ethical situations. Employees are persons, first and foremost, and therefore must be respected and never treated as means only. With this in mind, a morally defensible formulation of corporate policy, and interpretation of such policy in particular instances, can be more easily achieved.

References

Berlin, I: 1984, 'Two Concepts of Liberty,' in Michael Sandel (ed.), *Liberalism and Its Critics* (New York University Press, New York, NY), pp. 15–36.

Braybrooke, D.: 1987, *Meeting Needs* (Princeton University Press, Princeton, NJ).

Copp, D.: 1992, 'The Right to an Adequate Standard of Living: Justice, Autonomy and the Basic Needs,' in Ellen Frankel Paul, Fred D. Miller and Jeffrey Paul (eds.), *Economic Rights* (Cambridge University Press, Cambridge), pp. 231–261.

Desjardins, J. and R. Duska: 1987, 'Drug Testing in Employment,' *Business and Professional Ethics Journal* 6, 3–21.

Donaldson, T.: 1989, *The Ethics of International Business* (Oxford University Press, Oxford).

Donaldson, T. and T. W. Dunfee: 1995, 'Integrative Social Contracts Theory: A Communitarian Conception of Economic Ethics,' *Economics and Philosophy* 11, 82–112.

Ewing, D. W.: 1995, 'An Employee Bill of Rights,' in W. Michael Hoffman and Robert E. Frederick (eds.), *Business Ethics* (McGraw-Hill, New York), pp. 257–263.

Feinberg, J.: 1989, 'The Nature and Value of Rights,' in Morton E. Winston (ed.), *The Philosophy of Human Rights* (Wadsworth, Belmont, CA), pp. 61–74.

Freeman, R. E.: 1984, *Strategic Management: A Stakeholder Approach* (Pitman Publishing, Boston).

Gewirth, A.: 1978, *Reason and Morality* (University of Chicago Press, Chicago, IL).

Gewirth, A.: 1996, *The Community of Rights* (University of Chicago Press, Chicago, IL).

Hartman, E. M.: 1996, *Organizational Ethics and the Good Life* (Oxford University Press, Oxford).

Hohfeld, W. N.: 1919, *Fundamental Legal Conceptions as Applied in Judicial Reasoning*, Walter Wheeler Cook (ed.) (Yale University Press, New Haven, CT).

Kant, I: 1981, *Grounding for the Metaphysics of Morals*, James W. Ellington (Tr.) (Hackett, Indianapolis, IN).

Locke, J.: 1960, *Two Treatises of Government*, Peter Laslett (ed.) (Cambridge University Press, Cambridge).

McCall, J. J.: 1996, 'An Ethical Basis for Employee Participation,' in Joseph R. Desjardins and John J. McCall (eds.), *Contemporary Issues in Business Ethics* (Wadsworth, Belmont, CA), pp. 199–206.

Mill, J. S.: 1991, 'On Liberty,' in John Gray (ed.), *On Liberty and Other Essays* (Oxford University Press, Oxford), pp. 5–135.

Rawls, J.: 1971, *A Theory of Justice* (Harvard University Press, Cambridge, MA).

Raz, J.: 1987, *The Morality of Freedom* (Oxford University Press, Oxford).

Shue, H.: 1989, 'Security and Subsistence,' in Morton E. Winston (ed.), *The Philosophy of Human Rights* (Wadsworth, Belmont, CA), pp. 152–171.

Solomon, R. C.: 1992: *Ethics and Excellence* (Oxford University Press, Oxford).

Sumner, L. W.: 1987, *The Moral Foundation of Rights* (Oxford University Press, Oxford).

Thomson, J. J.: 1990, *The Realm of Rights* (Harvard University Press, Cambridge, MA).

Werhane, P. H.: 1985, *Persons, Rights, and Corporations* (Prentice-Hall, Englewood Cliffs, NJ).

Questions for Discussion:

1. What basic rights does Rowan believe employees have in the workplace? Do you agree? Would you add any to his list? Be treated as a person, safety, due process, Privacy.

2. On what basis does Rowan believe people have rights? In other words, how are these rights grounded? What does the Judeo-Christian view of human rights add to Rowan's understanding of these rights?

3. Do you agree with Rowan that what an employee does outside the workplace is none of the company's business? Why or why not?

4. Do you believe that employees are entitled to an appeal process when terminated? Does Rowan think this is an important right employees have? In some instances yes, the key is due process.

5. What do you think of Rowan's view of privacy in the workplace? Do you believe employees' privacy should be protected at work? On what basis?

Privacy, the Workplace and the Internet

Seumas Miller and John Weckert

Journal of Business Ethics 28 (2000): 255–65. Copyright © 2000 Kluwer Academic Publishers.

The coming into being of new communication and computer technologies has generated a host of ethical problems, and some of the more pressing concern the moral notion of privacy. Some of these problems arise from new possibilities of data collections, and software for computer monitoring. For example, computers can now combine and integrate data bases provided by polling and other means to enable highly personalized and detailed voter profiles.

Another cluster of problems revolves around the threat to privacy posed by the new possibilities of monitoring and surveillance. For example, telephone tapping, interception of electronic mail messages, minute cameras and virtually undetectable listening and recording devices give unprecedented access to private conversations and other private communications and interactions. Possibly the greatest threat to privacy is posed by the possibility of combining these new technologies and specifically combining the use of monitoring and surveillance devices with certain computer software and computer networks, including the Internet.

Concerns about the use of computer technology to monitor the performance and activity of employees in the workplace are not new (see Garson, 1988; and Zuboff, 1988), and are widely discussed from a variety of perspectives, frequently in computer ethics texts. Johnson (1995), and Forester and Morrison (1991) raise questions regarding the monitoring of work, while Langford (1995) and Severson (1997) both discuss the monitoring of employees' email. The works just cited mention arguments both from the point of view of employers and employees. Parker et al. take a different approach (1990). Their discussion is based on a survey taken of attitudes towards monitoring both employees' email and computer usage. Similar surveys have also been reported recently by Loch et al. (1998) and Hawk (1994). There are also a number of sociological examinations, including those by Perrolle (1996) and Rule (1996). An argument from the employees' point of view, highlighting employees' problems and concerns is given by Nussbaum (1989). A number of other important discussions are considered later in this paper.

These discussions are useful, but their purposes are different from the current one in this paper. Applied ethics is interdisciplinary by nature, so questions must be examined from a variety of perspectives. Some of the works just cited highlight the problems or perceived problems, some report on what people actually believe, and some give a sociological analysis. The concern in this paper is to examine the question of employee monitoring from a philosophical point of view. Hence the emphasis is on analysis and argument, not on original empirical research.

Provision of an adequate philosophical account of the notion of privacy is a necessary precursor to setting the proper limits of intrusion by the various new technologies. Such an account of privacy would assist in defining the limits to be placed on unacceptably intrusive applications of new technologies. Moreover it would do so in such a way as to be sensitive to the forms of public space created by these technologies and not unreasonably impede those new possibilities of communication and information acquisition which are in fact desirable. As always it is important to balance the rights of individuals against the needs of the community. On the one hand there is a fundamental moral obligation to respect the individual's right to privacy, on the other hand there are the legitimate requirements of, for example, employers to monitor the performances of their employees, and law enforcement agencies to monitor the communications and financial transactions of organised crime. Moreover the working out of these ethical problems is relative to a particular institutional and technological context. The question as to whether email, for example, ought to be assimilated to ordinary mail depends in part on the nature of the technology in question and the institutional framework in which it is deployed. Perhaps email messages sent on a company owned computer network ought to be regarded as public communications within the organisation however personal their content. These email messages, unlike ordinary mail, are always stored somewhere in the backup system owned by the company and are therefore accessible to the dedicated company cybersleuth (Magney, 1996). In this paper the discussion will be restricted to the notion of privacy with reference to computer monitoring in the workplace. First, an outline of the general notion of privacy.

The notion of privacy has proven to be a difficult one to adequately explicate. One account which has been influential is that by Parent:

> Privacy is the condition of not having undocumented personal knowledge about one possessed by others.... [P]ersonal knowledge ... consists of facts about a person which most individuals in a given soci-

ety at a given time do not want widely known about themselves (Parent, 1992, p. 92).

A problem with this definition is that personal knowledge and, therefore, privacy, is completely relativised to what people in a particular society, at a particular time, are prepared to disclose about themselves. Accordingly, if in some society everyone is prepared to disclose everything about themselves to everyone else, then they are still, on this account, in a condition of privacy. But they are surely not in a condition of privacy. Rather, they have chosen to abandon such a condition.

Presenting an alternative account is not easy, however, there are a number of general points that can be made (Miller, 1997; Benn, 1988; Warren and Brandeis, 1890). First, the notion of privacy has both a descriptive and a normative dimension. On the one hand privacy consists of not being interfered with, or having some power to exclude, and on the other privacy is held to be a moral right, or at least an important good. Most accounts of privacy acknowledge this much. For example, Warren and Brandeis gave an early and famous definition in terms of the right to be let alone. Naturally the normative and the descriptive dimensions interconnect. What ought to be must be something that realistically could be. The normative dimension of privacy is not a fanciful thing. The proposition must be rejected that the extent and nature of the enjoyment of rights to individual privacy is something to be determined by the most powerful forces of the day, be they market or bureaucratic forces. But it is equally important to avoid utopian sentimentality; it is mere self-indulgence to pine after what cannot possibly be.

Second, privacy is a desirable condition, power or moral right that a person has in relation to other persons and with respect to the possession of information by other persons about him/herself or the observation/perceiving of him/herself by other persons. The kind of "interference" in question is cognitive or perceptual (including perhaps tactile) interference.

Third, the range of matters regarded as private embraces much of what could be referred to as a person's inner self. A demand—as opposed to a request—by one person to know all about another person's thoughts, beliefs, emotions, and bodily sensations and states would be regarded as unacceptable. Naturally there are conditions under which knowledge concerning another person's inner self are appropriate. A doctor, counsellor, psychoanalyst or psychiatrist may need to know about a patient's bodily sensations and states, in so far as this was necessary for successful treatment and in so far as the patient had consented to be treated. Nevertheless such information while no longer unavailable to the doctor or other care worker, would still be unavailable to others, and for the care worker to disclose this information would constitute a breach of confidentiality, except perhaps to another who may be required to assist in the treatment.

Fourth, a person's intimate personal relations with other people are regarded as private. So while a lover might be entitled to know his/her lover's feelings toward him/her, others would not be so entitled. Indeed there would typically be an expectation that such information would not be disclosed by a lover to all and sundry.

Fifth, certain facts pertaining to objects I own, or monies I earn, are held to be private, at least in most Western societies, simply in virtue of my ownership of them. Ownership appears to confer the right not to disclose information concerning the thing owned. Or at least there is a presumption in favour of non-disclosure; a presumption that can be overridden by, for example, the public interest in tax gathering.

Sixth, certain facts pertaining to a person's various public roles and practices, including one's voting decisions are regarded as private. These kinds of facts are apparently regarded as private in part by virtue of the potential, should they be disclosed, of undermining the capacity of the person to function in these public roles or to compete fairly in these practices. If others know how I vote, my right to freely support a particular candidate might be undermined. If business competitors have access to my business plans they will gain an unfair advantage over me. If a would-be employer knows my sexual preferences he or she may unfairly discriminate against me.

Seventh, and more generally, a measure of privacy is necessary simply in order for a person to pursue his or her projects, whatever those projects might be. For one thing reflection is necessary for planning, and reflection requires privacy. For another, knowledge of someone else's plans can enable those plans to be thwarted. Autonomy requires a measure of privacy.

Equipped with this working account of privacy, including a basic taxonomy of the kinds of information regarded as private, let us now consider a number of ethical issues posed by computer monitoring and surveillance in the workplace.

Employers clearly have some rights in seeing that their employees are working satisfactorily. It is not only in the employer's interests that the required tasks are performed efficiently and well. It is also in the interests of other employees and in the interests of the general public. Employees do not want to have to work harder to support lazy or incompetent colleagues. Consumers do not want to buy sub-standard or overpriced products. But it does not follow from this that employees have no right to privacy when at work. Unfortunately, although some may say fortunately, the widespread use of computers has made workplace surveillance very easy.

Does this monitoring and surveillance matter? It is often defended by employers, who argue that it is in the interests of all. Employees who are not performing well are weeded out. Those doing their job well can be rewarded on objective criteria. In addition, and probably most importantly, it leads to more efficient and profitable businesses. But there are other important things in life besides efficiency and profitability. In particular, there is the right to privacy. As was indicated above, privacy considerations take a number of forms. All of these are conceivably relevant to employees in their place of work.

The existence of the right to privacy, and related rights such as confidentiality and auton-

omy, is sufficient to undermine extreme views such as the view that employees ought to be under surveillance every minute of the working day, or that should they be in a situation where every minute of the working day they suspect that they might be under surveillance, or that there should be surveillance of a nature or extent in respect of which the employees are ignorant. These extreme situations involve unjustified invasions of privacy. Employers have certain rights in respect of their employees, but there is no general and absolute right to monitor and control employees. This is obvious from the fact that employers are restricted in a whole range of ways by the rights of employees. Employers cannot imprison or rob their employees, and flogging in order to improve productivity is not generally condoned. The reason, obviously, why employers cannot imprison or rob (or flog), is that these activities are violations of a human's rights, and the fact that someone is your employee does not confer the right to violate those rights. Even in cases where explicit contracts have been agreed to, there are limits to which either party can go in order to ensure that the other party adheres to that contract.

So much is obvious. What is less obvious is the extent to which an employer can justifiably infringe an employee's right to privacy. It has already been argued that there is a right to privacy, and, other things being equal, employees have this right. The violation of the employee's right to privacy of concern in this paper is that posed by the electronic surveillance and monitoring of an employee's activities made easy by current computer technology, particularly networking. Keystrokes can be monitored for speed and accuracy, and the work on your screen may be brought up on the screen of another without your knowledge. Common software for accessing the Internet logs all activity, so that a record is kept of all visits to all sites, and email, listservers and so on can be monitored. A supervisor can fairly easily find who did what on the Internet. Notwithstanding these technical possibilities of infringing privacy, protection of privacy is high on the list of principles supported by many professional computing association codes of ethics (Barroso, 1997). A good example is found in the Association for Computing Machinery (ACM) code:

> Computing and communication technology enables the collection and exchange of personal information on a scale unprecedented in the history of civilization. Thus there is increased potential for violating the privacy of individuals and groups. It is the responsibility of professionals to maintain the privacy and integrity of data describing individuals . . .
>
> This imperative implies that only the *necessary amount of personal information* [emphasis added] be collected in a system, that retention and disposal periods for that information be clearly defined and enforced, and that personal information gathered for a specific purpose not be used for other purposes without consent of the individual(s). These principles apply to electronic communications, including electronic mail, and prohibit procedures that capture or monitor electronic user data, including messages, without the permission of users or bona fide authorization related to system operation and maintenance (1992).

(This code, it should be noted, is the code of a professional computing body, and hence is aimed at computer professionals who often have access to private information stored electronically, in their daily work of creating, managing and maintaining computer systems and networks. There is no implication that *only* computer professionals have responsibilities with respect to individual privacy.)

The quotation above makes it appear that employee monitoring by computer technology is frowned upon by the ACM, and that computer professionals should have no part of it, either in developing necessary software or involvement in the monitoring itself. It could be argued, however, that this surveillance of employees falls within the class of a "necessary amount of personal information"; necessary to the well-functioning of a business. In order to assess the justifiability of

computer monitoring, first some arguments for it will be considered, followed by a consideration of a number of criticisms.

Employees, as well as having at least a prima facie right to privacy, are also accountable to their employers because their employers have a right to a reasonable extent and quality of work output for the wages and salaries that they pay, and it is in the employees' interests (as well as the interests of employers) that their employers make a profit. Given potential conflict between these rights, perhaps an employees' right to privacy, *qua* employee, can, in a range of circumstances, be overridden. Three related types of justification are given, in terms of employers, customers, and employees. The most obvious is that with better monitored employees, profitability is greater, although this is sometimes couched in terms of better quality customer service. For example, "quality of service telemarketing monitoring" is the way that the Telemarketing Association portrays employee monitoring (*Direct Marketing*, 1993). The Computer Business and Equipment Manufacturers' Association puts it like this:

> the measurement of work by computer is a legitimate management tool that should be used wisely. Used appropriately, monitoring and related techniques, such as incentive pay or promotion based on productivity, can increase both an organization's effectiveness and the employee's ability to advance (Lund, 1992, p. 54).

Here the emphasis is not just on the employer, it is particularly on the benefit to the employee.

An interesting approach to computer monitoring is presented by DeTienne. She argues that this monitoring can be, not only quite benign, but useful to employees:

> Not only will these computers keep closer tabs on employees, but based on this added information, the computer will be able to help employees do their jobs more effectively. . . .
>
> Information gathered via computer monitoring will increasingly be used to coach

employees. Currently, many organisations use the information gathered as a basis for criticism. Companies will begin to realize that it is more motivating for employees to be coached rather than reproached (1993).

So the claim is that computer monitoring of employees has multiple benefits, at least potentially. It improves the quality of goods and services, and so is good for customers; it makes businesses more efficient, so profits rise, which benefits employers; and it helps employees get higher pay and promotion, and assists them in doing their jobs better. Given all these benefits, why is it questioned? There are two types of reasons, one type based on the unacceptable consequences to the organisation of monitoring and surveillance. Such consequences include ill health, stress and lowering of morale. The other type of reason concerns the harm to employees, including as a harm, infringement of employees' rights to privacy. Other harms relate to employees' wellbeing. There is evidence that computer monitored employees suffer health, stress and morale problems to a higher degree than other employees (Bewayo, 1996; Aiello and Kolb, 1996). If it does indeed generate these sorts of problems, then these problems must be weighed against the benefits. It might be countered that if the problems are too great, then monitoring will not make organisations more efficient, and so the practice will stop. Alternatively, the organisations who practice it will not be able to attract good employees, and so will be forced to discontinue it. One weakness of this counter is that workers are not always free to pick and choose their employers, particularly in times and places of high unemployment. Many will almost certainly prefer to work under conditions which they do not like, than to not work at all. Another flaw in the argument is that it is not necessarily true that practices which are detrimental to health and morale will lead to less efficiency, at least not in the short term. For example, forcing workers to work for long hours without rest over extended periods could increase productivity in the short term, but lead to longer term health problems. Raising the

levels of stress through continual monitoring could have the same effect. If the work requires a relatively low level of skill, and if there is unemployment, workers are easily replaceable. Treating workers in this fashion may not be good for a businesses' long term viability or profitability, but many businesses are not around for long. If the motive is short term profitability, long term effects are irrelevant. More importantly, treating workers in this fashion may be good for the profitability, long and short term, of that particular business. The problem may be the long term ill effects on the business sector in general, or on the specific industry sector in question.

The moral objection to computer monitoring is based on the principle that a right cannot be infringed without very good reason. It would be rare that greater efficiency or profitability would constitute such a good reason. There clearly are times when a person's privacy rights can be overridden. An unconscious and unconsenting hospital patient, for example, may need constant monitoring, but that is for the patient's own good. A prison inmate might also need constant monitoring, but that might be for the protection of the community. Monitoring of employees however, does not, in most circumstances, secure these fundamental rights to life and protection.

A defender of computer monitoring might argue that the moral problem only arises if employees have no input into the establishing of the monitoring system, or if they are not fully aware of its scope and implications. If these conditions are satisfied, there is no moral problem, because the employee has, in effect, consented to the system's use, by accepting employment under those conditions.

While this has some initial attraction, on closer examination it is not so plausible. One reason is the same as that discussed in connection with health and morale. When unemployment is high, or if the person badly needs a job, there is not much force in consent. It is rather a case of economic coercion. A second problem is that even if people do consent to some sort of treatment, it does not follow that it is moral to treat them in that manner. Slavery cannot be justified on the grounds that some slaves may not have minded their condition too much if they knew nothing better, and if they had always been taught that slavery was the natural order of things. Likewise, violation of privacy cannot be condoned simply because some employees are willing to accept it.

What can be made of the argument that employee monitoring can be to the benefit of the employees themselves? Their privacy is violated, but it is in a good cause. Three benefits to the employee have been suggested. One is that it can, if used properly, help them to improve their work practices. This might be true, but it would at best only justify short term monitoring, and only with the employee's consent. Perhaps the techniques and satisfaction of clumsy lovers could be improved by information gained from spying on their activities, but that hardly seems to justify spying. A second benefit is said to be that employees can be assessed on purely objective criteria, say number and accuracy of keystrokes. While objectivity is good, assessment of an employee's worth will usually have a substantial subjective element as well. A highly responsible or experienced person who types slowly may well improve the productivity of others. So at best this is a weak justification for infringement of privacy. Finally, it is argued that this monitoring will help get rid of "dead wood," workers who are not doing their fair share of the work. This will not only be good for the employer, but also for the other employees. However, while none of us want to support lazy and incompetent colleagues, it is not clear that this will not have countervailing effects, namely, on the hardworking and competent workers also thus monitored. There could, of course, be limited and targeted monitoring where there was good reason to believe that particular employees were not meeting reasonable standards. This would seem to be a far more reasonable policy. However, this is clearly not *general* monitoring and surveillance of the kind being discussed here. Supporting such colleagues is not good, but violation of privacy would, to many, seem even worse. (For discussion of these three

points see DeTienne, 1993; Lund, 1992; and Fenner and Lerch, 1993.)

A stronger argument for employing surveillance is the control of crime in the workplace, especially theft and financial fraud. Law enforcement agencies can have rights which override those of individuals in certain circumstances when it is in the public interest. Theft and fraud in the workplace are still theft and fraud, so some surveillance can be justified in order to apprehend culprits.

Another form of monitoring, perhaps less worrying, but often discussed, is that of monitoring employees' email. While this might be thought to be akin to opening private mail or listening in to private conversations, the argument is that because the system on which the email operates is owned by the employers, they have a right to read any messages (see Loch et al. 1992 for a discussion of a survey on this issue). But do they? The fact that two people are conversing in my house does not give me an automatic right to listen to what they are saying. But what if the two people are my employees? Does this make a difference? One argument that it does not, might go as follows: All I am paying for is my employees' labour. What they say to customers might be my business, but what they say to each other is not if it does not obviously and directly harm the business. Perhaps the cases are not analogous, because in the email case they are using my equipment, while in the other they are not. But what they say is still none of my business even if the consequences of what they say might be. The fact that they are continually having conversations might be overloading the equipment or hindering the work of others or themselves. Accordingly, banning or limiting private conversations might be justified. But this would not justify *monitoring* conversations. Perhaps this still misses the point. How will I know if the email is being used for private discussions unless I monitor it? I will not know unless I am told. But if no problems are being caused by overuse and so on, then there is no need to worry. If no harm is being caused by personal email, either to the computing equipment or to productivity, then monitoring what is said can have no purpose, except perhaps to satisfy curiosity. This is hardly a justification for violating a right. If there are problems such as the overloading of the system or inadequate work levels, then some steps may need to be taken, but even here actually reading messages would rarely be necessary. There could be a limit put on the length or number of messages, or the productivity of employees in question could be investigated. Employing people does not confer the right to monitor their private conversations, whether those conversations be in person or via email.

It might still be argued that what one employee says to a second employee might be my business as employer, if their conversation is work related. But even this cannot in general be correct. Consider the following three situations. First, if the two employees are, say, doctors in a private hospital, then their work related conversation might need to be protected by confidentiality. Second, what an employee is saying to a 'customer' might be protected by confidentiality, for example in the case of a lawyer working for a large corporation. In these circumstance a professional employee, that is, one who is a member of what is commonly thought of as a profession, for example, a medical doctor, lawyer or accountant, will need to be treated differently from a non-professional. Third, even non-professional employees need a measure of autonomy—conferred by privacy in the sense of non-interference and non-intrusion—in respect of one another and the public, if they are to take responsibility for their jobs and their performance in those jobs. Taking responsibility in this sense involves "being left alone" to do, or fail to do, the tasks at hand. Far from having the effect of ensuring that people do not make mistakes, intrusive and ongoing monitoring and surveillance might have the effect of causing employees to underperform because they are never allowed to take responsibility for outcomes, and therefore become lazy or engage in corrupt practices. Consider in this connection a salesman trying to convince a customer to buy a house, or a mechanic trying to figure out what is wrong with a car, or a supervi-

sor trying to instruct a new clerk. The conception of employees that those who favour monitoring or surveillance tend to have in mind seems to be those doing menial, repetitive jobs that do not require any autonomy or individual initiative or judgment in order to be performed.

The discussion so far in relation to the Internet, has concerned only email, but of course Internet access involves much more than just email. Some employees have, on their employer's computing equipment, almost unlimited access to material, particularly through the World Wide Web (WWW). Is it an unjustified invasion of privacy for employers to monitor their employees activity on the WWW, to check on the sites visited? Given costs, particularly in processing time, associated with activity on the WWW, some restrictions seem quite justifiable. It would be difficult to condemn an employer who prohibited access except for work-related tasks. Given general knowledge of this prohibition, the periodic checks of the sites accessed by employees is not unreasonable. More interesting problems arise in situations where employees require very free access in order to do their jobs properly, for example, many people involved in education. Universities, typically, allow their staff completely unfettered Internet access. Does the university then have a right to know how its employees are using this access? In general it would seem not. From a privacy perspective, there is no problem with restricting access to certain sites by the use of software. Monitoring sites visited, however, is not such an acceptable way of restricting access. Monitoring someone's use of the Internet in this way is a bit like monitoring library use, and it is instructive to look at how the library profession views the privacy issue.

Librarians have long been concerned about maintaining the privacy of library users' reading habits. The American Library Association puts its concern this way:

> The ethical responsibilities of librarians . . . protect the privacy of library users. Confidentiality extends to "information sought or received, and materials consulted, borrowed,

acquired," and includes database search records, reference interviews, circulation records, interlibrary loan records, and other personally identifiable uses of library materials, facilities, or services (*ALA Policy Manual*, 1996).

Why have librarians traditionally been so concerned about privacy? The reading habits of library users are the business of nobody except the user, but that in itself is not too important. My preference for unsugared, black tea rather than the sweet, white variety is also the business of nobody but me and the person making it for me, but worrying about the privacy of this information seems a bit extravagant. While much information about users which is stored in library databases might not be much more important than my preference in tea, in general, reading habits do reveal a little more about a person. It can be argued that what someone reads is very close to what he or she thinks, and therefore the ability to discover what is read is, in effect, the ability to find out what is thought.

It is not difficult to imagine situations where governments, advertising agencies or other groups could make use of this information for purposes which were not beneficial to the individual. For example, according to Million and Fisher, in the United States the Moral Majority attempted to obtain the names of school districts and individuals who had borrowed a film on sexual maturity from the Washington State Library (1986). Sometimes of course it might be beneficial to the community, for example when law enforcement agencies need information for criminal investigations. Borrowers, however, can be harmed if their records are not kept private. The burden of proof should be on those who want records made public, or at least available. The privacy of the individual can be overridden, but only to protect more important individual rights, or for the sake of very significant public goods (for further discussion see Weckert and Adeney, 1997).

Given that university librarians are part of the library profession, according to their own code of ethics, they are bound to keep library records private, including the borrowing records of university staff. From a professional librarian's point of view then, it would be an invasion of privacy for the university to check on an employee's borrowing record, even though the library is university owned and operated. It is difficult to see where the relevant difference lies is between the library and the Internet in this instance. Both are sources of information.

One complicating factor which rears its head in the context of email and Internet monitoring is vicarious liability, that is, the liability an employer might have for the actions of his or her employees. *Black's Law Dictionary* defines it thus:

> The imposition of liability on one person for the actionable conduct of another, based solely on a relationship between the two persons. Indirect or imputed legal responsibility for acts of another; for example, the liability of an employer for the acts of an employee . . . (1990).

Given this, it seems irresponsible of an employer not to monitor the email of employees or their use of the Internet in general. If this does not happen, the employer could be liable for breaches of the law with respect to, for example, defamation, copyright infringement and obscene material (Cutler, 1998). It does not follow from this however, that an employer has the right to monitor employee activity on the Internet which the employee could reasonably expect to be private. It does though, strengthen an employer's right to insist that his or her computing equipment is not to be used for anything apart from legitimate work related purposes. This policy must, of course, be made clear. It also might call into question the appropriateness of maintaining vicarious liability in some of these contexts. At any rate, the general point to be made here is that where an employer allows private email and other Internet activity, his vicarious liability does not necessarily legitimize monitoring of that activity.

Finally, should employers be able to monitor listservers which are on their computer systems? For employers in general, this will probably be a rare situation, but not for universities. Suppose that a university runs courses by distance education, something which is becoming increasingly common. The lecturer and students decide to establish a listserver to facilitate discussion, and to help overcome the isolation often felt by distance education students. Does the university have a right to monitor activity on that listserver without notifying the participants? It might be argued that they do, because the listserver is public in the same sense that a university lecture theatre is, and so any authorised university person has access. The analogy however, is not good. If someone enters a lecture theatre, he or she is there for all to see. There is no question of secrecy. Suppose now that the university monitors lectures, not by having staff attend, but rather by secretly installing cameras and microphones. The analogy here is closer, but the monitoring does not seem so benign. It might be objected that in the listserver case there is nothing secret. The university monitor enrolls, so it is not too difficult to discover the monitoring. Just look to see who is enrolled. But that is not the point. If there is to be monitoring, the onus for making it public should not be on those monitored, but on those monitoring.

Drawing an analogy between listservers and lecture theatres is misleading in any case. While it is true that authorised university staff can attend lectures in university owned buildings without violating anyone's right to privacy, nothing follows from this about secret listserver monitoring. Normally university lectures are not private. Anyone can come and listen. The situation changes a little with tutorials, where there is more interaction, and at private discussion between a lecturer and a student. It is not so clear that the university would be justified in authorising someone to monitor tutorials, without the tutors and students knowledge, or to monitor private student-lecturer discussions. The claim that this is justified simply because these activities are taking place on university property is dubious at best. Listservers seem more like tutorials than lectures. There is

some privacy. One cannot just look and see what is happening, as is possible with a newsgroup. One must enroll. Secret monitoring of class listservers then, can be seen as a violation of privacy rights, just as secret monitoring of tutorials would be.

Workplace monitoring is a practice which requires much more examination. Employers need an efficient and competent workforce in order to survive in a competitive environment, and customers demand and deserve high quality goods and services. The employees who produce these goods and services have a responsibility to work to the best of their ability for the financial reward that they receive, but they do not forfeit their rights to privacy by virtue of being employees. Although workplace monitoring can be justified in some circumstances, privacy is a moral right, and as such there is a presumption against its infringement. This paper has argued that some of the common justifications given for this monitoring do not withstand close scrutiny.

A number of questions remain to be researched, both empirical and analytical. One of these questions is the relationship between monitoring and trust in the workplace. It would appear that monitoring is a sign or distrust, and perhaps employees who know that they are being monitored, and hence not trusted, will become less trustworthy, in which case they will require more monitoring. Superficially at least, it appears that monitoring could precipitate a breakdown in trust, which in the longer term would probably lead to a less efficient workforce. But this requires investigation. Another issue is the role of vicarious liability in the violation of individual employee privacy. It seems that the current law (in countries which have it), or its interpretation, encourages, or even necessitates employee monitoring which is morally questionable. Perhaps the law requires modification in the light of contemporary computer technology. Privacy is perhaps the topic most discussed by those concerned about the social and ethical implications of computer technology. It deserves to be.

References:

ACM Code of Ethics and Professional Conduct: 1992, Section 1.7. http://www.acm.org/constitution/code.html (Read 25 July, 1998).

Aiello, John R. and Kathryn, J. Kolb: 1996, 'Electronic Performance Monitoring: A Risk Factor for Workplace Monitoring,' in S. L. Sauter and L. R. Murphy (eds.), *Organisational Risk Factors for Job Stress* (American Psychological Association), pp. 163–179.

ALA Policy Manual: 1996, Section Two (Position and Public Policy Statements), 52.4 Confidentiality of Library Records, gopher://ala1.ala.org:70/00/alagophviii/policy.hb (Read 25 July 1998).

Barroso Asenjo, P.: 1997, 'Key Ethical Concepts for the Internet and for Ethical Codes of Computer Professionals,' *Australian Computer Journal* 29, 2–5.

Benn, S. A.: 1988, *Theory of Freedom* (Cambridge University Press, Cambridge).

Bewayo, E.: 1996, 'Electronic Management: Its Downside Especially in Small Business,' in J. Kizza (ed.), *Social and Ethical Effects of the Computer Revolution* (McFarland and Co., Jefferson, NC), pp. 186–199.

Black, Henry Campbell: 1990, *Black's Law Dictionary*, 6th edition (West Publishing Co., St. Paul, MN), p. 1566.

Cutler, P. G.: 1998, 'E-mail: Employees and Liability', *Chemistry in Australia* (March, 1), 30–31.

DeTienne, K. B.: 1993, 'Big Brother or Friendly Coach,' *Futurist* 27, 33–37.

Direct Marketing: 1993, 'Telephone Monitoring Heads to Congress' (August 6), 6. Quoted in M. Levy, 'Electronic Monitoring in the Workplace: Power Through the Panopticon,' http://bliss.berkeley.edu/impact/students/mike/mike_ paper.html (Read 25 July 1998).

Fenner, Deborah B. and F. Javier Lerch: 1993, 'The Impact of Computerized Performance Monitoring and Prior Performance Knowledge on Performance Evaluation,' *Journal of Applied Social Psychology* 23, 573–601.

Forester, Tom and Perry Morrison: 1991, *Computer Ethics: Cautionary Tales and Ethical Dilemmas in Computing* (MIT Press, Cambridge, MA).

Garson, Barbara: 1988, *The Electronic Sweatshop* (Simon and Schuster, New York).

Hawk, Stephen, R.: 1994, *Journal of Business Ethics* 13, 949–957.

Johnson, Deborah G.: 1994, *Computer Ethics*, Second edition (Prentice Hall, Upper Saddle River, NJ).

Langford, Duncan: 1995, *Practical Computer Ethics* (McGraw-Hill, Maidenhead, Berkshire).

Loch, Karen D., Sue Conger and Effy Oz: 1998, 'Ownership, Privacy and Monitoring in the Workplace: A Debate on Technology and Ethics,' *Journal of Business Ethics* 17, 653–663.

Lund, J.: 1992, 'Electronic Performance Monitoring: A Review of the Research Issues,' *Applied Ergonomics* 23, 54–58.

Magney, J.: 1996, 'Computing and Ethics: Control and Surveillance Versus Cooperation and Empowerment,' in J. Kizza (ed.), *Social and Ethical Effects of the Computer Revolution* (McFarland and Co., Jefferson, NC), pp. 200–209.

Miller, S.: 1997 'Privacy and the Internet,' *Australian Computer Journal* 29, 12–15, for a similar discussion of the notion of the privacy.

Million, A. C. and K. N. Fisher: 1986, 'Library Records: A Review of Confidentiality Laws and Policies,' *Journal of Academic Librarianship* 11, 346–349.

Nussbaum, Karen: 1991, 'Computer Monitoring a Threat to the Right to Privacy?,' reprinted in Roy Dejoie, George Fowler and David Paradice, *Ethical Issues in Information Systems* (Boyd and Fraser Publishing Company, Boston).

Parent, P. "Privacy": 1992, in E. E. Cohen (ed.), *Philosophical Issues in Journalism* (Oxford University Press, New York), pp. 90–99.

Parker, Donn B., Susan Swope and Bruce N. Baker: 1990, *Ethical Conflicts in Information* and *Computer Science, Technology, and Business* (QED Information Sciences, Inc., Wellesley, MA).

Perrolle, Judith A.: 1996, 'Privacy and Surveillance in Computer-Supported Cooperative Work,' in David Lyon and Elia Zureik (eds.), *Computers, Surveillance, and Privacy* (University of Minnesota Press, Minneapolis), 47–65.

Rule, James, B.: 1996, 'High-Tech Workplace Surveillance: What's Really New?,' in David Lyon and Elia Zureik (eds.), *Computers, Surveillance, and Privacy* (University of Minnesota Press, Minneapolis), pp. 66–76.

Severson, Richard J.: 1997, *The Principles of Information Ethics* (M. E. Sharp, Armonk, NY).

Warren, S. and L. Brandeis: 1890, 'The Right to Privacy,' *Harvard Law Review* 4, 193–220.

Weckert, J. and D. Adeney: 1997, *Computer and Information Ethics* (Greenwood Publishing Group, Westport, Conn.).

Zuboff, Shoshana: 1988, *In the Age of the Smart Machine: The Future of Work and Power* (Basic Books, New York).

Questions for Discussion:

1. How do Miller and Weckert ground a right to privacy? Do you think that Judeo-Christian ethics recognizes an individual's right to privacy, and if so, on what basis?
2. How do Miller and Weckert define privacy?
3. Do you believe employees have a presumptive right to privacy in the workplace that can be overridden only with good reasons? Or do employees lose most rights to privacy when they enter the office or factory?
4. Do you agree with Miller and Weckert that companies do not have the right to monitor employees' email or Internet use? Why or why not? If you agree, would you have exceptions to this general rule? What would they be?

The Double Jeopardy of Sexual Harassment

J. H. Foegen

Business and Society Review 82 (Summer 1992). Copyright © 1992.

Biology prevents men and women from ignoring one another—in the workplace as elsewhere. Heightened sensitivity regarding sexual harassment has resulted from the Clarence Thomas confirmation hearings last year. Despite the admitted positive aspects, new awareness risks a productivity-reducing chill in the workplace climate. Most American companies can ill afford this as they compete internationally and pursue total quality management.

Last October, after controversial hearings concerning allegations of sexual harassment, the United States Senate confirmed Judge Clarence Thomas to the Supreme Court. The vote was fifty-two to forty-eight. Workplace fallout from those hearings will undoubtedly continue for a long time, as employers, supervisors, and workers of both genders try to accommodate greater sensitivity to an old problem made newly urgent. A potential danger is that either deliberately, or as an unconscious, knee-jerk reaction, males will in self-defense tend to ignore women coworkers. Wary of even possible charges of harassment, they will try to play it safe.

Much of the problem hinges upon definition; existing laws are helpful but hardly satisfactory. Though improving gradually, the laws remain less than helpful in specific situations. Equal Employment Opportunity Commission (EEOC) guidelines, which have been updated several times since 1980, flag two basic kinds of sexual impropriety. The blatant, now relatively uncontroversial kind involves a quid pro quo: sleep with me or else. The more subtle type, still arguable in its near-infinite ramifications, concerns "hostile environment." Offensive behavior not yet addressed satisfactorily under the law includes jokes, leers, displays of girlie calendars, and refusing to take "no" for an answer in dating.

In the typical legalese, the EEOC defined sexual harassment as: "unwelcome sexual advances, requests for sexual favors, and other verbal or physical contact or communication of a sexual nature when submission to such conduct is made either explicitly or implicitly a term or condition of an individual's employment; submission to or rejection of such conduct by an individual is used as a basis for employment decisions affecting such individual; or such conduct has the purpose or effect of unreasonably interfering with an individual's work performance, or creating an intimidating, hostile, or offensive work environment." Bringing such language down to earth, one of the nation's major labor unions, the United Auto Workers, spells things out more clearly in a brochure available from its women's department.

Noting that harassment violates Title VII of the Civil Rights Act, the union stresses that represented employees are also protected by the union's constitution, and often by negotiated contract language. All this is meaningless, however, unless the individual takes a stand, and says "no."

The UAW also notes that, while most of this undesirable contact is aimed at women, its policies also cover incidents in which men are victims, either of women or of other men.

Examples of nonverbal harassment are also cited. They include certain looks, gestures, leering, ogling, pictures, and cartoons. Physical offensiveness includes touching, pinching, rubbing, or "accidentally" brushing breasts or buttocks. The union advises members that, in addition to saying no, they should tell the offender they do not like what is going on. They should also document times, dates, and locations where harassment occurs, what was said or done to them, and their responses. Looking for other victims, sometimes people who were fired or who quit suddenly, is also advised, as is supporting others facing the problem.

Perhaps even more practical is the common-sense approach taken by Corning, the well-known kitchenware manufacturer. The company recommends that employees consider four questions, according to *The Economist*: Would you do it before your spouse or parents? Would you do it in front of a same-sex colleague? Would you like it reported in the local newspaper? Does it need saying or doing at all?

The courts, meanwhile, have tried to refine their concept of what is allowable. The test first evolved from a "reasonable man" standard to a more restrictive "reasonable person" one. And early last year a federal court in Florida ruled that the standard was what would be offensive in the perception of a reasonable woman.

Earlier, in the 1986 case, *Meritor Savings Bank v. Vinson*, the Supreme Court flagged possible employer liability if a policy on sexual harassment was absent. Many agree, however, that formal statements are not enough; preventative action is needed. Training sessions for both sexes are highly desirable, recognizing that too many people still do not realize that once-common practices are no longer acceptable.

The change impacting both genders today seems to hinge upon different perceptions between the sexes. During and after the Thomas confirmation hearings, countless stories were reported in the press. One consultant told *Business Week*, for example, that "When men look at sexual harassment, they tend to think of touching. Women tend to consider the hostile work environment—her chest being stared at, the sexual jokes." And syndicated columnist Ellen Goodman quoted a political scientist and law professor from the University of Michigan, who sees a related contrast: "Men see the sex first and miss the coercion. Women see the coercion and miss the sex." Regardless of seemingly intractable differences, the professor is not fatalistic about change. He says our justice system is convinced that empathy is possible. People can "get in another's head," given a willingness to do so.

Ignoring one another completely in the workplace, regardless of motivation, is of course unlikely, if not impossible. Such an extreme, however, is far from necessary. Even a degree of wariness can hinder productivity; people sense intuitively when interpersonal tension exists. Ample evidence can be found that such wariness is present already, with the end of the harassment controversy nowhere in sight.

Bewilderment about what is permissible continues to be reported—and what appears in print is undoubtedly only the tip of the iceberg. One manager, for example, told *Business Week* about a female colleague putting her hand lightly on a man's shoulder. Another woman rushed up and said excitedly, "Oh, no, don't do that!" Another woman at a large insurance company told the magazine, "In my office now, if we say something that could be misconstrued as sexist, the guys pop up and say, 'That's sexual harassment.'"

While the Hill-Thomas controversy was at its height, a *Washington Post* editor pointedly asked, "Can we women and men of the work force never again laugh together at the latest off-color joke? Can we not exchange compliments or (discreetly) discuss the physical attributes of passersby in the office halls?" Similarly, as Ellen Goodman reported, one boss greeted his secretary, "Good morning—or is that sexual harassment?" More likely than not, he was only half kidding; the ques-

tion can be seen as symbolic of a chilled atmosphere.

Perhaps most representative was the observation of an employee of the Union Pacific Railroad shortly after the Thomas hearings. "I have already noticed the difference at work. As a matter of fact, I asked a couple of ladies—they had even noticed the difference. Men are not speaking to them as . . . in the past," he told the Associated Press. He said he thought coworkers of both sexes were made nervous by the harassment issue.

Sex-Saturated Society

Behind the short-run feelings of unease created by greater awareness are at least two broad-scale problems that together offer a meaningful framework. The climate in which workplace harassment occurs is itself an issue. One editorial, which appeared in *The National Catholic Register*, was right on target: "Society cannot have it both ways. It cannot encourage and subsidize sleaze in art, film, literature, advertising, and television—and then expect to have work atmospheres that are free of sexual harassment. Our entire culture is so saturated and obsessed with sexual imagery that no one should be surprised when that obsession is expressed in the workplace." Individuals can, of course, control their actions; even in a sex-saturated society they do not have to harass coworkers. Still, a valid point is made.

Another wide-ranging aspect of the harassment issue concerns communication generally. Whatever deficiencies exist in an organization are magnified when an emotional issue like sexual behavior surfaces. Intentions are often misinterpreted; it is often hard to tell whether comments are innocent, intended to demean, or somewhere between. Unfortunately, this can also provide a handy rationalization for any who intend to harass. On the other hand, having to watch every word said can be irritating too, especially when no offense is meant. It seems as though the presumption of innocence until proved guilty has been turned on its head. It can be disconcerting.

Being on guard constantly against giving offense sexually inhibits all other communication too. You can never tell when someone might take something the wrong way. The situation can even deteriorate into another us-versus-them confrontation, much like that which exists between some labor unions and management. When total quality management is being stressed widely, such an atmosphere is counterproductive. Output, teamwork, competitiveness, and a pleasant work environment all suffer.

Without denying the problem's seriousness, it is instructive that confusion and wariness can fuse in a superficially humorous way. In one poll, for example, one in seven men responded that they would be offended if they were the object of sexual advances in the workplace; three-quarters of the polled women said so. But three-quarters of the men said they would be flattered.

This discussion should not be interpreted as defending sexual harassment by anyone at any time. The whole situation should, in fact, be a non-issue. For whatever perverse reasons, however, it remains one. Perhaps the bottom line must rest ultimately upon goodwill, once sufficient understanding has been achieved. While biology cannot be ignored, it controls intelligent employees of integrity only in a primitive sense. Those who, in fairness and good conscience, conduct themselves properly, can set the pace by being good examples. Any initial chill can disappear or remain negligible, given goodwill all around.

Questions for Discussion:

1. How would you define sexual harassment? In your view, what kinds of actions constitute a "hostile environment" in the workplace?
2. What are Corning's criteria for dealing with sexual harassment? Do you think these are helpful? Practical?
3. Do you agree with Foegen that the effort to reduce the incidence of sexual harassment in the workplace has created a "chilling effect" on relationships between men and women at work? If so, have you seen examples of this or experienced this yourself?
4. Do you agree with Foegen that "society cannot have it both ways" when it comes to allowing the bombardment of sexual imagery in the media and expecting the workplace to be free of sexual harassment? Why or why not?

CASE STUDIES

Case 7.1: Benefits for Spousal Equivalents

As president of a medium-sized engineering firm, you know how difficult it can be to recruit and retain good employees. Over the years, you have looked at a wide variety of compensation packages in order to remain competitive for good engineers and support staff. In recent years, you have become alarmed at how the cost of your company's medical benefits has increased, yet you know that it is difficult to be competitive for talent without providing these benefits. You have also committed yourself to treating your employees well, both in order to retain them and because you consider it consistent with your publicly stated and well-known Christian convictions about running the company.

In the past few years, your company has been doing business with a growing number of city governments. These are lucrative contracts, and you realize that once you have a good reputation with public officials, that part of your business could expand significantly. However, it comes with a requirement that your company offer benefits to spousal equivalents, which include both unmarried heterosexual couples and gay and lesbian couples. If you don't offer these benefits, your company will not be able to compete for these contracts in the future and will lose the current ones. You have a strong family values orientation that comes out of your Christian convictions, which are well known in the company and the community. You don't want to appear to condone couples living together outside of marriage, either heterosexual or homosexual, and you have major reservations about same-sex couples being treated as the equivalent of traditionally married couples. But you don't want to lose the city government business either.

Questions for Discussion:

1. What would you do if you had to make the decision about offering benefits to spousal equivalents? On what would you base your decision?
2. Do you think that offering the benefits is condoning a lifestyle that is immoral according to your Christian convictions? Why or why not?

3. Do you think it is fair to offer benefits to spouses and not to spousal equivalents? Why or why not?

Case 7.2: Conflicts of Conscience

You have been employed in sales for ACME Pharmaceuticals for the past twelve years. ACME is a mid-sized company which is a joint venture between two pharmaceutical giants. One of the parent companies is located in the United States, the other in Japan. At present you are the regional sales manager. Prior to selling your current product, a drug to treat gastrointestinal problems, you sold the company's synthetic hormone to obstetricians and gynecologists. It was used to treat many of the painful symptoms of endometriosis, a disease that affects the wall of the uterus. The hormone further treats a benign kind of uterine tumors called fibroids. This synthetic hormone has treated hundreds of thousands of women over the years and has enabled women of childbearing years to avoid a hysterectomy, thus preserving their ability to bear children. It has also enabled many women to avoid the crippling pain associated with endometriosis. But as is true with most pharmaceutical products, this synthetic hormone has some significant side effects. In this case, the side effects are hot flashes and bone loss, because the woman is put in a pseudo-menopausal state by taking the hormone.

In the past three years you have gained valuable insight into the strategy of bringing a new drug to the market. Your background and experience have made you the ideal person to assume a strategic position to launch a new product that your company acquired from the parent company in Japan. This new drug has all the benefits of the original synthetic hormone you have been selling but none of the side effects that are such a concern. The drug will be used in the same way, but it has an added feature. Because of its unique safety at high doses, it will also be used to terminate an unwanted pregnancy. Unlike RU–486, this drug is not designed solely, or even primarily, as an "abortion pill." Abortion rights groups are already putting pressure on the company to get the drug to market.

You are personally opposed to abortion and consider ending unwanted pregnancies morally very problematic. You don't see how you could participate in the sale of a drug that would be used in this way. Being the point person for the introduction of this drug to the market makes you very uncomfortable. In fact, you feel that you are involved in an immoral cooperation with a practice you believe to be wrong. You tell your supervisor about your views of this product and your views of abortion, and you request the company to appoint someone else because you have a conflict of conscience with this product. Your boss suggests that this is a career-limiting decision for you. You ask for a meeting with your boss and the vice president for human resources.

Questions for Discussion:

1. Do employees have a right to have their conscience respected in the workplace? Why or why not?
2. To what degree should companies accommodate employees when they have conflicts of conscience? What criteria should companies use when evaluating requests based on conscience?

Case 7.3: Family-Friendly Flex Policies

You are the vice president for human resources for a medium-sized company that prides itself on its family-friendly policies. Your company recently instituted a company-funded on-site day care center for employees with preschool children. The company has willingly honored the Family Leave Act, which grants employees up to twelve weeks of unpaid leave to attend to family matters such as the birth of a child or taking care of a seriously ill family member. A growing number of employees have taken advantage of these leaves. Other employees have successfully negotiated flexible working hours, freedom from most travel, and exemptions from being on call for evenings and weekends. To keep clients satisfied, you have noticed that supervisors sometimes shift the more demanding clients to employees who are not on a flex time arrangement, invariably, employees without children. You have also noticed that the childless employees are frequently the ones who pick up the slack for those with children who are leaving early to get kids to soccer games or who cannot work on weekends due to family commitments. Though you appreciate the commitment of parents, you wonder about the fairness of putting more work onto childless employees. You begin to wonder if these family-friendly policies actually discriminate against those employees who do not have children.

Recently, some of these employees have complained that they are bearing a disproportionate share of the workload. They see the flexible work schedules agreed to for colleagues and desire to have the same flexibility, though they do not have ill family members and they are not going to have children. They come to you arguing, "We have a life too," and want consideration for their requests for flex time too. One employee wants flex time for taking some courses in theology to help him be better at teaching a Bible study in his church. Another wants to train for a triathlon.

Questions for Discussion:

1. What would you tell these childless employees who request flex time similar to employees with children?
2. Does the reason for requesting the flex time matter? Is pressing them on the reason an invasion of privacy?
3. Are family-friendly policies such as the one at this company unfair? Do they discriminate against employees who have no children? Do you think companies should have policies such as these that are very helpful in retaining good employees with children? Explain.

COMMENTARY

Employee Rights

The discussion of employee rights began in earnest when David W. Ewing issued a proposed bill of rights to guide employers and empower employees in protecting proper worker rights. Modeled after the Bill of Rights to the U.S. Constitution, it outlines nine inviolable rights that employees have on the job:

1. No organization or manager shall discharge, demote or in other ways discriminate against any employee who criticizes in speech or in press, the ethics, legality or social responsibility of management actions.
2. No employee shall be penalized for engaging in outside activities of his or her choice after working hours, whether political, economic, civic, or cultural, nor for buying products and services of his or her choice for personal use, nor for expressing or encouraging views contrary to top management's on political, economic or social issues.
3. No organization or manager shall penalize an employee to carry out a directive that violates common norms of morality.

4. No organization shall allow audio or visual recordings of an employee's actions or conversations to be made without his or her prior knowledge and consent. Normally an organization requires an employee or applicant to take personality tests, polygraph examinations or other tests that constitute, in his opinion, an invasion of privacy.

5. No employee's desk, files, or locker may be examined in his or her absence by anyone but a senior manager who has sound reason to believe that the files contain information needed for a management decision that must be made in the employee's absence.

6. No employer organization may collect and keep on file information about an employee that is not relevant and necessary for efficient management. Every employee shall have the right to inspect his or her personnel file and challenge the accuracy, relevance, or necessity of data in it, except for personal evaluations and comments by other employees which could not reasonably be obtained if confidentiality were not promised. Access to an employee's file by outside individuals and organizations shall be limited to inquiries about the essential facts of employment.

7. No manager may communicate to prospective employers of an employee who is about to be or has been discharged gratuitous opinions that might hamper the individual from obtaining a new position.

8. An employee who is discharged, demoted, or transferred to a less desirable job is entitled to a written statement from management of its reasons for the penalty.

9. Every employee who feels that he or she has been penalized for asserting a right described in this bill shall be entitled to a fair hearing before an impartial official, board, or arbitrator. The findings and conclusions of the hearing shall be delivered in writing to the employee and management.

Ewing's bill raises some important questions about what rights employees have at work. Think about these as you reflect on the cases and readings in this chapter. For example, what employee rights do you think Ewing's bill appropriately protects? What rights does he propose to protect that you do not believe should be protected? Are there any other rights that you think employees have that Ewing's bill does not mention? In addition, do you think Ewing's bill of rights is realistic in today's competitive business environment? Remember, when first proposed, the economic environment was a bit different, and managers were not under the intense quarterly pressure from Wall Street to deliver profits in quite the same way as they are today. Ewing's bill of rights is the place where most of the discussion on employee rights begins. We will come back to it and evaluate the specific rights enumerated there after more reflection on the moral and theological basis for employee rights.

In approaching employee rights, we should be careful to distinguish between government's recognizing and empowering basic human rights, and exercising these rights in the workplace. For example, it is not unusual for companies to regulate free speech in its workplace, so that employees could be penalized for saying things that damage the company's reputation or cause problems with company morale. Many private organizations and colleges and universities have speech codes designed to restrict what is considered hate speech. The common criticism of these kinds of regulations is based on appeal to the First Amendment to the Constitution, which guarantees the right of free speech in society. What critics fail to recognize is that the right to free speech only applies to *government* restricting someone's speech or penalizing them for speaking their mind in public. Companies, however, are not the government, and there is nothing unconstitutional about regulating free speech in the workplace. It may be unwise or damaging to morale, but it is not unconstitutional. Of course, some aspects of the Bill of Rights may be applicable to private companies, but to apply them requires additional argument beyond their being part of the Constitution.

Human rights in general are premised on the unique dignity of human persons. John Rowan, in his article, suggests that there is something morally important about being a person—specifically that the person has goals and interests which are critical to human flourishing. Rowan suggests that when the minimal conditions are not present for persons to pursue their goals, something has gone wrong that needs fixing. For example, when someone does not have the minimum necessities of food, shelter, and health care to pursue his life goals, most people would agree that those conditions need rectifying. Rowan suggests that three basic rights follow from human dignity: a right to freedom, a right to well-being, and a right to equal treatment. In fact, Rowan summarizes human dignity under the notion of respecting these three basic rights.

From the perspective of Christian ethics, the best way to think about these "rights" is not in the classical liberal tradition of rights but as naturally flowing out of the concept of human dignity. Because human beings have essential dignity, these rights define how people should be treated. Think about how these implications of human dig-

nity might be applied to the workplace. Freedom involves a basic freedom from physical restraint (negative freedom) that would be violated when people are held against their will at work. One thinks of
sweatshops in which people are tied to their machinery and not
allowed to leave. This is a clear violation of freedom, which would
include the freedom to quit one's job when one chooses. A more subtle violation of freedom (what Rowan calls positive freedom) would
come when one is coerced by external forces. These are extreme violations of freedom that virtually everyone agrees are immoral and
ought to be illegal. However, one should recognize that employees
give up freedom voluntarily when they agree to a work contract. The
difficult question for employee rights is the degree to which the company has the right to ask employees to give up freedom in order to
fulfill their contract with the company. For example, to what degree
does the company have the right to regulate an employee's activities
when not on the job? Or take the situation in case 7.2—the conflicts
of conscience. To what degree does the employee have the right to
work in accord with the dictates of his or her conscience? Could the
company let someone go for these conflicts of conscience? Again,
remember to distinguish between the right of a private citizen in society to act according to conscience, and the right of an employee to
do so.

Rowan also suggests a right to well-being that emerges from
human dignity, but it is not clear that companies are obligated to
empower an employee's well-being. It is clearly ideal both for the
employee and the company if an employee can fulfill life goals in the
workplace. But as long as the work performed is not inherently dehu-
manizing, it does not seem that the company has the responsibility to
facilitate an employee's well-being. Many employees are dissatisfied
with their jobs and feel that what they do for a living does not contribute to their sense of well-being. That is consistent with the theological perspective of work under the curse of sin. It is clear that work
is inherently good, being instituted as part of creation, but it is also
subject to the effects of the entrance of sin into the world. This means
that any work has the potential to be alienating and to undercut one's
well-being as well as contribute to it. As Rowan suggests, what the
right to well-being requires is that the minimal conditions be in place
to pursue it, not that society or the company has the obligation to
ensure that well-being is achieved. Companies are not necessarily
doing anything unethical when employees are dissatisfied with their
work and find it undermining their well-being.

The final right that falls out of human dignity, the right to equal
treatment, does seem to relate directly to the workplace. Employees

are being treated in a way that undermines their dignity if they are treated unfairly, that is, if they are given unequal treatment compared to other employees. Of course, not all employees are situated equally. There are different levels of qualification, experience, and performance. But when situated similarly, employees are entitled to similar treatment.

From a Christian perspective, mere possessions of goals and interests is not sufficient to ground basic rights. Human beings are valuable and have intrinsic dignity because they are the special creations of their Creator God, and bear his image. Only with this theological grounding can rights be adequately grounded. If human beings are nothing more than the product of naturalistic evolution, there is nothing special or unique about them and nothing intrinsic to them that gives them dignity that should be respected. Regardless of one's worldview, most agree that human beings possess fundamental dignity. And most agree that though there are differences between rights in civil society and in the workplace, one does not forfeit all rights when entering the workplace.

Basic human dignity demands that persons be treated with the respect befitting someone made in God's image. Rowan suggests that "employees should at all times be treated in a way that respects them as persons." Think about Ewing's employee bill of rights. Which of these rights do you think necessarily emerge from the obligation to respect human dignity? Rowan suggests four: fair pay, safety, due process, and privacy. Ewing suggests others, such as a right to exercise one's conscience (#1, #2), and free speech (#1). Most of the rights Ewing enumerates have to do with privacy, both off and on the job.

Out of the notion of human dignity and basic fairness, the following aspects of workplace ethics should be recognized:

1. The terms of one's contract should be honored. No one should be treated with such disrespect as to have the formal agreement between employee and company ignored or violated.
2. Employees are to be paid fairly and in a timely fashion. One's wages should be determined by more than simply market forces. To have as the goal to pay the employee as little as one can get away with, without regard to needs or life circumstances, is a violation of his dignity. At the least, this involves the traditional "equal pay for equal work," assuming that the employees involved are equally qualified and equally experienced—that is, if they are equally situated and do equal work, they should receive equal pay.

3. Workplace safety should be insured. To subject employees to unnecessary risks, particularly without their knowledge, undermines their dignity and treats them as mere things, without regard for their health. To be sure, some jobs, such as law enforcement and fire fighting, have inherent risks. But safe working conditions are a minimal condition for respecting workplace dignity. If employees do undertake risks in doing their jobs, it should be with full disclosure prior to performing the job.

4. Some due process is necessary to ensure that employees are not treated solely as replaceable cogs in a profit-making machine. At the least, employees are owed a reason for their dismissal or demotion. Pure employment at will, which is the law in many states, violates this aspect of human dignity by treating employees as the equivalent of property, regarding them as the owners' to do with as they choose. Since it is generally easier for companies to fill positions than it is for laid-off employees to find new jobs, employees are owed some notice prior to termination of their employment, enabling them to transition to new jobs without undue hardship.

5. Respecting dignity involves creating and maintaining a workplace that is free of physical or sexual harassment. These forms of coercion treat the employee as an object to be manipulated rather than as a person to be respected and are thus inconsistent with the dignity befitting someone made in God's image.

6. Respecting human dignity also involves treating employees in a way that is discrimination free. That is, employees should not be subject to discrimination based on race, gender, or genetics, all factors that the employee cannot control. This would mean that the company should not use race, gender, or the results of genetic testing to deny or terminate employment or to demote a current employee.

7. There is a presumption of privacy in the workplace. Respecting someone's privacy follows from respecting their dignity in allowing them to keep their personal information private. This presumption can be overridden under certain conditions of the company's competing claim.

Christian ethics demands that employers treat employees with the decency and respect that they deserve as persons made in God's image. That means that Christian norms of compassion, not simply market forces, should help determine how employees are treated.

Employee Privacy

We agree with Miller and Weckert that there is a prima facie right to privacy in the workplace, that employees do not necessarily give up rights to privacy simply because they enter the office. However, a variety of balancing factors need to be taken into account. First, the right to privacy is balanced by the company's interest in holding employees accountable to reasonable output and quality of work. For example, this is the common practice of companies that monitor customer service departments to ensure that customers' needs are properly met. If monitoring is necessary for ensuring efficiency, then it can be justified, though Miller and Weckert raise a helpful point in their argument that such a practice may actually be harmful for morale and productivity in the long run.

Second, a right to privacy may be overridden when the company has probable cause to believe that a crime is being committed, or an action is being committed that is harmful to the company's interests. For example, if the management believes that company proprietary information is being leaked to competitors, the company has the right to investigate and may monitor email and other communications to determine the source of the leak. Or suppose the company believes that its Internet availability is being abused by employees using the Internet for personal business, or worse, for viewing pornography. The company has the right to monitor Internet use to insure that its resources are not being taken advantage of.

Third, a company has the right to override employee privacy when access to an employee's files or computer is necessary to make decisions in the employee's absence. There is little debate on this point, and most employees would not consider it an invasion of privacy if they were not available to provide information necessary to make important decisions.

These areas mentioned above concern invasions of privacy when the employee does not give consent or is not available to do so. The common practice of many companies is to disclose *prior to employment* that the employee's email, Internet use, computer use, and in some cases phone use will be monitored. We believe that this is different from the above situations in which privacy is explicitly overridden. In our view, the employee may be asked to relinquish some rights to privacy if properly informed prior to commencement of employment. Companies are justified in such preemployment disclosure because the employee can simply walk away from the job offer if this aspect of the terms is not acceptable. In the absence of this kind of disclosure, the employee enters the workplace with the expectation of privacy and may be in for quite a shock when routine monitoring occurs. This type of preemployment disclosure can be extended to other justifiable invasions of privacy that may be necessary due to the nature of the industry. For example, airline pilots, bus drivers, and operators of heavy equipment are routinely and randomly subjected to drug testing in the interests of public safety. Employees in these jobs are informed prior to employment that these tests are standard practice, and the employee can refuse employment if he or she believes that such tests constitute an intolerable invasion of privacy.

No discussion of employee rights would be complete without the corresponding discussion of the rights of the company. What rights does the employer have that may conflict with employee privacy? We would argue that companies have the right to have its job descriptions met and to assess employee performance according to the specifications of the job descriptions. Companies also have the right to protect against fraud and theft, both of company resources and time, and this may involve monitoring of some sort to ensure such protection. Finally, and somewhat controversially, companies have the right to protect against actions that would damage their reputation. This has to do with the area of an employee's private time. For example, a company has the right to terminate employment of someone who commits a crime while on his or her own time. Moreover, if a person engages in behavior that clearly harms the company's reputation, the company has the right to warn the person, and if the behavior continues, to terminate employment. For example, if an employee speaks out publicly in a way that is very critical of the company or portrays the company in a poor light, the company's reputation is harmed, and that may be sufficient reason to terminate employment.

Sexual Harassment

There is perhaps no other charge that strikes such fear and dread into the hearts of individuals in the workplace than the charge of sexual harassment. It is one of the few infractions of which a person can be guilty until proven innocent. Companies frequently feel the need to take harassment claims seriously, since the firm can be held liable for not stopping harassment of which it has knowledge. But this desire to take it seriously tends to undermine the rights of the accused to due process, which includes the opportunity to confront one's accuser and rebut the charges. Often employees accused of harassment are fired first and the company asks questions later. As a result, all it takes is the charge of sexual harassment to ruin a person's reputation, which at the least may take years to rebuild. At most, the charge alone can ruin a person's career with that particular company. This has resulted in a chilling effect on relations between the genders at work, precisely the opposite of what feminist advocates desired when they began to confront sexual harassment in the workplace.

Several issues must be resolved before fair and adequate laws can be put into place to safeguard both victims and those accused of sexual harassment. The first and perhaps the most difficult issue is the definition of sexual harassment. Many people cannot define it precisely, but they certainly know it when it occurs, particularly if it should happen to them. But an intuitive sense of when it occurs is inadequate, because it is much too subjective and puts too much power in the alleged victim. More objective criteria are needed to adequately assess when sexual harassment has genuinely occurred. Think about how you would define sexual harassment if you were a company's human resource manager responsible for drafting a policy for addressing sexual harassment.

A second issue is whether the current emphasis on sexual harassment has gone too far, resulting in frivolous accusations and a general stifling of interaction between men and women at work. There is no more effective way for employees to strike back at a boss or fellow employee who has hurt them than to charge them with harassment. As a result, there is a growing atmosphere of fear surrounding gender relations in the workplace, not exactly a desirable effect. Has the trend toward correcting sexual harassment in the workplace been pushed too far, or is the problem being addressed in proportion to the frequency with which it occurs? Has it produced unanticipated and unintended consequences that are not helpful to workplace morale and harmonious relationships between men and women at work?

A third critical issue is the way companies balance two legitimate concerns. It is clear that firms must take sexual harassment claims seriously, and a company that fails to deal with such an atmosphere is rightly held liable. But the firm must also be committed to employing due process for employees accused of harassment. The "fire first and ask questions later" approach surely indicates decisiveness about sexual harassment but, one must ask, at what price? If the price is the loss of due process for accused employees, is that too high a price to pay? Or is giving an employee access to due process only delaying dealing with the problem and giving companies a way to sweep employees' complaints about harassment under the rug?

A primary problem in defining sexual harassment is that women and men tend to perceive it very differently. What may be simply innocent joking and teasing for men may be offensive to women. What may be a culturally acceptable way of interacting for men may actually be threatening for women. So one question with defining sexual harassment is, from whose perspective should harassment be defined? The question implies that the victim's perception should set the standard.

The courts have defined two primary types of sexual harassment. The first is what is called "quid pro quo" harassment, in which sexual favors are demanded in exchange for job security or promotion. This is often called sexual extortion, and virtually everyone agrees that this constitutes the clearest and most egregious form of sexual harassment. But a second type has also been clarified. When the harassment produces a hostile working environment for the person victimized, that is also sexual harassment, and in most cases, justifiably so. The courts have held that a person who works in such an environment does not have to prove that he or she has been harmed in any way, either physically or emotionally, to establish that sexual harassment has occurred. While acknowledging that this aspect of the definition can be abused, we agree that unwanted sexual attention that creates a hostile work environment, particularly, but not exclusively, for women, constitutes sexual harassment and should be stopped.

The standard of the reasonable woman when it comes to defining harassment is a sound one and keeps it from being problematic had it been entirely subjective. Of course, if the reasonable woman standard is employed, then women must give fair warning to those who are treading on thin sexual harassment ice. It is unrealistic to expect men to be mind readers, particularly since the specifics of a reasonable standard are usually not spelled out, nor is it wise for any company's policy to become too specific in defining harassment. When it becomes too specific, then a firm runs the risk of being legalistic about sexual harassment, obeying the letter of the law and neglecting its spirit. Thus, before any charge of sexual harassment can be taken seriously, the alleged victim must take responsibility for saying no to any behavior that she finds sexually offensive. Once warned, alleged perpetrators are informed and can be held accountable for any similar violations with the same person in the future. The victim who suffers in silence cannot reasonably expect sexual harassment to stop, nor can the person hold any individual or company liable for harassment of which they have no awareness.

Of course, many people who do sexually harass women know it even without any warning. They know it is offensive, and frequently that is precisely the reason they engage in such behavior. But many co-workers, once warned, not only stop the offensive behavior but appreciate being told that their behavior was offensive. It is further incumbent on any company that intends to be sensitive to sexual harassment to have an adequate reporting system in place to empower victims to voice their complaints and to warn both the company and the perpetrator.

Thus, in general, sexual harassment is defined as behavior that either demands sexual favors in exchange for favorable treatment on the job, or creates a hostile working environment according to a reasonable woman standard. With this working definition, let's look at the following brief scenarios. Which of these would you say constitutes sexual harassment? Try to label them as "definitely harassment," "possibly harassment," and "definitely not harassment."

1. Being asked repeatedly for a date by a co-worker, all of which you turn down.
2. Putting your hand on a female co-worker's shoulder for a brief moment during a conversation.
3. Having calendar pinups of scantily clad women on the shop floor's bulletin board.
4. Reading soft porn in an out-of-the-way place at work during the lunch hour.
5. Telling sexual jokes in the presence of female co-workers.
6. Complimentary comments that are slightly suggestive about a person's appearance.
7. Looking a co-worker up and down during a conversation.

Companies that are trying to take sexual harassment seriously need to balance the concern for harassment with the effect that such concern has on employees. J. H. Foegen is surely correct in his observations about what the emphasis on sexual harassment has done to gender relations. He calls this a "productivity reducing chill in the workplace climate" that has undermined the original intent behind sexual harassment laws. Many men are justifiably nervous about relating to women at work, and some men are finding themselves going out of their way to avoid women in the workplace when they can. This is not only unfortunate for gender relations, but it also inhibits productivity and morale. Foegen points out that companies like Corning have issued some helpful general guidelines for avoiding sexual harassment situations:

1. Would you do or say the alleged harassment before your spouse or parents?
2. Would you do or say the alleged harassment in front of another same-sex colleague? (We would add to this "a colleague whom you respect," since some colleagues may actually encourage you in such behavior.)

3.   Would you like the alleged harassment reported in the newspaper?
4.   Does the alleged harassment need saying or doing at all?

These are very insightful questions that help eliminate harassment by putting responsibility on the one tempted to harass. Companies that are dealing with sexual harassment seriously have an interest in avoiding the chilling effect. One way to help alleviate the chill is to insist on clear, firm, and civil communication among employees when sexually offended. Both this emphasis on communication and an intolerance of sexual harassment must come from the top, both by example and policy. Foegen also insightfully points out the double standard that exists in a society that sponsors sex saturation in the media and yet expects the workplace to be free of sexual harassment.

Companies must also balance taking sexual harassment complaints seriously with due process for those charged with harassment. The "fire first and ask questions later" policy is unethical since it deprives employees of their right to confront their accusers and rebut the charges. It also potentially victimizes innocent employees and empowers people to use sexual harassment charges for purposes other than stopping sexual harassment. For people to use sexual harassment charges to strike back at people with whom they have grievances is unconscionable, and to be fair to all concerned, companies must institute a process for ensuring that people are not pronounced guilty before the evidence is heard. The tragic side effect of the recent sexual harassment sensitivity is that those unjustly charged or charged prior to fair warning have suffered severe and perhaps irreparable damage to their reputations. When that happens, genuinely innocent people are victimized. In the workplace as in the legal system, people should be innocent until proven guilty, particularly when the charge is sexual harassment.

EIGHT

Accounting and Finance

The accounting profession and particularly the AICPA [American Institute of Certified Public Accountants] have been almost oblivious to the words "public interest."

Arthur Levitt, former chairman of the
Securities and Exchange Commission[1]

If you think what my client did [in managing earnings] constitutes fraud, then every company in the Fortune 500 is engaged in fraud.

Wallace Timmeny, attorney
and former SEC staff member[2]

[1] Quoted in Paula Dwyer, "I Want It Crystal Clear Who's to Blame," *Business Week*, 25 September 2000, 166.

[2] Quoted in Carol J. Loomis, "Lies, Damned Lies and Managed Earnings," *Fortune*, 2 August 1999, 88.

INTRODUCTION

In the past few years, accounting and finance have dominated the discussion of business ethics. Accounting irregularities in many well-known and previously strong companies appear on the front pages of major business publications and have attracted a degree of public attention to business ethics that has not been seen since the days of Ivan Boesky and Michael Milken. The list of companies that have had to restate their earnings (as a result of correcting fraudulent accounting) has grown significantly over the past few years and includes companies that have become household names as a result of their fall into scandal and some even into bankruptcy. Companies such as Sunbeam, Waste Management, Enron, WorldCom, Tyco, Healthsouth, Global Crossing, Adelphia Communications, ImClone, and Xerox, to name a few, have all been under a cloud of suspicion; and some, such as Enron and WorldCom, have suffered precipitous declines, leaving employees and investors "holding the bag." Longtime accounting stalwart Arthur Andersen was implicated in the failed audits of Waste Management and particularly Enron, and was convicted of obstruction of justice for destroying materials relevant to the SEC's investigation. Business periodicals such as *Fortune* and *Business Week* have had cover stories calling for a restoration of trust in the financial reporting system.[3]

3 See, for example, Joseph Nocera, "System Failure," *Fortune*, 24 June 2002, 62–74; John Byrne, "Restoring Trust in Corporate America," *Business Week*, 24 June 2002, 31–44.

In the aftermath of the Enron debacle, some publications and business websites instituted regular "scandal watch" columns to track investigations and indictments. Most significantly, in late 2001 through 2002, the stock market sank to mid-1990s lows, erasing more than $7 trillion in investor holdings, depleting 401(k) accounts, and forcing many people nearing retirement to rethink their plans. There was a crisis of confidence among investors, who had grown increasingly skeptical of corporate earnings reports. Even when companies reported strong earnings, investors were asking, How do we know those numbers are true?

The crisis of confidence also struck at Wall Street. Investment banking houses were criticized for giving in to conflicts of interest that compromised their fiduciary duties to their clients. Analysts were cheerleading for their firm's investment banking clients instead of giving objective analysis. In addition, they were often selling stocks in their private accounts that they were touting as "strong buys" to the public. Merrill Lynch was fined roughly $100 million for breaching the "Chinese wall" that was supposed to separate analysts and bankers, trashing stocks privately that they were touting publicly. Furthermore, serious questions were raised about Wall Street's fairness in handling initial public offerings (IPOs). Critics assailed the major brokerage houses for giving preferential treatment to key institutional investors, often at the expense of the investing public and the startup companies that were going public.

Accounting scandals have also generated criticism of corporate governance.[4] The investing public and the SEC are demanding that corporate boards of directors be more involved in oversight of the company, holding management more accountable and serving the shareholders rather than the management. Boards of directors have long been criticized for allowing excessive CEO compensation. More recently, the audit committees of company boards, which are supposed to oversee the financial management of the company, have come in for harsh criticism for lack of oversight. Some groups are pushing for stronger liability for directors when debacles such as Enron occur.

4 John A. Byrne, "Special Report: How to Fix Corporate Governance," *Business Week*, 6 May 2002, 69–81.

The temptation to "cook the books" to make a company look like a better performer than it actually is has been around for some time. Watchdog groups such as the Securities and Exchange Commission (SEC), which regulates the stock markets and the stock activity of publicly traded companies, and public accounting firms, which audit companies regularly, are designed to assure the investing public that they can trust the financial statements that a company issues. In the past few years, there has been an alarming increase in the number of failed audits, where audit teams have failed to detect egregious errors.[5] In addition, the SEC has cracked down on what it considers accounting fraud, with more open investigations of accounting irregularities than ever before. In the past, the SEC was largely concerned about insider trading, and though that is still a concern, the SEC is now turning its attention to ensuring accuracy and uniformity in the financial statements a company issues.

Though the cases of clear fraud are the ones that make the headlines, they are the exception to the general rule. In general, new ways of doing business at times challenge the interpretation of current accounting practices (known as GAAP, or "generally accepted accounting principles"). This was true in the past as companies did business in space for the first time, or as health care companies wrestled with new ways of accounting for revenues, or as financial services firms accounted for increasingly complex products, and more recently, with e-commerce firms trying to figure out how to properly account for revenues when transactions are split between different parties. It takes some time for the accounting profession to react and carefully clarify how the standards should be applied to these new ways of conducting business.

To understand the pressures on management, and in particular on the company's financial officers, let's put a publicly traded company in a broader context. Think about four groups of individuals/institutions and how each group is involved in the process of investing and financial accountability. The first group is the *investing public*, which includes (1) individual investors, either through direct stock purchases or mutual funds; (2) institutional investors, such as pension fund managers and mutual fund managers; and (3) investment advisors, which include stockbrokers and financial planners. The second group is what we will call the *market makers*, which includes brokerage houses, investment banks, and stock analysts. This group of companies is commonly known as "Wall Street," since most of the major market makers are located on Wall Street or close to it in New York City. This group makes its money primarily by raising money for companies through its investment banking services and sales of stock to individuals and institutions. Market makers are very influential on the direction of the stock market, and the opinions of stock analysts can move the market up or down depending on the opinions they issue. The third group is the *executive management* of publicly traded companies, which includes the top executives and those who are accountable to

[5] See the example of MicroStrategy and its auditor, Price Waterhouse/Coopers, in Christopher H. Schmitt and Paula Dwyer, "Did the Auditors Cross the Line?" *Business Week*, 25 September 2000, 168–69. Other examples of companies that issued well-publicized restatements of their earnings in the aftermath of their audits include Cendant, McKesson HBOC, Columbia/HCA, Oxford Healthcare, Sunbeam, Greentree, Waste Management, and Riteaid. These were cited in the above article. See also Richard Melcher, "Where Are the Accountants?" *Business Week*, 5 October 1998, 144–46.

the board of directors. The board is ultimately responsible for the company's performance, though board members are traditionally distinct from the executive management. If the performance of management is not up to the investors' or analysts' expectations, then the investors can and often do sell the company's stock, sometimes sending its price downward and decreasing its market value. Thus, the management feels great pressure to meet those expectations, which are passed along to the final group involved in this process, the *accountants and chief financial officers*, who are responsible for preparing the company's financial statements. They are guided by basic accounting conventions and by the generally accepted accounting principles (GAAP), and have outside auditors who check the statements in order to assure the public that the statements are accurate and trustworthy.

To properly understand the story of the ethics of accounting and finance in the past few years, you need to see it in the context of all four of these important parties. The role of accountants/CFOs and executive management is often the focus of ethics discussions in finance and accounting. It is often said that the new ways of doing business over the Internet have created new challenges to ethics. But others hold that there is nothing about e-business that the accounting profession has not faced in the past when it comes to accounting for complicated transactions. The important side of this discussion is the pressure brought to bear on companies from the investing public and market makers.

What is genuinely new about the investment culture today is the change in emphasis from what might be called "value investing" in the past, to what is called "growth investing." Value investing refers to looking at the current profitability of a company based on its fundamentals such as its earnings per share. Growth investing refers to what a company might become in the future, regardless of its current profitability. This shift to growth investing is reflected in the growing short-term mentality of many investors, who are looking to turn a quick profit, and in some cases of the growing number of day traders, who are actually engaged in a practice analogous to gambling. This overemphasis on growth investing has generated a new way of evaluating a company's financial condition by focusing on revenue rather than profit and has provided new opportunities to manipulate financial statements to make a company's outlook look better than it actually is. This emphasis on growth investing explains why Internet companies that had never made a profit could command stock prices far in excess of their value, though with the collapse of the tech sector in recent years, Internet firms are no longer commanding such high valuations.

This shift to growth investing is not problematic per se, but in the past few years, especially with the wild growth of Internet stocks (and now their collapse), growth investing has been overemphasized. With the way the Internet bubble has burst, the emphasis has returned to more value investing. But what is clear is that the overemphasis on growth investing is an important part of the story that has put enormous pressure on executive management, and in turn on accountants and CFOs, to make a company's earnings appear as positive as possible and to do so on a quarterly basis. It is this pressure that has driven many of the ethical dilemmas and cases of outright accounting fraud that have been in the business headlines in the past few years. The pressure on financial professionals comes not only from their CEOs and boards of directors, but the ultimate source of that pressure is the investing public and the market makers who serve them. There are also ethical issues facing investment advisors, when they recommend growth investing at the expense of a more long-term value focus.

The area of accounting/finance ethics is very broad, and it is easy to get caught up in the technicalities of specific accounting practices. In this chapter our goal is to give you an overview of the various ethical issues that face accountants and financial professionals as well as some general principles for accounting with integrity. Some of the cases will put you in the place of the chief financial officer (CFO) of a company facing ethical decisions on how to report your company's earnings in its financial statements. Others will put you in the position of the outside auditor, and you will wrestle with the ethical pressures that come with that position, where you are paid by the company you are auditing but also have a responsibility to the public. Another set of issues comes more from the area of public policy for the financial professions. These issues go beyond what these individuals would face in the course of doing their jobs and have to do with ensuring independence and objectivity for auditors and stock analysts.

The reading in this chapter is a helpful overview of the issues that face financial professionals. It will introduce you to background concepts and principles that will give you the tools you need to address the various cases. Though the cases do involve professionals who make their living in accounting and finance, you don't need to be an accounting major or a CPA to make sense of this material. If you do have that background, then you may be able to anticipate other ethical issues that we have not mentioned. We would encourage you to apply the principles outlined in this chapter to those issues.

READING

Financial Ethics: An Overview

John Boatright

From *Ethics in Finance* (New York: Blackwell, 1999), 1–29.

The public's perception of ethics in finance is shaped by news stories of major scandals, such as these events from the past several decades.

- Wall Street was shaken in the late 1980s by the securities-law violations and the junk-bond market manipulations of Dennis Levine, Martin Siegel, Ivan Boesky, Michael Milken, and others. James B. Stewart, the author of *Den of Thieves*, calls their activities "the greatest criminal conspiracy the financial world has ever known."[1]

- In 1990, Michael Milken pleaded guilty to six felonies, for which he was sentenced to ten years in prison. Previously, Drexel Burnham Lambert, the firm that Milken had built into a junk-bond powerhouse, collapsed after Drexel officials admitted to six felonies and agreed to pay $650 million in a settlement with the Securities and Exchange Commission (SEC).

- The brokerage house E. F. Hutton was convicted in 1985 of 2,000 counts of mail and wire fraud for a check-kiting scheme in which the firm obtained interest-free use of more than $1 billion over a 20-month period by systematically overdrafting checking accounts at 400 banks. E. F. Hutton agreed to pay a fine of $2 million to settle the charges.

- Salomon Brothers was nearly destroyed in 1991 by charges that traders in the government securities division had attempted to execute a "squeeze" by rigging several auctions of US Treasury notes. The total cost of this scandal—including legal expenses and lost business, on top of a $290 million fine—has been estimated

at $1 billion. The firm discharged the people responsible for the bid rigging, as well as CEO John Gutfreund, who was unaware of the activity at the time. Gutfreund's offense was that he sat on the news for more than three months before reporting it to the Treasury Department.

- In the wake of massive losses on derivative transactions, Orange County in California sued its financial adviser Merrill Lynch for concealing the amount of risk that was involved in its investments. Procter & Gamble (P&G) eventually settled a suit with Bankers Trust after the bank agreed to forgive $200 million that P&G owed on failed derivative transactions. P&G's charges that Bankers Trust had misrepresented the investments was bolstered by damaging tapes, including some in which bank employees used the acronym ROF for "rip-off factor" to describe one method fleecing customers.

- Unauthorized trading by individuals has caused great losses at several banks and trading firms. Nick Leeson, a 28-year-old trader in the Singapore office of Barings Bank, destroyed this venerable British firm by losing more than $1 billion on futures contracts that bet the wrong way on the direction of the Japanese stock market. A Japanese trader in the New York office of Daiwa Bank hid losses of $1.1 billion over an 11-year period, and the acknowledged king of copper trading lost an estimated $2.6 billion for his employer, Sumitomo Corporation. Joseph Jett, a trader at the now-defunct firm Kidder Peabody, was accused in 1994 of faking

$350 in bond-trading profits in order to cover losses of $85 million.

- Prudential Securities admitted in 1994 that crimes had been committed in the sale of limited partnerships during the 1980s and agreed to pay fines and penalties in excess of $700 million. Previously, the securities firm had settled a class action suit for $90 million, in which investors who had been defrauded were paid eight cents on the dollar for their losses.[2] The parent company, Prudential Insurance, continues to face multiple class action suits over charges that insurance agents "churned" client accounts and used false and misleading sales tactics.

These scandals not only undermine the public's confidence in financial markets and financial institutions but fuel a popular image of the financial world as one of greed. A 1996 poll reveals that a majority of respondents agree with the claim that most people on Wall Street "would be willing to break the law if they believed they could make a lot of money and get away with it" and that they care only about "making money and absolutely nothing else."[3] This image is not entirely undeserved, of course. Ivan Boesky delighted a commencement audience of business school students at the University of California at Berkeley with the assurance that greed is "all right." "I think greed is healthy," he said. "You can be greedy and still feel good about yourself."[4]

Although these examples of egregious wrongdoing and naked greed rivet our attention, they give a misleading picture of the level of ethics in finance. People in finance engage in an array of activities that involve the handling of financial assets. Not only does the welfare of everyone depend on the care and use of these assets, but millions of financial transactions take place each day with a high level of integrity. However, there are ample opportunities in finance for some people to gain at others' expense. Simply put, finance concerns other people's money (OPM), and OPM invites misconduct. Professionals in the financial services industry—such as stockbrokers, bankers, financial advisers, mutual fund and pension managers, and insurance agents—have a responsibility to the clients they serve. Financial managers in corporations, government, and other organizations have an obligation to manage the financial assets of their employers well. Everyone else involved in finance, from financial analysts to market regulators, fills positions of trust that carry certain duties.

The ethics of an occupation or a profession is best understood not by examining the worst conduct of its members but by attending to the conduct that is commonly expected and generally found. What are the standards that people in finance ought to observe? How should the inevitable ethical dilemmas in financial activities be resolved? These fundamental questions are not easily answered, and the attempt to answer them is the main task of this book. This chapter lays the groundwork for the ones that follow by explaining the need for ethics in finance and providing an overview of the main problems of finance ethics. A comprehensive treatment of ethics in finance is, of necessity, long and involved because of the diversity of financial activities and the range of ethical issues that they raise. However, there is little that is unique to financial ethics. The ethical dilemmas of finance take different forms in other areas of business and the professions, such as medicine and law. Thus, our discussion of ethics in finance can be facilitated by drawing on the well-developed fields of business and professional ethics.

The Need For Ethics In Finance

Some cynics jokingly deny that there is any ethics in finance, especially on Wall Street. This view is expressed in a thin volume, *The Complete Book of Wall Street Ethics*, which claims to fill "an empty space on financial bookshelves where a consideration of ethics should be."[5] Of course, the pages are all blank! However, a moment's reflection reveals that finance would be impossible without ethics. The very act of placing our assets in the hands of other people requires immense trust. An untrustworthy stockbroker or insurance agent, like an untrustworthy physician or attorney, finds few takers for his or her services.

Financial scandals shock us precisely because they involve people and institutions that we should be able to trust.

Financial ethics is about far more than trust. However, a complete account of the need for ethics in finance is not possible in a few words. First, finance is not a clearly identifiable occupation or profession. Like medicine, law, engineering, accounting, and so on, finance involves a highly technical body of knowledge, but people who are trained in finance engage in a much wider range of activities. Accountants, by contrast, do much the same work in every setting, and the different accounting functions—public and management accounting or external and internal auditing—raise similar ethical problems that can be identified and addressed in a code of ethics. Thus, accounting ethics, like the ethics of medicine, law, and engineering, focuses on the ethical problems of a relatively uniform activity. Although codes of ethics exist for some specific fields in finance, such as financial advisers and insurance underwriters, the idea of a single code of ethics for everyone in finance is impractical.

Second, the ethics of finance is concerned not solely with the ethical problems of individuals in a specific occupation or profession but also with problems in financial markets and financial institutions. Because market regulation is concerned with fairness, financial ethics must address the question, What are fair trading practices? The financial services industry handles vast assets for clients. The ethical treatment of clients and the responsible handling of assets raise many issues in financial ethics. Finance is also a function in every business enterprise and in many nonprofit organizations and governmental units. Corporate financial managers are responsible for myriad decisions, from how best to raise and invest capital to the planning of mergers and acquisitions. Public finance, on the other hand, is concerned largely with raising and disbursing funds for governmental purposes. These tasks raise ethical dilemmas of personal conduct, as well as broad questions of public policy, when corporate and public financial decisions affect society.

Markets, clients, and personal dilemmas

Despite the diversity of financial roles and activities, an understanding of the need for ethics in finance can be developed around three broad themes.

1. *Ethics is needed in financial markets.* Financial transactions typically take place in markets and presuppose certain moral rules and expectations of moral behavior. The most basic of these is a prohibition against fraud and manipulation, but, more generally, the rules and expectations for markets are concerned with fairness, which is often expressed as a level playing field. The playing field in financial markets can become "tilted" by many factors, including unequal information, bargaining power, and resources. In addition to making one-time economic exchanges, participants in markets also engage in financial contracting whereby they enter into long-term relations. These contractual relations typically involve the assumption of fiduciary duties or obligations to act as agents, and financial markets are subject to unethical conduct because of opportunistic behavior by fiduciaries and agents. Finally, market transactions between two parties often have third-party effects, which is to say that they affect others. This is especially true of investment decisions by corporations and financial institutions. Thus, fairness in financial markets includes some consideration of the social impact of financial activity and the responsibility of financial decision makers to balance the competing interests of various groups.

2. *Ethics is needed in the financial services industry.* The financial services industry is the most visible face of finance and the aspect that affects ordinary citizens most directly. As an industry, it has an obligation to develop products that fit people's needs and to market them in a responsible manner, avoiding, for example, deceptive or coercive sales tactics. In addition, organizations that provide financial services typically deal with individuals as clients. A reputation for ethical behavior is crucial in gaining the confidence of clients, but, more importantly, a firm owes certain duties to clients. For example, a stockbroker or an insurance agent is (or should be) more than an

order-taker or a peddler in a buyer-seller environment. Such a person is offering to put special skills and knowledge to work for the benefit of others. The people who make such an offer become fiduciaries and agents who have an obligation to subordinate their own interests to those of clients. Some financial service providers may even be characterized as professionals who have stringent professional duties like those of physicians and lawyers. The main duties of professionals are to perform services with competence and due care, to avoid conflicts of interest, to preserve confidentiality, and to uphold the ideals of the professions.

3. *Ethics is needed by finance people in organizations.* The vast majority of people in finance are employees of an organization, and they and their organizations encounter the full range of ethical problems that occur in business. These include personal ethical dilemmas, such as the situation of the financial manager of a corporation who is instructed to overstate the return on a project in order to gain its approval, or the analyst in a brokerage firm who is pressured to withdraw a planned "sell" recommendation for the stock of a company that is also a client of the firm. Individuals who are aware of or involved in unethical and/or illegal conduct face the difficult dilemma of whether to become a *whistleblower.* Consider, for example, the situation of an employee of an investment banking firm who learns that a bribe was made to city officials to secure the business of underwriting a municipal bond offering. What is such a person obligated to do—or free to do? Now that finance is global, people in finance encounter the dilemmas that result from different practices and standards in other countries. Organizations, too, face all of these problems and must develop procedures and policies that address such topics as reporting alleged misconduct and operating abroad.

Ethics and finance theory

The need for ethics, as it has been explained so far, focuses on the practice of finance, but finance is also a theoretical body of knowledge upon which the practical application depends. Many important decisions are based on finance theory, but the contribution of theory is usually thought to be purely technical. The theory of finance is limited to answering questions about what will happen if certain decisions are made. Decision makers can be guided by this knowledge in choosing the most effective means to a given end, but the choice of ends—which belongs to the realm of ethics—is separate from finance theory. In short, finance theory, as commonly conceived, is concerned with means; ethics with ends.

Most finance theorists would insist, moreover, that finance is an objective science that depends solely on observable facts and assumes nothing about moral values. Finance theory, in other words, is completely value-free. The point is often expressed by saying that finance theory is a *positive* science which contains only statements that are verifiable by empirical evidence. Positivists hold that all sciences should exclude normative statements, which is to say statements that express a value judgment.[6]

This picture of finance theory as a purely technical, value-free science that is concerned solely with means and not ends oversimplifies a more complex reality. Financial managers often make decisions that involve both means and ends without being aware of the value commitments that are implicit in the choice of ends. The general assumptions and specific doctrines of finance theory also shape managers' perceptions of what needs to be done and how best to proceed. Thus, even if finance is concerned only with technical matters, it is very easy to slip from saying "This is" to "This ought to be." For example, the fundamental tenet of finance that the objective of the firm is to maximize shareholder wealth is very much a normative statement about what businesses *ought* to do. A complete account of the need for ethics in finance must consider, then, the ethical consequences of acting on the basis of finance theory.

Why the law is not enough

Finance is perhaps the most heavily regulated area of American business. Not only is the basic framework established by major legislative enactments, but Congress and state legislatures have also created innumerable regulatory bodies with the power to set and enforce rules. Many questionable industry practices are challenged in court, so that the judiciary plays a prominent role in determining the boundaries of acceptable conduct. And most markets and exchanges have their own private rule-setting and rule-enforcement bodies. In view of this extensive regulation, people in finance might well assume that law is the only guide. Their motto might be: "If it's legal, then it's morally okay." This motto is inadequate for many reasons. As a former SEC chairman observed, "It is not an adequate ethical standard to aspire to get through the day without being indicted."[7] A certain amount of self-regulation is necessary, not as a replacement for legal regulation, but as a supplement for areas which the law cannot easily reach and as an ideal for rising above the law.[8]

First, the law is a rather crude instrument, and it is not suited for regulating all aspects of financial activities, especially those that cannot be reduced to precise rules. For example, a law against conflicts of interest would be difficult to draft, and indeed such conflicts are not illegal except when they involve the violation of a fiduciary duty or constitute fraud. Because of the variety of conflicts, rules designed to prevent them can be effective only if individuals obey the spirit as well as the letter of these rules. Second, the law often develops as a reaction to activities that are considered to be unethical. It would be perverse to encourage people in finance to do anything that they want until the law tells them otherwise. Besides, the law is not always settled, and many people who thought that their actions were legal, though perhaps immoral, have ruefully discovered otherwise. Third, merely obeying the law is insufficient for managing an organization or for conducting business because employees, customers, and other groups expect, indeed demand, ethical treatment. The attitude that only the law applies to financial activities invites even more legislation, litigation, and regulatory attention. Self-regulation—by indi-

viduals, organizations, and markets—is not only a more effective means for securing ethical conduct on some matters but also a shrewd strategy for avoiding more onerous legal regulation.

Ethics And Financial Markets

Market transactions constitute a large portion of financial activity. Many of these are one-time trades that take place in organized exchanges, such as stock markets, commodities markets, futures or options markets, currency markets, and the like. We have already noted that the main ethical problems in market transactions arise from unfair trading practices, such as those involving fraud and manipulation, and from the unlevel playing field that can result from unequal information and other inequalities. Furthermore, financial activity includes long-term contractual relations, in which individuals and organizations become fiduciaries and agents, with the duties or obligations that attend these roles. . . .

Financial contracting raises some additional ethical problems that are not easily settled. In the standard model of contracting, the terms of a contract specify the conduct required of each party and the remedies for noncompliance. In short, there is little "wiggle room" in a well-written contract. However, many contractual relations in finance and other areas fall short of this ideal, because actual contracts are often vague, ambiguous, incomplete, or otherwise problematic. The result is uncertainty and disagreement about what constitutes ethical (as well as legal) conduct. This section examines four areas in which financial contracting gives rise to ethical problems. These areas consist of the following: implicit contracts, imperfect contracting, remedies for breaches, and the balancing of competing interests.

Implicit contracts

The main terms of contracts are typically expressed in writing or in spoken words. No matter how detailed the agreement, however, some understandings still remain unexpressed and must be inferred. The law recognizes both *express* (written and oral) contracts and *implied* contracts, the latter of which include all manner of legally enforceable agreements. Beyond what is legally enforceable as a contract lie innumerable tacit understandings that have moral, if not legal, force. Financial affairs and business generally would be impossible if every detail of a transaction had to be specified in an express contract. Much is left implicit out of necessity. However necessary implicit contracts may be, they are the source of two ethical problems. One is that whatever is left implicit is subject to differing interpretations and disagreements, and the other is that insofar as they cannot be legally enforced, implicit contracts may be breached with impunity.

Corporations make innumerable implicit contracts with employees, customers, suppliers, and other stakeholder groups. Thus, companies are able to attract talented employees with promises of job security and loyal customers with warranties and other guarantees. Companies often gain valuable community support with pledges to be good corporate citizens. Employees and their employers may interpret guarantees of job security differently, so that a laid-off employee might consider the action to be a breach of an implicit promise. Similarly, customers might accuse a manufacturer of bad faith in failing to replace an arguably defective product. Because they can be broken without legal consequences, implicit contracts facilitate opportunistic behavior. One alleged abuse of implicit contracts occurs in successful hostile takeovers when raiders are able to finance the deal by capturing the value of the implicit contracts that the target firm has made to various groups, most notably employees and local communities. The raiders do not necessarily deny that the former managers made certain promises, but contend that the new management is not bound by these commitments.

Imperfect contracting

Although the parties to a contract attempt to strike the best bargain possible under the circumstances, they often fail to do so because of inherent limitations in our cognitive abilities. The most notable of these limitations are incomplete knowledge, bounded rationality,[9] and lack of knowledge of future contingencies. That is, contractors seldom possess all of the information that they need to make rational choices; they usually lack the ability to process even the information that is available to them; and no one can anticipate and plan for all eventualities.

One of the problems that imperfect contracting creates is that the parties may fail to negotiate contracts that produce the maximal benefit for each. Another problem is that it is difficult in some situations to specify the terms of a contract precisely because the relation itself may be too complex and uncertain to permit careful planning. Both of these problems are cited in arguments for the fiduciary duty of management to serve the interests of shareholders. Employees, customers, suppliers, and other constituencies can write reasonably precise contracts that have predictable results. Shareholders—according to this argument—cannot write such precise contracts, and so considerable managerial discretion is required to serve the shareholders' interests.

Remedies for breaches

Contracting involves two elements: (1) the planning of the relation, with attention to all of the situations that can be foreseen; and (2) the specification of the remedies that are available in the event that one party fails to perform accordingly. There is some evidence that individuals and business firms carefully plan the relation but neglect to provide for breaches.[10] As a result, many ethical and legal disputes concern the available remedies. Suppose, for example, that an employer who has made guarantees of job security as part of an implicit contract terminates a group of employees with three months' severance pay. If the implicit contract includes no provision for severance pay, then employees may grumble about inadequate compensation, while the managers may feel that they have treated the employees fairly. The ethical issue is, What is fair compensation? And in the absence of any contractual agreement, some standard must be sought in more general ethical principles.

A closely related problem is the standard for performance. Remedies can be invoked only when one party has failed to live up to the agreement, but whether this has occurred may be disputed. If the terms of a contract are utterly precise, then noncompliance may be easy to determine, but contracts for more open-ended situations may call not for specific actions (such as, "Do X!") but a best effort ("Try to do Y!"). Whether a party has met the "best effort" test requires some standard.[11]

The balancing of competing interests

Financial decision makers often have an identifiable obligation, such as a fiduciary duty, to serve the interests of a particular party, but this obligation does not exclude a responsibility to consider the impact of a decision on others. The extent of this responsibility, however, is open to question. If the primary obligation of a corporate finance officer, for example, is to serve the interests of shareholders, then should the fact that a decision will result in layoffs or plant closures be taken into account? It is tempting for financial managers to make purely financial judgments and leave the more difficult task of balancing interests to others, but such a neat division of responsibility is not always possible.

Furthermore, financial institutions serve many publics and wield immense power in our society. At one extreme, financial institutions have produced devastating social harm through reckless, "public be damned" activities, some of which constitute criminal conspiracies. In recent years, the savings and loan crisis, the collapse of the Bank of Credit and Commerce International (BCCI), and money laundering by otherwise respectable banks have been prominent in the financial news. Just as manufacturing firms have an obligation to avoid destructive consequences, such as polluting the environment, so too must financial institutions take care that their form of business does not inflict similar harm. Even in their normal activities, financial institutions are called upon to balance competing interests, not only in the distribution of benefits and harms but, perhaps more significantly, in the distribution of financial

risk. Whose interests should be taken into account in making these decisions? How should competing interests be reconciled?

Many of the harms that business firms inflict on society are *externalities* or spillover effects, which are costs of production that are not borne by the producer but passed along to others. Pollution is a common externality from manufacturing, but financial activities are also capable of producing externalities. Of all financial activities, decisions about investment . . . have the greatest potential for socially harmful consequences. Consider, for example, the impact that bank lending practices have on community development. Insofar as banks engage in *redlining*—the alleged practice of denying mortgages and home-improvement loans for properties in deteriorating neighborhoods, figuratively outlined in red on a map—they actively contribute to the process of urban decay. Banks have also been accused of discrimination by treating racial groups differently in the loan approval process. Both redlining and loan discrimination are addressed by federal legislation, such as the Home Mortgage Disclosure Act (HMDA) of 1975 and the Community Reinvestment Act (CRA) of 1977, but evidence of redlining and discrimination persists. On an international scale, the lending practices of multinational banks, especially the World Bank, exert a powerful influence on less-developed countries (LDCs), and so they need to exercise a high degree of responsible conduct.

The Financial Services Industry

The financial services industry provides a vast array of financial services and products to individuals, businesses, and governments. The industry itself primarily comprises major financial institutions, such as commercial banks, savings and loan companies, securities and investment banking firms, mutual fund and pension fund providers, financial planners, and insurance companies. Private partnerships, such as hedge funds, and publicly traded investment management firms, such as Warren Buffet's Berkshire Hathaway, further expand the definition of a financial services firm. In the United States, these institutions have been separated to some extent by law. The Glass–Steagall Act of 1933, for example, prohibits commercial banks from engaging in investment banking, and vice versa, but these legal barriers have been broken by new financial instruments that blur the lines between different financial institutions, and by the globalization of finance that enables institutions to operate differently abroad.

Firms in the financial services industry fulfill many useful purposes. They enable individuals, businesses, and governments to save and borrow, to invest for a return and to have access to capital, to insure against misfortune, and to effect major changes, such as mergers and acquisitions. These benefits are made possible by specialized services, such as the research of a stock analyst, the guidance of an investment planner, or the investment ability of a mutual fund or pension manager. The financial services industry also provides benefits through the creation of innovative products. Thus, insurance serves to reduce risk by pooling assets; money-market funds allow small investors to invest in large-denomination commercial paper, while mutual-stock funds enable people of limited means to hold a diversified portfolio; and home-equity loans turn an otherwise illiquid asset into a liquid liability. In recent years, securities that bundle a group of assets, such as a pool of mortgages, and derivatives, which are contracts whose value is "derived" from some underlying asset, have created new opportunities, as well as far-reaching changes.

In providing these services and products, financial services firms operate primarily as financial *intermediaries*, which is to say that they use their capital to support the provision of services rather than to trade and invest on their own behalf. For example, banks receive their revenue largely from fees charged to customers. As intermediaries which still operate in markets, financial services firms encounter virtually all of the ethical problems of market transactions and financial contracting that are presented above. Because financial services are provided to clients in a contractual relationship, most ethical issues are concerned with a firm's obligation to clients, whether

these be individuals or organizations. Some practices in the client–provider relation are clearly unethical and even illegal, but others are more controversial; and every practice involves a gray area in which the lines of acceptable and unacceptable conduct are not easily drawn.

This section examines, first, the ethical problems in the financial services industry that concern the treatment of individual clients and the general public. This is followed by a consideration of the ethical issues that arise in managing financial services firms, including the special concerns of institutional investors, such as mutual fund and pension fund managers.

Serving individual clients

The ethical objections to so-called bucket-shop or boiler-room operations are obvious. In these scams, cold-calling con artists attempt to sell securities of dubious value to naive investors, using high-pressure sales tactics and false or deceptive sales pitches. Respectable brokers and agents eschew such unsavory practices. They employ much more refined ones instead.

False and misleading claims

The ethical treatment of clients requires salespeople to explain all of the relevant information truthfully, and in an understandable and nonmisleading manner. One observer complains that brokers, insurance agents, and other salespeople have developed a new vocabulary that obfuscates rather than reveals.

> Walk into a broker's office these days. You won't be sold a product. You won't even find a broker. Instead, a "financial adviser" will "help you select" an "appropriate planning vehicle," or "offer" a menu of "investment choices" or "options" among which to "allocate your money." ... [Insurance agents] peddle such euphemisms as "private retirement accounts," "college savings plans," and "charitable remainder trusts." ... Among other linguistic sleights of hand in common usage these days: saying tax-free when, in

fact, it's only tax-deferred; high yield when it's downright risky; and projected returns when it's more likely in your dreams.[12]

Salespeople avoid speaking of commission, even though this is the source of their remuneration. Commission on mutual funds is "front-end" or "back-end loads"; and insurance agents, whose commission can approach 100 percent of the first year's premium, are not legally required to disclose this fact—and they rarely do. The agents of one insurance company represented life insurance policies as "retirement plans" and referred to the premiums as "deposits."[13]

Deception

False claims are capable of being disproved—although individual clients may not have easy access to the evidence—but deception is often a matter of interpretation. Promotional material for a mutual fund, for example, may be accurate but misleading if it emphasizes the strengths of a fund and minimizes the weaknesses. Past performance figures can be carefully selected and displayed in ways that give a misleading impression. Deception can also occur when essential information is not revealed. Thus, an investor may be deceived when the sales charge is rolled into the fund's annual expenses, which may be substantially higher than the competition's, or when the projected hypothetical returns do not reflect charges that are revealed elsewhere in the promotional material. As these examples suggest, true claims may lead a typical investor to hold a mistaken belief. Whether the claims are responsible for the false belief, however, or whether the investor has jumped too quickly to a false conclusion, is obviously a matter for further investigation.

Concealment of information

Deception aside, what information *ought* to be disclosed to a client? Salespeople are not obligated to provide complete details on every product, and clients have some responsibility to seek out information on their own. Questions about disclosure arise in virtually all buyer–seller relations, and sev-

eral different principles apply. For example, in many states, the seller of a house is required by law to reveal hidden termite damage. The rationale for a legal obligation to disclose the damage is twofold: first, the information is *material*, that is, it concerns a fact that has a significant bearing on the buyer's decision; and, second, the information cannot be readily obtained by the buyer. Of course, the buyer could hire a termite inspector, and so the law reflects the judgment that a buyer should not have to incur this expense when the information can be provided at less cost by the seller. In short, legislators have determined that a housing market is more efficient under a rule of seller disclosure than under a rule of *caveat emptor* ("let the buyer beware").

The Securities Act of 1933 requires the issuer of a security to disclose all material information, which is defined as information about which an average prudent investor ought reasonably to be informed or to which a reasonable person would attach importance in determining a course of action in a transaction. The rationale for this provision of the Securities Act is both fairness to investors, who have a right to make decisions with adequate information, and the efficiency of securities markets, which requires that investors be adequately informed. Most financial products, including mutual funds and insurance policies, are accompanied by a written prospectus that contains all of the information that the issuer is legally required to provide.

Churning, suitability, and risk

In addition to the obligation of any seller to avoid deception and to provide sufficient information, people in the financial services industry have additional obligations which derive from their role as fiduciaries or agents. The most prominent of these obligations are: to avoid excessive trading that generates commission but does not benefit the client (called "churning"), to recommend only suitable investments, and to disclose the level of risk.

Churning may be committed by a broker who executes multiple trades or trades with higher than usual commission for the purpose of generating more commission. In addition, an insurance agent may engage in churning by advising a client to exchange an old life insurance policy for a new one when there is little additional benefit for the policyholder but a handsome commission for the agent. Although the ethical and legal wrongs of churning are easily identified, the definition is not as self-evident. Clients who suffer losses from frequent trades often claim that their accounts were churned, but clients who gain are seldom known to complain about a broker's active trading. How can we determine whether a broker executed unwise trades solely for the commission or engaged in aggressive trading that merely turned out badly? . . .

Suitability and risk disclosure are closely related. The obligation to recommend only suitable investments for a client includes judgments of the appropriate level of risk among many other factors. In addition, brokers, agents, and other salespeople have an obligation to inform clients about the riskiness of investments. Both obligations are problematic for at least three reasons. First, is the relation merely a buyer–seller relation or an agent–principal relation? If a customer places an order with a broker to buy 100 shares of IBM stock, then, under most circumstances, the broker is being paid to execute the order and has no obligation to judge the suitability of the investment or to disclose any risk. On the other hand, if a client asks for investment advice, then the broker has an obligation to recommend only suitable investments and to explain the risk involved. Many relations fall between these poles, so that the obligations of the broker are unclear. The nature of the relation may also be a source of misunderstanding, as when a client believes that he or she is obtaining investment advice while the broker views his or her role as that of a salesperson.

Second, how far do these obligations extend? If a broker has refrained from recommending an unsuitable investment and advised the client of the significant risk, what is the broker's obligation for a client who insists on making the investment anyway? To refuse to make the trade and thereby

protect a client from his or her own poor judgment would be *paternalistic*. Paternalism—which may be defined as limiting people's liberty for their own good—is generally suspect and in need of justification. Thus, requiring people to save for their retirement through Social Security is criticized for interfering in people's investment decisions, but the system is upheld on the grounds that many people lack the discipline to save. On the other hand, legalized gambling permits people to throw away their life savings at the roulette tables of Las Vegas. Should unsophisticated investors be allowed to make similar bets on complex derivatives, for example? Or do they deserve to be protected by investment professionals, who, after all, would not wish to be compared with Las Vegas croupiers?[14]

Third, judgments of suitability and risk are obviously open to interpretation. Whether an investment is suitable for a client depends on the client's financial objectives and risk preferences, the total risk and reward of the investment, and a comparison with other available investment opportunities. Although some investments are clearly unsuitable for any given client, others may fall into a gray area in which reasonable disagreement is possible. How unsuited need an investment be to be unsuitable?

The integrity of products

The financial products that firms offer to their clients and the general public should meet certain standards of integrity. Not only should they be accurately represented—which is to say, firms should avoid false, misleading, or deceptive claims and disclose relevant information, including the level of risk—but they should also be fairly priced and offer sound value. In addition, financial services firms perform a valuable function when they create innovative products that meet special needs.

Among the many charges against Prudential Securities were allegations that the properties in real estate and energy limited partnerships were of dubious value, and that the packagers of the partnerships engaged in kickbacks, self-dealing, and other questionable practices. The firm was also accused of inflating the payouts of some of money-losing partnerships by returning investors' capital under the guise of "partnership distributions." Thus, Prudential Securities did not merely engage in illegal sales practices, such as representing these highly risky partnerships as safe investments, but developed financial products of questionable integrity.

Managing financial institutions

Financial services firms are themselves businesses, and as such, they confront managers with typical business problems. However, the nature of the business raises special ethical concerns in the management of financial institutions. And institutional investors, such as mutual funds and pension funds, because of their large holdings, face additional ethical issues about their investment decisions.

Institutional clients

The obligations of financial services firms to individual clients that are discussed above apply to institutional clients as well. Although institutional clients are usually more sophisticated and better able to protect their own interests, they are still owed accurate and complete information and competent, reliable service. The losses on derivative transactions by Orange County, California, and by Procter & Gamble, show that even sophisticated investors may be unable to understand complex financial instruments, and are vulnerable to fleecing as much as naive individual investors. In addition, the size and complexity of transactions with institutional clients create special opportunities for misconduct that show the need for additional safeguards. For example, the constant need of cities to float bonds creates a lucrative municipal bond-underwriting business for many firms, and the greatest amount of business goes to the firms with the best relations with countless city governments. Until the practice was restricted by an industry agreement, political contributions to city officials were essential for gaining access, and the leading firms still devote great

resources to currying favor with city officials who are in a position to throw business their way.

In one widely publicized incident, Mark S. Ferber, a politically well-connected partner in the distinguished firm Lazard Frères, was selected to oversee the financing of a $6 million project to clean up Boston harbor, and in this capacity he had the power to recommend the firms who would raise the money. In a secret agreement, Merrill Lynch, which obtained much of the business, agreed to split the underwriting fees with Lazard Frères, and over a four-year period, the two firms split $6 million in fees. In addition, Mr Ferber received $2.6 million in retainer payments, while Merrill Lynch garnered millions more from other clients of Mr. Ferber which were steered to Merrill Lynch. An SEC commissioner described the fee-splitting arrangement as outrageous and declared: "I hire an investment adviser to give me prudent objective advice and they have a financial incentive to skew the business to a particular party? That's troubling, and if I were a client, I'd have a fit."[15]

Merrill Lynch and Lazard Frères denied that the secret agreement was improper or that they had any obligation to reveal it. Mr. Ferber said, "I'm not telling you it's pretty. But there is no violation of my fiduciary responsibilities."[16] A federal judge disagreed and sentenced Ferber to 33 months in prison, in addition to a $1 million fine and a lifetime ban from the securities industry. Merrill Lynch and Lazard Frères each paid $12 million to settle charges brought by the SEC. In a parting shot, the judge chastized the firms and their lawyers for creating an environment that fostered rampant graft and corruption. As for the obligation to disclose conflicts of interest, the judge concluded, "And if this sorry lot of municipal bond attorneys do not understand it, let me spell it out: it is required that every potential conflict of interest be disclosed in writing and in detail."[17]

Conflicts of interest

Of the many instances of conflict of interest in financial services firms, two are worth noting specifically. First, research analysts who work for brokerage and investment banking firms are torn occasionally between the integrity of their research and the interest of the firm. Brokerage firms are loath to offend powerful clients by lowering a "buy" recommendation to "hold" or (worse) "sell." Analysts who uncover unfavorable information that could cause a drop in the price of a client's stock are not infrequently pressured by their firm to keep quiet—or threatened after the fact with retaliation by the errant company. One writer observes: "Because of a 'shoot the messenger' syndrome, it is always risky for an analyst to issue a negative report. He or she may be coerced by the investment bankers and could be cut off from the company contact."[18] In firms that underwrite initial public offerings (IPOs), the evaluation of the analysts is often lower than the rosy projections of the corporation's finance department and the firm's investment banking group. A firm that underwrites an IPO cannot issue a recommendation on the stock in the first 25 days, but after this "quiet period," the research department is expected to issue a "buy" recommendation as a "booster shot."[19] Reputable firms attempt to shield their research analysts from improper pressure, but the conflicting interests of researchers and underwriters are an unavoidable source of tension.

A second instance of conflict of interest that has received great attention concerns personal trading by fund managers. In 1995, John Kaweske, a former money manager for Invesco Funds Group, paid $115,000 to settle an SEC complaint that he had not reported 57 personal trades for himself and his wife, as required by the company's rules. Although it is not illegal for fund managers to trade, the SEC holds that they should not use their position for personal gain. Mutual fund companies are required by law to have policies and procedures on personal trading, although the details are left to each company. At Fidelity Investments, for example, fund managers are barred from buying or selling a stock for their own portfolio within seven days of trading the same stock for their funds; they must hold personal stocks for at least two months; and they cannot sell short any stock that Fidelity owns. The Fidelity policy has been criticized for encouraging fund managers to invest in stocks that are *not* in their portfolio, and that is a problem because managers can save the best prospects for themselves. The problem of personal trading by fund managers and the possible solutions raise complex issues. . . .

Supervision and arbitration

Wrongdoing can occur in any organization. A key test of ethics is the organizational response. Do supervisory managers look the other way or even wink and nod at unethical sales practices by subordinates that benefit the firm? What controls are in place to detect and punish those who violate company rules? Do compensation systems and other incentives foster unethical and even illegal behavior? A legal obligation of anyone in a supervisory capacity in a securities firm is to supervise subordinates with an appropriate degree of care.

Many rogue traders, such as Nick Leeson at Barings Bank and Joseph Jett at Kidder Peabody, insist that their activities were known to and condoned by their superiors, who also stood to gain by the success of these "star" traders. A former Metropolitan Life manager complained that he repeatedly warned his supervisors of widespread misconduct by the company's sales force.[20] The manager reported that nothing was done during the 1987–90 period to prevent the payment of millions of dollars in unearned sales commission that resulted when salespeople short of their goal for the year sold large policies to friends and relatives in late December. Although the buyers had no intention of keeping the policies and would return them within the 10-day free-trial period, the sale was credited for the calendar year, and the salesperson received a year-end bonus. Reportedly, top-level executives at Prudential Bache Securities were also aware of pervasive problems at the Dallas branch that were costing clients millions of dollars, but they failed to crack down because the branch was among the firm's most profitable.[21]

A major weapon of victims in most industries is the lawsuit. People who are injured by defective products, for example, can sue for actual losses as well as punitive damage. Investors, by contrast, are forced by the securities industry to waive the right to sue and to abide by the results of arbitration. This system is intended to resolve disagreements quickly, fairly, and inexpensively. In practice, however, some investors who have lost their life savings to dishonest and incompetent brokers have been denied any compensation. Opponents of the practice charge that arbitrators, who do not need to know or follow relevant laws, are often industry insiders who fail to obtain critical documents and admit irrelevant information into the process. Arbitrators' decisions, which do not need to be explained, are largely immune to appeal. Employees of securities firms are also required to submit disputes to arbitration. As a result, some women whose charges of sexual harassment have been dismissed by unsympathetic male arbitrators are unable to seek redress in the courts.[22] A congressional critic of arbitration in the securities industry has remarked, "Christians had a better chance against the lions than many investors and employees will have in the climate being created."[23]

Consumers are increasingly losing the right to sue banks, credit card companies, mortgage lenders, insurers, and other providers of financial services.[24] Many consumers are unaware that they have lost the right to sue, and those who object to compulsory arbitration are told to "take it or leave it." Compulsory arbitration can also be a headache for financial services firms. In particular, the securities industry has been concerned about large punitive damages. In response to both industry concerns and the objections of investors, an arbitration policy task force, which was formed by the National Association of Securities Dealers (NASD), issued a report in 1996 that made 70 recommendations for overhauling the system of compulsory arbitration.[25] . . .

Institutional investors

Trading in financial markets is now dominated by institutions such as mutual funds, insurance companies, pension funds, and private trusts and endowments. The managers of these large invest-

ment portfolios have the obvious duties of all fiduciaries, and these duties are detailed in specific legislation. Thus, the Employee Retirement Income Security Act (ERISA) of 1974 imposes very specific fiduciary duties on the managers of private pension funds. However, institutional investors encounter two unique problems that result from their role as shareholders of public corporations.

First, should institutional investors make investment decisions solely on the basis of financial factors, or should they consider socially desirable objectives? In 1994, the California Public Employees' Retirement System (CalPERS), which controls $80 billion in assets, announced that it would take into account how a corporation treats its employees in making investment decisions. The decision was based on a study which showed that companies with recommended employment practices outperformed the average for their industries by 7.5 percent, and companies with poor practices consistently lagged behind industry averages.[26] Considering the treatment of employees, therefore, is sound financial decision making, but the use of such factors involves a departure from standard balance-sheet analysis. Writing in support of the CalPERS decision, former Secretary of Labor Robert B. Reich observed:

> Measures of success in the capital management business have become more complicated, less dependent on traditional measures of corporate performance, and more reliant on factors previously considered intangibles. . . . The difficulty of measuring these concepts on a balance sheet simply requires analysts to look a little harder to fully assess a company's prospects.[27]

Some mutual funds, pension plans, and endowments go beyond the CalPERS position and engage in *socially responsible investing*. The aim of socially responsible investors is to hold stocks only in corporations that treat employees well, protect the environment, contribute to communities, produce safe, useful products, and, in general, exercise social responsibility. In particular, all socially responsible investors avoid the stocks of companies involved with tobacco, alcohol, and gambling (so-called "sin stocks"), and some screen out companies that are engaged in defense contracting, nuclear energy, and business with oppressive foreign regimes. Socially responsible funds enable people who are concerned with where their money is going and how it is used to invest with a clear conscience. Churches, universities, and foundations want their investment decisions to be consistent with the values that they espouse. The right of fund managers to engage in socially responsible investing is unproblematic as long as the goals are understood and accepted by the appropriate parties. Thus, pension plans in which contributors are free to choose among socially responsible and conventional stock funds raise no ethical concerns. But do the managers of a pension plan with a single fund have a right to reject all tobacco stocks, for example? Whether fund managers can effectively screen for social responsibility and whether socially responsible funds produce satisfactory returns are further questions. . . .

Second, as major shareholders in numerous corporations, institutional investors must decide what role they are going to play in corporate governance. In voting on shareholder proposals, the election of directors, amendments to the bylaws or charter, or any other matters, should institutional investors use the same purely financial criteria that guided the initial investment decision? Should they be traditional, passive investors or should they become more active participants in corporate affairs? How closely should they monitor the performance of the officers and directors of a corporation, and what should they do in the event of lagging performance? Dissatisfied individual shareholders have the option of selling their stock and switching their investment to another company. However, institutional investors are often "locked into" an investment and have no choice but to push for major changes. In recent years, institutional investors have forced CEO changes at such giant companies as American Express, Borden, General Motors, IBM, Kodak, and Westinghouse. The term *relationship investing* has been coined to describe this development. The arguments for and against relationship invest-

ing . . . concern primarily the impact of this movement on corporate governance. Some proponents believe that more active institutional investors have the potential to restore shareholder control, while opponents are more skeptical.

Individuals in Organizations

The ethical dilemmas that arise for *individuals* in finance are typically not questions that confront the profession as a whole, such as whether a sales practice is deceptive or whether insider trading is unfair. Rather, they test one's own personal values, moral beliefs, and commitment to right action that arise from working in an organization. In short, they are organizational challenges to an individual's *integrity*.

Organizational pressures

Some of the most difficult dilemmas of business life occur when individuals become aware of questionable behavior by others or are pressured to engage in it themselves. In a survey of 30 recent Harvard University MBA graduates, many of the young managers reported that they had received "explicit instructions from their middle-manager bosses or felt strong organizational pressures to do things that they believed were sleazy, unethical, or sometimes illegal."[28] A survey of more than one thousand graduates of the Columbia University business school revealed that more than 40 percent of the respondents had been rewarded for taking some action they considered to be "ethically troubling," and 31 percent of those who refused to act in ways they considered to be unethical believed that they were penalized for their choice, compared to less than 20 percent who felt they had been rewarded.[29] The Harvard graduates do not believe that their superiors or their organizations are corrupt. The cause is rather intense pressure to get a job done and to gain approval. Ethical and even legal restraints can get lost when the overriding message is "Just do it!"

Unethical behavior can also be fostered by the culture of an organization. In *Liar's Poker*, an amusing exposé of the author's brief stint as a trader at Salomon Brothers, Michael Lewis describes the coarse pranks of a group who occupied the back row of his training class.

> There was a single trait common to denizens of the back row, though I doubt it occurred to anyone: They sensed that they needed to shed whatever refinements of personality and intellect they had brought with them to Salomon Brothers. This wasn't a conscious act, more a reflex. They were the victims of the myth, especially popular at Salomon Brothers, that a trader is a savage, and a great trader is a great savage.[30]

In the culture that Michael Lewis describes, ethical behavior is not readily fostered. He continues: "As a Salomon Brothers trainee, of course, you didn't worry too much about ethics. You were just trying to stay alive. You felt flattered to be on the same team with the people who kicked everyone's ass all the time."[31]

Wrongdoing also occurs in large organizations when responsibility is diffused among many individuals and no one person is "really" responsible. The check-kiting scheme at E. F. Hutton, for example, apparently began as an attempt to squeeze a little more interest income from the "float" that inevitably occurs when checks are written on one interest-bearing account and deposited into another. No one person created or orchestrated the practice, and yet the firm, through the actions of many individuals, defrauded banks of millions. When the check-kiting scheme began, few people were aware of the extent of the activity, and it continued, no doubt, because anyone who intervened would have had to acknowledge the existence of the fraud and take responsibility for the loss of the extra income. In addition, the participants could assure themselves that their own actions did not do any significant harm.

Leadership and ethics

Although individuals bear some responsibility for their own behavior, the leaders of firms and those in other leadership positions have a responsibility for the environment in which unethical conduct takes place. In a *Harvard Business Review* article, Lynn Sharp Paine writes:

> Rarely do the character flaws of a lone actor fully explain corporate misconduct. More typically, unethical business practice involves the tacit, if not explicit, cooperation of others and reflects the value, attitudes, beliefs, language, and behavioral patterns that define an organization's operating culture. . . . Managers who fail to provide proper leadership and to institute systems that facilitate ethical conduct share responsibility with those who conceive, execute, and knowingly benefit from corporate misdeeds.[32]

The bond-trading scandal at Salomon Brothers, for example, was not due merely to the willingness of the head of the government bond-trading department to violate the treasury auction rules; it resulted, in large measure, from the aggressive trading culture of the firm, from a poorly designed compensation system, and from a lack of internal controls. At Salomon Brothers, some units had negotiated compensation systems in which members shared a bonus pool equal to a percentage of the total profits, while managers in other units received lesser amounts that were based, in part, on the overall performance of the firm. This system placed no cap on the bonuses of some traders and encouraged them to maximize profits without regard for the profitability of the whole firm. In addition, there were few controls to detect irregular trading by the managers of the most profitable units. The task for the new leadership of Salomon included a thorough overhaul of the whole organization.

Ultimately, the level of ethics in finance depends on a complex interplay of the personal integrity of individuals, ethical leadership by people in positions of responsibility, and an understanding of the ethical issues that arise in finance. . . . [These ethical issues] must be understood in order to settle questions about right and wrong conduct in finance. Knowing how financial activity ought to be conducted is an essential first step toward ensuring a high level of ethics in finance, but this knowledge is of little use without personal integrity and ethical leadership.

Notes

1. James B. Stewart, *Den of Thieves* (New York: Simon & Schuster, 1991), 15.

2. For a detailed account of the scandal at Prudential Securities (formerly Prudential Bache), see Kurt Eichenwald, *Serpent on the Rock* (New York: HarperCollins, 1995).

3. Tom Herman "Survey Says Many Think Selfishness, Greed Are Widespread on Wall Street," *Wall Street Journal*, October 18, 1996, B3. In the survey, 52 percent of the respondents disagreed with the statement, "In general, people on Wall Street are as honest and moral as other people," but 69 percent agreed that Wall Street performs a service that is "absolutely essential."

4. Quoted in Stewart, *Den of Thieves*, 223.

5. Jay L. Walker [pseudonym], *The Complete Book of Wall Street Ethics* (New York: William Morrow, 1987).

6. The physical sciences are generally considered to be purely positive, but whether the social sciences can or should be value-free is a subject of much dispute. Economics, for example, is divided into two distinct branches: positive economics, which is allegedly value-free, and normative economics, which explicitly assumes value judgments.

7. The remark is by former SEC Chairman Richard Breeden, quoted in Kevin V. Salwen, "SEC Chief's Criticism of Ex-Managers of Salomon Suggests Civil Action Is Likely," *Wall Street Journal*, November 20, 1991, A10.

8. For a discussion of the limits of law, see Christopher D. Stone, *Where the Law Ends: The Social Control of Corporate Behavior* (New York: Harper & Row, 1975).

9. The term *bounded rationality* is due to Herbert Simon, "A Behavioral Model of Rational Choice," in *Models of Man: Social and Rational* (New York: John Wiley & Sons, 1957), 241–60. Because of cognitive limitations, human beings cannot act in complex situations as the rational decision makers presupposed by economic theory. According to Simon, organizations serve to overcome the limited rationality of individual actors.

10. Stewart Macaulay, "Non-contractual Relations in Business: A Preliminary Study," *American Sociological Review* 28 (1963), 55–67.

11. A proposal for such a standard is presented in Charles J. Goetz and Robert E. Scott, "Principles of Relational Contracts," *Virginia Law Review*, 67 (1981), 1089–150.

12. Ellen E. Schultz, "You Need a Translator for Latest Sales Pitch," *Wall Street Journal*, February 14, 1994, C1.

13. Michael Quint, "Met Life Shakes Up Its Ranks," *New York Times*, October 29, 1994, C1.

14. The protection of "at risk" investors can be addressed not only by suitability rules but also by rules for securities transactions. Thus, SEC rules limit private placements and other "exempt transactions," that is, transactions exempt from some provisions of securities law, to "accredited investors." . . .

Whether more sweeping restrictions to exclude "at risk" investors from securities markets are necessary is examined in Robert E. Frederick and W. Michael Hoffman, "The Individual Investor in Securities Markets: An Ethical Analysis," *Journal of Business Ethics*, 9 (1990), 579–89.

15. SEC commissioner Richard Y. Roberts, quoted in Leslie Wayne, "A Side Deal and a Wizard's Undoing," *New York Times*, May 15, 1994, Sec. 3, 1.

16. Wayne, "A Side Deal and a Wizard's Undoing," Sec. 3, 8.

17. Quoted in Craig T. Ferris, "Ferber Judge's Words Are Chilling Indictment of Muni Industry," *The Bond Buyer*, January 21, 1997, 27.

18. Patrick J. Regan, "Analyst, Analyze Thyself," *Financial Analysts Journal*, July–August 1993, 10.

19. W. Powers, "Why Hot, New Stocks Get Booster Shots," *Wall Street Journal*, February 10, 1993, C1.

20. Cynthia Crosson, "Met Brass Had Warnings on Abuses: Ethics Mgr.," *National Underwriter*, January 23, 1995, 3, 41.

21. The details are contained in a two-part series by Kurt Eichenwald, "Misplaced Trust: A Tale of Texas Brokers." "Commissions are Many, Profits Few," *New York Times*, May 24, 1993, C1, C3; and "Prudential's Firm Within a Firm," *New York Times*, May 25, 1993, C1, C19.

22. For examples, see Margaret A. Jacobs, "Riding Crops and Slurs: How Wall Street Dealt with a Sex Bias Case," *Wall Street Journal*, June 9, 1994, A1, A8.

23. Margaret A. Jacobs and Michael Siconolfi, "Investors Fare Poorly Fighting Wall Street—And May Do Worse," *Wall Street Journal*, February 8, 1995, A1.

24. Barry Meier, "In Fine Print, Customers Lose Ability to Sue," *New York Times*, March 10, 1997, A1, C7.

25. *Securities Arbitration Reform*, Report of the Arbitration Policy Task Force to the Board of Governors, National Association of Securities Dealers, Inc., January 1996.

26. Statement by Robert B. Reich, in "Should Investors Look Beyond the Bottom Line?" *Business and Society Review*, Fall 1994, 7.

27. "Should Investors Look Beyond the Bottom Line?" 7–8.

28. Joseph L. Badaracco, Jr., and Allen P. Webb, "Business Ethics: A View from the Trenches," *California Management Review*, 37 (Winter 1995), 8.

29. "Doing the 'Right' Thing Has Its Repercussions," *Wall Street Journal*, January 25, 1990, B1.

30. Michael Lewis, *Liar's Poker: Rising Through the Wreckage on Wall Street* (New York: W. W. Norton, 1989), 41.

31. *Liar's Poker*, 70.

32. Lynn Sharp Paine, "Managing for Organizational Integrity," *Harvard Business Review*, March–April 1994, 106.

CASE STUDIES

Case 8.1: Audit Adjustments

You are a CPA/auditor for a multinational CPA firm. You are the senior auditor on an annual audit of a manufacturing company. The company was a small subsidiary of a larger firm located on the east coast. As with many parent-subsidiary relationships, there was a tremendous amount of pressure on the subsidiary company's management to reach certain projected sales goals for the year. Because of this, the climate at the manufacturing subsidiary was tense. You and your audit team were engaged to perform an audit of the year-end financial statements of the subsidiary company.

During the course of the audit, you performed a sales cutoff test to ensure that all sales transactions at year end were recorded in the proper period. Considering the pressure on management to reach its sales goals, you were keenly aware of the possibility of sales being recorded prior to the actual shipping date. The sales cutoff test revealed numerous shipments made in the following year which were recorded as sales on the books in the year under audit. This method of recording sales resulted in significantly higher revenues for the year than were actually made. This method of accounting for these sales was reported to the controller of the company.

As the auditor, you have a responsibility both to the client and to those who might make decisions based on the company's financial statements, such as banks and investors. The parent company was a longstanding auditing client of the firm and had recently signed a lucrative consulting contract with the consulting division of the firm. You informed the controller of the company that a proper recording of the sales transactions would require an adjustment significantly reducing sales for the year. The controller then discussed the matter with the president of the company. During a follow-up meeting with management, the president attempted to downplay the significance of the matter, stating that they were immaterial errors. He then suggested that the way the sales were recorded was inconsequential, not misleading, and thus the revenue adjustment was unnecessary. He pointed out to you that numerous firms in the industry record their sales in this manner and that he was not suggesting you do anything that other companies in the industry do not also do. He encouraged you to issue a clean report.

Source: Mike McNamee et al., "Accounting Wars," *Business Week*, 25 September 2000, 157–66.

Questions for Discussion:

1. What do you think is the ethically correct thing to do—to insist on the revenue adjustment, or to issue a clean report as the company president has requested?
2. If you insisted on making the revenue adjustment and the company refused to comply with your decision and threatened to take their auditing and consulting business elsewhere, what would you do?
3. If your boss insisted that you comply with the company's way of recording their sales and issue a clean report, what would you do?
4. Do you think there is a conflict of interests facing the auditing firm by doing the auditing of a company with whom they have an ongoing consulting contract? Why or why not?

Case 8.2: The New Insiders

You are the Vice-President of Research and Development at TechCom, a small company that manufactures high-speed devices for e-business, which the company claims will revolutionize networking applications. The technology is both for established companies that augment traditional sales with Internet sales and companies that do business exclusively on the Web. The company recently went public, and the stock price has increased dramatically due to speculation that its technologies will soon be completed and will gain widespread acceptance.

You are one of the ten key executives who own stock in the company and have options to acquire additional shares that when sold would result in a substantial profit. The current market value of your stock in the company, which you are free to sell without restriction, accounts for 95 percent of your total net worth even after paying the taxes that would be due. Friends and family members have strongly advised you to sell some of your shares to diversify your portfolio and to secure your family's financial future, namely your retirement and the college education of your children.

The company's founder, Jack Smith, has recently dropped some not-so-subtle hints that he would be very disappointed in members of senior management who sold all or substantial portions of their stock.

Smith suggests that, to the extent that such sales have to be reported publicly, the disclosure might send the wrong signal to the market and negatively affect the stock price. He further suggests that such a sale by any one member of the executive team would be an act of disloyalty to the others on the team by diminishing the value of their shares. Finally, Smith suggests that selling one's shares at present would be foolish, since the stock is bound to go higher in the future. You have your doubts about that, since as VP for Research and Development, you are not as optimistic as the company's founder about your products revolutionizing the networking industry. The company has disclosed both technology and market risks in all required public filings, but the market appears to be ignoring this information.

> *Sources*: Erick Schoenfeld, "Misadventures in the ME-FIRST Economy," *Fortune*, 20 March 2000, 100–120.

Questions for Discussion:

1. What factors should you consider in determining to sell all or part of your stock in the company? How should the financial security of your family be weighed against loyalty to the company and your fellow executives?
2. If you decide to sell some of your shares, based on both your desire to take care of your family financially and your doubts about the technology, does that constitute insider trading? Why or why not?
3. Is the company founder doing anything unethical by putting pressure on the executive team not to sell any shares? Why or why not?
4. Imagine yourself as the founder and CEO of the company. Six months and a few days after the IPO, you decide to sell 20 percent of your holdings in the company. In the vast majority of cases there is a binding contract between the IPO underwriters, and all insiders—such as key management and all shareholders who held shares prior to the IPO—must hold stock issued publicly for six months before selling. The stock is still at a high level, thanks to strong company public relations efforts to "sell" the prospectus of the company to the investing public. You net a profit of roughly $200 million. Do you think the CEO has a conflict of interest in his sale of his stock? Why or why not?

Case 8.3: Stock Analysts and Investment Bankers

You are a stock market analyst for a major Wall Street investment banking firm specializing in selected technology stocks, including some startup companies. Your job is to research the companies you cover, stay abreast of developments that may affect the companies, and issue objective opinions about the company's stock. Though some investment banking houses prohibit their analysts from owning stock in companies they cover, yours does not, and you do own stock in some of the companies that you consider good investments. You are careful to disclose this when you comment on these companies, either in the media or for the in-house material you generate for the firms' clients. You have been careful to avoid the appearance of a conflict of interest when it comes to your own personal portfolio.

In the past few months, your firm has more aggressively targeted companies in your specialized area for investment banking business, that is, helping companies raise capital through a variety of means, including stock offerings and various types of debt, such as bonds. You know that this is the part of the firm's business that is the most profitable. You have issued lukewarm views of some of the companies in your area recently, downgrading some from your previous recommendations of "strong buy" to simply "buy" or to "hold." You realize that it is rare in your position to issue a recommendation to "sell," so a "hold" is about as negative as you issue, and is standard in the industry. Recently, one of the investment banking partners has encouraged you to support the investment banking efforts more wholeheartedly. Specifically, two companies are merging, and your firm is arranging the merger and coordinating the capital necessary to make it happen. You are not so sure that the merger is a good long-term situation and you are hesitant to endorse it, but you are getting pressure from the investment bankers working on the merger to "get on the team" and issue an opinion supportive of the merger.

Sources: Jeffrey Laderman, "Wall Street's Spin Game," *Business Week*, 5 October 1998, 148–56; Peter Elkind, "Where Mary Meeker Went Wrong," *Fortune*, 14 May 2001, 69–82; Thomas S. Mulligan, "Amid Criticism, Wall St. Offers Analyst Guidelines," *Los Angeles Times*, 13 June 2001, C1, 5.

Questions for Discussion:

1. Do you consider the request to support the merger a conflict of interests? Why or why not? What would you do in the face of the partner's pressure to issue a supportive opinion of the

upcoming merger, knowing that failure to do so would likely be a backward step in your career?

2. Do you think stock analysts should be prohibited from owning stock in the companies they cover? Or should they be free to "put their money where their mouth is" and stand behind their recommendations?

COMMENTARY

The world of accounting and finance is complex and has a variety of ethical issues that merit our reflection. The first of these has to do with the accountants and financial managers of a company. These are the issues that have received most of the public attention in the past few years. They have to do with how a company represents itself in its financial statements, the traditional issues relating to accountants and chief financial officers. Under this heading we will discuss principles for accounting with integrity and isolate a handful of specific accounting techniques that raise ethical questions. We will further address the broader issue of the independence and objectivity of auditors. A second group of issues has to do not so much with a company's financial statements as with broader questions about the integrity of the financial markets. These include the issues of insider trading and stock analysts' objectivity.

In the aftermath of the accounting and stock market scandals we have mentioned, Congress acted to make changes in existing law. The Sarbanes-Oxley Act of 2002 was a step in the right direction.[6] It requires greater transparency in financial reporting, strengthens the role of the board of directors—especially the audit committee—and reduces the potential for conflicts of interest on the part of accounting firms. Some of the specifics include restriction of non-audit services during the time of the audit, rotation of lead audit partner every five years, and a one-year required interim prior to an auditor's being hired by the client. This new law, combined with more aggressive prosecution of accounting fraud by the federal government and the SEC, promises to do a better job of protecting the investing public. However, as we will show in this chapter, the law alone is not sufficient to ensure that confidence in the system is restored. There is an important place for ethics and character to provide what the law cannot.

[6] The entire Sarbanes-Oxley Act can be referenced in a variety of ways. A summary is available at the website for the American Institute of Certified Public Accountants (AICPA) at www.aicpa.org /info/sarbanesoxley_ summary (17 May 2004).

I. Principles for Accounting with Integrity

Accountants and financial managers are professionals with a high degree of technical expertise that the general public does not have. That places them in a position of great power to mislead their clients and others who are dependent on their information. The people who rely on their reports and opinions are placing a high degree of trust in their expertise and in their integrity. As John Boatright rightly points out in his survey of financial ethics, ethics is needed precisely because the financial services industry is built on trust. Even though there is widespread skepticism about Wall Street ethics and some consider it the newest oxymoron, millions of transactions in the capital markets are handled smoothly because trust is assumed between the parties. Without a high degree of trust, people would be unwilling to put their money at risk in various investments. This degree of trust is critical in broader circles too. For example, large institutional investors are increasingly unwilling to invest the capital at their disposal in countries that do not respect the rule of law because they cannot trust that their investments will be handled properly. Moreover, they cannot trust that the best products will be the most competitive in the market when unethical practices such as bribery are customary.

Think about the necessity for ethics and integrity in the various parts of the financial services industry. When you invest your money with a financial advisor or stockbroker, you are trusting that he or she will invest your money properly, will give you reliable advice, and will look out for your best financial interests. You trust that his opinion will not be colored by his own self-interest. When a banker considering loaning money to a company reads their financial statements, he or she trusts that the statements are truthful as they are presented. This is particularly true if the statements have been audited by an outside auditor. In these cases, the public who use the financial statements to make decisions about loans or investments, is trusting that when the auditors sign off on the financial statements, they are telling the truth about the company's financial condition and not concealing important information. Until recently, when a stock analyst issued a recommendation on a specific stock, the public took those recommendations at face value. If there was skepticism about them, it was because the opinion was wrong as often as it was right, not that the analysts' recommendations were not objective, as is alleged today. But the average person investing in the stocks still trusts that the analysts are not being self-serving when they issue recommendations. Ethics is critical for industries that function on trust. Without ethics, trust in the capital markets would be diminished and people would, as a result, be less willing to put their money at risk, thus depriving companies of badly needed investment capital.

The world of accounting and finance is an example of what the law calls "fiduciary" relationships. This means that the accounting/ financial professional has a special obligation to his or her clients: to seek their best financial interests even if it conflicts with his or her own self-interest. To put it another way, the self-interest of the professional is not to be placed ahead of advancing the interest of the client. The fiduciary is not to engage in practices that advance their interests to the detriment of the client. Physicians, lawyers, and mental health professionals also operate with fiduciary obligations that make ethics critical for these relationships of trust to function effectively.

Boatright also points out that the law is not sufficient to regulate the relationships of trust necessary for the financial services industry to operate properly. He rightly observes that the conventional wisdom in many business circles is that "if it's legal, then it's moral." In many cases, what this actually means is that a practice is acceptable as long as one does not get caught. We would suggest that the law is the moral minimum, and with rare exceptions for civil disobedience, it is unethical to violate the law. However, ethics certainly involves more than mere compliance with the law. Avoiding indictment is a worthy goal, but surely ethics requires more than that.

Questions of ethics in the financial arena involve going beyond what the letter of the law requires. How far one must go beyond the law is the crucial issue for ethics. Boatright is clearly correct when he points out the shortcomings in reliance on the law to ensure trust in the fiduciary relationships. No law can be crafted that would be specific enough to cover all the possible violations. In addition, the more specific the law, the more potential loopholes it contains. Human nature being what it is, inevitably professionals in this area will search diligently for these loopholes and end up missing the spirit of the law, while perhaps being in compliance with the letter of the law. Though there are clear laws and SEC rules that govern the financial markets, Boatright is correct to insist on self-regulation as the key to maintaining the integrity of the industry.

Accounting with integrity is critical, particularly for publicly traded companies, whose investors rely on these published financial statements to make their investment decisions. Since capital moves so rapidly in today's digital age, there is great pressure on companies to put their best foot forward in their financial statements or else face the possibility of being punished by Wall Street. The American Institute of Certified Public Accountants (AICPA), which sets standards and partners with the SEC to enforce them, has a clear code of ethics that governs internal accountants and external auditors. Underlying the AICPA code of ethics are a handful of core moral principles. Keep in mind when reviewing these principles and working your way through the cases that it is easy to get bogged down in accounting details and miss the big picture. What follows is the overall principles that govern accounting with integrity.

First, what the AICPA code of ethics is fundamentally about is the prevention of deception, based on the principle of truth telling, which is ultimately grounded in the ninth of the Ten Commandments, which prohibits bearing false witness. The original setting for this command was a trial in which a witness was sworn to tell the truth. In many cases, someone's life depended on his or her veracity as a witness. Though CPAs are not generally in court as formal witnesses, their role as guardian of the company's financial statements surely puts them in an equally formal position and is analogous to the courtroom witness setting of the ninth commandment. The CFO of a publicly traded company or the CPA who audits them is duty bound to bear witness to the truth about the company's financial condition. Intentional misstatements are analogous to perjury on the witness stand. Of course, the ninth commandment also grounds the general principle of truth telling in everyday life, but is specifically applied to accounting by analogy. This principle is recognized as valid in virtually every culture, regardless of its religious beliefs, and is clearly a part of virtually all moral traditions.

Thus, the financial professional is bound by the ethical norm of *truth telling*. This involves forthright and accurate financial accounting, following the more rigid norms of the generally accepted accounting principles (GAAP). In fact, perhaps the best measure of the integrity of a company's financial statements comes from the perspective of the investor. A key question to ask in this regard is: If the one preparing the financial statements of the company were an investor, would he/she feel misled by the way in which the statements were prepared and the figures were presented? Or, to put the key question more bluntly, when considering how the financial statements are prepared, is the intent to mislead investors about the company's financial health? Or to put it another way, if you were an investor, would you be getting all the necessary information for understanding the company's performance during the period in question?[7] The same questions can apply to auditors. If the auditor were an investor, would he/she feel misled by the statements under review? Would he/she have all the critical information needed to accurately assess the company's performance? The investing public expects integrity and accuracy in

7 These were the suggestions of legendary investor Warren Buffet, encouraging corporate boards to force auditors to state their true opinions. Cited in "Put Bite Into Audit Committees," *Fortune*, 2 August 1999, 90.

financial statements and audits. There is no room for puffery or bluffing when it comes to financial disclosure. However, some of these issues of how to account for specific revenues and costs are difficult and involve legitimate gray areas in which professionals working in good faith can disagree. Generally, it takes the accounting profession some time to wrestle with new challenges and new ways of doing business and to carefully consider how the rules could be clarified.

A second principle that underlies the AICPA code of ethics is to *avoid conflicts of interest* that could compromise one's objectivity and independence from the company one is analyzing. One application of this principle is that auditors have for some time been prohibited from owning stock in companies that they audit to avoid an obvious potential conflict of interest. Further potential conflicts of interest include the auditor whose company has other, non-auditing business, such as consulting, with the client, which might tempt the auditor not to alienate a profitable consulting client. In fiduciary relationships that are dependent on trust, objectivity is critical. Fiduciary relationships, by definition, are to be uncolored by these kinds of potential conflicts. This is a crucial principle for integrity in the financial services and accounting areas.

A third principle that is not specifically included in the code of ethics but is relevant has to do with relativism in the defining of standards. Just because an accounting practice is the industry standard does not necessarily make it morally right. One should *beware of "industrial relativism,"* in which the industry defines standards for itself. To be sure, GAAP and the AICPA code of ethics are generally accepted by the profession. But a particular, and perhaps novel, interpretation of GAAP is often justified with the observation that such a practice is "common in the industry." That observation has no specific normative value. Just because it is an accepted practice, it does not follow that it should be. For example, if it is accepted practice that earnings are smoothed out and some put into reserves to save for a poor performing quarter, that is irrelevant to the moral assessment of the practice. The question should be, Is that a misleading practice? not Is everyone else doing it? University of Chicago accounting professor Katherine Schipper suggests that there is a difference between what is acceptable and what is appropriate.[8] One hopes that auditors would uphold rigorous standards instead of allowing those who push the envelope to set the industry standard.[9] Of course, it may be that new ways of doing business do demand new ways of accounting. It may be that some GAAP rules are out of date and need to be changed. Our point here is that an industry standard is only descriptive, and a moral norm does not necessarily follow from such a description.

[8] Cited in Richard Melcher, "Where Are the Accountants?" *Business Week*, 5 October 1998, 146.

[9] Ibid.

Specific Issues for Accounting with Integrity: Managed Earnings

There are a wide variety of accounting mechanisms that can make a company appear more profitable than it actually is. Most of these are not illegal and are broadly within the GAAP guidelines. But with increasing pressure on companies to meet earnings expectations, the need to manage a company's earnings carefully has increased. Many of these practices are widely used, particularly among new economy companies. They argue that they are not doing anything improper, but that new ways of doing business require new accounting rules or new interpretations of generally accepted principles. What follows below is a look at some of the recent accounting practices about which the SEC is raising questions. Keep in mind the overriding principles for accounting with integrity and form your own evaluation of the ethics of these practices.

Cookie Jar Reserves

When companies report fluctuations in earnings from quarter to quarter, it can be disastrous for their stock prices, and it can cause catastrophic decreases in a company's market capitalization, that is, the total value of its investment capital. This is the reason for the practice of holding back a portion of the company's earnings in a given quarter and "saving it for a rainy day."[10] In other words, the company will not report all of its earnings in the quarter, typically a quarter in which it has done well, and save the reserve in the "cookie jar" for a quarter in which they fall short of expectations. The annual earnings may be the same as if the earnings were not managed in this way. But from quarter to quarter, the company's earnings are being smoothed out in order to avoid damaging fluctuations. This too is a common practice in most Fortune 500 companies. It is not unusual for companies to be advised to treat their earnings in this way.[11]

This practice is also called "managed earnings," and there is debate about the degree to which this is misleading to investors. The long-run picture is not any different, since earnings are simply reallocated to different quarters. But investors can be misled in that the company is both cushioning poor quarters (some call it "dimming the signals") and underreporting positive quarters. The counter argument is often that quarterly reporting requirements are themselves misleading, that the company's financial picture may be different over the long run, and that managing earnings is a way to accurately present the long-term earnings of the company most accurately. Also the company

10 The best-known case so far of the SEC prosecuting a company for managed earnings is the case of the chemical firm W. R. Grace, settled in 1998 with Grace admitting no wrongdoing. Cited in "SEC Files First Suit in Its Accounting Fraud Fight," *Los Angeles Times*, 23 December 1998, C3.

11 One stock analyst suggested that companies should consider "hiding earnings for future use" and that "if you don't play the game, you're going to get hurt." Cited in Loomis, "Lies, Damned Lies and Managed Earnings," 92.

could argue that it is acting to protect investors from these stock price variations, and thus managing earnings is actually in the shareholders' interest.

Revenue Recognition Techniques

During the Internet boom, with so many new economy companies struggling to make a profit, there had to be new ways of evaluating a company's prospects and progress. So instead of looking at earnings, investors, investment advisers, and analysts focused on revenues to guide them in assessing a company's business. These are important because even small increases in revenue can mean a rising stock price, new investors, and increased net worth for the company's founders and principal stockholders. This emphasis on revenue is actually what is new, since companies have wrestled with how to properly account for revenues for some time. Many industries, such as defense contractors with multiple subcontractors involved, or health care organizations with mandated reductions from insurance companies, have wrestled with how to account for gross revenues accurately. What is truly new is the emphasis on revenues as the benchmark of a company's progress and of its investment-worthiness. As mentioned in the introduction to the chapter, this is a result of the shift in investment priorities from value investing to growth investing, in which the goal is short-term growth in the stock as opposed to longer term value. These new ways of recognizing revenue are a result of this new emphasis that admittedly has tempered since the tech bubble burst in 2000–2001. Evaluate these ways of accounting for revenues in view of the principles of accounting with integrity.

One common way to increase revenues reported for a given period is to book sales early.[12] That is, to record a sale as revenue prior to shipping the product is one way to make revenues appear greater than they actually are. GAAP rules are clear that sales (and costs) are to be recorded in the period in which they occurred. But new economy executives argue that many of their sales do not fit traditional GAAP rules and thus can be recorded prior to shipping. A second way to enhance revenues is to report the entire sales price as revenue when in fact, the website would only be entitled to a commission or some other small part of the total sales price as a fee for their service.[13] For example, websites that book travel arrangements such as air fare, hotel rooms, and rental cars can and do report the entire gross amount paid to the site as revenue, and the cost to the site of the tickets that it brokers as costs. The overall profit that the company makes is the same, but both revenues and costs are substantially higher. For companies

[12] One can also book costs late. Though this does not affect revenue, it does affect a company's earnings for a particular quarter or year.

[13] This practice is described in Jeremy Kahn, "Presto Chango! Sales are Huge!" *Fortune,* 20 March 2000, 92.

that are evaluated on the basis of revenue instead of earnings, this has the potential to be misleading. It is analogous to traditional travel agencies booking the total amount received for tickets as revenue and the cost of the tickets to the agency as expense. Though it is true that the bottom line remains the same, revenues are greatly exaggerated. Proponents of these travel sites argue that they actually buy the tickets and assume the risk of owning the tickets, making them more analogous to a retail operation and its "cost of goods sold" category as a cost.

A similar method of revenue recognition is the way discounts, coupons, and rebates are used. Typically, when discounts are given, the amount of revenue booked is determined by the price received after the discount. But many new economy companies offering substantial price breaks record the full amount of the sale as revenue, and the rebate or discount is recorded as a marketing cost. Again, the bottom line is unaffected, but the amount of revenue booked is inflated. Proponents argue that this is not misleading since earnings are not changed, but in many cases, these companies show losses consistently, and revenues are critical in evaluating their future prospects. This too has the potential to be misleading to investors.

Many online companies that depend on advertising for the majority of their revenue count barter revenue as sales.[14] Barter deals, primarily in which advertising space on a website is traded for ad time on TV or radio, are common in media companies. Barter is a useful method of advertising for startup companies because it allows them to advertise their site on major media outlets without outlays of cash. However, it also provides a way to inflate revenues when barter is booked as sales. The gray area comes in determining the value of the barter. GAAP rules state that barter revenue must be recorded at their fair value. But determining that value is tricky when website ad space may not have been sold for cash for very long (or at all), which is different from traditional barter used by major media, where the value of the ad space is easy to determine because of the long precedent of selling it for cash. Not so with many online companies, which allows for the fair value of the barter to be inflated well beyond its worth.

A final way in which revenues can be enhanced is the way marketing and fulfillment costs are recorded.[15] Fulfillment costs typically refer to the costs associated with a retail operation, such as warehousing goods, handling, and shipping expenses. Many new economy companies record these as marketing costs instead of the permanent costs of conducting business. The advantage of doing this is to enable the company to hide normal operating expenses in categories such as marketing expenses that could be considered by investors and analysts as temporary spikes in costs due to one-time aggressive marketing

14 Ibid., 94.

15 Ibid., 96.

campaigns. In addition, marketing expenses can be treated in reverse, though not affecting revenues, but making the company appear more profitable than it actually is. For example, America On Line would periodically send out millions of its software programs free to potential customers. They reasoned that since the subscriber is usually with the company for some time, they could defer the cost of those expenses over the life of the customer with the company instead of when the CDs were purchased. This enabled AOL to defer what should have been recorded as periodic costs over a much longer period, thereby preventing initial drags on earnings, making them look more profitable initially than they were. The net result was to sustain investor optimism about its prospects, keeping its stock price high and eventually putting it in the position of having the resources to buy out a media giant like Time-Warner.

All the above revenue recognition practices have the potential to mislead investors and can violate GAAP principles that suggest that costs and revenues be recorded in the period in which they occur. For traditional companies, which are evaluated on the basis of earnings, the impact is not as great, since with many of these practices the bottom line is not affected. But for companies being evaluated by a different standard, it is critical that revenues be accurately represented. One should be careful to focus on both of the important ethical issues, the techniques for revenue recognition, and the emphasis that drives the focus on revenues, which is the shift from value to growth investing. One can argue that it is just as important to evaluate the shift in outlook as it is to evaluate the specific techniques for recognizing revenue. Ultimately, it is the pressure from the investing public that is driving financial professionals' use of many of these techniques.

Specific Issues for Accounting with Integrity: Auditor Independence

CPAs who audit a company's financial statements have responsibilities to the client and to the public that they must carry out simultaneously. The client has hired them to perform the audit, or annual check of the accuracy of the company's books. But when the company is publicly traded, the auditors have another responsibility, that is, to the investing public, to ensure that the company's statements accurately represent its financial condition to the investors. This puts the auditor in a potentially precarious position if the results of the audit reveal something negative about the company. There is an inherent conflict of interests that must be carefully managed. The client pays for the auditing service and can easily dismiss the auditor and hire another one if the results are not satisfactory to the company. The auditor must be aware of this potential and cannot compromise the accuracy of the audit for fear of losing the client's business for future audits. The stakes can be high, for when companies have to restate their earnings through revised financial statements, investor confidence is usually shaken and the stock price goes down, often dramatically, causing investors to lose substantial amounts of money. This is even more of a problem when the auditors actually help the client to misstate its financial condition.[16] This situation opens the auditors up to being sued by the investors to recover their losses.

The potential conflicts of interest for auditors is complicated by another factor. Their employer, the accounting firm, provides a variety of consulting services to the companies they audit, including tax counsel, compensation systems, and financial information systems; and they can even be a sales agent for the products of the companies they audit.[17] In fact, under SEC rules that now require accounting firms to disclose the amount of consulting fees earned from audit clients, it has become clear that auditing constitutes only a small part of the fees paid by a specific client. The vast majority of fees earned from companies by accounting firms is for various consulting services, not auditing. Imagine the scenario in which an audit team has to tell a lucrative consulting client that its books have been handled improperly in some way or that the team will not approve accounting practices that make the company appear more profitable than it actually is. The risk to the accounting firm is not just the loss of the client's auditing business but the loss of millions of dollars in consulting fees if the accounting firm is fired.

SEC rules are already clear that auditors cannot own stock in the companies they audit, a necessary first step in ensuring independence. The SEC further insists that accounting firms cannot audit and consult for the same clients at the same time and remain independent in their audits. The SEC argues that when accounting firms combine auditing and other services, they cannot be truly independent. The Big Five accounting firms counter that the expertise required by the consulting side of their business actually makes them better auditors. The reason for this is that the consulting side of their business brings specialists in specific companies and industries that are necessary for accurate auditing. There is such a wide range of businesses that require audit services that it is unrealistic to expect that auditors can understand the intricacies of their clients without the consulting expertise that the accounting firms brings. The accounting firms further argue that without their lucrative consulting services, they will not be able

[16] For example, see the SEC allegations that Arthur Andersen helped Waste Management overstate its income in excess of $1 billion. Andersen paid $7 million in fines to settle the SEC's charges. In addition, PriceWaterhouseCoopers (PWC) paid $55 million to settle a class action lawsuit filed by shareholders in MicroStrategy. Cited in Marianne Lavelle, "Auditors Exposed! Cozy Deals Alleged!" *US News and World Report*, 23 July 2001, 40–42.

[17] For example, Andersen has a contract with IBM to help companies install IBM's e-business software. Cited in Mike McNamee, Paula Dwyer, and Christopher Schmitt, "Accounting Wars," *Business Week*, 25 September 2000, 158–59.

to retain the industry's most qualified people, and as a result, the quality of auditing will decline.

Some accounting firms have already spun off their consulting units or have erected more of a wall between consulting and auditing. But even those firms that have spun off consulting units have begun to rebuild new consulting services. Consulting and auditing will be mixed for the foreseeable future, bringing the potential for a conflict of interest that may not necessarily compromise audits but must be managed carefully. At the least, the SEC rule that requires companies to disclose the consulting fees paid to its auditing firm is a good start. Moreover, the audit committee of the company board of directors needs to function as more than a rubber stamp of the audit; it should exercise substantial oversight to ensure that the audit is not compromised by a conflict of interest. The committee should ask the following questions of the auditors to help them manage the potential conflict of interest: (1) If the auditor were an investor, would he/she have received the essential information accurately presented to understand the company's financial condition? (2) If the auditor were solely responsible for preparing the company's financial statements, would he/she have done anything differently? [18]

18 Taken from the advice of investor Warren Buffet, cited in "Put Bite Into Audit Committees," *Fortune*, 2 August 1999, 90.

II. Integrity in the Financial Markets

Issues for accountants and CFOs, though timely and prominent in the news, do not exhaust the issues relating to integrity in the area of finance. There are other issues that are not specifically related to accounting but are critical to the structure and integrity of the financial markets, namely the stock markets and investment banking industry, which are the vehicles through which companies raise the capital necessary to grow and thrive. Two specific issues will be addressed here, one of them the subject of years of discussion and the other a fairly new issue that arose with the late 1990s stock market boom and the prominence of initial public offerings (IPOs) issued by companies going public for the first time. The first of these, the issue of insider trading, has been around for some time. It made headlines in the 1980s in the operations of notorious financiers such as Ivan Boesky and Michael Milken. Even though these larger-than-life figures no longer dominate the headlines, insider trading is still a critical issue underlying the integrity of the financial markets. A second and newer issue has to do with the objectivity of stock market analysts. This issue emerged in the 1990s during the Internet boom, and the SEC has issued new rules aimed at ensuring that analysts stay objective and not be too closely tied to their firms' investment banking business.

A. Insider Trading

While the concept sounds technically complex, the practice of insider trading is relatively simple to understand. With large amounts of money at stake, tidbits of private information about company activities become invaluable. All one has to do is find out about important developments shortly before they are announced to the public and either purchase or "sell short"[19] some shares of the company stock, and a fortune can be made instantly. Other "insiders" have been more than willing to steal tips, sell them, tip off friends and relatives, and trade on them for their own profit. Insider trading received widespread public attention in the late 1980s because of Boesky and Milken; and even more recently, well-known figures like Martha Stewart have been accused of profiting from trading on insider information.

Insider trading is generally defined as using significant facts about a company that have not been made public to trade securities or releasing such information for a profit. Insider trading is illegal for two primary reasons. The first is that it violates a company's property rights, of which confidential information is a prime example. As such, private information should be treated in the same manner as other corporate assets. Since the corporation "owns" the information, employees who trade on it or disseminate it without permission are engaging in theft of company property. However, if a company agrees to give permission to its employees to trade on such information, no theft of property has occurred. And if this is announced to shareholders and the general public at large, it is indeed hard to imagine how anyone would be defrauded by such actions. Furthermore, many remote tippees and other "outsiders" have not purposefully or maliciously—or in some cases, even knowingly—acquired insider information. Consequently, they have not stolen anyone's property, nor have they breached any fiduciary responsibilities to the corporation or its shareholders.

The second rationale is based on much broader goals of fairness and equity in the securities market. Insider trading is prohibited within this framework to ensure that all investors who trade on the securities market are playing on a "level playing field" in terms of access to information. From this perspective, it would seem wrong for anyone to trade on this type of information, regardless of how it is acquired. If the second rationale of fairness is consistently applied, it would seem that anyone trading on nonpublic information, no matter how they acquired it, should be held criminally liable for trading on the information because it is unfair. Thus, even if a grandmother overheard two executives conversing in a train station and sold her shares in a company to

19 Selling short refers to the practice of trading stocks by betting that the price will go down rather than up. The client borrows stock and repays the debt with stock that is sold at a lower price, thus making a profit.

avoid losing her retirement assets, she could be guilty of transgressing the line of fairness.

In addition, though fairness in terms of a level playing field is important, total fairness is an unrealistic aim. Some sophisticated investors will always find information that others will not. For example, many market professionals such as mutual fund managers and analysts constantly search for new information about companies as part of their responsibilities to shareholders. While they are not legally entitled to "inside" information such as an impending takeover or the date of new product releases that have not been made public, they have timely access to more accurate information than does the typical small investor. In many cases, market professionals and other large individual investors can have access to high-ranking officials of companies in which they are interested in investing. However, there is a difference between insider information and hard work, since insiders are privy to information that other resourceful investors or analysts are not, no matter how hard they work, short of bribing someone or stealing it in another way.

But the line between insider information and good analysis may be less clear than one would like to think.[20] If fairness is really the goal, then it would seem that anyone trading on such information, no matter how they attained it, should be criminally liable. However, in related scenarios that we could all envision, it seems obvious that some remote tippees should not be criminally liable for their actions. While the situation described above is "unfair," it is hard to imagine that our fictitious grandmother who overhears two executives talking and trades on the information to avoid losses in her retirement portfolio has been malicious in her actions.

Some defenders of insider trading have argued that it is essentially a "victimless crime" and that, in fact, many outsiders will benefit from the moves of insiders. Clearly, though, we can all think of situations in which non-insiders can get hurt. For example, if insiders knew about an impending negative legal judgment against a company and dumped their shares before the public announcements, investors who subsequently bought these shares would be financially hurt by the deals. Conversely, investors would be buying overvalued shares when trading on insider information that is considered good news for the company.

If, however, insider trading were made legal and all investors were made aware of this, it would be hard to imagine how anyone would then be defrauded in the cases like the proceeding one, since all participants would then be privy to the rules. However, there are other critical reasons why the practices should remain illegal. Permitting them would erode the trust that is critical to a vibrant economy. For example, one effect that legalization of these practices would have is

20 John C. Coffee Jr., "Outsider Trading, That New Crime," *Wall Street Journal*, 14 November 1990.

that they would serve to severely lessen the number of participants in the securities industry.

It is hard to imagine that the many small investors whose finances make up a sizable portion of the total dollars invested would want to participate in transactions in which they could not acquire crucial information in order to be a rational actor in the market. Buying stocks while knowing that others have critical information that you cannot acquire would be akin to buying a car without the ability to find information on its repair record, fuel efficiency, or potential resale value. When only insiders and those who pay them or are tipped off by them are in possession of critical information, the whole basis for fair competition would be thwarted. Position and the ability to pay for information instead of fair competition would be the determining factors for success. Specifically, profiting from investments would then have very little to do with research and analysis, traditional tools that even small investors can utilize. Since the legalized selling of information would allow tips to go to the highest bidder, success in the market would then be based on position in crucial organizations and the ability to pay large sums for information. Trust would eventually erode to the point where only a few actors would willingly place their money into the securities industry, a critical source of funds for corporate improvement and innovation. The competitive ability of our whole economy would then suffer severely.

In a further blow to corporate competitiveness and well-being, significant fiduciary relationships may be jeopardized by allowing companies to permit insider trading among their employees. If insider trading were permitted, employees would likely turn their attention from their daily management duties and jockey for position in order to maximize the use of insider information.[21]

In sum, while significant clarification should be made to insider trading laws, these activities should remain illegal. Permitting their practice would undermine the very foundations of trust which are central to a thriving, growing economy. Without trust in the basic fairness of the system, investors are not likely to place their funds in the market, thus depriving companies of the capital they need for growth and competitiveness. Furthermore, managers would be placed in positions where conflicts of interest would only be magnified.

21 Jennifer Moore, "What Is Really Wrong with Insider Trading?" *Journal of Business Ethics* (September 1990): 171–82.

B. Stock Analysts' Objectivity

Another side of the financial services industry that has come under scrutiny for conflicts of interest is the role of the stock analyst. Generally employed by the large investment banking houses on Wall

Street, analysts are supposed to give out objective, unbiased advice to the investment community about stocks and companies that are about to go public. Analysts are usually specialists in specific industries, such as Internet stocks or bank stocks or a limited number of companies across certain industries. At present, there is increasing skepticism about analysts' objectivity and a growing recognition that their research and recommendations have been compromised by self-serving agendas.[22]

Analysts face at least three potential conflicts of interest, all of which call for careful management in order to maintain the integrity of their recommendations. The first is the potential conflict between the analyst's financial self-interest and the objectivity of his or her recommendations. That is, analysts can artificially affect the price of a stock by their recommendation to buy or hold the stock, and if they own that stock, they can benefit financially. As a result, some investment banking firms have prohibited analysts from owning stock in the companies they cover. But the counter argument to this is that analysts should "put their money where their mouth is." That is, analysts owning stock in companies they cover might actually demonstrate that an analyst is willing to stand behind his/her recommendations.

A second potential conflict has to do with the analyst's relationship with his/her employer. Most of the revenue generated by the investment banking houses on Wall Street comes from their involvement in mergers/acquisitions and initial public offerings (IPOs). They reap substantial fees from helping companies raise money for mergers or raise operating capital through IPOs. Increasingly, analysts are viewed as an aid in the recruitment of investment banking clients. In order to recruit and maintain investment banking relationships, they rely on analysts' making positive recommendations about the companies they serve. If the firm's analysts are issuing negative recommendations on companies with whom the investment bankers are doing business, that could negatively affect the investment banking business of the firm. There is great pressure on analysts to issue research opinions that support the investment banking activities of the firm. Analysts have been fired when their recommendations are seen to undermine the firm's investment banking relationships. There is pressure to highlight the good news and downplay the bad news of the companies with whom the firm is involved in investment banking. This conflict of interests is a serious one and clearly undermines the objectivity of the analyst's opinion. On the other hand, the analysts and the investment bankers can work together. If the analyst likes a company he is covering, he can suggest that the firm ought to pursue the company as an investment banking client. But far too many times

22 See for example, Jeffrey Laderman, "Wall Street's Spin Game," *Business Week*, 5 October 1998, 148–56.

"the tail wags the dog," and the analyst is expected to issue a research opinion that supports the investment banking deal.

A third potential conflict of interest affects the way the analyst is able to do his/her job. It is not uncommon for the companies covered by analysts to cut off access to company personnel and key information if the analysis has been negative on the company. As a result, it is rare for analysts to issue "sell" recommendations, and the euphemism for "sell" has become "hold" or "neutral." There are numerous examples of analysts issuing "buy" recommendations for fear of losing access to key information. This too is a key conflict, since losing access makes it much more difficult for the analyst to do his or her job properly.

The Securities Industry Association, responding to some of the criticism of analysts' objectivity and perhaps anticipating SEC investigations, has recommended the following guidelines for analysts:[23]

1. Use the full spectrum of ratings for a stock, including "sell."[24]
2. Analysts should not report to the investment banking department of the firm.
3. Analysts should be paid based on the accuracy of their recommendations, not on their ability to attract investment banking business.
4. Analysts should not personally trade a stock while preparing research on that company or within a reasonable time period after issuing a recommendation.
5. Analysts should not trade against their recommendations, i.e., selling shares that they have recommended to "buy."
6. Analysts should disclose personal investments or business relationships (analysts and their firms) with the company being analyzed.

[23] Taken from Thomas S. Mulligan, "Amid Criticism, Wall St. Offers Analyst Guidelines," *Los Angeles Times*, 13 June 2001, C1, 5.

[24] Recent studies from Thomson/First Call that track analysts' recommendations have shown that the percentage of "sell" recommendations is very small, less than 2 percent of all recommendations issued (ibid., C5).

Conclusion: Restoring Trust in the Financial Markets

Trust is essential for a functioning economic system, particularly the operation of the financial markets. When investors no longer trust in the fair play of the markets, they will take their capital and invest it in areas in which they are assured of fairness. Investors must be able to trust a company's earnings reports, stock analysts' recommendations, the auditors' affirmations, the fiduciary responsibilities of investment bankers, and the oversight of the board of directors if they are to restore confidence in the markets.

Ultimately, restoring trust is not a matter of extrinsic motivations such as more regulations and stiffer penalties for noncompliance. These are important, but the SEC already has volumes of rules and guidelines. And there are more coming. Rules alone are not adequate because they cannot cover all the possibilities and there will always be loopholes in the law. This is a good example of why ethics is so important. Alexander Solzhenitsyn put it this way: "A society with no other scale but the legal one is not quite worthy of man. The letter of the law is too cold and formal an atmosphere of moral mediocrity, paralyzing man's nobler impulses." As you will see later in this book, this is why companies need programs in ethics rather than simply compliance. Ethics empowers our nobler impulses, and character is crucial to leadership. Trust is restored by character, not simply by obedience to rules and regulations. Increasingly, the investing public is demanding that trust be restored, and the corporate leadership is seeing that trust is essential for a system that functions in a healthy way.

NINE

Marketing and Advertising

Everybody everywhere wants to modify, transform, embellish, enrich, and reconstruct the world around him—to introduce into an otherwise harsh or bland existence some sort of purposeful and distorting alleviation. Civilization is man's attempt to transcend his animality; and this includes both art and advertising.

Theodore Levitt

We buy all the right stuff and yet have no more friends, lovers, excitement, or respect than before.

John Waide

INTRODUCTION

Advertising plays a significant and unquestionable role in stimulating economic growth and the attainment of higher living standards. Yet taken as a whole, it continues to be a highly controversial business activity because of its seemingly ever-expanding presence, its alleged power to influence consumers into making unnecessary purchases, and its promotion of a materialistic worldview.

From humble beginnings in the form of leaflets and catalogs, advertising has undoubtedly expanded its reach in a number of impressive ways. In addition to traditional media forms, ads are now directed to potential customers while they are surfing the Internet (banners and pop-ups), watching movies (paid product placements), refueling automobiles (video screens at gas pumps), and making use of public restrooms (billboards placed within view of toilets and lavatories). Some experts estimate that Americans are exposed to 3,000 advertising messages daily.[1]

[1] In addition to traditional media sources such as television, billboards, print, and the Internet, consumers also see ads in the form of "brands" worn on clothing and placed on products.

2 Critics allege that as citizens of developing countries rapidly buy into a materially based vision of the "good life," cultural conflict and economic and environmental damage will occur. For a well-articulated account of these and related criticisms see, David C. Korten, *When Corporations Rule the World*, Kumarian Press, 1995.

In recent years, advertising has also extended its reach geographically and demographically. Ads promoting Western products are routinely seen in developing countries, contributing to cultural changes as they appear.[2] Furthermore, young children are also the targets of advertising campaigns. Some advertisers see them both as having a strong influence in regular family purchasing decisions and as potential loyal long-term customers.

The methods used by advertisers seem limitless. Common emotions and psychological insecurities are routinely appealed to for the purpose of selling more products and/or services. For example, psychological terrain such as sexual satisfaction through promiscuity is regularly used to pitch a product or service. Products ranging from alcoholic beverages to shampoo are now sold through appeals to overt sexual power. Advertising also extends to the spiritual sphere of human life. By promoting a message that "ultimate" questions such as personal meaning and satisfaction can be answered through the ownership of the right goods and services, the traditional bounds of religion are transgressed.

With all of these criticisms, the moral status of advertising seems obvious. However, several arguments can be advanced in its favor. At a minimum, advertising can be said to have tremendous usefulness because of the role it plays in promoting economic growth. It is not a stretch to conclude that if the scope of advertising were sharply curtailed, consumer spending and thereby product sales would slow. In turn, a large-scale economic domino effect could occur, slowing the growth of local and national economies, and ultimately the interconnected global economic system.

A defense of the intrinsic nature of advertising can also be offered. Some advertisers portray it as a benign cultural mirror of consumer values. Seen in this light, advertising is "information" packaged in a manner that is demanded by the consuming public. People respond to particular appeals and/or visions of the good life. This is the case because advertising truly reflects their often latent but nevertheless real desires, and not because it has some mysterious and/or astonishing power to manipulate. Consumers are willing participants who demand more than just the pure utility offered by products or services. Poetic descriptors and fancy packaging are a part of the "mix" of what is purchased.

Given these negative and positive aspects of advertising, can it be employed in a manner that is consistent with Christian ethics? Or, given its ubiquitous presence and increasingly questionable methods, is it primarily an immoral enterprise? With respect to individual campaigns, are some types of appeal legitimate while others are not? This chapter will address some of these tensions by evaluating advertising and developing broad guidelines for how it can be used in an ethical manner.

The first article in this chapter is Theodore Levitt's classic defense of advertising, "The Morality (?) of Advertising." In it Levitt argues that consumers want excitement to enliven their otherwise mundane lives. Quoting T. S. Eliot, he notes that "human kind cannot bear very much reality." Therefore, advertising merely responds to true consumer demands, which are often latent, but are nonetheless real.[3]

Author Rodney Clapp disagrees with such a benign assessment, arguing in "Making Consumers" that consumers are not "born" as such. People do not naturally consume as a way of life. Rather, a brief look at history suggests that they had to be taught to do so, with early twentieth-century advertising serving as one of their primary instructors. Advertising, Clapp argues, continues today to create new needs in consumers, not merely to respond to existing ones.

In "The Making of Self and World in Advertising," author John Waide criticizes associative advertising based on how it might impact human character. Waide notes that he is not concerned with advertising's alleged power to manipulate or create new needs as much as with the kind of people and the type of world that is shaped through the proliferation of associative advertising.

[3] To be sure, Levitt's arguments predate the most recent expansion of global capitalism.

READINGS

The Morality (?) of Advertising

Theodore Levitt

Harvard Business Review (July–August 1970): 84–92. Copyright © 1970.

In curbing the excesses of advertising, both business and government must distinguish between embellishment and mendacity.

The present controversy over the regulation of advertising may well result in restrictive legislation of some kind, but it is by no means clear how this should be set up. This article presents a philosophical treatment of the human values of advertising as compared with the values of other "imaginative" disciplines. It is designed to provoke thought about the issues at stake....

This year Americans will consume about $20 billion of advertising, and very little of it because we want it. Wherever we turn, advertising will be forcibly thrust on us in an intrusive orgy of abrasive sound and sight, all to induce us to do something we might not ordinarily do, or to induce us to do it differently. This massive and persistent effort crams increasingly more commercial noise into the same, few strained 24 hours of the day. It has provoked a reaction as predictable as it was inevitable: a lot of people want the noise stopped, or at least alleviated.

And they want it cleaned up and corrected. As more and more products have entered the battle for the consumer's fleeting dollar, advertising has increased in boldness and volume. Last year, industry offered the nation's supermarkets about 100 new products a week, equal, on an annualized basis, to the total number already on their shelves. Where so much must be sold so hard, it is not surprising that advertisers have pressed the limits of our credulity and generated complaints about their exaggerations and deceptions.

Only classified ads, the work of rank amateurs, do we presume to contain solid, unembellished fact. We suspect all the rest of systematic and egregious distortion, if not often of outright mendacity.

The attack on advertising comes from all sectors. Indeed, recent studies show that the people most agitated by advertising are precisely those in the higher income brackets whose affluence is generated by the industries that create the ads.[1] While these studies show that only a modest group of people are preoccupied with advertising's constant presence in our lives, they also show that distortion and deception are what bother people most.

This discontent has encouraged Senator Philip Hart and Senator William Proxmire to sponsor consumer-protection and truth-in-advertising legislation. People, they say, want less fluff and more fact about the things they buy. They want description, not distortion, and they want some relief from the constant, grating, vulgar noise.

Legislation seems appropriate because the natural action of competition does not seem to work, or, at least not very well. Competition may ultimately flush out and destroy falsehood and shoddiness, but "ultimately" is too long for the deceived—not just the deceived who are poor, ignorant, and dispossessed, but also all the rest of us who work hard for our money and can seldom judge expertly the truth of conflicting claims about products and services.

The consumer is an amateur, after all; the producer is an expert. In the commercial arena, the consumer is an impotent midget. He is certainly not king. The producer is a powerful giant. It is an uneven match. In this setting, the purifying power of competition helps the consumer very little—especially in the short run, when his money is spent and gone, from the weak hands into the strong hands. Nor does competition among the sellers solve the "noise" problem. The more they compete, the worse the din of advertising.

A Broad Viewpoint Required

Most people spend their money carefully. Understandably, they look out for larcenous attempts to separate them from it. Few men in business will deny the right, perhaps even the wisdom, of people today asking for some restraint on advertising, or at least for more accurate information on the things they buy and for more consumer protection.

Yet, if we speak in the same breath about consumer protection and about advertising's distortions, exaggerations, and deceptions it is easy to confuse two quite separate things—the legitimate purpose of advertising and the abuses to which it may be put. Rather than deny that distortion and exaggeration exist in advertising, in this article I shall argue that embellishment and distortion are among advertising's legitimate and socially desirable purposes; and that illegitimacy in advertising consists only of falsification with larcenous intent. And while it is difficult, as a practical matter, to draw the line between legitimate distortion and essential falsehood, I want to take a long look at the distinction that exists between the two. This I shall say in advance—the distinction is not as simple, obvious, or great as one might think.

The issue of truth versus falsehood, in advertising or in anything else, is complex and fugitive. It must be pursued in a philosophic mood that might seem foreign to the businessman. Yet the issue at base *is* more philosophic than it is pragmatic. Anyone seriously concerned with the moral problems of a commercial society cannot avoid this fact. I hope the reader will bear with me—I believe he will find it helpful, and perhaps even refreshing.

What Is Reality?

What, indeed? Consider poetry. Like advertising, poetry's purpose is to influence an audience; to affect its perceptions and sensibilities; perhaps even to change its mind. Like rhetoric, poetry's intent is to convince and seduce. In the service of that intent, it employs without guilt or fear of criticism all the arcane tools of distortion that the literary mind can devise. Keats does not offer a truthful engineering description of his Grecian urn. He offers, instead, with exquisite attention to the effects of meter, rhyme, allusion, illusion, metaphor, and sound, a lyrical, exaggerated, distorted, and palpably false description. And he is thoroughly applauded for it, as are all other artists, in whatever medium, who do precisely this same thing successfully.

Commerce, it can be said without apology, takes essentially the same liberties with reality and literality as the artist, except that commerce calls its creations advertising, or industrial design, or packaging. As with art, the purpose is to influence the audience by creating illusions, symbols, and implications that promise more than pure functionality. Once, when asked what his company did, Charles Revson of Revlon, Inc. suggested a profound distinction: "In the factory we make cosmetics; in the store we sell hope." He obviously has no illusions. It is not cosmetic chemicals women want, but the seductive charm promised by the alluring symbols with which these chemicals have been surrounded—hence the rich and exotic packages in which they are sold, and the suggestive advertising with which they are promoted.

Commerce usually embellishes its products thrice: first, it designs the product to be pleasing to the eye, to suggest reliability, and so forth; second, it packages the product as attractively as it feasibly can; and then it advertises this attractive package with inviting pictures, slogans, descriptions, songs, and so on. The package and design are as important as the advertising.

The Grecian vessel, for example, was used to carry liquids, but that function does not explain why the potter decorated it with graceful lines and elegant drawings in black and red. A woman's compact carries refined talc, but this does not explain why manufacturers try to make these boxes into works of decorative art.

Neither the poet nor the ad man celebrates the literal functionality of what he produces. Instead, each celebrates a deep and complex emotion which he symbolizes by creative embellishment—a content which cannot be captured by literal description alone. Communication, through advertising or through poetry or any other medium, is a creative conceptualization that implies a vicarious experience through a language of symbolic substitutes. Communication can never be the real thing it talks about. Therefore, all communication is in some inevitable fashion a departure from reality.

Everything Is Changed . . .

Poets, novelists, playwrights, composers, and fashion designers have one thing more in common. They all deal in symbolic communication. None is satisfied with nature in the raw, as it was on the day of creation. None is satisfied to tell it exactly "like it is" to the naked eye, as do the classified ads. It is the purpose of all art to alter nature's surface reality, to reshape, to embellish, and to augment what nature has so crudely fashioned, and then to present it to the same applauding humanity that so eagerly buys Revson's exotically advertised cosmetics.

Few, if any, of us accept the natural state in which God created us. We scrupulously select our clothes to suit a multiplicity of simultaneous purposes, not only for warmth, but manifestly for such other purposes as propriety, status, and seduction. Women modify, embellish, and amplify themselves with colored paste for the lips and powders and lotions for the face; men as well as women use devices to take hair off the face and others to put it on the head. Like the inhabitants of isolated African regions, where not a single whiff of advertising has ever intruded, we all encrust ourselves with rings, pendants, bracelets, neckties, clips, chains, and snaps.

Man lives neither in sackcloth nor in sod huts—although these are not notably inferior to tight clothes and overheated dwellings in congested and polluted cities. Everywhere man rejects nature's uneven blessings. He molds and repackages to his own civilizing specifications an otherwise, crude, drab, and generally oppressive reality. He does it so that life may be made for the moment more tolerable than God evidently designed it to be. As T. S. Eliot once remarked, "Human kind cannot bear very much reality."

. . . Into Something Rich and Strange

No line of life is exempt. All the popes of history have countenanced the costly architecture of St. Peter's Basilica and its extravagant interior decoration. All around the globe, nothing typifies man's materialism so much as the temples in which he preaches asceticism. Men of the cloth have not been persuaded that the poetic self-denial of Christ or Buddha—both men of sackcloth and sandals—is enough to inspire, elevate, and hold their flocks together. To amplify the temple in men's eyes, they have, very realistically, systematically sanctioned the embellishment of the houses of the gods with the same kind of luxurious design and expensive decoration that Detroit puts into a Cadillac.

One does not need a doctorate in social anthropology to see that the purposeful transmutation of nature's primeval state occupies all people in all cultures and all societies at all stages of development. Everybody everywhere wants to modify, transform, embellish, enrich, and reconstruct the world around him—to introduce into an otherwise harsh or bland existence some sort of purposeful and distorting alleviation. Civilization is man's attempt to transcend his ancient animality; and this includes both art and advertising.

. . . And More Than "Real"

But civilized man will undoubtedly deny that either the innovative artist or the *grande dame* with *chic* "distorts reality." Instead, he will say that artist and woman merely embellish, enhance, and illuminate. To be sure, he will mean something quite different by these three terms when he applies them to fine art, on the one hand, and to more secular efforts, on the other.

But this distinction is little more than an affectation. As man has civilized himself and developed his sensibilities, he has invented a great variety of subtle distinctions between things that are objectively indistinct. Let us take a closer look at the difference between man's "sacred" distortions and his "secular" ones.

The man of sensibility will probably canonize the artist's deeds as superior creations by ascribing to them an almost cosmic virtue and significance. As a cultivated individual, he will almost certainly refuse to recognize any constructive, cosmic virtues in the productions of the advertisers, and he is likely to admit the charge that advertising uniformly deceives us by analogous techniques. But how "sensible" is he?

And by Similar Means . . .

Let us assume for the moment that there is no objective, operational difference between the embellishments and distortions of the artist and those of the ad man—that both men are more concerned with creating images and feelings than with rendering objective, representational, and informational descriptions. The greater virtue of the artist's work must then derive from some subjective element. What is it?

It will be said that art has a higher value for man because it has a higher purpose. True, the artist is interested in philosophic truth or wisdom, and the ad man in selling his goods and services. Michelangelo, when he designed the Sistine chapel ceiling, had some concern with the inspirational elevation of man's spirit, whereas Edward Levy, who designs cosmetics packages, is interested primarily in creating images to help separate the unwary consumer from his loose change.

But this explanation of the differences between the value of art and the value of advertising is not helpful at all. For is the presence of a "higher" purpose all that redeeming?

Perhaps not; perhaps the reverse is closer to the truth. While the ad man and designer seek only to convert the audience to their commercial custom, Michelangelo sought to convert its soul. Which is the greater blasphemy? Who commits the greater affront to life—he who dabbles with man's erotic appetites, or he who meddles with man's soul? Which act is the easier to judge and justify?

. . . For Different Ends

How much sense does it really make to distinguish between similar means on the grounds that the ends to which they are directed are different—"good" for art and "not so good" for advertising? The distinction produces zero progress in the argument at hand. How willing are we to employ the involuted ethics whereby the ends justify the means?

Apparently, on this subject, lots of people are very willing indeed. The business executive seems to share with the minister, the painter, and the poet the doctrine that the ends justify the means. The difference is that the businessman is justifying the very commercial ends that his critics oppose. While his critics justify the embellishments of art and literature for what these do for man's spirit, the businessman justifies the embellishment of industrial design and advertising for what they do for man's purse.

Taxing the imagination to the limit, the businessman spins casuistic webs of elaborate transparency to the self-righteous effect that promotion and advertising are socially benign because they expand the economy, create jobs, and raise living standards. Technically, he will always be free to argue, and he *will* argue, that his ends become the means to the ends of the musician, poet, painter, and minister. The argument which justifies means in terms of ends is obviously not without its subtleties and intricacies.

The executive and the artist are equally tempted to identify and articulate a higher rationale for their work than their work itself. But only in the improved human consequences of their efforts do they find vindication. The aesthete's ringing declaration of "art for art's sake," with all its self-conscious affirmation of selflessness, sound shallow in the end, even to himself; for, finally, every communication addresses itself to an audience. Thus art is very understandably in constant need of justification by the evidence of its beneficial and divinely approved effect on its audience.

The Audience's Demands

This compulsion to rationalize even art is a highly instructive fact. It tells one a great deal about art's purposes and the purposes of all other communication. As I have said, the poet and the artist each seek in some special way to produce an emotion or assert a truth not otherwise apparent. But it is only in communion with their audiences that the effectiveness of their efforts can be tested and truth revealed. It may be academic whether a tree falling in the forest makes a noise. It is *not* academic whether a sonnet or a painting has merit. Only an audience can decide that.

The creative person can justify his work only in terms of another person's response to it. Ezra Pound, to be sure, thought that "... in the [greatest] works the live part is the part which the artist has put there to please himself, and the dead part is the part he has put there ... because he thinks he *ought* to—i.e., either to get or keep an audience." This is certainly consistent with our notions of Pound as perhaps the purest of twentieth-century advocates of art for art's sake.

But if we review the record of his life, we find that Pound spent the greater part of his energies seeking suitable places for deserving poets to publish. Why? Because art has little merit standing alone in unseen and unheard isolation. Merit is not inherent in art. It is conferred by an audience.

The same is true of advertising: if it fails to persuade the audience that the product will fulfill the function the audience expects, the advertising has no merit.

Where have we arrived? Only at some common characteristics of art and advertising. Both are rhetorical, and both literally false; both expound an emotional reality deeper than the "real"; both pretend to "higher" purposes, although different ones; and the excellence of each is judged by its effect on its audience—its persuasiveness, in short. I do not mean to imply that the two are fundamentally the same, but rather that they both represent a pervasive, and I believe *universal*, characteristic of human nature—the human audience *demands* symbolic interpretation in everything it sees and knows. If it doesn't get it, it will return a verdict of "no interest."

To get a clearer idea of the relation between the symbols of advertising and the products they glorify, something more must be said about the fiat the consumer gives to industry to "distort" its messages.

Symbol and Substance

As we have seen, man seeks to transcend nature in the raw everywhere. Everywhere, and at all times, he has been attracted by the poetic imagery of some sort of art, literature, music, and mysticism. He obviously wants and needs the promises, the imagery, and the symbols of the poet and the priest. He refuses to live a life of primitive barbarism or sterile functionalism.

Consider a sardine can filled with scented powder. Even if the U.S. Bureau of Standards were to certify that the contents of this package are identical with the product sold in a beautiful paisley-printed container, it would not sell. The Boston matron, for example, who has built herself a deserved reputation for pinching every penny until it hurts, would unhesitatingly turn it down. While she may deny it, in self-assured and neatly cadenced accents, she obviously desires and needs the promises, imagery, and symbols produced by hyperbolic advertisements, elaborate packages, and fetching fashions.

The need for embellishment is not confined to personal appearance. A few years ago, an electronics laboratory offered a $700 testing device for sale. The company ordered two different front panels to be designed, one by the engineers who developed the equipment and one by professional industrial designers. When the two models were shown to a sample of laboratory directors with Ph.D.'s, the professional design attracted twice the purchase intentions that the engineer's design did. Obviously, the laboratory director who has been baptized into science at M.I.T. is quite as responsive to the blandishments of packaging as the Boston matron.

And, obviously, both these customers define the products they buy in much more sophisticated terms than the engineer in the factory. For a woman, dusting powder in a sardine can is not the same product as the identical dusting powder in an exotic paisley package. For the laboratory director, the test equipment behind an engineer-designed panel just isn't as "good" as the identical equipment in a box designed with finesse.

Form Follows the Ideal Function

The consumer refuses to settle for pure operating functionality. "Form follows function" is a resoundingly vacuous cliché, which like all clichés, depends for its memorability more on its alliteration and brevity than on its wisdom. If it has any truth, it is only in the elastic sense that function extends beyond strict mechanical use into the domain of imagination. We do not choose to buy a particular product; we choose to buy the functional expectations that we attach to it, and we buy these expectations as "tools" to help us solve a problem of life.

Under normal circumstances, furthermore, we must judge a product's "non-mechanical" utilities before we actually buy it. It is rare that we choose an object after we have experienced it; nearly always we must make the choice before the fact. We choose on the basis of promises, not experiences.

Whatever symbols convey and *sustain* these promises in our minds are therefore truly functional. The promises and images which imaginative ads and sculptured packages induce in us are as much the product as the physical materials themselves. To put this another way, these ads and packagings describe the product's fullness for us: in our minds, the product becomes a complex abstraction which is, as Immanuel Kant might have said, the conception of a perfection which has not yet been experienced.

But all promises and images, almost by their very nature, exceed their capacity to live up to themselves. As every eager lover has ever known, the consummation seldom equals the promises which produced the chase. To forestall and sup-

press the visceral expectation of disappointment that life has taught us must inevitably come, we use art, architecture, literature, and the rest, and advertising as well, to shield ourselves, in advance of experience, from the stark and plain reality in which we are fated to live. I agree that we wish for unobtainable unrealities, "dream castles." But why promise ourselves reality, which we already possess? What we want is what we do *not* possess!

Everyone in the world is trying in his special personal fashion to solve a primal problem of life—the problem of rising above his own negligibility, of escaping from nature's confining, hostile, and unpredictable reality, of finding significance, security, and comfort in the things he must do to survive. Many of the so-called distortions of advertising, product design, and packaging may be viewed as a paradigm of the many responses that man makes to the conditions of survival in the environment. Without distortion, embellishment, and elaboration, life would be drab, dull, anguished, and at its existential worst.

Symbolism Useful and Necessary

Without symbolism, furthermore, life would be even more confusing and anxiety-ridden than it is *with* it. The foot soldier must be able to recognize the general, good or bad, because the general is clothed with power. A general without his stars and suite of aides-de-camp to set him apart from the privates would suffer authority and credibility as much as perfume packaged by Dracula or a computer designed by Rube Goldberg. Any ordinary soldier or civilian who has ever had the uncommon experience of beginning in the same shower with a general can testify from the visible unease of the latter how much clothes "make the man."

Similarly, verbal symbols help to make the product—they help us deal with the uncertainties of daily life. "You can be sure ... if it's Westinghouse" is a decision rule as useful to the man buying a turbine generator as to the man buying an electric shaver. To label all the devices and embellishments companies employ to reassure the prospective customer about a product's quality with the pejorative term "gimmick," as critics tend to do, is simply silly. Worse, it denies, against massive evidence, man's honest needs and values. If religion must be architectured, packaged, lyricized, and musicized to attract and hold its audience, and if sex must be perfumed, powdered, sprayed, and shaped in order to command attention, it is ridiculous to deny the legitimacy of more modest, and similar, embellishments to the world of commerce.

But still, the critics may say, commercial communications tend to be aggressively deceptive. Perhaps, and perhaps not. The issue at stake here is more complex than the outraged critic believes. Man wants and needs the elevation of the spirit produced by attractive surroundings, by handsome packages, and by imaginative promises. He needs the assurances projected by well-known brand names, and the reliability suggested by salesmen who have been taught to dress by Oleg Cassini and to speak by Dale Carnegie. Of course, there are blatant, tasteless, and willfully deceiving salesmen and advertisers, just as there are blatant, tasteless, and willfully deceiving artists, preachers, and even professors. But, before talking blithely about deception, it is helpful to make a distinction between things and descriptions of things.

The Question of Deceit

Poetic descriptions of things make no pretense of being the things themselves. Nor do advertisements, even by the most elastic standards. Advertisements are the symbols of man's aspirations. They are not the real things, nor are they intended to be, nor are they accepted as such by the public. A study some years ago by the Center for Research in Marketing, Inc. concluded that deep down inside the consumer understands this perfectly well and has the attitude that an advertisement is an ad, not a factual news story.

Even Professor Galbraith grants the point when he says that ". . . because modern man is exposed to a large volume of information of varying degrees of unreliability . . . he establishes a system of discounts which he applies to various sources almost without thought. . . . The discount becomes

nearly total for all forms of advertising. The merest child watching television dismisses the health and status-giving claims of a breakfast cereal as 'a commercial.' "[2]

This is not to say, of course, that Galbraith also discounts advertising's effectiveness. Quite the opposite: "Failure to win belief does not impair the effectiveness of the management of demand for consumer products. Management involves the creation of a compelling image of the product in the mind of the consumer. To this he responds more or less automatically under circumstances where the purchase does not merit a great deal of thought. For building this image, palpable fantasy may be more valuable than circumstantial evidence."[3]

Linguists and other communications specialists will agree with the conclusion of the Center for Research in Marketing that "advertising is a symbol system existing in a world of symbols. Its reality depends upon the fact that it is a symbol . . . the content of an ad can never be real, it can only say something about reality, or create a relationship between itself and an individual which has an effect on the reality life of an individual."

Consumer, Know Thyself!

Consumption is man's most constant activity. It is well that he understands himself as a consumer.

The object of consumption is to solve a problem. Even consumption that is viewed as the creation of an opportunity—like going to medical school or taking a singles-only Caribbean tour—has as its purpose the solving of a problem. At a minimum, the medical student seeks to solve the problem of how to lead a relevant and comfortable life, and the lady on the tour seeks to solve the problem of spinsterhood.

The "purpose" of the product is not what the engineer explicitly says it is, but what the consumer implicitly demands that it shall be. Thus the consumer consumes not things, but expected benefits—not cosmetics, but the satisfactions of the allurements they promise; not quarter-inch drills, but quarter-inch holes; not stock in companies, but capital gains; not numerically controlled milling machines, but trouble-free and accurately smooth metal parts; not low-cal whipped cream, but self-rewarding indulgence combined with sophisticated convenience.

The significance of these distinctions is anything but trivial. Nobody knows this better, for example, than the creators of automobile ads. It is not the generic virtues that they tout, but more likely the car's capacity to enhance its user's status and his access to female prey.

Whether we are aware of it or not, we in effect expect and demand that advertising create these symbols for us to show us what life *might* be, to bring the possibilities that we cannot see before our eyes and screen out the stark reality in which we must live. We insist, as Gilbert put it, that there be added a "touch of artistic verisimilitude to an otherwise bald and unconvincing narrative."

Understanding the Difference

In a world where so many things are either commonplace or standardized, it makes no sense to refer to the rest as false, fraudulent, frivolous, or immaterial. The world works according to the aspirations and needs of its actors, not according to the arcane or moralizing logic of detached critics who pine for another age—an age which, in any case, seems different from today's largely because its observers are no longer children shielded by protective parents from life's implacable harshness.

To understand this is not to condone much of the vulgarity, purposeful duplicity, and scheming half-truths we see in advertising, promotion, packaging, and product design. But before we condemn, it is well to understand the difference between embellishment and duplicity and how extraordinarily uncommon the latter is in our times. The noisy visibility of promotion in our intensely communicating times need not be thoughtlessly equated with malevolence.

Thus the issue is not the prevention of distortion. It is, in the end, to know what kinds of distortions we actually want so that each of our lives, is, without apology, duplicity, or rancor, made bearable. This does not mean we must accept out of hand all the commercial propaganda to which we are each day so constantly exposed, or that we must accept out of hand the equation that effluence is the price of affluence, or the simple notion that business cannot and government should not try to alter and improve the position of the consumer vis-à-vis the producer. It takes a special kind of perversity to continue any longer our shameful failure to mount vigorous, meaningful programs to protect the consumer, to standardize product grades, labels, and packages, to improve the consumer's information-getting process, and to mitigate the vulgarity and oppressiveness that is in so much of our advertising.

But the consumer suffers from an old dilemma. He wants "truth," but he also wants and needs the alleviating imagery and tantalizing promises of the advertiser and designer.

Business is caught in the middle. There is hardly a company that would not go down in ruin if it refused to provide fluff, because nobody will buy pure functionality. Yet, if it uses too much fluff and little else, business invites possibly ruinous legislation. The problem therefore is to find a middle way, and in this search, business can do a great deal more than it has been either accustomed or willing to do:

- It can exert pressure to make sure that no single industry "finds reasons" why it should be exempt from legislative restrictions that are reasonable and popular.
- It can work constructively with government to develop reasonable standards and effective sanctions that will assure a more amenable commercial environment.
- It can support legislation to provide the consumer with the information he needs to make easy comparison between products, packages, and prices.
- It can support and help draft improved legislation on quality stabilization.
- It can support legislation that gives consumers easy access to strong legal remedies where justified. It can support programs to make local legal aid easily available, especially to the poor and undereducated who know so little about their rights and how to assert them.

- Finally, it can support efforts to moderate and clean up the advertising noise that dulls our senses and assaults our sensibilities.

It will not be the end of the world or of capitalism for business to sacrifice a few commercial freedoms so that we may more easily enjoy our own humanity. Business can and should, for its own good, work energetically to achieve this end. But it is also well to remember the limits of what is possible. Paradise was not a free-goods society. The forbidden fruit was gotten at a price.

Notes

[1] See Raymond A. Bauer and Stephen A. Greyser, *Advertising in America: The Consumer View* (Boston, Division of Research, Harvard Business School, 1968), see also Gary A. Steiner, *The People Look at Television* (New York, Alfred A. Knopf, Inc., 1963).

[2] John Kenneth Galbraith, *The New Industrial State* (Boston, Houghton Mifflin Company, 1967), 325–26.
[3] Ibid., 326.

Questions for Discussion:

1. Do you agree with Levitt that the embellishment of products provided by advertising is necessary and a good thing for society? Why or why not?
2. Do you agree with Levitt that there is an important difference between embellishment and duplicity? How would you distinguish between the two?

The Making of Self and World in Advertising

John Waide

Journal of Business Ethics 6 (1987), 73–79. Copyright © 1987 D. Reidel Publishing Co.

In this paper I will criticize a common practice I call associative advertising. The fault in associative advertising is not that it is deceptive or that it violates the autonomy of its audience—on this point I find Arrington's arguments persuasive.[1] Instead, I will argue against associative advertising by examining the virtues and vices at stake. In so doing, I will offer an alternative to Arrington's exclusive concern with autonomy and behavior control.

Associative advertising is a technique that involves all of the following:

1. The advertiser wants people[2] to buy (or buy more of) a product. This objective is largely independent of any sincere desire to improve or enrich the lives of the people in the target market.
2. In order to increase sales, the advertiser identifies some (usually) deep-seated non-market good for which the people in the target market feel a strong desire. By "non-market good" I mean something which cannot, strictly speaking, be bought or sold in a marketplace. Typical non-market goods are friendship,

acceptance and esteem of others. In a more extended sense we may regard excitement (usually sexual) and power as non-market goods since advertising in the U.S.A. usually uses versions of these that cannot be bought and sold. For example, "sex appeal" as the theme of an advertising campaign is not the market-good of prostitution, but the non-market good of sexual attractiveness and acceptability.

3. In most cases, the marketed product bears only the most tenuous (if any) relation to the non-market good with which it is associated in the advertising campaign. For example, soft drinks cannot give one friends, sex, or excitement.

4. Through advertising, the marketed product is associated with the non-market desire it cannot possibly satisfy. If possible, the desire for the non-market good is intensified by calling into question one's acceptability. For example, mouthwash, toothpaste, deodorant, and feminine hygiene ads are concocted to make us worry that we stink.

5. Most of us have enough insight to see both (a) that no particular toothpaste can make us sexy and (b) that wanting to be considered sexy is at least part of our motive for buying that toothpaste. Since we can (though, admittedly, we often do not bother to) see clearly what the appeal of the ad is, we are usually not lacking in relevant information or deceived in any usual sense.

6. In some cases, the product actually gives at least partial satisfaction to the non-market desire—but only because of advertising.[3] For example, mouthwash has little prolonged effect on stinking breath, but it helps to reduce the intense anxieties reinforced by mouthwash commercials on television because we at least feel that we are doing the proper thing. In the most effective cases of associative advertising, people begin to talk like ad copy. We begin to sneer at those who own the wrong things. We all become enforcers for the advertisers. In general, if the advertising images are effective enough and reach enough people, even preposterous marketing claims can become at least partially self-fulfilling.

Most of us are easily able to recognize associative advertising as morally problematic when the consequences are clear, extreme, and our own desires and purchasing habits are not at stake. For example, the marketing methods Nestlé used in Africa involved associative advertising. Briefly, Nestlé identified a large market for its infant formula—without concern for the wellbeing of the prospective consumers. In order to induce poor women to buy formula rather than breast-feed, Nestlé selected non-market goods on which to base its campaigns—love for one's child and a desire to be acceptable by being modern. These appeals were effective (much as they are in advertising for children's clothing, toys, and computers in the U.S.A.). Through billboards and radio advertising, Nestlé identified parental love with formula feeding and suggested that formula is the modern way to feed a baby. Reports indicate that in some cases mothers of dead babies placed cans of formula on their graves to show that the parents cared enough to do the very best they could for their children, even though we know the formula may have been a contributing cause of death.[4]

One might be tempted to believe that associative advertising is an objectionable technique only when used on the very poorest, most powerless and ignorant people and that it is the poverty, powerlessness, and ignorance which are at fault. An extreme example like the Nestlé case, one might protest, surely doesn't tell us much about more ordinary associative advertising in the industrialized western nations. The issues will become clearer if we look at the conceptions of virtue and vice at stake.

Dewey says "the thing actually at stake in any serious deliberation is not a difference of quantity [as utilitarianism would have us believe], but what kind of person one is to become, what sort of self is in the making, what kind of a world one is making."[5] Similarly, I would like to ask who we become as we use or are used by associative advertising. This will not be a decisive argument. I have not found clear, compelling, objective principles—only considerations I find persuasive and which I expect many others to find similarly persuasive. I will briefly examine how associative advertising affects (a) the people who plan and execute marketing strategies and (b) the people who are exposed to the campaign.

(a) Many advertisers[6] come to think clearly and skillfully about how to sell a marketable item by associating it with a non-market good which people in the target market desire. An important ingredient in this process is lack of concern for the well-being of the people who will be influenced by the campaign. Lloyd Slater, a consultant who discussed the infant formula controversy with people in both the research and development and marketing divisions of Nestlé, says that the R & D people had made sure that the formula was nutritionally sound but were troubled or even disgusted by what the marketing department was doing. In contrast, Slater reports that the marketing people simply did not care and that "those guys aren't even human" in their reactions.[7] This evidence is only anecdotal and it concerns an admittedly extreme case. Still, I believe that the effects of associative advertising[8] would most likely be the same but less pronounced in more ordinary cases. Furthermore, it is quite common for advertisers in the U.S.A. to concentrate their attention on selling something that is harmful to many people, e.g., candy that rots our teeth, and cigarettes. In general, influencing people without concern for their well-being is likely to reduce one's sensitivity to the moral motive of concern for the well-being of others. Compassion, concern, and sympathy for others, it seems to me, are clearly central to moral virtue.[9] Associative advertising must surely undermine this sensitivity in much of the advertising industry. It is, therefore, *prima facie* morally objectionable.

(b) Targets of associative advertising (which include people in the advertising industry) are also made worse by exposure to effective advertising of this kind. The harm done is of two kinds:

(1) We often find that we are buying more but enjoying it less. It isn't only that products fail to live up to specific claims about service-life or effectiveness. More often, the motives ("reasons" would perhaps not be the right word here) for our purchases consistently lead to disappointment. We buy all the right stuff and yet have no more friends, lovers, excitement or respect than before. Instead, we have full closets and empty pocket books. Associative advertising, though not the sole cause, contributes to these results.

Associative advertising tends to desensitize its practitioners to the compassion, concern, and sympathy for others that are central to moral virtue and it encourages its audience to neglect the cultivation of non-market virtues.

---

(2) Associate advertising may be less effective as an advertising technique to sell particular products than it is as an ideology[10] in our culture. Within the advertising which washes over us daily we can see a number of common themes, but the most important may be "You are what you own."[11] The quibbles over which beer, soft drink, or auto to buy are less important than the overall message. Each product contributes its few minutes each day, but we are bombarded for hours with the message that friends, lovers, acceptance, excitement, and power are to be gained by purchases in the market, not by developing personal relationships, virtues, and skills. Our energy is channeled into careers so that we will have enough money to *be* someone by buying the right stuff in a market. The not very surprising result is that we neglect non-market methods of satisfying our non-market desires. Those non-market methods call for wisdom, compassion, skill, and a variety of virtues which cannot be bought. It seems, therefore, that insofar as associative advertising encourages us to neglect the non-market cultivation of our virtues and to substitute market goods instead, we become worse and, quite likely, less happy persons.

To sum up the argument so far, associative advertising tends to desensitize its practitioners to the compassion, concern, and sympathy for others that are central to moral virtue and it encourages its audience to neglect the cultivation of non-market virtues. There are at least five important objections that might be offered against my thesis that associative advertising is morally objectionable.

First, one could argue that since each of us is (or can easily be if we want to be) aware of what is going on in associative advertising, we must want to participate and find it objectionable. Accordingly, the argument goes, associative advertising is not a violation of individual autonomy. In order to reply to this objection I must separate issues.

(a) Autonomy is not the main, and certainly not the only, issue here. It may be that I can, through diligent self-examination neutralize much of the power of associative advertising. Since I can resist, one might argue that I am responsible for the results—*caveat emptor* with a new twist.[12] If one's methodology in ethics is concerned about people and not merely their autonomy, then the fact that most people are theoretically capable of resistance will be less important than the fact that most are presently unable to resist.

(b) What is more, the ideology of acquisitiveness which is cultivated by associative advertising probably undermines the intellectual and emotional virtues of reflectiveness and self-awareness which would better enable us to neutralize the harmful effects of associative advertising. I do not know of specific evidence to cite in support of this claim, but it seems to me to be confirmed in the ordinary experience of those who, despite associative advertising, manage to reflect on what they are exposed to.

(c) Finally, sneer group pressure often makes other people into enforcers so that there are penalties for not going along with the popular currents induced by advertising. We are often compelled even by our associates to be enthusiastic participants in the consumer culture. Arrington omits consideration of sneer group pressure as a form of compulsion which can be (though it is not always) induced by associative advertising.

So far my answer to the first objection is incomplete. I still owe some account of why more people do not complain about associative advertising. This will become clearer as I consider a second objection.

Second, one could insist that even if the non-market desires are not satisfied completely, they must be satisfied for the most part or we would stop falling for associative advertising. This objection seems to me to make three main errors:

(a) Although we have a kind of immediate access to our own motives and are generally able to see what motives an advertising campaign uses, most of us lack even the simple framework provided by my analysis of associative advertising. Even one who sees that a particular ad campaign is aimed at a particular non-market desire may not see how all the ads put together constitute a cultural bombardment with an ideology of acquisitiveness—you are what you own. Without some framework such as this, one has nothing to blame. It is not easy to gain self-reflective insight, much less cultural insight.

(b) Our attempts to gain insight are opposed by associative advertising which always has an answer for our dissatisfactions—buy more or newer or different things. If I find myself feeling let down after a purchase, many voices will tell me that the solution is to buy other things too (or that I have just bought the wrong thing). With all of this advertising proposing one kind of answer for our dissatisfactions, it is scarcely surprising that we do not usually become aware of alternatives.

(c) Finally, constant exposure to associate advertising changes[13] us so that we come to feel acceptable as persons when and only when we own the acceptable, fashionable things. By this point, our characters and conceptions of virtue already largely reflect the result of advertising and we are unlikely to complain or rebel.

Third, and perhaps most pungent of the objections, one might claim that by associating mundane marketable items with deeply rooted non-market desires, our everyday lives are invested with new and greater meaning. Charles Revson of Revlon once said that "In the factory we make cosmetics: in the store we sell hope."[14] Theodore Levitt, in his passionate defense of associative advertising, contends that[15]

> Everyone in the world is trying in his [or her] special personal fashion to solve a primal problem of life—the problem of rising above his [or her] own negligibility, of escaping from nature's confining, hostile, and unpredictable reality, of finding significance, security, and comfort in the things he [or she] must do to survive.

Levitt adds, "Without distortion, embellishment, and elaboration, life would be drab, dull, anguished, and at its existential worst."[16] This objection is based on two assumptions so shocking that his conclusion almost seems sensible.

(a) Without associative advertising would our lives lack significance? Would we be miserable in our drab, dull, anguished lives? Of course not. People have always had ideals, fantasies, heroes, and dreams. We have always told stories that captured our aspirations and fears. The very suggestion that we require advertising to bring a magical aura to our shabby, humdrum lives is not only insulting but false.

(b) Associative advertising is crafted not in order to enrich our daily lives but in order to enrich the clients and does not have the interests of its audience at heart. Still, this issue of intent, though troubling, is only part of the problem. Neither is the main problem that associative advertising images somehow distort reality. Any work of art also is, in an important sense, a dissembling or distortion. The central question instead is whether the specific appeals and images, techniques and products, enhance people's lives.[17]

A theory of what enhances a life must be at least implicit in any discussion of the morality of associative advertising. Levitt appears to assume that in a satisfying life one has many satisfied desires—*which* desires is not important.[18] To propose and defend an alternative to his view is beyond the scope of this paper. My claim is more modest—that it is not enough to ask whether desires are satisfied. We should also ask what kinds of lives are sustained, made possible, or fostered by having the newly synthesized desires. What kind of self and world are in the making, Dewey would have us ask. This self and world are always in the making. I am not arguing that there is some natural, good self which advertising changes and contaminates. It may be that not only advertising, but also art, religion, and education in general, always synthesize new desires.[19] In each case, we should look at the lives. How to judge the value of these lives and the various conceptions of virtue they will embody is another question. It will be enough for now to see that it is an important question.

> **There is another legitimate concern besides that of autonomy and behavior control—whether the advertising will tend to influence us to become worse persons.**

Now it may be possible to see why I began by saying that I would suggest an alternative to the usual focus on autonomy and behavior control.[20] Arrington's defense of advertising (including, as near as I can tell, what I call associative advertising) seems to assume that we have no standard to which we can appeal to judge whether a desire enhances a life and, consequently, that our only legitimate concerns are whether an advertisement violates the autonomy of its audience by deceiving them or controlling their behavior. I want to suggest that there is another legitimate concern—whether the advertising will tend to influence us to become worse persons.[21]

Fourth, even one who is sympathetic with much of the above might object that associative advertising is necessary to an industrial society such as ours. Economists since Galbraith[22] have argued about whether, without modern advertising of the sort I have described, there would be enough demand to sustain our present levels of production. I have no answer to this question. It seems unlikely that associative advertising will end suddenly, so I am confident that we will have the time and the imagination to adapt our economy to do without it.

Fifth, and last, one might ask what I am proposing. Here I am afraid I must draw up short of my mark. I have no practical political proposal. It seems obvious to me that no broad legislative prohibition would improve matters. Still, it may be possible to make small improvements like some that we have already seen. In the international arena, Nestlé was censured and boycotted, the World Health Organization drafted infant formula marketing guidelines, and finally Nestlé agreed to change its practices. In the U.S.A., legislation prohibits cigarette advertising on television.[23] These are tiny steps, but an important journey may begin with them.

Even my personal solution is rather modest. *First*, if one accepts my thesis that associative advertising is harmful to its audience, then one ought to avoid doing it to others, especially if doing so would require that one dull one's compassion, concern, and sympathy for others. Such

initiatives are not entirely without precedent. Soon after the surgeon general's report on cigarettes and cancer in 1964, David Ogilvy and William Bernbach announced that their agencies would no longer accept cigarette accounts and *New Yorker* magazine banned cigarette ads.[24] *Second*, if I am even partly right about the effect of associative advertising on our desires, then one ought to expose oneself as little as possible. The most practical and effective way to do this is probably to banish commercial television and radio from one's life. This measure, though rewarding,[25] is only moderately effective. Beyond these, I do not yet have any answers.

In conclusion, I have argued against the advertising practice I call associative advertising. My main criticism is twofold: (a) Advertisers must surely desensitize themselves to the compassion, concern, and sympathy for others that are central emotions in a virtuous person, and (b) associative advertising influences its audience to neglect the nonmarket cultivation of our virtues and to substitute market goods instead, with the result that we become worse and, quite likely, less happy persons.

Notes

[1]Robert L. Arrington, "Advertising and Behavior Control," *Journal of Business Ethics*, 3–12.

[2]I prefer not to use the term "consumers" since it identifies us with our role in a market, already conceding part of what I want to deny.

[3]Arrington, 8.

[4]James B. McGinnis. *Bread and Justice* (New York: Paulist Press, 1979), 224. McGinnis cites as his source INFACT Newsletter, September 1977, 3. Formula is often harmful because poor families do not have the sanitary facilities to prepare the formula using clean water and utensils, do not have the money to be able to keep up formula feeding without diluting the formula to the point of starving the child, and formula does not contain the antibodies which a nursing mother can pass to her child to help immunize the child against common local bacteria. Good accounts of this problem are widely available.

[5]John Dewey, *Human Nature and Conduct* (New York: Random House, 1930), 202.

[6]This can be a diverse group including (depending upon the product) marketing specialists, sales representatives, or people in advertising agencies. Not everyone in one of these positions, however, is necessarily guilty of engaging in associative advertising.

[7]This story was told by Lloyd E. Slater at a National Science Foundation Chatauqua entitled "Meeting World Food Needs" in 1980–1981. It should not be taken as a condemnation of marketing professionals in other firms.

[8]One could argue that the deficiency in compassion, concern, and sympathy on the part of advertisers might be a result of self-selection rather than of associative advertising. Perhaps people in whom these moral sentiments are strong do not commonly go into positions using associative advertising. I doubt, however, that such self-selection can account for all the disregard of the audience's best interests.

[9]See Lawrence A. Blum, *Friendship, Altruism and Morality* (Boston: Routledge and Kegan Paul, 1980) for a defense of moral emotions against Kantian claims that emotions are unsuitable as a basis for moral judgment and that only a purely rational good will offers an adequate foundation for morality.

[10]I use "ideology" here in a descriptive rather than a pejorative sense. To be more specific, associative advertising commonly advocates only a part of a more comprehensive ideology. See Raymond Guess, *The Idea of a Critical Theory* (Cambridge University Press, 1981), 5–6.

[11]For an interesting discussion, see John Lachs, "To Have and To Be," *Personalist* 45 (Winter 1964), 5–14; reprinted in

John Lachs and Charles Scott, *The Human Search* (New York: Oxford University Press, 1981), 247–55.

[12]This is, in fact, the thrust of Arrington's arguments in "Advertising and Behavior Control."

[13]I do not mean to suggest that only associative advertising can have such ill effects. Neither am I assuming the existence of some natural, pristine self which is perverted by advertising.

[14]Quoted without source in Theodore Levitt, "The Morality (?) of Advertising," *Harvard Business Review*, July–August 1970; reprinted in Vincent Barry, *Moral Issues in Business*, (Belmont, CA: Wadsworth Publishing Company, 1979), 256.

[15]Levitt (in Barry), 252.

[16]Levitt (in Barry), 256.

[17]"Satisfying a desire would be valuable then if it sustained or made possible a valuable kind of life. To say this is to reflect the argument that in creating the wants he [or she] can satisfy, the advertiser (or the manipulator of mass emotion in politics or religion) is necessarily acting in the best interests of his [or her] public." Stanley Benn, "Freedom and Persuasion," *Australasian Journal of Philosophy* 45 (1969); reprinted in Beauchamp and Bowie, *Ethical Theory and Business*, second edition (Englewood Cliffs, NJ: Prentice Hall, 1983), 374.

[18]Levitt's view is not new. "Continual success in obtaining those things which a man from time to time desires—that is to say, continual prospering—is what men call felicity." Hobbes, *Leviathan* (Indianapolis: Bobbs-Merrill, 1958), 61.

[19]This, in fact, is the principal criticism von Hayek offered of Galbraith's argument against the "dependence effect." F. A. von Hayek, "The Non Sequitur of the 'Dependence Effect,'" *Southern Economic Journal*, April 1961; reprinted in Tom L. Beauchamp and Norman F. Bowie, *Ethical Theory and Business*,

second edition (Englewood Cliffs, New Jersey: Prentice Hall, 1983), 363–66.

[20]Taylor R. Durham, "Information, Persuasion, and Control in Moral Appraisal of Advertising," *The Journal of Business Ethics* 3, 179. Durham also argues that an exclusive concern with issues of deception and control leads us into errors.

[21]One might object that this requires a normative theory of human nature, but it seems to me that we can go fairly far by reflecting on our experience. If my approach is to be vindicated, however, I must eventually provide an account of how, in general, we are to make judgments about what is and is not good (or life-enhancing) for a human being. Clearly, there is a large theoretical gulf between me and Arrington, but I hope that my analysis of associative advertising shows that my approach is plausible enough to deserve further investigation.

[22]The central text for this problem is *The Affluent Society* (Houghton Mifflin, 1958). The crucial passages are reprinted in many anthologies, e.g., John Kenneth Galbraith. "The Dependence Effect," in W. Michael Hoffman and Jennifer Mills Moore, *Business Ethics Readings and Cases in Corporate Morality* (New York: McGraw-Hill, 1984), 328–33.

[23]"In March 1970 Congress removed cigarette ads from TV and radio as of the following January. (The cigarette companies transferred their billings to print and outdoor advertising. Cigarette sales reached new records.)" Stephen Fox, *The Mirror Makers: A History of American Advertising and Its Creators* (New York: William Morrow and Co., 1984), 305.

[24]Stephen Fox, 303–4.

[25]See, for example, Jerry Mander, *Four Arguments for the Elimination of Television* (New York: Morrow Quill Paperbacks, 1977).

Questions for Discussion:

1. What is associative advertising? What is Waide's assessment of it? Do you agree?
2. Do you agree with Waide that associative advertising encourages people to consider market commodities as solutions to non-market needs? Explain your answer.

Making Consumers

Rodney Clapp

From "Why the Devil Takes Visa," *Christianity Today* (7 October 1996): 18–20.

It would be a gross distortion to act as if Protestantism alone invented and sustained consumer capitalism, though Protestantism's effects are significant if we are to understand the influence of consumerism on Christians. Still, it is crucial to note other historical factors essential to the birth and growth of consumerism. In terms of the push and pull of the everyday economy, historians are agreed that production-oriented capitalism moved on to become consumption-oriented capitalism because capitalism itself was so successful.

Until the twentieth century, most American homes were sites not only of consumption but of production. Even as late as 1850, six out of ten people worked on farms. They made most of their own tools; they built their homes and barns; they constructed their furniture; they wove and sewed their clothes; they grew crops and animals, producing food and drink; they chopped wood and made candles to provide heat and light. One nineteenth-century Massachusetts farmer, for instance, produced so much of what he needed at home that he never spent more than $10 a year.

The Industrial Revolution changed all that, very quickly. As the factory system and mass production came to dominance over the space of decades, it displaced home production by cheaply producing a host of commodities formerly made at home, driving out cottage industry and forcing millions into wage labor. From 1859 to 1899, the value of manufactured goods in the United States shot from $1.9 billion to $13 billion. Factories grew from 140,000 to 512,000.

Rather suddenly, this economic system could produce many more goods than the existing population, with its set habits and means, could afford and consume. For instance, when James Buchanan Duke procured merely two Bonsack cigarette machines, he could immediately produce 240,000 cigarettes a day—more than the entire U.S. market smoked. Such overproduction was the rule, not the exception, throughout the economy. From flour manufacturers to stovemakers, there was a widespread and acute recognition that the amount of goods available had far surpassed the number of buyers for those goods. Further, new products emerged for which markets needed to be developed. For instance, when Henry P. Crowell of Quaker Oats (benefactor of Moody Bible Institute, where a building is named after him) built an automated mill in 1882, most Americans ate meat and potatoes, not cereal, for breakfast.

There was, in short, a huge gap between production and consumption. How to close it? Industrial production's momentum had already built up, so cutting production was not feasible. Manufacturers decided instead to pump up consumption, to increase demand to meet supply. But they realized consumption was a way of life that had to be taught and learned. People had to move away from habits of strict thrift toward habits of ready spending. To be adequate consumers, they had to depart from a dependence on traditional skills, on production by families and artisans and local merchants. They had to learn to trust and rely on a multitude of products and services manufactured and promoted from far away by complete strangers.

By trial and error, manufacturers arrived at methods for reshaping people's economic habits. They instituted money-back guarantees and credit buying. They created brand names and mascots to give their mass-produced goods an appealing "personality." They introduced mail order and, as in the case of Sears, coached and reassured semiliterate customers to order by post ("Tell us what you want in your own way, written in any language, no matter whether good or poor writing, and the goods will promptly be sent to you"). And, of course, they advertised.

The Cultivation of Consumers

Many other factors were important in the rise of consumerism, but since advertising is the most insistent and undisguised face of advanced consumption, it merits special attention.

Until the late nineteenth century, advertising had been mainly informational. Advertising pages in eighteenth-century newspapers looked like the classifieds in today's papers. There were no pictures and, rather like news items, the ads simply did such things as announce when a shipment of rice would arrive from the Carolinas. But faced with a mass market and the crises of overproduction, manufacturers by the late nineteenth century initiated an advertising revolution. New advertising departed the realm of pure information, incorporating images and a host of persuasive tactics. It was, and remains, a primary tool in teaching people how to be consumers.

Early twentieth-century advertising, for instance, was used by Colgate to teach people who had never heard of toothpaste that they should brush their teeth daily. King Gillette, the inventor of the disposable razor, coaxed men to shave daily and to do it themselves, not see a barber. Thus his ads included shaving lessons, with leads such as "Note the Angle Stroke." Eastman Kodak advertising tutored the masses in making the portable camera their "family historian." Food manufacturers published cookbooks training housewives to cook with exact measures of (branded) products. Newly enabled by preservatives and far-flung distribution networks, Domino Gold Syrup sought in 1919 explicitly to "educate" people that syrup was not only for wintertime pancakes. Said the sales manager, "Our belief is that the entire year is syrup season and the people must be educated to believe this is a fact."

The effectiveness of advertising in selling any specific product remains debatable. What cannot be doubted is that early advertising successfully

introduced an expansive array of products and services, playing a key role in the replacement of traditional home production by store-bought commodities. Furthermore, advertising and related media have served and still serve as important shapers of an ethos that has the good life attained through acquisition and consumption, and that would have its inhabitants constantly yearning for new products and new experiences.

Indeed, advertisers soon recognized that they must not simply cater to pre-existing needs, but create new needs. As Crowell of Quaker Oats noted, "[My aim in advertising] was to do educational and constructive work so as to awaken an interest in and create a demand for cereals where none existed." And as *The Thompson Red Book on Advertising* put it more generally in 1901, "Advertising aims to teach people that they have wants, which they did not recognize before, and where such wants can be best supplied." Consequently, one newspaper reader in 1897 said that not so long ago people "skipped [ads] unless some want compelled us to read, while now we read to find out what we really want."

Advertisers did not act alone in training consumers. Government began in the early twentieth century to solidify and boost the newly emerged strength of business corporations, capping this alliance with Herbert Hoover's expansion of the Department of Commerce in the 1920s. Schools quite self-consciously cooperated with corporations in molding young consumers.

One 1952 Whirlpool short-subject film, for instance, featured three teenage girls around a kitchen table, at work on a report about the emancipation of women. Did emancipation equal winning the vote? Assuming property and other legal rights? No, the girls decide, as the host rises from the table to attend a shiny washing machine. Real emancipation came with release from the drudgery of chores, with washing machines and dryers that liberated women from clotheslines and "dark basements." *Business Screen* magazine gave clear instruction for the film's use in its review: "Some good clean selling takes place during this half-hour. The film will have special appeal to women's groups of all kinds and to home economics classes from teenage on up."

Consumers, in short, were made, not born.

The Deification of Dissatisfaction

Into the nineteenth century, then, advertising and consumption were oriented to raw information and basic needs. It was only in the late nineteenth and then the twentieth century, with the maturation of consumer capitalism, that a shift was made toward the cultivation of unbounded desire. We must appreciate this to realize that late modern consumption, consumption as we now know it, is not fundamentally about materialism or the consumption of physical goods. Affluence and consumer-oriented capitalism have moved us well beyond the undeniable efficiencies and benefits of refrigerators and indoor plumbing. Instead, in a fun-house world of ever-proliferating wants and exquisitely unsatisfied desire, consumption entails most profoundly the cultivation of pleasure, the pursuit of novelty, and the chasing after illusory experiences associated with material goods.

Sex appeal sells everything from toothpaste to automobiles. (Recently, a cancer-detection ad on the back of a Christian magazine headlined, "Before you read this, take your clothes off." Then, in fine print, it counseled how to do bodily self-examinations.) Often, cigarette and alcohol ads do not even depict their product being consumed, but instead prime us to associate them with robust cowboys and spectacular mountain vistas. By 1989, the American Association of Advertising Agencies explicitly stated that consumer *perceptions* "are a fundamental part of manufacturing the product—as much as size, shape, color, flavor, design, or raw materials."

In 1909, an advertising manager for Winton Motor Cars representing the old school had declared, "When a man buys an automobile he purchases a specific entity, made of so much iron, steel, brass, copper, leather, wood, and horsehair, put together in a specific form and manner.... Why attract his attention to the entity by something that is foreign thereto? Has the car itself not sufficient

merit to attain that attention? Why suggest 'atmosphere,' which is something he cannot buy?"

But by 1925, "atmosphere" no longer seemed beyond the reach of the market. In that year advertising copywriter John Starr Hewitt wrote, "No one has ever in his life bought a mere piece of merchandise—per se. What he buys is the satisfaction of a physical need or the gratification of some dream about his life."

In the same year, Ernest Elmo Calkins, the cofounder of the Calkins and Holden ad agency, observed, "I have spent much of my life trying to teach the business man that beauty has a dollars-and-cents value, because I feel that only thus will it be produced in any quantity in a commercial age." Calkins recognized that, in his words, "Modernism offered the opportunity of expressing the inexpressible, of suggesting not so much the motor car as speed, not so much a gown as style, not so much a compact as beauty." All, of course, with a dollars-and-cents value attached.

Thus speed, style, beauty, sex, love, spirituality have all become for the modern consumer categories to be evoked and sampled at will by selecting from a vast array of products, services, and commodified experiences. Colin Campbell considers contemporary tourism a prime example. Tourism as an industry and a commodity depends for its survival on an insatiable yearning for "ever-new objects to gaze at." The same can be said for shopping, spectator sports, concert-going, movie-viewing, and other quintessential "consumer" activities. "Modern consumers will desire a novel rather than a familiar product because this enables them to believe that its acquisition and use will supply experiences they have not encountered to date in reality." Moreover, as those many now blissfully lost in cyberspace will attest, reality can be decidedly more inconvenient and less purely pleasurable than virtual reality.

In 1627, Francis Bacon's *New Atlantis* dreamed of a utopia in which technology could adjust growing seasons and create synthetic fruit tastier and better looking than natural fruit. In our culture, the New Atlantis has, after a fashion, come into being, and its plenty includes cosmetically enhanced fruit, artificial sweeteners, nonalcoholic beer, and fat-free junk food.

Yet, as Campbell reminds us, actual consumption is "likely to be a literally disillusioning experience, since real products cannot possibly supply the same quality of perfected pleasure as that which attends imaginatively enjoyed experiences." So we modern consumers are perpetually dissatisfied. Fulfillment and lasting satisfaction are forever just out of reach. And if we cannot escape completely to cyberspace, we reach for and grab again and again the product or commodified experience that provides temporary pleasure.

We are profoundly schooled and thousands of times daily reinforced—remember, the average American is exposed to more than three thousand sales messages daily—in an insatiability that is, as the theologian Miroslav Volf remarks, "unique to modernity." Insatiability itself is as old as humanity, or at least the fall of humanity. What is unique to modern consumerism is the idealization and constant encouragement of insatiability—the deification of dissatisfaction.

Economics and the consumerism it serves is, as the economist Robert Nelson candidly admits, "our modern theology." Modernity is that age that has believed in the future against the past, in limitless progress that would eliminate not just the practical but the moral and spiritual problems of humanity. Many of the major concerns and practices of classical Christianity were accordingly redefined along economic lines. Material scarcity and the resulting conflict over precious resources were seen as the sources of human sinfulness. So economic progress and the building of consumer societies has "represented the route of salvation to a new heaven on earth." Economic efficiency has for many replaced the providence of God.

Christian missionaries traveled to spread the gospel; economic theology has missionaries such as the Peace Corps and international development agencies, delivering the good news of "economic progress, rational knowledge, and human redemption." Christianity saw the coming of Christ as history's supreme revelatory moment. Economic theology, or a theology of consumption, considers it to be the discoveries of modern science and technology. And twentieth-century religious wars are no longer fought between Roman Catholics and various Protestants, but "among men often inspired by Marxist, fascist, capitalist, and still other messages of economic salvation" (Robert Nelson).

The Importance of Character

"Whoever has the power to project a vision of the good life and make it prevail," the historian William Leach writes, "has the most decisive power of all. In its sheer quest to produce and sell goods cheaply in constantly growing volume and at higher profit levels, American business, after 1890, acquired such power and has kept it ever since."

Since consumer capitalism—today not just in America but around the world—so effectively promotes its version of the good life, and since consumers are made rather than born, a Christian response demands a consideration of character.

Every culture or way of life requires a certain kind of person—a "character" with fitting attitudes, skills, and motivations—to sustain and advance the good life as that culture knows it. Thus Sparta was concerned to shape its citizens in the character of the warrior; Aristotle hoped for a polity that would make aristocrats; and twentieth-century America charged its public schools with the task of instilling the American way of life in their students.

In the postwar boom days of 1955, retailing analyst Victor Lebow echoed his advertising predecessors, declaring, "Our enormously productive economy . . . demands that we make consumption our way of life, that we convert the buying and use of goods into rituals, that we seek our spiritual satisfaction, our ego satisfaction, in consumption. . . . We need things consumed, burned up, worn out, replaced, and discarded at an ever increasing rate."

Can there be any doubt that we now live in the world Lebow prophesied and desired? That shopping has become a conspicuous ritual profoundly indicative of our social ethic is facetiously but tellingly betrayed in such slogans as "I shop, therefore I am," and "They came, they saw, they did a little shopping," scrawled on the Berlin Wall shortly after East Germans were allowed to pass freely into West Germany.

Planned obsolescence, installment buying, and credit cards—all creations of this century—were key means to making consumption a way of life. Now, as with President Bush a few years ago, public officials dutifully appear on the evening news buying a pair of socks to inaugurate the Christmas season.

Our language is one significant indication that consumption is a way of life. We are encouraged to see and interpret more and more of our activities in terms of consumption. In the language of marketers, people who go to movies are not "audiences," but "consumers"; those who go to school are no longer "students," but "educational consumers." People who visit a physician are no longer "patients," those who go to church are no longer "worshipers," those who go to libraries and bookstores are no longer "readers," those who go to restaurants are no longer "diners." All are as frequently designated "consumers."

The church must examine and challenge consumerism at exactly this point. What sort of people does consumer capitalism want us to be? What are the key character traits of the consumer par excellence? And how do these stack up against the standards and aims of Christian character?

Questions for Discussion:

1. What do you think of Clapp's assessment of American consumer culture? Do you think he is correct, or has he overstated the case? Explain your answer.
2. Why do you think there is such a taboo on discussing what we do with our money?
3. Do you think it is necessary as a Christian to resist the consumer culture? If so, what would you suggest as some practical ways to get started?

CASE STUDIES

Case 9.1: Diamonds Are Forever

One popular advertisement for engagement rings sponsored by the DeBeers Diamond Company poses the following question to men planning proposal: "Is two-months salary too much to spend?"

Many suitors take "two-months salary" as an unwritten rule of etiquette and as a measurement of how well they've faired in the jewelry aspect of courtship. However, "two months" is not written in any well-known traditional books on wedding etiquette. It seems to simply be an extremely effective creation of the DeBeers Company, which controls a large share of the world diamond market.

While wedding rings were traditionally regarded as symbols of vows to lifelong commitment, today they symbolize wealth and, at least to some, how much the suitor loves his bride-to-be. Givers and receivers of the glittering objects can be regularly comparing the caret weight and cost of their "symbols" with friends and family members.

This seems like a clear situation in which the diamond business has violated consumer autonomy by creating a new "need" through exploiting the basic human desire to fit in and impress others. For some potential suitors, simply saying no in the face of social pressures is difficult. But advertisers would probably respond that they are simply fulfilling latent human desires rather than creating them.

Questions for Discussion:

1. Is the prevalence of the belief of the "two-months salary rule" proof of the power of advertisers to create needs by exploiting human insecurity? Why or why not?
2. If so, does this unjustly violate the autonomy of consumers?

Case 9.2: School-Based Marketing

Many major corporations sponsor in-school promotional programs. *Channel One*, the news and "current events" television program seen in 40 percent of the nation's schools is laced with commercials. Some organizations market in a more subtle way by providing curricular materials splashed with the company's logo or products. For example, an exercise that purports to teach third-graders math has them counting Tootsie Rolls. Others advertise outright by purchasing billboard space in the schools and on the sides of school buses.[4]

One of the more controversial practices is the arrangement of exclusive deals between school districts and soft-drink companies. In exchange for large cash payments, school districts give the companies exclusive rights to aggressively sell their products on campuses. Rival companies have sometimes competed for these rights, driving up the price of the contracts into the millions of dollars. For example, school district officials in Colorado Springs signed an agreement with Coca-Cola under which the school district will receive $8.4 million over ten years, with the chance to earn more if it exceeds its requirement of selling 70,000 cases of Coke products a year.[5]

Critics fear that in order to meet these types of incentives, schools will move vending machines to where students will be allowed virtually unlimited access to Coke products all day, which could lead to nutrition problems. A recent medical study published in *The Lancet* (a medical journal) linked obesity to soft drink consumption, and a report from the U.S. Agriculture Department raised concerns that soda was replacing school lunches (often paid for by taxpayers) for many children.[6]

Supporters of these contracts argue that they represent a novel way to increase resources for financially strapped school districts, especially in places such as Colorado Springs where voters have not passed a tax levy to support schools for over two decades.

However, opponents of these arrangements are alarmed about the increase of commercialism in schools, once a safe haven from advertising. In addition to current sales of products, critics see these attempts as means of cultivating the loyalty of a young captive audience by "branding" teenagers at an early age. Other critics look at the long-term horizon and see a trend toward an increasing dependence on corporate funding for schools, which may discourage public prioritization of education and reinforce the distinctions between wealthy and poor school districts.[7]

[4] For further examples of school-based marketing, see the PBS film, *Affluenza*.

[5] Steve Manning, "Students for Sale," *The Nation*, 27 September 1999.

[6] Marc Kaufman, "Coca-Cola Tries to Cap Exclusive School Deals, *Washington Post*, 14 March 2001, A2.

[7] Manning, "Students for Sale."

Question for Discussion:

Should advertisers stay out of schools and respect them as a "commercial free" zone? If not, what limits should they abide by in attempting to advertise to school-aged children and teenagers?

COMMENTARY

With rapid advances in technology and increasingly close economic connections across the globe, the presence and influence of advertising has impressively expanded. Many business leaders see an unprecedented opportunity to increase the size and scope of markets, while critics bemoan the prospect of increased intrusions into the physical, psychological, and spiritual dimensions of life.

While the physical ubiquity of advertising is controversial, it is largely a secondary issue. The mere spread of advertising would be at worst an annoyance if commercial communications possessed little in the way of real power to alter behavior. Thus, the more important foundational issues to be considered are advertising's power and persuasiveness, and the methods it employs.

Some criticisms of these dimensions of advertising merit serious consideration. Rodney Clapp is correct to point out that while individual ads have questionable amounts of influence, the aggregated message of advertising encourages a philosophy of shallow consumerism. As an ethos of "instant gratification" spreads into other areas of life, spiritual and moral values necessary to sustain meaningful relationships, such as family and community ties, can erode.

John Waide also correctly inquires about the type of world we are making through associative advertising. He asks if advertising "will tend to influence us to become worse persons." Instead of the cultivation of virtues, he asserts, advertising contributes to a culture in which people seek security in material goods that promise non-market goods such as friendship and joy. It is obvious that there is no way for market goods to fulfill these deep needs of human beings. While advertising cannot be blamed for creating shallow values, it undoubtedly perpetuates them.

While these criticisms are valid, persuasive advertising is not necessarily at odds with Christian values. An outright rejection of the enterprise is much too simplistic. Advertising has played an irreplaceable role in raising standards of living across the globe. While the needs of people should not be reduced to economic terms, increased life spans, improved physical health, educational achievement, and other measures of human well-being often accompany economic development.

Examining the intrinsic nature of advertising, Theodore Levitt is probably correct that advertising may not be as pernicious as some observers allege. Consumers often demand the use of "symbolic communications" by advertisers. Advertising packages products and services in a manner that appeals to the often latent, but real desires of consumers. Repeat purchases serve as one piece of evidence that some desires are, in fact, met.

While advertising may not be as powerful as some critics would suggest, however, neither is it as benign as some of its supporters portray it. It is a business practice that should be approached with caution. The critical moral challenge is to appropriately manage the real tension inherent in preserving and enhancing the legitimate social contributions of advertising while curbing its morally questionable elements.

Advertising is undoubtedly a powerful force that can influence and persuade by appealing to human desires in questionable ways. Some defenses of advertising, such as Levitt's, assume that a good life is one in which many desires are satisfied but stop short of asking if some desires are more legitimate or important than others. Indeed, it seems critical to ask if an appeal to *any* emotion, insecurity, or need, just because people have it, is as morally neutral as Levitt implicitly assumes.

Most would agree that appeals to healthy needs met with good products and services serve an important and justifiable function in a robust and growing economy. For example, commercials for long-distance telephone services, in which keeping in touch with friends and family is emphasized, is a legitimate social function that can be met. Furthermore, many public service advertisements portray the consequences of tobacco, drug, and alcohol abuse. There is little debate over whether the prevention of substance abuse is a service worth selling through appeals to healthy amounts of human fear.

In contrast, some campaigns clearly traverse the bounds of healthy persuasion. For example, many messages capitalize on insecurities about not fitting in. Others actively cultivate dissatisfaction through comparative statements about taste and/or status. More overtly, some campaigns attempt to appeal to raw sexual power. In many of the ads, the product itself is not the primary focus. Rather, provocatively dressed actors or models are used to grab attention and to lead the consumer to associate the product with sexual power or feelings. A disturbing aspect of these campaigns is that appeals to these parts of the psyche seem so unnecessary. There are countless examples of campaigns that rely instead on more appropriate expressions of creativity.

Some advertisers defend the use of these avenues by stating that they reflect cultural values rather than create them. Thus, in reality, advertising simply gives consumers what they want. Indeed, advertisements have to reflect cultural values to some degree, or they would be dismissed outright. But is the simple reflection of societal values morally sufficient? Are advertisers free from any moral responsibility to appeal to healthier parts of the human psyche?

The practice of responsible advertising surely suggests limits. Appealing to an insecurity, fear, or desire simply because it can be successfully targeted is morally deficient. Although advertisements do not create questionable social values, they can and do powerfully reinforce them. Furthermore, the claim that advertising merely "reflects reality" is untruthful. The physical beauty of portrayed products and people is often enhanced by computer technology, creating a type of unreality. Advertising can be described as a distorted mirror, at best.

Businesses that seek to be ethical in terms of the methods of appeal employed must respect human well-being and the "world" that they are making. As John Waide states it, creating ads that "influence people without concern for their well-being is likely to reduce one's sensitivity to the moral motive of concern for the well-being of others."

This is all the more the case when attempting to sell products to vulnerable members of a target audience who do not meet a "reasonable consumer" standard.[8] For example, young children are becoming constant targets of a wide variety of advertising, including traditional broadcast media, packaging, and product placement. Most pernicious is the attempt to "brand" children at an early age in the attempt to create loyal long-term consumers.[9] These attempts work against the interests of parents and create family conflicts. Clearly, children cannot be expected to bear the responsibilities accorded to a rational consumer in the marketplace. Thus, in almost all cases, children should be off limits as targets of commercial messages.

Ethical considerations should also place limits on the physical reach of advertising. Commercial messages are now often seen in places once deemed off limits. In addition to the new venues discussed in this chapter's introduction, school-age children now see advertising on *Channel One*, in hallways, and in the form of overtly branded "learning" materials.

In all likelihood, technology will continue to embolden and empower advertising. The mixing and matching of information found in powerful computer databases will allow advertisers to come ever closer to the once unimaginable goal of tailoring messages to *individual* consumers.

With the possibility for damaging effects on both our individual and collective identities, a Christian response to advertising is necessarily cautious and critical. It is our firm belief, however, that advertising is not in and of itself contrary to Christian ethics. It can be practiced in a responsible manner. The following guidelines, while

[8] The "reasonable consumer" standard is widely used when trying to determine what a consumer should have known in legal disputes over advertising, particularly accusations of false and misleading campaigns.

[9] In the film *Affluenza*, cameras record a session of a conference called "Kid Power." The conference is not about empowering children, but about how to successfully market products and services to them. One presenter uses terms such as "branding them and owning them" in reference to children.

admittedly broad, can be used to help develop ads in a morally responsible manner:

First, advertising should be open and honest. While it is unfair to accuse most advertisements of deception, since most consumers can see through their claims, some campaigns can be misleading. Businesspeople who use advertising must be sensitive to claims or graphics that could mislead the audience.

Second, appeals should be made to healthier parts of the human psyche. Sexuality and insecurities such as social acceptance are part of our natural makeup. However, they should not be taken advantage of in order to make a sale. Healthy values such as true friendship and physical and social well-being are more appropriate means to reach an audience.

Third, advertisers should be mindful of the vulnerable. The interpretative lenses of children, the elderly, new immigrants, and perhaps citizens of developing nations who have yet to develop the sophistication to see through messages we take for granted must be taken into consideration.

Fourth, advertising should be "broadcast" (and "narrow cast" in the case of customized data base–driven marketing) in the least invasive manner possible. To a large degree, a person's "space" and when it becomes violated is a culturally defined matter. Therefore, it is difficult to give set guidelines without being unduly and inappropriately legalistic. The more important point is that each culture has a point where "sacred" space may be violated. For sound moral (and business) reasons, advertisers would do well to respect these boundaries.

TEN

Environmental Stewardship

The environmental crisis is fundamentally a crisis of the West's anthropocentric philosophical and religious orientations and values.

George Sessions[1]

The Judeo-Christian peoples were probably the first to develop on a large scale a pervasive concern for land management and an ethic of nature.

Rene Dubos[2]

1 George Sessions, Introduction (to Part II, "Deep Ecology"), in Michael Zimmerman, ed., *Environmental Philosophy: From Animal Rights to Radical Ecology* (Englewood Cliffs, N.J.: Prentice Hall, 1993), 161.

2 Rene Dubos, *A God Within* (New York: Scribner's, 1972), 161.

INTRODUCTION

In the past twenty-five years, the environmental movement has succeeded at raising public awareness of the various dangers to the environment posed by industry, development, and population growth. Movements such as Greenpeace and Earth First reflect more radical views, but it is clear that movements such as these have made significant inroads with the general public and particularly with those who make environmental policy. The result has been substantial progress in halting the spread of environmental damage as well as a backlash against what is becoming more widely perceived as environmental extremism. Though the environmentalists have been routinely opposed by business and industry leaders, the public has recently become more aware of the extremes of environmentalism and appears to desire a more balanced view of society's environmental responsibility. For example, the way endangered species such as the gnatcatcher, the spotted owl, and the kangaroo rat are protected at the expense of jobs, communities, and individual property rights has become troubling for many who see that the environment has become an end in itself and is being protected to an extreme at the expense of other important social goods.

To be sure, there have been cases of egregious environmental negligence in recent years that have justifiably stimulated a growing concern for the environment. The oil spill of the Exxon Valdez in Prince William Sound off the coast of Alaska left damage that will likely never be fully repaired despite the millions of dollars Exxon committed to the cleanup efforts. The nuclear disasters at Three Mile Island and Chernobyl illustrate the dangers of nuclear power and the need for extremely careful control of such power plants. The destruction of the Amazon rain forests seems to many to be a rampant and random destruction of a unique environmental habitat to make room for economic development in Latin America. Even the North American Free Trade Agreement (NAFTA) passed in the mid-1990s was controversial because of what many people perceive as lower environmental standards in Mexico. They fear that the agreement will allow American businesses to export their air and water pollution along with their products and jobs to areas that care more about economic development than about environmental protection.

Environmental awareness is even becoming more fashionable, with a wide variety of "green products" being advertised for their environmental sensitivity. These products range from biodegradable laundry detergent and other types of household cleaners to a wide variety of recycled products, particularly paper products made from recycled paper. Some green products, such as certain environmentally sensitive fashions and cosmetics, are even considered chic.[3] The well-publicized British body products chain "The Body Shop," which specializes in environmentally sensitive facial and body care products, has been very profitable since the late 1980s and early 1990s. The success of these products has prompted the charge that these companies are simply using environmental awareness as a marketing strategy and actually care very little for the environment. But the CEOs of many of these companies appear genuinely concerned for the environment and developed their products out of their environmental interest.

The central issue that this chapter addresses is how to maintain a proper balance between environmental protection and economic growth. Many protective environmental measures come at the expense of economic growth, and many economic development projects come at the expense of the environment. Environmental issues are thus often stated in terms of jobs versus the environment. There seems to be an almost inherent conflict between an expanding business and the environment. This is particularly acute for the underdeveloped countries of the Third World, who argue that they should be able to set their own priorities and not be bound to the developed first world's standards of environmental protection. How one balances con-

[3] Rose Marie Turk, "Lean, Mean and Green," *Los Angeles Times*, 25 April 1995, E1.

cern for the environment, particularly endangered species, with concerns about human well-being is at the heart of this issue that all too frequently pits business against environmental activists. Some of the cases in this chapter will challenge you to articulate how you would balance economic growth and the environment.

The readings in this chapter address a more fundamental issue, how one should view the environment. These are questions of one's worldview, which are philosophical and theological questions. The way one views the environment reveals one's philosophical and theological assumptions—about God, the natural world, and human beings' place vis-à-vis nature. As you read the selections in this chapter, be aware of the deeper assumptions underlying each view. Michael Hoffman outlines a view that is increasingly popular, especially in many religious circles, known as *biocentrism*. In his article, he argues that the environment has intrinsic value and should be respected irrespective of what it can contribute to human beings. He is critical of the long-standing view known as *homocentrism*, which holds that the environment only has instrumental value in what it can contribute to human development and well-being. By contrast, Thomas Sieger Derr offers an insightful critique of biocentrism and outlines a Christian approach to the environment. He also responds to the view, widely held in environmentalist circles, that Christian ethics is responsible for the misuse of the environment.

READINGS

Business and Environmental Ethics[1]

W. Michael Hoffman

Business Ethics Quarterly 1, no. 2 (1991): 169–84. Copyright © 1991.

Business has an ethical responsibility to the environment which goes beyond obeying environmental law.

The business ethics movement, from my perspective, is still on the march. And the environmental movement, after being somewhat silent for the past twenty years, has once again captured our attention—promising to be a major social force in the 1990s. Much will be written in the next few years trying to tie together these two movements. This is one such effort.

Concern over the environment is not new. Warnings came out of the 1960s in the form of burning rivers, dying lakes, and oil-fouled oceans. Radioactivity was found in our food, DDT in mother's milk, lead and mercury in our water. Every breath of air in the North American hemisphere was reported as contaminated. Some said these were truly warnings from Planet Earth of eco-catastrophe, unless we could find limits to our growth and changes in our lifestyle.

Over the past few years Planet Earth began to speak to us even more loudly than before, and we began to listen more than before. The message was ominous, somewhat akin to God warning Noah. It spoke through droughts, heat waves, and forest fires, raising fears of global warming due to the buildup of carbon dioxide and other gases in the atmosphere. It warned us by raw sewage and medical wastes washing up on our beaches, and by devastating oil spills—one despoiling Prince William Sound and its wildlife to such an extent that it made us weep. It spoke to us through increased skin cancers and discoveries of holes in the ozone layer caused by our use of chlorofluorocarbons. It drove its message home through the rapid and dangerous cutting and burning of our primitive forests at the rate of one football field a second, leaving us even more vulnerable to greenhouse gases like carbon dioxide and eliminating scores of irreplaceable species daily. It rained down on us in the form of acid, defoliating our forests and poisoning our lakes and streams. Its warnings were found on barges roaming the seas for places to dump tons of toxic incinerator ash. And its message exploded in our faces at Chernobyl and Bhopal, reminding us of past warnings at Three Mile Island and Love Canal.

Senator Albert Gore said in 1988: "The fact that we face an ecological crisis without any precedent in historic times is no longer a matter of any dispute worthy of recognition."[2] The question, he continued, is not whether there is a problem, but how we will address it. This will be the focal point for a public policy debate which requires the full participation of two of its major players—business and government. The debate must clarify such fundamental questions as: (1) What obligation does business have to help with our environ-

mental crisis? (2) What is the proper relationship between business and government, especially when faced with a social problem of the magnitude of the environment crisis? And (3) what rationale should be used for making and justifying decisions to protect the environment? Corporations, and society in general for that matter, have yet to answer these questions satisfactorily. In the first section of this paper I will briefly address the first two questions. In the final two sections I will say a few things about the third question.

I.

In a 1989 keynote address before the "Business, Ethics and the Environment" conference at the Center for Business Ethics, Norman Bowie offered some answers to the first two questions.

> Business does not have an obligation to protect the environment over and above what is required by law; however, it does have a moral obligation to avoid intervening in the political arena in order to defeat or weaken environmental legislation.[3]

I disagree with Bowie on both counts.

Bowie's first point is very Friedmanesque.[4] The social responsibility of business is to produce goods and services and to make profit for its shareholders, while playing within the rules of the market game. These rules, including those to protect the environment, are set by the government and the courts. To do more than is required by these rules is, according to this position, unfair to business. In order to perform its proper function, every business must respond to the market and operate in the same arena as its competitors. As Bowie puts this:

> An injunction to assist in solving societal problems [including depletion of natural resources and pollution] makes impossible demands on a corporation because, at the practical level, it ignores the impact that such activities have on profit.[5]

If, as Bowie claims, consumers are not willing to respond to the cost and use of environmentally friendly products and actions, then it is not the responsibility of business to respond or correct such market failure.

Bowie's second point is a radical departure from this classical position in contending that business should not lobby against the government's process to set environmental regulations. To quote Bowie:

> Far too many corporations try to have their cake and eat it too. They argue that it is the job of government to correct for market failure and then they use their influence and money to defeat or water down regulations designed to conserve and protect the environment.[6]

Bowie only recommends this abstinence of corporate lobbying in the case of environmental regulations. He is particularly concerned that politicians, ever mindful of their reelection status, are already reluctant to pass environmental legislation which has huge immediate costs and in most cases very long-term benefits. This makes the obligations of business to refrain from opposing such legislation a justified special case.

I can understand why Bowie argues these points. He seems to be responding to two extreme approaches, both of which are inappropriate. Let me illustrate these extremes by the following two stories.

At the Center's First National Conference on Business Ethics, Harvard Business School Professor George Cabot Lodge told of a friend who owned a paper company on the banks of a New England stream. On the first Earth Day in 1970, his friend was converted to the cause of environmental protection. He became determined to stop his company's pollution of the stream, and marched off to put his new-found religion into action. Later, Lodge learned his friend went broke, so he went to investigate. Radiating a kind of ethical purity, the friend told Lodge that he spent millions to stop the pollution and thus could no longer compete with other firms that did not follow his example. So the company went under, 500 people lost their jobs, and the stream remained polluted.

When Lodge asked why his friend hadn't sought help from the state or federal government for stricter standards for everyone, the man replied that was not the American way, that government should not interfere with business activity, and that private enterprise could do the job alone. In fact, he felt it was the social responsibility of business to solve environmental problems, so he was proud that he had set an example for others to follow.

The second story portrays another extreme. A few years ago "Sixty Minutes" interviewed a manager of a chemical company that was discharging effluent into a river in upstate New York. At the time, the dumping was legal, though a bill to prevent it was pending in Congress. The manager remarked that he hoped the bill would pass, and that he certainly would support it as a responsible citizen. However, he also said he approved of his company's efforts to defeat the bill and of the firm's policy of dumping wastes in the meantime. After all, isn't the proper role of business to make as much profit as possible within the bounds of law? Making the laws—setting the rules of the game—is the role of government, not business. While wearing his business hat the manager had a job to do, even if it meant doing something that he strongly opposed as a private citizen.

Both stories reveal incorrect answers to the questions posed earlier, the proof of which is found in the fact that neither the New England stream nor the New York river was made any cleaner. Bowie's points are intended to block these two extremes. But to avoid these extremes, as Bowie does, misses the real managerial and ethical failure of the stories. Although the paper company owner and the chemical company manager had radically different views of the ethical responsibilities of business, both saw business and government performing separate roles, and neither felt that business ought to cooperate with government to solve environmental problems.[7]

If the business ethics movement has led us anywhere in the past fifteen years, it is to the position that business has an ethical responsibility to become a more active partner in dealing with social concerns. Business must creatively find ways to become a part of solutions, rather than being a part of problems. Corporations can and must develop a conscience, as Ken Goodpaster and others have argued—and this includes an environmental conscience.[8] Corporations should not isolate themselves from participation in solving our environmental problems, leaving it up to others to find the answers and to tell them what not to do.

Corporations have special knowledge, expertise, and resources which are invaluable in dealing with the environmental crisis. Society needs the ethical vision and cooperation of all its players to solve its most urgent problems, especially one that involves the very survival of the planet itself. Business must work with government to find appropriate solutions. It should lobby for good environmental legislation and lobby against bad legislation, rather than isolating itself from the legislative process as Bowie suggests. It should not be ethically quixotic and try to go it alone, as our paper company owner tried to do, nor should it be ethically inauthentic and fight against what it believes to be environmentally sound policy, as our chemical company manager tried to do. Instead business must develop and demonstrate moral leadership.

There are examples of corporations demonstrating such leadership, even when this has been a risk to their self-interest. In the area of environmental moral leadership one might cite DuPont's discontinuing its Freon products, a $750-million-a-year-business, because of their possible negative effects on the ozone layer, and Proctor and Gamble's manufacture of concentrated fabric softener and detergents which require less packaging. But some might argue, as Bowie does, that the real burden for environmental change lies with consumers, not with corporations. If we as consumers are willing to accept the harm done to the environment by favoring environmentally unfriendly products, corporations have no moral obligation to change so long as they obey environmental law. This is even more the case, so the argument goes, if corporations must take risks or sacrifice profits to do so.

This argument fails to recognize that we quite often act differently when we think of ourselves

as *consumers* than when we think of ourselves as *citizens*. Mark Sagoff, concerned about our over-reliance on economic solutions, clearly characterizes this dual nature of our decision making.[9] As consumers, we act more often than not for ourselves; as citizens, we take on a broader vision and do what is in the best interests of the community. I often shop for things I don't vote for. I might support recycling referendums, but buy products in non-returnable bottles. I am not proud of this, but I suspect this is more true of most of us than not. To stake our environmental future on our consumer willingness to pay is surely shortsighted, perhaps even disastrous.

I am not saying that we should not work to be ethically committed citizen consumers, and investors for that matter. I agree with Bowie that "consumers bear a far greater responsibility for preserving and protecting the environment than they have actually exercised,"[10] but activities which affect the environment should not be left up to what we, acting as consumers, are willing to tolerate or accept. To do this would be to use a market-based method of reasoning to decide on an issue which should be determined instead on the basis of our ethical responsibilities as a member of a social community.

Furthermore, consumers don't make the products, provide the services, or enact the legislation which can be either environmentally friendly or unfriendly. Grass roots boycotts and lobbying efforts are important, but we also need leadership and mutual cooperation from business and government in setting forth ethical environmental policy. Even Bowie admits that perhaps business has a responsibility to educate the public and promote environmentally responsible behavior. But I am suggesting that corporate moral leadership goes far beyond public educational campaigns. It requires moral vision, commitment, and courage, and involves risk and sacrifice. I think business is capable of such a challenge. Some are even engaging in such a challenge. Certainly the business ethics movement should do nothing short of encouraging such leadership. I feel morality demands such leadership.

II.

If business has an ethical responsibility to the environment which goes beyond obeying environmental law, what criterion should be used to guide and justify such action? Many corporations are making environmentally friendly decisions where they see there are profits to be made by doing so. They are wrapping themselves in green where they see a green bottom line as a consequence. This rationale is also being used as a strategy by environmentalists to encourage more businesses to become environmentally conscientious. In December 1989 the highly respected Worldwatch Institute published an article by one of its senior researchers entitled "Doing Well by Doing Good" which gives numerous examples of corporations improving their pocketbooks by improving the environment. It concludes by saying that "fortunately, businesses that work to preserve the environment can also make a buck."[11]

In a recent Public Broadcast Corporation documentary entitled "Profit the Earth," several efforts are depicted of what is called the "new environmentalism" which induces corporations to do things for the environment by appealing to their self-interest. The Environmental Defense Fund is shown encouraging agribusiness in Southern California to irrigate more efficiently and profit by selling the water saved to the city of Los Angeles. This in turn will help save Mono Lake. EDF is also shown lobbying for emissions trading that would allow utility companies which are under their emission allotments to sell their "pollution rights" to those companies which are over their allotments. This is for the purpose of reducing acid rain. Thus the frequent strategy of the new environmentalists is to get business to help solve environmental problems by finding profitable or virtually costless ways for them to participate. They feel that compromise, not confrontation, is the only way to save the earth. By using the tools of the free enterprise system, they are in search of win-win solutions, believing that such solutions are necessary to take us beyond what we have so far been able to achieve.

I am not opposed to these efforts; in most cases I think they should be encouraged. There is certainly nothing wrong with making money while protecting the environment, just as there is nothing wrong with feeling good about doing one's duty. But if business is adopting or being encouraged to adopt the view that good environmentalism is good business, then I think this poses a danger for the environmental ethics movement—a danger which has an analogy in the business ethics movement.

As we all know, the position that good ethics is good business is being used more and more by corporate executives to justify the building of ethics into their companies and by business ethics consultants to gain new clients. For example, the Business Roundtable's *Corporate Ethics* report states:

> The corporate community should continue to refine and renew efforts to improve performance and manage change effectively through programs in corporate ethics . . . corporate ethics is a strategic key to survival and profitability in this era of fierce competitiveness in a global economy.[12]

And, for instance, the book *The Power of Ethical Management* by Kenneth Blanchard and Norman Vincent Peale states in big red letters on the cover jacket that "Integrity Pays! You Don't Have to Cheat to Win." The blurb on the inside cover promises that the book "gives hard-hitting, practical, *ethical* strategies that build profits, productivity, and long-term success."[13] Whoever would have guessed that business ethics could deliver all that! In such ways business ethics gets marketed as the newest cure for what ails corporate America.

Is the rationale that good ethics is good business a proper one for business ethics? I think not. One thing that the study of ethics has taught us over the past 2500 years is that being ethical may on occasion require that we place the interests of others ahead of or at least on par with our own interests. And this implies that the ethical thing to do, the morally right thing to do, may not be in our own self-interest. What happens when the right thing is not the best thing for the business?

Although in most cases good ethics may be good business, it should not be advanced as the only or even the main reason for doing business ethically. When the crunch comes, when ethics conflicts with the firm's interests, any ethics program that has not already faced up to this possibility is doomed to fail because it will undercut the rationale of the program itself. We should promote business ethics, not because good ethics is good business, but because we are morally required to adopt the moral point of view in all our dealings—and business is no exception. In business, as in all other human endeavors, we must be prepared to pay the costs of ethical behavior.

There is a similar danger in the environmental movement with corporations choosing or being wooed to be environmentally friendly on the grounds that it will be in their self-interest. There is the risk of participating in the movement for the wrong reasons. But what does it matter if business cooperates for reasons other than the right reasons, as long as it cooperates? It matters if business believes or is led to believe that it only has a duty to be environmentally conscientious in those cases where such actions either require no sacrifice or actually make a profit. And I am afraid this is exactly what is happening. I suppose it wouldn't matter if the environmental cooperation of business was only needed in those cases where it was also in business self-interest. But this is surely not the case, unless one begins to really reach and talk about that amorphous concept "long-term" self-interest. Moreover, long-term interests, I suspect, are not what corporations or the new environmentalists have in mind in using self-interest as a reason for environmental action.

I am not saying we should abandon attempts to entice corporations into being ethical, both environmentally and in other ways, by pointing out and providing opportunities where good ethics is good business. And there are many places where such attempts fit well in both the business and environmental ethics movements. But we must be careful not to cast this as the proper guidelines for business' ethical responsibility. Because when it is discovered that many ethical actions are not necessarily good for business, at least in the short-run, then the rationale based on self-interest will come up morally short, and both ethical movements will be seen as deceptive and shallow.

III.

What is the proper rationale for responsible business action toward the environment? A minimalist principle is to refrain from causing or prevent the causing of unwarranted harm, because failure to do so would violate certain moral rights not to be harmed. There is, of course, much debate over what harms are indeed unwarranted due to conflict of rights and questions about whether some harms are offset by certain benefits. Norm Bowie, for example, uses the harm principle, but contends that business does not violate it as long as it obeys environmental law. Robert Frederick, on the other hand, convincingly argues that the harm principle morally requires business to find ways to prevent certain harm it causes even if such harm violates no environmental law.[14]

However, Frederick's analysis of the harm principle is largely cast in terms of harm caused to human beings and the violation of rights of human beings. Even when he hints at the possible moral obligation to protect the environment when no one is caused unwarranted harm, he does so by suggesting that we look to what we, as human beings, value.[15] This is very much in keeping with a humanistic position of environmental ethics which claims that only human beings have rights or moral standing because only human beings have intrinsic value. We may have duties with regard to nonhuman things (penguins, trees, islands, etc.) but only if such duties are derivative from duties we have toward human beings. Nonhuman things are valuable only if valued by human beings.

Such a position is in contrast to a naturalistic view of environmental ethics which holds that natural things other than human beings are intrinsically valuable and have, therefore, moral standing. Some naturalistic environmentalists only include other sentient animals in the framework of being deserving of moral consideration; others include all things which are alive or which are an integral part of an ecosystem. This latter view is sometimes called a biocentric environmental ethic as opposed to the homocentric view which sees all moral claims in terms of human beings and their interests. Some characterize these two views as deep *versus* shallow ecology.

The literature on these two positions is vast and the debate is ongoing. The conflict between them goes to the heart of environmental ethics and is crucial to our making of environmental policy and to our perception of moral duties to the environment, including business. I strongly favor the biocentric view. And although this is not the place to try to adequately argue for it, let me unfurl its banner for just a moment.

A version of R. Routley's "last man" example[16] might go something like this: Suppose you were the last surviving human being and were soon to die from nuclear poisoning, as all other human and sentient animals have died before you. Suppose also that it is within your power to destroy all remaining life, or to make it simpler, the last tree which could continue to flourish and propagate if left alone. Furthermore you will not suffer if you do not destroy it. Would you do anything wrong by cutting it down? The deeper ecological view would say yes because you would be destroying something that has value in and of itself, thus making the world a poorer place.

It might be argued that the only reason we may find the tree valuable is because human beings generally find trees of value either practically or aesthetically, rather than the atoms or molecules they might turn into if changed from their present form. The issue is whether the tree has value only in its relation to human beings or whether it has a value deserving of moral consideration inherent in itself in its present form. The biocentric position holds that when we find something wrong with destroying the tree, as we should, we do so because we are responding to an intrinsic value in the natural object, not to a value we give to it. This is a view which argues against a humanistic

environmental ethic and which urges us to channel our moral obligations accordingly.

Why should one believe that nonhuman living things or natural objects forming integral parts of ecosystems have intrinsic value? One can respond to this question by pointing out the serious weaknesses and problems of human chauvinism.[17] More complete responses lay out a framework of concepts and beliefs which provides a coherent picture of the biocentric view with human beings as a part of a more holistic value system. But the final answer to the question hinges on what criterion one decides to use for determining moral worth—rationality, sentience, or a deeper biocentric one. Why should we adopt the principle of attributing intrinsic value to all living beings, or even to all natural objects, rather than just to human beings? I suspect Arne Naess gives as good an answer as can be given.

> Faced with the ever returning question of "Why?," we have to stop somewhere. Here is a place where we well might stop. We shall admit that the value in itself is something shown in intuition. We attribute intrinsic value to ourselves and our nearest, and the validity of further identification can be contested, and *is* contested by many. The negation may, however, also be attacked through a series of "whys?" Ultimately, we are in the same human predicament of having to start somewhere, at least for the moment. We must stop somewhere and treat where we then stand as a foundation.[18]

In the final analysis, environmental biocentrism is adopted or not depending on whether it is seen to provide a deeper, richer, and more ethically compelling view of the nature of things.

If this deeper ecological position is correct, then it ought to be reflected in the environmental movement. Unfortunately, for the most part, I do not think this is being done, and there is a price to be paid for not doing so. Moreover, I fear that even those who are of the biocentric persuasion are using homocentric language and strategies to bring business and other major players into the movement because they do not think they will be successful otherwise. They are afraid, and undoubtedly for good reason, that the large part of society, including business, will not be moved by arguments regarding the intrinsic value and rights of natural things. It is difficult enough to get business to recognize and act on their responsibilities to human beings and things of human interest. Hence many environmentalists follow the counsel of Spinoza:

> . . . it is necessary that while we are endeavoring to attain our purpose . . . we are compelled . . . to speak in a manner intelligible to the multitude. . . . For we can gain from the multitude no small advantages. . . .[19]

I understand the temptation of environmentalists employing a homocentric strategy, just as I understand business ethicists using the rationale that good ethics is good business. Both want their important work to succeed. But just as with the good ethics is good business tack, there are dangers in being a closet ecocentrist. The ethicists in both cases fail to reveal the deeper moral base of their positions because it's a harder sell. Business ethics gets marketed in terms of self-interest, environmental ethics in terms of human interest.

A major concern in using the homocentric view to formulate policy and law is that nonhuman nature will not receive the moral consideration it deserves. It might be argued, however, that by appealing to the interests and rights of human beings, in most cases nature as a whole will be protected. That is, if we are concerned about a wilderness area, we can argue that its survival is important to future generations who will otherwise be deprived of contact with its unique wildlife. We can also argue that it is important to the aesthetic pleasure of certain individuals or that, if it is destroyed, other recreational areas will become overcrowded. In this way we stand a chance to save the wilderness area without having to refer to our moral obligations to respect the intrinsic value of the spotted owl or of the old-growth forest. This is simply being strategically savvy. To trot out our deeper ecological moral convictions runs the risk of our efforts being ignored, even ridiculed, by business leaders and policy makers. It also runs head-on against a barrage of counter arguments that human interests take precedence over nonhuman interests. In any event it will not be in the best interest of the wilderness area we are trying to protect. Furthermore, all of the above homocentric arguments happen to be true—people will suffer if the wilderness area is destroyed.

In most cases, what is in the best interests of human beings may also be in the best interests of the rest of nature. After all, we are in our present environmental crisis in large part because we have not been ecologically intelligent about what is in our own interest—just as business has encountered much trouble because it has failed to see its interest in being ethically sensitive. But if the environmental movement relies only on arguments based on human interests, then it perpetuates the danger of making environmental policy and law on the basis of our strong inclination to fulfill our immediate self-interests, on the basis of our consumer viewpoints, on the basis of our willingness to pay. There will always be a tendency to allow our short-term interests to eclipse our long-term interest and the long-term interest of humanity itself. Without some grounding in a deeper environmental ethic with obligations to nonhuman natural things, then the temptation to view our own interests in disastrously short-term ways is that much more encouraged. The biocentric view helps to block this temptation.

Furthermore, there are many cases where what is in human interest is not in the interest of other natural things. Examples range from killing leopards for stylish coats to destroying a forest to build a golf course. I am not convinced that homocentric arguments, even those based on long-term human interests, have much force in protecting the interests of such natural things. Attempts to make these interests coincide might be made, but the point is that from a homocentric point of view the leopard and the forest have no morally relevant interests to consider. It is simply fortuitous if nonhuman natural interests coincide with human interests, and are thereby valued and protected. Let us take an example from the work of Christopher Stone. Suppose a stream has been polluted by a business. From a homocentric point of view, which serves as the basis for our legal system, we can only correct the problem through finding some harm done to human beings who use the stream. Reparation for such harm might involve cessation of the pollution and restoration of the stream, but it is also possible that the business might settle with the people by paying them for their damages and continue to pollute the stream. Homocentrism provides no way for the stream to be made whole again unless it is in the interests of human beings to do so. In short it is possible for human beings to sell out the stream.[20]

I am not saying that human interests cannot take precedence over nonhuman interests when there are conflicts. For this we need to come up with criteria for deciding on interspecific conflicts of interests, just as we do for intraspecific conflicts of interest among human beings.[21] But this is a different problem from holding that nonhuman natural things have no interests or value deserving of moral consideration. There are times when causing harm to natural things is morally unjustifiable when there are no significant human interests involved and even when there are human interests involved. But only a deeper ecological ethic than homocentrism will allow us to defend this.

Finally, perhaps the greatest danger that biocentric environmentalists run in using homocentric strategies to further the movement is the loss of the very insight that grounded their ethical concern in the first place. This is nicely put by Lawrence Tribe:

> What the environmentalist may not perceive is that, by couching this claim in terms of human self-interest—by articulating environmental goals wholly in terms of human needs and preferences—he may be helping to legitimate a system of discourse which so structures human thought and feeling as to

erode, over the long run, the very sense of obligation which provided the initial impetus for his own protective efforts.[22]

Business ethicists run a similar risk in couching their claims in terms of business self-interest.

The environmental movement must find ways to incorporate and protect the intrinsic value of animal and plant life and even other natural objects that are integral parts of ecosystems. This must be done without constantly reducing such values to human interests. This will, of course, be difficult, because our conceptual ideology and ethical persuasion is so dominantly homocentric; however, if we are committed to a deeper biocentric ethic, then it is vital that we try to find appropriate ways to promote it. Environmental impact statements should make explicit reference to nonhuman natural values. Legal rights for nonhuman natural things, along the lines of Christopher Stone's proposal, should be sought.[23] And naturalistic ethical guidelines, such as those suggested by Holmes Rolston, should be set forth for business to follow when its activities impact upon ecosystems.[24]

At the heart of the business ethics movement is its reaction to the mistaken belief that business only has responsibilities to a narrow set of its stakeholders, namely its stockholders. Crucial to the environmental ethics movement is its reaction to the mistaken belief that only human beings and human interests are deserving of our moral consideration. I suspect that the beginnings of both movements can be traced to these respective moral insights. Certainly the significance of both movements lies in their search for a broader and deeper moral perspective. If business and environmental ethicists begin to rely solely on promotional strategies of self-interest, such as good ethics is good business, and of human interest, such as homocentrism, then they face the danger of cutting off the very roots of their ethical efforts.

Notes

[1]This paper was originally presented as the Presidential Address to the *Society for Business Ethics*, August 10, 1990, San Francisco, CA.

[2]Albert Gore, "What Is Wrong With Us?" *Time* (January 2, 1989), 66.

[3]Norman Bowie, "Morality, Money, and Motor Cars," *Business, Ethics, and the Environment: The Public Policy Debate,* edited by W. Michael Hoffman, Robert Frederick, and Edward S. Petry, Jr. (New York: Quorum Books, 1990), 89.

[4]See Milton Friedman, "The Social Responsibility of Business Is to Increase Its Profits," *The New York Times Magazine* (September 13, 1970).

[5]Bowie, 91.

[6]Bowie, 94.

[7]Robert Frederick, Assistant Director of the Center for Business Ethics, and I have developed and written these points together. Frederick has also provided me with invaluable assistance on other points in this paper.

[8]Kenneth E. Goodpaster, "Can a Corporation Have an Environmental Conscience," *The Corporation, Ethics, and the Environment*, edited by W. Michael Hoffman, Robert Frederick, and Edward S. Petry, Jr. (New York: Quorum Books, 1990).

[9]Mark Sagoff, "At the Shrine of Our Lady of Fatima, or Why Political Questions Are Not All Economic," found in *Business Ethics: Readings and Cases in Corporate Morality*, 2nd edition, edited by W. Michael Hoffman and Jennifer Mills Moore (New York: McGrawHill, 1990), 494–503.

[10]Bowie, 94.

[11]Cynthia Pollock Shea, "Doing Well By Doing Good," *WorldWatch* (November/December, 1989), 30.

[12]*Corporate Ethics: A Prime Business Asset*, a report by The Business Roundtable, February, 1988, 4.

[13]Kenneth Blanchard, and Normal Vincent Peale, *The Power of Ethical Management* (New York: William Morrow and Company, Inc., 1988).

[14]Robert Frederick, "Individual Rights and Environmental Protection," presented at the Annual Society for Business Ethics Conference in San Francisco, August 10 and 11, 1990.

[15]Frederick.

[16]Richard Routley, and Val Routley, "Human Chauvinism and Environmental Ethics," *Environmental Philosophy*, Monograph Series, No. 2, edited by Don Mannison, Michael McRobbie, and Richard Routley (Australian National University, 1980), 121ff.

[17]See Paul W. Taylor, "The Ethics of Respect for Nature," found in *People, Penguins, and Plastic Trees*, edited by Donald VanDe Veer and Christine Pierce (Belmont, California: Wadsworth, 1986), 178–83. Also see R. and V. Routley, "Against the Inevitability of Human Chauvinism," found in *Ethics and the Problems of the 21st Century*, edited by K. E. Goodpaster and K. M. Sayre (Notre Dame: University of Notre Dame Press, 1979), 36–59.

[18]Arne Naess, "Identification as a Source of Deep Ecological Attitudes," *Deep Ecology*, edited by Michael Tobias (San Marcos, California: Avant Books, 1988), 266.

[19]Benedict de Spinoza, "On the Improvement of the Understanding," found in *Philosophy of Benedict de Spinoza*, translated by R. H. M. Elwes (New York: Tudor Publishing Co., 1936), 5.

[20]Christopher D. Stone, "Should Trees Have Standing?—Toward Legal Rights for Natural Objects," found in *People, Penguins, and Plastic Trees*, 86–87.

[21]Stone, 83–96.

[22]Lawrence H. Tribe, "Ways Not to Think about Plastic Trees: New Foundations for Environmental Law," found in *People, Penguins, and Plastic Trees*, 257.

[23]Stone, 83–96.

[24]Holmes Rolston, III, *Environmental Ethics* (Philadelphia: Temple University Press, 1988), 301–13.

Questions for Discussion:

1. Do you agree with Hoffman's claim that the environment has value in and of itself? Why or why not?

2. Do you believe that a homocentric view of the environment reflects what Hoffman calls "human chauvinism"? Explain your answer.

3. Does Hoffman hold to the view that the environment should take precedence over human needs? How would you balance those competing interests?

4. Do you believe that animals have rights that should be protected? Plants? Nonliving things? On what basis?

The Challenge of Biocentrism

Thomas Sieger Derr

From *Creation at Risk: Religion, Science and Environmentalism,* ed. Michael Cromartie (Grand Rapids: Eerdmans, 1995), 85–104.

At first glance I might appear to be an unlikely person to be critical of the environmental movement in any way. A sometime countryman, I usually know where the wind is and what phase of the moon we're in. I take good care of my small woodland, and I love my dogs. My personal predilections carry over into public policy, too. I champion the goals of reducing the waste stream, improving air and water quality, preserving the forests, protecting wildlife. I think of environmentalism as in some form a necessary and inevitable movement.

But by current standards that does not make me much of an environmentalist, for I am profoundly unhappy with the direction of current environmental philosophy, and most especially because I am a Christian. My trouble stems partly from the determination of mainstream environmentalism to blame Christianity for whatever ecological trouble we are in. This is a piece of historical nonsense that apparently thrives on repetition, so that every time it appears in print more people feel free to quote the source as authoritative, and each reference has a further multiplier effect.

Although a canard of this sort cannot surely be traced to a single source, probably the closest we can come to its origin is an essay by the late, formidable medieval historian Lynn White, Jr., called "The Historical Roots of Our Ecologic Crisis," which appeared in *Science* in 1967 and has since enjoyed virtually eternal life in anthologies.[1] It is cited as evidence of the need for an alternative religion, as for example by George Sessions, premier philosopher of the currently popular "Deep Ecology" movement: "The environmental crisis [is] fundamentally a crisis of the West's anthropocentric philosophical and religious orientations and values."[2]

It is not so much that White himself blamed Christianity; he was far too careful a historian for that, and he wrote, moreover, as a Christian and an active churchman. But his essay was used by others to promote darker purposes.

To be sure, White gave them ammunition. He traced the modern technological exploitation of nature back through the ages to the famous "dominion" passage in Genesis 1:28, which gives humanity some form of supremacy over the rest of creation. Because, he argued, technology is now ecologically "out of control," it is fair to say that "Christianity bears a huge burden of guilt" for this result. We need to reject "the Christian axiom that nature has no reason for existence save to serve man." We must overcome our "orthodox Christian arrogance toward nature." White even gave his blessing to the counterculture's espousal of alternative religions: "More science and more technology are not going to get us out of the present ecologic crisis until we find a new religion, or rethink our old one. . . . The hippies . . . show a sound instinct in their affinity for Zen Buddhism and Hinduism, which conceive the man-nature relationship as very nearly the mirror image of the Christian view."

Is Christianity really the ecological culprit? And did White really say that it is? The answer to both questions is no.

Many scholars have concluded that Christianity made an important contribution to the rise of science and technology in the West, but to make it the only cause would be too much. Yes, the doctrine of creation separates nature from God, makes it not itself divine, and suggests strongly that inquiry into its workings is a pious study of the mind of the Maker. That way of looking at the world surely abets the scientific and technological culture. But it is not a *sufficient* condition for the appearance of that culture, which did not arise in lands dominated by Eastern Christianity but only in the Latin West, and then only after a millennium. Nor is it a *necessary* condition, for science flourished without benefit of Christianity in China, ancient Greece, and the medieval Islamic world.

Neither can we say that it is chiefly Christian lands that are environmentally heedless. Ecological destruction like overgrazing and deforestation, sometimes enough to cause the fall of civilizations, has been committed by Egyptians, Persians, Romans, Aztecs, Indians, and even Buddhists. This probably comes as a surprise to no one except those gullible Westerners who romanticize other cultures of which they know very little. There is, for example, a noted Western ecologist who, despising his own civilization, extols "the Eastern and gentle Pacific cultures in which man lives (or lived) a leisurely life of harmony with nature."[3] That could only have been written by someone who knows nothing of the sorry, violent history of those peoples.

What, then, does produce the technological society? And what causes ecological pillage? As to technology, we may guess at primitive origins in simple artisanship and the domestication of animals; the natural human quest for labor-saving devices; trade and commerce with other societies where these developments are further advanced; or just the natural momentum of technological change, once started in however small a way. Other likely suspects include geography, climate, population growth, urbanism, and democracy. To this mix add the idea that the world is an intelligible order ruled by general principles, which we received from the ancient Greeks, mediated powerfully (as A. N. Whitehead asserted[4]) by the medieval insistence on the rationality of God; or perhaps the rise of purely *secular* philosophy celebrating human mastery over nature, as in Bacon, Descartes, and Leibnitz. That is quite a list. Given this wealth of candidates, it would be impossible to sort out what the primary influences really are, and even White acknowledged that the causes are finally mysterious.

As for the causes of ecological harm, we may cite first the simple fact that there are more people on the earth than ever before, and their search for food and shelter frequently assaults the world around them. It is, notably, not only the factories of the developed nations, but the daily gathering and burning of wood for fuel by rural people in the Third World, along with the depredations of their domestic animals, that have damaged the world's soils and dirtied its air (which in the Third World is far more polluted than ours). Of course industrial development has caused ecological damage, but much of that is the result of ignorance and error, mistakes often quite correctable. Noisy voices in the environmental movement attribute the damage to corporate greed, and the more fanciful among them go searching for deeper roots in capitalist culture, which in turn they find spawned by Christian theology in some form. It is simpler and surely more accurate to say that human self-seeking is a constant in our natures that no culture, no matter what its religion, has managed to eliminate.

Lynn White really did not blame Christianity for our environmental difficulties. By "orthodox Christian arrogance toward nature" he did *not* mean, he later said, that arrogance toward nature is orthodox Christian doctrine, only that presumably orthodox Christians have been arrogant toward nature. By "the Christian axiom that nature has no reason for existence save to serve man" he meant, he claimed, that some Christians have *regarded* it as an axiom, not that it is a matter of true faith.[5] Qualifications like these really vitiate the apparent argument in his "Historical Roots" essay, which was that Christians were heedless of nature *because* they were Christians. But on reflection, after absorbing the storm, White retreated to saying only that Christians, like human beings everywhere, found it possible to misappropriate certain elements from their religious tradition to serve their selfish ends.

Having talked with White at some length about his essay, I believe that, although he may have been pleased at the notice it received, he was also disturbed at the way it was used. He was only half joking when he wrote me about the "theology of ecology," saying, "Of course, I claim to be the founder!" But surely he would disown many of his offspring.

The Christian Approach to Nature

What is the *real* orthodox Christian attitude toward nature? It is, in a word, stewardship. We are trustees for that which does not belong to us. "The earth is the Lord's, and the fullness thereof; the world and they that dwell therein" (Ps. 24:1). The implications of this idea for environmentalism are profound and, I think, wholly positive. They have been spelled out in different ways by many writers, including Douglas John Hall in *The Steward*, Loren Wilkinson and his colleagues in *Earthkeeping in the Nineties*, and my own book of twenty years ago, *Ecology and Human Need*.[6]

The rough historical evidence suggests that this theoretical obligation has not been without its practical results. For example, some Christian lands in Europe have been farmed in an ecologically stable manner for centuries. Rene Dubos says flatly, "The Judeo-Christian peoples were probably the first to develop on a large scale a pervasive concern for land management and an ethic of nature."[7] Clarence Glacken, one of the most patient and exhaustive historians of these matters, concludes from his survey of the vast literature, "I am convinced that modern ecological theory . . . owes its origin to the design argument," the idea so prominent in Christian theology of all ages that the complexity of the world is the work of a creator God.[8] Lynn White knew this, too. And in the past it has been common for even the ecological critics of Christianity to say that the Christians' problem is only that they did not take their own doctrines seriously enough.

What is new in our world today is a rejection of this semi- or pseudo-irenic view and its replacement by a root-and-branch attack on the doctrine of stewardship itself by that increasingly powerful and pervasive school of environmental thought known as biocentrism. There are many variations of biocentrism, of course, and one must be careful not to overgeneralize. But it is fair to say of nearly all varieties that they find the idea of stewardship repulsively anthropocentric, implying as it plainly does that human beings are in charge of nature, meant to manage it for purposes that they alone are able to perceive. Stewardship, says Richard Sylvan (ex-Routley), means "Man as tyrant."[9] May we think of ourselves as the earth's gardeners? Bad metaphor: gardening is controlling the earth's fecundity in a way that nature, left to its own devices, would not do. Human design is wrongly imposed.

The problem is simply compounded by Christian theism, which places human beings at the apex of nature by design of the ultimate giver of life. Made, as we say, in the image of God, we give ourselves license to claim that our interests as a species take precedence over those of the rest of creation; stewardship of the creation means mainly that we should manage it so that it sustains us indefinitely. Nature is made for us, as we are made for God. Here, say the biocentrists, is the bitter harvest of anthropocentrism: human selfishness, parochialism, chauvinism, "speciesism" (the awful term Peter Singer uses of those who reject animal rights), moral naïveté, a profanation of nature, self-importance and pride carried to their extreme. Regarding humankind as of more inherent worth than other species is, says Paul Taylor, like regarding noblemen of more inherent worth than peasants. A claim to human superiority is "a deep-seated prejudice, . . . a wholly arbitrary claim . . . an irrational bias in our own favor."[10] Lynn White was right after all: it is simply arrogance.

Rights in Nature

What do the biocentrists propose instead? Their most fundamental proposition is that nature itself, the life process as a whole, is the primary locus of value. Within that process all species have value, intrinsic value, just because they *are*, because they would not *be* if they did not have an appropriate niche in the ecology of the whole. And if they have intrinsic value, we must say that they have rights of some sort, claims on us for appropriate treatment, an integrity of their own that is not available for our mere willful disposition.

Notice that the alleged rights of non-human entities do not depend on their possession of any attributes, like rationality or language or even sentience. That would be subtle anthropocentrism, say the biocentrists. It would make a semblance to human characteristics the test of value—a mistake made by many of the animal-rights advocates and one that separates them from the biocentrists. We must say instead that all entities have value simply in themselves. They have their own purposes, or "good," which they value, either consciously or unconsciously. Their value, and their consequent rights, depend solely on their essential need to be themselves, on their own "vital interests."[11]

This is, incidentally, the way a biocentrist would dispose of the animal-rights argument that human infants or mentally defective human beings may be surpassed by animals in certain qualities, such as intelligence or adaptability, and yet we would not (or most of us would not) deny human rights to these human beings; so why not give animals rights? The answer, says the biocentrist—and here, for once, I would agree—is that rights inhere in a class or species, and not in the possession of certain qualities that individuals in that species possess. My difference, as I will make plain in a moment, is that I would not extend rights below the human level.[12]

Intrinsic Value in Nature

Since the assertion that the natural world has rights we must honor begins with the claim that the natural world has intrinsic value, let us spend a moment on this prior claim. No one, to my knowledge, has worked harder or with greater care to establish this idea—that natural entities have value independent of human beings (or, for that matter, independent of God, whom he does not mention)—than Holmes Rolston.[13] If, as I will claim, even *his* most careful and gracefully expressed formulations cannot stand, then one may suppose the biocentrists' foundations generally are weak.

To Rolston, the ability to support life is a natural good that the earth possesses without us, which means that the human experience of satis-faction is not necessary to have a "good." The earth is able to produce value without us. We recognize the presence of that objective value when we value our natural science, "for no study of a worthless thing can be intrinsically valuable."[14] Organisms are living beings and hence have a good for themselves, maintaining their own life; and this good is a value that can claim our respect. In fact, "the living individual . . . is per se an intrinsic value."[15]

Rolston admits that the human participant supplies value to an object: "No value can in principle . . . be altogether independent of a valuing consciousness. . . . If all consciousness were annihilated at a stroke, there would be no good or evil, . . . no right or wrong; only impassive phenomena would remain." However, "to say that something is valuable means that it is able to be valued, if and when human valuers come along, but it has this property whether or not humans . . . ever arrive." The value is already in the thing, hence "intrinsic." Rolston does not like any account of value in natural things that depends on human psychology. He wants the value to emerge from nature directly, so that we can value the object "for what it is in itself." Value may increase with the attention of human beings, but it is present without them. Thus his theory is "biocentric."[16]

On the contrary, I argue that, with the important theistic exception noted below, we human beings *supply* the value, that nature is valuable because we find it so. There is no value without a valuer. Values are for someone or some thing. A thing can provide value to someone, and in that sense it possesses value, i.e., the capacity to provide value for someone. That is not the same as "intrinsic" value, which is value in and for the thing itself, whatever anyone makes of it. The mere fact that we value studying a particular thing does not make that thing intrinsically valuable; it makes it valuable *for us*. Someone may find it valuable for his peace of mind to finger worry beads, but that does not mean that we must accord those beads intrinsic value. Some elderly recluses have been known to save newspapers for years, valuing the accumulating mountain highly. But that does not make these old papers *intrinsically* valuable. Mosquitos or bacteria may have a goal or drive for themselves in perpetuating their life; but that is quite different from having an *intrinsic* value that other, conscious beings are required to acknowledge.

The attempt of Rolston and other biocentrists—J. Baird Callicott, for example—to distinguish between human appreciation of nature's intrinsic value, and the value that human beings add to nature by appreciating it, strikes me as hairsplitting. It is much more compelling and credible to say simply that a natural object may generate value for us not by itself but only in conjunction with our situation. We supply the value; the object contributes its being. Value is not a term appropriate to it in isolation, by itself.

The Amorality of Nature

The discussion of value takes a different course if we are theists who accept the doctrine of creation as the foundation of our environmental philosophy, or theology. We may rightly say, as James Nash does, that all creatures must reflect their Maker in some way and that a presumption of value in their favor is not unreasonable.[17] This is not to say that natural entities have intrinsic value; their value still depends on the valuer. But here the valuer is other than human beings. God bestows the value, which still does not belong to the object as such.

This is a well-developed idea with impeccable Thomist credentials; yet it does not solve our ecological problem. If anything, it makes the problem more difficult. To say that "God saw everything that he had made, and behold, it was very good" establishes well our obligation to respect the natural world; it is the foundation of our stewardship duty, of course. But we still face, and in a peculiarly painful form (for it raises the ancient problem of theodicy), the observable amorality of nature and its frequent hostility to us. That nature is full of what we perceive as violence and ugliness is beyond dispute. It is the realm of the food chain, of brute struggle and painful death. Sur-

prisingly, no one has put it more candidly and vividly than Rolston himself:

> Wildness is a gigantic food pyramid, and this sets value in a grim, deathbound jungle. Earth is a slaughterhouse, with life a miasma rising over the stench. Nothing is done for the benefit of another. . . . Blind and ever urgent exploitation is nature's driving theme.[18]

Worse yet, from our point of view, nature is frequently hostile to our human lives. From violent storm to volcanic eruption to drought to killer viruses, to say nothing of the cosmic possibilities that could end our lives in one great, sudden bang, the natural world is certainly not unambiguously our friend.

Can one read an ethic out of this natural behavior? Not likely, or at least not an ethic that any Christian could for a moment tolerate. It is not that nature is immoral, for to say that would be to read our human values into this world. But nature is certainly amoral, and we would not begin to derive our ethical standards from its actions. Nevertheless the biocentrists, bound to locate value primarily in this amoral world, find something to cherish there, something that rises above the brutality of the food chain, something that relativizes the ugliness. Some choose the harmony that they profess to see behind the apparent chaos, the patterns that repeat themselves, the balances that are restored. Other biocentrists admire nature's vitality, fecundity, and regenerative power, its strength, endurance, and dynamism, even in the midst of its fury. New life emerges from rotting carcasses and burned forests. "Ugliness," says Rolston, "though present at time in particulars, is not the last word. . . . Over time nature will bring beauty out of this ugliness."[19]

But seeing it that way is a matter of choice. Harmony in an ecosystem is only apparent, superficial. There are emergent forces that triumph, species that disappear, balances that are permanently upset. To see harmony is to look selectively. Harmony, like beauty, is mostly in the eye of the beholder. If it is natural power and regenerative strength that enthrall us, we can love the rapid reproduction of cancer cells, or the terrible beauty of a tornado. We can love what kills us. Over time, nature means to destroy this world. The death of our sun might be beautiful if there were anyone to see it, I suppose, even though it would mark the end of planet earth. We can appreciate the natural facts any way we choose. To say it once again: we supply the value.

But what shall we say to those theists who reply that surely God must value what he has made? Can we discern what God intends for the creation?

Faced with the puzzle of natural evil and the ancient lineage of the problem of theodicy, and bearing in mind the centuries of false prophets who have claimed to know God's will all too well, I think we must be very, very modest in answering this question. Given the centrality of the divine-human drama in Christian faith, given its proclamation of the redemptive event addressed to humankind, I am certainly willing to say—more than willing, in fact, insistent upon saying—that our focus must be on human life, and that our task with the earth is to sustain the conditions for human life for as far into the future as our wits and strength allow. But I am not willing to go much beyond that. I am not willing to guess at what the earth's good is, or, to put it better, to guess at what God intends for the earth, which by definition would be its good.

A Calculus of Rights

The biocentrists are much less modest. They do claim to know the good of nature. If I may turn the tables on them, I would say they are far more daring, even impudent, in their claims to know the purposes of nature (or of God with nature, if they are theists) than are traditional Christians. Building on their theory of intrinsic value in natural entities, the biocentrists tell us that there are severe limits on what we may do with the natural world. In search of a strong position that will have sufficient force to restrain human selfishness, many of them, though not all, adopt the language of rights. Nature has rights, and thus has claims

against us, much as we human beings claim rights that other human beings may not transgress.

But at once they plunge us into a realm of competing rights. Whose rights take precedence? When may they be violated, and by whom? May we eat meat? experiment on animals in laboratories? spread agricultural pesticides? use antibiotics? dam rivers? May a cat kill a mouse? In order to solve these conflicts and save the whole concept from reduction to absurdity, its defenders propose an inequality of rights, or even a complete disjunction between our obligations to one another and to the natural world.

Constructing a calculus of variable rights for different levels of existence is no simple task, however. Nash, who calls himself a Christian biocentrist and who, for his theological care, deserves to be exempted from many of the faults of the larger movement, does it by using "value-creating" and "value-experiencing" as the criteria for relevant differences, with rights diminishing as we descend a scale established by the relative presence of these capacities. Thus he hopes to solve conflicts of rights by "appropriate adjustments for the different contexts."[20] Rolston similarly would have the rights of animals and other natural entities "fade over a descending phylogenic spectrum."[21] These systems give priority in rights to human beings, a lesser preference to creatures merely sentient, and still less to non-sentient entities.

More radical versions of rights in nature take a Schweitzer-like approach, avoiding all killing of "lesser" forms of life except under threat to our own lives, and then only with a profound sense of sorrow for this necessary evil. How many times have we heard it said in recent years, with wondering admiration, that American Indians, those supposed ecological paragons, apologized to their game before killing it? An Irish pacifist once told me, with appropriate sardonic tone, that political assassination in Ireland was so common it was considered a normal part of the political process rather than murder in the sense of violating the sixth commandment; "but," he added, "it is doubtful whether the victims appreciated the distinction." And so also the caribou, slain by an Indian arrow tipped with a profound apology.

Faced with these tangles, even the biocentrically inclined must be tempted to give up on rights language. Rolston verges on the cynical when he admits that rights may after all be merely "a cultural discovery, really a convention" that does not translate to ecosystems, but that it may be politically useful to use the term anyway. "It is sometimes convenient rhetorically but in principle unnecessary to use the concept of rights at all."[22] What matters is the power of the restraint, and the language may be adjusted as necessary.

Reining in Rights

With all due respect to the intellectual strength and agility of the biocentric arguments, I would slice through their Gordian tangles by limiting "rights" to intrahuman affairs. "Rights" is a political and social term in the first instance, applicable only to human society, often enshrined in a fundamental document like a constitution, or embedded in the common law. As a metaphysical term, the transcultural phrase "human rights" applies to that which belongs to human beings by their very nature, i.e., not by their citizenship. Theologically, we guarantee human rights neither by our nature nor by our citizenship but by the radical equality of the love of God, the concept of "alien dignity," a grace bestowed on us that does not belong to our nature as such. In none of these forms has nature participated in rights.

Biocentrists sometimes seek to redress what to them are these deficiencies in the history of ideas by what I will call the argument from extension. "Rights," they point out, originally applied only to male citizens; but just as rights were gradually extended to women, to slaves, and finally to all other human beings, so it is a logical extension of this political liberalism to extend rights now to nonhuman creatures and even to agglomerations like ecosystems. Or, if the forum is not politics but Christian ethics, one could argue that the command to love our neighbors must now apply to non-human "neighbors," our "co-siblings of cre-ation,"[23] or that the justice we are obliged to dispense to the poor and oppressed must now be extended to oppressed nature, or even that the enemies we are asked to love may include nature in its most hostile modes.

Although I appreciate the generous spirit of this line of argument, I think it involves a serious category mistake. Non-humans cannot have the moral status that only human beings possess, by our very natures. It is not irrelevant that the command to love our neighbors, in its original context, does in fact *not* apply to non-humans. An "extension" amounts to a substantial misreading of the text. Our obligations to the natural world cannot be expressed this way.

Another use of the idea of extension, one that occurs in Nash and in a different way in Paul Santmire,[24] is to argue that ultimate redemption is meant not only for humankind but also for the natural world, indeed the whole cosmos. That would imply much about our treatment of nature, our companion in cosmic redemption. The Incarnation confers dignity not only on us but on the whole material world: the divine takes on not only human flesh but material being in general. Certain New Testament passages are suggestive here—Romans 8:18–25, Colossians 1:15–20, Revelation 21:1—and Eastern Orthodox theology has formally incorporated this notion.

This is a theological idea of considerable gravity, and it deserves to be taken seriously. Nevertheless the doctrine is only vaguely expressed and appears to faith as hope, a hope made legitimate by faith, but a hope without details. Indeed, if we are to be scientifically honest, it is a "hope against hope," given the secular geological wisdom about the death of planet earth in fire and ice. The doctrine of eschatological renewal cannot tell us much about the care of nature beyond what we already know from our stewardship obligation, that we are to preserve this world as a habitat fit for humanity. The natural details of a redeemed environment are beyond our ken. Our trust in God for the eternal Presence beyond death does not require the preservation of these rocks and rills, these woods and templed hills. Again we find ourselves behind the veil of ignorance: we simply do not know nature's divine destiny.

In short, and in sum thus far, I believe it would be more consistent, more logical, and conceptually much simpler to insist that nature has neither intrinsic value nor rights. And I believe this is true whether we are secular philosophers or Christian theologians, whether we speak with the tongues of men or of angels.

Policy Consequences of Biocentrism

It is time now to ask what is practically at stake in this disagreement. What are the policy consequences of the biocentrists' position, for which they seek the vocabulary of rights or other strong language? What is denied to us thereby that would be permitted from the viewpoint of Christian humanism?

Since the biocentrists will not allow us to use nature as we see fit for ourselves, but insist that it has rights or at least claims of its own against us, their general recipe is that it should be left alone wherever possible. There is of course disagreement about the details and the exceptions, but the presumption is in favor of a hands-off policy. That is the *prima facie* rule: Let nature take its course. The burden of proof is on us to show why we should be allowed to impose our wills on natural processes.

Concretely this means we should take the necessary measures to protect existing species for their own sakes, not because they might offer something to us in the form of, say, aesthetic pleasure or possible future medicinal benefits. The Endangered Species Act should be vigorously defended and enforced; and its conflicts with human desires—the spotted owl vs. the timber industry, the snail darter vs. the Tennessee dam—should be settled in favor of the species threatened. The state will have to intervene to protect the species and the land, which means limitations on a landowner's use of his own property. After all, the wild animals and plants on the land should have their freedom, too.

Especially should we preserve and expand wild lands, the necessary larger habitats needed for these species, even though human beings may desire the land for other purposes, like farming. When it comes to such conflicts, mankind ought to lose. Arne Naess, founder of the Deep Ecology school (which is a form of biocentrism tending to argue the equal worth of all natural entities), says with astonishing frankness, "If [human] vital needs come in conflict with the vital needs of nonhumans, then humans should defer to the latter."[25]

We should also leave alone those injured wild creatures that we are tempted to save—the baby bird fallen from its nest, the wounded animal we come upon in the forest, the whale trapped by the ice. Intervention in natural processes is wrong whether the motives are benevolent or not. The species is strengthened by the premature extinction of its weaker members. Respecting nature's integrity means not imposing our soft-hearted human morality upon it. We should let forest fires burn and have their way with the wild creatures.

We should not build monuments in the wild. No more Mount Rushmores, no Christ of the Andes, no railroads up Mount Washington, and probably no more wilderness roads or ski lifts.

We should suspend genetic engineering in agriculture and animal husbandry and not permit there anything we would not permit among human beings. We should not take animal lives in teaching biology or medicine, and certainly not in testing cosmetics. Zoos and botanical gardens are suspect; better that the species there displayed should live in the wild. We should not keep pets. (There go my Springers.)

What about recreational hunting or fishing? Some biocentrists frown upon it as human interference with nature and unnecessary to our diet besides; but others would permit it as simply a form of predation, which is a fact of nature and not subject to our moral scrutiny. And by this same token there would be no moral obligation for us to become vegetarians. In fact, and rather awkwardly, even plants have a "good of their own" in the biocentric theory, which leads to some mental agility to sort out their permissible uses. It is all right to eat them, of course, for that is nature's way; but "frivolous" uses (Halloween pumpkins? Christmas trees?) are questionable. One suspects that even flower gardens would be a dubious activity, which may be why the biocentric literature rarely if ever mentions them.

Although we are in principle to leave nature alone, we are obligated to restore that which we have harmed. This form of intervention is acceptable because it is guided by the principle that pristine nature, before human impact, is somehow ideal. Here again the calculus of permissibility has to be rather finely tuned. It might be wrong to plant trees in a natural desert, for example, but obligatory to plant them if human activity had contributed substantially to creating that desert. Obviously this principle can be carried to extremes. Paul Shephard has seriously suggested that we in this country all move to the coasts and restore the land between to its pre-human condition, in which we would be permitted only as hunter-gatherers, like our most primitive ancestors. Few biocentrists would go anywhere near this far, but the principle is there. The argument is about the movable boundaries.

Stalking the Elusive Limits

My criticism of these limits begins with their vagueness and ambiguity, which is spiced with a generous dash of arbitrariness. Species, we are told, should be allowed to exist until the end of their natural "evolutionary time"; but how can we know when that time has arrived? We human beings should not take more than our "due" or occupy more than our "fair share" of land or exceed our "limits" in technological grasp; but these terms cannot even begin to be specified. What can be done with any creature turns on its degree of neural complexity, or some other hierarchical principle; but such distinctions will never be clear and are subject to a lot of pure arbitrariness. In the end I suspect that these measures are not in nature, but in ourselves. The lines are drawn according not to objective natural differences but to human preferences: human beings supply the values.

The matter of species disappearance is also confused. Leaving nature alone means allowing natural extinctions. Are we then to allow species to vanish, intervening only to save those threatened by human activity? (Yes, says Rolston. New life arises from the old when the demise is natural, but artificial extinction is "without issue."[26]) Or is it our responsibility to preserve as many species as possible, no matter what threatens them? Isn't domestication, far from being harmful interference with the wild, a useful way to preserve species? In defense of all of us dog owners, I note that many creatures have thrived because of the human presence—mice and rats, famously, and raccoons, and of course all species bred as pets or for agricultural utility.

The degree of simplicity of life is another matter of confusion. Some biocentrists would allow a fairly complex civilization. Others, like the bioregionalists, would turn their backs on the global economy and live in a locally sustainable way, even reverting to a simple agricultural economy. The movement as a whole can offer us very little real guidance about our permissible impact on the natural world. While it would allow us to feed and clothe and house ourselves, it would require of us some degree of self-limitation because of our exceptional talents, including particularly our talent for reproducing ourselves. But it is very difficult to tell what this directive might mean beyond the generalized complaint that we are too clever and thus exceed our space too readily. We have to pretend we are less, in effect, so that the other creatures may be more; but how and how much are quite unspecifiable.

The practical problems with the theory are many and are mainly intractable. They are also mostly unnecessary. Inevitably, once rights for non-human entities are proposed, the situation becomes impossibly complex. Absent this proposition, matters become much clearer, though solutions are seldom completely evident. We are still in for a process of experiment, of trial and error, mistake and correction. We have a lot to learn, mostly from science. But with a focus on human welfare we will have a reasonably clear idea how to use our knowledge; the complexities will be simpler, the conflicts easier to resolve.

Biocentric Fatalism: Many Must Die

There is one final, serious problem with bio-centrism, and that is its fatalism. Biocentrists take their cues as to what *ought* to be from what *is*, and thus base their views of an acceptable future on what will happen if we let the natural world follow its own laws as far as possible. If an organism exists, the biocentrist presumes it has an important ecological niche and should be left alone. "Natural kinds are good kinds until proven otherwise."[27] If it is an ecological misfit it will perish naturally anyway, and we should not regret its demise. Death may be bad for individuals, but it is good for the system.

Should this ecological "wisdom," if that is the word, be applied to Homo sapiens? Because the whole direction of biocentric thought is to answer this question affirmatively, and because the consequences are so fearsome for most people's sensitivities, it is hard to find candid replies. When they do come out, ordinary ethical opinion, unenlightened by this new environmental realism, is apt to be appalled. Should we curtail medicine so that more of us may die "naturally" and earlier? Yes. Should we refrain from feeding the hungry, so that population will not exceed its boundaries? Yes, said the "lifeboat school," and especially its helmsman Garrett Hardin, whose bluntness is plainly an embarrassment to the current generation of biocentrists. Or consider J. Baird Callicott's rendering of William Aiken's questions as direct statements: "Massive human diebacks would be good. It is our duty to cause them. It is our species duty, relative to the whole, to eliminate 90 percent of our numbers."[28]

Even Lynn White, that most humane and Christian man, walked up to the edge of this moral abyss. Human beings are crowding out earth's other species, our "comrades" on the planet, and a balance needs to be restored. How shall we do this? Shall individual human beings be sacrificed, in defiance of traditional Christian ethics, if some killing will save many species? White hesitated, he said, to "light candles before the saints requesting a new Black Death" to give us, like fourteenth-century Europe before us, a "tragic respite" from our ecological peril. Almost visibly he drew back from the fearful answer; and yet with only slight obliqueness he said it: Many must die.[29]

To be sure, and to be fair, many biocentrists recoil from the social implications of their theory. It is only the biocentric egalitarians, for whom all life is of equal value, who are driven to these fearful antihuman conclusions. For the others, their schema of hierarchical differentiation allows them to claim a different level of moral behavior among human beings, different from that between human beings and the natural world, and certainly different from natural amorality. Callicott insists that "humanitarian obligations in general come before environmental duties." Rolston calls it "monstrous" not to feed starving human beings, though he would let overpopulated wild herds die.

But the boundaries between nature and culture are blurred and repeatedly crossed, as the examples of White and Hardin show well enough. Callicott acknowledges that the conflicts are a "difficult and delicate question." Nash calls them "immensely complicated." Rolston says that ecological "fitness" means and implies different things in nature than it does for human beings, but (let the reader beware) the two meanings have similarity, too; they are "homologous" or "analogous." "This biological world that *is* also *ought* to be; we must argue from the natural to the moral. . . . So much the worse for those humanistic ethics no longer functioning in, nor suited to, their changing environment."[30] Apparently one can, in a way, import ethics from nature to culture.

And that is precisely the ethical problem. Without a secure anchor in humanism, Christian or otherwise, biocentrism risks great moral evils. At the extreme, it appears actually indifferent to human destiny. Paul Taylor says that as members of a biotic community we must be impartial toward all species, our own included: that in fact we are unnecessary to other species that would be helped by our extinction. Thomas Berry is similarly minded: "The human species has, for some thousands of years, shown itself to be a pernicious presence in the world of the living on a unique and universal scale."[31] Since species must be allowed their "evolutionary time" and then die, and because this process is "good," the human species, too, must expect to perish; and from nature's point of view, that will be normal. If nature were capable of regret, there would be no regret for our passing. The ecosystem will survive as well or better without us at the top of the food chain. But since nature is amoral, we must say that our extinction is of no moral significance in nature.

Would God care? The whole direction of our faith says that God would indeed care, which suggests strongly that we should oppose biocentrism and not anticipate the demise of our species with equanimity. I admit that this is a conviction of faith. What God really is about I would not dare to say I knew.

Whether such modesty is becoming or not, it eludes the biocentrists, who seem to know more than I do about the ultimate principles that rule the universe. Here, for example, is Carol Christ:

> We are no more valuable to the life of the universe than a field [of flowers]. . . . The divinity that shapes our ends is an impersonal process of life, death, and transformation. . . . The life force does not care more about human creativity and choice than it cares about the ability . . . of moss to form on the side of a tree. The human species, like other species, might in time become extinct, dying so that other lives might live.[32]

Rolston is only moderately more hopeful: the evolutionary system is "not just a random walk" but "some kind of steady, if statistical heading." In the extinction of some species and the appearance of new ones "a hidden principle seems to be at work, organizing the cosmos in a coherent way." But that is scant comfort to human beings, who come very late to the story and are only "short-sighted and arrogant" if they think it was meant for them.[33] Rolston is quite fatalistic about our destiny: recognizing that there is nothing necessary or inevitable about our appearance on earth, we will simply have to accept the overall course of evolution as good, no matter where it eventually goes.[34]

James Gustafson, a justly celebrated ethicist, has written similarly that we should not count on humanity's being at the apex of creation nor consider that human good trumps the good of nonhuman nature. Our disappearance would not be bad "from a theocentric perspective," which acknowledges that "the source and power and order of all of nature is not always beneficent in its outcomes for the diversity of life and for the well-being of humans as part of that." "The Divine . . . [is] the ultimate source of all human good, but does not guarantee it." Such ruminations have led Nash to characterize Gustafson's "God" as "a non-conscious and nonmoral ordering power without intention, volition, or cognition. . . . This power sustains the universe, apparently unintentionally, but lacks the purposive, benevolent, or redemptive qualities to seek the good of individuals, the human species, otherkind, or the whole cosmos. . . . This perspective seems close to atheism or pantheism."[35]

The ecological ethic emerging from biocentric fatalism, such as it is, is simply to enjoy the earth's fecundity, to laugh and weep and celebrate all life, whether it is our life or not. "Humanity's highest possibility is to bear witness to and participate in the great process of life itself."[36] And so the biocentrist love affair with a mysterious Natural Process cultivates, inevitably, indifference to the human prospect.

It is, of course, a bit odd for biocentrists to view humanity as just another species serving out its evolutionary time, when with the same voice they must also acknowledge that we are a very special species, endowed with enormous power over the environment. We cannot renounce this power, either. It is ours to use for good or ill, and so they urge us to use it in a self-limiting way to preserve the rest of the environment and to care for the other creatures of the earth. Notice that the message is anthropocentric in spite of itself: our great power engenders our great responsibility. But that, of course, is precisely the Christian ethic of dominion and stewardship.

I do not know where the human story will end. But, as I think William Faulkner, that great literary icon of my college generation, said in accepting the Nobel Prize, "I decline to accept the end of man." I think that my efforts ought to be bent to perpetuating human life, and that that goal ought to be the overriding test of our ecological conduct.

In arguing otherwise, large sections of the environmental movement are on the wrong track. In the name of its own humanistic faith, Christianity ought to criticize these environmentalists, rather than scramble to say, "Me, too." What is historic and traditional in our valuation of Creation is a perfectly sufficient guide to sound ecology.

Notes

1. Lynn White, Jr., "The Historical Roots of Our Ecologic Crisis," *Science*, 155 (March 10, 1967): 1203–7.

2. George Sessions, "Introduction" (to Part II, "Deep Ecology"), in Michael Zimmerman, ed., *Environmental Philosophy: From Animal Rights to Radical Ecology* (Englewood Cliffs, N.J.: Prentice Hall, 1993), 161.

3. Paul Ehrlich and Richard L. Harriman, *How to Be a Survivor* (New York: Ballantine, 1971), 129.

4. Alfred North Whitehead, *Science and the Modern World* (New York: Macmillan, 1950 [original 1925]).

5. Lynn White, "Continuing the Conversation," in Ian G. Barbour, ed., *Western Man and Environmental Ethics* (Reading, Mass.: Addison-Wesley, 1973). Also private conversations.

6. Douglas John Hall, *The Steward: A Biblical Symbol Come of Age* (Grand Rapids: Eerdmans, 1990). Loren Wilkinson et al., *Earthkeeping in the Nineties: Stewardship of Creation* (Grand Rapids: Eerdmans, 1991). Thomas Sieger Derr, *Ecology and Human Need* (Philadelphia: Westminster, 1973 and 1975).

7. Rene Dubos, *A God Within* (New York: Scribner, 1972), 161. See pp. 157–61 for his argument against White's thesis.

8. Clarence Glacken, *Traces on the Rhodian Shore: Nature and Culture in Western Thought from Ancient Times to the End of the Eighteenth Century* (Berkley: University of California, 1967), 423.

9. Richard Sylvan, "Is There a Need for a New, an Environmental Ethic?" in Zimmerman, *Environmental Philosophy*, 13–14.

10. Paul Taylor, "The Ethics of Respect for Nature," in Zimmerman, *Environmental Philosphy*, 78–80.

11. Biocentrists and animal-rights activists are further and seriously separated by the former's focus on saving individuals, and the latter's giving priority to species. A biocentrist, who is indifferent to suffering in the wild (just part of the natural ecosystem, which is good), would allow, even encourage, the death of weaker individuals so that the species as a whole may flourish. For this a leading animal-rights advocate, Tom Regan, has fastened upon biocentrism the charming sobriquet "eco-fascism" (*The Case for Animal Rights* [Berkeley: University of California, 1983], 262). But biocentrists reject this "humanitarian ethic" as misplaced in nature. It is not a true environmental ethic. Thus Mark Sagoff: "Mother Nature is so cruel to her children she makes Frank Perdue look like a saint" ("Animal Liberation and Environmental Ethics: Bad Marriage, Quick Divorce," in Zimmerman, *Environmental Philosophy*, 89–92).

12. Not all biocentrists reject the argument from defective human beings, however. Kenneth Goodpaster uses it to deny that "moral considerability" should be restricted to humans because they are rational. He extends moral status beyond humans, and beyond animals, too, to all that is alive ("On Being Morally Considerable," in Zimmerman, *Environmental Philosophy*, 54, 56).

13. Systematically in Holmes Rolston, *Environmental Ethics: Duties to and Values in the Natural World* (Philadelphia: Temple University Press, 1988).

14. Ibid., 9.

15. Ibid., 100.

16. Ibid., 112–16.

17. James A. Nash, *Loving Nature: Ecological Integrity and Christian Responsibility* (Nashville: Abingdon, 1991), 99. See also his essay "Biotic Rights and Human Ecological Responsibility," in *The Annual of the Society of Christian Ethics, 1993*, 137–62.

18. Rolston, *Environmental Ethics*, 218.

19. Ibid., 240–41.

20. Nash, *Loving Nature*, 176, 181; "Biotic Rights," 150–51, 158–59. Nash would not award rights to abiotic entities, only organisms; and thus he rejects the term "rights of nature," though granting, like Rolston, that "the term remains rhetorically valuable" ("Biotic Rights," 148).

21. Rolston, *Environmental Ethics*, 48.

22. Ibid., 50–51.

23. Larry Rasmussen's phrase, defending the extension of neighbor love even to inorganic nature; in Wesley Granberg-Michaelson, ed., *Tending the Garden: Essays on the Gospel and the Earth* (Grand Rapids: Eerdmans, 1987), 199. For an anti-theological version of the extension argument, see J. Baird Callicott, following his hero, the much-cited Aldo Leopold, *In Defense of the Land Ethic* (Albany: State University of New York, 1989), 80–82.

24. H. Paul Santmire, *The Travail of Nature: The Ambiguous Ecological Promise of Christian Theology* (Philadelphia: Fortress, 1985). Nash, *Loving Nature*, 124–33.

25. Arne Naess, "The Deep Ecological Movement: Some Philosophical Aspects," in Zimmerman, *Environmental Philos-*

ophy, 203. George Sessions is less severe but, as a "biocentric egalitarian," will give us no more than equality with nature: non-human entities have "equal inherent value or worth along with humans" ("Deep Ecology and Global Ecosystem Protection," in Zimmerman, *Environmental Philosophy*, 236).

26. Rolston, *Environmental Ethics*, 155. That is not, strictly speaking, quite true. Nature has a way of restoring devastated land, whether it be laid waste by a volcano or an atomic bomb test. Extinction of species on a grand scale is simply the way of nature, and always has been, since well before human life appeared.

27. Rolston, *Environmental Ethics*, 103.

28. Hardin's essay "The Tragedy of the Commons" (*Science*, December 13, 1968) is still routinely cited and anthologized, as are the conclusions he drew from it in another essay, "Living on a Lifeboat" (*Bioscience* 24, 1974). But harshest of all is *Exploring New Ethics for Survival: The Voyage of the Spaceship Beagle* (Baltimore: Penguin, 1973), which is virtually invisible today. The quotation from William Aiken is from his essay "Ethical Issues in Agriculture," in Tom Regan, ed., *Earthbound: New Introductory Essays in Environmental Ethics* (New York: Random House, 1984), 269; cited in Callicott, *In Defense of the Land Ethic*, 92. This is not Aiken's position, though Callicott's alterations make it appear to be so. Aiken says that these statements, which in his essay are questions, would be those of a position he calls "eco-holism," an extreme stance that he suggests may be ascribed to Paul Taylor among others, and which he rejects in favor of a more humanistic one. On page 272 he outlines a scale of comparative value much like Nash's, one that favors human beings.

29. Lynn White, "The Future of Compassion," *The Ecumenical Review* 30, no. 2 (April 1978): 108.

30. Rolston, *Environmental Ethics*, 329; Rolston, "Challenges in Environmental Ethics," in Zimmerman, *Environmental Philosophy*, 136; Nash, "Biotic Rights," 159; Callicot, *In Defense of the Land Ethic*, 93–94.

31. Taylor, "Ethics of Respect for Nature," 71, 81. Berry, in Zimmerman, *Environmental Philosophy*, 174.

32. Carol Christ, "Rethinking Theology and Nature," in Irene Diamond and Gloria Feman Orenstein, eds., *Reweaving the World: The Emergence of Ecofeminism* (San Francisco: Sierra Club, 1990), 68.

33. Rolston, *Environmental Ethics*, 185–86, 195–98 (quoting in part P. C. W. Davies).

34. Ibid., 344–45.

35. James Gustafson, *A Sense of the Divine: The Natural Environment from a Theocentric Perspective* (Cleveland: Pilgrim Press, 1994), chaps. 1 and 3 in the unpaginated manuscript. Nash, *Loving Nature*, 233–34, n. 10, commenting on Gustafson's *Theocentric Ethics*, vol. 1 (Chicago: University of Chicago Press, 1981), 106, 183–84, 248–50, 270–73.

36. Michael Zimmerman, "Deep Ecology and Ecofeminism: The Emerging Dialogue," in Diamond and Orenstein, *Reweaving the World*, 140. Zimmerman, like Naess and Sessions, is a "biocentric egalitarian"; thus: "Humanity is no more, but also no less, important than all other things on earth" (ibid.).

Questions for Discussion:

1. How does Derr's position on the environment differ from Hoffman's?
2. What are the elements of Derr's Christian approach to nature?
3. Do you agree with Derr that biocentrism leads to impractical and dangerous extremes? Why or why not?
4. Do you agree with Derr's claim that the environment has neither rights nor intrinsic value? Why or why not?

CASE STUDIES

Case 10.1: Heap-Leach Mining in Latin America

You are the founder of a small company that manufactures, sells, and installs irrigation equipment worldwide. You have typically sold your products in the Middle East, but when the Gulf War broke out in 1991, your company nearly went bankrupt. As a result, you have looked to other parts of the world for new business, particularly for your main application, drip systems for agriculture. You have discovered that a market for your agricultural products exists in Latin America, and you are now doing roughly $4 million in annual sales. But agricultural business conditions are unstable, and you cannot count on these revenues from year to year. You have also discovered that your irrigation products made for agriculture can be used in various types of mining projects, which would be a more stable source of revenue.

One such process is known as "heap-leach mining." It is a process by which copper and other minerals are extracted by applying chemicals by drip irrigation systems over large areas of freshly piled earth, known as heap-leach pits. The earth to be mined is taken from the hillsides and mountainsides, placed on large pond liners, and then treated with chemicals such as cyanide. The cyanide dissolves the non-metallic elements, leaving you with fresh ore. The heap-leach pit is contained by the pond liners so that the cyanide and other chemicals used don't leak into the water supply. You have developed technology that would be able to monitor the surrounding soils to be sure that the chemicals were not contaminating the ground water.

You have projected annual sales from mining projects to be roughly $2 million and a profit of $400,000. These additional sales would create new jobs and would prosper you and your partners. The products were very well received at a mining show in Chile. You had prepared a working demonstration of the heap-leach pit, complete with all the monitoring equipment and drip irrigation equipment. The mining officials took you to some of the areas that would be mined by this method. You were surprised by how pristine the beautiful environment was in the mining areas, and you knew that the process of mining these areas would forever change the beautiful landscape.

In fact, you believe that these areas are some of the prettiest countryside in the world, and your equipment would be involved in destroying the aesthetic value of this area. You liken it to some of the ways in which forests were harvested by clear-cutting, a method that leaves a terrible environmental eyesore in some very beautiful areas in the Pacific Northwest of the United States. Yet you also are responsible for creating sales for your company. This is a potentially lucrative market that you can not afford to ignore.

Questions for Discussion:

1. How would you balance your environmental responsibility with your opportunity to earn a profit and create jobs, particularly for many impoverished people in Latin America? To what degree are you obligated to maintain the local environment as a part of your Christian environmental stewardship?

2. You noticed at the product demonstration at the mining show in which you introduced your products that the mining companies were not particularly interested in your control features and monitoring equipment. This concerns you because you realize that even if you bundle the products together, you cannot be sure the companies will use the monitoring equipment. Does this change the way you would balance environmental responsibility and job creation? Does it make a difference that the government has less restrictive environmental laws and invites business as a way to provide jobs?

Case 10.2: Yew Trees and Cancer Cures

You are an executive for a large pharmaceutical company that has been working on various cancer treatments for some time. Some of the products your company has developed are successfully treating various kinds of cancers, but none of them offer a cure. They only arrest the growth of the cancer cells, putting the patients into remission. These drugs extend patients' lives, raise their quality of life, and though they have side effects, patients are informed of these and consider them acceptable tradeoffs for how they slow the cancer. Unfortunately, some cancers, such as ovarian cancer, are very aggressive and are resistant to the chemotherapy agents available on the market.

Your company has developed an experimental drug, not yet approved by the Food and Drug Administration (FDA), known as taxol. It is made from a rare Pacific Northwest yew tree. To ensure that enough taxol is made available to the thousands of women who suffer from ovarian cancer, you realize that tens of thousands of yew trees would have to be cut down. This would devastate some of the most beautiful forests of the Pacific Northwest and would ruin the habitat of the endangered spotted owl. Successful development and distribution of taxol would also be very profitable for the company.

Sources: Alexander Hill, *Just Business*, 185; Marilyn Chase, "New Cancer Drug May Extend Lives at the Cost of Rare Trees," *Wall Street Journal*, 9 April 1991, A1.

Questions for Discussion:

1. How would you balance human needs and environmental concerns in this case? Which needs should take priority? On what basis do you set the priorities?
2. If there are other ways to obtain taxol that are more expensive and would significantly raise the cost of the drug for cancer patients, are you obligated to use that alternative source if it would preserve forests? If the alternative drug had unpleasant side effects for the patients that taxol does not, would that change the way you balance human needs and the environment?
3. How do you think a person who holds a biocentric view of the environment would resolve this dilemma?

Case 10.3: Animal Testing for Perfumes

Your company manufactures cosmetics, shampoos, and a variety of perfumes and colognes. You routinely test your products on animals and consider it important for ensuring that your customers do not have allergic or other adverse reactions to the chemicals in your products. The animals have a variety of reactions, some benign and others harmful. Some are painful and can even cause death, though your company does its best to alleviate the animals' pain and will put some to sleep humanely when they are close to dying. You have recently heard of a growing number of body care product companies that have decided not to use animal testing. You realize that they are getting good public relations value out of that policy, and you wonder if that's all it is—simply marketing. You wish that the animals used in your testing did not suffer like they sometimes do, but you also realize that animal testing is a reliable indicator of when human beings will have problems with one of your company's products.

Questions for Discussion:

1. Do you believe that the animals used in these experiments have rights that need to be protected? Why or why not?
2. Do you think the company is obligated to use other methods besides animals to test its products, even if they are not nearly as effective? Or do you see no problem with the use of animals in this way?
3. Would your answer be any different if your company were manufacturing pharmaceutical products instead of cosmetics? Why or why not?

COMMENTARY

The conflict between business and the environment involves maintaining the difficult balance between jobs and economic growth and environmental protection. Clearly there are extremes and rhetoric on both sides of the issue. Environmentalists are wrong when they insist on doomsday scenarios, suggesting that society is at the brink of an environmental Armageddon. Business leaders are likewise wrong when they insist that there is no environmental problem for which it is worth sacrificing economic growth. It is a given that there are environmental problems that need urgent attention, particularly in Eastern Europe and the Third World, though some, such as global warming and the ozone problem, have undoubtedly been overstated and may not even be issues at all. But it is also true that in many ways the environment is healthier today than at any time in the past fifty years. For example, the air in smog-ridden Southern California is likely cleaner than at any time in the past four decades. Environmentalists point out that results like this mean that their emphasis and strong government regulation is working and should be continued just as aggressively as in the past. But business leaders point to the condition of the environment as evidence that the days of grave environmental concern are past, thus justifying a rethinking of the balance, tilting it back toward economic growth, development, and less government interference to protect the environment at the expense of business.

Biblical Parameters for Environmental Ethics

The Bible sets the primary parameters for a Judeo-Christian environmental ethic. In the creation account in Genesis 1–2, God is the sovereign over creation who proclaimed it good at every stage but also proclaimed it "very good" after the creation of human beings on the final day of creation. Because God is the Creator, the creation has value. God's conclusion that his creation was good reflected the notion that it has value simply because it is the object of a loving and creative God who invested it with value. Its value is further reflected by the promise of ultimate redemption that extends to creation.

Human beings are not the only recipients of God's redemption. The Bible is clear that creation is at present awaiting its redemption, when it too will have the curse of sin removed (Romans 8:19–22; Ephesians 1:10; Colossians 1:20). In other words, there is hope for the creation as well as for the human beings who inhabit it. God is said to care for creation and for its creatures in passages that have little if anything to do with the interests of human beings (Psalm 104). The environment should be seen from a theocentric perspective, with God at the center and the environment having value because it is the special creation of God. Thus, the environment has intrinsic value because God has created it and it reflects his glory (Psalm 19:1–2). But it also has God-ordained instrumental value for human beings, and there is nothing wrong with human beings responsibly using the earth for their benefit. Nor is there anything necessarily wrong with placing human well-being as the higher priority when it conflicts with environmental concern.

A proper theocentric view reflects both God as creator and human beings as beneficiaries of the environment. This is not the same thing as a homocentric view, proponents of which suggest that the environment has only instrumental value in terms of the ways it can benefit human beings. Such a homocentric view, Hoffman argues, runs the risk of neglecting God's place as creator and sustainer of the world, can be reduced in practice to human narcissism over the environment, can lead to scarcity due to overuse of resources, and risks over-reliance on technology to resolve all environmental problems.[4]

Ironically, most of the proponents of biocentrism hold to the worldview of evolutionary naturalism, that is, that the world came into being apart from any activity of a transcendent, intelligent being such as God. If the earth is nothing more than the product of natural forces, then it is unclear on what basis biocentrists attribute value to it. In fact, if naturalistic evolution is true, then the earth has no intrinsic value, natural processes are clearly amoral, and there is no basis on

[4] Alexander Hill, *Just Business* (Downers Grove, Ill.: InterVarsity Press, 1997), 186–88.

which to attribute rights to any part of the environment, including human beings.

However, the Genesis account is clear that the earth was incomplete without human beings. Creation was not completed until human beings were formed and placed on the earth in relationship to each other and to God. Human beings are portrayed by Genesis as the pinnacle of creation. Moreover, in Genesis God clearly gives human beings dominion over the creation, as illustrated by their naming the animals as an exercise of their dominion. The creation is God's gift to humankind to be used for his benefit. That is the implication of the command to subdue the earth in order to control it and use it for good. The sciences, medicine, technology, and business are some of the avenues used by human beings to extend dominion over the earth. After the entrance of sin into the world, however, the exercise of dominion became more difficult and complicated. It was possible to abuse the creation and exercise dominion over it to bring harm instead of good.

After the Fall, dominion took on the added dimension of reversing the effects of the entrance of sin. For example, medicine is an extension of human beings' dominion over creation, alleviating one of the primary effects of the entrance of sin, which is disease. Similarly, business and commerce are the extension of human dominion over the creation by providing the means of making goods and services plentiful, allowing an outlet for human creativity, initiative, and vocation.[5] They also serve to alleviate scarcity of goods, one of the effects of the entrance of sin. But the privilege of dominion over the environment is always balanced by the responsibility to be a good steward over that which has been entrusted. Thus, the Cornwall Declaration is appropriately titled with the terms "environmental stewardship."[6]

Human beings do not own the environment. It clearly belongs to God (Psalm 24:1–2), and the property laws of the Old Testament reflect God's ultimate ownership of the earth (Leviticus 25:23). Humanity was commanded by God to subdue the earth, for its own benefit. Dominion is not equated with tyranny. Dominion is caring and responsible trusteeship over the earth. To be sure, this privilege has been abused due to the entrance of sin into the world. Greed has replaced legitimate self-interest, and dominion over the environment has repeatedly motivated mankind to rape the environment, thereby abandoning, for the sake of profit, human beings' rightful place as stewards and caretakers of the creation. Strip mining, clear-cutting of forests, and gill netting the ocean floor are examples of greed-motivated neglect of the environment that leaves it blighted and its inhabitants in jeopardy. However, Derr is correct when he argues that these

5 See Robert Sirico, "The Entrepreneurial Vocation," in chapter 2.

6 "The Cornwall Declaration on Environmental Stewardship," in *Environmental Stewardship in the Judeo-Christian Tradition*, ed. Michael B. Barkey (Grand Rapids: Acton Institute, 2000), xi–xv.

abuses are a deviation from the Judeo-Christian ethic, not something that follows directly from it, as many environmentalists claim. To suggest that Christian ethics is responsible for giving license for environmental destruction is historically inaccurate, and it ignores the many contributions of Judaism and Christianity to responsible environmentalism.[7]

Human beings' dominion over creation and the command to subdue the earth clearly imply that development that brings creation under their control and for their benefit is a good thing from God's perspective. Peter J. Leithart insightfully points out that the environmentalist ideal of a return to the pristine undeveloped wilderness is not necessarily a biblical ideal. He suggests a contrast between the biblical notion of dominion and the contemporary environmentalist ideal:

> More precisely, in God's wisdom, man best guards the world precisely by subduing it. . . . Wild animals become safe and serviceable only after they are made submissive to human rule. Land becomes more productive under human care. Art and architecture are possible only because of human effort to transform the material of creation. Subduing the earth brings safety, prosperity and beauty. As the earth is subdued, it becomes something worth guarding; it becomes a sanctuary. By contrast, should man fail to exercise this royal mandate, the world will be less productive, safe and beautiful. This pattern implies a very different perspective from that of contemporary environmentalism. Instead of guarding the pristine creation, humanity is called to guard the world once it has been subdued to human rule, once it has been transformed into something like a sanctuary. Man guards the garden and the city, not the wilderness.[8]

Humanity's dominion is clearly seen as a good thing from the perspective of Scripture. It is debatable how much development contributes to the beauty of creation, and Leithart likely overstates how much beauty comes out of development. Most people would prefer an undeveloped wilderness to a city for sheer aesthetics. But that does not undermine his primary point, that development was originally a good thing, though, like everything else in creation, corrupted by sin, which makes abuses and excesses inevitable. Conversely, the natural environment prior to the entrance of sin was very different from the undisturbed wilderness after the Fall. As the biocentrist Holmes Ralston points out (cited by Derr), "Wildness is a gigantic food pyramid, and this sets value in a grim, deathbound jungle. Earth is a slaughterhouse, with life a miasma rising over the stench. Nothing is done for

7 James Nash, "A Response," in Michael Cromartie, ed., *Creation at Risk? Religion, Science and Environmentalism* (Grand Rapids: Eerdmans, 1995), 106.

8 Peter J. Leithart, "Snakes in the Garden: Sanctuaries, Sanctuary Pollution and the Global Environment," *Stewardship Journal* (Fall 1993): 24–32.

the benefit of another. Blind and urgent exploitation is nature's driving theme."[9]

This point can probably be taken a step further. A good case can be made that the environmental ideal of a pristine, undisturbed wilderness is actually parallel in the Bible to land that is under God's curse.[10] For example, when the prophets describe the land of Israel and the land of many of its neighbors as under God's curse, there is a remarkable similarity to the ideal held up by environmentalists as the goal of their movement and the environmental policy they hope to shape. Furthermore, Leithart insightfully suggests that the ultimate ideal in the Bible, the eternal state, is crafted, not from the metaphor of the undisturbed wilderness, but from that of the *city*. The eternal state is referred to as the heavenly city (Revelation 21–22).[11] Thus, it would appear that development is not inherently problematic, nor is the pristine environment inherently as good as the environmental movement seems to assume. This is not to suggest that human dominion has not been corrupted by sin and the environment not abused. But to insist that development is somehow inherently a problem is not consistent with the biblical account of humanity's relationship with creation.

Assessment of Biocentrism

This biblical emphasis on human dominion over the creation helps us to evaluate the popular paradigm for environmentalism suggested by Michael Hoffman known as biocentrism, or deep ecology. Deep ecologists hold that the environment can and should be protected for its own sake, not for how it can benefit human beings. Many environmentalists and religious groups with environmental concerns have adopted this view and have given it strongly spiritual overtones. Movements such as creation spirituality and the Mother Earth movement, outgrowths of biocentrism, are actually forms of ancient paganism, in which the creation was revered and worshiped. Eco-terrorism is sometimes referred to as a form of worship, and there is an emphasis on bonding with the earth in many of these movements.

All of these manifestations of biocentrism have much in common with various forms of idolatry condemned by the Bible. To be sure, God reveals himself in the creation (Psalm 19:1), and the earth does belong to the Lord (Psalm 24:1). But the earth is not the Lord. Nowhere does the Bible or any Judeo-Christian ethic that is consistent with the Bible equate worship of the creation with worship of the Creator. In fact, one of the purposes of the Genesis account of creation was to distance Hebrew theology from the Canaanite religions

9 Holmes Ralston, *Environmental Ethics: Duties to and Values in the Natural World* (Philadelphia: Temple University Press, 1988), 218.

10 For further details on this see E. Calvin Beisner, *Prospects for Growth: A Biblical View of Population, Resources and the Future* (Westchester, Ill.: Crossway, 1990).

11 Leithart, "Snakes in the Garden."

of the Middle East, most of which worshiped the creation or parts of it. The creation account in the Bible is very clear that God stands over and above the creation. He is not to be identified with creation, nor is creation to be worshiped instead of him. Certainly human beings honor God when we properly care for his creation, exercising our role as stewards over it. But human beings also honor God when they exercise dominion over creation, developing it and harnessing it for the benefit of humanity.

The biblical notion of God as creator giving value to the earth and giving human beings dominion over creation would suggest that a theocentric view of the environment is more consistent with Judeo-Christian ethics than a biocentric ethic. There is no reason why a proper theocentric view of the environment, with God as creator investing the earth with value and entrusting human beings with responsible dominion over the earth, cannot produce a genuine environmental concern. Most people are motivated to take care of the environment because it belongs to God and is his creation, but also for the more homocentric reason that there is something left to pass on to the next generations.

A second concern with biocentrism is that it appears to lead to the notion of trees, plants, and animals having parallel rights with human beings. Hoffman suggests that nonhuman living things are also integral parts of the ecosystem that have intrinsic value. Human beings with rights do not stand above animals and plants, lacking such rights. Rather, all are part of a more holistic system in which all things are valued equally. This would seem to lead to the idea that animals and trees have rights that should be protected. We would not want to suggest that animals, for example, have no interests that are worthy of protection. We would hold that cruelty to animals is immoral, but we would stop short of insisting that animals have intrinsic rights. There is a good deal of debate over animal rights that is beyond the scope of this discussion, but at the least we would suggest that animals and plants are not rights bearers, but that animals may nevertheless have some interests that protect them from cruelty.

The problem with the way biocentrists view plants and animals is that it presents a system that is very difficult to live with consistently. If plants and trees have rights, then basic questions about what one will have for dinner are problematic. To be fair, Hoffman does hold that with clear criteria, human interests can take precedence over the environment, but he does not spell these criteria out. Once one admits that animals and trees have rights, then it would seem to be difficult to draw the necessary lines that would justify promoting human interests ahead of those of the rest of the ecosystem. In our view, a theocentric view balanced by the responsibility of stewardship for the creation avoids many of those problems.

Derr points out a third difficulty for biocentrism: the extremes to which it leads when practiced consistently. Not only does it make for public policy ambiguities when it comes to balancing competing rights, a task that Derr rightly calls hopelessly complicated. But to live out one's biocentrism consistently, Derr suggests, involves what he calls "biocentric fatalism." That is, for example, if overpopulation threatens the environment and the ongoing existence of certain species of animals, then it is not clear that human well-being would take priority. In fact, some have argued that when core human interests conflict with core nonhuman interests, human interests must give way. It may even be that in some cases, as Derr points out, some biocentrists even suggest a "thinning of the herd" of human beings in order to safeguard the environment. Most would regard this as a chilling prospect, as do some biocentrists, but to be consistent, one would have to admit to that possibility.

Balancing Jobs versus the Environment

However, the broad biblical parameters of dominion and stewardship are not particularly helpful when it comes to balancing jobs versus the environment in specific cases. The cases of the spotted owl and gnatcatcher are difficult ones, and balancing jobs and the environment is a challenge in both those cases. What makes them particularly difficult is that the birds in view are threatened with extinction for the sake of economic development. How should extinction of certain species of animals be viewed by someone committed to stewardship of the environment? A good case can be made for protecting species threatened by extinction because each species is a part of God's creative order with a part to play in maintaining it. But others argue that there is no moral obligation to protect species of animals and plants. Wilfred Beckerman, in "The Case for Economic Growth,"[12] argues that thousands of species of animals have naturally become extinct over the ages, and that if it happened naturally without any intervention of human beings, how can it be so problematic when it happens and humanity benefits from the economic development? Furthermore, he insists that even if the world does run out of some natural resources, society will likely get along just fine without it as it had for centuries before these raw materials were discovered. Many people apply this kind of reasoning to the spotted owl and the gnatcatcher, suggesting that in a few years, no one will notice their disappearance. Certainly compromises such as the one reached

12 Published in *Public Utilities Fortnightly*, 26 September 1974, 357–62.

in the gnatcatcher case that allowed developers to use some of the bird's habitat in exchange for protecting other parts of the habitat was a way to have environmental protection and economic development at the same time, though neither to the degree to which its advocates desired. With the spotted owl, new studies have demonstrated that the owl nests just as well in new growth forests as in the old growth ones, again providing basis for a compromise that lets loggers stay in business and protects the owl at the same time. In those cases where no compromise is available and when existence of a species is in conflict with the existence of communities dependent on an industry affected by the presence of the species, then one can argue that the people thrown out of work will recover from their fate. They will get new jobs, relocate if necessary, and get on with their lives. But the extinct species will not recover from extinction. On the other hand, it can also be argued that the communities that are destroyed by endangered species listings may not recover, and with their loss, something valuable to human society and community will have been lost.

This conflict between jobs and the environment is particularly acute in developing countries. Many third world countries insist that it is unfair to hold them to developed countries' standards of environmental protection. They argue that they should be allowed to set their own standards for protecting the environment, reflecting their national priorities, presumably biased toward economic growth at the expense of the environment. They suggest that it is hypocritical of the developed world to impose their standards on the developing nations, since the developed countries had the benefits of developing without current environmental standards. This is perhaps one area where economic growth can and should be pursued and environmental protection be allowed to take a lower place on the scale of priorities, since the livelihood of many people living on the precipice of poverty is at stake. If a nation's pollution could all be contained within their borders and they would pay all the costs of cleanup or live with the consequences, then that would probably be fair. However, pollution inevitably spills over borders, affecting people who have no say in the matter. Economists call these "externalities," and a significant problem in third world environmental ethics is who pays for the externalities.

Balancing jobs/development and the environment involves careful weighing of a number of factors. Except in unusual cases, one cannot be an absolutist about environmental issues. Resolving these issues involves a balance between two good things. It is simply not feasible, financially or in terms of lifestyle, to protect the environment in an optimal way without regard to how that will affect jobs and communities. Nor is it possible to have as much development as possible without regard to potential environmental damage. It is simply too costly to even clean up all environmental damage. Environmental ethics involves balancing of two morally praiseworthy goals—providing jobs and protecting the environment. The moral principles that undergird both of these goals come into conflict at times. That is what makes these issues so difficult.

Resolving environmental issues involves weighing the principles of exercising dominion over the earth and environmental stewardship. Properly balancing these depends on factors that include the degree of risk to the environment, which includes both the probability of damage and the level of damage to the environment, the benefits of development to the community, and the amount of loss sustained if the development project is curtailed. For example, in the heap-leach mining case, if the buyers of the irrigation systems were not interested in the monitoring equipment, that could bring a degree of risk to the environment that could endanger people's lives. The owner of the company should think very carefully about going forward with the sale without the monitoring equipment. In that case, it would seem that the risks to the environment would be significant and would outweigh any benefits in terms of jobs for the community. Conversely, in the spotted owl case, the harm to the logging communities was substantial, and it was found that the owl could nest in new growth forests. If that were not possible, one could make a case that the risk to the owl was outweighed by the risk to the communities that were greatly dependent on the logging industry for their livelihood. Or in the case of the Exxon Valdez, the oil tanker that ran aground in Prince William Sound in Alaska, one could argue that the expense in building double-hulled tankers would be justified if it would prevent the catastrophe involved in an oil spill. Or consider that gill netting the ocean floor to fish for tuna and other types of fish brings such destruction of the habitat that it outweighs any benefit in terms of jobs and income for the fishing industry.

A further factor is whether or not a compromise is feasible, as in the case of the gnatcatcher and the housing developers. Compromise is often in short supply in these discussions between radical environmentalists and business leaders. Companies facing these balancing decisions should clearly regard the environment as a stakeholder to whom they have responsibilities. The business executive operating out of a Judeo-Christian worldview should bear in mind both that "the earth is the LORD's" (Psalm 24:1) and that business activity is part of the exercise of human dominion over the earth.

Market-Based Environmental Policies

However one balances jobs versus the environment, there is also debate over the most effective means to accomplish that balance. The essential difference is between those who advocate a command style approach to environmental protection and those who advocate a market style approach. Critics of government regulation cite the repeated failures of government to protect the environment and suggest that in many cases government policy has actually produced the opposite effect from what was intended.

Though market incentives are not available to address every environmental problem, the market can be very effective in encouraging environmental protection by offering incentives for people to safeguard it. For example, in some countries in sub-Sahara Africa, elephants are prized for their ivory tusks and are thus endangered. Some countries take a command approach and prohibit poaching of elephants and sale of ivory. Since it is so profitable, there are more poachers than the government can police. But some countries have taken a market approach and allowed the villages around the elephants' habitat to trade in ivory and share the profit. They have financial incentive to keep the herds well populated, and in those countries the number of herds is rising. To be sure there are limits on how much ivory can be "harvested," but there is a more powerful incentive, financial self-interest, that motivates the people in the area to safeguard the herds.

A second example of market incentives involves air pollution. The Los Angeles basin is one of the most heavily polluted areas in the United States, and the local Air Quality Management District (AQMD) has set guidelines for businesses and automobiles in conjunction with the federal Clean Air Act. These guidelines set limits on the total amount of air pollution allowed in the area. But the AQMD also allocates "pollution credits" to the businesses in the area that indicate their acceptable pollution level. The AQMD also allows companies to buy and sell their pollution credits, so that companies would have incentive to reduce pollution and sell their credits to those who need them. The net amount of pollution being created is the same. Advocates of a market-oriented environmental policy suggest a similar approach to recycling and reducing the amount of trash by charging fees for trash collection based on the amount of trash a household generates.

For protecting environmentally sensitive areas, the government should either sell the land or turn over its maintenance to the environmental groups intent on seeing the land remain undeveloped. This approach enabled environmentalists to safeguard the wilderness area of Laguna Canyon in southern California and keep it free from development. At the least, when the government lists a species as endangered and declares its habitat off limits, it should compensate those who own the land by paying them fair market value for it. This is the normal procedure when government takes land to build highways. It is called the right of "eminent domain." But when the government exercises eminent domain, it is obligated to compensate the property owners for the loss of their property. Fairness dictates that the same procedure should be followed in dealing with environmentally sensitive areas.

ELEVEN

Technology in the Workplace

Technology giveth and technology taketh away.

Neil Postman

You already have zero privacy—get over it.

Scott McNealy, chairman and CEO, Sun Mircosystems

INTRODUCTION

During the last several decades, information technology has been harnessed to enhance business activities in dramatic ways. Organizations have used computing power to greatly increase production and distribution efficiencies, to extend their geographical reach far beyond national boundaries, and to collect and aggregate data to make more informed decisions regarding economic conditions, suppliers, competitors, employees, and customers.

Consumers who have access to computers have also experienced tremendous increases in economic power. With the staggering amount of data now readily available on the Internet, information gaps have been closed and bargaining ability greatly increased. Buyers can now easily compare prices and share information about the quality of products, services, and retailers, giving them greater leverage in transactions.

While the gains offered by technology have been impressive and widely experienced by those with access, it is critical to acknowledge the fact that there are real costs accrued as the price of achievement. As several critics remind us, technology always has unintended and not so obvious consequences.[1]

In the specific arena of the workplace, for example, some applications of technology are criticized for their negative impact on people, particularly employees and consumers. With respect to both

[1] For a lengthy discussion of the unintended consequences of technology, see Edward Tenner, *Why Things Bite Back: Technology and the Revenge of Unintended Consequences* (New York: Vintage Books, 1996).

groups, new technology permits information to be collected, stored, aggregated, and disseminated cheaply and quickly. The information can then be used for good or ill purposes, sometimes both in the same application.

New, inexpensive software, for example, allows for the monitoring of employee behavior in previously unimagined ways. Performance-based information such as the number of calls answered or key strokes made per increment of time is easily gathered. In addition, information such as phone and electronic mail messages, websites visited, and amount of time spent at particular sites is easily accessible to employers who may wish to track productivity and/or compliance with company policies. Even more powerful are inexpensive programs known as "key loggers" that permit the recording of each key stroke on a computer, including those which have been erased or edited.

While an organization should protect its interests and hold employees accountable, ethical questions persist about how far organizations should go to keep tabs on employees. In gathering data, information of a highly personal nature could be collected and wrongly used. These types of questions are particularly important to consider since technology continues to rapidly improve. In the near future, it seems that "panoptic" power will be available and employee (and consumer) behavior will become increasingly transparent and observable.

The focus of this chapter will be on evaluating technology and its applications to the workplace. Among the critical questions to consider are: Should a particular application be used just because technology permits it? If not, by which criteria should the use of technology be judged as "appropriate"? Is technology merely a "value neutral" tool, or is it values laden with a "bias" of its own?

The reading selections in this chapter offer some helpful insights into developing answers for these questions. In the first article, "Is Technology (ever) Evil?" David Gill evaluates the adequacy of a popular way of viewing technologies as merely "neutral" tools that are strictly dependent on the innate goodness (or evil) of the people who use them for their moral status. In contrast to this view, Gill argues that technology itself is embedded with values, some helpful and others harmful.

The second article, "Five Big Issues in Today's Technological Workplace," focuses on workplace issues. In it, Albert Erisman, a former Boeing executive, and now director of the Institute for Business, Technology and Ethics (www.ethix.org), discusses five areas in which there are significant challenges in making the "business case" for a new technology while simultaneously benefiting the people who may be affected by its application in the workplace.

The final article, "LittleBrother Is Watching You" by Miriam Schulman, addresses the specific issue of privacy and information gathering in the workplace. Schulman presents specific arguments on both sides of the issue and offers insight on some possible middle ground.

The case studies in this chapter present scenarios in which employers use technology either to enhance profitability or to protect their assets (theft prevention). However, some aspects of employee privacy may be invaded in the process. The discussion questions ask you to weigh the legitimacy of these applications of technology and to consider specific limits and guidelines.

READINGS

Is Technology (ever) Evil?

David Gill

Ethix (December 1999): 11.

In the October 19, 1999, issue of *InfoWorld*, editor Sandy Reed discussed our Institute for Business, Technology, and Ethics. She did a nice job and we appreciate both the encouragement and the publicity.

However, she began her column by saying that Al Erisman comes from the side that says "technology is good" and that I come from the side that says that "technology is evil." There is an element of truth to this way of representing Al and me and how we got into this project together; but it is misleading if we leave it at that.

I can't imagine ever saying simply that "technology is evil." What I oppose is "technopoly" or "technologism"—the unquestioned dominance and centrality of technology in human life. One way to put it is that technology is great in the tool box of life, but terrible on the throne of life.

———

Ethics is the study of matters of good and evil (or "bad") and right and wrong. What qualifies

something as ethically/morally "bad" or "evil"? It is that something is actually or potentially harmful to human life. Even if your ethics and morality are based on faith and religion, the reason why something is morally prohibited (by God or religion) is because it is harmful to human life.

Is technology (ever) actually or potentially harmful to human life? That is a question that interests me. Some of you will immediately think "If you put the question that way, then almost anything is potentially bad or evil!" Exactly! (The flip side is also important: almost anything is potentially beneficial to human life in some way, and thus potentially "good.") The moral life consists of wrestling with such questions, not in mindless conformity to some simplistic rules.

We are used to thinking about the ethics of technology in a simpler era, when technology was a matter of simple "tools." Technology, we think, is like a hammer. Its moral evaluation depends entirely on how it is used by people. Pounding nails to build a house is good; hitting your opponent over the head is bad. Morality is a matter of the intentions and actions of individuals; the instruments are morally neutral. Many today use that same logic to assess computers, genetic engineering, or any other technology.

This approach was a little naive even in the case of a hammer (someone once said "to a man with a hammer, everything looks like a nail"—i.e., the design of a hammer is already embedded with intentions and possible beneficial and harmful uses). But it is radically naive in the case of more complex technologies like automobiles or computers and networks.

Automobiles and computers are not merely "neutral" tools depending on whether their users are good or bad people. They bring both good and bad impacts into peoples' lives. Technology is not good or evil; it is good and evil. It is beneficial to human life in certain respects and harmful in others. Technology does not come into empty spaces in human life (there are none); it comes into spaces already occupied by other things; technologies replace things (sometimes earlier, less desirable technologies; sometimes conversation; etc.).

> *Technology is not good or evil;*
> *it is good and evil.*

The question is "what is the cost" of this new technology? What will it replace? What will it require in the future? What positive and negative uses will its presence incline and empower me to pursue? What are its "side effects?"

The primary values that are characteristic of technological thinking are "change," "power," "speed," "rationality," "measurability," and "efficiency." Judged only by its own internal values, "good" technologies are ones that change our world by increasing speed, power, and efficiency in ways that are rational and measurable (quantifiable).

My argument is, first, that all technological developments "bite back" and have hidden costs which we must attend to, and, second, that the core internal values of technology are inadequate as a general philosophy of life (what I would call "technologism").

So technology is not simply evil, but it is a terrible mistake if we give all technology a free "pass" on ethics. Sometimes such critical questioning will lead us to create compensations and defenses around certain technologies; other times it will send us back to the drawing board to develop better technologies with fewer negative features; but sometimes, I believe, it may lead us to say "no" to technology and choose a non-technological, inefficient, weak, slow, irrational, immeasurable, unchanged mode of existence and relationship. And that, on occasion, is good.

Questions for Discussion:

1. What do you think of Gill's assertion that all technologies have hidden costs and unintended consequences—in other words, that technologies have the capacity to "bite back"?
2. Do you agree that it may be better sometimes to "say 'no' to technology and choose a non-technological, inefficient, weak, slow, irrational, immeasurable, unchanged mode of existence and relationship"? Why or why not?

Five Big Issues in Today's Technological Workplace

Albert M. Erisman

Ethix (March/April 2002): 4–5.

What is the Institute for Business, Technology, and Ethics trying to accomplish? Briefly, it is to help businesses (and the professions) figure out the best way to get value from information technology for the good of the business without sacrificing people and ethical values along the way. Put another way, it is to create ways that businesses and the professions can use technology that will allow people to thrive and will also bring business value.

The problem is tough because of the rapid change of information technology, offering potential new solutions almost every day. Business pressures often undermine the opportunity to think clearly about unintended consequences from these new solutions. This may lead to solutions that undermine people and fail to deliver on the promised business value.

> *There are two reasons to consider people as a part of business solutions using technology: caring about people and caring about business.*

Many companies and institutions fail to consider the people side of the problem and focus only on business value. Interestingly, when the use of technology undermines people on the job, it also undermines the business because people are vital to business success. So there are two reasons to consider people as a part of business solutions using technology: caring about people and caring about business.

I would argue that doing the right thing by people should be a good enough motivation. However, presenting a new idea to business under pressure (that is, almost any business today) usu-

ally requires a "business case." So our goal is to examine problem areas where technology could produce transformation and develop strategies that bring value to the business while creating good environments for people (customers, employees, the community).

I will identify five areas where we can get more specific about these objectives.

Family-Friendly Business

As business is under pressure today, so too are families. In many families both parents need to work. This means parents face the challenge of balancing their workload, making time for each other and the children, not to mention their community and personal lives. Single parents have additional pressure points.

From the parents' point of view, it would be desirable to have the flexibility to juggle schedules, appointments, and school issues. Information technology makes it possible to provide flexible schedules, work from home, monitoring connections to day care centers, and the like. It would seem that these tools could be a great help to families.

But where is the value of all this for the business? Certainly, peace of mind for the employee makes it possible for them to give more creative energy to the job. Most literature on "knowledge work" today suggests this. But knowledge work can often be broken into tasks that can be done independently, *allowing work and other activity to mix*. For particularly intense knowledge work, the person will think about the problem a good deal of the time, *even in so-called personal time*. Capturing this "real estate of the brain" should be a great benefit to any business.

Making life easier for the employee has a benefit for both the employee and the business.

Similarly, distractions arising from family breakdown are very costly for both. The problem here, as in the other issues I will outline, is that many institutions have not thought carefully about what policies are appropriate for the business in managing knowledge workers.

Work Time and Personal Time

We live in an increasingly connected world with telecommunications, e-mail, pagers and cell phones. This enables people to work from almost anywhere. This technology allows for the collapse of boundaries between work and home. It allows the possibility of telecommuting (doing much of the work from home via the Internet). It allows a company to have its employees on call at all hours of the day or night. It also allows for employees to surf the web from the office, do the "paper" work for a mortgage from the office, or keep track of stocks through the company computer system.

With all of these possibilities, what are the appropriate responses for businesses and for individual employees?

Many companies look at telecommuting as an option only in the case of emergency. They want to set strict boundaries for what can be done from company-owned computing resources, but haven't considered strict boundaries in terms of expecting employees to be on call. Other companies look at telecommuting as a way to save the cost of office space, but are naïve about the issues of trust and serendipity that are lost when employees do not see each other face-to-face.

One early pioneering company encouraged employees to use company resources for personal work, as long as they were doing it on their own time. They argued that the time spent keeping bowling scores for their church on the data base program at work motivated them to learn the program and made them more productive for the company. "The database program and the PC don't wear out," an executive told me. "This has got to be a win-win."

Doctors have a history of managing the expectation of who is on call, what is expected, and when a person is "off duty." Companies have had much less history of structuring "on call" work for their network engineers.

Monitoring

Technology allows for the close monitoring of employees, whether it is websites visited, keystrokes, or (in the case of a truck driver) location and speed of the vehicle. Should there be limits on monitoring of employees or should the company have the right to monitor in any way it chooses? What disclosure should the company make to their employees on the monitoring they do?

Here again there are multiple things to consider. The company can easily argue that these people are doing work for the company and should follow the rules. Unauthorized behavior can be tracked, so why not?

The upside of monitoring is that it enables the company to quickly identify the person surfing porn sites at the office, and this appears to be a significant problem. So, too, is speeding and lack of required rest for truckers on the road.

The downside of this is what the "big brother" environment does to creative people. Does excessive monitoring actually inhibit creativity? If it is true that most people (90% or higher) will be trying to do the right thing, is it worth creating an oppressive environment in order to catch the small number of people who would abuse the rules?

Technology Transition

Projects that introduce new information technology often lead to changes in the way the companies implement their business processes. Resistance to change from people within the company is one of the largest barriers to the success of these projects. Sometimes this resistance is legitimate when plans don't account for needed "details" unseen by the company leaders. What do companies do to overcome resistance to change? Are there strategies companies could use to make the changes easier to implement and more successful?

Few companies have policies related to change in jobs from technology-based initiatives, except in the case of union work in a manufacturing setting. Often the union rules were reactionary as an organized way to fight off change, rather than working toward a "win-win" solution.

Thinking creatively about these and related issues is a requirement for business in the 21st century.

Technology has enabled "reengineering" projects that have had a significantly high failure rate because of these issues. Some authors have even equated reengineering and downsizing because the first often results in the second. It is time for serious discussion of technology transition because of its tremendous business and people impact.

Globalization

Globalization of a company leads to many changes in its culture. One is simply dealing with multiple cultures among its employees and customers. A second is creating an environment for leadership when the boss can't simply "drop by" each area of the company. Then there are issues of law that become challenging across country boundaries. What are ways that information technology can be used to support and augment traditional leadership responsibilities? How should these be used for greatest effectiveness?

Some companies are exploring parts of this big issue: dealing with loss of jobs when work is sent outside the country; creating collaborative teams around the world that can shorten cycle time in product development by passing work across the time zones; outsourcing "night shift" customer service to allow worldwide twenty-four-hour support.

Summary

These five problem areas represent a start at addressing issues in the workplace in our technological era. New tools and ideas made possible by changes in information technology are best used to do something new, not just automate the past. There are both new possibilities and new pitfalls. Thinking creatively about these and related issues is a requirement for business in the 21st century.

In this context we take business in its broadest terms, because almost any of these issues could be recast in thinking about the future university, medical services area, or government activity.

Question for Discussion:

In the five areas that Erisman mentions, do you think the technological transformations he envisions are essentially good things? Or do they have some "bite back" capacities about which you are concerned?

LittleBrother Is Watching You

Miriam Schulman

Business and Society Review 100/101 (1998): 65–69. Copyright © 1998 by the Center for Business Ethics at Bentley College.

Last year, a software package came on the market that allows employers to monitor their workers' Internet use. It employs a database of forty-five thousand Web sites that are categorized as "productive," "unproductive," or "neutral" and rates employees based on their browsing. It identifies the most frequent users and the most popular sites. It's called LittleBrother.

Though the title is tongue-in-cheek, Little-Brother does represent the tremendous capabilities technology has provided for employers to keep track of what their workforce is up to. There are also programs to search e-mail and programs to block objectionable Web sites. Beyond installing monitoring software, your boss can simply go into your hard drive, check your cache to see where you've been on the Net, and read your e-mail.

Did you delete that message you sent about his incompetence? Not good enough. The e-mail trash bin probably still exists on the server, and there are plenty of computer consultants who can retrieve the incriminating message.

All told, such monitoring is a widespread—and growing—phenomenon. Looking just at e-mail, a 1996 survey by the Society for Human Resource Management found that 36 percent of responding companies searched employee messages regularly and 70 percent said employers should reserve the right to do so.

The Law

Legally, employees have little recourse. The most relevant federal law, the 1986 Electronic Communications Privacy Act, prohibits unauthorized interception of various electronic communications, including e-mail. However, the law exempts service providers from its provisions, which is commonly interpreted to include employers who provide e-mail and Net access, according to David Sobel, legal counsel for the Electronic Privacy Information Center in Washington, D.C. A federal bill that would have required employers at least to notify workers that they were being monitored failed to come to a vote from 1993 to 1995.

The situations in the courts is similar. "There aren't many cases, and they tend to go against the employee," according to Santa Clara University (SCU) professor of law Dorothy Glancy. "Often, court opinions take the point of view that when the employees are using employers' property—the employers' computers and networks—the employees' expectation of privacy is minimal." When courts take this view, Glancy continues, "if employees want to have private communications, they can enjoy them on their own time and equipment."

In a presentation on employee monitoring, Mark S. Dichter and Michael S. Burkhardt of the law firm Morgan, Lewis & Bockius explain that courts have tried to balance "an employee's reasonable expectation of privacy against the employer's business justification for monitoring."

For example, in *Smyth* v. *Pillsbury Co.*, Michael Smyth argued that his privacy was violated and he was wrongfully discharged from his job after his employers read several e-mails he had exchanged with his supervisor. In the electronic messages, among other offensive references, he threatened to "kill the backstabbing bastards" in sales management.

The court ruled that Smyth had "no reasonable expectation of privacy" on his employer's system, despite the fact that Pillsbury had repeatedly assured employees that their e-mail was confidential. In addition, the court held that the company's interest in preventing "inappropriate and unprofessional" conduct outweighed Smyth's privacy rights.

Privacy as a Moral Matter

But the fact that employee monitoring is legal does not automatically make it right. From an ethical point of view, an employee surely does not give up all of his or her privacy when entering the workplace. To determine how far employee and employer moral rights should extend, it's useful to start with a brief exploration of how privacy becomes a moral matter.

Michael J. Meyer, SCU professor of philosophy, explains it this way: "Employees are autonomous moral agents. Among other things, that means they have independent moral status defined by some set of rights, not the least of which is the right not to be used by others as a means to increase overall welfare or profits."

Applying this to the workplace, Meyer says, "As thinking actors, human beings are more than cogs in an organization—things to be pushed around so as to maximize profits. They are entitled to respect, which requires some attention to privacy. If a boss were to monitor every conversation or move, most of us would think of such an environment as more like a prison than a human workplace."

But, like all rights, privacy is not absolute. Sometimes, as in the case of law enforcement, invasions of privacy may be warranted. In "Privacy, Morality and the Law," William Parent, also a philosophy professor at SCU, sets out six criteria for determining whether an invasion of privacy is justifiable:

1. For what purpose is the undocumented personal knowledge sought?
2. Is this purpose a legitimate and important one?
3. Is the knowledge sought through invasion of privacy relevant to its justifying purpose?
4. Is invasion of privacy the only or the least offensive means of obtaining the knowledge?
5. What restrictions or procedural restraints have been placed on the privacy-invading techniques?
6. How will the personal knowledge be protected once it has been acquired?[1]

These questions can offer guidance as we consider both sides of the controversy.

The Case for Workplace Monitoring

If an employer uses a software package that sweeps through office computers and eliminates games workers have installed, few people will feel such an action is an invasion of privacy. Our comfort with this kind of intrusion suggests that most of us don't fault an employer who insists that the equipment he or she provides be used for work, at least during working hours.

Why, then, should we balk when an employer tries to ensure that his equipment is not being used to surf non-job-related Web sites? Hours spent online browsing the recipe files of Epicurious are no less a breach of the work contract than game playing.

"The underlying principle is value for money," says Joseph R. Garber, a columnist for *Forbes* magazine. "If you don't deliver value for money, in some sense, you're lying." Garber gives this illustration: If we hired someone to paint our house and they didn't do the northern wall, we would feel moral outrage. Similarly, if we pay workers to give a good day's work and they are, instead, surfing X-rated Web sites, we are also morally outraged.

Such "cyberlollygagging" is no small problem. A study by Nielsen Media Research found that employees at major corporations such as IBM, Apple, and AT&T logged onto the online edition of *Penthouse* thousands of times a month.

Beyond worry about lost productivity, employers have legitimate concerns about the use of e-mail in thefts of proprietary information, which, according to the "Handbook on White Collar Crime," account for more than $2 billion in losses a year.[2] The transfer of such information can be monitored by programs that search employee e-mails for suspect word strings or by employers simply going into the employee's hard drive and reading the messages.

In a case last year, a former employee of Cadence Systems was charged with stealing proprietary information and intending to bring it to the rival software maker Avant! According to prosecutors, before leaving Cadence, he e-mailed a file containing five million bytes to a personal e-mail account. Such large messages suggested that he might be sending source code for the company's products and prompted Cadence to contact the police.

Electronic communications can pose other dangers for employers besides breached security and lost productivity. More and more, employers are being held legally liable for the atmosphere in the workplace. Although the case was ultimately dismissed, employers worry about litigation like the $70 million suit brought by Morgan Stanley employees who claimed that racist jokes on the company's electronic mail system created a hostile work environment.

Sexual harassment cases also often hinge on allegation of a hostile work environment, which might be evidenced by employees downloading or displaying pornographic material from the Web or sending off-color e-mails. "The days of guys putting naked bunnies up on their computer screens are gone because that's actionable stuff," Garber comments.

To prevent such abuses, Garber argues, employers need to be allowed to monitor: "We can't make corporations responsible for stopping unacceptable forms of behavior and then deny them the tools needed to keep an eye out for that behavior."

The Case against Workplace Monitoring

Consider this scenario: It's lunch hour. An employee writes a note to her boyfriend. She puts it in an envelope, affixes her own stamp, and drops it in the basket where outgoing mail is collected. Does the fact that the pencil and paper she used belong to her employer give her boss the right to open and read this letter?

Although most people would answer no, that's just the argument employers are making to defend monitoring e-mail, according to the Electronic Privacy Information Center's Sobel: Employers claim that because they own the computer, they have the right to read the e-mail it produces.

The situation is complicated by the fact that work and personal life are not as clearly delineated as they once were, owing, in part, to the very tech-

nologies that are being monitored. Employees may telecommute, doing much of their business through e-mail and the Net. Often they work a good deal more than forty hours a week. If they take a moment to send a message to Aunt Margaret in Saskatoon, do they not have a right to expect their e-mail will be confidential?

"Most people don't work eight to five," says Anthony Pozos, senior vice president for human resources and corporate service at Amdahl Corp. "We pay people to do a job; we don't really pay by time increment. Employees probably do use our e-mail or Web access for personal matters, it's analogous to using the telephone. People do sometimes need to do personal things on the job, but as long as it doesn't interfere with work, that should be okay."

Another ethical consideration in the debate is fairness. Usually, it's not corporate higherups who are subject to monitoring, but line workers. That's particularly true when it comes to keystroke monitoring, a form of electronic surveillance that measures the speed of data entry. According to an article in Public Personnel Management, "The majority of employees being electronically monitored are women in low-paying clerical positions."[3]

Then there's Parent's question about whether the invasion of privacy (represented by monitoring) is the only or the least offensive means of obtaining the information employers seek. In a survey conducted by *PC World*, slightly more than half of the executives interviewed were opposed to monitoring employees' Internet use. Scott Paddock, manager of PC Brokers, told the magazine, "First, I trust my employees; that's why they work for me. If there were to be any problems with an employee, those problems would present themselves without the need for me to get involved in cloak-and-dagger shenanigans. And second, if I spent time monitoring their Web usage, I would be just as guilty of wasting time as my behavior implies they are."[4]

Trust is often mentioned by opponents of monitoring as a major ethical issue. As Rita C. Manning writes in the *Journal of Business Ethics*, "When we look at the workplaces in which surveillance is common, we see communities in trouble. What is missing in these communities is trust."[5]

If, Manning continues, employers create trust, employee behavior "will conform to certain norms, not as a result of being watched, but as a result of the care and respect which are part of the communal fabric."[6]

Some Possibilities for Common Ground

It is possible to moot many of these ethical issues by arguing that monitoring all comes down to a question of contract. That is the view of David Friedman, an economist and professor at SCU's School of Law. "There isn't an agreement that is morally right for everybody. The important thing is what the parties agree to," he says. "If the employer gives a promise of privacy, then that should be respected." If, on the other hand, the employer reserves the right to read e-mail or monitor Web browsing, the worker can either accept those terms or look elsewhere for employment, Friedman continues.

Friedman's argument doesn't address the problems of lower-income workers who may not have a choice about whether to accept a job or, if they do, may be choosing between entry-level positions where monitoring is a feature of the work environment. But he does point to an area where some common ground may exist between opponents and proponents of monitoring. Most parties

to the debate agree that the companies should have clear policies on electronic surveillance and that these should be effectively communicated to employees.

A recent study by International Data Corporation suggests that such clarity does not currently prevail. A survey of employees at 110 businesses showed that 45 percent thought their company had no policy on e-mail at all. Most of those who did know the company policy had either learned it by word of mouth or were directly involved in writing it.[7]

Spelling out company policy "is our bottom line," says Sobel. "We would like to see an outright prohibition on e-mail monitoring in the workplace, but, at the very least, there needs to be notice to employees if that's the policy."

Pozos believes that involving employees in the creation of monitoring policy is also a way to find common ground. By bringing employees and managers together to develop principles and guidelines for electronic mail, Amdahl was able to create a policy that was acceptable to both sides, Pozos says.

In any case, employers who reserve the right to monitor should attend to the considerations Parent proposes, ensuring at least that the monitoring serves a legitimate purpose and follows clear procedures to protect a worker's personal life from unnecessary prying, either by LittleBrother or by Big Brother.

Notes

1. William A. Parent, "Privacy, Morality and the Law," *Philosophy and Public Affairs* 12 (fall 1983): 269.

2. Paul S. Greenlaw and Cornelia Prudeanu, "The Impact of Federal Legislation to Limit Electronic Monitoring," *Public Personnel Management* 26 (22 June 1997): 227.

3. Ibid., p. 227.

4. Jim A. Martin, "Is Monitoring Legal?" *PC World*, November 1997.

5. Rita C. Manning, "Liberal and Communitarian Defenses of Workplace Privacy," *Journal of Business Ethics* 6 (1997): 817.

6. Ibid., p. 817.

7. *Computing Canada*, 31 March 1997.

Questions for Discussion:

1. How do you balance concerns for privacy with business concerns about employee productivity that might show a need for workplace monitoring?
2. What is your evaluation of William Parent's six criteria for determining whether invasions of privacy are justified?

CASE STUDIES

Case 11.1: Customer Service and Privacy

Executives for a company engaged in providing express delivery and courier services have implemented a new computer program to improve customer service and driver productivity and safety. The program employs GPS (Global Positioning System) technology that can track the exact location of company trucks and vans. It allows the company to engage in "real time" tracking of shipments. Customers can log onto the company website, locate their shipments in transit, and receive an estimated arrival time.

Company executives have also discovered that the program can be used to track data about driver behavior. Since the company's business is based in large part on speed of delivery and the fact the company is liable for damage caused by company vehicles involved in accidents, executives welcome the use of tools that provide additional information about efficiency and safety.

After using the technology for a few months, managers have reprimanded and/or fired a few drivers for violating company policy on speeding, running errands on company time, and length of breaks. In response, many of the remaining drivers have complained that the program functions as an "electronic leash" and that it affects their ability to concentrate on safe driving since they are acutely aware of the fact that they are being so closely monitored.

Questions for Discussion:

1. Evaluate the use of this type of technology. How should the employer's need to hold employees accountable be balanced with trust and employees' need for some freedom at work?
2. What guidelines should be established to allow the legitimate use of this type of technology?

Case 11.2: To Catch a Thief

Executives of a small software development firm have long suspected that one of their employees has been stealing company secrets via computer. In order to develop a legal case against the suspect, they have investigated various options for fact gathering. After finding that surveillance cameras are impractical and raise serious legal questions, they turned to a computer program that would monitor keystrokes on employees' computers.

To avoid tipping off the suspect, the program (purchased for $99) was installed on the computers of everyone in his workgroup. The installation occurred after work hours and was packaged with other "upgrades" to avoid suspicion. The program, which is virtually detection proof, tracks every keystroke made on a computer on which it is installed, even erased and/or corrected ones.

After using the program for several weeks, it became clear the suspected thief has not been stealing secrets from the company. However, he and several other members of his workgroup were playing the game *Mercenary* during their work shifts. These employees have been given stern reprimands by their supervisor.

Another employee was recorded sending a negative email about a company executive to a new employee of the firm. "Sam is a first-class jerk! I can't stand working for him. He has no people skills whatsoever," she began. However, she backed over the entire message and replaced it with "Sam is very task-oriented. He doesn't spend too much time on personal issues because he values being efficient with his time." While the corrected message was the one that was sent, the program recorded all of the keystrokes made, even the "erased" ones. Sam, the executive referred to in the email is the company's chief technology officer. He was informed of her message and has been treating her differently since.

Questions for Discussion:

1. Evaluate the use of this type of technology. How should the company's need to protect its interests be balanced with trust and employee's need for some freedom at work?
2. What guidelines should be established to allow the legitimate use of this type of technology?

COMMENTARY

The advances made in the marketplace through new applications of technology have been impressive. New methods of conducting transactions and novel business models almost unimaginable just a few years ago are now a mainstream part of our economy. For example, E-Bay has found a highly successful niche by bringing buyers and sellers together through technology without the traditional business functions of taking actual ownership of merchandise and/or operating production facilities.

Companies can also efficiently reduce labor costs and provide round-the-clock service by using technology to shift labor overseas. Without knowing it, for example, Americans wishing to check their credit card balances may seamlessly reach call service centers located in India staffed by locals with made-up English names.[2]

Information technology also permits companies to search worldwide for lower costs on raw materials and capital, higher returns on investments, and more profitable markets in which to sell their goods. Management, design, manufacturing, and distribution functions of products can also be separated by geographical distances not permissible in the not-too-distant past because of the monitoring and information exchange abilities provided by computers.

These types of efficiency gains are impressive and illustrate the promise offered by technological innovation. However, caution must be taken in order to avoid falsely painting a picture in which only the positive aspects of technology are portrayed. When the advances become the sole points of emphasis, technology can become an almost unchallenged organizing principle, or what David Gill refers to as "technologism."

From a Christian perspective, technology must be critically evaluated and not judged by its internal logic alone. As Gill and others have observed, technology often has a cost or "bite back" effect. To be sure, Christian reflection does not have to be "technophobic," or "neo-Luddite" in nature. In fact, in their proper place, technological innovations can be viewed as wondrous gifts of the Creator. However, the possible and real negative impacts of technological applications must be honestly recognized and assessed so that ethics drives and limits technology and not the other way around. Email, for example, is a helpful medium in some instances, but it can be a hindrance to relationships and community if it serves as a thoughtless substitute for communications that should be conducted on a face-to-face basis.

[2] As reported in the video series *Commanding Heights*, Episode Three: The New Rules of the Game, Heights Productions Inc., 2002.

With respect to other applications of computers in the workplace, Albert Erisman wisely points out that the "business case" for a new technology can inhibit the ability of people in the organization to thrive. Sometimes the two agendas can be brought together so that they are complementary rather than adversarial goals, as Erisman points out. Yet in other instances the two are not so easily merged. Acknowledgement must be made that clear tradeoffs are involved and a perfect balance may not be possible.

One of the areas in which tensions arise in the contemporary workplace is in the use of technological tools for purposes of employee monitoring. As information becomes easy and inexpensive to collect, combine, and use in decision making, the interests of employers and employees can collide in intense ways. As Miriam Schulman points out, employers generally want value for money or a "fair day's work for a fair day's pay" and want to protect company assets from theft or legal liability. In addition to the traditional reasons of assuring good customer service and physical safety, employers now monitor employees in order to protect themselves from legal liability for sexual harassment (through email or visits to adult websites); use of computers for illegal purposes such as theft, hacking, or sabotage; and wasting time "on the clock" through personal use of computers. Recent surveys show that the majority of employers now monitor computer use to some degree.

While these are legitimate reasons to use monitoring tools, employees may feel intruded upon. Employees want to be trusted, and they dislike the feeling of being watched, even if they are doing nothing at odds with company policies and procedures. Furthermore, most employees want and expect some degree of privacy and the ability to use email and Internet access in the workplace for reasonable personal matters.

By what criteria might Christian ethics deem a use of technology in this regard appropriate? Fairness is the first standard that comes to mind. On the side of employers, some degree of monitoring is appropriate. Accountability and the protection of company assets are morally appropriate goals. There are indeed employees who steal, have poor work habits, or who could expose the company to legal liability through sexual harassment or dangerous driving of company vehicles. Given advance notice of policies to employees, reasonable means, and overall due process, monitoring is fair, given the fact that companies are paying employees to work and to enhance company assets.

However, there are also negative consequences to these applications of technology. Some company policies are too stringent, and some means of data collection are overly invasive both in terms of ethics and managerial efficiency. As Erisman points out, the lines between work time and personal time are becoming increasingly blurred, especially with "knowledge workers." If companies expect employees to work from home on some evenings (and to use personal computers on company business), or to be "on call" during "off work" hours, then fairness dictates that employees should be allowed to spend a reasonable amount of time during "working hours" on personal matters.

With respect to data gathering on employee activities, a general rule of "the least invasive means possible" is best. Most employees are reasonable and understand when there are legitimate reasons for monitoring behavior. However, the "big brother" feeling created by overly invasive means leads to a threatening environment where the worst is assumed. Most employees do not respond well to a culture of distrust.

Since so much of organizational activity is done through technological means in the contemporary workplace, a vast amount of data is recorded. Data collected and stored for one reason could be used or aggregated for purposes outside of original intentions. Some of this information may be highly personal in nature. While such data may be recorded legitimately (for legal liability purposes, for example), organizations seeking to be ethical in their dealings must have clear policies regarding their review, dissemination, and use. Such data should only be retrieved if reasonable and just grounds exist to suspect an employee of violating company policies.

Using specific technologies such as "key logging" software outside of highly specific instances is questionable. Everyone has had the experience of beginning an email message, erasing portions of it, and then sending a rephrased message. Nobody would want the erased words to be recorded and read. The ability to record such data is tantamount to a "thought police" level of monitoring.

In many instances the results intended by monitoring can be achieved with less invasive means. Counting key strokes and/or checking time spent surfing the Web, for example, may be unnecessary. The efficiency of some workers can be checked through other measures such as progress toward specific project goals.

The use of computers for employee monitoring in the workplace is a good example of why it is necessary to critically evaluate technology by standards other than its ability to accomplish something in an efficient, powerful, or novel manner. While it may seem like a waste of time to "philosophize" or "theologize" about technology, asking critical questions allows us to define appropriateness and set limits. Otherwise, as noted author and social critic Neil Postman reminds us, we will be used by technology, rather than be users of it.[3]

3 Neil Postman, *Technopoly: The Surrender of Culture to Technology* (New York: Vintage Books, 1993).

TWELVE

Moral Leadership in Business

Why should my conscience bother me? . . . I just do as I'm told, and I'd advise you to do the same.

Statement made to Kermit Vandivier
during a scandal involving aircraft brakes[1]

In fact, ethics has everything to do with management.

Lynn Sharp Paine, Harvard Business School[2]

[1] Kevin Vandivier, "Why Should My Conscience Bother Me?" in Robert Heilbroner, *In the Name of Profit* (New York: Doubleday, 1972), 3–31.

[2] Lynn Sharp Paine, "Managing for Organizational Integrity," *Harvard Business Review* (March–April 1994).

INTRODUCTION

There is much more to business ethics than individuals making good ethical decisions. Business ethics is often described under the broader term of "organizational ethics," suggesting that ethics has to do with organizations as well as with individuals. That is, an organization such as a company can have moral responsibilities and can exercise influence on its employees simply by virtue of their being in the organization. Implicit in this is the notion that organizations can, by a variety of both formal and informal mechanisms, either empower or discourage employees from following the dictates of conscience.

In this chapter, we want you to wrestle with the ways in which organizations can affect individuals in their moral decision making, either for better or for worse. We would argue that individual moral decision making in the context of an organization is much more complex than moral decision making in private life. Organizational pressures can be brought to bear on employees to compromise values that have no analogy in private life and in strictly individual decision

423

making. The important issue we want to raise in this chapter is how a company, in its formal structure and informal practices, can be a place that encourages and supports ethical behavior.

In "Creating and Encouraging Ethical Corporate Structures," Patrick Murphy offers specific policy measures that companies can implement to encourage ethical behavior. He argues that since "ethical business practices stem from ethical corporate culture," managers must introduce several critical components to create and sustain a culture that enhances ethics. Among these components are corporate credos, ethics programs, and codes of conduct that provide specific guidance to employees in various business areas.

We would not suggest, however, that organizational factors are solely responsible for an employee's moral behavior. We recognize that personal character plays a significant role in one's ethical behavior on the job and that character is formed largely outside the workplace by other significant influences such as parents, religious background, education, mentors, and prominent peers. Virgil Smith, in his article "The Place of Character in Corporate Ethics," points out the need for character and personal integrity along with institutional mechanisms to encourage ethical behavior. Smith critiques the recent literature on management and ethics that emphasizes systems while neglecting personal character as the heart of an economic system. In pointing us back in the direction in which we started this book, Smith asserts that "system" and social control will likely fail in the absence of personal virtue and trust, which are critical elements to a successful and moral commercial system. One of the cases in this chapter ("How Much Does Character Count?") will help you wrestle with the specific link between character and performance on the job.

Finally, Kermit Vandivier writes in the first person about his experiences in a famous case of fraud that occurred in the context of trying to win a defense industry subcontract. While this episode occurred almost thirty years ago, the issues are still relevant. In Vandivier's case, his company was faced with tremendous competitive pressures and a strong desire to beat the competition to win a critical contract, making the plant he worked at ripe for ethical compromise. His description is eye-opening, and it insightfully illustrates many of the factors outlined by the other authors in this chapter. We suggest that you read it as a case study by placing yourself in his situation. Imagine yourself facing the conflict of conscience, family obligations, and authority. How do you think you would react?

READINGS

Creating and Encouraging Ethical Corporate Structures

Patrick E. Murphy

Sloan Management Review 30, no. 2 (Winter 1989): 81–87. Copyright © 1989 by the Sloan Management Review Association.

[1]What is an ethical company? This question is not easy to answer. For the most part, ethical problems occur because corporate managers and their subordinates are *too* devoted to the organization. In their loyalty to the company or zest to gain recognition, people sometimes ignore or overstep ethical boundaries. For example, some sales managers believe that the only way to meet ambitious sales goals is to have the sales reps "buy" business with lavish entertaining and gift giving. This overzealousness is the key source of ethical problems in most business firms.

Employees are looking for guidance in dealing with ethical problems. This guidance may come from the CEO, upper management, or immediate supervisors.[2] We know that ethical business practices stem from an ethical corporate culture. Key questions are: How can this culture be created and sustained? What structural approaches encourage ethical decision making? If the goal is to make the company ethical, managers must introduce structural components that will enhance ethical sensitivity.

In this paper, I examine three promising and workable approaches to infusing ethical principles into business:

- corporate credos that define and give direction to corporate values;
- ethics programs where company-wide efforts focus on ethical issues; and
- ethical codes that provide specific guidance to employees in functional business areas.

Below I review the virtues and limitations of each and provide examples of companies that successfully employ these approaches.

Corporate Credos

A corporate credo delineates a company's ethical responsibility to its stakeholders; it is probably the most general approach to managing corporate ethics. The credo is a succinct statement of the values permeating the firm. The experiences of Security Pacific Corporation (a Los Angeles–based national bank that devised a credo in 1987) and of Johnson & Johnson illustrate the credo approach.

Security Pacific's central document is not an ethical code per se; rather, it is six missionlike commitments to customers, employees, communities, and stockholders. The credo's objective is "to seek a set of principles and beliefs which might provide guidance and direction to our work." . . .

More than 70 high-level managers participated in formulating a first draft of the commitments. During this process, senior managers shared and analyzed examples of ethical dilemmas they had faced in balancing corporate and constituent obligations. An outside consultant, hired to manage the process, helped to draft the language. Ultimately more than 250 employees, from all levels of the bank, participated in the credo formulation process via a series of discussion groups.

Once the commitments were in final form, management reached a consensus on how to communicate these guiding principles to the Security Pacific organization. Credo coordinators developed and disseminated a leader's guide to be used at staff meetings introducing the credo; it contained instructions on the meeting's format and on showing a videotape that explained the credo and the process by which it was developed. At the meetings, managers invited reactions by posing these questions: What are your initial feelings about what you have just read? Are there any specific commitments you would like to discuss? How will the credo affect your daily work? Employees were thus encouraged to react to the credo and to consider its long-run implications.

Security Pacific's credo was recently cited as a model effort, and it serves internally both as a standard for judging existing programs and as a justification for new activities.[3] For example, the "commitment to communities" formed the basis for a program specifically designed to serve low-income constituents in the area. However, this credo should not be considered the definitive approach to ethics management. First, the credo could be interpreted simply as an organizational mission statement, not as a document about ethics. Indeed, the examples supporting the credo and the videotape itself do stress what might just be called good business practice, without particular reference to ethical policies. And second, the credo has not been in place long enough for its impact to be fully assessed.

Table 1	The Credo of Security Pacific Corporation

Commitment to Customer

The first commitment is to provide our customers with quality products and services which are innovative and technologically responsive to their current requirements, at appropriate prices. To perform these tasks with integrity requires that we maintain confidentiality and protect customer privacy, promote customer satisfaction, and serve customer needs. We strive to serve qualified customers and industries which are socially responsible according to broadly accepted community and company standards.

Commitment of Employee to Employee

The fourth commitment is that of employees to their fellow employees. We must be committed to promote a climate of mutual respect, integrity, and professional relationships, characterized by open and honest communication within and across all levels of the organization. Such a climate will promote attainment of the Corporation's goals and objectives, while leaving room for individual initiative within a competitive environment.

Commitment to Employee

The second commitment is to establish an environment for our employees which promotes professional growth, encourages each person to achieve his or her highest potential, and promotes individual creativity and responsibility. Security Pacific acknowledges our responsibility to employees, including providing for open and honest communication, stated expectations, fair and timely assessment of performance and equitable compensation which rewards employee contributions to company objectives within a framework of equal opportunity and affirmative action.

Commitment to Communities

The fifth commitment is that of Security Pacific to the communities which we serve. We must constantly strive to improve the quality of life through our support of community organizations and projects, through encouraging service to the community by employees, and by promoting participation in community services. By the appropriate use of our resources, we work to support or further advance the interests of the community, particularly in times of crisis or social need. The corporation and its employees are committed to complying fully with each community's laws and regulations.

Commitment of Employee to Security Pacific

The third commitment is that of the employee to Security Pacific. As employees, we strive to understand and adhere to the corporation's policies and objectives, act in a professional manner, and give our best effort to improve Security Pacific. We recognize the trust and confidence placed in us by our customers and community and act with integrity and honesty in all situations to preserve that trust and confidence. We act responsibly to avoid conflicts of interest and other situations which are potentially harmful to the corporation.

Commitment to Stockholder

The sixth commitment of Security Pacific is to its stockholders. We will strive to provide consistent growth and a superior rate of return on their investment, to maintain a position and reputation as a leading financial institution, to protect stockholder investments, and to provide full and timely information. Achievement of these goals for Security Pacific is dependent upon the successful development of the five previous sets of relationships.

Any discussion of corporate credos would be incomplete without reference to Johnson & Johnson, whose credo is shown in Table 2. This document focuses on responsibilities to consumers, employees, communities, and stockholders. (The current J&J president, David Clare, explains that responsibility to the stockholder is listed last because "if we do the other jobs properly, the stockholder will always be served.") The first version of this credo, instituted in 1945, was revised in 1947. Between 1975 and 1978, chairman James Burke held a series of meetings with J&J's 1,200 top managers; they were encouraged to "challenge" the credo. What emerged from the meetings was that the document in fact functioned as it was intended to function; a slightly reworded but substantially unchanged credo was introduced in 1979.

Over the last two years, the company has begun to survey all employees about how well the company meets its responsibilities to the four principal constituencies. The survey asks employees from all fifty-three countries where J&J operates questions about every line in the credo. An office devoted to the credo survey tabulates the results, which are confidential. (Department and division managers receive only information pertaining to their units and composite numbers for the entire firm.) The interaction at meetings devoted to discussing these findings is reportedly very good.

Does J&J's credo work? Top management feels strongly that it does. The credo is often mentioned as an important contributing factor in the company's exemplary handling of the Tylenol crises several years ago. It would appear that the firm's commitment to the credo makes ethical business practice its highest priority. One might question whether the credo is adequate to deal with the multitude of ethical problems facing a multinational firm; possibly additional ethical guidelines could serve as reinforcement, especially in dealing with international business issues.

When should a company use a corporate credo to guide its ethical policies? They work best in firms with a cohesive corporate culture, where a spirit of frequent and unguarded communication exists. Generally, small, tightly knit companies find that a credo is sufficient. Among large firms, Johnson & Johnson is an exception. J&J managers consciously use the credo as an ethical guidepost; they find that the corporate culture reinforces the credo.

When is a credo insufficient? This approach does not offer enough guidance for most multinational companies facing complex ethical questions

---

Table 2   Johnson & Johnson Credo

We believe our first responsibility is to the doctors, nurses, and patients, to mothers and all others who use our products and services. In meeting their needs everything we do must be of high quality. We must constantly strive to reduce our costs in order to maintain reasonable prices. Customers' orders must be serviced promptly and accurately. Our suppliers and distributors must have an opportunity to make a fair profit.

We are responsible to our employees, the men and women who work with us throughout the world. Everyone must be considered as an individual. We must respect their dignity and recognize their merit. They must have a sense of security in their jobs. Compensation must be fair and adequate and working conditions clean, orderly, and safe. Employees must feel free to make suggestions and complaints. There must be equal opportunity for employment, development, and advancement for those qualified. We must provide competent management, and their actions must be just and ethical.

We are responsible to the communities in which we live and work and to the world community as well. We must be good citizens—support good works and charities and bear our fair share of taxes. We must encourage civic improvements and better health and education. We must maintain in good order the property we are privileged to use, protecting the environment and natural resources.

Our final responsibility is to our stockholders. Business must make a sound profit. We must experiment with new ideas. Research must be carried on, innovative programs developed and mistakes paid for. New equipment must be purchased, new facilities provided, and new products launched. Reserves must be created to provide for adverse times. When we operate according to these principles, the stockholders should realize a fair return.

in different societies, for firms that have merged recently and are having trouble grafting disparate cultures, and for companies operating in industries with chronic ethical problems. A credo is like the Ten Commandments. Both set forth good general principles, but many people need the Bible, religious teachings, and guidelines provided by organized religion, as well. Similarly, many companies find that they need to offer more concrete guidance on ethical issues.

Ethics Programs

Ethics programs provide more specific direction for dealing with potential ethical problems than general credos do. Two companies—Chemical Bank and Dow Corning—serve as examples. Although the thrust of the two programs is different, they both illustrate the usefulness of this approach.

Chemical Bank, the nation's fourth largest bank, has an extensive ethics education program. All new employees attend an orientation session at which they read and sign off on Chemical's code of ethics. (This has been in existence for thirty years and was last revised in May 1987.) The training program features a videotaped message from the chairman emphasizing the bank's values and ethical standards. A second and more unusual aspect of the program provides in-depth training in ethical decision making for vice presidents.[4]

The "Decision Making and Corporate Values" course is a two-day seminar that occurs away from the bank. Its purpose, according to a bank official, is "to encourage Chemical's employees to weigh the ethical or value dimensions of the decisions they make and to provide them with the analytic tools to do that." This program began in 1983; more than 250 vice presidents have completed the course thus far. Each meeting is limited to twenty to twenty-five senior vice presidents from a cross-section of departments; this size makes for a seminarlike atmosphere. The bank instituted the program in response to the pressures associated with deregulation, technology, and increasing competition.

The chairman always introduces the seminar by highlighting his personal commitment to the program. Most of the two days is spent discussing case studies. The fictitious cases were developed following interviews with various Chemical managers who described ethically charged situations. The cases are really short stories about loan approval, branch closings, foreign loans, insider trading, and other issues.[5] They do not have "solutions" as such; instead, they pose questions for discussion, such as, Do you believe the individual violated the bank's code? Or, What should X do?

Program evaluations have yielded positive results. Participants said they later encountered dilemmas similar to the cases, and that they had developed a thinking process in the seminar that helped them work through other problems. This program, while it is exemplary, only reaches a small percentage of Chemical's 30,000 employees. Ideally, such a program would be disseminated more widely and would become more than a one-time event.

Dow Corning has a long-standing—and very different—ethics program. Its general code has been revised four times since its inception in 1976 and includes a seven-point values statement. The company started using face-to-face "ethical audits" at its plants worldwide more than a decade ago. The number of participants in these four-to-six-hour audits ranges from five to forty. Auditors meet with the manager in charge the evening before to ascertain the most pressing issues. The actual questions come from relevant sections in the corporate code and are adjusted for the audit location. At sales offices, for example, the auditors concentrate on issues such as kickbacks, unusual requests from customers, and special pricing terms; at manufacturing plants, conservation and environmental issues receive more attention. An ethical audit might include the following questions.

- Are there any examples of business that Dow Corning has lost because of our refusal to provide "gifts" or other incentives to government officials at our customers' facilities?
- Do any of our employees have ownership or financial interest in any of our distributors?
- Have our sales representatives been able to undertake business conduct discussions with

distributors in a way that actually strengthens our ties with them?

- Has Dow Corning been forced to terminate any distributors because of their business conduct practices?
- Do you believe that our distributors are in regular contact with their competitors? If so, why?
- Which specific Dow Corning policies conflict with local practices?

Developing a structure is not sufficient by itself. The structure will not be useful unless it is supported by institutionalized managerial processes.

John Swanson, manager of Corporate Internal and Management Communications, heads this effort; he believes the audit approach makes it "virtually impossible for employees to consciously make an unethical decision." According to Swanson, twenty to twenty-three meetings occur every year. The Business Conduct Committee members, who act as session leaders, then prepare a report for the Audit Committee of the board. He stresses the fact that there are no shortcuts to implementing this program—it requires time and extensive interaction with the people involved. Recently the audit was expanded; it now examines internal as well as external activities. (One audit found that some salespeople believed manufacturing personnel need to be more honest when developing production schedules.) One might ask whether the commitment to ethics is constant over time or peaks during the audit sessions; Dow Corning may want to conduct surprise audits, or develop other monitoring mechanisms or a more detailed code.

When should a company consider developing an ethics program? Such programs are often appropriate when firms have far-flung operations that need periodic guidance, as is the case at Dow Corning. This type of program can deal specifically with international ethical issues and with peculiarities at various plant locations. Second, an ethics program is useful when managers confront similar ethical problems on a regular basis, as Chemical Bank executives do. Third, these programs are useful in organizations that use outside consultants or advertising agencies. If an independent contractor does not subscribe to corporate credo, the firm may want to use an ethical audit or checklist to heighten the outside agency's sensitivity to ethical issues.

When do ethics programs come up lacking? If they are too issue centered, ethics programs may miss other, equally important problems. (Dow's program, for example, depends on the questions raised by the audit.) In addition, the scope of the program may limit its impact to only certain parts of the organization (e.g., Chemical Bank). Managers who want to permanently inculcate ethical considerations may be concerned that such programs are not perceived by some employees as being long term or ongoing. If the credo can be compared with the Ten Commandments, then ethics programs can be likened to weekly church services. Both can be uplifting, but once the session (service) is over, individuals may believe they can go back to business as usual.

Tailored Corporate Codes

Codes of conduct, or ethical codes, are another structural mechanism companies use to signal their commitment to ethical principles. Ninety percent of Fortune 500 firms, and almost half of all other firms, have ethical codes. According to a recent [*sic*] survey, this mechanism is perceived as the most effective way to encourage ethical business behavior.[6] Codes commonly address issues such as conflict of interest, competitors, privacy, gift giving and receiving, and political contributions. However, many observers continue to believe that codes are really public relations documents, or motherhood and apple pie statements; these critics claim that codes belittle employees and fail to address practical managerial issues.[7]

Simply developing a code is not enough. It must be tailored to the firm's functional areas (e.g., marketing, finance, personnel) or to the major line of business in which the firm operates. The rationale for tailored codes is simple. Functional areas or divisions have differing cultures and needs. A consumer products division, for example, has a relatively distant relationship with customers, because it relies heavily on advertising to sell its products. A division producing industrial products, on the other hand, has fewer customers and uses a personal, sales-oriented approach. A code needs to reflect these differences. Unfortunately, very few ethics codes do so.

Several companies have exemplary codes tailored to functional or major business areas. I describe two of these below—the St. Paul Companies (specializing in commercial and personal insurance and related products) and International Business Machines (IBM).

The St. Paul Companies revised their extensive corporate code, entitled "In Good Conscience," in 1986. All new employees get introduced to the code when they join the company, and management devotes biannual meetings to discussing the code's impact on day-to-day activities. In each of the five sections, the code offers specific guidance and examples for employees to follow. The statements below illustrate the kinds of issues, and the level of specificity, contained in the code.

- Insider Information. For example, if you know that the company is about to announce a rise in quarterly profits, or anything else that would affect the price of the company's stock, you cannot buy or sell the stock until the announcement has been made and published.
- Gifts and Entertainment. An inexpensive ballpoint pen, or an appointment diary, is a common gift and generally acceptable. But liquor, lavish entertainment, clothing, or travel should not be accepted.
- Contact with Legislators. If you are contacted by legislators on matters relating to the St. Paul, you should refer them to your governmental affairs or law department.

The "Employee Related Issues" section of the code is the most detailed; it directly addresses the company's relationship to the individual, and vice versa. This section spells out what employees can expect in terms of compensation (it should be based on job performance and administered fairly), advancement (promotion is from within, where possible), assistance (this consists of training, job experience, or counseling) and communications (there should be regular feedback; concerns can be expressed without fear of recrimination). It also articulates the St. Paul Companies' expectation of employees regarding speaking up (when you know something that could be a problem), avoiding certain actions (where the public's confidence could be weakened), and charting your career course.

The company also delineates employee privacy issues. The code outlines how work-related information needed for hiring and promotion is collected. (Only information needed to make the particular decision is gathered; it is collected from the applicant/employee where possible. Polygraphs are not used.) The St. Paul informs employees about what types of information are maintained. Finally, information in an individual's file is open to the employee's review.

The code covers other important personnel issues in depth, as well. It touches on equal opportunity by mentioning discrimination laws, but the emphasis is on the company recognition of past discrimination and its commitments to "make an affirmative effort to address this situation in all of its programs and practices." Data acquired from the St. Paul supports this point. Between 1981 and 1986, hiring and promotion increased 60 percent for minorities in supervisory positions and 49 percent for women in management—even though overall employment rose only about 3 percent during this time. In addition, the code informs employees that the company will reimburse all documented business expenses. And it covers nepotism by stating that officers' and directors' relatives will not be hired; other employees' relatives can be employed, so long as they are placed in different departments.

Being an ethical company requires providing clear guidelines for employees. The St. Paul Companies' extensive discussion of personnel policies does just that. Employees may strongly disapprove of certain policies, but they are fully informed. The termination policy, for example, states that employment is voluntary and that individuals are free to resign at any time; the company, too, can terminate employees "at any time, with or without cause." Some people may consider that policy unfair or punitive, but at least the rules of the game are clear. One limitation of the code is that all sections are not uniformly strong. For example, the marketing section is only one paragraph long and contains few specifics.

The second illustration is of a code tailored to the company's major line of business. IBM's "Business Conduct Guidelines" were instituted in the 1960s and revised most recently in 1983 [*sic*]. New employees receive a copy and certify annually that they abide by the code. It has four parts; the most extensive section is entitled "Conducting IBM's Business." Since IBM is, at its core, a marketing and sales organization, this section pertains primarily to these issues.

Six subsections detail the type of activities IBM expects of its sales representatives. First, "Some General Standards" include the following directives, with commentaries: do not make misrepresentations to anyone, do not take advantage of IBM's size, treat everyone fairly (do not extend preferential treatment), and do not practice reciprocal dealing. Second, "Fairness in the Field" pertains to disparagement (sell IBM products on their merits, not by disparaging competitors' products or services). In addition, it prohibits premature disclosure of product information and of selling if a competitor already has a signed order. Third, "Relations with Other Organizations" cautions employees about firms that have multiple relationships with IBM (deal with only one relationship at a time, and do not collaborate with these firms).

The fourth and fifth sections address "Acquiring and Using Information for or about Others." The code spells out the limits to acquiring information (industrial espionage is wrong) and to using information (adverse information should not be retained). Employees must determine the confidentiality of information gathered from others. The final section outlines IBM's policy on "Bribes, Gifts, and Entertainment." The company allows customary business amenities but prohibits giving presents that are intended to "unduly influence" or "obligate" the recipient, as well as receiving gifts worth more than a nominal amount.

One might contend that it is easy for a large, profitable company like IBM to have an exemplary code. On the other hand, one could also argue that a real reason for the company's continued success is that its sales representatives do subscribe to these principles. Is this a perfect code? No. The gifts area could use more specificity and, even though the company spends millions of dollars a year on advertising, that subject is not addressed in any section of the code. Further, IBM's legal department administers the code, which may mean that problems are resolved more by legal than ethical interpretation.

When should a company use a tailored code of ethics? If a company has one dominant functional unit (like IBM), or if there is diversity among functional areas, divisions, or subsidiaries, then a tailored code might be advisable. It allows the firm to promulgate specific and appropriate standards. Tailored codes are especially useful to complex organizations because they represent permanent guidelines for managers and employees to consult.

When should they be avoided? If a firm's leaders believe specific guidelines may be too restrictive for their employees, then a tailored code is an unsatisfactory choice. Codes are not necessary in most small firms or in ones where a culture includes firmly entrenched ethical policies. If a credo is similar to the Ten Commandments, and programs are similar to religious services, then tailored credos can be considered similar to the Bible or to other formal religious teachings. They provide the most guidance, but many people do not take the time to read or reflect on them.

Conclusion

My research on ethics in management suggests several conclusions that the corporate manager may wish to keep in mind.

- **There Is No Single Ideal Approach to Corporate Ethics.** I would recommend that a small firm start with a credo, but that a larger firm consider a program or a tailored code. It is also possible to integrate these programs and produce a hybrid: in dealing with insider trading, for example, a firm could develop a training program, then follow it up with a strongly enforced tailored code.[8]

- **Top Management Must Be Committed.** Senior managers must champion the highest ethical postures for their companies, as James Burke of J&J does. This commitment was evident in all the companies described here; it came through loud and clear in the CEOs' letters, reports, and public statements.

- **Developing a Structure Is Not Sufficient by Itself.** The structure will not be useful unless it is supported by institutionalized managerial processes. The credo meetings at Security Pacific and the seminars at Chemical Bank are examples of processes that support structures.

- **Raising the Ethical Consciousness of an Organization Is Not Easy.** All the companies mentioned here have spent countless hours—and substantial amounts of money—developing, discussing, revising, and communicating the ethical principles of the firm. And in fact there are no guarantees that it will work. McDonnell Douglas has an extensive ethics program, but some of its executives were implicated in a recent defense contractor scandal.

In conclusion, let me add that managers in firms with active ethics structures—credos, programs, and tailored codes—are genuinely enthusiastic about them. They believe that ethics pay off. Their conviction should provide others with an encouraging example.

Notes

[1]The author would like to thank Bernard Avishai, Gene Laczniak, Michael Mokwa, Lee Tavis, and Oliver Williams, C.S.C., for their helpful comments on an earlier version of this article.

[2]P. E. Murphy and M. G. Dunn, "Corporate Culture and Marketing Management Ethics" (Notre Dame, IN: University of Notre Dame, working paper, 1988).

[3]R. E. Berenbeim, *Corporate Ethics* (New York: The Conference Board, research report no. 900, 1987), 15, 20–22.

[4]A more detailed discussion of Chemical's comprehensive program, and of Johnson & Johnson's, appears in *Corporate Ethics: A Prime Business Asset* (New York: Business Roundtable, February 1988).

[5]One of the case studies appears in "Would You Blow Whistle on Wayward Colleague?" *American Banker*, 17 June 1988, 16.

[6]Touche Ross, *Ethics in American Business* (New York: Touche Ross & Co., January 1988).

[7]Berenbeim (1987), 17.

[8]G.L. Tidwell, "Here's a Tip—Know the Rules of Insider Trading," *Sloan Management Review*, Summer 1987, 93–99.

Questions for Discussion:

1. What is your reaction to the corporate credo for Security Pacific Corporation? What, if anything, would you take issue with in the credo?

2. What do you think of the idea of an ethics audit for a company? Do you think Murphy's questions for such an audit are helpful? What would you add to the questions you would ask an organization if you were conducting an audit like this?

3. How important do you think the commitment of management is to maintaining an environment conducive to ethics? What specific things can management do to foster such an environment?

The Place of Character in Corporate Ethics

Virgil Smith

Previously unpublished article, copyright © 1996 by Virgil Smith.

Introduction

Much has been written lately to provide various suggestions for assuring that decision making in organizations is done ethically.[1] These suggestions essentially revolve around the task of creating an ethical corporate culture through structural means (codes of ethics, corporate credos, ethics audits, ethics policies, etc.). While the structures in an organization are extremely important to assure ethical corporate behavior, there is a fundamental prerequisite that must take place in order for these structures to come into existence. The prerequisite is that those individuals who control the establishment or modification of the organization's structures (i.e., top management), must possess an overriding desire for an ethical organizational culture. The desire for ethics must have a very high priority because these top managers must establish the structures, and then act in consistently ethical ways themselves.

It takes effort, time, and money to establish and maintain organizational structures. Top management must believe that ethics is important enough to justify the considerable expenditure of resources necessary to achieve these structures. Yet, that is not the most difficult requirement. To establish structures which encourage ethical behavior will not, by itself, succeed in creating an ethical culture. The second requirement is that top managers must personally act ethically. Not only is this second requirement generally understood in the ethics literature (for instance, each of the other articles in this chapter mention it),[2] but it is also a scriptural principle.[3]

It is therefore impossible for an organization to develop an ethical culture without top managers who are individually ethical. It is reasonable to expect the organizational structures and corporate culture to affect the ethical behaviors of individuals lower down in the organization, as long as the top managers are ethical. However, it is not reasonable to expect the structures and culture to affect the ethical behaviors of unethical top managers, since the top managers are the very ones who instigate and create those structures and culture. That is, the top managers are the "guardians" of the social systems we call "organizational structures," so, the question becomes, "Who guards the guardians?" That is the question I wish to address in this paper.

When we are dealing with organizational ethics, the question boils down to this: "How can we be sure that top managers care enough about ethics to go to all the trouble of building ethics into the organization?" In order to explore this issue, we must first understand that the problem is not new, and it goes well beyond the boundaries of the organization. In fact, the problem is endemic to the people living in groups, but it drastically increased in scope with the beginnings of modern commerce. By the early 1500s commercial activity was expanding from a community affair, where individuals bought and sold from other individuals that they had known and lived with most of their lives (Tawney, 1926). The new world coming about consisted of the much more impersonal, increasingly complex, and radically enlarged scope of commerce that is normal today.

What is important in this for our discussion is what this new world was doing to business ethics. When you deal with your neighbor, the commercial transaction is normally governed by interpersonal trust based on individual ethical standards. However, in modern commercial systems, transactions tend to be between individuals who are strangers, between an individual and an organization, or between organizations. In each of these cases, it is difficult to rely on individual ethical standards to control the transaction (i.e., to keep one party from taking unfair advantage of the other). In each case we are likely to be dealing with a relatively unknown individual whose personal ethical standard is also relatively unknown.

If we cannot rely on our intimate knowledge of the personal trustworthiness of the individual with whom we do business, how can we be assured that we are not taken advantage of? Essentially, we must seek some force outside the individual person that we can rely on to control the transaction. That force might be the structures and culture of the organization the individual acts for,[4] or in a more generic sense, it might be societal systems that are put in place in order to control commercial (and other) interactions. A number of societal systems have been put in place for this purpose. Examples would include the economic, monetary, and legal systems.

Can Private Sin Lead to Public Righteousness?

If the social system corrects for the individual behaviors of the participants in the system, then greed, envy, and avarice can be allowed to run free in commercial life, with no impairment of the economic system's ability to provide for the physical needs of the society. However, in a very practical sense, individual sin run amok would change the way commerce would have to be carried out. If, as a participant in the system, I know you are likely to be motivated solely by your own cravings, the last thing I will do is trust you in our commercial dealings. Yet I need to be able to trust you. As a simple example, many commercial transactions require an agreement today for actions that will not be carried out until later. For instance, shares of stock are normally traded on the stock exchanges on a hand signal, and the paperwork may not catch up for several days.

If we feel we cannot fully trust those we are dealing with, we can create systems to help out. In the case of the stock transaction, we can create stock exchanges with a limited and costly membership. The stock exchange can police its own members by denying membership to any who abuse the privilege. In other words we substitute trust in a system for trust in the individuals we face day to day in the marketplace. The question is whether systems can totally replace individual trust. This debate is alive and well in the scholarly business literature today. Trust in a person has generally been termed "interpersonal trust" while trust in the system can perhaps be best described (following Luhmann, 1979; and Zucker, 1986), as "system trust."

System trust is not centered on an individual. Rather, it is centered on some aspect of a larger social system that people are willing to put confidence in. Thus we "trust in democracy," or "trust in the law," or, "trust in the market," or, trust in an organization's reputation, which is backed by its structures and culture. We trust these systems to assure proper outcomes that result from our interactions with other people and organizations. Interpersonal trust, on the other hand, is essentially a choice by one person to trust another person based on that person's perceived trustworthiness. Since interpersonal trust is placed in a person, it is necessary to discuss in more detail the necessary characteristics of the person we are choosing to put our trust in. There are two general aspects to a person's trustworthiness—ability and character.

The Role of Ability and Character in Interpersonal Trust

Ability is the technical competence or capacity to perform whatever task the person is being trusted for. Character, on the other hand, has been defined as fiduciary responsibility (Barber, 1983), ethical values (Morgan & Hunt, 1993), commitment and loyalty (Silver, 1985), and willingness of the one trusted to do the task he or she is being trusted for (Coleman, 1990). Of the two considerations of ability and character, character seems to generally demand more of our attention when deciding whether or not to trust another person. This is because there are, almost always, numerous physical manifestations of a person's ability available in the environment. These may include specific schooling for the task, certification, past success at similar tasks, etc.

Assessing a person's character is not so easy. Certification may occasionally be an aid if it includes a code of conduct that is policed by the certifying body, and if the code relates to the task at hand (Zucker, 1986). Likewise, organizational structures and a culture that enforces trustworthy behavior may be seen in the organization's reputation in the marketplace. In both cases, however, we are substituting system trust for interpersonal trust. Therefore, if we are to rely only on interpersonal trust, we must rely on personal experience with, and reputation of, the person we are seeking to do business with (Alchian & Demsetz, 1772; Anderson & Weitz, 1989; Good, 1988; Tsui, 1984; Weigelt & Camerer, 1988). Personal experience is normally considered the most reliable of these options, but, at best, the potential truster can only infer sufficient character for the present situation from past situations. Thus character is more difficult to assess than ability, and this is where system trust, at least theoretically, has some advantages.

The Place and Value of System Trust

System trust is substantially different from interpersonal trust in that a personal relationship between parties is not needed in order for system trust to operate. Some authors argue that this "depersonalizing" of trust makes it superior to interpersonal trust because it is less individual and situation specific (e.g., Luhmann, 1979; Zucker, 1986). So the character issue assumes much less importance in everyday usage of system trust, and primary attention is focused on the abilities and capabilities of the system (Barber, 1983). Instead of trusting a person to control the uncertain future, we trust the system to control the uncertain future.

Thus, for instance, we find it easy to discriminate between the politician, whom we may not trust (an interpersonal trust issue), and the political system, which we do trust (a system trust issue). However, as Sitkin and Roth (1993) point out, the value issues do not go away, even though the ability issues are dealt with. They argue that systems use legalistic remedies, such as formalized rules and contracts, which are able to deal with

ability issues but not the character issues, and thus cannot take the place of interpersonal trust.

Is Interpersonal Trust Needed?

Many scholars have argued that because the economic world has become increasingly complex with the advent of capitalism and the modern organization, it is too difficult to create the kind of relationships necessary to form, and to rely on, interpersonal forms of trust (see for instance, Eisenstadt & Roniger, 1984; Hawthorn, 1988; Luhmann, 1979; Silver, 1985; and Zucker, 1986). They conclude that this is the reason that there is a general decline in interpersonal trust in the modern world.[5]

Some writers essentially advocate abandoning interpersonal trust altogether, and increasing our reliance on forms of system trust (for example, Baumol, 1975; Luhmann, 1979; Meyer, 1983; and Zucker, 1986), because it is much easier to ascertain ability than character, and system trust reduces, or (they argue) eliminates the need for character (Dunn, 1988; Holzner, 1973). There is also the fact that a betrayal by a person tends to destroy interpersonal trust, but system trust is more resistant to betrayal. For instance, Luhmann says:

> The shift to system trust . . . makes trust diffuse and thereby resistant; it becomes almost immune to individual disappointments, which can always be explained away and passed off as a special case, while personal trust can be sabotaged by trivial treacheries. (1979: 56–57)

The question remains, however, whether system trust can totally, or even substantially, take the place of interpersonal forms of trust in the marketplace.

System Trust Used Alone Will Fail

The most perfect form of system trust, that all other systems attempt to emulate, is purported to be the neoclassical market system—the system that is argued to remove the necessity for personal morality in commercial situations. The market system, the argument goes, allows each person to pursue his or her own self-interest through "greed, envy, and avarice," as Adam Smith put it, with the paradoxical outcome being the betterment of all. As Robert Heilbroner, an economic historian says, "What [Adam Smith explained] was 'the invisible hand,' as he called it, whereby 'the private interests and passions of men' are led in the direction 'which is the most agreeable to the interest of the whole society'" (Heilbroner, 1980:52, citing Smith, 1937[1776]:423).

Yet, as some social scientists have lately pointed out, the idea of the market working to control the outcomes emanating from greed, envy, and avarice has never truly been questioned and has no substantive empirical support (Barber, 1977; Mahoney, Huff & Huff, 1993). In actuality, the market system cannot do away with the necessity for personal morality for the simple reason that the market system (as described by Adam Smith) has never existed, and cannot exist in anything like its pure form. This is also why its outcomes have not been empirically verified.

Most introductory economics texts begin by mentioning, in a more or less complete form, the assumptions behind the theory of the market. Those assumptions are (1) that there exists an almost infinite number of buyers, (2) facing an equally large number of sellers, (3) all selling an identical product, and (4) that there is free and perfect information available to the buyers and sellers. These books do not usually mention the more modern-day requirement, that the buyers and sellers have the ability to process all of the information they freely and perfectly receive. It is fairly obvious to see that these conditions do not exist and never have existed in any actual economy.

By the previous discussion I am not attempting to argue that the market system is useless. It obviously does produce some pressures, and considerable pressures in some cases, in the directions indicated by Adam Smith. For this we should be thankful. It does not however, in and of itself, truly control commercial actions. It must rely on other forces of control—other systems, or interpersonal trust—to work.

Mahoney et al. argue that, in reality, Adam Smith's concept of the invisible hand depended

in his day on "human virtue and a common social ethic" (1993:6). Barber (1977) agrees with this assessment and concludes that the market system works only because it is embedded within the social environment. It is to a large extent, then, the social environment, made up of all the individual human relationships that revolve around interpersonal trust, in some form, that allows the market to work in any meaningful way. Thus the market system can aid in the control of commerce, but it cannot force control by itself and, moreover, depends on the underlying social ethic for its effect.

A Matter of Basic Principles

A further proof of the inadequacies of the market system derives from the fact that, while interpersonal relationships based on trust may exist within a market system, and may do so quite happily, the market cannot, in itself, create trust or substitute for it. A well-known economist says in this regard:

> Now trust has a very important pragmatic value, if nothing else. Trust is an important lubricant of a social system. It is extremely efficient; it saves a lot of trouble to have a fair degree of reliance on other people's word. Unfortunately this is not a commodity which can be bought very easily. If you have to buy it, you already have some doubts about what you've bought. Trust and similar values, loyalty or truth-telling, are examples of what the economist would call "externalities." They are goods, they are commodities; they have real, practical, economic value; they increase the efficiency of the system, enable you to produce more goods or more of whatever values you hold in high esteem. But they are not commodities for which trade on the open market is technically possible or even meaningful. (Arrow, 1974:23)

Social Systems Cannot Replace Interpersonal Trust

A social system, such as the market, can therefore enhance and aid the underlying social ethic of individuals but cannot take its place. This is for two reasons: (1) both interpersonal and system trust depend on trustworthiness, and (2) system trust is inextricably intertwined with interpersonal trust. The first of these is fairly easily explained. The general level of interpersonal trust relies on the general level of interpersonal trustworthiness (Dasgupta, 1988). That is, if people don't find others they deem trustworthy, they will be forced to trust less. Likewise, if the systems are not perceived to be trustworthy, people will not place their trust in them and system trust will decrease. While system trust is more resilient to betrayal than interpersonal trust, even system trust will fail in the face of consistent, repeated duplicity.

The second reason why system trust cannot stand on its own is built on the first. When system trust is low, interpersonal trust becomes riskier, so it becomes less used (Lewis & Weigert, 1985). This is because the risk inherent in an act of interpersonal trust is commonly mitigated through the use of system trust. For instance, contracts are utilized in most market transactions. Contracts act to reduce the risk of interpersonal trust by clarifying the agreement between the parties (a communications based, interpersonal trust issue) and providing an option should one party to the transaction prove untrustworthy (a system trust issue).

In order to take advantage of the option provided by the contract, one must put one's trust in the legal system, where the contract can be adjudicated for damages or specific performance can be ordered. Thus if the parties trust the legal system, the risk of betrayal is lessened. The point here is that if people question the trustworthiness of the judicial (or any other) system, it will not be perceived to mitigate the risk inherent in interpersonal trust and interpersonal trust will not occur as often.

Likewise, low interpersonal trust affects the workings of system trust (Fox, 1974). This is so because the mechanistic structures of systems can never, in and of themselves, take the place of character. As Silver puts it, "Conceptions of trust that turn on anonymity, interchangeability of persons, and standardization of performances are not con-

cerned with moral qualities" (1985:64). Even secular scholars are forced to the conclusion that the character issues of trust are inherently moral issues (see, for example, Gabarro, 1978; Morgan & Hunt, 1993; or Ring & Van de Ven, 1992).

While it is true that system trust does not generally rely on character, the character of at least one person or group is central to its proper functioning. Someone has to control and safeguard the system from breakdown. These are the "guardians" of the system. For the legal system in the U.S. the primary safeguards are embodied in Congress and the Supreme Court. For our monetary system it is the Federal Reserve Board, and ultimately Congress. For ethical organizational structures and cultures it is the top managers of the organizations. The only system hypothesized not to have a guardian is the market system. That is why Adam Smith needed to create the concept of "an invisible hand" (Smith, 1937 [1776]:423).

In actual practice, one can easily question the sufficiency of the market to control its own outcomes. If it were sufficient, it would have been unnecessary for governments down through the centuries to regularly intervene in the market's workings. For instance, in the United States today, we have substituted the government for the market in many areas,[6] and by doing this, we have substituted a specific guardian system for one that neoclassical economics held needs no guardian. Therefore, if all systems in which we would trust, even the market system, need a human guardian, sooner or later, the question becomes, who guards the guardians?

A general lessening of interpersonal trustworthiness will eventually (or perhaps immediately) affect the guardians of the systems. If the guardians are not personally trustworthy, the system they guard is open to attack through the guardian. At that point the systems will become corrupt and cease to safeguard what they were created to protect. An illustration of this point comes from the Paine (1994) articles in which she says of one company studied, "While the [ethical] values are used as a firm reference point for decision making and evaluation in some areas of the company, they are still viewed with reservation in others. Some managers do not 'walk the talk,' employees complain" (1994:116).

Likewise, an increase in interpersonal trustworthiness will cause the guardians to be more trustworthy, and the systems they guard will become more trustworthy. Therefore, interpersonal trustworthiness has a high positive correlation with system trustworthiness, and it is not possible to rely solely on system trust to regulate the dealings of people.

A Win-Win Versus Win-Lose View of the Market

There is an additional factor that occurs when a society loses sight of the need for interpersonal trust, and it can be seen at work in how views of the market system have changed over time. Barber points out that the earliest proponents of the concept of the market saw it as a win-win proposition, where everyone could be better off. Before long, however, the concept of the market had been transformed into a zero-sum, win-lose proposition (Barber, 1977). The transformation works in this way. If we believe in the need for interpersonal trust in commercial dealing, we must, perforce, also see the market as a win-win situation. This is because trust is a reciprocal relationship which is destroyed by a betrayal of the trust (Akerstrom, 1991; Johnson-George & Swap, 1982). If one party is forced to lose while the other wins in a commercial transaction, any trust between them will be effectively betrayed and destroyed.

If our commercial relationship is based on trust, we are effectively barred from participating in zero-sum transactions. But, happily, win-win situations are by far the most plentiful in a commercial society.[7] Think of the last time you went out to dinner, or to buy yourself a new suit of clothes. Would you have completed the purchase if you had not believed you would benefit from the exchange? Likewise, do you think the seller would have offered the goods for sale if he had not believed the exchange was to his benefit?

On the other hand, look at the results if you rely on the impersonal force of, for instance, a contract to create a desirable result for yourself. You now do not care whether the other party to the transaction wins or loses. The controlling force that is applied should the contract need to be sued upon is the law of the land with all of its coercive methods.[8] In the case of a lawsuit, there is only one possibility available to the parties. One will win and the other will lose. If we take this attitude toward our commercial interactions, the other party inevitably becomes "the enemy." Our only ethic becomes survival of the fittest, and we will do anything necessary to make sure that we survive. We have only to look around us today, to see many people that display exactly this attitude toward the commercial world in which they engage. The one who seeks to act Christianly in business should stay far from this perception of the commercial world.

The Need for Personal Ethics in the Market

The conclusions reached here argue an overwhelming need for those in the commercial system who hold forth a godly virtue. Since effective ethical organizational systems of structure and culture are instigated and maintained only by top managers who have strong personal ethical standards, this is particularly important at the top levels of organizations. With no sustaining example of biblical ethics in business, interpersonal trust will inevitably decline, and declining trust in the balance of the society's systems will ensue, followed by the eventual breakup of the society itself. Therefore Christians should not forsake the world of commerce. Rather, they should follow the example provided by a group of Christians in the 1500s, who, seeing the modern forms of commerce emerging around them with all of the potential for ethical abuse, believed that it was the Christian's responsibility to, "show the world how to do it right" (Packer, 1995).

Conclusion

The argument pursued in this paper is that the notion of the market, or any social system for that matter, having to exercise control because of the sin of man, is flawed in several ways. While the market and other social systems have important roles to play in governing the behavior of people, all social systems become ineffectual if not upheld through the underlying ethic and trustworthiness of their participants. The sinfulness of man will never allow for a perfect human system.

From the perspective of the specific topic of this paper—business ethics—an individual organization, over the long run, will be only as ethical as its top manager.[9] Therefore, if we desire to have ethi-

cal organizations, we must have ethical people who have the ability and willingness to lead them. For this reason, Christians, who are seeking to live by a biblical ethic, should not shun the field of business, and they should not shun positions of power within business organizations. Those business organizations that truly desire to have an ethical culture will be actively seeking such people,[10] and it is not unreasonable to expect that God may desire for some of them to eventually be "guardians" of the system.

References

Akerstrom, M. (1991). *Betrayal and Betrayers: The Sociology of Treachery*. New Brunswick, N.J.: Transaction Publishers.

Alchian, A. A., and H. Demsetz (1972). Production, information costs, and economic organization. *American Economic Review* 62(5), 777–95.

Anderson, E., and B. Weitz (1989). Determinants of continuity in conventional industrial channel dyads. *Marketing Science*, 8(4), 310–23.

Arrow, K. J. (1974). *The Limits of Organization*, New York, NY: W.W. Norton.

Barber, B. (1977). Absolutization of the market: Some notes on how we got from there to here. In G. Dworkin, G. Bermant and P.G. Brown, eds., *Markets and Morals* (15–31). Washington D.C.: Hemisphere Publishing Corp.

Barber, B. (1983). *The Logic and Limits of Trust*. New Brunswick, N.J.: Rutgers University Press.

Baumol, W. J. (1975). Business responsibility and economic behavior. In E. S. Phelps, ed., *Altruism, Morality, and Economic Theory* (45–56). New York: Russell Sage Foundation.

Coleman, J. S. (1990). *Foundations of Social Theory*. Cambridge, MA: The Belknap Press.

Dasgupta, P. (1988). Trust as a commodity. In D. Gambetta, ed., *Trust: Making and Breaking Cooperative Relations* (49–72). New York, NY: Blackwell.

Dunn, J. (1988). Trust and political agency. In D. Gambetta, ed., *Trust: Making and Breaking Cooperative Relations* (73–93). New York, NY: Blackwell.

Eisenstadt, S. N., and L. Roniger (1984). *Patrons, Clients and Friends: Interpersonal Relations and the Structure of Trust in Society*. Cambridge, UK: Cambridge University Press.

Ferrell, O. C., and J. Fraedrich (1990). Understanding pressures that cause unethical behavior in business. *Business Insights*, 1–4.

Fox, A. (1974). *Beyond Contract: Work, Power and Trust Relations*. London, UK: Faber and Faber Limited. Gabarro, J. J. (1978). The development of trust, influence, and expectations. In A. G. Athos and J. J. Gabarro, eds., *Interpersonal Behavior: Communication and Understanding in Relationships* (290–303). Englewood Cliffs, N.J.: Prentice Hall, Inc.

Good, D. (1988). Individuals, interpersonal relations, and trust. In D. Gambetta, ed., *Trust: Making and Breaking Cooperative Relations* (pp. 111–26). New York, N.Y.: Blackwell.

Heilbroner, R. L. (1980). *The Worldly Philosophers* (5th ed.). New York, N.Y.: Simon and Schuster, Inc.

Hochreich, D. J., and J. B. Rotter (1970). Have college students become less trusting? *Journal of Personality and Social Psychology*, 15 (211–14).

Holzner, B. (1973). Sociological reflections on trust. *Humanitas*, 9(3), 333–45.

Johnson-George, C., and W. C. Swap (1982). Measurement of specific interpersonal trust:

Construction and validation of a scale to assess trust in a specific other. *Journal of Personality and Social Psychology*, 43(6), 1306–1317.

Lewis, J. D., and A. J. Weigert (1985). Social atomism, holism, and trust. *The Sociological Quarterly*, 26(4), 455–71.

Luhmann, N. (1979). *Trust and Power.* Chichester, UK: John Wiley and Sons, Inc.

Mahoney, J. T., A. S. Huff, and J. O. Huff (1994). Toward a new social contract theory in organization science. *Journal of Management Inquiry*, 1–35.

Meyer, J. W. (1983). Organizational factors affecting legalization in education. In J. W. Meyer and W. R. Scott, eds., *Organizational Environments: Ritual and Rationality* (217–32). Beverly Hills, Calif.: Sage.

Morgan, R. M., and S. D. Hunt (1993). Commitment and trust in relationship marketing [Working Paper] (1–45). Texas Tech University.

Murphy, P. E. (1989). Creating ethical corporate structures. *Sloan Management Review*, 30(2), 81–87.

Packer, J. I. (1995). [A Seminar on the Puritans, conducted from 1/3/95 to 1/13/95 by Dr. J. I. Packer, at Biola University]. La Mirada, California.

Paine, L. S. (1994). Managing for organizational integrity. *Harvard Business Review*, March-April, 106–117.

Ring, P. S., and A. H. Van de Ven (1992). Structuring cooperative relationships between organizations. *Strategic Management Journal, 13*, 483–98.

Silver, A. (1985). "Trust" in social and political theory. In G. Suttles and M. Zald, eds., *The Challenge of Social Control* (52–67). Norwood, N.J.: Ablex.

Sitkin, S. B., and N. L. Roth (1993). Explaining the limited effectiveness of legalistic "remedies" for trust/distrust. *Organization Science, 4*(3), 367–92.

Smith, A. (1937 [1776]). *An Inquiry into the Nature and Causes of the Wealth of Nations.* New York, N.Y.: Random House.

Tawney, R. H. (1926). *Religion and the Rise of Capitalism: A Historical Study.* London: John Murray.

Tsui, A. S. (1984). A role set analysis of managerial reputation. *Organizational Behavior and Human Performance, 34*, 64–96.

Weigelt, K., and C. Camerer (1988). Reputation and corporate strategy: A review of recent theory and applications. *Strategic Management Journal, 9*, 443–54.

Wrightsman, J. B., and N. J. Baker (1969). *Where have all the idealistic, imperturbable freshmen gone?* Proceedings of the 77th Annual Convention of the American Psychological Association (vol. 4, 299–300).

Zucker, L. G. (1986). Production of trust: Institutional sources of economic structure, 1840–1920. In B. Staw and L. L. Cummings, eds., *Research in Organizational Behavior* (vol. 8, 53–111). Greenwich, Conn: JAI Press.

Notes

[1]See Ferrell & Fraedrich, 1990; Murphy, 1989; and Paine, 1994.

[2]Ferrell and Fraedrich say, "Most experts agree that the chief executive officer and vice-president level executives set the ethical tone for the entire organization" (1990:27). Murphy says, "Senior managers must champion the highest ethical postures for their companies. . . . This commitment was evident in all the companies described here; it came through loud and clear in the CEOs' letters, reports, and public statements" (1989:217). Paine states, "Above all, organizational ethics is seen as the work of management" (1994:111), and further notes in one of the case studies, "While the [ethical] values are used as a firm reference point for decision making and evaluation in some areas of the company, they are still viewed with reservation in others. Some managers do not 'walk the talk,' employees complain" (1994:116).

[3]For instance, Proverbs 29:12 states, "If a ruler listens to lies, all his officials become wicked." (New International Version)

[4]If the organization has a reputation for ethical dealings and has established a culture that encourages ethical dealings, we

can assume that this person, who acts on behalf of the organization, will act ethically because of the organizational constraints placed upon his or her individual behavior.

[5]There is empirical evidence to support the hypothesis that interpersonal trust has recently been on the decline, at least in the United States. See, for instance, Coleman (1990), Hochreich and Rotter (1970), and Wrightsman and Baker (1969).

[6]One needs only think of antitrust laws, regulated industries, or the last time the nation threatened an embargo over another nation's "dumping" their goods in our market to get the idea.

[7]We can of course turn any win-win situation into a win-lose situation if we insist on treating it that way, and some market participants seem to have a habit of doing this. Therefore, the business practitioner acting with a good ethic must watch out for this type of person or company.

[8]It is interesting to note in this regard, that the controlling force of a social system always is coercion or the threat of coercion.

[9]It is possible that an organization could have ethical individual members and unethical top managers, but it seems unrealistic for this circumstance to last long, as Proverbs 29:12 (cited in a previous note) indicates. Constant frustration of their ethical desires should cause the ethical members to leave the firm, to be replaced eventually by unethical members.

[10]As Paine mentions regarding Wetherill Associates' pursuit of an ethical culture, "the company . . . take special care to hire people willing to support right action" (1994:117).

Questions for Discussion:

1. In your opinion, should character be a concern of a company, or should such concerns be left to other institutions such as families, religious organizations, and community groups?
2. Spell out the differences between system trust and interpersonal trust.
3. Do you agree that personal ethics is necessary in the marketplace? Why or why not?
4. Do you agree that trust in an organization can reduce costs? If so, give some examples of how that might work.

"Why Should My Conscience Bother Me?"

The Aircraft Brake Scandal

Kermit Vandivier

From *In the Name of Profit*, ed. Robert Heilbroner et al. (New York: Doubleday, 1972), 3–31. Copyright © 1972.

The B. F. Goodrich Co. is what business magazines like to speak of as "a major American corporation." It has operations in a dozen states and as many foreign countries, and of these far-flung facilities, the Goodrich plant at Troy, Ohio, is not the most imposing. It is a small, one-story building, once used to manufacture airplanes. Set in the grassy flatlands of west-central Ohio, it employs only about six hundred people. Nevertheless, it is one of the three largest manufacturers of aircraft wheels and brakes, a leader in a most profitable industry. Goodrich wheels and brakes support such well-known planes as the F111, the C5A, the Boeing 727, the XB70 and many others. Its customers include almost every aircraft manufacturer in the world.

Contracts for aircraft wheels and brakes often run into millions of dollars, and ordinarily a contract with a total value of less than $70,000, though welcome, would not create any special stir of joy in the hearts of Goodrich sales personnel. But purchase order P-23718, issued on June 18, 1967, by the LTV Aerospace Corporation, and ordering 202 brake assemblies for a new Air Force plane at a total price of $69,417, was received by Goodrich with considerable glee. And there was good reason. Some ten years previously, Goodrich had built a brake for LTV that was, to say the least, considerably less than a rousing success. The brake had not lived up to Goodrich's promises, and after experiencing considerable difficulty, LTV had written off Goodrich as a source of brakes. Since that time, Goodrich salesmen had been unable to sell so much as a shot of brake fluid to LTV. So in 1967, when LTV requested bids on wheels and brakes for the new A7D light attack aircraft it proposed to build for the Air Force, Goodrich submitted a bid that was absurdly low, so low that LTV could not, in all prudence, turn it down.

Goodrich had, in industry parlance, "bought into the business." Not only did the company not expect to make a profit on the deal; it was prepared, if necessary, to lose money. For aircraft brakes are not something that can be ordered off the shelf. They are designed for a particular aircraft, and once an aircraft manufacturer buys a brake, he is forced to purchase all replacement parts from the brake manufacturer. The $70,000 that Goodrich would get for making the brake would be a drop in the bucket when compared with the cost of the linings and other parts the Air Force would have to buy from Goodrich during the lifetime of the aircraft. Furthermore, the company which manufactures brakes for one particular model of an aircraft quite naturally has the inside track to supply other brakes when the planes are updated and improved.

Thus, that first contract, regardless of the money involved, is very important, and Goodrich, when it learned that it had been awarded the A7D contract, was determined that while it may have slammed the door on its own foot ten years before, this time, the second time around, things would be different. The word was soon circulated throughout the plant: "We can't bungle it this

time. We've got to give them a good brake, regardless of the cost."

There was another factor which had undoubtedly influenced LTV. All aircraft brakes made today are of the disk type, and the bid submitted by Goodrich called for a relatively small brake, one containing four disks and weighting only 106 pounds. The weight of any aircraft part is extremely important. The lighter a part is, the heavier the plane's payload can be. The four-rotor, 106-pound brake promised by Goodrich was about as light as could be expected, and this undoubtedly had helped move LTV to award the contract to Goodrich.

The brake was designed by one of Goodrich's most capable engineers, John Warren. A tall, lanky blond and a graduate of Purdue, Warren had come from the Chrysler Corporation seven years before and had become adept at aircraft brake design. The happy-go-lucky manner he usually maintained belied a temper which exploded whenever anyone ventured to offer any criticism of his work, no matter how small. On these occasions, Warren would turn red in the face, often throwing or slamming something and then stalking from the scene. As his coworkers learned the consequences of criticizing him, they did so less and less readily, and when he submitted his preliminary design for the A7D brake, it was accepted without question.

Warren was named project engineer for the A7D, and he, in turn, assigned the task of producing the final production design to a newcomer to the Goodrich engineering stable, Searle Lawson. Just turned twenty-six, Lawson had been out of the Northrup Institute of Technology only one year when he came to Goodrich in January 1967. Like Warren, he had worked for a while in the automotive industry, but his engineering degree was in aeronautical and astronautical sciences, and when the opportunity came to enter his special field, via Goodrich, he took it. At the Troy plant, Lawson had been assigned to various "paper projects" to break him in, and after several months spent reviewing statistics and old brake designs, he was beginning to fret at the lack of challenge.

When told he was being assigned to his first "real" project, he was elated and immediately plunged into his work.

The major portion of the design had already been completed by Warren, and major assemblies for the brake had already been ordered from Goodrich suppliers. Naturally, however, before Goodrich could start making the brakes on a production basis, much testing would have to be done. Lawson would have to determine the best materials to use for the linings and discover what minor adjustments in the design would have to be made.

Then, after the preliminary testing and after the brake was judged ready for production, one whole brake assembly would undergo a series of grueling, simulated braking stops and other severe trials called qualification tests. These tests are required by the military, which gives very detailed specifications on how they are to be conducted, the criteria for failure, and so on. They are performed in the Goodrich plant's test laboratory, where huge machines called dynamometers can simulate the weight and speed of almost any aircraft. After the brakes pass the laboratory tests, they are approved for production, but before the brakes are accepted for use in military service, they must undergo further extensive flight tests.

Searle Lawson was well aware that much work had to be done before the A7D brake could go into production, and he knew that LTV had set the last two weeks in June, 1968, as the starting dates for flight tests. So he decided to begin testing immediately. Goodrich's suppliers had not yet delivered the break housing and other parts, but the brake disks had arrived, and using the housing from a brake similar in size and weight to the A7D brake, Lawson built a prototype. The prototype was installed in a test wheel and placed on one of the big dynamometers in the plant's test laboratory. The dynamometer was adjusted to simulate the weight of the A7D and Lawson began a series of tests, "landing" the wheel and brake at the A7D's landing speed, and braking it to a stop. The main purpose of these preliminary tests was to learn what temperatures would

develop within the brake during the simulated stops and to evaluate the lining materials tentatively selected for use.

During a normal aircraft landing the temperatures inside the brake may reach 1000 degrees, and occasionally a bit higher. During Lawson's first simulated landings, the temperature of his prototype brake reached 1500 degrees. The brake glowed a bright cherry-red and threw off incandescent particles of metal and lining material as the temperature reached its peak. After a few such stops, the brake was dismantled and the linings were found to be almost completely disintegrated. Lawson chalked this first failure up to chance and, ordering new lining materials, tried again.

The second attempt was a repeat of the first. The brake became extremely hot, causing the lining materials to crumble into dust.

After the third such failure, Lawson, inexperienced though he was, knew that the fault lay not in defective parts or unsuitable lining material but in the basic design of the brake itself. Ignoring Warren's original computations, Lawson made his own, and it didn't take him long to discover where the trouble lay—the brake was too small. There simply was not enough surface area on the disks to stop the aircraft without generating the excessive heat that caused the linings to fail.

After the third such failure, he knew that the fault lay not in defective parts or unsuitable lining material but in the basic design of the brake itself.

The answer to the problem was obvious but far from simple—the four-disk brake would have to be scrapped, and a new design, using five disks, would have to be developed. The implications were not lost on Lawson. Such a step would require the junking of all the four-disk-brake subassemblies, many of which had now begun to arrive from the various suppliers. It would also mean several weeks of preliminary design and testing and many more weeks of waiting while the suppliers made and delivered the new subassemblies.

Yet, several weeks had already gone by since LTV's order had arrived, and the date for delivery of the first production brakes for flight testing was only a few months away.

Although project engineer John Warren had more or less turned the A7D over to Lawson, he knew of the difficulties Lawson had been experiencing. He had assured the young engineer that the problem revolved around getting the right kind of lining material. Once that was found, he said, the difficulties would end.

Despite the evidence of the abortive tests and Lawson's careful computations, Warren rejected the suggestion that the four-disk brake was too light for the job. Warren knew that his superior had already told LTV, in rather glowing terms, that the preliminary tests on the A7D brake were very successful. Indeed, Warren's superiors weren't aware at this time of the troubles on the brake. It would have been difficult for Warren to admit not only that he had made a serious error in his calculations and original design but that his mistakes had been caught by a green kid, barely out of college.

Warren's reaction to a five-disk brake was not unexpected by Lawson, and, seeing that the four-disk brake was not to be abandoned so easily, he took his calculations and dismal test results one step up the corporate ladder.

At Goodrich, the man who supervises the engineers working on projects slated for production is called, predictably, the projects manager. The job was held by a short, chubby and bald man named Robert Sink. A man truly devoted to his work, Sink was as likely to be found at his desk at ten o'clock on Sunday night as ten o'clock on Monday morning. His outside interests consisted mainly of tinkering on a Model-A Ford and an occasional game of golf. Some fifteen years before, Sink had begun working at Goodrich as a lowly draftsman. Slowly, he worked his way up. Despite his geniality, Sink was neither respected nor liked by the majority of the engineers, and his appointment as their supervisor did not improve their feelings about him. They thought he had only gone to high school. It quite naturally rankled

those who had gone through years of college and acquired impressive specialties such as thermodynamics and astronautics to be commanded by a man whom they considered their intellectual inferior. But, though Sink had no college training, he had something even more useful: a fine working knowledge of company politics.

Puffing upon a Meerschaum pipe, Sink listened gravely as young Lawson confided his fears about the four-disk brake. Then he examined Lawson's calculations and the results of the abortive tests. Despite the fact that he was not a qualified engineer, in the strictest sense of the word, it must certainly have been obvious to Sink that Lawson's calculations were correct and that a four-disk brake would never have worked on the A7D.

But other things of equal importance were also obvious. First, to concede that Lawson's calculations were correct would also mean conceding that Warren's calculations were incorrect. As projects manager, he not only was responsible for Warren's activities, but, in admitting that Warren had erred, he would have to admit that he had erred in trusting Warren's judgment. It also meant that, as projects manager, it would be he who would have to explain the whole messy situation to the Goodrich hierarchy, not only at Troy but possibly on the corporate level at Goodrich's Akron offices. And, having taken Warren's judgment of the four-disk brake at face value (he was forced to do this since, not being an engineer, he was unable to exercise any engineering judgment of his own), he had assured LTV, not once but several times, that about all there was left to do on the brake was pack it in a crate and ship it out the back door.

There's really no problem at all, he told Lawson. After all, Warren was an experienced engineer, and if he said the brake would work, it would work. Just keep on testing and probably, maybe even on the very next try, it'll work out just fine.

Lawson was far from convinced, but without the support of his superiors there was little he could do except keep on testing. By now, housings for the four-disk brake had begun to arrive at the plant, and Lawson was able to build up a production model of the brake and begin the formal qualification tests demanded by the military.

The first qualification attempts went exactly as the tests on the prototype had. Terrific heat developed within the brakes and, after a few, short, simulated stops, the linings crumbled. A new type of lining material was ordered and once again an attempt to qualify the brake was made. Again, failure.

Experts were called in from lining manufacturers, and new lining "mixes" were tried, always with the same result. Failure.

It was now the last week in March 1968, and flight tests were scheduled to begin in seventy days. Twelve separate attempts had been made to formally qualify the brake, and all had failed. It was no longer possible for anyone to ignore the glaring truth that the brake was a dismal failure and that nothing short of a major design change could ever make it work.

In the engineering department, panic set in.

In the engineering department, panic set in. A glum-faced Lawson prowled the test laboratory dejectedly. Occasionally, Warren would witness some simulated stop on the brake and, after it was completed, troop silently back to his desk. Sink, too, showed an unusual interest in the trials, and he and Warren would converse in low tones while poring over the results of the latest tests. Even the most inexperienced of the lab technicians and the men who operated the testing equipment knew they had a "bad" brake on their hands, and there was some grumbling about "wasting time on a brake that won't work."

New menaces appeared. An engineering team from LTV arrived at the plant to get a good look at the brake in action. Luckily, they stayed only a few days, and Goodrich engineers managed to cover the true situation without too much difficulty.

On April 4, the thirteenth attempt at qualification was begun. This time no attempt was made

to conduct the tests by the methods and techniques spelled out in the military specifications. Regardless of how it had to be done, the brake was to be "nursed" through the required fifty simulated stops.

Fans were set up to provide special cooling. Instead of maintaining pressure on the brake until the test wheel had come to a complete stop, the pressure was reduced when the wheel had decelerated to around 15 mph, allowing it to "coast" to a stop. After each stop, the brake was disassembled and carefully cleaned, and after some of the stops, internal brake parts were machined in order to remove warp and other disfigurations caused by the high heat.

By these and other methods, all clearly contrary to the techniques established by the military specifications, the brake was coaxed through the fifty stops. But even using these methods, the brake could not meet all the requirements. On one stop the wheel rolled for a distance of 16,000 feet, nearly three miles, before the brake could bring it to a stop. The normal distance required for such a stop was around 3,500 feet.

On April 11, the day the thirteenth test was completed, I became personally involved in the A7D situation.

I had worked in the Goodrich test laboratory for five years, starting first as an instrumentation engineer, then later becoming a data analyst and technical writer. As part of my duties, I analyzed the reams and reams of instrumentation data that came from the many testing machines in the laboratory, then transcribed it to a more usable form for the engineering department. And when a new-type brake had successfully completed the required qualification tests, I would issue a formal qualification report.

Qualification reports were an accumulation of all the data and test logs compiled by the test technicians during the qualification tests, and were documentary proof that a brake had met all the requirements established by the military specifications and was therefore presumed safe for flight testing. Before actual flight tests were conducted on a brake, qualification reports had to be delivered to the customer and to various government officials.

On April 11, I was looking over the data from the latest A7D test, and I noticed that many irregularities in testing methods had been noted on the test logs.

Technically, of course, there was nothing wrong with conducting tests in any manner desired, so long as the test was for research purposes only. But qualification test methods are clearly delineated by the military, and I knew that this test had been a formal qualification attempt. One particular notation on the test logs caught my eye. For some of the stops, the instrument which recorded the brake pressure had been deliberately miscalibrated so that, while the brake pressure used during the stops was recorded as 1000 psi (the maximum pressure that would be available on the A7D aircraft), the pressure had actually been 100 psi!

I showed the test logs to the test lab supervisor, Ralph Gretzinger, who said he had learned from the technician who had miscalibrated the instrument that he had been asked to do so by Lawson. Lawson, said Gretzinger, readily admitted asking for the miscalibration, saying he had been told to do so by Sink.

I asked Gretzinger why anyone would want to miscalibrate the data-recording instruments.

"Why? I'll tell you why," he snorted. "That brake is a failure. It's way too small for the job, and they're not ever going to get it to work. They're getting desperate, and instead of scrapping the _____ thing and starting over, they figure they can horse around down here in the lab and qualify it that way."

An expert engineer, Gretzinger had been responsible for several innovations in brake design. It was he who had invented the unique brake system used on the famous XB70. A graduate of Georgia Tech, he was a stickler for detail and he had some very firm ideas about honesty and ethics. "If you want to find out what's going on," said Gretzinger, "ask Lawson, he'll tell you."

Curious, I did ask Lawson the next time he came into the lab. He seemed eager to discuss the A7D and gave me the history of his months of frustrating efforts to get Warren and Sink to change the brake design. "I just can't believe this is really happening," said Lawson, shaking his head slowly. "This isn't engineering, at least not what I thought it would be. Back in school, I thought that when you were an engineer, you tried to do your best, no matter what it cost. But this is something else."

He sat across the desk from me, his chin propped in his hand. "Just wait," he warned. "You'll get a chance to see what I'm talking about. You're going to get in the act, too, because I've already had the word that we're going to make one more attempt to qualify the brake, and that's it. Win or lose, we're going to issue a qualification report!"

I reminded him that a qualification report could only be issued after a brake had successfully met all military requirements, and therefore, unless the next qualification attempt was a success, no report would be issued.

"You'll find out," retorted Lawson. "I was already told that regardless of what the brake does on the test, it's going to be qualified." He said he had been told in those exact words at a conference with Sink and Russell Van Horn.

This was the first indication that Sink had brought his boss, Van Horn, into the mess. Although Van Horn, as manager of the design engineering section, was responsible for the entire department, he was not necessarily familiar with all phases of every project, and it was not uncommon for those under him to exercise the what-he-doesn't-know-won't-hurt-him philosophy. If he was aware of the full extent of the A7D situation, it meant that matters had truly reached a desperate stage—that Sink had decided not only to call for help but was looking toward that moment when blame must be borne and, if possible, shared.

Also, if Van Horn had said, "regardless what the brake does on test, it's going to be qualified," then it could only mean that, if necessary, a false qualification report would be issued! I discussed this possibility with Gretzinger, and he assured me that under no circumstances would such a report ever be issued.

"If they want a qualification report, we'll write them one, but we'll tell it just like it is," he declared emphatically. "No false data or false reports are going to come out of this lab."

On May 2, 1968, the fourteenth and final attempt to qualify the brake was begun. Although the same improper methods used to nurse the brake through the previous tests were employed, it soon became obvious that this too would end in failure.

When the tests were about half completed, Lawson asked if I would start preparing the various engineering curves and graphic displays which were normally incorporated in a qualification report. "It looks as though you'll be writing a qualification report shortly," he said.

I flatly refused to have anything to do with the matter and immediately told Gretzinger what I had been asked to do. He was furious and repeated his previous declaration that under no circumstances would any false data or other matter be issued from the lab.

"I'm going to get this settled right now, once and for all," he declared. "I'm going to see Line [Russell Line, manager of the Goodrich Technical Services Section, of which the test lab was part] and find out just how far this thing is going to go!" He stormed out of the room.

In about an hour, he returned and called me to his desk. He sat silently for a few moments, then muttered, half to himself, "I wonder what the hell they'd do if I just quit?" I didn't answer and I didn't ask him what he meant. I knew. He had been beaten down. He had reached the point when the decision had to be made. Defy them now while there was still time—or knuckle under, sell out.

"You know," he went on uncertainly, looking down at his desk, "I've been an engineer for a long time, and I've always believed that ethics and integrity were every bit as important as theorems and formulas, and never once has anything happened to change my beliefs. Now this . . . Hell, I've got two sons I've got to put through school and I just . . ." His voice trailed off.

He sat for a few more minutes, then, looking over the top of his glasses, said hoarsely, "Well, it looks like we're licked. The way it stands now, we're to go ahead and prepare the data and other things for the graphic presentation in the report, and when we're finished, someone upstairs will actually write the report.

He didn't believe what he was saying, and he knew I didn't believe it either. It was an embarrassing and shameful moment for both of us.

"After all," he continued, "we're just drawing some curves, and what happens to them after they leave here, well, we're not responsible for that."

He was trying to persuade himself that as long as we were concerned with only one part of the puzzle and didn't see the completed picture, we really weren't doing anything wrong. He didn't believe what he was saying, and he knew I didn't believe it either. It was an embarrassing and shameful moment for both of us.

I wasn't at all satisfied with the situation and decided that I too would discuss the matter with Russell Line, the senior executive in our section.

Tall, powerfully built, his teeth flashing white, his face tanned to a coffee-brown by a daily stint with a sun lamp, Line looked and acted every inch the executive. He was a crossword-puzzle enthusiast and an ardent golfer, and though he had lived in Troy only a short time, he had been accepted into the Troy Country Club and made an official of the golf committee. He had been transferred from the Akron offices some two years previously, and an air of mystery surrounded him. Some office gossips figured he had been sent to Troy as the result of some sort of demotion. Others speculated that since the present general manager of the Troy plant was due shortly for retirement, Line had been transferred to Troy to assume that job and was merely occupying his present position to "get the feel of things." Whatever the case, he commanded great respect and had come to be well liked by those of us who worked under him.

He listened sympathetically while I explained how I felt about the A7D situation, and when I had finished, he asked me what I wanted him to do about it. I said that as employees of the Goodrich Company we had a responsibility to protect the company and its reputation if at all possible. I said I was certain that officers on the corporate level would never knowingly allow such tactics as had been employed on the A7D.

"I agree with you," he remarked, "but I still want to know what you want me to do about it."

I suggested that in all probability the chief engineer at the Troy plant, H. C. "Bud" Sunderman, was unaware of the A7D problem and that he, Line, should tell him what was going on.

Line laughed, good-humoredly. "Sure, I could, but I'm not going to. Bud probably already knows about this thing anyway, and if he doesn't, I'm sure not going to be the one to tell him."

"But why?"

"Because it's none of my business, and it's none of yours. I learned a long time ago not to worry about things over which I had no control. I have no control over this."

I wasn't satisfied with this answer, and I asked him if his conscience wouldn't bother him if, say, during flight tests on the brake, something should happen resulting in death or injury to the test pilot.

"Look," he said, becoming somewhat exasperated, "I just told you I have no control over this thing. Why should my conscience bother me?"

His voice took on a quiet, soothing tone as he continued. "You're just getting all upset over this thing for nothing. I just do as I'm told, and I'd advise you to do the same."

He had made his decision, and now I had to make mine.

I made no attempt to rationalize what I had been asked to do. It made no difference who would falsify which part of the report or whether the actual falsification would be by misleading numbers or misleading words. Whether by acts of commission or omission, all of us who contributed to the fraud would be guilty. The only question left for me to decide was whether or not I would become a party to the fraud.

Before coming to Goodrich in 1963, I had held a variety of jobs, each a little more pleasant, a little more rewarding than the last. At forty-two, with seven children, I had decided that the Goodrich Company would probably be my "home" for the rest of my working life. The job paid well, it was pleasant and challenging, and the future looked reasonably bright. My wife and I had bought a home and we were ready to settle down into a comfortable, middle-age, middle-class rut. If I refused to take part in the A7D fraud, I would have to either resign or be fired. The report would be written by someone anyway, but I would have the satisfaction of knowing I had had no part in the matter. But bills aren't paid with personal satisfaction, nor house payments with ethical principles. I made my decision. The next morning, I telephoned Lawson and told him I was ready to begin on the qualification report.

In a few minutes, he was at my desk, ready to begin. Before we started, I asked him, "Do you realize what we are going to do?"

"Yeah," he replied bitterly, "we're going to screw LTV. And speaking of screwing," he continued, "I know now how a whore feels, because that's exactly what I've become, an engineering whore. I've sold myself. It's all I can do to look at myself in the mirror when I shave. I make me sick."

I was surprised at his vehemence. It was obvious that he too had done his share of soul-searching and didn't like what he had found. Somehow, though, the air seemed clearer after his outburst, and we began working on the report.

I had written dozens of qualification reports, and I knew what a "good" one looked like. Resorting to the actual test data only on occasion, Lawson and I proceeded to prepare page after page of elaborate, detailed engineering curves, charts, and test logs, which purported to show what had happened during the formal qualification tests. Where temperatures were too high, we deliberately chopped them down a few hundred degrees, and where they were too low, we raised them to a value that would appear reasonable to the LTV and military engineers. Brake pressure, torque values, distances, times—everything of consequence was tailored to fit the occasion.

Occasionally, we would find that some test either hadn't been performed at all or had been conducted improperly. On those occasions, we "conducted" the test—successfully, of course—on paper.

For nearly a month we worked on the graphic presentation that would be a part of the report. Meanwhile, the fourteenth and final qualification attempt had been completed, and the brake, not unexpectedly, had failed again.

During that month, Lawson and I talked of little else except the enormity of what we were doing. The more involved we became in our work, the more apparent became our own culpability. We discussed such things as the Nuremberg trials and how they related to our guilt and complicity in the A7D situation. Lawson often expressed his opinion that the brake was downright dangerous and that, once on flight tests, "anything is liable to happen."

I saw his boss, John Warren, at least twice during that month and needled him about what we were doing. He didn't take the jibes too kindly but managed to laugh the situation off as "one of those things." One day I remarked that what we were doing amounted to fraud, and he pulled out an engineering handbook and turned to a section on laws as they related to the engineering profession.

He read the definition of fraud aloud, then said, "Well, technically I don't think what we're doing can be called fraud. I'll admit it's not right, but it's just one of those things. We're just kinda caught in the middle. About all I can tell you is, Do like I'm doing, make copies of everything and put them in your SYA file."

"What's an 'SYA' file?" I asked.

"That's a 'save your _____' file." He laughed.

Although I hadn't known it was called that, I had been keeping an SYA file since the beginning of the A7D fiasco. I had made a copy of every scrap of paper connected even remotely with the A7D and had even had copies of 16mm movies that had been made during some of the simulated stops. Lawson, too, had an SYA file, and we both

maintained them for one reason: Should the true state of events on the A7D ever be questioned, we wanted to have access to a complete set of factual data. We were afraid that should the question ever come up, the test data might accidentally be "lost."

We finished our work on the graphic portion of the report around the first of June. Altogether, we had prepared nearly two hundred pages of data, containing dozens of deliberate falsifications and misrepresentations. I delivered the data to Gretzinger, who said he had been instructed to deliver it personally to the chief engineer, Bud Sunderman, who in turn would assign someone in the engineering department to complete the written portion of the report. He gathered the bundle of data and left the office. Within minutes, he was back with the data, his face white with anger.

"That _____ Sink's beat me to it," he said furiously. "He's already talked to Bud about this, and now Sunderman says no one in the engineering department has time to write the report. He wants us to do it, and I told him we couldn't."

The words had barely left his mouth when Russell Line burst in the door. "What the hell's all the fuss about this _____ report?" he demanded loudly.

Patiently, Gretzinger explained. "There's no fuss. Sunderman just told me that we'd have to write the report down here, and I said we couldn't. Russ," he went on, "I've told you before that we weren't going to write the report. I made my position clear on that a long time ago."

Line shut him up with a wave of his hand and, turning to me, bellowed, "I'm getting sick and tired of hearing about this _____ report. Now, write the _____ thing and shut up about it!" He slammed out of the office.

Gretzinger and I just sat for a few seconds looking at each other. Then he spoke.

"Well, I guess he's made it pretty clear, hasn't he? We can either write the thing or quit. You know, what we should have done was quit a long time ago. Now, it's too late."

Somehow, I wasn't at all surprised at this turn of events, and it didn't really make that much difference. As far as I was concerned, we were all up to our necks in the thing anyway, and writing the narrative portion of the report couldn't make me any more guilty than I already felt myself to be.

> *All the time we were working on the report, I felt, deep down, that somewhere, somehow, something would come along and the whole thing would blow over.*

Still, Line's order came as something of a shock. All the time Lawson and I were working on the report, I felt, deep down, that somewhere, somehow, something would come along and the whole thing would blow over. But Russell Line had crushed that hope. The report was actually going to be issued. Intelligent, law-abiding officials of B. F. Goodrich, one of the oldest and most respected of American corporations, were actually going to deliver to a customer a product that was known to be defective and dangerous and which could very possibly cause death or serious injury.

Within two days, I had completed the narrative, or written portion of the report. As a final sop to my own self-respect, in the conclusion of the report I wrote, "The B. F. Goodrich P/N 2-1162-3 brake assembly does not meet the intent or the requirements of the applicable specification documents and therefore is not qualified."

This was a meaningless gesture, since I knew that this would certainly be changed when the report went through the final typing process. Sure enough, when the report was published, the negative conclusion had been made positive.

One final and significant incident occurred just before publication.

Qualification reports always bear the signature of the person who has prepared them. I refused to sign the report, as did Lawson. Warren was later asked to sign the report. He replied that he would "when I receive a signed statement from Bob Sink ordering me to sign it."

The engineering secretary who was delegated the responsibility of "dogging" the report through publication told me later that after I, Lawson, and

Warren had all refused to sign the report, she had asked Sink if he would sign. He replied, "On something of this nature, I don't think a signature is really needed."

On June 5, 1968, the report was officially published and copies were delivered in person to the Air Force and LTV. Within a week, flight tests were begun at Edwards Air Force Base in California. Searle Lawson was sent to California as Goodrich's representative. Within approximately two weeks, he returned because some rather unusual incidents during the tests had caused them to be canceled.

His face was grim as he related stories of several near crashes during landings—caused by brake troubles. He told me about one incident in which, upon landing, one brake was literally welded together by the intense heat developed during the test stop. The wheel locked, and the plane skidded for nearly 1500 feet before coming to a halt. The plane was jacked up and the wheel removed. The fused parts within the brake had to be pried apart.

Lawson had returned to Troy from California that same day, and that evening, he and others of the Goodrich engineering department left for Dallas for a high-level conference with LTV.

That evening I left work early and went to see my attorney. After I told him the story, he advised that, while I was probably not actually guilty of fraud, I was certainly part of a conspiracy to defraud. He advised me to go to the Federal Bureau of Investigation and offered to arrange an appointment. The following week he took me to the Dayton office of the FBI, and after I had been warned that I would not be immune from prosecution, I disclosed the A7D matter to one of the agents. The agent told me to say nothing about the episode to anyone and to report any further incident to him. He said he would forward the story to his superiors in Washington.

A few days later, Lawson returned from the conference in Dallas and said that the Air Force, which had previously approved the qualification report, had suddenly rescinded that approval and was demanding to see some of the raw test data taken during the tests. I gathered that the FBI had passed the word.

Omitting any reference to the FBI, I told Lawson I had been to an attorney and that we were probably guilty of conspiracy.

"Can you get me an appointment with your attorney?" he asked. Within a week, he had been to the FBI and told them of his part in the mess. He too was advised to say nothing but to keep on the job, reporting any new development.

Naturally, with the rescinding of Air Force approval and the demand to see raw test data, Goodrich officials were in a panic. A conference was called for July 27, a Saturday morning affair at which Lawson, Sink, Warren and myself were present. We met in a tiny conference room in the deserted engineering department. Lawson and I, by now openly hostile to Warren and Sink, ranged ourselves on one side of the conference table while Warren sat on the other side. Sink, chairing the meeting, paced slowly in front of a blackboard, puffing furiously on a pipe.

The meeting was called, Sink began, "to see where we stand on the A7D." What we were going to do, he said, was to "level" with LTV and tell them the "whole truth" about the A7D. "After all," he said, "they're in this thing with us, and they have the right to know how matters stand."

"In other words," I asked, "we're going to tell them the truth?"

"That's right," he replied. "We're going to level with them and let them handle the ball from there."

"There's one thing I don't quite understand," I interjected. "Isn't it going to be pretty hard for us to admit to them that we've lied?"

"Now, wait a minute," he said angrily. "Let's don't go off half-cocked on this thing. It's not a matter of lying. We've just interpreted the information the way we felt it should be."

"I don't know what you call it," I replied, "but to me it's lying, and it's going to be _____ hard to confess to them that we've been lying all along."

He became very agitated at this and repeated his "We're not lying," adding, "I don't like this sort of talk."

I dropped the matter at this point, and he began discussing the various discrepancies in the report.

We broke for lunch, and afterward, I came back to the plant to find Sink sitting alone at his desk, waiting to resume the meeting. He called me over and said he wanted to apologize for his outburst that morning. "This thing has kind of gotten me down," he confessed, "and I think you've got the wrong picture. I don't think you really understand everything about this."

Perhaps so, I conceded, but it seemed to me that if we had already told LTV one thing and then had to tell them another, changing our story completely, we would have to admit we were lying.

"No," he explained patiently, "we're not really lying. All we were doing was interpreting the figures the way we knew they should be. We were just exercising engineering license."

During the afternoon session, we marked some forty-three discrepant points in the report: forty-three points that LTV would surely spot as occasions where we had exercised "engineering license."

After Sink listed those points on the blackboard, we discussed each one individually. As each point came up, Sink would explain that it was probably "too minor to bother about," or that perhaps it "wouldn't be wise to open that can of worms," or that maybe this was a point that "LTV just wouldn't understand." When the meeting was over, it had been decided that only three points were "worth mentioning."

Similar conferences were held during August and September, and the summer was punctuated with frequent treks between Dallas and Troy, and demands by the Air Force to see the raw test data. Tempers were short and matters seemed to grow worse.

Finally, early in October 1968, Lawson submitted his resignation, to take effect on October 25. On October 18, I submitted my own resignation, to take effect on November 1. In my resignation, addressed to Russell Line, I cited the A7D report and stated: "As you are aware, this report contained

numerous deliberate and willful misrepresentations which, according to legal counsel, constitute
fraud and expose both myself and others to criminal charges of conspiracy to defraud.... The
events of the past seven months have created an
atmosphere of deceit and distrust in which it is
impossible to work...."

> *"The events of the past seven
> months have created an atmos-
> phere of deceit and distrust in
> which it is impossible to work."*

On October 25, I received a sharp summons to
the office of Bud Sunderman. As chief engineer at
the Troy plant, Sunderman was responsible for the
entire engineering division. Tall and graying,
impeccably dressed at all times, he was capable of
producing a dazzling smile or a hearty chuckle or
immobilizing his face into marble hardness, as the
occasion required.

I faced the marble hardness when I reached his
office. He motioned me to a chair. "I have your
resignation here," he snapped, "and I must say you
have made some rather shocking, I might even say
irresponsible, charges. This is very serious."

Before I could reply, he was demanding an
explanation. "I want to know exactly what the
fraud is in connection with the A7D and how you
can dare accuse this company of such a thing!"

I started to tell some of the things that had
happened during the testing, but he shut me off
saying, "There's nothing wrong with anything
we've done here. You aren't aware of all the things
that have been going on behind the scenes. If you
had known the true situation, you would never
have made these charges." He said that in view of
my apparent "disloyalty" he had decided to accept
my resignation "right now," and said it would be
better for all concerned if I left the plant immediately. As I got up to leave he asked me if I
intended to "carry this thing further."

I answered simply, "Yes," to which he replied,
"Suit yourself." Within twenty minutes, I had
cleaned out my desk and left. Forty-eight hours

later, the B. F. Goodrich Company recalled the
qualification report and the four-disk brake,
announcing that it would replace the brake with
a new, improved, five-disk brake at no cost to
LTV.

Ten months later, on August 13, 1969, I was the
chief government witness at a hearing conducted
before Senator William Proxmire's Economy in
Government Subcommittee of the Congress's
Joint Economic Committee. I related the A7D
story to the committee, and my testimony was
supported by Searle Lawson, who followed me to
the witness stand. Air Force officers also testified,
as well as a four-man team from the General
Accounting Office, which had conducted an
investigation of the A7D brake at the request of
Senator Proxmire. Both Air Force and GAO inves-
tigators declared that the brake was dangerous
and had not been tested properly.

Testifying for Goodrich was R. G. Jeter, vice-
president and general counsel of the company,
from the Akron headquarters. Representing the
Troy plant was Robert Sink. These two denied any
wrongdoing on the part of the Goodrich Company, despite expert testimony to the contrary by
Air Force and GAO officials. Sink was quick to
deny any connection with the writing of the
report or of directing any falsifications, claiming
to be on the West Coast at the time. John Warren
was the man who supervised its writing, said Sink.

As for me, I was dismissed as a high-school
graduate with no technical training, while Sink
testified that Lawson was a young, inexperienced
engineer. "We tried to give him guidance," Sink
testified, "but he preferred to have his own convictions."

About changing the data and figures in the
report, Sink said: "When you take data from several different sources, you have to rationalize
among those data what is the true story. This is
part of your engineering know-how." He admitted
that changes had been made in the data, "but only
to make them more consistent with the overall
picture of the data that is available."

Jeter pooh-poohed the suggestion that anything improper occurred, saying: "We have thirty-

odd engineers at this plant . . . and I say to you that it is incredible that these men would stand idly by and see reports changed or falsified. . . . I mean you just do not have to do that working for anybody. . . . Just nobody does that."

The four-hour hearing adjourned with no real conclusion reached by the committee. But, the following day the Department of Defense made sweeping changes in its inspection, testing and reporting procedures. A spokesman for the DOD said the changes were a result of the Goodrich episode.

The A7D is now in service, sporting a Goodrich-made five-disk brake, a brake that works very well, I'm told. Business at the Goodrich plant is good. Lawson is now an engineer for LTV and has been assigned to the A7D project. And I am now a newspaper reporter.

At this writing, those remaining at Goodrich are still secure in the same positions, all except Russell Line and Robert Sink. Line has been rewarded with a promotion to production superintendent, a large step upward on the corporate ladder. As for Sink, he moved up into Line's old job.

Questions for Discussion:

1. In your opinion, did Vandivier do the right thing by blowing the whistle on his employer? Why or why not? If you were in the same situation, would you have done anything differently? Defend your answer.
2. What factors within the organizational setting contributed to the situation's getting so out of hand before anything was done about it? What factors contributed to a "buck passing" mentality of moral responsibility? Do the same conditions exist in other organizations in which you have been employed or involved?
3. If Vandivier would have claimed that he was simply obeying orders, would this be an adequate moral justification for his actions? Why or why not? Can you think of a situation in which you could justify "just obeying orders" to do something immoral or illegal?

CASE STUDIES

Case 12.1: Billing Practices and the Bankruptcy Courts

Sears had a problem with its credit card accounts. Though the company has always had to deal with its share of bad debts, they were seeing the problem in a new way. An increasing number of its cardholders were declaring personal bankruptcy, keeping the goods purchased on credit from Sears, and not having to pay their balances. To be sure, some of what these people owed Sears was being repaid, but in a variety of different arrangements. For example, some were making monthly payments less than what they were being billed. Others were settling their accounts for substantially less than they owed, and some never were going to pay their debt to Sears. The law requires that when someone declares personal bankruptcy, the bankruptcy court oversees the restructuring of the person's debt and assigns to different creditors a place on the priority list that will determine when and how much of the debt gets repaid. All subsequent billing and collection efforts for the account must go through the bankruptcy court. Companies cannot continue to bill customers who have declared bankruptcy without clearance from the bankruptcy court.

Beginning in Massachusetts, the bankruptcy court found that Sears had been making attempts at collection from customers who had been given bankruptcy protection without the court's permission or awareness. As the investigation unfolded, it revealed that thousands of Sears' customers had been billed in this way. With many, Sears had simply continued to bill them as though they had never declared bankruptcy, even though it was a violation of bankruptcy law. Sears' collections employees were understandably upset that so many people were in essence getting free merchandise from Sears. At first, Sears claimed that the operation was confined to a small group of employees operating outside company guidelines. Subsequent investigations revealed a much more widespread problem that indicated the approval of management. Sears was eventually required to pay roughly $60 million in back payments and fines.

Source: "The Sorry Side of Sears," *Newsweek*, 22 February 1999, 31–43.

Questions for Discussion:

1. Why do you think the employees involved at Sears violated the law in this way? What conditions do you think may have been present at Sears to permit, or even to encourage, this kind of illegal behavior?
2. What pressures do you think were on employees who saw a problem to not blow the whistle on the company?
3. What policies and procedures would you put in place at a company like Sears to help ensure that these practices do not occur again?

Case 12.2: How Much Does Character Count?

You serve on the board of directors of a medium-sized, publicly traded manufacturer of computer software. The company has experienced double-digit growth for the past five years with a corresponding rise in the stock price, substantially increasing your net worth and the net worth of the other board members. Most people, both inside the company and in the investment community, believe the reason for this growth is the performance of the company's CEO, who was hired by the board about seven years ago. The CEO is a charismatic leader and effective manager whose vision has motivated the executives and sales staff. He has instituted a variety of changes that the employees have appreciated, such as broadening the employee stock option program. His leadership has provided stable jobs and wealth for many employees who have taken advantage of the stock option program.

The CEO has a charming personality, which frequently turns flirtatious. It is widely known that he has had multiple affairs, and there have been rumors of romantic relationships with female employees from time to time. Employees sometimes wonder why his wife stays with him. Though they admire his business skills, they have reservations about his character. The board has been nervous about his personal life, but the company has been doing so well that no one on the board has thought it appropriate to mention anything to him.

The most recent affair has caught the board off guard. This time the affair was with a much younger employee of the company and has become more public. They were seen together at a charity function in the area last month, and recently they were seen leaving a company function together. He is a public figure, and they are concerned about the effect on the company's public relations, particularly since the company employs numerous women and since some of its best customers are companies run by women. The board has new concerns about the "character issues" of their CEO and have called a meeting to discuss what, if anything, they should do about it.

Source: Suzy Wetlaufer, "A Question of Character," *Harvard Business Review* (September/October 1999): 31–43.

Questions for Discussion:

1. Do you think the board has a legitimate concern about the personal character of the CEO? Why or why not?
2. What are the risks to the company of ignoring the character issues of the CEO? Conversely, what are the risks of confronting the CEO about these issues?
3. To what degree should the board take into account the character of the CEO in evaluating his ability to lead the company? Do you think character makes a difference in his performance, or is it irrelevant? How does the article by Virgil Smith earlier in this chapter contribute to your answer?
4. Does the character flaw in the CEO make a difference if the company's target market for its product is women in an industry such as fashion or cosmetics? Why or why not?

COMMENTARY

Organizations of all varieties have a greater stake than ever in developing and implementing policies that encourage ethical behavior within their ranks. In a climate of economic downturns, increased competition, and downsizing, temptations to cut ethical corners are greater than ever. The resulting damage caused by revelations of immoral behavior on the part of executives and employees can have a lasting impact on public trust and internal morale. Moreover, the law now considers contributions by management and the organization to individual transgressions of law. Companies can be punished and/or given leniency according to the steps that they have taken to either encourage or prevent misconduct on the part of their employees. As a result, companies are implementing policies that encourage ethical behavior in the workplace. Some firms have started ethics and compliance offices and have hired ethics executives to staff them. Many others pay consultants to provide ethics awareness and training sessions for their employees. Most companies have at least written ethical concerns into their mission statements and have developed detailed corporate codes of conduct governing specific situations that employees may face in the course of their duties.

Despite the money being poured into these efforts, some critics wonder whether or not ethics can truly be "taught" and fostered within the context of corporations.[3] To these critics, ethics is something that is learned at our parents' knee. Consequently, it is reasoned that in the absence of values in ones upbringing, it is too late to try to teach ethics to employees during a day- or week-long training session. However, Aristotle reminds us that although ethics start with a good upbringing, they develop during the course of life through practical experience and critical reflection. Thus, while perhaps we would put it less strongly than Lynn Sharp Paine's assertion that "ethics has *everything* to do with management," we believe corporations can and do have a very real impact on the beliefs and behaviors of their members through both formal and informal mechanisms.

Fostering good ethics is not simply a matter of hiring morally upright people in the hope that their values will guide the organization's decisions. In many scandals, it is not "bad apples" in the form of rogue individuals or executives who explicitly set out to defraud the public, though that is often the explanation given to the public. Rather, it is usually a combination of organizational and environmental factors that play the biggest role in creating the "bad barrel" that leads to unethical actions. Let's think about some of the organizational factors that can exercise influence on individuals in the workplace to violate their consciences and do unethical or even illegal actions.

In almost every well-publicized scandal in the business world, a group of well-educated and respected participants get caught in actions that seem to go beyond the bounds of how they would act as individuals. Co-workers, family members, neighbors, and fellow church congregants usually express shock and disbelief that the people they know as responsible employees, spouses, and citizens could actually commit illegal and immoral acts. How is it that otherwise good, moral people in reputable organizations can get caught up in actions that would undoubtedly violate their individual consciences? How is it that illegal and immoral acts with dire consequences can occur with no one willing to assume moral responsibility?

One possible explanation to these pressing questions is the nature and structure of groups and organizations. For years, sociologists and psychologists have undertaken detailed studies of these entities and their affects on the beliefs and behaviors of their individual members. If they are accurate, their conclusions are startling

3 See, for example, Andrew Bartlett and David Preston, "Can Ethical Behavior Really Exist in Business?" *Journal of Business Ethics* 23 (2000): 199–209.

because they have found that individual members of groups will often commit acts of evil in violation of their own beliefs for the sake of obeying authority and going along with the group. One of the contributing factors to this dynamic is known as "group think" which is defined as "a mode of thinking that people engage in when they are deeply involved in a cohesive in-group, when the members' strivings for unanimity override their motivation to realistically appraise alternative courses of actions . . . group think refers to the deterioration of mental efficiency, reality testing, and moral judgment that results from in-group pressures."[4]

4 Irving L. Janus, *Victims of Group Think* (Boston: Houghton Mifflin, 1972), 9.

When group think occurs, the morality of a group decision or action goes unquestioned by the individuals within it. Consequently, scenarios like that which occurred during Watergate can readily happen. Experts believe that other contributing factors to these scenarios include some forms of hierarchy where responsibility for actions typically get diffused both up and down the chain of command and "buck passing" becomes the modus operandi. Thus, disastrous decisions can be made with no one taking responsibility for their consequences.

Undoubtedly, these dynamics have a direct relevance for business ethics. Although we have focused mainly on ethical issues and decision making up until this point in this book, correct courses of action are not debated and undertaken in a social vacuum. Most business decisions and transactions are made within the context of organizational and group pressures. Consequently, most of us have faced or will face similar situations during careers in a variety of professions. As such, we must be aware of the effect of organizational pressures on the morals and actions of individual members. The two following incidents are prime examples of these dynamics at work:

First, during a famous incident during the Vietnam War, a U.S. army task force entered the village of Mylai in search of Vietcong soldiers. Instead of armed guerrillas, the members of Task Force Barker only found unarmed women, children, and old men. In the stress and paranoia of jungle warfare, members of the task force proceeded to kill between four and six hundred villagers. One platoon, under the command of Lieutenant William L. Calley Jr., herded villagers into groups of twenty to forty or more and then slaughtered them by rifles, machine guns, and grenades. What stood out most about this episode is the fact that only one person in the whole task force voiced objection to the mayhem that occurred despite the fact that perhaps as many as two hundred soldiers witnessed the incident. In the year that followed this tragedy, no one attempted to report this crime. Eventually, six people were brought to trial and only one person, Lieutenant Calley, was ever convicted of wrongdoing.[5]

5 Scott Peck, "Mylai: An Examination of Group Evil," in *People of the Lie* (New York: Simon & Schuster/Touchstone, 1983), 212–53.

Second, in the months leading up to the space shuttle *Challenger* disaster, executives at Morton Thiokol and NASA had ample evidence and warnings by several key engineers that O-ring failure would likely lead to an explosion shortly after ignition. Yet after repeated warnings, and knowing that several lives were at stake and that a disaster loomed, a decision was made to proceed with the launch. On January 28, 1986, the *Challenger* exploded seventy-three seconds into flight, killing the seven astronauts aboard.

Military and business organizations need a high level of group cohesion. Teamwork, unity, and cooperation are intangible factors that can have a tremendous bearing on success. However, the critical issue is whether there is a point where too much of a good thing makes the exercise of moral courage more difficult. With the many examples of group think that have occurred, we must ask if there is something about the structure of some organizations and the social makeup of individuals that contributes to a potentially volatile mixture. Are these instances explainable by a simple lack of moral courage on the part of the individuals involved, or is there something about the unique nature of organizations that may explain, though not excuse, what appears to be a fairly consistent pattern of behavior?

In many business ethics scandals that have come to light, the individuals involved typically absolve themselves of moral culpability by claiming that someone else was ultimately responsible for what occurred. For example, in many of these cases the first response of corporate executives is to lay the blame at the feet of "rogue individuals" who were acting without company permission and knowledge. These individuals in turn claim that they were unaware of the consequences of their actions because they did not have the big picture and were "only following orders." While the fallen nature of humanity undoubtedly contributes to a lack of moral courage in the presence of the potential for significant financial gains, we must ask if there is something in the structure of organizations that contributes to this lack of moral responsibility.

Many corporations have socialization processes to inculcate organizational values and instruct them in the "company way." This socialization process continues more informally as the organization seeks to create loyalty and commitment on the part of the employees. Many of these informal practices of the corporate culture serve to reinforce specific behaviors through peer pressure, rewards, and punishment. Those who play by the rules are rewarded through praise, promotions, and pay increases. Non-team players are discouraged through threats of embarrassment, demotion, and the potential of being fired. Of course, loyalty and commitment are good things that companies are correct to encourage and that contribute to their ability to run smoothly. But at what point do these traits become group think and inhibit critical thinking and moral courage?

In addition to peer pressure, the deck is further stacked against ethics in many companies by the nature of hierarchical organization. The specialization of tasks and the division of labor that comes with bureaucratic structures cripples many employees from seeing the larger contexts and consequences of their actions. As we mentioned earlier, when scandals are revealed and investigated, those at the top often blame those on lower rungs. Those on the bottom are routinely told, as Kermit Vandivier was in "Why Should My Conscience Bother Me?" that they don't have the big picture and that it will be top management's responsibility if anything happens. Thus, it is easier to "leave the driving to others" and claim they were only following orders than to assume responsibility. Buck passing then becomes the norm.

The experience of Vandivier at the Troy, Ohio, Goodrich plant is a good illustration of the institutional factors that can work against someone who desires to exercise moral courage. Competition in conjunction with group think and the demands of authority can create enormous pressures on an individual to abandon conscience for the sake of the perceived well-being of the group. The authority of higher-level employees had many in the organization simply shifting responsibility to others. Peer pressure and hierarchy further added to the deck-stacking effect. Adding to the reality of competing loyalties in the equation, Vandivier mentions his struggle over family obligations. "But bills are not paid with personal satisfaction, nor house payments with ethical principles," he states. Undoubtedly, the ability to stand up for what's right is often compounded by painful tradeoffs. The prospect of unemployment in these situations is real.

While this particular case occurred in the 1960s, investigations of fraud still regularly make news. Thus, the principles involved are still very relevant. If you were in Vandivier's position, how do you think you would respond?

As the Nuremberg trials established, simply obeying authorities is not an ample moral or legal excuse for transgressing ethical principles. While the prospect of losing one's job and house are painful realities, Christians are promised divine providence in pursuing the right course of action. Furthermore, we are never guaranteed home ownership or a middle-class lifestyle. There are, indeed, tradeoffs to being morally courageous. If it were easy, everyone would stand up for what's right.

Despite the best efforts of companies, there will always be maverick individuals or "bad apples" who will inevitably choose the shortest path to quick gain. However, as the articles in this chapter make clear, corporations can do much to create a climate that supports ethical decisions. Peer pressure and socialization can work both ways, to encourage as well as discourage moral courage.

First, let us examine some of the *formal* mechanisms that encourage ethical behavior. These include reporting relationships and incentive systems. Though the tall command-and-control organizational structures of the rational bureaucratic model are a dying breed, all organizations still maintain some type of hierarchy in order to determine chain of command and reporting relationships. While it is true that flat structures that empower employees to make quick decisions are swiftly becoming the norm, there are still levels of authority and division according to specialization within every organization of size. Thus, some employees are privy to larger and longer-term views than others. This can create a climate in which some employees only see a small part of the total picture. Thus, "buck passing" of moral responsibility up and down the chain of command can easily become the norm.

The case of Sears Auto Centers is an example of this phenomenon.[6] As a result of numerous complaints and a statewide undercover operation, the state of California found that Sears was overcharging its customers by recommending unnecessary auto repair work on an average of $235 per customer. In this situation, employees were inadvertently encouraged to commit fraud because the only way for them to meet sales goals established by higher management was to unnecessarily replace car parts. It appears that no individual schemed to defraud the public. Rather, miscommunication and differing goals of the various levels of the organization directly contributed to a climate that was ripe for misconduct. Furthermore, although we cannot know for sure, employees who complained were probably told that they should simply follow the policy and "do their jobs" because they didn't have the big picture in their grasp. To avoid these situations, corporations must open communication channels up, down, and across the corporate ladder so that the big picture is conveyed downward, and upward feedback is welcomed. Furthermore, individual actors must be rewarded and held responsible for group-based decisions. Moral responsibility should not be diluted to the point where it is the "system" and not individuals who are held accountable for specific actions.

In addition to hierarchy, incentive systems can also foster a climate in which customer interests are readily sacrificed for commissions and higher profits. Any beginning-level textbook on psychology or organizational behavior and management includes a chapter on how individuals "learn" at a basic level through rewards and punishment.

6 See Paine, "Managing for Organizational Integrity."

Although not every person is a "rational actor" in a purely economic sense, many employees will act in a manner that is most rewarding in terms of finances and career progression. Unethical behaviors will likely occur if they are rewarded. Thus, corporate policies must be critically examined to see if they make it in the financial interest of employees to behave unethically. Honest sales practices that are truly in the best interest of consumers can just as easily be rewarded as those that are not.

In addition to these formal mechanisms, informal ones such as corporate culture and the socialization process further serve to perpetuate behaviors. Financial incentives to cheat are even more likely to occur when compounded by peer pressure. While individuals ultimately have responsibility for their own choices and actions, employees are often socialized into the norms and culture of an organization. In so doing, they will often take cues from the surrounding environment to determine what is acceptable or even expected behavior. For example, if co-workers and executives regularly engage in practices that disregard the law, such as padding expense accounts or copying software illegally, the message that these are acceptable norms within the organization will be communicated loud and clear.

Every organization has a culture with its own stories, creeds, and norms for behavior that develops over a period of time. Narrative and stories can be powerful guides for action and socialization because they communicate much about an organization's values. For example, the pariah of a company tale may be one who possessed a moral voice and dared speak out against some unethical practices.

Usually company management plays a significant role in developing the culture by telling these stories, developing creeds, and articulating and enforcing the company's values. If, however, company leadership does not articulate and model the values, a culture will evolve all on its own. Thus, the critical question is whether that culture will be one that fosters or actively discourages ethical behaviors on the part of employees. To have a better chance at the former, company leadership must be proactive in helping to shape the moral values of the corporate culture that develops. Although the saying "It starts at the top" sounds like a well-worn cliché, company leadership, especially the CEO, is the critical values setter for the company. His or her attitude toward ethics will often set the tone for the whole organization, both in what is said and what is modeled. Clearly, when that which is modeled is somehow different than the message that is articulated verbally, it is an enormous setback for an ethical environment, since employees do what their superiors do, not what they say, when words and deeds conflict.

Company executives can also play a role in the shaping of culture through the development of creedal statements, the implementation of training programs, and the articulation of specific guidelines for employees. Efforts in these arenas will undeniably contribute to the infusing of ethics into the company climate. However, creeds and codes are insufficient if they are not enforced through formal mechanisms such as performance reviews and compensation and promotion-related decisions. In fact, many critics have remarked that ethics codes and training programs are really no more than mere "window dressing" that serves as a useful public relations tool to ward off scrutiny and governmental interference. Indeed, many companies that are caught crossing ethical and legal lines have mission statements that claim ethics as a high priority. Thus, the developed creeds and codes must be lived as well as preached. If the stated values have no teeth to them or if they see executives betray them, some employees will swiftly catch on and will likely revert to the behaviors that are "really" rewarded.

Moreover, a legalistic devotion to a codified compliance program is insufficient. Ethics must become a key part of strategic planning and objectives through the cultivation of integrity as the governing ethic. An ethic of integrity and trust that goes beyond mere legalistic compliance is a much better way of encouraging moral corporate climates. Compliance programs usually generate a negative "police state" environment, where employees fear authority structures and ethics is perceived as a top-down product created by management to catch employees and serve as liability protection.

In contrast, an "integrity strategy" encourages all employees to take ownership of ethics as a total corporate objective. Managers at all levels and across functions must be involved for a successful implementation of an integrity ethic. Involving managers at all levels in the discussion serves to raise awareness and foster a sense of ownership of the objectives. We would add that even non-managerial employees must be involved in the dialogue. Environments of truly open two-way communications must be carefully cultivated if all employees are to be free to stand up to group and peer pressures.

Phenomena such as group think and blind obedience to authority can only be minimized by a climate that truly values diversity of opinions. As Sears and other companies have found out, it is often employees at the lowest level of the hierarchy for whom ethical decisions are most salient, since they are the ones in the trenches. Furthermore, many organizations are successful for the very reason that they value innovative and creative thinking that falls outside of the so-called box created by an overabundance of group cohesion and outdated company

norms and expectations. Thus, a climate where communication channels are open and feedback is welcome will likely contribute to both
the financial and the ethical well-being of a company.

In summary, it is within the financial self-interest of companies to
create moral corporate climates. They can encourage these environments by the infusion of values through corporate culture and through
the modeling of integrity on the part of executives who set the tone
for the whole organization. However, talk of ethics in mission statements, creeds, and codes becomes empty if it is not seen as part of the
long-term objectives. Ethics must be rewarded through formal policies such as performance reviews and promotion decisions. Organizations must begin on the path to the creation of ethical climates by
taking a long-term view and making ethics a key component of strategic planning. Only then will ethics filter downward and become a matter of day-to-day operating policy.

Our goal in this chapter has been to explain, not excuse, the conditions for unethical behavior that occur in some organizations. If education can accomplish anything, it can raise our awareness about our
tendencies to conform and show us ways that we can avoid these types
of actions. An awareness of our propensity to go against our own moral
convictions in the face of authoritarian and social pressures can be one
step in the path of allowing us to stand for that which is morally right.

CONCLUSION

Business, Virtue, and the Good Life

Much of this book has addressed, from a variety of perspectives, the conflicts that arise when a company's pursuit of profit collides with its obligation to its community. That community may include the company's employees, the environment, the consumers of its products and services, or the general public. Many texts in business ethics would leave you with the impression that resolving these conflicts is all there is to the matter. Yet we have tried to show that there are other issues about personal moral development, responsibility, and decision making that are crucial for a full-orbed discussion of business ethics. To put it in terms of moral theory, action-oriented theories of morality are helpful but not sufficient to address the critical component of business ethics and the person. It takes the additional influence of more virtue-oriented emphases in ethics to round out our discussion.

Many approaches to virtue are connected with conceptions of the "good life" and the good society. What constitutes a good life is a critical question that anyone who spends forty to fifty hours a week working in business should consider. More specifically, what place do business and the pursuit of profit have in a person's conception of the good life? What place *should* they have? How should a person's religious faith help form that conception? These are important questions that merit serious personal reflection, not only for a well-rounded discussion of business ethics, but for a well-rounded personal life.

In his book *God and Mammon in America*, sociologist Robert Wuthnow discloses that religious faith, though still important in questions of economic life, exercises an ambivalent and therapeutic influence.[1] He suggests that the impact of religious views has been weakened by cultural trends toward greater secularization and that, as a result, they no longer shape our views on economic life as much as they reinforce

[1] Robert Wuthnow, *God and Mammon in America* (New York: Free Press, 1994), 5.

465

choices made on the basis of prevailing market orientation. He suggests that "we look to religion, therefore, to make us happy about our preferences, not to channel them in specific directions."[2]

We suggest that if the biblical record is any guide, its strong emphasis on faith as influencing one's economic life compels religious believers to think through more carefully how their faith impacts life in the workplace, and summons their places of worship to be better equipped to provide such guidance. Readers of this book who are heading for vocational ministry can do their congregations a significant service by being able to address coherently the issues that most businesspeople will face regularly in their places of work. We have tried here to provide such guidance for those making this pilgrimage and for those who assist them.

We challenge you to think more carefully about how you view your workplace experience, whether as a calling or as a career. Earlier in this book we distinguished between these two and encouraged you to consider what is your calling and to pursue that, in contrast to pursuing only a career. You may encounter some tensions between fulfilling your calling and making the kind of living you feel you need in order to provide for a family. We are not suggesting a simplistic injunction such as "do what you love and the money will follow." But we are urging you not to blindly follow the career orientation that is prevalent in the marketplace today. There is more to your calling than your position in the organization, your prospects for advancement, and your earning potential. Your attitudes and values in your working years are just as important—if not more so—than how you advance your career by moving up a corporate ladder.

We also challenge you to think more carefully about how business fits into your conception of the good life. What constitutes a good life for you? What do your religious beliefs suggest constitutes a good life? How does your definition of success fit with your conception of the good life? The way many people would regard success has more to do with your position and income than with the contribution you have made to your community and the kind of person you have become. That is the orientation of the career, not the calling. To be sure, being recognized and appropriately rewarded for quality work is a reasonable expectation, but if that does not occur—or if it does not occur according to your timetable—it is not uncommon, then, to become disillusioned with your work. By contrast, for someone who adopts a calling orientation toward work, the job is considered inherently valuable and motivating, and advancement—though important—is not the all-consuming passion of one's professional life. We find it difficult to consider people a success, irrespective of their position and net worth, if they have compromised important personal beliefs and virtues and have been less, rather than more, of the person God would have them to become.

From the perspective of Judeo-Christian ethics, the good life involves living out our calling with excellence, becoming more godly in personal character, being committed to our family and community, and living out goals that are consistent with our calling. This is a very different conception from that which dominates the marketplace today—placing value on a person and one's life based on position, prestige, and net worth. A person may well achieve those marks while at the same time pursuing the good life, as defined by Judeo-Christian ethics. But position, prestige, and net worth are not the constituent elements of the good life. The writer of the book of Ecclesiastes put it this way: "A man can do nothing better than to eat and drink and find satisfaction in his work. This too, I see, is from the hand of God" (Eccl. 2:24).

CREDITS

The authors are grateful to the publishers and copyright owners for permission to reprint the articles that appear in the Readings of this book.

CHAPTER 1

"Is Business Bluffing Ethical?" by Albert Z. Carr. Reprinted by permission of *Harvard Business Review* (January/February 1968). Copyright © 1967 by the President and Fellows of Harvard College; all rights reserved.

"Why Be Honest If Honesty Doesn't Pay?" by Amar Bhide and Howard H. Stevenson. Reprinted by permission of *Harvard Business Review* (September/October 1990). Copyright 1990 by the President and Fellows of Harvard College; all rights reserved.

"Companies Are Discovering the Value of Ethics," by Norman Bowie. *USA Today Magazine* (January 1998): 22–24. Copyright © 1998 Society for the Advancement of Education. Copyright © 2000 Gale Group.

CHAPTER 2

"Christ and Business," by Louke van Wensveen Siker, *Journal of Business Ethics* 8 (1989): 883–88. Copyright © 1989 Kluwer Academic Publishers. Reprinted by permission of Kluwer Academic Publishers.

"The Entrepreneurial Vocation," by Fr. Robert Sirico. Copyright © 1996. The Rev. Robert A. Sirico is president of the Acton Institute for the Study of Religion and Liberty, 161 Ottawa Avenue N.W., Suite 301, Grand Rapids, Michigan 49503. (616) 454-3080.

"Tough Business: In Deep, Swift Waters," by Steve Brinn, " *Vocatio* 2 no. 2 (July 1999): 3–6. Copyright © 1999.

CHAPTER 3

"The Bible and Culture in Ethics," by Bernard T. Adeney, in *Strange Virtues: Ethics in a Multicultural World* (Downers Grove, IL: InterVarsity Press, 1995), 79–105.

"Business Ethics," by Alexander Hill, in *The Complete Book of Everyday Christianity*, ed. by Robert J. Banks and R. Paul Stevens (Downers Grove, IL: InterVarsity Books, 1998). Copyright © 1997 by Robert Banks and

CHAPTER 4

CHAPTER 5

CHAPTER 6

CHAPTER 7

CHAPTER 8

"Financial Ethics: An Overview," by John Boatright, in *Ethics in Finance* (New York: Blackwell, 1999), 1–29.

CHAPTER 9

"The Morality (?) of Advertising," by Theodore Levitt. Reprinted by permission of *Harvard Business Review* (July/August 1970). Copyright © 1970 by the President and Fellows of Harvard College; all rights reserved.

"The Making of Self and World in Advertising," by John Waide, *Journal of Business Ethics* 6 (1987), 73–79. Copyright © 1987 D. Reidel Publishing Co. Reprinted by permission of Kluwer Academic Publishers.

"Making Consumers," by Rodney Clapp, from "Why the Devil Takes Visa," *Christianity Today* (7 October 1996).

CHAPTER 10

"Business and Environmental Ethics," copyright © W. Michael Hoffman. Reprinted from *Business Ethics Quarterly*, vol. 1, no. 2 (April 1991): 169–84. Copyright © 1991.

"The Challenge of Biocentrism," by Thomas Sieger Derr, in Michael Cromartie, ed., *Creation at Risk: Religion, Science and Environmentalism* (Grand Rapids: Eerdmans, 1995), 85–104.

CHAPTER 11

"Is Technology (ever) Evil?" by David Gill, *Ethix* (December 1999): 11.

"Five Big Issues in Today's Technological Workplace," by Albert M. Erisman, *Ethix* (March/April 2002): 4–5.

"LittleBrother Is Watching You," by Miriam Schulman, *Business and Society Review* 100/101 (1998): 65–69. Copyright © 1998 by the Center for Business Ethics at Bentley College. Reprinted by permission.

CHAPTER 12

"Creating and Encouraging Ethical Corporate Structures," by Patrick E. Murphy. Reprinted from *Sloan Management Review*, 30:2, Winter 1989, pp. 81–87, by permission of publisher. Copyright © 1989 by the Sloan Management Review Association. All rights reserved.

"The Place of Character in Corporate Ethics," by Virgil Smith. Copyright © 1996 by Virgil Smith. Previously unpublished article published with permission of the author.

" 'Why Should My Conscience Bother Me?' The Aircraft Brake Scandal," by Kermit Vandivier, from *In the Name of Profit* by Robert Heilbroner, 3–31. Copyright © 1972 by Doubleday. Used by permission of Doubleday, a division of Bantam Doubleday Dell Publishing Group, Inc.

ABOUT THE AUTHORS

Scott B. Rae (Ph.D., University of Southern California) is professor of Christian ethics at Talbot School of Theology, Biola University. He is the author of numerous articles and six books, including *Moral Choices: An Introduction to Ethics* (Zondervan) and *Body and Soul: Human Nature and the Crisis in Ethics* (InterVarsity Press). He is a consultant for ethics for five Southern California hospitals. He is a fellow of the Wilberforce Forum and the Center for Bioethics and Human Dignity.

Kenman Wong (Ph.D., University of Southern California) is professor of business ethics at the School of Business and Economics, Seattle Pacific University, where he has won several awards for excellence in teaching and scholarship. He is the author of *Medicine and the Marketplace* (University of Notre Dame Press) and has published articles in journals such as the *Journal of Business Ethics, Journal of Management Education,* and *Science and Engineering Ethics.* He was employed with a leading management and technology consulting firm before entering the academic profession.